MW00883110

# Change & Chance Embraced

## ACHIEVING AGILITY WITH SMARTER FORECASTING IN THE SUPPLY CHAIN

(Edition: August 4, 2024)

HANS LEVENBACH, PhD

 Professional development: Certified Professional Demand Forecaster (CPDF®), *www.cpdftraining.org*

# Contents

## Chapter 1 - Why Demand Forecasting is So Crucial to Supply Chain Planners and Managers

## Chapter 2 -Smarter Forecasting Is Mostly about Data:

### Improving Data Quality through Data Exploration and Visualization    37

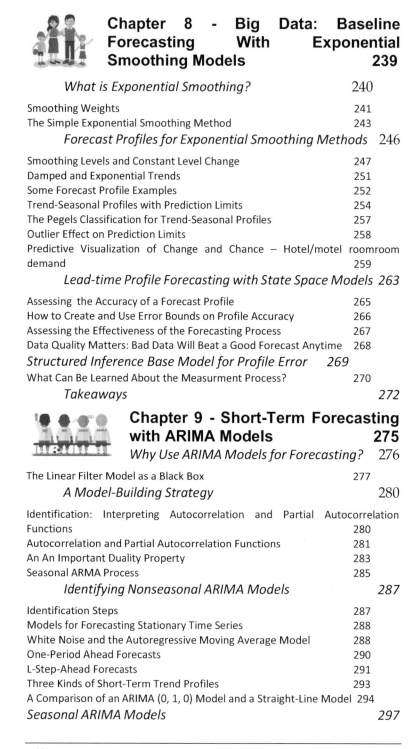

## Chapter 13 - Creating a Database Framework for Agile Forecasting and Performance Management    407

# Preface

For some time now, the use of computerized and improved statistical forecasting methodologies have greatly enhanced the productivity and effectiveness of forecasting in business, government and private sectors around the world. This development is in part driven by the changing and uncertain nature in competitive markets, global economic disruptions, financial objectives, shifting demographics, and operational environments facing a business enterprise.

The clear need for improved business planning to reduce costs, increase profitability and enhance customer satisfaction, for instance, has increased the desire to apply better forecast modeling approaches to the planning and management of **change and chance (*uncertainty*)** in the supply chain.

Fortunately for supply chain practitioners, data-driven predictive analytics have greatly simplified and speeded up the way we can make their planning forecasts. Ready access to large data sources, automated statistical modeling, cheap computing and increasingly sophisticated quantitative techniques have given rise to a wide variety of modern data-intensive techniques that can be applied in a relatively short time at a reasonable cost. Still, practitioners and managers can be easily overwhelmed by a plethora of forecasting techniques that are easily misunderstood or not well implemented in software. Moreover, the manager and end-user of the forecasting process have been offered little training in how to make more effective and appropriate use of these powerful (often inadequately documented) techniques in real-world situations.

## Demand Forecasting: A Data-Centric Process

Up to recent times, **business forecasting** has been closely linked to economic and financial analysis. During the 1980's, for instance, economic forecasting suffered from a lack of credibility, media ridicule and shortcomings in accuracy goals. Nowadays, the meaning of business forecasting has broadened considerably to include forecasting a *consumer* demand for products and services throughout a supply chain from supplier of raw material to consumer of finished goods. Called **demand forecasting**, it generally attempts to predict future consumer/customer demand for a company's goods and services under uncertainty.

The modern $21^{st}$ century focus is directed more to forecasting the disaggregated elements of product demand for supplying warehouses, distributors, channels, customer accounts, and consumers than to economic- and financial-driven aggregates. **Demand forecasting**, within the context of this book, means that the firm attempts to predict the *right* amount of the *right* product to be in the *right* place at the *right* time for the *right* price, which is one of the underpinnings of what is now known as **demand forecasting and replenishment planning** for the supply chain.

By presenting a unified and practical orientation to demand forecasting, this book aims to prepare a practicing forecaster or student learning about demand forecasting to become a productive professional. To this end, I present the most widely accepted, currently practiced quantitative and qualitative techniques in business forecasting. The principal unifying theme of this book is the presentation of forecasting as a **process**, rather than a series of disconnected techniques. A further unifying theme is a constant emphasis on the role and importance of looking at data, or **exploratory data analysis**, as practiced by statisticians and scientists.

The industrial examples and computer spreadsheet exercises included herein are also consistent with the goal of preparing the reader for the immediate practice of demand forecasting as a data-driven process.

## What Is New?

This book is a complete revision of my 2005 book **Forecasting – Practice and Process for Demand Management** and its 1984 predecessor **The Modern Forecaster,** coauthored with James P. Cleary. Although basic principles underlying the demand forecasting process have not changed, a sea change has occurred to forecasting in the business environment from top-down macroeconomic forecasting to bottom-up operational forecasting. This has meant a realignment of major topics as well as the introduction of new material based on bottom-up data structures for large database applications.

## Scope

In this book, I have introduced the following:

- Establishment of a *structured data framework* for an agile demand forecasting process. Specific methodologies and practical techniques are presented within the context of the overall process.
- Selection of the forecasting and analytical techniques *most appropriate* for any given problem, based on *forecast profiles*, rather than model fitting. The techniques discussed, many representing current state-of-the-art, are the ones that have proved to be most useful and reliable to practicing forecasters.
- *Exploratory analysis of historical data* before attempting to create models and forecasts. Computer-generated graphical

displays enable you to see in a picture what you might otherwise have to glean from a spreadsheet.

- Performance of *diagnostic analyses on both fit and forecast errors*. To determine what the unexplained variation might tell us about the adequacy of the model and the uncertainty in the forecast, I stress the importance and usefulness of displaying residual diagnostics and forecast error distributions. Residuals and forecast errors from hold-out samples are emphasized throughout as essential in all phases of an agile forecasting process.

- Using *robust/resistant methods* to complement traditional methods. Experience with a wide variety of realistic applications has convinced me that data are rarely well behaved enough for the direct application of standard statistical assumptions. The robust/resistant methods produce results that are less impacted by departures from conventional normality assumptions and to the distortions caused by a few outlying or unusual data values. By creating both traditional and robust/resistant results, the practitioner is in a better position to decide which are the most useful for the problem at hand.

- Refocusing the attention of practitioners away from the *mechanistic execution of computer software* and *the excessive manipulation of model fit parameters* toward a greater understanding of data, data quality, forecast profiles and performance, and business context.

- *Embracing forecast numbers with measured uncertainty* in forecasting as a key ingredient to achieving agility and credibility with demand forecasting among planning organizations and with trading partners. The field sales input, collaboration with partners and customers, and the Sales and Operations process helps assure that the forecaster's role as *advisor* achieves forecast accuracy, credibility, and acceptance with management and forecast-users.

This book describes a number of basic, well-established and proven forecasting methodologies that are applicable to a wide variety of real-world business applications. The practicing demand forecaster will find that the techniques explained in this book provide preliminary models necessary to achieve improvements in data quality before building increasingly complex models. Likewise, managers and end users of forecasts will find in this book a comprehensive treatment of how to evaluate basic forecasting approaches. In addition, the material offers a guide (including checklists) to using, interpreting, and communicating practical forecasting results.

For the practicing forecaster and planner, student, and researcher, the book will be of interest because it extends the basic principles to meet the need of the experienced forecaster. The development of the book progresses in a natural fashion from the basic, most-widely used techniques to the more sophisticated, less familiar algorithms. In this progression, the book includes up-to-date statistical forecasting tools in exploratory data analysis, intermittent lead-time demand forecasting, elements of robust/resistant estimation, exception handling and root-cause diagnostics, state-space forecasting models, and structured, relational database management for forecasting decision support.

This book shows how to analyze and forecast variables by emphasizing basic forecasting techniques. It begins the analysis with traditional approaches and follows them with resistant (those that safeguard against outliers and unusual values) and robust (those that safeguard against departures from classical normality assumptions) alternatives to the same problems. More advanced techniques, including the ARIMA (Autoregressive-Integrated-Moving Average) models based on the Box-Jenkins methodology, and some dynamic regression and econometric modeling with multiple variables, are considered as well. However, some more esoteric techniques, such as neural networks, vector autoregression, and GARCH, are not included because they appear to be more relevant in applications to financial business and macroeconomic forecasting.

Many examples are drawn from the experience of practicing forecasters, teachers and consultants in industry. My personal experience suggests that modern demand forecasting applications contain a common thread independent of the particular supply chain or industry. That is, the characteristics of the data and the structured modeling steps required are vital to the understanding of any forecasting technique. However, as I stress throughout the book, the context of the business problem must not be forgotten; it plays a vital role throughout the forecasting endeavor. Data sets from a variety of real company sources have also been used throughout to make certain points or illustrate a particular technique.

## Coverage

My experience suggests that, in practice, the failure of many forecasting efforts begins with flaws in the quality and handling of data rather than in the lack of modeling sophistication. Thus, my objective has been to place greater emphasis on data-analytic methodology (much of it intuitive and graphical) as a key to improved demand forecasting.

A number of forecasting techniques useful to students and researchers of forecasting are not covered in great detail in this book. The omitted techniques are typically used when quantitative data are scarce or nonexistent. As an example, the whole field of technological forecasting, which requires grounding in probabilistic (in contrast to data-analytic) statistical concepts, is not treated. Because this book deals with exploratory data analysis along with confirmatory modeling, I have emphasized techniques for which a reasonable amount of data is available or can be collected.

The focus and emphasis on formal statistical approaches for empirical work in most forecasting books are rooted in the days of limited computing power and data storage capability. Much of the subject matter in those texts are mathematically elegant; others are designed to make it easy for the instructor to provide packaged lectures, problem exercises and test questions. My experience in the corporate world suggests that statistical theory tends to be over-emphasized at the expense of data quality with real data. Although not grounded as firmly in theory, simpler approaches can frequently do as well as, and at times surprisingly better than, their complex cousins.

The computer has made it feasible to warehouse lots of relevant data in 'big data' repositories and process complex predictive analytic algorithms in a flash, or in the cloud, as the case may be. We are now able to effectively analyze ever-larger amounts of data, much of this through graphical means and data mining techniques from data warehouses/cloud-based data repositories, in shorter timeframes than ever before. We are entering the petabyte (PB = $10^{15}$ bytes) era on the way to the yottabyte (YB = $10^{24}$ bytes) of data storage capability. The availability of relevant data, simple paradigms, and the experience of individual demand forecasters needs to be more balanced than ever before.

Economics, mathematics and mathematical statistics have provided much of the formal underpinnings and rationale in the demand forecasting practice before the widespread availability of desktop computing power. As a result, certain statistical tools, such as hypothesis testing, are omitted from this book. In fact, formal hypothesis testing is not really required for demand forecasting because confidence measures and prediction intervals give, for all practical purposes, identical results and are closer to the business realities. I understand this goes along with some recent trends occurring in statistics curricula for business students.

## Courseware

The material in this book can be used for turnkey courses and training workshops for enhancing the professional skills of forecasters performing the demand forecasting function in supply chain environments. I can suggest three courses here:

## A. Introduction to Demand Forecasting (IDF)

**Target population:** This course is intended for entry-level forecasters and forecast users requiring a working knowledge and understanding of market and demand forecasting in the modern supply chain. This course is also recommended for managers in sales, marketing, budgeting, human resources and operational organizations, who require an appreciation in the use of quantitative and qualitative forecasting techniques.

**Description:** IDF is designed to provide the hands-on skills for dealing effectively with the principles and techniques of data analysis, graphical presentation and interpretation of forecasting models and results. The course focuses on those forecasting techniques for products and services that have become the most widely accepted and prominently used by forecasters in industry. Topics are drawn from chapters 1 - 8 , 12, 14.

## B. Data Analysis and Forecast Modeling (DAFM)

**Target Population:** This course is intended for intermediate forecasters and analysts with some background and experience in quantitative analyses. This course is also recommended for managers in sales, marketing, budgeting, human resources and operational organizations, who require a sound foundation in the use of statistical modeling tools for macro-level forecasting applications.

**Description**: DAFM is designed to provide the enhanced statistical skills for understanding the theoretical and empirical foundations upon which data analysis and statistical forecasting models are based. This course focuses on skill-based techniques for exploratory data analysis, data quality, data visualization, trend/seasonal time series models, regression/econometric applications, residuals and forecast error analysis, and presentation of results occurring in a broad range of industrial forecasting applications. Topics are drawn from the following chapters: 1- 11.

## C. Agile Demand Forecasting (ADF)

**Target Population:** This course is intended for the experienced forecasters and analysts with at least two years of active involvement in demand forecasting at the corporate level. Some background and experience in quantitative modeling and analysis is highly desirable.

**Description:** ADF is designed to provide automated, databased forecasting simulations of real-world demand forecasting applications in the cloud. The material covers techniques for exploratory data analysis, data quality, database management, predictive visualization, chance distributions, intermittent demand, automated forecast modeling, regression/econometric modeling, residual analysis, and presentation of results occurring in a broad range of demand forecasting applications in industry. Topics are drawn from the following chapters: 1- 14.

Other options for using this material include:

- **Train-the-Trainer Services**. Enable organizations to achieve a quick, effective start-up of training to provide timely services for new hires, organizational changes or redeployment of resources.
- **Customized Training**. Courses can be adapted to provide specific modules addressing the needs of distinct audiences involved in forecasting: power users, casual users of forecasts, managerial users, and new hires.
- **On-site Training**. Same courses held at a corporate training facility.
- **Training an Installed Base on software upgrades**. Provide continuity of usage of forecasting software systems adopted by forecasting organizations.

## Organization

This book is divided into five parts. The first part **framing the Demand Forecasting Process** is comprised of four chapters on how to start making a forecast, introducing the demand forecasting process along with preliminary data analysis, a classification of forecasting techniques, and forecast accuracy measurement. The three chapters of Part II cover **Exploring Historical Data** with chapters on characterizing demand variability in terms of: seasonality, trend, and the uncertainty factor; dealing with seasonal fluctuations, and forecasting trend-cycles with turning points. The next two chapters in Part III concern **Automated Forecasting Techniques: The State-Space Approach** with chapters on baseline forecasting with exponential smoothing models and the comprehensive Box-Jenkins methodology for the ARIMA family of univariate linear models. In Part IV on **Creating Causal Forecasting Models**, two chapters cover demand forecasting with classical data-generating regression models, intermittent demand forecasting with the new *Structured Inference Base* (**SIB**) models, and gaining credibility through root cause analysis and exception handling. These techniques are used primarily for short-term, operational forecasting applications with causal factors. Part V (**Improving Forecasting Agility with the PEER Process**) examines the analytic and management needs for acquiring agility in demand forecasting performance. These three chapters deal with delivering the final forecast numbers; creating a data framework for Agile Forecasting® and decision support, and blending Agile Forecasting® with an integrated business planning process.

## DEDICATION
*I would very much like to thank my wonderful wife Suzanne and my family, for their patience and understanding of yet another distraction into writing a book.*

# Acknowledgments

I am deeply indebted to my friend and former co-author Jim Cleary, who collaborated on this book project for over 30 years. Without his earlier contributions to the practice and teaching of demand forecasting in the Bell System, this book and its earlier versions would never have seen the light of day.

More recently, I have been inspired and influenced by my new friend and namesake Hans Amell, who, as a strong proponent of agile approaches to mastering uncertainty in the business world, has just published a thought-provoking book *Mastering Agility – Successfully Navigating Uncertainty,* co-authored with Kurt Larsson.

One contributor from my 40+-year association with the *International Institute of Forecasters (IIF)* has enabled me to include a variety of Excel-based tools that form the basis for the hands-on portions of the CPDF® professional development (www.cpdftraining.org) workshops for supply chain practitioners that I have been conducting for more than a decade around the world: Professor Everette S. Gardner, Jr. (University of Houston) was instrumental in introducing spreadsheet forecasting tools for students and practitioners. Dr. Gardner also pioneered and implemented the first automated statistical forecasting algorithms that illustrate many of the practical forecasting and data analytic tools used throughout this book. Also, Professor Len Tashman, (University of Vermont) generously provided examples from his work on forecast accuracy measurement and forecast simulation methods.

In addition, I appreciate the encouragement, support, and feedback from a number of *IIF* members, former colleagues and thought leaders whose ideas helped shape the vision of this book: James Alleman (U of Colorado), Scott Armstrong (Wharton U), Bill

Brelsford (Bell Labs), Simon Conradie (Noetic Consulting, South Africa), Lew Coopersmith (Rider College), Isis Santos Costa (Rocket.Chat, Brazil), Estela Bee Dagum (U of Bologna, Italy), Lorraine Denby (Bell Labs), Robert Fildes (Lancaster U, UK), Wil Gorr (Carnegie Mellon U), Rob Hausman (AT&T), Jon Kettenring (Bell Labs), Anne Koehler (Miami U), Larry Lapide (MIT), Michael Lawrence (U New South Wales, Australia), Spyros Makridakis (INSEAD, France), Elliott Mandelman (Consultant), Keith Ord (George Washington U), Stephen Parkoff (Consultant), Roy Pearson (College of William and Mary). Robert Samohyl (UFSC, Brazil), Paul Savage (Iona College), Bill Williams (Bell Labs), and Lilian Wu (IBM Research).

Among forecasting and business planning professionals I have worked with, I should mention Lori Appelhans (Skil-Bosch), Chuck Biggar (IBM), Sharon Boyer (Blommer Chocolate), Erin Bromley-Gans (UTi, South Africa), Ron Buchanan (Haemonetics), Len Digristina (Kodak), Jared Endicott (Verizon Wireless), Mohsen Hamoudia (Orange, France), Tae Yoon Lee (SAS Inst.), Mark Luther (Volvo NA), Christine Mathers (AT&T), Cynthia McClain (Haemonetics), Kirshnee Moodley (UTi, South Africa), Danie Payne (Eskom, South Africa), Blake Reuter (Bell Labs), Leon Schwartz (Pitney Bowes), Rachel Seligman (Pfizer), Jon Senior (Darlington Fabrics), Bill Sichel (Revlon), Otto Tomasek (Bell Canada), Amy Waters (Coca Cola Bottling NY), and Pete Weber (IBM).

Forgive me for an unintended senior moment if I left someone out.

**Hans Levenbach, PhD**                    **December, 2021**

# WHY DEMAND FORECASTING IS SO CRUCIAL TO SUPPLY CHAIN PLANNERS

The Supply Chain

### 1. Analyzing Customer Demand: What should we make and when?

Based on customer demand, product design, cost, and pricing considerations, the ice cream manufacturer (as in Cases 1A, 3A–8A, 10A, 13A–15A) sets the supply chain in motion. For instance, cocoa beans for making chocolate will be sourced from Africa or South America.

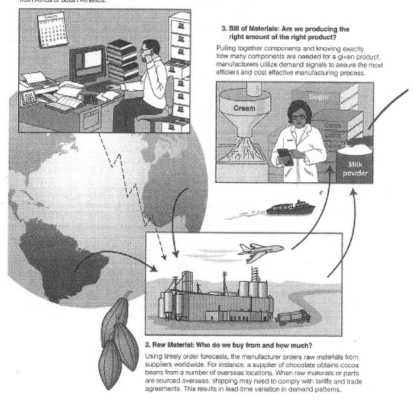

### 3. Bill of Materials: Are we producing the right amount of the right product?

Pulling together components and knowing exactly how many components are needed for a given product, manufacturers utilize demand signals to assure the most efficient and cost effective manufacturing process.

### 2. Raw Material: Who do we buy from and how much?

Using timely order forecasts, the manufacturer orders raw materials from suppliers worldwide. For instance, a supplier of chocolate obtains cocoa beans from a number of overseas locations. When raw materials or parts are sourced overseas, shipping may need to comply with tariffs and trade agreements. This results in lead-time variation in demand patterns.

# AND MANAGERS IN THE GLOBAL SUPPLY CHAIN
# OF AN ICE CREAM MANUFACTURER

**4. Assembly: How do we make the final product?**

As parts move along the assembly line, subassemblies are transformed into finished goods. Inventory and shipping information is communicated throughout the channel to distribution and retail/wholesale sites.

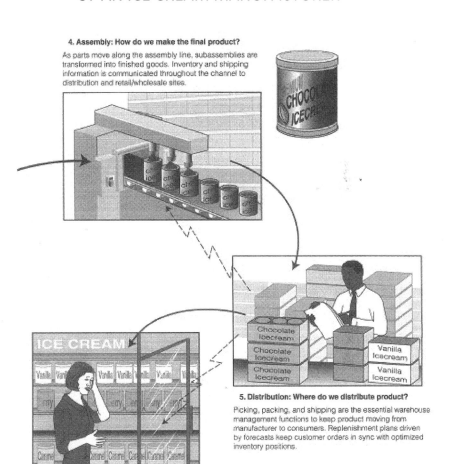

**5. Distribution: Where do we distribute product?**

Picking, packing, and shipping are the essential warehouse management functions to keep product moving from manufacturer to consumers. Replenishment plans driven by forecasts keep customer orders in sync with optimized inventory positions.

**6. Retail/Wholesale: What is the proper assortment and allocation of merchandise in stores?**

Accurate forecasts assure that the right amount of the right product is available to consumers when they need it. Poor forecasts can lead to overstocks, out-of-stocks and loss of profit.

# 1

## Why Demand Forecasting is So Crucial to Supply Chain Planners and Managers

*The earth is degenerating these days. Bribery and corruption abound. Children no longer mind parents. Every man wants to write a book, and it is evident that the end of the world is approaching fast.*

ATTRIBUTED TO AN ANCIENT TEXT

This introductory chapter describes

- what a demand forecasting process is
- why it is a necessary discipline for demand planners and managers to become familiar with
- a new role for demand managers in a modern, consumer data-driven supply chain
- how, when, where, and by whom the demand forecasting job is done
- the systematic steps for an agile execution of the demand forecasting process in the supply chain

As you begin to read this book, you may find it helpful to keep the following in mind:

- A grasp of economics, demographics, computer science and statistics, although necessary for a demand forecaster, will not in itself ensure successful demand forecasting practices.
- For the best results, apply such knowledge within a sound framework—a demand-forecasting process.

- Following a sound process, which describes the sequence of activities to be followed, can reduce chances of inadvertently overlooking a key step.
- The omission of a key step, whether deliberate or inadvertent, can jeopardize a forecaster's credibility, and credibility is a forecaster's livelihood.

After reading this chapter, you should be able to

- create a visual representation of your business in relation to sources of demand for products and services in the industry and how it links to the consumer (end user) or customer (organization/account)
- understand the motivation behind exploring and quantifying sources of variation in demand
- create graphical representations of the variation in demand in terms of seasonality (economic consumer habit), trend (demographic consumer growth), and other quantifiable factors, including uncertainty.

## Inside the Crystal Ball

A wise person once said that he/she who lives by the crystal ball soon learns to eat ground glass. The same sage left this advice for all managers pressed to provide their corporate bosses with projections: Give them a number or give them a date, but never give them both. Unfortunately, those in the business of forecasting the **demand** for products and services must provide both numbers and a timeline.

## Determinants of Demand

Economists have long attempted to determine what causes people to behave as they do in the marketplace. Over the years, one aspect of this research has evolved into a theory of demand. In theory, demand expresses the inverse relationship between price and quantity; it shows the maximum amount of money consumers are willing and able to pay for each additional unit of some commodity, or the maximum amount of the commodity they are willing and able to purchase at a given price.

There may not be enough of the commodity available to satisfy the demand. Economists concern themselves not with a single item purchased by members of a group (a market) but rather with a continuous flow of purchases by that group. Therefore, demand is expressed in terms of the amount desired per hour, per day, per month, or per year.

There are a number of **determinants of demand**. The demand for international holiday tourism, for instance, is known to depend on a number of factors including (a) the origin population (the higher the number of people resident in a country, the greater the number of trips taken abroad), (b) origin country real income and personal disposable income, (c) cost of travel to the destination and the cost of living for the tourist in the destination, and (d) a relative price index relating substitution between tourist visits to a foreign destination and domestic tourism.

## Demand Forecasting Defined

The simplest definition of forecasting is that it is a process that has as its objective the prediction of future events or conditions. More precisely, forecasting attempts to predict change in the presence of uncertainty. Demand Forecasting is all about *change* and *chance*. If future events represented only a quantifiable change from historical events, future events or chance conditions could be readily predicted through quantitative projections of historical patterns into the future. Methodologies that are used to describe historical events with mathematical equations (or models) for the purpose of predicting future events are classified as quantitative modeling techniques. However, there is much more to forecasting than projecting past trends.

Experience and intuitive reasoning quickly reveal that future events or chance conditions are not solely a function of historical patterns. Demand varies with tastes, total market size, average income, distribution of income, the price of the good or service, and the prices of competing and complementary goods.

Even familiar abstractions such as trend, cycle, and seasonality, although extremely useful to business planners, cannot be completely relied upon when it comes to predicting future events. In addition, in the commercial world, goods and services are bought by individuals for innumerable reasons. Therefore, demand forecasting must include other ingredients to complement quantitative modeling techniques.

A demand forecast is not an end product but rather an input to an integrated business planning process. A demand forecast provides advice to planners and decision-makers as to what is likely to happen under an assumed set of circumstances. Often, a forecast is a prediction of future values of one or more variables under "business as usual" conditions. In planning activities, this is often referred to as the status quo or the **baseline**. Forecasts are also required for a variety of "what if" situations and for the formulation of business plans to alter base case projections that have proved unsatisfactory.

> *Demand forecasting is the process of predicting future consumer and customer demand for a firm's goods and services with quantified uncertainty.*

## Why Demand Forecasting?

Forecasting for demand planning and management in the supply chain generally attempts to predict future consumer/customer demand for a firm's goods and services. Customers tend to be loosely defined as either consumers (individuals at checkout counters) or accounts through which goods or services are ordered. For some time, this process had been closely linked to sales and marketing. Within the corporation, sales forecasting has suffered from a lack of credibility, corporate ridicule, and shortcomings in accuracy. Within the marketplace, business media have commented on the inability of economic forecasters to predict recessions, as per the 1996 Fortune writer who said, "The biggest problem with macro-economic forecasters is that they generally can't tell us what we most want to know."

So, why bother with forecasting? It is generally recognized that accurate, credible forecasts are necessary to provide significant improvements in manufacturing, distribution, and the operations of retail firms. Over time, demand forecasting has become much more focused on the disaggregate elements of product demand for supplying warehouses, distributors, channels, and consumers than on economic and financially driven aggregates. In recent times, the scope of demand forecasting has broadened to include forecasting more detailed, micro elements of the demand for goods and services from socio-geographic and microeconomic, behavioral patterns of consumers. Data-driven demand forecasting of the *right* amount of the *right* product in the *right* place at the *right* time and at the *right* price is one of the underpinnings of a **demand management** practice in the supply chain.

The starting point for the forecasting process is to identify all the things that are needed to put a forecast together. These are inputs. Typical inputs include finding sources of **data** about the item to be forecast; obtaining information about external conditions, that is, about factors in the environment influencing a forecast; determining the needs of the user of the forecast; gathering the human and financial resources required to produce a forecast; and listing projection techniques. These are inputs not only to the forecasting process but also to the forecaster's judgment, which is applied throughout the process. The forecasting process also requires knowledge about the outputs of the process: formatting the output of the final product, presenting the forecast to the forecast users, and evaluating forecast errors on an ongoing basis.

> *The forecast user will generally specify the format of the forecast output and collaborate with the forecaster about the kinds of analyses and/or variables that should be considered.*

Once forecasting needs have been identified, a data-gathering network capable of continuously providing pertinent information about market conditions must be established. The data that have been gathered are then placed into some form of a relational database or **forecast decision support platform** (FDSP) for ease of analysis (to be discussed in Chapter 13). Data gathering and analysis can be very time-consuming and should both precede and follow the production of the forecast.

The end product of the forecasting process is clearly the forecast itself. A forecast should not be considered permanent or never changing. The dynamic nature of any market (i.e., consumer demands for goods and services) dictates that the forecasting process be revisable and repeatable at some future time. Because the value of any forecast is based on the degree to which it can provide advice in a decision-making process, the view of a market and its demands on a company within that marketplace (as expressed in terms of a forecast) must be current to be credible. In the next section, we describe the demand forecasting process as an integral part of a supply chain.

## The Role of Demand Forecasting in Data-Driven Supply Chains

Traditionally, much of the responsibility for forecasting in corporations resides with Sales Forecasters (*Sell what you can make*). After all, they are closest to knowing what customer needs are. However, that role prescribed a process of determining what the business is expected to sell, based on what it could produce. The function of the sales forecaster represents an internally driven, traditional push paradigm of the supply chain.

In a **traditional** supply chain, product flows through a system from one level to another (Figure 1.1) in a linear fashion. Driven by manufacturers and suppliers, the traditional supply chain is the furthest away from the ultimate consumer or end user. Each operating unit tends to maintain its own forecast information system (mostly in spreadsheets) and communication flows that occur between individual departments (referred to as **silos**).

In the 21$^{st}$ century, dominated by global economics and eCommerce, the term supply chain has taken on a broader meaning. The **Council of Supply Chain Management Professionals** (CSCMP) (*http://cscmp.org*) defines a supply chain as the "material and informational interchanges in the logistical process stretching from acquisition of raw materials to delivery of finished products to the end user. All vendors, service providers and customers are links in the supply chain." This definition is a mouthful, but it underlies the recognition that competition is no longer limited to individual companies vying against each other.

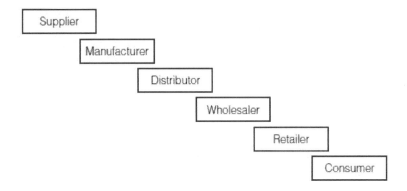

Figure 1.1 Traditional supply chain: Sell what you can make.

*A traditional supply chain is any sequential set of business operations leading from raw material through conversion processes, storage, distribution, and delivery to an end customer or consumer. In the 21st century data-driven supply chain, demand information flows in the reverse direction as well.*

## Sell What You Can Make

• Assume predictable, continuous demand

• Efficient process

• No external drivers of demand

## Make What You Can Sell

• Assume unpredictable, discontinuous demand

• Adaptive process

• Both internal and external drivers of demand

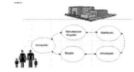

Figure 1.2 Traditional (Sell What You Can Make) vs. consumer data-driven (Make What You Can Sell) supply chains.

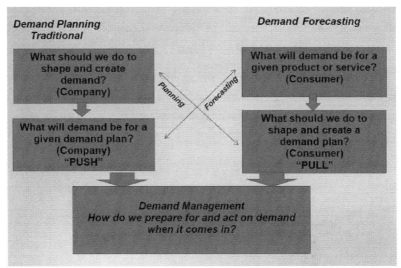

Figure 1.3 A paradigm shift: A traditional Demand Management (DM) process *(left flowchart)* versus a consumer-driven 21st Century DM process *(right flowchart)*. Source of left flowchart – Larry Lapide (MIT)

In the context of a 21st century consumer-driven "pull" supply chain (e.g., e-commerce), the demand forecaster makes detailed statements about future demand for products and services in the face of uncertainty. A demand forecast is not just a number, outcome or task. It is part of an ongoing process directly affecting sales, marketing, inventory, production and all other aspects of the modern supply chain (Figures 1.2 and 1.3).

Demand forecasting and planning is the process that drives inventory levels to improve a company's ability to replenish or fulfill product to meet customer (and ultimate consumer) needs in a timely and cost-effective way. If forecasting does not have a good link to drive inventory stocks, improving it won't necessarily improve customer service levels or reduce costs (Figure 1.4).

*An effective forecaster can start with a simple demand theory without having to build complex models.*

Demand managers must then reconcile their planning approaches with the assumptions for the future so that the most credible methodology will produce accurate and reliable forecasts. The Demand Management (DM) process makes use of computerized intelligence to synchronize and optimize essential elements of manufacture and distribution.

Demand planners and managers use item-level (disaggregated) forecast data from a number of sources to create a clear view of what product demand is likely to be, and then link inventory and replenishment processes to that future view. This bottom up-demand forecast incorporates a logical and coherent series of steps that, if performed in a consistent, management-supported fashion, can improve forecasting effectiveness, reliability and credibility throughout the supply chain (Figure 1.5).

> *Demand management (DM) refers to getting the right amount of the right product to where it is needed, while managing unproductive inventory levels to achieve maximum return on assets.*

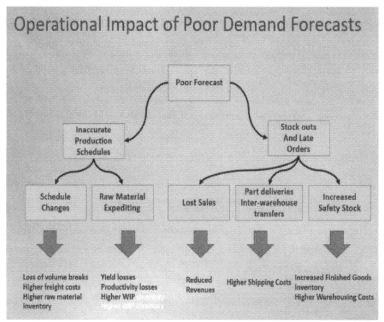

Figure 1.4 Operational impact of poor forecasts in the supply chain (courtesy Simon Conradie – Noetics Business Consulting, RSA

## Is Demand Forecasting Worthwhile?

The process of demand forecasting is not an exact science; it is more like an art form. As with any worthwhile art form, the forecasting process is definitive and systematic and is supported by a set of special tools and techniques that are dependent upon human informed judgment and experience.

An effective demand forecaster can develop a simple demand theory without having to build complex models. For example, you may be required to project the sales of a product or service per household.

A total sales forecast can be obtained by multiplying the forecast of this ratio by an independent forecast of the number of households. In this way, an important relationship can be modeled that uses relatively simple methods. This gives a first approximation, which can provide valuable and timely information to decision-makers.

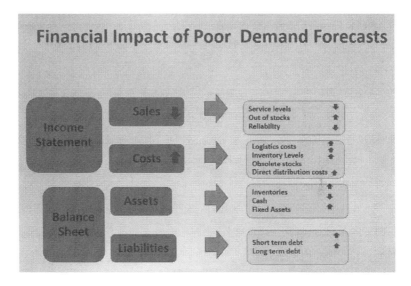

Figure 1.5 Financial impact of poor forecasts in the supply chain (Courtesy Simon Conradie – Noetric Business Consulting, RSA).

The demand forecaster is an **advisor**. The completed forecast must meet the requirements of the end user in terms of timeliness, format, methodology, and presentation. In the forecaster end-user relationship, the end-user has **domain expertise** about the environment surrounding the problem and variables that should be considered. The forecaster is knowledgeable about the forecasting process and specific forecasting techniques and models most appropriate for the problem. In most multi-national firms, the volume and complexity of required forecasts is usually sufficient to support a well-trained, professional demand forecasting staff.

*The demand forecaster is an advisor, not just a producer of numbers.*

## Who Are the End Users of Demand Forecasts in the Supply Chain?

The diversity of business activities creates work for many kinds of planners, or end users of forecasts; each with a special set of problems.

The problems may be viewed in terms of the impact of poor forecasting on a business function and a time horizon for that function.

- **Executive managers** are concerned with current performance but even more concerned with future direction - strategic planning. In which markets should the business operate over the next five to 30 years? An executive manager must identify and analyze key trends and forces that may affect the formulation and execution of strategies, including economic trends, technological developments, regulatory climates, market conditions, and assessment of potential competitors.
- **Financial managers** are concerned with financial planning, for which they need short-term (one to three months), medium-term (up to 24 months), and long-term (more than two years) forecasts. For example, cash flow projections are needed to negotiate lines of credit in the short term and estimates for capital investment for planning in the long term (Figure 1.5).
- **Sales and marketing managers** are concerned with short- and long-term forecasts of demand of products and services. Forecasting techniques suited to products and services have existed for some time. In forecasting a *new* product or service, these techniques are applicable if analogous products exist or if careful market trials can be conducted. The demand for the product can then be related to the economic or demographic profiles of the **population** in the market areas. These relationships can then be used to predict the product's acceptance and profitability in other areas having their own economic and demographic characteristics.
- **Planners of competitive strategies** use forecasting techniques to forecast the total market - for example, total gasoline consumption, passenger-miles of traffic between cities, automobile purchases by size (sedan, compact, and subcompact), and computer storage requirements. Given the total market, each firm within it will then estimate its market share on the basis of product differences, price, advertising, quality of service, market coverage (including the size of the sales force), geography, and other factors specific to the market for the product or service. In many cases, market share is also estimated by using quantitative modeling approaches.
- **Production and inventory managers** are often concerned with very short-term forecasts (hours, days, weeks). Production managers use forecasts to plan raw material and capacity requirements and schedule resources for manufacturing. In

inventory management, exponential smoothing models find extensive application. (This important technique is like a weighted moving average, in which the most current data are given the greatest weight.) For extremely complex inventory systems, these models can produce many forecasts with varying degrees of uncertainty, which are closely monitored for unusual deviations between estimated and actual inventories. Sometimes deviations can be interpreted as event-driven and can be modeled to alter demand projections. Large deviations are flagged as exceptions, for future scrutiny and reevaluation of the forecast-generating model.

## Learning from Industry Examples

Throughout this book, we will examine practical forecasting problems from the author's broad experience as a practitioner in industry, consultant to forecasting organizations, and instructor to managers and students interested in learning about demand forecasting. Where appropriate, we also use time series (historical data about changes through time) from real-world sources to illustrate forecasting techniques and models and to compare or contrast results.

*A time series is a set of chronologically ordered values of historical data, such as the sales revenue received by month, units shipped by week, or energy consumed per hour or day for an extended period.*

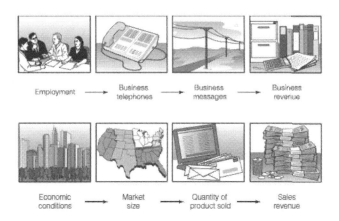

Figure 1.6 Sales-revenue forecasting example for telecommunications.

The telecommunications industry illustrates a number of considerations common to many market-based forecasting applications (Figure 1.6 top frames). The global market that generates business telecom revenues may be viewed, in part, as the number of business telephones from which calls can be made. Messages (calls) are regarded as the quantity of service rendered (or product sold).

The forecasting problems, borrowed from industrial experience, arise from the requirement for accurate, timely, and reliable forecasts of demand, sales revenues, product shipments, and services; throughout we develop forecasts of these items from actual data under realistic assumptions.

The correspondence between revenues and messages is not one-to-one because additional factors, such as the geographical location of the parties and duration of calls, cause variation in the revenue per message. In general, the overall state of the economy, as measured by an economic indicator such as nonfarm employment, is known to influence the demand for business telecom service (Figure 1.6 bottom frames)

## Examples of Product Demand

As an example of product demand, consider the market for selling books online or in bookstores. The college textbook publishing industry is a particularly challenging area for demand forecasters. College textbooks, like fashion products, are highly polished products. They require years of preparation and are geared for a very limited yet noncaptive market. Accurately forecasting the potential demand for each title seems crucial. To provide book publishers with some assistance in conceptualizing the role of demand forecasting in the textbook industry, it is useful to create a visual representation or model of the publishing industry (Figure 1.7, *left frame*).

 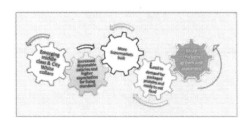

Figure 1.7 (*left*): Demand for e-books. (*right*): Demand for fast foods.

In another example, the economic growth in China in recent years has created a rapidly growing middle class and city white-collar jobs. These expanding demographics have increased disposable incomes that help raise living standards. People seek food that is both high in protein and convenient to the consumer. Supermarket chains expand and establish more stores to meet the demand, resulting in the increase of the consumption for ready-to-eat packaged foods. A Consumer-Packaged Goods (CPG) manufacturer supplies more and varied products, such as chicken, for the fast-foods (FMCG) market to fulfill the demand from consumers (Figure 1.7, *right frame*).

Different measures of economic activity, such as interest rates, industrial production, the unemployment rate, gross domestic product (GDP), volume of imports versus exports, and inflation rates, have special significance in other industries to help determine the size of some market at a designated time and place.

The revenue-quantity relationship, in the most general sense, is similar to that encountered in forecasting revenues from passenger miles of transportation, mortgage commitments from housing starts, expenditures for goods and services purchased during tourism travel, tax revenues from retail sales, and revenues from barrels of crude oil after refining. In each instance, the revenue depends on the mix of the products sold or services provided. However, for financial planning purposes, accurate aggregate revenue forecasts can often be derived without the necessity of forecasting every product or product combination and multiplying that by a sales price.

The CPG industry provides a somewhat broader sales and operational (S&OP) forecasting application, in which inventory, bills of material, routings, lead times, and customer orders must be accurately forecasted in a timely way before schedules and plans can be effectively established. Sales and operational forecasting incorporate the business plan, sales plan, production plan, and marketing plans into one information source. Detailed demand forecasts are prepared as inputs for planning inventory, establishing customer service, and determining production loads. They must be created at a disaggregated level in order to account for the product and customer detail required for manufacturing operations.

In the retail industry, department store sales may be influenced by a number of regional economic variables such as the **consumer price index**, average weekly earnings, and the unemployment rate. Retailers may also feel that the number of shopping days between Thanksgiving and Christmas has a major impact on the Christmas holiday sales volume, so their needs tend to be expressed by accurate disaggregated unit forecasts. Likewise, the shifting Ramadan holiday period will impact sales volumes reported for the month the holiday occurs.

Market planning and forecasting at electric utilities require demand and energy models, where demand refers to the level of electricity consumption at a particular instant in time and place, and energy refers to the level of total use of electricity over a given period of time. Residential electricity consumption is highly influenced by weather, economic, and demographic factors. Weather influences are measured by heating degree-days and cooling degree-days. The economic factors used are price and disposable income, and the demographic influences include size and age of dwelling, age of family residents, number and type of electrical appliances, and type of space and water heating equipment.

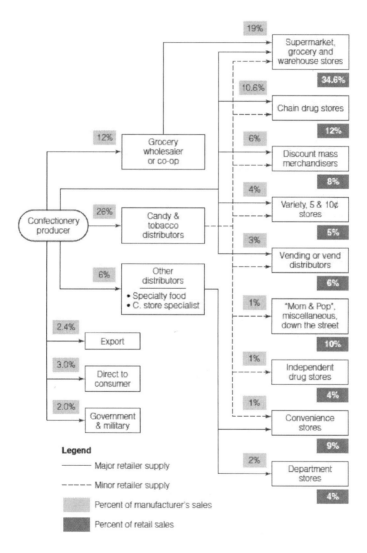

Figure 1.8 Comprehensive view of a U.S. confectionary packaged goods producer.

> *Demand forecasting for Sales and Operations planning (S&OP) drives marketing, sales, logistics, production, and financial plans to determine disaggregated production plans of product demand or services*

Figure 1.8 depicts a broad visualization of a packaged goods producer (retailer sums to 92.6%). The manufacturer produces a product for export, direct sales to consumers, the government, and the military; and sales to an extensive network of retailers. A grocery wholesaler or co-op retailer might distribute the product to supermarkets, grocery stores, and warehouse stores. Other distributors sell the product to chain drug stores, discount mass merchandisers, and variety stores. The entities being forecast are often product groupings segmented by geography (sales region or market zone) and customer-specific categories (warehouses, channels, or accounts).

> *Credible forecasting means that you will never have to be certain.*

## The Demand Planner's Dilemma: Is a Forecast Just a Number or Something More?

Consider the demand for building products—for Turkey in this example, or any other published forecast of a product or service around the world. You might find a forecast as depicted in Figure 1.9. The overall growth rate in 2010 is stated as 11.5%. For 2011–2015, it is projected to be 14.5%. The actual numbers are not of interest here. We want to focus on what was omitted. As stated, the implications are that this forecast is projected to have a accuracy of + or − 0%, either exactly right or totally wrong. This is not credible.

### FORECASTS FOR TURKISH BUILDING MATERIALS INDUSTRY

| 2010: | ➤ PRODUCTION VOLUME | : 68,1 BILLION TL |
| | ➤ OVERALL GROWTH RATE | : 11,5 % |
| 2011-2015: | ➤ GROWTH RATE | : 14,5% |

Source: ENR & IMSAD Research Report, Distribution Network and Channels in Building Materials Sector, 2011

Figure 1.9 Is a forecast just a number? Growth rates without uncertainty.

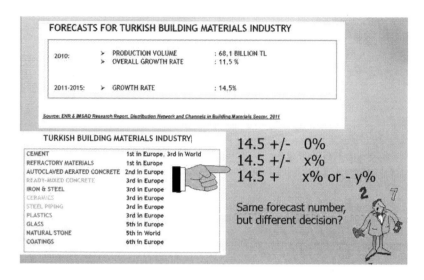

Figure 1.10 When a single forecast can lead to potentially different decisions, because of unspecified uncertainty.

What would a credible forecast be? Why is it necessary to be able to quantify uncertainty for a forecast? Depending on decisions made based on the forecast, it should be apparent that the same forecast number could also be (14.5%: + 1.5% or– 1.5%), or say (14.5%: + 1% or– 3%) as shown in Figure 1.10. These could have different implications as

forecast advice for demand and supply chain planners. Thus, credible demand forecasts are incomplete without a stated measure of uncertainty. Yet the prevailing forecast question asked of demand planners by managers in supply chain organizations today is "What is the number?!!"

Tens of thousands of years ago, if you asked a group of tribe members and community leaders to raise their right hand if they believed the earth was flat, all hands would go up. Yet, today some people would do so, but if you were to ask a group of supply chain planners and managers today whether they believe a forecast is just a number, most hands would go up also. What is wrong with this picture? Today most people would not raise their hand for a flat earth theory, but they do appear to believe that a forecast is just a number. A *flat earth mindset* among demand planners and forecast practitioners still prevails.

Imagine taking a long airplane trip between Chicago and Shanghai. On the cabin screens, you can follow your flight on the flat earth map in front of you. Following a best *flat earth* forecast of fuel needed would take you along a *straight line* on this map. But, why does the pilot not follow your forecasted number of the amount of fuel needed? The airplane appears to be flying a much 'longer' flight that is curved. How accurate would that appear to a flat-earth forecast planner or manager?

While we know a curvature dimension must be added to a flat earth model to be accurate, should demand planners and managers continue believing and behaving as if a demand **forecast is just a number**, ignoring the **uncertainty factor** as an essential **dimension of variability**?.

> *Uncertainty is a certain factor in demand forecasting and should not be ignored in an agile forecasting process.*

## *Creating a Structured Forecasting Process*

Suppose that you are responsible for making a forecast of the demand for a product or service in your company for use during the next few hours, days, weeks, months, quarters, or even years. How do you begin to plan your work? You start by defining a process that works for your environment like this:

1. **Define Objectives and Requirements:** Clearly define the objectives of the forecasting and planning application. Understand the specific requirements such as forecast horizon, granularity, and data sources.

2. **Data Collection and Preparation:** Gather historical data relevant to the forecasting problem. Clean and preprocess the data to handle missing values, outliers, and inconsistencies.

3. **Select Forecasting Methods:** Choose a range of forecasting methods suitable for the problem at hand. This could include statistical learning (SL) methods (e.g., ARIMA, exponential smoothing, linear regression), machine learning (ML) algorithms (e.g., nonlinear regression, classification, neural networks), or a combination of both.

4. **Baseline Model:** Establish a baseline model to benchmark the performance of other forecasting methods. This could be a simple method like N1 Naive forecasting or N2 Seasonal Naive forecasting.

5. **Model Training and Evaluation:** Train each forecasting model on a portion of the historical data and evaluate its performance on a separate validation set. As a start, use basic metrics such as Mean Absolute Error (MAE), Mean Squared Error (MSE), or others relevant to the specific objectives.

6. **Cross-Validation:** Employ cross-validation techniques such as k-fold cross-validation to assess the generalization performance of the models and ensure they are not overfitting to the training data.

7. **Ensemble Methods:** Explore ensemble methods such as model averaging or stacking to combine the predictions from multiple forecasting models. This can often improve forecast accuracy and robustness.

8. **Forecast Visualization:** Visualize the forecasted values alongside the actual data to gain insights into the performance of the forecasting methods. Identify any patterns, trends, or anomalies.

9. **Iterative Improvement:** Continuously refine and fine-tune the forecasting models based on the validation results and feedback from stakeholders. This may involve adjusting parameters, experimenting with different algorithms, or incorporating additional features.

10. **External Validation:** Validate the forecasting models on unseen data or in real-world scenarios to confirm their effectiveness and efficiency in practical applications. Monitor the performance over time and update the models as necessary.

11. **Documentation and Communication:** Document the validation process, including the chosen methods, evaluation results, and any assumptions made. Communicate the findings and recommendations to stakeholders as necessary.

The specific operations for each stage of the forecasting process are diagrammed in a flowchart below. We emphasize the iterative nature of the forecasting process. Note that each stage has a feedback loop, indicating the need to allow for time in the forecasting cycle to iterate back to the beginning of a stage, perhaps once or twice (at most). This is also a design criterion for implementing a forecast decision support platform (FDSP) (to be described in Chapter 13).

# The PEER Methodology: A Structured Demand Forecasting Process

Under PEER, the four key stages in which forecasting is done are prepare, execute, evaluate, and reconcile.

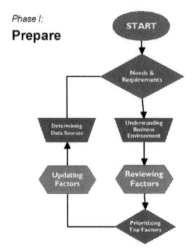

*Phase I:*

**Prepare**

**PEER Phase I: Prepare.** Of primary importance when we prepare a forecast is that better forecasts result when the proper process has been meticulously followed. At this stage, we try to identify and understand the context and data framework in which the forecast is to be developed. Note that each phase has a feedback loop, indicating that it may be necessary to loop back to the beginning of a phase at times.

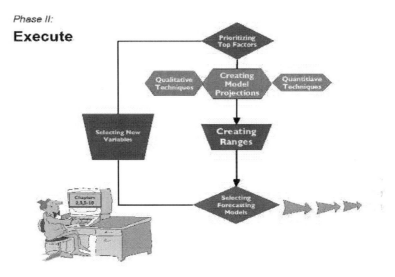

**PEER Phase II: Execute.** Once the forecasting context and a data framework have been established, we can turn to the execution stage. A systematic execution of a forecasting methodology leads to a better understanding of the factors that influence demand for a product or service. The demand forecaster who has a good handle on demographic, economic, political, geo-location-specific, competitive, and pricing considerations will develop the necessary expertise to make the most credible forecasts of the demand for a company's products and services.

**PEER Phase II: Evaluate.**

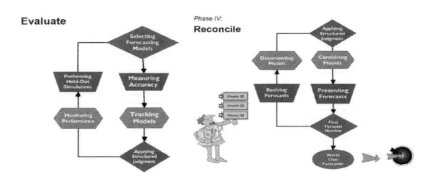

The forecasting cycle is typically an iterative process. Once the forecasting models are built, we still need to turn our attention to an evaluation stage before posting forecasts. How well have the models performed in the past? The process of forecasting focuses attention on evaluating forecasts and using the right methodology for a given forecast (for example, not using short-term methods for long-term forecasts)

**PEER Phase IV: Reconcile.** During the forecasting cycle, we could be  making changes to the models, projections and assumptions behind our forecasts. But in the end, we need to come up with a final forecast (embracing change and chance); essentially a set of assumptions and numbers on which the company can build its future plans. Instead of focusing on the plans they hope will result from a forecast, forecast managers and users must reconcile their planning approaches so that the most credible methodology will produce accurate forecasts. Selecting the right forecasting methodology is the focus of Chapter 3.

Together these stages make up the PEER methodology.

## *Case Example: A Consumer Electronics Company*

GLOBL (a fictitious company) is one of the leading international providers of consumer technology products to a broad range of worldwide customers. GLOBL's mission is to provide

- development, manufacturing, and sales of educational technology products
- development and sales of hardware and software systems to support these products
- a broad range of customer-support services ranging from demonstrations, training, consulting, and ongoing maintenance.

**The demand forecaster's role**. You have just been hired by GLOBL as a demand forecaster. You have received some on-site training and have visited various overseas offices to learn about the scope of the job, which is extensive. Your responsibilities are to provide forecasting services to all GLOBL business units. You must appropriately serve all aspects of GLOBL businesses, including planning for demand and supply, marketing, sales and operations, finance, new product development and introduction, and corporate strategy.

Your manager has observed that, as with any business function, there are not nearly enough forecasting resources to address all the potential needs at GLOBL. Thus, careful evaluation and prioritization of forecasting work activities must be done. Also, there is a great opportunity to become more agile by better synchronizing some of the forecasting services now separately performed for each GLOBL business area.

Your initial assignment is to the demand/supply planning area of GLOBL, and your first product forecasting responsibility is a set of high-tech consumer products. However, over the first five years in their careers, it is usual in GLOBL for forecasters to be rotated through several diverse product and services assignments—as well as different aspects of particular business areas.

Your job description as a demand forecaster includes

- forecasting the demand for a group of GLOBL's products
- providing regular coordinated communications with the development, sales, and marketing groups
- developing reliable modeling approaches to predict sales volumes providing periodic, objective, and credible forecasts to the sales and operations planning (S&OP) process, which will use this forecast for production and capacity planning over the subsequent six months
- providing monthly forecast updates and related information for revenue planning
- presenting and defending forecasts to senior management, as required
- reviewing forecasting performance
- on an ongoing basis with your user groups and information sources to identify areas needing improvement

## PEER Step 1: **PREPARE** by Identifying Factors Likely to Affect Changes in Demand

The first two activities of the Preparation phase involve defining the parameters that will govern the forecast and making first choices among alternative factors or drivers of demand. First, the forecaster identifies the forecast users and their information needs. For example, revenue forecasts are needed by a business to determine the expected net income and return on investment for a base case. You want to be certain that you have an understanding of which products or services should be measured in your forecast. These considerations help the forecaster answer the question: Can cost-effective, timely and agile forecasts be provided to assist planners or managers in making their decisions?

Next, a forecaster's own practical needs must be recognized; if they are overlooked, the credibility of the forecast will be diminished. Thus, you should consider your time, administrative support needed, expenses for computerized forecast production, and costs related to field visits.

A demand forecaster also needs information about the business environment in which a company operates: Which factors have affected the demand for a product or service in the past and are likely to affect the demand in the future?

For example, in the consumer goods industry, the demand for a product is forecast along with a measure of the effect (**price elasticity**) a change in price of a product will have on its demand. Or the demand forecaster may need to consider demographic, economic, and market factors: factors such as income, market potential, and fashion and consumer habits are usually an integral part of a formal demand theory:

- *Income* measures a consumer's ability to pay for a company's goods or services. The price of its goods or services and the prices of its competitors are certainly important.
- The *market potential* represents the total market for products or services being forecast. This might be the number of households or business establishments.
- *Fashion and consumer habit* are crucial because innovation and change create new products and services, thus causing people's tastes and habits to change. These changes must be monitored. For example, the introduction of air transportation caused people to change travel habits; the resulting impact on the railroad industry was tremendous. Also, the introduction of computers and smart phones has impacted people's work habits.

## The GLOBL Product Lines

Although GLOBL develops, manufactures, and sells a broad range of consumer products, you have three product lines, or families of products, for which you will develop forecasts (Figure 1.11):

- **Product line A** is a family of consumer products for early childhood development. The consumers for these products are preschool children in the autism spectrum. Their needs are for educational toys, games, and devices that allow them to better adapt to their environment and enhance their growth potential within the community.
- **Product line B** is a family of consumer products for academia and institutions of higher learning. The consumers for these products are students requiring specialized learning devices and educational materials to allow them to cope more effectively and competitively in a general academic environment.
- **Product line C** is a family of consumer products for the occupationally challenged. The consumers for these products are

adults in the workforce requiring customized aids for enhancing their productivity in the workplace.

## Product Lines

- *iFunBuddy* is a tablet designed for children with autism preloaded with specialized developmental and learning apps

- *iHearBuddy* is a tablet provides university students with disabilities a learning aid such as translating lectures

- *iWorkBuddy* caters for specialized needs of the workforce with disabilities

Figure 1.11 "*i*-Buddy" product line for GLOBL— iFunBuddy, iHearBuddy, and iWorkBuddy.

## The Marketplace for GLOBL Products

There are five major players in the worldwide educational technology marketplace, plus another dozen niche players. GLOBL has a centralized market intelligence staff that is responsible for overall marketplace trends and outlooks, keeping track of competitive activities and market share, and performing specialized marketplace studies as required by sales, marketing, and product development.

- **GLOBL Product Development**. GLOBL does all the development work on the three product lines you will be forecasting. This means that GLOBL maintains a development staff whose responsibilities include evaluating and tracking customer requirements for educational products, determining and prioritizing what needs may be best pursued by GLOBL, designing and developing products to meet these needs, determining go-to-market strategies for these products, tracking GLOBL product performance versus objectives, and enhancing products required to meet GLOBL objectives.
- **GLOBL Sales Force and Channel Strategy**. GLOBL has a worldwide team of dedicated product sales specialists. There are also a number of business partners who sell GLOBL products, often along with other products and services. There is a strong focus on

increasing the use of web-based facilities to exploit e-business sales.

- **GLOBL Manufacturing**. GLOBL performs manufacturing activity for the products you forecast. Worldwide manufacturing supply/demand planning is performed centrally for all products, although there are several manufacturing sites for each product.

## GLOBL Product and Strategy Details

➢ **Product line A** sells into the preschool market. In recent years, product line A has seen dramatically increased use to support Web-based applications.

➢ **Product line B** sells into the academic market and institutions of higher learning. Although GLOBL has been in the market for quite a few decades, the original versions of this line were introduced just over 36 months ago. Sales have been normal for the past year. Two years ago, there was an unexpected upswing in demand in quarter 3, which caused big manufacturing problems. A dedicated sales force does over 90% of sales and has grown significantly in size over the past three years. There are currently plans for a further strengthening of the sales budget due to concern that GLOBL is still number three in this marketplace. This sales force operates off a quota system with sales contests scheduled approximately once a year, usually in the last quarter. Selling in this marketplace depends on establishing good relationships with the educational institutions. GLOBL's competitors appear to be more successful at this. You have difficulties getting solid information on the product line's sales activities from the sales force.

➢ **Product line C** sells into the commercial workplace market. It spans a wide range of occupational functions in industry, supporting complex needs across many business applications. Product line C has seen modest growth over the past several years; new and esoteric applications in many commercial marketplaces are driving a niche market. GLOBL has divided its sales efforts between its own sales force and its business partners in roughly a 30-70 split. Good contacts with traditional customers have been key to sales success. However, forward-looking strategists are beginning to be concerned regarding the trends to mutual e-procurement initiatives in these customers.

In addition to these demand factors, supply considerations should also be taken into account. In forecasting regulated services (such as residential waste management or power utility in some areas), it is important to recognize that a corporate charter requires a company to serve consumer demand. Its management does not have the option of meeting only a part of the demand. In competitive industries, where this is not so, the demand forecaster and the forecast user must evaluate the interaction of demand and supply before arriving at the final forecast.

> *The problem-definition step concludes with a determination of the costs versus benefits of the alternative solutions. The forecaster must look for solutions in which the benefits exceed the costs. But has the forecaster been adequately prepared to measure costs and benefits?*

## PEER Step 2: **EXECUTE** to Select a Forecasting Technique

Many different forecasting techniques are available ranging from elementary smoothing methods to time series and regression models. A forecasting model is a job aid for forecasters: it creates a simplified representation of reality. The forecaster tries to include in the representation those factors that are critical and to exclude those that are not. This process of stripping away the non-essential and concentrating on the essential is like peeling an onion and is the essence of forecast modeling.

> *A forecasting technique is a simplified representation of reality for making projections.*

Although abstract, models permit the forecaster to estimate the effects of important future events or trends. In the cable TV industry, for example, there are thousands of reasons why subscribers want their homes connected or disconnected for use of the Internet or to place calls over a digital network. It is beyond the scope of the forecaster to deal with all these reasons. Therefore, a forecaster attempts to distill these many influences down to a limited number of the most pertinent factors.

In a particular place, such as Detroit, Michigan, the forecasting model might look like Figure 1.12. This model assumes that the automobile industry creates jobs for people, who then buy homes or rent apartments and want cable services. The demand forecaster's job, for instance, is to determine the relationships among employment levels, household growth, land use, and cable service demand along with a quantification of uncertainty.

Mathematical equations are used to develop models that represent a real-world situation. For a cable TV service model, such an equation might take the form

$$CTV\ demand = b_0 + b_1\ (Employment) + b_2\ (Number\ of\ housing\ starts) +\ random\ error$$

where $b_0$, $b_1$, and $b_2$ are coefficients determined from historical data.

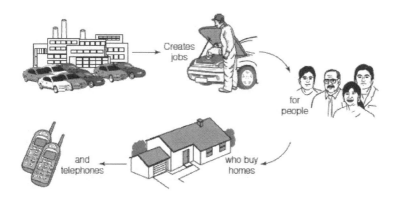

Figure 1.12 Forecasting model of the demand for residential CTV services in Detroit`

Models such as these simplify the analysis of some problems, but, of course, do not account for all the factors that cause people to behave as they do. Notice that the model summarized in the equation does not include information on the prices of other goods and services, but does include the uncertainty factor.

As another example, consider tourism demand forecasting. International tourism has grown very rapidly over the past few decades and has become a major part of the global trade. Tourism demand measures a visitor's use of a quantity of a good or service; such measures commonly found in tourism forecasting include number of visitors to a destination, number of transportation passengers, and amount of tourism expenditures. Some factors that are known to affect tourism demand include personal disposable income, travel costs, natural and human-made disasters, and weather (Figure 1.13, *top*).

To get a measure of the nature of demand variability and uncertainty, Figure 1.13 (*bottom*) shows that the total variability in the data (as determined from a preliminary STI_Classification technique, explained later in Chapter 5, Appendix A) is comprised of 86.6 % seasonality, 12.1 % trend and 1.3% irregular (unknown, other than trend/seasonal effect).

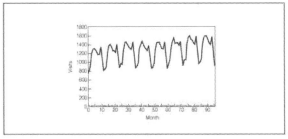

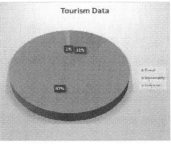

Figure 1.13 Time plot (*top*) and STI classification: trend-seasonal decomposition pie chart (bottom) of monthly tourism demand in a metropolitan area: Trend (12%), Seasonal (78%) and Other (1%). (*Data Source*: D.C.Frechtling, *Practical Tourism Forecasting*(1996)

The primary driver in this example is seasonality, so we will use a model with a seasonal/trend **forecast profile** (e.g. Holt-Winters, to be discussed in Chapter 8, or the ARIMA (011) (011)$_{12}$ "airline" model, to be discussed in Chapter 9) should be on top of the list of techniques to be considered. Forecasters need to understand the factors driving consumer demand and consumer trends in their areas in order to create a demand forecast for a product or service. What other factors of demand or domain knowledge might you need to quantify the remaining irregular variation? Modeling and projection techniques are tangible and structured, just like the forecasting process.

A credible modeling approach should be able to produce uncertainty measurement and reproducible results. As the analytical engine of a forecasting model, these techniques provide the basis for understanding **forecast profiles** and **forecast error** impacts (Forecast error is conventionally defined as Actual–Forecast). Models perform similar tasks regardless of the data they use; although some inputs to the forecasting process depend on the context of the given situation, projection techniques do not. For this reason, the forecaster must exercise sound judgment in selecting and using the projection techniques that yield the credible **forecast profiles**. Through a systematic process of elimination, the forecaster can identify those projection techniques that will provide the greatest reliability in the development of the forecast output.

There is a trade-off between simplicity and completeness in every model-building effort. Multi-equation causal models (Chapter 10) are commonly used to approximate the relationships between retail consumption and its drivers: price, advertising spending, coupons, competitive influences and seasonality.

Because seasonality is such a dominant factor, the data are often seasonally adjusted first before modeling begins (Figure 1.14). On the premise that there is a strong relationship between consumer purchases and factory shipments, a related causal model around factory shipments would include among its drivers' retail consumption, merchandising, trade allowances, and promotional lift variables.

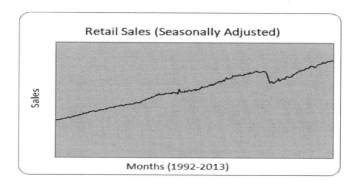

Figure 1.14 Time plot of monthly retail sales, adjusted for seasonal variations, trading-day, and holiday differences. *Source :* (https://www.census.gov/retail/marts/www/download/text/adv4400 0.txt)

In this book, we analyze and forecast variables by emphasizing **exploratory data analysis** (EDA) for assuring data quality and basic forecasting techniques for generating credible and reliable forecasting profiles. We begin the analysis with traditional approaches and supplement them with **resistant** (those that safeguard against unusual values, like outliers) and **robust** (those that safeguard against departures from classical normality modeling assumptions) alternatives to the same problem. More advanced techniques, including the autoregressive, integrated, moving average (ARIMA) models, based on the Box-Jenkins methodology, dynamic regression and some econometric modeling with multiple variables and equations, will be considered as well.

> *There are numerous alternative ways of generating any forecast. Selecting a forecasting technique is a systematic procedure for producing and analyzing forecasts.*

## PEER Step 3: **EVALUATE** Forecasting Models

With a data framework in place to process, analyze and manage data, the demand forecaster completes the forecast techniques selection step. Next, the forecaster starts to create forecasts with each selected method. After executing the forecast modeling step, the demand forecaster evaluates each technique. The forecast model evaluation step is called **diagnostic checking** and often results in modifications of the initial models until acceptable models are obtained. This phase involves accuracy measurement based on forecast error analysis (to be discussed in Chapter 4).

## PEER Step 4: **RECONCILE** Final Forecasts

After completing the evaluation of forecasting models (to be discussed in Chapter 11),

- informed judgment, important throughout the process, is used to create forecast adjustments and select the forecast values and uncertainty ranges from among the possible candidates
- estimates are made about the reliability of the forecast in terms of prediction limits, and presentations are made to gain the acceptance of the forecast
- the forecasts are monitored to ensure their continuing relevance, and forecast changes are proposed when necessary

## *Getting Insights into Forecasting New Demand for Products and Services*

One objective of a smarter forecasting process is to identify and evaluate systematically all factors, which are most likely to affect the course of demand for products and services. What can we do for *new* demand for which there are no historical patterns? The demand forecaster should identify *measurable* variables for factors affecting the quantity demanded for a market or region of interest, using comparable products or services for which there are historical data

Based on the forecaster's domain knowledge and the recent history of GLOBL product line B, called *i*HearBuddy, the forecaster may be able to advise that if the business can capture 7% of the educational market, it will yield a monthly internal rate of return of 21.5%.

The business planners have designed the daily production requirements, equipment, manpower, and facility requirements based on these sales targets. Recent recessionary trends have been a concern, and now the planners would like to backtrack and see what the outlook of the consumer electronics industry is before embarking on the new venture.

The information on the industry would indicate whether this product is still a wise investment. The demand factors and consumption trends that need to be investigated include price, income, demographics, advertising, and regulation.

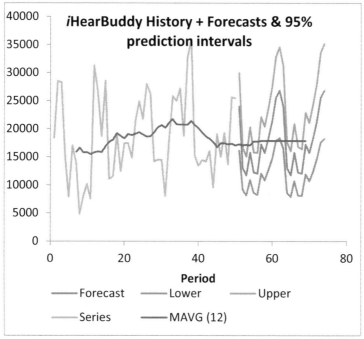

Figure 1.15 Predictive visualization of IHearBuddy product demand: monthly time series of a seasonal product in GLOBL product line B, showing history, forecast profile (change), prediction limits (chance), and moving average smoothing of history and forecasts.

Figure 1.15 is a **predictive visualization** of iHearBuddy (a learning aid for foreign language students that translates lectures). The plot shows historical data values, a trend/seasonal forecast profile with prediction limits based on the Additive Holt-Winters model, coded ETS (A,A,A); see Chapter 8 for details. It clearly shows a dominant seasonal pattern (reflecting *consumer habits*?) and a less pronounced trend pattern (reflecting *consumer demographics*?).

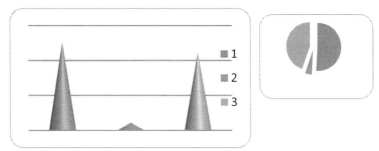

Figure 1.16 Pie chart and cone chart as alternative ways to depict total variation in the demand variable in terms of (1) seasonality (51%), (2) trend (4%), and (3) other (45%). Exploratory decomposition display of GLOBL product iHearBuddy created with Excel Data Analysis add-in for two-way ANOVA without Replication.

In Figure 1.16, the three ETS components are displayed as pie- and cone charts to visualize the relative contribution of the trend and seasonal variation to the total variation. Using an exploratory year-month decomposition method, calculated with the "Two-way ANOVA without Replication" routine in the Excel Data Analysis add-in (described in Chapter 8), we can make the interpretation that the data made up of 51% Seasonality, 4% Trend, and 45% Other.

As an exploratory step, the demand forecaster could now make some insightful assumptions for product line B. The dominant seasonality can be quantified by consumer habit factors, such as number of holidays and School openings/closings, driving the demand for Product Line B. The trend relates to the underlying growth of the student population and can be quantified by the age-cohorts of student consumers, for example.

The "Other" component (45%) still contains information about everything else not attributable to consumer habits (seasonality) and consumer demographics (trend). This could include promotions, economic cycle, unusual events and random error.

In a modeling environment, we first characterize the trend/seasonality with a time series forecasting model with a trend/seasonal forecast profile (e.g., Holt-Winters exponential smoothing or an ARIMA (011) $(011)_{12}$ "airline" model; these are in the same family of the State Space Forecasting models discussed in Chapters 8 and 9.)

The model residuals (Actual minus Fit) can be analyzed and used to quantify the remaining factors with causal (regression) models, for example. This iterative process is like peeling an onion to uncover *change* and *chance*. The models give insight into the appropriate forecast profile (*change*) while forecast errors (Actual minus Forecast) from holdout samples can be used to get insight into the uncertainty factor (*chance*). In this sense, we characterize uncertainty as a **certain factor**.

Oveall Impact

| Factor | Past changes | Current impact | Change in upcoming periods | Max. influence that the factor can have (+/- %) |
|---|---|---|---|---|
| Economy | + 3% | - 1% | - 5% | +/- 10% |
| Demographics | + 2% | + 2% | + 1% | +/- 3% |
| Price Index re Competition | - 4% | - 4% | - 6% | +/- 8% |
| Income | + 8% | + 6% | - 3% | +/- 16% |
| Advertising | - 2% | - 8% | + 2% | +/- 8% |

| Impact in the Period | | Current | Future |
|---|---|---|---|
| Factor | Direction (+/-) | Intensity (1-5) 1 = Low | Intensity (1-5) 1 = Low |
| Economy | + | 1 | 1 |
| Demographics | + | 4 | 2 |
| Price Index re Competition | - | 3 | 3 |
| Income | + | 2 | 5 |
| Advertising | + | 5 | 4 |

Figure 1.17 Illustrative factor matrices for trend and seasonal drivers of demand for GLOBL product line B.

The impact of the dominant drivers of demand can be summarized in a Factor Impact Matrix (Figure 1.17), along with a predictive visualization of the historical and future impact of a driver of demand (Figure 1.18). To monitor a time history for the impact of drivers on demand on an ongoing basis, we create factor matrices for the Immediate Past, Present and Future. The time periods should be representative of the current context or situation. For example, one could use lead-times for inventory or production.

The direction would indicate the impact a factor would have on demand if it were increasing or decreasing. For example, price increases would tend to result in decreases (-) in demand, while increases in holidays and festivals would tend to increase (+) the demand for electronics products. The quantification of the resulting impact is based on informed judgment and domain expertise and signifies the intensity on a numerical scale, say 1 to 5.

### The Impact of the Best Factors

| The historical impact of a factor over the past few periods | The factor's effect on projected demand in the current period | The expected future impact of a factor on demand | The overall impact of the top factors | Proportion to circle area | |
|---|---|---|---|---|---|
| | | | | Intensity | Radius (x2) |
| | | | | 1 | 1 |
| | | | | 2 | 1.414213562 |
| | | | | 3 | 1.732050808 |
| | | | | 4 | 2 |
| | | | | 5 | 2.236067977 |

Figure 1.18 A predictive visualization of the impact of a driver of demand.

To summarize the impact of a driver on demand, we create a **predictive visualization** of the driver or factor by relating the score to the size of a dartboard surface. Use the relationship of Area $= \pi \, (\text{radius})^2$ to determine the size of the circles shown in Figure 1.18. For instance, for a score of 5, the circle should appear five times larger than the one with a score of 1. To get the correct visual effect, you can accomplish this as follows: Score 1 ➔ radius 1, Score 2 ➔ radius √ 2. Score 3 ➔ radius √ 3, Score 4 ➔ radius 2 and Score 5 ➔ √ 5. If you have deeper domain knowledge, you can extend the scale to 7 or 11.

**Uncertainty is a certain factor in characterizing change and chance.**

## A Comprehensive Checklist for General Forecasting:

*http://www.cgdev.org/doc/ghprn/Demand_Forecasting_Principl es,Sept-06.pdf*

✓  Have I identified the principal customers/decision-makers of the forecast and do I clearly understand their needs?

✓ Have I understood and clearly communicated the purpose of the forecast and the decisions that will be affected by the forecast?

✓ Have I created a **forecasting process that is independent of plans and targets**?

✓ Have I understood the political considerations and taken measures to protect the process from political interference? Is my process transparent?

✓ Have I understood the broader environment in which the forecasting process is occurring?

✓ Have I created the forecast in the context of market and policy trends, portfolio of investments, and new product developments by suppliers? Have I clearly communicated this context?

✓ Have I created a dynamic forecasting process that incorporates and will reflect changes in the market and in public policy as they occur?

✓ Have I selected the techniques that are most appropriate for the forecast problem and data available? Do I understand how to apply the various techniques that are most suitable? Have I obtained decision-makers' agreement on the techniques?

✓ Does my methodology reflect the appropriate level of accuracy and detail that is needed for the forecast? Have I explicitly identified prediction intervals in the forecast?

✓ Have I made my forecast assumptions clear and explicitly defined them for those who will use the forecast? Do I understand the data and their limitations? Have I searched for data from multiple sources and gathered both qualitative and quantitative data? Am I using these different types of data appropriately?

A checklist is good advice because it appears to be broadly applicable to all forecasting functions.

## Takeaways

➢ The systematic structure of a **smarter forecasting** process establishes the foundation on which the most important ingredient (human judgment and intuition) is based.

➢ The purpose of a **smarter forecasting** process is to identify and evaluate systematically all factors, which are most likely to affect the course of demand.

➢ Problem definition is necessary to define what is to be done, design a data framework and establish the criteria for successful completion of the project or forecast.

➢ The four **PEER** phases of the **smarter forecasting** process are independent of the item to be forecast and the input parameters.

➢ Exploratory data analysis, forecasting, and model-building should only begin after all agreements have been reached.

➢ Lastly, demand forecasting is a **complex process**. Complex processes require checklists for effective execution.

# 2

# Smarter Forecasting Is Mostly about Data
## Improving Data Quality through Data Exploration and Visualization

*Time series analysis consists of all the techniques that, when applied to time series data, yield, at least sometimes, either insight or knowledge, AND everything that helps us choose or understand these procedures.*

JOHN W. TUKEY, pioneer data scientist
(1980)

This chapter deals with the statistical basis for data analysis in demand forecasting. As in the modeling process presented in Chapter 1, you will find that

- as a statistical methodology, much data analysis in demand forecasting is informal and exploratory
- data analysis is open-ended and iterative in nature
- the steps may not always be clearly defined
- the nature of the process depends on what information is revealed at various stages. At any given stage, various possibilities may arise, some of which will need to be explored separately.

However, it is important to realize in forecasting demand that

- an understanding of historical data will be enhanced when we can identify key patterns in a time series
- data visualizations are beneficial in describing the shape or distribution of data patterns, model residuals, forecast errors and forecast accuracy measures
- assuming unrealistic distributions for forecast errors can lead to misleading results when assessing forecasting performance. Most testing procedures implicitly assume that the underlying data follow a *normal distribution,* and this is mostly not the case in demand forecasting applications
- analyzing data is part of the smarter forecasting process. For example, when data contain trends, contain seasonal patterns, or have outliers, the use of some commonly used projection techniques, such as moving averages is inappropriate. The moving average forecast over any horizon is always level. Theoretically, there is no means of determining an uncertainty factor. The moving average forecast is just not smart enough anymore to belong in a forecaster's toolkit.
- the use of accuracy performance measurements that make use of the arithmetic mean (e.g., MAE, MAPE, sMAPE, MASE) for forecast performance measurement can yield misleading results, because such data rarely follow conventional statistical assumptions.

## Smarter Forecasting Is Mostly about Data

When a multidisciplinary research study group at Princeton University undertook a study of the paired uses of electricity and gas in townhouses, it contacted the residents of Twin Rivers, a nearby planned community in New Jersey. Over a five-year study period, it learned how to eliminate three-quarters of the energy used by the furnace in quite ordinary, reasonably well-built townhouses, as chronicled in *Saving Energy in the Home: Princeton's Experiments at Twin Rivers,* edited by Robert H. Socolow (Cambridge, MA: Ballinger, 1977). The purpose of the Princeton study, during a winter in the mid-1970s, was to examine differences in energy use and make comparisons with structural aspects of the 152 individual townhouses and the behavioral aspects of their inhabitants.

As an applied statistician (a.k.a. data scientist), I took great delight in being a participant and was intrigued by later looking at the results and the data from the study. I was a resident at Twin Rivers at the time, not realizing that some new analysis techniques used on the data would eventually be published in 1977 in the ground-breaking book *Exploratory Data Analysis* by data science pioneer John W. Tukey (1915–2000).

The data were gathered automatically through a special device that was hooked up to the landline telephones and the energy sources in the home. There were questions to be answered periodically about our lifestyle, the details of which have long escaped my memory. Nevertheless, some novel uses of charting techniques with schematic data plots (data visualization) can be found throughout this book. These techniques, new at the time, have now become a familiar part of many business statistics books.

## Exploring Data Patterns

Studying the patterns in the data improves the forecaster's chances of successfully modeling data for forecasting applications. Through exploratory data analysis (EDA), a demand forecaster can start the important task of finding factors (drivers of demand) that are generally quantitative in nature.

Tukey likens EDA to detective work: "A detective investigating a crime needs both tools and understanding. If he/she has no fingerprint powder, the detective will fail to find fingerprints on most surfaces. If detectives do not understand where criminals are likely to have put their fingers, they will not look in the right places." A planned forecasting and modeling effort that does not include provisions for exploratory data analysis often misses the most interesting and important results; although it is only a first step, not the whole story.

> *Exploratory data analysis means looking at data, absorbing what the data are suggesting, and using various summaries and display methods to gain insight into the process generating the data.*

Many business forecasting books describe a variety of classical ways to summarize data. For the practitioner, an entertaining yet informative cartoon guide covering these is Gonick and Smith's *A Cartoon Guide to Statistics,* published in 1993. For example, the familiar histogram is widely used in practice. In addition, there are a number of lesser-known techniques that are specifically useful for analyzing large quantities of data that have become accessible as a result of the increased flexibility in data management, computer processing, and predictive analytics. Because of their potential value to demand forecasting, we describe them in some detail.

## Learning by Looking at Data Patterns

Because most forecasting techniques require data, a forecaster analyzes the availability of data from both external (outside the company) and internal (within the company or its industry) sources. For example, one potential source of **internal data** is a corporate data warehouse or **E**nterprise **R**esource **P**lanning (ERP) system, which normally contains a rich history of product sales, shipments, prices, revenues, expenses, capital expenditures, and marketing programs.

The availability of **external data** is improving rapidly. Most of the required demographic factors (age, race, sex, households, and so forth), forecasts of **economic indicators**, and related variables can be readily obtained from computerized data sources and from industry and government publications on the Internet.

With the explosion of Internet websites, potential sources of valuable data are becoming limitless. With unstructured data, the need for data mining tools has become a necessity for exploring potential sources of data for consumer-data analyses and predictive modeling purposes.

## *Data Exploration as an Essential Data Quality Check in Forecasting*

The analysis of data for forecasting purposes requires a careful consideration of the quality of data sources. **Data quality** is important for modeling, because a model based on historical data will be no better than the quality of its data source. Moreover, forecast accuracy is directly impacted by unexamined data.

Definitions may vary because of changes in the structure of an organization, accounting procedures, or product and service definitions. As part of the forecasting process, throughout this book various kinds of demand data will be related to economic/demographic indicators, survey data, and other external data in a number of examples and spreadsheet exhibits.

There are several criteria that can be applied to data to determine their appropriateness for modeling:

- **Accuracy:** Proper care must be taken that the required data are collected from a reliable source with proper attention given to accuracy. **Survey data** exemplify the need to ensure accurate data:

Survey data are collected by government agencies and research firms from questionnaires and interviews to determine future plans of consumers and businesses. The **consumer confidence index** in Figure 2.1 is the result of a survey made by the Conference Board (https://www.conference-board.org/data/consumerconfidence.cfm).

Figure 2.1 Time plot of the Conference Board's Consumer Confidence Index US (1977 – 2014) (Units: 1985 = 100 - *Source*: https://www. Conference-board.org/); the variation in the Consumer Confidence Index shows the dominant 89% trend-cycle effect.

These data have certain limitations because they reflect only the respondents' anticipation (what they expect others to do) or expectations (what they themselves plan to do), not firm commitments. Nevertheless, such information may be regarded as a valuable aid to forecasting demand directly or as an indication of the state of consumer confidence concerning the economic outlook.

Based on an STI_Classification (cf. *MS Excel Data Analysis Add-in > ANOVA: Two-Factor without Replication> SS column expressed as %)*, we determine that the total variability in the data is made up of 1% seasonality (Month effect), 89% trend-cycle (Year effect) and 10% unknown. When modeling we can ignore models with seasonal forecast profiles, like the Holt-Winters exponential smoothing family, but when using these data as an explanatory factor or driver of demand in causal models, we recognize its value in explaining primarily economic cycle and trending behavior.

- **Conformity**. The data must adequately represent the phenomenon for which it is being used. If the data purport to represent economic activity, the data should show upswings and downswings in accordance with past historical **business cycle** fluctuations. Data that are too smooth or too erratic may not adequately reflect the patterns desired for modeling.

The Federal Reserve Board **Index of Industrial Production** (Figure 2.2) is an example of a cyclical indicator of the economy. It is evident that the data are consistent with economic expansions and contractions (to be discussed in Chapter 7). The index of industrial production measures changes in the physical volume of the output of manufacturers, mineral suppliers, and electric and gas utilities. The index does not cover production on farms, in the construction industry, in transportation, or in various trade and service sectors.

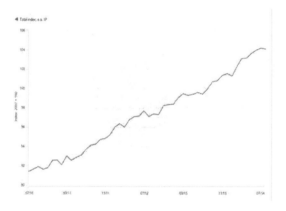

Figure 2.2 Time plot of the monthly seasonally adjusted index of industrial production from the Federal Reserve Board, July 2010–August 2014 (Units: 2007 = 100). (*Source*: Board of Governors of the Federal Reserve System - *http://www.federalreserve.gov/*)

Since the U.S. Federal Reserve Board (FRB) first introduced the index in 1920, it has been revised from time to time to take account of the growing complexity of the US economy, the availability of more data, improvements in statistical processing techniques and refinements in methods of analyses. Such indices are now widely available in many other national economies.

The STI_Classification of the original (unadjusted) FRB Index of Industrial Production suggests that the total variability in the data is made up of 10% seasonality (Month effect), 89% trend-cycle (Year effect) and 1% irregular (Not identified). When using these data as an explanatory factor or driver of demand in causal models, we recognize its value in explaining primarily trend and economic cycles.

- **Timeliness**. It takes time to collect data. Data collected, summarized, and published on a timely basis are of greatest value to the forecaster. Often preliminary data are available first, so that the time delay before the data are declared official may become a significant factor. Demographic data may fall into this category for many users. The monthly housing starts data shown in Figure 2.3 are demographic data reported by contractors and builders for use by government and private industry. Such external data are of course, subject to adjustment because of data collection delays and reporting inaccuracies.

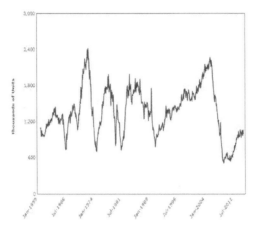

Figure 2.3 Time plot of monthly U.S. new housing starts (seasonally adjusted annual rates). (*Source*: *www.census.gov*)

Figure 2.4 Time plots of monthly new housing units started in the United States (seasonally adjusted annual rates for periods 1960–1969 and 2004–2013). (Source: www.census.gov)

Once a factor has been identified as a key driver of demand, we should not assume that its usefulness is good for all times. Data need to be analyzed on an ongoing basis for quality assurance. For example, a preliminary STI_Classification, while useful to assess the strength of a seasonal or trend-cycle effect, can point to a change in the composition of components of variability. For the ten-year period 1960–1969 (Figure 2.4 left frame), the total variability in the data is made up of 0.1 % seasonality, 64.5% trend and 35.4% irregular (unknown).

On the other hand, for the ten-year period 2004–2013 (Figure 2.4 right frame), the total variability in the data is made up of 0.3 % seasonality, 96.5% trend and 3.2% irregular (unknown). Because these are seasonally adjusted data, no significant seasonal effect can be present. The non-trending variability in the early period, masked by the deep dip, is suggested by the high irregular contribution. When using these data as an explanatory factor or driver of demand in causal models, we recognize its value in explaining primarily economic and demographic consumer behavior.

- **Consistency**. Data must be consistent throughout the period of their use. When definitions change, adjustments need to be made in order to retain logical consistency in historical patterns. The monthly demand for refrigerator sales, shown in Figure 2.5, is an example of internal data that would be made available to a demand forecaster of a consumer goods manufacturer. It shows a consistent (seasonal with business cycle?) pattern. If the data pattern shows abrupt level changes or unusual variation, the forecaster should check into how the data are defined.

In Figure 2.5 (*left frame*), the total variability in the refrigerator data is made up of 81% seasonality, 7% trend and 12% Other (unknown). It can be seen that the second seasonal peak appears unusually low (domain expert's explanation: lack of inventory resulting in lost sales). A simple interpolation between the seasonal peaks makes the data more representative of the demand.

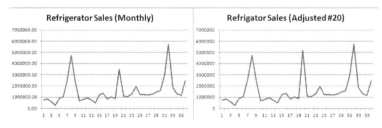

Figure 2.5 Time plots of monthly revenues of home refrigerator sales in a foreign currency.

It is important to recognize that modeling with unexamined data can distort the expected forecast profile (*change*) as well as the uncertainty (width of the prediction limits: *chance*). With the adjustment, the total variability in the data is now made up of 87%

seasonality, 4% trend and 9% Other (unknown). The seasonality is still dominant but the unknown component, comprised of the uncertain variation is significantly reduced—the impact of just a single data point!

When using these data as demand in causal models, we recognize the need for explanatory factors explaining primarily seasonality or habit in consumer behavior, along with a measure of the nature of the uncertainty (Other).

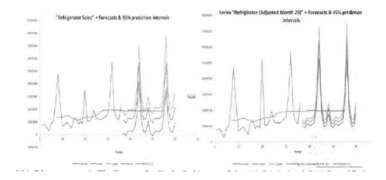

Figure 2.6 Improvement in the forecast profile for refrigerator sales for original (*left*) and outlier-adjusted (*right*) period #20.

The consequences of jumping into the modeling phase before thoroughly investigating the quality of the data and checking for anomalies can be quite severe. For instance, if we blindly applied a credible trend-seasonal model (e.g., Holt-Winters exponential smoothing or an ARIMA (011) (011)$_{12}$ "airline" model) to the original data, we would see that the seasonal peak months plateau and the uncertainty range is wide; on the other hand, with a single point adjustment based on informed judgment and the same trend-seasonal model, the results become much more credible and practical (Figure 2.6). Not only is the forecast profile representative of what may lie in the future, but the prediction limits have become much narrower, indicating a tamed (reduced) uncertainty. The variability in the *Other* category of the exploratory STI_Classification is reduced and our forecasts become more precise.

> **Bad Data Will Beat a Good Forecast Every Time. (Paraphrasing W. Edwards Deming)**

## Data Visualization

Why are graphical displays so useful in forecasting? A graphical display is often easier to interpret than the tabular forms of the same data in a spreadsheet or report. Graphical displays are flexible in their ability to reveal alternative structures present in data or to show relationships among variables. A wise choice in the scale of a graphical display can also make the difference between seeing something important in the data or missing it altogether. For example, rates of growth and changing rates of growth tend to be easier to interpret from graphs with a logarithmic scale than with an arithmetic scale. Why?

Data visualization software tools have given us virtually unlimited power to display data but less on guidance on how to display data most

effectively. Although forecasters have always used graphics for analysis and presentation, the principles for effective visual data analyses and presentation are still evolving. Search, for example, for Bill Cleveland's *The Elements of Graphing Data* (1994, rev. ed.), Naomi Robbins's *Creating More Effective Graphs* (2005), and Ed Tufte's (*left*) masterfully produced *The Visual Display of Quantitative Information* (1983), *Envisioning Information* (1990), *Visual Explanations* (1990) and *Beautiful Evidence* (2006), and more recently Alberto Cairo's *The Truthful Art: Data, Charts, and Maps for Communication* (2016), and *Storytelling with Data: A Data Visualization Guide for Business Professionals* (2015) by Cole Nussbaumer Knaflic.

The R package **forecast** provides methods and tools for displaying and analyzing univariate time series forecasts including exponential smoothing via state space models and automatic ARIMA modelling. This package is being replaced and upgraded with the **fable** package.

## Time Plots

**Time plots** (or sequence plots) are charts that show values arranged sequentially in time. If data are recorded at equal time intervals, the corresponding values must be plotted at equally spaced time intervals. These time intervals may be hours, days, weeks, months, quarters, or years.

Time plots provide a useful initial step in the forecast modeling process. Many macroeconomic variables, such as the nonfarm employment (Figure 2.7), industrial production, and gross domestic product (GDP), are dominated by a strong trend, so time plots offer an opportunity to make visual comparisons of their growth patterns.

> *A time plot is a graph in which the data values are shown sequentially in time.*

When a time series is re-expressed (transformed) into another form more useful for a particular analysis, the time plot often shows why a new form may give better results. When analyzing trending data, for example, the percentage changes of a given time series reveal growth rates over time.

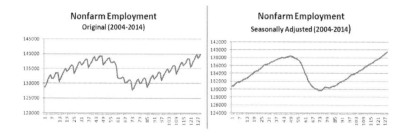

Figure 2.7 Time plots of U.S. nonfarm employment, 2004–2014, original (*left*) and seasonally adjusted (*right*). (Source: U.S. Dept. of Labor, Bureau of Labor Statistics, www.bls.gov)

Figure 2.7(b) shows a plot of the seasonally adjusted U.S. Nonfarm Employment. The establishment payroll survey, the **Current Employment Statistics** (CES) survey, is based on a sample of 400,000 business establishments nationwide. According to the **Bureau of Labor Statistics** website (*www.bls.gov*), the "CES Employment is the total number of persons on establishment payrolls employed full or part time who received pay for any part of the pay period which includes the 12th day of the month. Temporary and intermittent employees are included, as are any workers who are on paid sick leave, on paid holiday, or who work during only part of the specified pay period. A striking worker who only works a small portion of the survey period, and is paid, would be included as employed under the CES definitions. Persons on the payroll of more than one establishment are counted in each establishment. Data exclude proprietors, self-employed, unpaid family or volunteer workers, farm workers, and domestic workers." The nonfarm employment series (Figure 2.7) could be used as a potential driver of demand in a regression model for a consumer product, like home refrigerator sales.

## Scatter Diagrams

We can visually display a relationship between pairs of variables in a **scatter diagram**. When the values of a time series (or variable) are paired with corresponding values of a related time series (or variable), a relationship between the variables can be depicted in a scatter diagram. One variable is plotted on the horizontal scale and the other variable is plotted on the vertical scale. Such a plot is a valuable tool for exploring linearity in the relationship between two or more sets of variables.

> *A scatter diagram is a plot in which paired values of two variables are plotted on the same diagram.*

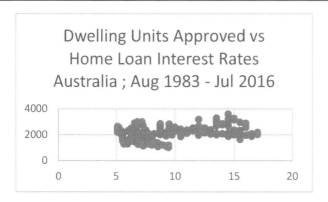

Figure 2.8 Scatter diagram of private dwelling units approved (*vertical axis*) in NSW, Australia, versus home loan interest rates (*horizontal axis*) for a 33-year historical period.

The scatter diagram in Figure 2.8 relates monthly, seasonally adjusted private dwelling units approved and home loan interest rates data for a 33-year period. Forecasts of housing starts are used for plans for expansions or cutbacks within the construction industry. They are also used for forecasts of goods and services used by the home buyer, such as refrigerators and TV, telephone, and internet cable access. Here it may be difficult to suggest a simple forecasting relationship because of the wide dispersion of points.

As a prelude to **linear regression** modeling (finding the line that best fits the points of the scatter diagram; to be discussed in Chapter 10), we may search for variables that are related to one another. If a variable has been plotted against another variable that is dependent on it (as a driver of demand), we may see a functional relationship between the two variables. As part of the modeling process, scatter diagrams can suggest if certain relationships among variables can be assumed to be linear on the basis of physical, economic, or intuitive hypotheses. This is not automatic.

The analyst needs to graphically explore different relationships, such as lagging interest rates or segmenting portions of the data in Figure 2.8 (say, less than 8% and greater than 8% loan rate) with the guidance of an economist or industry domain expert.

After **regression analysis**, scatter diagrams play a diagnostic role in the graphical analysis of **residual series** (Actual–Fit) to help verify that assumptions are reasonable and that a proposed statistical model provides an adequate fit to the data.

Whenever the scatter diagram does not suggest a clear relationship between the variables, it can be useful to look at **transformations** (log, square root, Box-Cox) of these variables as well (to be discussed in Chapter 11). For annual (trending) data, it often makes sense to look at the relationship between changes or growth rates (percentage changes) of variables to be forecast. Figure 2.9 shows the relationship between the period-over-period changes in a U.S. housing starts and mortgage rates variable, as shown by the clear downward pattern.

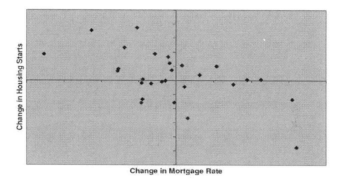

Change in Housing Starts

Change in Mortgage Rate

Figure 2.9 Scatter diagram of changes in annual housing starts versus changes in annual mortgage rates for a 29-year period.

For forecasting annual housing starts, this suggests that modeling the relationship between changes in the variable (Figure 2.9) might be more promising for forecasting housing starts than a model based on the original volumes (Figure 2.8).

*A transformation is a mathematical operation to enhance the analysis, display, and interpretation of data.*

## Displaying Data Distributions

Suppose that we have been asked to evaluate the performance of a product over a 52-week horizon using a conventional measure of accuracy given by the **Absolute Percentage Error** (100*(|A-F|)/A), where A = Actual and F = Forecast. The vertical bars denote taking absolute values. The Absolute Percentage Error (APE) is a widely used accuracy measure in demand planning and forecasting applications. The focus here is on the nature of the numbers, not whether it is the appropriate measure for the problem.

The data in Figure 2.10, collected during a year, make up a time series calculated after a forecast is made for a 52-week horizon and the APE is calculated weekly after the actuals for the week are reported. The following questions are to be answered: What is the most typical accuracy? (Where are most of the results concentrated or centered?) What is a typical APE? How much variability is there in the APE data? Are there any extreme or unusual values—values that do not seem to fit the bulk of the data?

| Week | Absolute Percentage Error (APE) | Week | Absolute Percentage Error (APE) | Week | Absolute Percentage Error (APE) | Week | Absolute Percentage Error (APE) |
|---|---|---|---|---|---|---|---|
| 1 | 11 | 14 | 14 | 27 | 11 | 40 | 37 |
| 2 | 10 | 15 | 10 | 28 | 10 | 41 | 11 |
| 3 | 23 | 16 | 5 | 29 | 16 | 42 | 8 |
| 4 | 7 | 17 | 21 | 30 | 8 | 43 | 12 |
| 5 | 9 | 18 | 30 | 31 | 8 | 44 | 11 |
| 6 | 13 | 19 | 4 | 32 | 7 | 45 | 40 |
| 7 | 14 | 20 | 13 | 33 | 10 | 46 | 27 |
| 8 | 4 | 21 | 11 | 34 | 6 | 47 | 17 |
| 9 | 4 | 22 | 6 | 35 | 10 | 48 | 3 |
| 10 | 3 | 23 | 32 | 36 | 6 | 49 | 20 |
| 11 | 23 | 24 | 10 | 37 | 6 | 50 | 12 |
| 12 | 9 | 25 | 11 | 38 | 6 | 51 | 18 |
| 13 | 7 | 26 | 9 | 39 | 22 | 52 | 38 |

Figure 2.10 Accuracy measurement on a product for 52 weeks.

## Overall Behavior of the Data

Firstly, we will start by describing the overall behavior of the APE data in Figure 2.10. It is apparent that the way the data are displayed (Figure 2.10) is not very enlightening. To describe the overall behavior of the data, we may decide to condense the raw data by placing the numbers into cells or classes. These classes can be either numerical or attributive in nature. Our data can be easily grouped into numerical classes of three successive APE values (Figure 2.11).

| Interval (%) | Number of APEs | Relative Percentage of APEs | Cumulative Percentage of APEs |
|---|---|---|---|
| 3–5 | 6 | 12 | 12 |
| 6–8 | 11 | 21 | 33 |
| 9–11 | 15 | 29 | 62 |
| 12–14 | 6 | 12 | 73 |
| 15–17 | 2 | 4 | 77 |
| 18–20 | 2 | 4 | 81 |
| 21–23 | 4 | 8 | 89 |
| 24–26 | 0 | 0 | 89 |
| 27–29 | 1 | 2 | 91 |
| 30–32 | 2 | 4 | 95 |
| 33–35 | 0 | 0 | 95 |
| 36–38 | 2 | 4 | 99 |
| 39–41 | 1 | 2 | 100 |

Figure 2.11 Frequency distribution of accuracy measurements on a product for 52 weeks. (*Source*: Data in Figure 2.10)

The procedure for counting the number of occurrences of a given characteristic in a grouping of data gives rise to frequencies. These frequencies, when considered as fractions, can be displayed as a relative frequency distribution (Figure 2.11. column 3). The relative percentage of total number of APEs contained in each class suggests that 9%–11% is the typical or most frequent weekly APE.

Most of the data are clustered within 3%–14%. The one APE falling in the 39%–41% bracket looks very unusual, and all values greater than 26% look suspect because they are so far from the apparent average. Perhaps there were extenuating circumstances that caused these accuracy measurements to be so great. But how does the analyst determine if some of the APEs are truly unusual? Can the overall behavior of the data be described?

A grouping interval must be selected before tallying the data; this interval will depend on the range of variation, the number of data values, and the palatability of the display to the user. In Figure 2.11, the intervals have a width of 3%. An interval of 1% or 2% would have resulted in a long table without providing added information.

The groupings should be uniquely defined so that there is no ambiguity about which cell a given tally belongs in. The relative frequencies are then determined by counting the number of data values in a cell and dividing by total number of data values recorded. In the first cell, for example, there are six APEs out of 52, giving a relative frequency of about 12%. This information is then appropriately summarized as a relative frequency distribution in the third column.

The last column in Figure 2.11 is another relative frequency distribution, the cumulative percentage of APEs. Once the 27%–29% is reached, over 90% of the data have been counted. This reinforces the suspect nature of the remaining data. A relative frequency distribution should be displayed as a cumulative frequency distribution when we are interested in quantities such as the proportion of APEs below (or above) a given standard value or when we are investigating whether a distribution follows some particular mathematical form (see the section on quantile-quantile plots).

A bar chart of the frequency distribution can take the form of a histogram. In a histogram, data are plotted as bars rather than as a single chart line. The bins in a histogram are intervals suitably chosen to make a meaningful distribution of frequencies. A good rule of thumb is to select eight to 15 equally spaced intervals.

There are a very few large APEs (greater than 25%) and the APEs around the median (10%) are the most typical. The distribution is said to have a tail skewed to the right because a number of values are far above the median. However, the shape of the histogram can be sensitive to the choice of class intervals. It is often desirable to try out several different class intervals to be certain that the results appear reasonable. It has become preferable to display such data in stem-and-leaf displays rather than histograms, because they are more informative.

## Stem-and-Leaf Displays

Stem-and-leaf displays, attributed to data scientist John Tukey in his aforementioned EDA book, are useful because they show inherent groupings; show asymmetrical trailing off data going farther in one direction than another; highlight unexpected values; show approximately where the values are centered; and show approximately how widely the values are spread.

| Tens Digit | Unit Digit | Number of Absolute Percentage Errors |
|---|---|---|
| 0 | 33444566666777888999 | 20 |
| 1 | 00000111111223344678 | 21 |
| 2 | 012337 | 6 |
| 3 | 0278 | 4 |
| 4 | 0 | 1 |
| 5 | | 0 |
| 6 | | 0 |
| 7 | | 0 |
| 8 | | 0 |
| 9 | | 0 |

Figure 2.12 Stem-and-leaf display of 52 weekly accuracy measurements. (*Source*: Data in Figure 2.10)

Figure 2.12 shows the stem-and-leaf display for the absolute percentage errors (APE) in Figure 2.11. The stem is the vertical column; its divisions are multiples of 10. The leaves are the horizontal rows of numbers; each of the numbers in a leaf represents a unit digit. For example, the first number is 3 (# 10 in Figure 2.10). The tens digit is 0 and the unit digit is 3. By entering each number in this manner and ordering the numbers, we get a visual impression of the distribution of the data as well as an ordering of the data.

Frequent values stand out (e.g., 10% and 11%) as do atypical values and values that are absent or missing. For example, there are no values in the 45%–49% range. Notice that the leaves have been ordered. The right-hand column provides a count that is useful as a check that all the APE values are entered. A cumulative count will also turn out to be useful in the quick calculation of certain statistics, such as the Interquartile Range (IQR).

*A stem-and-leaf diagram is a device for depicting frequencies as well as actual values in a simple display.*

| Range | Unit Digit | Number of Absolute Percentage Errors |
|---|---|---|
| 0–4 | 33444 | 5 |
| 5–9 | 566666777888999 | 15 |
| 10–14 | 000000111111223344 | 18 |
| 15–19 | 678 | 3 |
| 20–24 | 01233 | 5 |
| 25–29 | 7 | 1 |
| 30–34 | 02 | 2 |
| 35–39 | 78 | 2 |
| 40–44 | 0 | 1 |
| 45–49 | | 0 |

*Median = ( 26th + 27th value )/2 =*   Total = 52
*(10 + 11) / 2 = 10.5*

Figure 2.13 Stem-and-leaf display with split stem. (*Source*: Data in Figure 2.10)

When the data are concentrated, as these are, it is often desirable to split each tens unit of the stem into two ranges (0%–4% and 5%–9%). This is illustrated in Figure 2.13. The absence of data in the 45%–49% range becomes more apparent. Additional information can be added by using symbols to identify various qualities of data that may be helpful in understanding differences in data. For example, a circle might be used to indicate that an APE value represented the peak seasonal week (whose peak may be harder to predict).

Choosing the number of lines L for a stem-and-leaf display is analogous to determining the number of intervals or the interval width for a histogram. A useful formula for the maximum L when n is less than 100 is; for *n* greater than 100 the formula L = 10 log10 n is recommended, where L is taken as the largest integer not exceeding the right-hand side of the expression. For our example, *n* = 52, so we have 2 (52) ½ = 14.4. Thus a 10-line stem-and-leaf display for the APE data seems satisfactory.

## Box Plots

When describing a frequency distribution, the pth percentile is the value that exceeds p% of the data. The median is the 50th percentile; that is, it is the value that exceeds 50% of the data. For example, the frequency distribution shows that the median of the Absolute Percentage Errors (MdAPE) is 10.5%. The average of the APEs is the MAPE (= 13.3%). The distribution does not have a symmetrical shape, so it is advisable to summarize the central tendency with more than one number.

Although percentiles can be used to describe a frequency distribution, it is often desirable to summarize a distribution with the smallest set of values possible. Rather than displaying a sequence of percentiles, we can use the box plot, popularized by John Tukey. The box plot concisely depicts the median, the upper and lower quartiles (the 75th and 25th percentiles), and the two extremes of any group of data.

> *A box plot is a display based on a five-number summary of a frequency distribution, consisting of the median, upper, and lower quartiles and two extreme values in a data set.*

A box plot for the APE data is shown in Figure 2.14. Fifty percent of the data values are tightly grouped (these are depicted by the box, which includes all data falling between the 25th and 75th percentiles); these quartiles were also named hinges. The upper tail appears longer than the lower tail.

The mean value, in this case, is slightly higher than the middle line of the box. The upper extreme value appears to be an outlier because it is so far away from the bulk of the data. Because there may be values along the whisker (the vertical line), this conclusion needs to be confirmed by additional analyses. This plot gives a surprising amount of information for such a simple display.

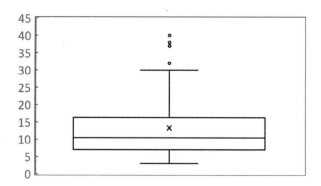

Figure 2.14 Box plot of absolute percentage error (APE) data. (Source: Data in Figure 2.10)

The simple box plot summarizes the distribution in terms of five quantities. In addition, the distance between the quartiles is called the Interquartile range (IQR) and is a measure of dispersion.

A single comprehensive box plot may not be enough by itself. One weakness is its inability to identify or discern data with different populations. Figure 2.15 shows box plots of the absolute percentage errors for three products for three successive years. It shows that there are really two distributions: APEs for the first two products and APEs for the third product. A single box plot would mask these differences.

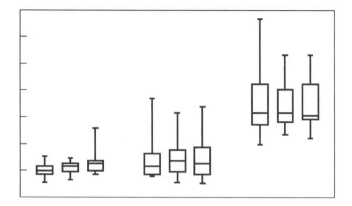

Figure 2.15 Box plots of monthly absolute percentage errors (APE) for three products over three years.

## Quantile-Quantile Plots

When the quantiles (or percentiles) of one distribution are plotted in a scatter diagram against the quantiles of the second distribution, we get a quantile-quantile (Q-Q) plot. If two data sets have the same probability distribution, the Q-Q plot is linear (looks like a straight line). For example, the quantiles of an empirical data set can be compared to the quantiles of the standard normal distribution ($\mu = 0$, $\sigma = 1$) to test for normality. Such a display is known as a normal probability plot.

> ***The quantile-quantile (Q-Q) plot is used to determine whenever two data sets have the same probability distribution.***

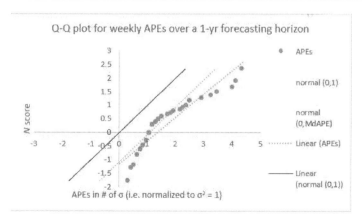

Figure 2.16 Normal probability plots in which the data are not normally distributed.

Figure 2.16 shows a normal probability plot for a situation in which the data are not normally distributed. When the distribution of the data is right-skewed, the highest values tend to be far from the center and the lowest values tend to be close to the center. Thus, the highest and lowest values both exceed the expected normal deviates. For left-skewed data distributions, the highest and lowest values tend to be less than expected normal deviates. The pattern weaves around the line in the case of light- and heavy-tailed data distributions.

A normal probability plot for the APE data (Figure 2.10) is shown in Figure 2.16. This plot shows an upper tail in the empirical distribution that is much longer than that of the normal distribution. The tails of many data sets are longer than those of the normal distribution, but generally by less than in this example.

## *Creating Data Summaries (Resistant and Robust!)*

To get a better understanding of patterns and structure in data, we extract some essential features from the data and summarize them with a few meaningful numbers. These summary measures are called statistics.

Summary statistics are commonly used for simply describing some aspect of the data that needs to be highlighted for a particular application, such as measures of bias, dispersion, variability, measured uncertainty: summarizing salient features of a frequency distribution, such as percentiles for setting safety stock; comparing two or more frequency distributions; and confirming an analysis, such as calculating prediction intervals on forecasts and determining confidence limits for model parameters.

Unusual or atypical values, called outliers, occur quite frequently in data used by demand planners and forecasters. Summary statistics based on averaging, most notably the arithmetic mean and standard deviation, are quite sensitive to outliers, and should be supplemented by non-traditional alternatives whenever decisions based on demand forecasts are to be made.

A statistic is said to be resistant if a change in a small fraction of the data will not produce a large distortion of a total calculated value - it is resistant to weird or unusual values. Statistics based on the median or arithmetic mean of truncated data appear to be much more resistant to outliers than the arithmetic mean (commonly called the average). The arithmetic mean is clearly not resistant because its value can be changed by arbitrarily increasing only one of its terms. The median, on the other hand, is quite resistant.

A seminal study on measures of location and their properties under varying realistic assumptions of distribution is found in the Princeton Robustness Study (Dave Andrews and six authors in 1972 published Robust Estimation of Location: Survey and Advances); however, insufficient attention has been given to date in appropriately handling outliers in forecasting best practices in supply chain organizations, especially with regard to accuracy measurement.

| *An outlier is an unusual or atypical value in a data set.* |
| --- |

## Centrality

The location, or central tendency, of a dataset is the center of the data when they are arranged in order of size; this is the typical or average measurement. The most commonly used measure of central tendency is the familiar arithmetic mean or sample average (the sum of n data values $\{Y_1, Y_2, ..., Y_n\}$ divided by $n$).

In the next chapter, we encounter this statistic when we define the moving average of p successive values $\{Y_t, Y_{t-1}, ..., Y_{t-(p-1)}\}$ of a time series by $(Y_t + Y_{t-1} + Y_{t-2} + ... + Y_{t-(p-1)})/p$, where $Y_t$ is the actual value at time t and $p$ is the number of values included in the average. This is the quantity we name P_MAVG for this smoothing method.

Another familiar measure of central tendency is the median. The median is the middle value when the data are arranged in order from lowest to highest.

The reason that no single measure of central tendency is always the best is that each measure can provide its own perspective and insight, and in practice outliers or unusual values can seriously distort the representativeness of certain statistics, such as the commonly used arithmetic mean.

| *The central tendency or location of a set of data is a middle, typical value in the data set.* |
| --- |

## Resistant Centrality: The Trimmed Mean

One simple way to make the arithmetic mean less sensitive to outliers is first to delete, or trim, a proportion of the data from each end and then calculate the arithmetic mean of the remaining numbers. Such a statistic is called a trimmed mean. The midmean, for example, is a 25% trimmed mean because 25% of the data values have been trimmed from each end (i.e., the mean is taken of the values between the 25th and 75th percentiles). The deletion of values is based on their order, but the deleted values are not necessarily the extreme values. For the sample of 12 absolute percentage errors in Figure 2.17, the midmean is $(2.1 + 2.6 + 2.6 + 3.1 + 3.7 + 4.7)/6 = 3.1$, a fairly typical value.

## Variability

In addition to measures of central tendency, certain measures of variability (also called measures of spread or dispersion) are also useful. Some commonly used examples are the range and standard deviation and variations of these. The range is simply the difference between the largest and smallest value in a set of data. To measure variability, we need to consider how far away numbers are from their typical value, such as the arithmetic mean or median. Then, to summarize variability in the data, we can square or take absolute values of these deviations and seek a typical value for these deviations. This is a measure of spread or dispersion.

> **Spread or variability in a data set is a measure of dispersion around the measure of central tendency.**

The most familiar measure is the sample standard deviation, which is the square root of the (sample) variance. For a sample of values $\{Y_1, Y_2, \ldots Y_n \}$, the sample variance is the sum of squared deviations from the sample mean divided by $n - 1$. Although the standard deviation is by far the most familiar measure of variability, it is not always the most effective. Like the sample mean, it can be very misleading when there are outliers.

Taking, instead, the absolute deviations from the mean and average the result is better, because a large absolute deviation is not as extreme as a squared deviation. This gives rise to the mean absolute deviation (MAD) statistic. However, because it is an arithmetic mean, the MAD statistic may still not be sufficiently resistant to outliers. In comparing these measures, the practical consequences of using inappropriate assumptions about the data can be more damaging than the uncritical reliance on theoretical approximations.

> **A sample standard deviation is a conventional measure of spread.**

## Resistant Variability: Median Absolute Deviation from the Median

To ensure lower sensitivity to outliers, the median absolute deviation (MdAD is a viable alternative to the sample standard deviation and MAD. The calculation of a MdAD is illustrated in Figure 2.17. The data represent 12 monthly APE values. The MdAD is calculated by first sorting the data from smallest to largest (column 2) and picking the median, which is $(2.6 + 3.1)/2 = 2.85\%$, because there is an even number of data values. Absolute deviations from the median are calculated next (column 3), and the result is reranked (column 4). The midvalue of the latter set of numbers is the MdAD $(0.95 + 1.25)/2 = 1.1$.

## Resistant Variability: The Interquartile Range

The interquartile range (IQR) is the difference between the 75th and 25th percentile positions in the ordered dataset. For example, the dataset in Figure 2.17 consists of twelve absolute percentage errors $\{1.1, 1.6, 4.7, 2.1. 3.1, 32.7, 5.8. 2.6. 4.8, 1.9, 3.7. 2.6.$ Calculations for Q1 and Q3 are taking the position of data as their values, resulting in the IQR = 2.9%

- 1st quartile = value of position from rounded ¼(n+1) = 13/4 = 3.25 → 3rd value: 1.9%
- 3rd quartile = value of position from rounded ¾ (n+1) = 39/4 = 9.75 → 10th value: 4.8%
- the 25th percentile position is the rounded ¼(n+1) = 13/4 = 3.25, so the 3rd point, whose value is 1,9%.
- the 75th percentile position is the rounded ¾ (n+1) = 39/4 = 9.75, so the 10th point, whose value is 1,9%.

When we deal with forecast accuracy in practice, a demand forecaster typically reports averages of quantities based on forecast errors (squared errors, absolute errors, percentage errors, etc.). To properly interpret a measure of forecast accuracy, we must also be sensitive to the role of unusual values in these calculations. Over the twelve-monthly periods, the mean absolute percentage error (MAPE = 5.6%) can be interpreted as a typical percentage error for a month. The median absolute percentage error (MdAPE = [2.6 + 3.1]/2 = 2.9%), on the other hand, is an outlier-resistant measure and gives quite a different answer.

Note that the arithmetic mean has been distorted by the outlying value 32.7%. The arithmetic mean of the numbers when we exclude the outlier is 3.1% and, like the MdAPE, appears to be much more typical of the underlying data. Overall, an average absolute percentage error for the 12 months is more likely to be around 3% per month than around 6% per month, in this example.

| Position | | Q1 | | | Q2 | | Q3 | | | | | Data Summary | | Outlier Effect | |
|---|---|---|---|---|---|---|---|---|---|---|---|---|---|---|---|
| | 1 | 2 | 3 | 4 | 5 | 6 | 7 | 8 | 9 | 10 | 11 | 12 | | | | |
| Percentile (%) | 8 | 17 | 25 | 33 | 42 | 50 | 58 | 67 | 75 | 83 | 92 | 100 | | | | |
| APEs (ranked) (%) | 1.1 | 1.6 | 1.9 | 2.1 | 2.6 | 2.6 | 3.1 | 3.7 | 4.7 | 4.8 | 5.8 | 32.7 | Mean | 5.6 | +80% | (MAPE) |
| Q1, Q2 (Median), Q3 | | | 1.9 | | | 2.85 | | | 4.8 | | | | Median | 2.9 | +10% | (MdAPE) |
| Midmean | | | | 2.1 | 2.6 | 2.6 | 3.1 | 3.7 | 4.7 | | | | Midmean | 3.1 | +11% | |
| Squared Deviations from the Mean | 19.9 | 15.7 | 13.4 | 12.0 | 8.8 | 8.8 | 6.0 | 3.5 | 0.7 | 0.6 | 0.1 | 736.7 | MSD | 68.8 | +3297% | |
| Absolute Deviations from the Mean | 4.5 | 4.0 | 3.7 | 3.5 | 3.0 | 3.0 | 2.5 | 1.9 | 0.9 | 0.8 | 0.2 | 27.1 | MAD | 4.6 | +278% | |
| Absolute Deviations from the Median | 1.8 | 1.25 | 0.95 | 0.8 | 0.3 | 0.3 | 0.3 | 0.5 | 1.9 | 2.0 | 3.0 | 29.9 | MdAD | 1.1 | +10% | |
| (ranked) | 0.3 | 0.3 | 0.3 | 0.8 | 0.9 | 0.95 | 1.25 | 1.8 | 1.9 | 2.0 | 3.0 | 29.9 | | | | |

| Position | | Q1 | | | Q2 | | Q3 | | | | Data Summary | | |
|---|---|---|---|---|---|---|---|---|---|---|---|---|---|
| | 1 | 2 | 3 | 4 | 5 | 6 | 7 | 8 | 9 | 10 | 11 | | |
| Percentile (%) | 9 | 18 | 27 | 36 | 45 | 55 | 64 | 73 | 82 | 91 | 100 | | |
| APEs (ranked) (%) | 1.1 | 1.6 | 1.9 | 2.1 | 2.6 | 2.6 | 3.1 | 3.7 | 4.7 | 4.8 | 5.8 | Mean | 3.1 (MAPE) |
| Q1, Q2 (Median), Q3 | | | 1.9 | | | 2.6 | | | 4.7 | | | Median | 2.6 (MdAPE) |
| Midmean | | | | 2.1 | 2.6 | 2.6 | 3.1 | 3.7 | | | | Midmean | 2.8 |
| Squared Deviations from the Mean | 4.0 | 2.2 | 1.4 | 1.0 | 0.2 | 0.2 | 0.0 | 0.4 | 2.6 | 2.9 | 7.3 | MSD | 2.0 |
| Absolute Deviations from the Mean | 2.0 | 1.5 | 1.2 | 1.0 | 0.5 | 0.5 | 0.0 | 0.6 | 1.6 | 1.7 | 2.7 | MAD | 1.2 |
| Absolute Deviations from the Median | 1.5 | 1.0 | 0.7 | 0.5 | 0.0 | 0.0 | 0.5 | 1.1 | 2.1 | 2.2 | 3.2 | MdAD | 1.0 |
| (ranked) | 0.0 | 0.0 | 0.5 | 0.5 | 0.7 | 1.0 | 1.1 | 1.5 | 2.1 | 2.2 | 3.2 | | |

Figure 2.17 Calculation of the median absolute deviation from the median (MdAD), based on the 12 observations (*top panel*) and with the outlier (32.7) removed (*bottom panel*).

Among most demand planners, the MAPE is routinely reported for planning purposes to summarize forecasting performance. What should a demand planner and forecast practitioner do in practice? It is always best to calculate and compare multiple measures for the same quantity to be estimated, just to be assured that you are not misled by the conventional average calculation. If the measures are practically close, you report the conventional measure. If not, you check out the APEs for anything that appears unusual. Then work with domain experts to find a credible rationale (stock outs, weather, strikes, etc.)

We can scale MdAD and IQR by dividing by 0.6745 and 1.349, respectively, giving the unbiased median absolute deviation (UMdAD) and the unbiased interquartile range (UIQR. The divisors used for scaling are empirically derived so that, for normally distributed data, this scaling makes these measures good approximations of their theoretical counterpart $\sigma$ (the population standard deviation) if the number of values can be assumed to be very large.

**The MAD, MdAD, and IQR are other useful measures of spread.**

# Detecting Outliers with Resistant Measures

Outliers in forecast errors and other sources of unusual data values should never be ignored or deleted in the accuracy measurement process. With the measurement of bias, for example, the calculation of the mean forecast error ME (the arithmetic mean of Actual [A] minus Forecast [F]) will drive the estimate towards the outlier. An otherwise unbiased pattern of performance can be distorted by just a single unusual value.

Although the arithmetic mean is the traditional estimator of central tendency, forecasters and business planners should not accept it uncritically. As our example shows, one outlier can have an undue effect on the arithmetic mean and pull an estimate of the bulk of data away from a representative or typical value.

The values that do not seem to fit can be filtered out by a simple rule. In Tukey's terminology, a step is defined as 1.5 times the IQR. Inner fences are values one step above the 75th percentile and one step below the 25th percentile:

- Lower inner fence = 25th percentile - 1.5 IQR
- Upper inner fence = 75th percentile + 1.5 IQR

Outer fences are values two steps above and below these percentiles:
- Lower outer fence = 25th percentile - 3.0 IQR
- Upper outer fence = 75th percentile + 3.0 IQR

A value outside an inner fence can be an outlier, but a value outside an outer fence is much more likely to be one. The choice of 1.5 is arbitrary, but it seems to work well, in practice.

For the (APE) data (Figure 2.10), we find that
- Lower inner fence = 7 - 1.5 (9) = - 7
- Upper inner fence = 16 + 1.5 (9) = 30

Outer fences are determined as
- Lower outer fence = -20
- Upper outer fence = 43

According to the inner fence rule, there are five potential outliers (30%, 32%, 37%, 38% and 40%).

Alternatively, we can also calculate the median +/- 3 UMdAD, which gives (10.5 − 3* [3.5/0.6745}) = -5% and 10.5 + 3*[3.5/0.6745}) = 26%) and find the same five outliers plus an additional one (27%).

Using the *conventional approach*, on the other hand, by adding and subtracting 3 standard deviations from the mean results in the calculations:

Lower limit = mean − 3 standard.deviations = 13.3 − 3*9.1 = -14
Upper limit = mean + 3 standard.deviations = 13.3 + 3*9.1 = 41

Using three standard deviations rule to determine the cutoffs results in no outliers identified. The MAPE is 13.3 and the MdAPE = 10.5. A good rule is to always calculate both and report the MAPE only when the two measures are close, in practice, taking into account the business context of the application. Otherwise, closely scrutinize the underlying data.

## The Need for Nonconventional Methods

The need for a nonconventional approach to estimation is motivated by two problems. First, a forecaster never has an accurate knowledge of the true underlying distribution of the random errors in a model. Second, even slight deviations from a strict parametric model can give rise to poor performance in statistical forecasting with classical (i.e., associated with the ordinary least-squares method) estimation techniques. Estimators that are less sensitive to these factors are often referred to as robust.

*Big Data sets with numerous unusual values have become more prevalent in planning systems for forecasting replenishments of SKUs (stock-keeping units) for inventory, production, and distribution planning applications. Outliers will become more common.*

There appear to be many meanings of the word robustness in the statistical literature. In the context of estimation, robustness of efficiency means that parameter estimates are highly efficient not only under idealized (usually normal) conditions but also under a wide class of nonstandard circumstances. The 1972 Princeton Robustness Study was an early effort to analyze systematically this concept for estimates of location. Estimates that have robust efficiency are often very resistant to outliers. This can be a very valuable consideration because real-world demand data (typically non-negative) are typically non-normal and possess hard-to-detect outlying or unusual data values. This is the challenge for the smarter forecaster. (a.k.a, *data detective*)

> *What we desire, for best practices, are robust/resistant procedures that are resistant to outlying values and robust against non-normal characteristics in the data distribution, so that they give rise to estimates that are more reliable and credible than those based on normality assumptions.*

## M-Estimators

The M-estimation method can be used to reduce automatically the effect of outliers by giving them a reduced weight when we compute the typical value for the data. The method is based on an estimator that makes repeated use of residuals in an iterative procedure. This estimator, called an M-estimator, is the maximum likelihood estimate (a good statistical property to possess) for the location parameter of a heavy-tailed distribution. Basically, the distribution attributed to Peter J. Huber (b. 1934), behaves like a normal distribution in the middle range and like an  exponential distribution in the tails. Thus, the bulk of the data appears normally distributed but there is a greater chance of having extreme values in the data.

## A Numerical Example

We will work out an example of calculating an M-estimate based on a small set of (ordered) data corresponding to 15 forecast errors on weekly forecasts: {- 67, - 48, 6, 8, 14, 16, 23, 24, 28, 29, 41, 49, 56, 60, 75}.

The first step in data analysis is to investigate the data graphically. Note there are a couple of negative values due to over-forecasting, - 67 and - 48. We might then prepare a Q-Q plot. If the data are normally distributed, they should lie along a straight line. The Q-Q plot can also be used to get a quick-and-dirty robust estimate of the $(\mu, \sigma)$ parameters of the normal distribution. By eyeballing a straight line through the bulk of the points on the Q-Q plot, you can determine that the Y-intercept at X = 0 and the slope of the line correspond to estimates of μ and σ, respectively.

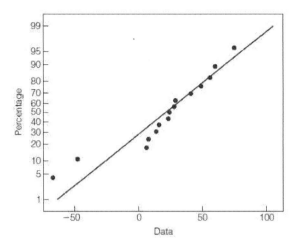

Figure 2.18 Q-Q plot for the example data set (mean = 20.93; standard deviation = 36.46

$$\theta_0 = \text{Median} = 24$$

$$s = \text{MdAD} / 0.6745 = 17/0.6745 = 25.20$$

$$Ks = 50.40$$

$$\theta_1 = \left[\sum_i W_i^2 y_i \middle/ \sum_i W_i^2\right] = 357.38/14.24 = 25.13$$

$$s = \text{MdAD} / 0.6745 = 17.13 / 0.6745 = 25.40$$

$$Ks = 50.80$$

$$\theta_2 = \left[\sum_i W_i^2 y_i \middle/ \sum_i W_i^2\right] = 358.72/14.25 = 25.17$$

$$V(\theta) = \left[\sum_i W_i^4 (y_i - \theta_2)^2 / (n^*)^2\right]^{1/2}$$

$$= \left[\sum_i W_i^4 (y_i - 25.17)^2 / (13)^2\right]^{1/2} = 8.28$$

where $n^* = $ number of observations receiving full weight

Figure 2.19 Calculations of the Huber M-estimator of location (K = 2, and $\theta_0$ = 24, median).

The plot (figure 2.18) indicates that the two negative values are indeed extreme, and the general pattern drawn by the data, with many points distancing from the reference line, indicate the normality assumption as not valid. On the other hand, the ordinary least-squares estimates, calculated from the data, are $\mu = 20.93$ and $\sigma = 37.74$, which could be used to superimpose a straight line with intercept 20.93 and slope 37.74 on the Q-Q plot. As can be seen from Figure 2.18, the straight line determined from the least-squares estimates does not represent the bulk of the data on the Q-Q plot very well.

Figures 2.19 and 2.20 show the calculations for the Huber M-estimator of location and its corresponding standard error for our data set {- 67, - 48, 6, 8, 14, 16, 23, 24, 28, 29, 41, 49, 56, 60, 75}. The median of the data is 24. Column 2 is the difference between the raw data and the median. The median absolute deviation is 17; it is the median of the absolute value of this column (the eighth largest absolute value in column 2). An approximate unbiased scale statistic is the UMdAD = MdAD/0.6745 = 25.2.

The results for the mean, the 0.25-trimmed mean (midmean), and the Huber M-estimator are shown in Figure 2.20:

| $Y_{(i)}$ | $Y_{(i)} - \theta_0$ | $w_{i1}^2$ | $Y_{(i)} - \theta_1$ | $w_{i2}^2$ |
|---|---|---|---|---|
| −67 | −91 | 50.4/91 | −92.13 | 50.8/92.13 |
| −48 | −72 | 50.4/72 | −73.13 | 50.8/73.13 |
| 6 | −18 | 1 | −19.13 | 1 |
| 8 | −16 | 1 | −17.13 | 1 |
| 14 | −10 | 1 | −11.13 | 1 |
| 16 | −8 | 1 | −9.13 | 1 |
| 23 | −1 | 1 | −2.13 | 1 |
| 24 | 0 | 1 | −1.13 | 1 |
| 28 | 4 | 1 | 2.87 | 1 |
| 29 | 5 | 1 | 3.87 | 1 |
| 41 | 17 | 1 | 15.87 | 1 |
| 49 | 25 | 1 | 23.87 | 1 |
| 56 | 32 | 1 | 30.87 | 1 |
| 60 | 36 | 1 | 34.87 | 1 |
| 75 | 51 | 50.4/51 | 49.87 | 1 |

Figure 2.20 Calculations of the Huber M-estimator of location (K = 2, and $\theta_0$ = 24, median).

On a final technical note, V(θ) is the estimated standard deviation (standard error) of the location estimator and should not be confused with the estimated standard deviation of the data values.

| ¤ | Mean¤ | Midmean¤ | M-estimator¤ |
|---|---|---|---|
| θ¤ | 20.93¤ | 25.78¤ | 25.17¤ |
| V(θ)¤ | 9.74¤ | 7.37¤ | 8.28¤ |

We have now shown several times that the arithmetic mean (and hence any moving average) is very sensitive to outliers (extreme values) in the data. Both the trimmed mean and Huber M-estimator provide estimates that are less sensitive to these extreme values and thus offer some protection. The standard error of the M-estimator is somewhat smaller than the corresponding standard error of the arithmetic mean.

However, the standard error for the midmean is significantly smaller. This is somewhat expected since computations for the midmean begin by trimming (Winsorizing) 40% of the data, this 40% being the most extreme values (three from each end). However, these values still have some effect on (but less than on **least squares**) the Huber M-estimator because their associated weight is not zero.

The M-estimator can also be used in regression analysis (Chapter 10) to weight extreme values so that they cannot unduly distort estimates in regression relationships.

## Are There More Reliable Measures Than the MAPE?

Among practitioners, it is a jungle out there trying to understand the role of the APEs in the measurement of forecast accuracy. *Forecast accuracy* is commonly measured and reported by just the **M**ean **A**bsolute **P**ercentage **E**rror (MAPE), which is the same no matter which definition of forecast error one uses.

The M-estimation method, can be used to automatically reduce the effect of outliers by appropriately down- weighting values 'far away' from a typical MAPE.  The method is based on an estimator that makes repeated use of the underlying data in an iterative procedure. In the case of the MAPE, a family of robust estimators, called *M-estimators,* is obtained by minimizing a specified function of the absolute percentage errors (APE). Alternate forms of the function produce the various M-estimators. Generally, the estimates are computed by iterated weighted least squares.

It is worth noting that the **Bisquare**-weighting scheme is more severe than the **Huber** weighting scheme. In the bisquare scheme, all data for which $| e_i | \leq Ks$ will have a weight less than 1. Data having weights greater than 0.9 are not considered extreme. Data with weights less than 0.5 are regarded as extreme, and data with zero weight are, of course, ignored. To counteract the impact of outliers, the bisquare estimator gives zero weight to data whose forecast errors are quite far from zero.

What we need, for best practices, are *robust/resistant procedures* that are resistant to outlying values and robust against non-normal characteristics in the data distribution, so that they give rise to estimates that are more reliable and credible than those based on normality assumptions.

Taking a data-driven approach with APE data to measure accuracy, we can create more useful TAPE (Typical APE) measures. However, we recommend that you start with the MdAPE for the first iteration. Then use the Huber scheme for the next iteration and finish with one or two more iterations of the Bisquare scheme. The Huber-Bisquare-Bisquare Typical APE (HBB TAPE) measure has worked quite well for me in practice and can be readily automated even in a spreadsheet. This is worth testing with your own data to convince yourself whether a Mean APE should remain King of the accuracy jungle!!

> The *Huber-Bisquare-Bisquare* Typical APE (HBB TAPE) measure has worked quite well in practice

## *Why Is the Normal Distribution So Important?*

Statistical analyses usually proceed along the following lines:

- Postulate a probability model, including unknown parameters, for a situation involving uncertainty.
- Use data to estimate the unknown parameters in the model.
- Plug the estimated parameters into the model and make calculations.

For a normal distribution with (population) mean $\mu$ and standard deviation $\sigma$, we know from introductory statistics that the interval ($\mu$ - 1.64 $\sigma$, $\mu$ + 1.64 $\sigma$) contains 90% of the distribution. Similarly, there is approximately a 68% probability that a random observation from a normal distribution will be between plus and minus one standard deviation $\sigma$ of the mean $\mu$. This well-known normal distribution, which is deeply rooted in statistical theory, looks symmetrical and is completely specified by the two (population) parameters ($\mu,\sigma$).

> *In inferential statistics, probability models are used to make assumptions about the probability that a certain portion of the data will fall within a specified range.*

One reason why forecasters use histograms is to get a sense of how closely historical demand, forecast errors, or model residuals resemble a normal (bell shaped) probability distribution. For example, we might assume that weekly changes in inventory stock follow a normal distribution. Using historical data to estimate the mean and standard deviation of the assumed distribution, we then use the model to predict future changes in inventory. When we look at 52 weekly changes in inventory over a year, we are considering a sample of size 52 from a hypothetical population of all weekly changes in inventory.

The normality assumption is widely used among practitioners and is justified primarily for the following reasons:

- Observed experimental data are often represented reasonably well by a normal distribution. This can be verified by the use of empirical frequency distributions or various normal probability plotting techniques.
- When the data are not normally distributed, it is theoretically possible to find a transformation of the data that renders the distribution normal. Although this is not always practical, sometimes a very simple transformation (such as taking the logarithm or square root of the data) results in residuals that appear approximately normal.
- Fortunately, the normality assumption permits us to apply a very extensive (although not always realistic), often simple, and quite elegant set of statistical tests to a multitude of statistical forecasting problems.

*In the words of Tukey: Practice dictates a choice between what can be done and should be done. In the absence of anything better, normality usually implies what can be done.*

Much statistical theory used in demand forecasting is built on a mathematical foundation that is often not justified in the practice of demand planning. For determining a typical value and variability from well-behaved data (usually implying they are normally distributed), the arithmetic mean and sample variance can be shown to be "best" (i.e., the estimators have optimal theoretical properties) if the data can be viewed as a random sample from the normal distribution. Least-squares techniques are not only not "best," but their results can be very misleading when the data deviate even a little from normality assumptions. Because of this, smarter forecasters need to adopt forecasting procedures that are robust against non-normal characteristics in the data to avoid producing misleading results.

## Case Example: GLOBL Product Line B Sales in Region A

The GLOBL forecaster introduced in Chapter 1 is trying to get some insight into the demand patterns of product line B (academia challenged) in a specific region by performing an exploratory data analysis. The data table that follows contains four years of monthly sales of Product Line B consumer electronics products (in units) in Region A:

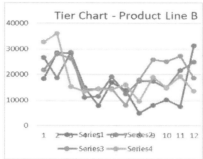

1.  Create a time plot, and examine the pattern in terms of the seasonal, trend, business cycle variation. Show the annual variations by constructing a *tier chart* for each year (total four). How would you characterize the seasonality? Is the seasonality regular? Can you improve the display by identifying chart junk (horizontal lines necessary?) and missing axis labeling?

| Product Line B | | Year | | |
|---|---|---|---|---|
| | 18416 | 26668 | 21777 | 32705 |
| | 28517 | 18678 | 27999 | 36078 |
| | 28279 | 28564 | 26272 | 15235 |
| | 15014 | 11092 | 14192 | 13428 |
| | 7914 | 11538 | 14516 | 14451 |
| Month | 17008 | 19182 | 14454 | 14169 |
| | 13914 | 12445 | 8019 | 16059 |
| | 4870 | 17409 | 17995 | 9550 |
| | 8015 | 17416 | 25838 | 19072 |
| | 10168 | 14848 | 25020 | 14996 |
| | 7526 | 21601 | 27224 | 19264 |
| | 31296 | 24908 | 18752 | 13676 |

2. Construct a preliminary STI_Classification and quantify the contribution of trend and seasonal to the total variation.

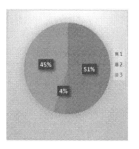

> **Results**: Row effect (Seasonality) = 51%, Column effect (Trend-Cycle) = 4%, Unexplained = 45%. Comment on how you may need to improve the visual for more effective presentation.

| | Count | Sum | Average | Median | St.·Dev· | UMdAD |
|---|---|---|---|---|---|---|
| Jan. | 4 | 99566 | 24892 | 24223 | 6214 | 6117 |
| Feb. | 4 | 111272 | 27818 | 28258 | 7125 | 5989 |
| Mar. | 4 | 98350 | 24588 | 27276 | 6318 | 1699 |
| Apr. | 4 | 53726 | 13432 | 13810 | 1689 | 1176 |
| May | 4 | 48419 | 12105 | 12995 | 3120 | 2208 |
| Jun. | 4 | 64813 | 16203 | 15731 | 2361 | 2105 |
| July | 4 | 50437 | 12609 | 13180 | 3401 | 2679 |
| Aug. | 4 | 49824 | 12456 | 13480 | 6356 | 6260 |
| Sep. | 4 | 70341 | 17585 | 18244 | 7347 | 6243 |
| Oct. | 4 | 65032 | 16258 | 14922 | 6257 | 3579 |
| Nov. | 4 | 75615 | 18904 | 20433 | 8288 | 5901 |
| Dec. | 4 | 88632 | 22158 | 21830 | 7629 | 8326 |

3. Calculate the 12 monthly averages and medians and comment on the pattern of these measures of central tendency. Do you find any unusual values or pattern within the monthly patterns?

4. Contrast the standard deviation and a resistant alternative such as UMdAD.

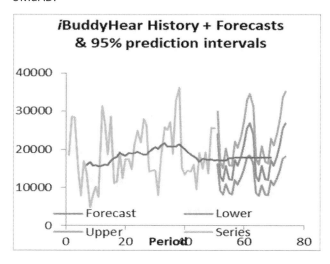

5.  Create a visual summary of *change* **&** *chance* for management and planning colleagues and explain your findings in non-technical language.

## *Takeaways*

> ➤ The importance of using **exploratory data analysis** and **visualization** tools based on a sound statistical foundation for all phases of demand forecasting cannot be overemphasized.

> ➤ For exploratory as well as confirmatory analysis, a number of data summary statistics are recommended: measures, such as the arithmetic mean, median, and trimmed mean, used to describe central tendency; measures of dispersion, such as the standard deviation, median absolute deviation from the median, and range; box plots, which are a convenient way of visually displaying a five-number summary of a distribution; scatter diagrams, which are a useful tool for looking for linear associations between pairs of variables.

> ➤ **Outlier limits** based on measures resistant to unusual, out-of-distribution values.

> ➤ Summaries are necessary to quantify information inherent in the shape or distribution of data. We plot frequency distributions to show what percentage of the total number of data each interval contains, and cumulative frequencies or percentiles can be used to determine whether a data set follows a normal probability distribution.

> ➤ When assumptions are not satisfied, a statistical analysis can give misleading results and unreliable (and likely inaccurate) forecasting results. When an exploratory data analysis suggests the data are non-normal with unusual values, robust and resistant methods should be considered as a complement to conventional approaches and displayed together.

# 3

# Predictive Analytics: Selecting Useful Forecasting Techniques

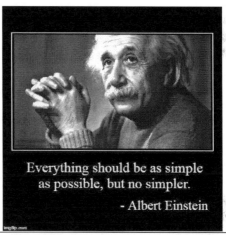

Everything should be as simple as possible, but no simpler.

\- Albert Einstein

This chapter provides an overview of the most widely used forecasting techniques available for solving demand forecasting problems. One of the first things you will need when you start putting a forecasting model together is a listing of projection techniques. We describe a way of classifying projection techniques into qualitative and quantitative approaches. Whatever the technique, you need to start the selection process with

- a statement of the forecasting problem in terms of the stages of a product/service life cycle
- an economic theory stating what changes will affect demand for a product or service
- a gathering of market intelligence from field sales forecasters, market research studies, and competitive analyses
- a listing of plans for new products and special events or promotions.

## *All Models Are Wrong. Some Are Useful*

M any different forecasting techniques are available, ranging from elementary smoothing methods to more complex ARIMA and econometric models. How are we to select the most appropriate one for a particular situation? Firstly, there is no best forecasting model, only appropriate and credible models for the context to which they are being applied. How can we expect to derive accurate forecasts before we have asked the right questions? Delving straight into the methods and models is no substitute for a careful examination of the data first, followed with the listing of the pros and cons of what is available. Attributed to the world-renowned statistician George E. P. Box (1919–2013) is the saying, "*All models are wrong. Some are useful*".

In most circumstances, a demand forecaster will be well advised to develop multiple models in a given situation and maintain them as the best selection. For what performs best in one instance may very well rank lower in the next forecasting cycle.

Forecasting techniques can be classified as either **qualitative** or **quantitative**. This distinction may have no bearing on the accuracy of the forecast achievable by a particular approach. What is the difference between a qualitative and quantitative technique? To describe what one of two mutually exclusive things are, we only need to define one. It is easier to define quantitative as something that involves *mostly* numbers and *some* judgment. Then, the concept of qualitative is the opposite—*mostly* judgment and *some* numbers.

> *Quantitative techniques are characterized by a rigorous data acquisition procedure along with a mechanical application of techniques. Qualitative techniques may lack rigorous data acquisition and involve techniques that are more intuitive and requiring more human judgment.*

## Qualitative Techniques

Qualitative techniques provide a framework within which running models (including forms of quantitative analyses, such as decision trees and data mining) are brought to bear on a particular forecasting problem. The objective of a qualitative technique is to bring together in a logical, unbiased, and systematic way all information and judgments that relate to the demand variables of interest. These techniques use informed judgment and rating schemes to turn qualitative information into numeric estimates.

Familiar qualitative techniques include the panel of consensus, Delphi method, market research (focus groups), surveys, visionary forecasts, and historical analogies. Treatments of these subjects can be found in forecasting textbooks, Wikipedia pages, and other search results available online. A brief description of some of these qualitative techniques follows.

**Panel consensus.** Perhaps the most widely practiced qualitative technique, a panel consensus can be as simple as having managers sit around a conference table and decide collectively on the forecast for a product or service. Bringing executives from various business disciplines together increases the amount of relevant information available to the decision makers.

A further advantage of the approach is the speed with which forecasts can be obtained, particularly in the absence of complete historical or market data. This advantage may be offset by the lack of accountability for the forecast.

Also, the typical problems of group dynamics become apparent here and are compounded by the relative ranks in management. Unfortunately, the person with the best insight may not have sufficient weight to sway the whole group decision.

**Delphi method.** This method is used to obtain the consensus of a panel of experts about a problem or issue. The Delphi method attempts to avoid the possible negative aspects associated with group dynamics (e.g., suppression of minority opinions, domination by strong individuals who may be incorrect, unwillingness to change public positions, and bandwagon effects). Therefore, instead of bringing these experts together in a debating forum, the Delphi method relies on the distribution of questionnaires to the experts with an admonishment not to discuss the problem among themselves. They may not know who the other members of the panel are, and they are not provided with individual opinions or estimates.

The initial questionnaire may be used to state the problem and to obtain preliminary estimates and reasons or assumptions behind them. The responses are then summarized and fed back to the panel. Members with widely differing estimates are asked to review the responses and, if appropriate, revise their estimates. Through several iterations it may be possible to refine the differences among experts to a usable range of opinion. However, there is no attempt to force an expert to accept the majority opinion. If an expert feels strongly about another position and can articulate it persuasively, the method provides a range of opinion, which may be desirable in conditions of high uncertainty.

Criticisms of the Delphi method include questions about panel members' true level of expertise, the clarity (or outright vagueness) of questionnaires, and the reliability of forecasts.

**Historical analogue**. This method uses the history of similar products as a reasonable guide in situations such as the introduction of a new product. For example, the introduction of digital television into households can be related to the earlier introduction of color television; perhaps the type of growth curve is comparable here.

The depletion of natural resources may be viewed similarly. Wood burning was replaced by coal, which was replaced by oil. As oil resources are eventually depleted, and if nuclear power continues to face problems, we find that solar and wind technology will become a serious energy alternative.

Historical analogues may also be useful in the shorter term when a new product replaces and improves on its predecessor. For example, each new generation of computers can be evaluated in terms of price and performance relative to the existing market. Comparing the current improvements in price and performance with previous new product introductions, given their rate of price and performance improvement, can suggest the appropriate introduction or replacement rate.

**Surveys**. Business surveys have been widely used throughout the world to measure economic movements such as manufacturing production in a country. The variables used in these surveys are typically qualitative in nature with only a few responses possible, such as Larger, Smaller, and Unchanged.

Some examples of variables used in a manufacturing production survey include volume of production, production capacity, prices, orders, purchases, and time of deliveries. The responses are then further calibrated into barometer-type series in which the difference between larger and smaller responses is summarized.

The resulting series are reported by central statistical agencies for use by business economists and managers to get a pulse of the overall economy in relation to their own particular industry sector.

**Visionary technological forecasting**. This approach offers a variety of techniques that attempt to predict future technological trends. Often, a set of "S" curves are constructed from data representing factors such as speed, efficiency, horsepower, and density to predict the characteristics of the next generation of technological products. For example, the capacity of a memory chip to store a given number of bits of information can be plotted over time (often using semi-logarithmic scales).

By extrapolating this growth curve, the forecaster in effect predicts the next breakthrough. Similarly, the constant dollar cost per chip can be plotted and extrapolated. Because there are relatively few data values for most items being forecast, significant judgment is required and assumptions must be developed and evaluated. There are physical and theoretical limits to certain factors such as speed not exceeding the speed of light and efficiency not exceeding a certain value.

**Morphological research**. This method attempts to identify all possible parameters that may be part of the solution to a problem. A (multidimensional) box is created showing all possible combinations of parameters. Each possibility is then individually evaluated. By determining the number of parameters by which the proposed technology differs from present technology, we can evaluate which breakthroughs are most likely to occur.

**Role playing**. In a role-playing scenario, several panel members are assigned the role of the competitor. (One of the potential drawbacks of using the Delphi and panel consensus techniques for forecasting demand is that the competitor is typically not represented.) Several panel members are made responsible for developing information about the competitor and for creating competitor strategies and reaction plans. In a simulated forecasting session, assumptions developed by the home team are challenged by the competition.

The separation of roles may allow a greater range of possibilities to be explored and more realistic assumptions to be developed than would otherwise occur.

**Decision trees**. Decision trees are used to help decide upon a course of action from a set of alternative actions that could be taken. Alternative actions are based on selected criteria such as maximization of expected revenues and minimization of expected costs.

The method uses probability theory to assess to the odds for the alternatives. In most cases, however, the probability assessments are subjective in nature and cannot be tested for validity. Decision trees are frequently used in making pricing and product-planning decisions and for developing hedging policies to protect against future currency changes in international financing arrangements

. Consider a simple situation in which a firm is deciding how to respond to a published request for bids for 1000 units of a nonstandard product. The firm's managers believe there is a 30% chance of winning the contract with a bid of $1000 per unit and a 70% chance of losing the contract to a competitor. A win would result in $1 million in revenue (1000 units x $1000/unit). At a price of $750 per unit, the probability of a win is expected to be 60%. A win of $750 would result in $750000 in revenue.

> *Qualitative techniques are most commonly used in forecasting something about which the amount, type, and quality of data are limited.*

If the decision is made to go with a bid of $1000/unit, the expected value is equal to the probability of a win (0.3) multiplied by the revenue ($1 million) plus the probability of loss (0.7) multiplied by the revenue ($0), or $300000. Similarly, for the alternative $750 bid the expected value is (0.6) ($750000) + (0.4) ($0), or $450000. If the managers' expected probabilities are correct, a lower bid would yield more revenue.

The profit margin for the alternative bid is smaller but the probability of winning the bid is substantially increased. If a firm has little available capacity, a $1000 bid might be appropriate. If it wins the bid, the job will be very profitable. If they lose the bid, they still have plenty of business. A firm with a smaller backlog of orders on hand may be more interested in keeping the volumes up to help maintain revenues and operating efficiencies.

## Quantitative Approaches

If appropriate and sufficient data are available, then quantitative techniques can be employed. Quantitative techniques can be classified into two more categories: **stochastic (statistical)** and **deterministic**.

**Deterministic methods.** These methods incorporate the identification and explicit determination of relationships between the variable being forecast and other influencing factors. Deterministic techniques include anticipation surveys, growth curves, leading indicators (Chapter 7), and input-output tables.

**Input-output analysis.** This method was developed by Nobel laureate Wassily Leontief (1905–1999) as a method for quantifying relationships among various sectors of the economy. This forecasting approach, generally used for long-range forecasts, can be used to answer one or more of the following questions: What is happening in the economy or industry sector? What is important about different aspects of the economy or industry sectors? How should we look at the economy or industry sectors? How should we look at changes in the economy or industry sectors?

**Dynamic systems modeling**. This branch of modelling involves building evaluation models that replicate how systems operate and how decisions are made. In a business environment, the analyst models the flows of orders, materials, finished goods, and revenues and subsystems are developed for functional areas such as marketing/selling, pricing, installation/maintenance, research, product development, and manufacturing.

> *Quantitative approaches are often classified into statistical and deterministic.*

The information and operational **feedback** systems are also modeled. The objective might be to evaluate alternative policies to determine the combination of policies and strategies that will result in growth in assets employed and profitability.

Pioneered by Jay Forrester (1918-2016), the equations that describe the system are not based on correlation studies; rather, they are descriptive in nature.

For example, the number of salespeople this month equals the number last month plus new hires minus losses. Equations are then developed describing how hires and losses are determined If an individual salesperson can sell a given amount of product, the desired sales force equals the desired total sales divided by the quota per salesperson. Hires are initiated when the actual sales force size falls below the desired level.

In a similar manner, a set of equations is developed that represents the behavior of the system or business. **Assumptions** are established and the model is exercised using an evaluation language incorporated in computer software. A properly developed model should be able to simulate past behavior and provide insights into strategies that can improve the performance of the system.

## Self-Driven Forecasting Techniques

**Statistical (stochastic) techniques.** These techniques focus entirely on patterns, pattern changes, and disturbances caused by random influences. This book extensively treats quantitative techniques as **methods** (moving averages and time series decomposition) and **models** (State Space and regression analysis), with the distinction being that models explicitly include a random error assumption as the *certain* uncertainty component.

Within statistical techniques, there are essentially two approaches. The first approach is best illustrated by a **time series decomposition** method, discussed in Chapter 5. The primary assumption on which this methodology is based is that the historical data can be decomposed into several *unobservable* components, such as trend, seasonality, cycle, and irregularity, and that these components can then be analyzed and projected by component into the future. A *self-driven* forecast is then obtained by combining the projections for the individual components.

> *A decomposition method is an approach to forecasting that regards a time series in terms of a number of unobservable components, such as trend, cycle, seasonality, and irregularity.*

An underlying assumption made in a time series approach is that the factors that caused demand in the past will persist into the future. Time series analysis then helps to identify trends in the data and the growth rates of these trends. For instance, the prime determinant of trend for many consumer products is the growth in the numbers of households.

Time series analysis can also help identify and explain cyclical patterns repeating in the data roughly every two, or three, or more years - commonly referred to as the business cycle. A **business cycle** is usually irregular in depth and duration and tends to correspond to changes in economic expansions and contractions.

*Trend, seasonality, and cycle are only abstractions of reality. These concepts help us think about how to structure data and models for them.*

Other uses of time series analysis include inventory forecasts dealing with daily or weekly shipments of units over short-term sales cycles or lead times, sales forecasts dealing with dollar-based volumes on a monthly to annual basis (this also includes seasonality, which is related to weather and human customs), and forecasts dealing with quarterly and annual economic time series.

A second approach comprises a set of time series techniques that include the model-based approaches associated with the State-Space (an integrated family of exponential smoothing and ARIMA models) and econometric modeling methodologies, discussed in Chapters 8 and 9.

*A model-based approach to forecasting represents the situation usually in terms of mathematical equations with stochastic error terms.*

The *econometric approach* may be viewed as a cause-effect methodology. Its purpose is to identify the drivers responsible for demand. The econometric models of an economy, for example, can be very sophisticated and represent one extreme of econometric modeling. These models are built to depict the essential quantitative relationships that determine output, income, employment, and prices.

The Detroit model, illustrated in Figure 1.12 in Chapter 1, is an example of how an econometric system is used in the telecommunications industry. The growth in revenues might be analyzed, projected, and related to business telephones in service, a measure that is related to the level of employment.

It should not necessarily be assumed that the drivers that caused demand in the past will persist in the future; rather, the factors believed to cause demand are identified and forecast separately.

It is general practice in econometric modeling to remove only the seasonal influence in the data prior to modeling. The trend and cyclical movements in the data should be explicable by using economic and demographic theory.

There is often a finer distinction made within the model-based approaches: (a) the Box-Jenkins (ARIMA) methodology versus (b) the econometric approaches. Although they share similarities in their mathematical formulations, these two model-based approaches offer significant practical differences in the way relationships among variables are constructed and model parameters are interpreted.

As part of a final selection, each technique must be rated by the demand forecaster in terms of its general reliability and applicability to the problem at hand, relative value in terms of effectiveness as compared to other appropriate techniques, and relative performance (accuracy) level. With selection criteria established, the forecaster can proceed to produce a list of potentially useful extrapolative techniques. An understanding of the data and operating conditions is the forecaster's primary input now. This knowledge must, however, be supplemented by a thorough knowledge of the techniques themselves.

## Combining Forecasts is a Useful Method

**Rule-based forecasting** employs dozens of empirical rules to model a time series for forecasting. These rules are distilled from published empirical research, surveys of professional forecasters, and recorded sessions with forecasting experts. The result of a rule-based forecasting procedure is a combining forecasting method.

A number of extrapolative procedures are fit to a time series, such as a random walk, a least-squares trend line, or an exponential smoothing method. At each forecast lead-time, the methods' projections are averaged by a set of rules that determines how to give weights to the various components of the combined model. For example, a possible rule is that the weight assigned to the random walk component of the combined model is raised, from a base of 20%, if recent trends depart from the global trend, there are shifts detected in the level of the series, or the series is considered suspicious in that it seems to have undergone a recent change in pattern.

Incorporating informed judgment into the extrapolations can further enhance rule-based procedures, which an exponential smoothing technique is unable to do directly.

> *A rule-based forecast is based on empirical rules to model a time series for forecasting.*

## Informed Judgment and Modeling Expertise

When describing complexity, clearly no single approach can be considered universally adaptable to any given forecasting situation. The assumptions and theories on which the extrapolative techniques are based limit their appropriateness, reliability, and credibility. The forecaster should be careful to avoid using techniques for which the data characteristics do not match the assumptions of the method.

Bear in mind first that a greater number of techniques are appropriate for the time horizon one year ahead than are appropriate for two-year-ahead forecasts. As we approach forecasts two or more years out, exponential smoothing and ARIMA time series models become less applicable.

Also apparent is that more techniques handle trending data than handle cyclical data. If we assume a turning point will occur in the second year, exponential smoothing and trending models are no longer adequate, because they do not have the appropriate forecast profile.

In terms of accuracy of a forecast for the one-year-ahead horizon, the State Space approach (exponential smoothing and ARIMA models), regression analysis and econometrics are the most useful. If there is a turning point expected in the forecast period, univariate exponential smoothing and ARIMA models may not be useful.

If we consider time constraints and the desire to present an easily understood technique, the exponential smoothing and linear regression approaches should also be considered tor two-year-ahead forecasts. Different conclusions might result, however, when

- shorter time horizons are involved
- data gathering and computational costs are important
- accuracy requirements are less stringent
- time is not a constraint
- the ease of understanding and explaining forecasting approaches is extremely important.

## A Multimethod Approach to Forecasting

The purpose of using more than one technique is to ensure that the forecasting approach will be as flexible as possible and that the forecaster's judgment (which is so critical to the demand forecasting process) is not overly dependent on one particular forecasting technique. It is not uncommon to see forecasters develop a search for one "best" forecasting technique and then use that technique almost exclusively, even in an ongoing forecasting process. Such a preference can become easily established because of the highly specialized nature of some of the techniques.

One of the lasting myths about forecasting is that complex models should be more accurate than simple models. Some forecasters uncritically prefer the most sophisticated statistical techniques that can be found. Remember Einstein's quote at the head of this chapter: "Everything should be made as simple as possible, but not simpler."

The accuracy of an extrapolative technique, however, is not necessarily a direct function of the degree of its sophistication. In many cases, this tendency can greatly reduce the effectiveness and credibility of a forecasting model because complex models may become unbelievable when unexpected pattern changes occur in the time series. A simpler model, on the other hand, may remain relatively unaffected by the change.

We recommend that two or more approaches be used every time to describe the historical behavior of the data and to predict future behavior. In essence, this allows us to evaluate alternative views of the future.

## Some Supplementary Approaches
## Market Research

Market research is often conducted to determine market potential, market share, desirable or unfavorable product attributes, responses to changes in price or terms and conditions, customer preferences, and key factors that customers consider important in deciding among a variety of purchase or lease products from alternative vendors.

The old adage that "a problem well defined is half-solved" is especially true in marketing research. In the early stages of a market research project, the objectives may be fairly well defined but the nature of the specific questions to be asked may be less well defined. Often small focus groups (three to ten potential respondents, randomly selected) are brought together to discuss the questions. A moderator directs the session. By asking specific questions and directing the discussion, the moderator determines whether the respondents understand the questions, believe other issues are important (leading to additional questions), and whether the project should continue. The moderator then makes recommendations for field work: questionnaire development, testing; and surveying.

*The American Marketing Association defines market research as the systematic gathering, recording, and analysing of data about problems in the marketing of goods and services.*

It is important to remember that the results of market research do not predict the future. Instead, market research studies may be used to identify the characteristics of existing users (income, age, product's life cycle position, nature of business, number of establishments, etc.).

They may also be useful to estimate market potentials by gathering similar data about customers or potential customers. An example of this approach using regression models is illustrated in Chapter 10, in which variables are selected based on previous market research studies combined with available data sources.

## New Product Introductions

As competitive pressures mount, companies are driven to introduce new products at an ever-increasing pace. It is not uncommon to see a 20%–60% turnover of product assortment in many companies. Promotional and new product forecasts are initially based on the analogous product history of similar products and finalized by consensus with input from marketing, sales, finance, distribution, and manufacturing. Other studies, such as intent-to-purchase market research studies may also be used to firm up the forecast. For the initial period, a borrowed model from an analogous product can be used for forecasting. When approximately six values of historical data become available, smoothing and time series methods become effective for short-term trending.

Many products have direct predecessors—products that have become outdated, gone out of style, or become unprofitable. Demand for a new product can be estimated by inheriting the historical pattern of its predecessor and using exponential smoothing models for forecasting. For products that have no predecessors or analogs, an estimate of demand can be correlated to a forecast of the overall size of the product line. Then, by projecting a mix ratio for the new product, we can obtain a historical profile that can be used with a smoothing model for updates and monitoring.

## Promotions as Special Events

Manufacturers spend much time and effort trying to find ways to market their products. What does a manufacturer hope to gain from a promotion? Trade promotions are an important part of a manufacturer's plan to increase profitability and sales to retailers. Promotions are widely used in a number of industries to stimulate additional demand for a product or service. In the consumer goods industry, where promotional campaigns are used to maintain or gain additional market share, companies spend a significant amount of advertising money to beat out the competition. As a result, sales demand patterns for promoted products can create very wide swings in the data.

The effect of a promotion introduces several stages in addition to the normal pattern of demand. Before an announced promotional campaign, the demand for a product might fall below expected levels due to the drop in demand as consumers anticipate the advantage of a promotional price. During the promoted period, a promotional blip may result from the increased demand for the product along with a pull-ahead amount for the demand that would have been there after the promotion ended. After the close of a promotional campaign, demand might drop again below normal levels for a short period as the forward buy dissipates and demand returns to normal patterns. These patterns differ across promotions in type, intensity, and duration.

# Sales Force Composites and Customer Collaboration

In a typical demand forecasting situation, forecasts from a field sales force may need to be reconciled with a centralized, administrative forecast. In this process, information flowing from the field includes specific customer developments (key accounts), pricing strategies, and market information.

> *The sales force composite is the compilation of estimates from the salespeople adjusted for expected changes in demand and presumed biases.*

Feedback from the central staff typically deals with relevant economic developments, the competitive environment, corporate promotional plans, capacity constraints, and new product information. Although tactical in nature, the informed judgment of the field sales force plays a crucial role the sales and operations planning (S&OP) process in formulating a consensus forecast for production planning and in setting sales quotas.

To gain additional cost savings and efficiencies, some companies and their customers collaborate in the demand forecasting and planning process by sharing information and co-managing processes. **Collaborative Planning, Forecasting and Replenishment** (CPFR), a trademark of GS1 US) is a concept that aims to enhance supply chain integration by supporting and assisting joint practices.

CPFR seeks cooperative management of inventory through joint visibility and replenishment of products throughout the supply chain. For instance, a consumer goods manufacturer can collaborate with a retailer to share supply and demand forecasts for certain product lines. The retailer develops demand forecasts for the product line in its stores and the manufacturer produces to meet that demand; this can benefit both sides of the partnership in increased sales and market share.

## Neural Nets for Forecasting

The **artificial neural network** (ANN) is a means of processing complex data when a problem is not fully understood or well specified. Many forecasting problems suffer from noisy and incomplete data, which do not lend themselves to formal modeling approaches. Neural nets are inspired by the architecture of the human brain, which processes complex data using interconnected neurons and processing paths; these interconnections are simulated in a computer program. Each neuron takes many input signals, and then, based on an internal weighting system, produces a single output that is typically sent as input to another neuron. The neurons are tightly integrated and organized into different layers.

> *A neural net, or artificial neural network, is a processing architecture derived from models of neuron interconnections of the human brain.*

In a forecasting application, the input layer can receive multiple inputs (e.g., the drivers of the forecasted item) and the output layer produces the projections of the item of interest. Usually, one or more hidden layers are sandwiched in between the two. This structure makes it impossible to predict or know the exact flow of the data, but allows the system to learn and generalize from experience. A neural net is useful because it can be exposed to large amounts of data and discover patterns and relationships within them.

## *A Product Life-Cycle Perspective*

**Product development**. A product life cycle begins with the decisions made and actions taken before the product is introduced. The feasibility and marketability of a new product will depend on the availability of the appropriate technology, R&D funding, product designs, resource allocation, and business strategies. Figure 3.1 provides broad recommendations for forecasting techniques related to a product's life cycle.

The techniques used to forecast a product's future in the early stages are included in the Delphi method, market research related to the characteristics of the market and consumers' willingness to pay, panel consensus, visionary forecasts, historical analogs, decision trees, and other techniques that can be applied with little or no historical data about the product concept

> *The life cycle of a successful product is characterized by a number of stages: product development, product introduction, rapid growth, mature stage, fall-off, and abandonment.*

**Product introduction**. Product introduction begins the next phase of the **product life cycle**. Quite often, supply limitations, **pipeline supply backups**, and lack of customer awareness result in only a gradual buildup of the quantity of products sold. High marketing costs will often result in net losses. High failure rates may also place increased demands on manufacturing test and repair resources. A period of time will be required for the product to gain acceptance in the marketplace. At this stage, qualitative techniques, such as Delphi and panel consensus, and market-research estimates may be more useful.

**Rapid growth**. The next stage in the life of a successful product is rapid growth. The product fills a need not otherwise met in the marketplace, or its price-performance characteristics are superior to its competitors, and it is adopted rapidly; faster, in fact, than would be accounted for by average growth in market or economic conditions.

The growth period is characterized by increasing sales, and profits begin to rise. With historical data at hand, statistical (time series) techniques become applicable. If fewer than 18 months of historical data are available, exponential smoothing models may be tried. For longer stretches of data, ARIMA models may be preferable. If 24 months or more of data become available, research shows that the performance of ARIMA models become superior to exponential smoothing models.

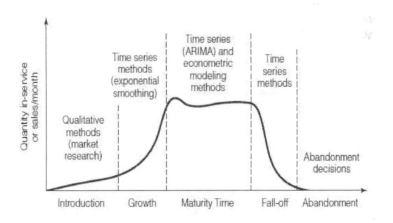

Figure 3.1 The life cycle of a product.

**Mature stage**. As the product enters a mature stage or steady state, competition is intense and marginal competitors will usually drop out of the market. During the maturity phase, intense competition coupled with increased price reductions and advertising costs will squeeze profits. Cost-reduction efforts focused on the reduction of material costs can be employed to increase profits.

With adequate data available on sales, prices, economic factors, market size, and so forth, econometric modeling techniques can be applied. Econometric models offer an explanatory capability that the univariate time series models lack. Whether this is an important consideration depends on the circumstances that have created the need for the forecast; in the mature phase, a product is frequently modified or its price adjusted to maintain its competitiveness.

**Fall-off.** As new technology or other competitive products with superior price-performance characteristics also enter the market, the demand for the mature product falls off at a rate greater than can be attributed to economic or market size considerations. Consideration is given to whether the product will become obsolete or be enhanced in the near future.

Enhancing an existing product will extend the maturity phase at a much lower cost than designing a new product design. Once again, time series techniques may be more responsive in projecting the rapid decline of the product's sales.

**Abandonment** In the final stage of the life cycle, the product is about to be abandoned. It is no longer profitable, and its past history may not help in determining when it will be withdrawn. Financial considerations, or plans to introduce a new product to customers, will determine the product's fate. The pruning of losing products is a strategy employed by corporate turnaround specialists to get losing companies back on track.

## A Prototypical Forecasting Technique: Smoothing Historical Patterns

In today's world of Big Data, many, forecasting practitioners use spreadsheets to create forecasts for the products and services in their company, despite the database limitations of spreadsheets. Why is this so? Granted that with spreadsheet add-ins, simple as well as complex algorithms can be implemented in effective and time saving ways. Computing power is cheap and storage is plentiful, which has created greater acceptance of statistical forecasting models and sophisticated modeling algorithms among practitioners.

Experience has shown that simple techniques can do quite well, while the more sophisticated techniques often do not do any better, at least not enough to justify the time and financial investments required to get the added benefits. One should follow Einstein's words at the start of this chapter.

Next, we introduce an intuitive approach to smoothing historical patterns that allows us to motivate the basic concept of *smoothing* that underlies so many forecasting techniques. Most often, **simple smoothing** refers to a procedure of taking weighted sums of data in order to smooth out very short-term irregularities. To smooth a time series in which the effect of seasonality and the impact of any irregular variation need to be diminished or eliminated, we must perform some type of smoothing operation.

To demand forecasters, smoothed data reveal information about secular trends (those of long duration) and economic cycles, which need to be understood and projected using a set of assumptions about the future. Smoothed data are also required in econometric modeling in order to have meaningful estimates of changes for many economic time series.

> *A smoothing technique is a procedure that uses weighted sums of data to create a projection or to smooth irregularities in data.*

Smoothed data are easy to interpret. A plot of a smoothed employment series or of a smoothed industrial production series provides insight into the state of the economy.

Percentage changes, which are calculated from *transformations* or re-expressions of smoothed data, are readily interpreted by laypersons and corporate managers and gives insight into changes in business or the economy. Percentages based on unadjusted series, on the other hand, behave too erratic to be practically useful.

> *A transformation is a mathematical operation to enhance the analysis, display, and interpretation of data.*

When we interpret differences between unadjusted and smoothed historical data, we are often able to model relationships in quantitative (statistical) terms. When these differences are less important or irrelevant in a given analysis, then we use smoothing to remove them. In macroeconomics, the seasonal component is often removed, and then the notions of trend-cycle and turning point become important factors to analyze from the smoothed data.

At times, unadjusted data and smoothed data may indicate movement in opposite directions because of a technical feature in the smoothing method. As demand forecasters gain experience, these anomalies can be properly interpreted and their meaning adequately communicated to forecast users. It is also worth noting that certain sophisticated time series models, known as ARIMA models (described in Chapter 9) do not require smoothed data as inputs, yet can produce useful forecasting results.

## Smoothing with Moving Averages

A widely used technique for revealing patterns in time series over the short term is based on averaging a sliding window of values over time, known as the **moving average**. This technique is used to smooth historical data in which the effect of seasonality and the impact of randomness can be minimized or eliminated. The result is a smoothed value that gets used as a *heuristic, self-driven forecast* for the immediate future. In doing so, we note that too much smoothing will cause a delayed or even unnoticed change in direction in the data.

When calculating simple averages for smoothing, forecasters need to use discretion and match the degree of smoothing to each particular application. We caution that the calculations can be seriously distorted by outliers. A moving average output with an outlier will be distorted around the point of an outlier.

> *A simple moving average is a smoothing technique in which each value carries the same weight.*

**Moving medians** can be used to complement moving averages, when you need to be concerned about the impact of outliers on the smoothed pattern. The main advantage of a moving median compared to moving average smoothing is that outliers adversely influence results to a lesser extent. Thus, if there are outliers in the data, median smoothing typically produces smoother curves than moving average-based smoothing on the same moving window width.

Moving medians can be effective in separating or estimating a promotional impact (lift) from a baseline forecast. Moving averages have a tendency, in this situation, to follow the promotion peaks and troughs, which reduce the effectiveness of separating the promotion effect from the baseline series.

The main disadvantages of median smoothing are that in the absence of clear outliers it may produce more "jagged" curves than moving average and it does not allow for weighting.

> *Moving median smoothing, compared to moving average smoothing, is more resistant to outliers.*

As a basic algorithm, the moving average is widely used as a forecasting tool. However, it should be noted that a multistep (*lead-time*) forecast with a moving average procedure **will always be level**, no matter what the underlying pattern is in the historical data shows.

In fact, the projections depend only on the data within the latest window used in the calculations.

The most rudimentary smoother using moving averages is the *unweighted* moving average, in which each value of the historical data carries the same weight in the smoothing algorithm. Because these moving averages are so readily used in spreadsheets, they will have names, similar to a variable name in a software program. This will help us distinguish them from other kinds of moving averages.

For *n* values of a set of historical data $\{Y_1, \ldots, Y_n\}$, the three-term moving average (3_MAVG$_t$) has the formula

$$3\_MAVG_t = (Y_t + Y_{t-1} + Y_{t-2})/3$$

In general, the *p*-term moving average (P_MAVG$_t$) is given by

$$P\_MAVG_t = (Y_t + Y_{t-1} + Y_{t-2} + \ldots + Y_{t-(p-1)})/p$$

where $Y_t$ denotes the actual (observed) value at time *t*, and *p* is the number of values included in the average. This moving average technique is so basic and important in demand forecasting that we give it the name $P\_MAVG_T$, a *P*-term simple moving average projection starting from the time period *t = T*.

As long as no trending is expected in the immediate future or no seasonality is present, this is a readily understood, elementary approach for carrying out a level point forecast without having uncertainty assumptions. A forecast made at a specific point in time *t = T* for the *next* period is obtained by setting the forecast equal to the value of the moving average at time *t = T*: $Y_T(1) = P\_MAVG_T$.

> *The one-period-ahead forecast $Y_t$ (1) of a moving average technique is based on a simple average of the current period's value $Y_t$ and the previous t - (p - 1) values.*

The forecast *m* steps ahead is the *m*-period-ahead forecast, given by a repetition of the one-period-ahead point forecast $Y_T(m) = Y_T(1)$. The set of values MAVG-m = $\{Y_T(1), Y_T(2), Y_T(3), Y_T(4), \ldots Y_T(m)\}$ is called a **forecast profile**; it produces a constant-level profile, in this case. Thus, the MAVG moving average technique can only produce constant-level profiles from any historical pattern. If level future values are expected, this may be an acceptable, but limited, approach to use.

> *The forecast profile is the set of m-period-ahead forecasts produced by a forecasting technique.*

In Chapter 5, a *centered* moving average plays a key role, when creating a seasonal decomposition with the Ratio-to-Moving Average (RMA) method. The *p*-term *centered* moving average (**P_CMAVG**) is given by

$$P\_CMAVG_t = (Y_{t-m} + Y_{t-m+1} + \ldots + Y_{t-1} + Y_t + Y_{t+1} + \ldots + Y_{t+m})/p)$$

where the $Y_t$ values denote the actual (observed) values and $p$ is the number of values included in the average. In this formula, $p$ is an odd integer and $m = (p - 1)/2$. In other words, we are using $(p - 1)/2$ values on either side of $Y_t$ to produce a smoothed value of $Y_t$. For example, the three-term centered moving average (**3_CMAVG**) has the formula

$$3\_CMAVG_t = (Y_{t-1} + Y_t + Y_{t+1})/3$$

The larger the value of p, the smoother the moving average becomes. If $p$ is even, as is the case in smoothing quarterly data ($p = 4$) or monthly data ($p = 12$), there is no middle position to place the smoothed value. In that case, we place it right after the observed value or, alternatively, take another centered two-period moving average.

---

*A centered moving average can be used to smooth unwanted fluctuations in a time series.*

---

Figure 3.2, we take the first 36 values of monthly Champagne sales in the first column and display a centered 12-term moving average in the second column. Note that the first value of the moving average is centered on value 7 (=18.8) of Champagne sales. A two-term centered moving average of column 2 results in the values shown in column 3. The first value of this moving average is centered on value 6 of the original data (=26.4). Finally, the time plot in Figure 3.3 illustrates the smoothness of the final result.

| Champagne | 12_CMAVG | 2_12_CMAVG |
|---|---|---|
| 15 | | |
| 18.7 | | |
| 23.6 | | |
| 23.2 | | |
| 25.5 | | |
| 26.4 | | 29.75 |
| 18.8 | 29.75 | 29.9115 |
| 16 | 30.3958 | 30.3677 |
| 25.2 | 30.9292 | 30.9646 |
| 39 | 31.6042 | 31.6625 |
| 53.6 | 32.5125 | 32.475 |
| 67.3 | 33.2708 | 33.2625 |
| 24.4 | 33.9958 | 33.951 |
| 24.8 | 34.5417 | 34.5344 |
| 30.3 | 35.0583 | 35.101 |
| 32.7 | 35.7458 | 35.7875 |
| 37.8 | 36.6 | 36.7625 |
| 32.3 | 38.1042 | 38.0198 |
| 30.3 | 39.2708 | 39.1042 |
| 17.6 | 39.7708 | 39.8073 |
| 36.0 | 40.4167 | 40.3875 |
| 44.7 | 40.9458 | 40.8563 |
| 68.4 | 41.1167 | 41.1698 |
| 88.6 | 41.5 | 41.5073 |
| 31.1 | 41.9125 | 41.8698 |
| 30.1 | 42.1542 | 42.1302 |
| 40.5 | 42.3 | 42.3406 |
| 55.2 | 42.6083 | 42.6885 |
| 39.4 | 43.2375 | 43.3177 |
| 39.9 | 44.1875 | 43.95 |
| 32.6 | | 44.1875 |
| 21.1 | | |
| 36.0 | | |
| 52.1 | | |
| 76.1 | | |
| 103.7 | | |

Figure 3.2 Monthly Champagne sales: 2-term of a 12-term cantered moving average (n = 36).

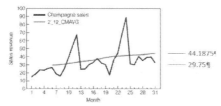

Figure 3.3Time plot of monthly Champagne sales: 2-term of a 12-term moving average smoothing. (Source: Figure 3.6).

| ¤ | Fit-Errors | $Y_{T+1}-Y_T(1)$ | $Y_{T+2}-Y_T(2)$ | $Y_{T+3}-Y_T(3)$ |
|---|---|---|---|---|
| T=-28¤ | 35.2–42.6=-7.4 | 39.4–42.6=-3.2 | 39.9–42.6=-2.7 | 32.6–42.6=-10.0 |
| T=-29¤ | 39.4–43.2=-3.8 | 39.9–43.2=-3.3 | 32.6–43.2=-10.6 | 21.1–43.2=-22.1 |
| T=-30¤ | 39.9–44.2=-4.3 | 32.6–44.2=-11.6 | 21.1–44.2=-23.1 | 36.0–44.2=-8.2 |

Figure 3.4 Fit versus forecast errors for 12_MAVG of monthly Champagne sales. (*Source*: Fig. 3.2; *n* = 36)

Figure 3.5 shows a comparison of the forecast errors found in Figure 3.8 with the corresponding NF1 forecast errors. Because the data are trending in this stretch of the time series, the NF1 performs better than a one-period-ahead moving average projection. Similar calculations can be made for the other forecast horizons. In short, a moving average is not appropriate for projecting trending, also known as non-stationary, data. We discuss the evaluation of forecast errors in more detail in Chapter 4.

| | Fit Errors | $Y_{T+1}-Y_T(1)$ | $Y_{T+2}-Y_T(2)$ | $Y_{T+3}-Y_T(3)$ |
|---|---|---|---|---|
| T = 28 | 35.2-40.5 = -5.3 | 39.4-40.5 = -1.1 | 39.9-40.5 = -0.6 | 32.6-40.5 = -7.9 |
| T = 29 | 39.4-35.2 = 4.2 | 39.9-35.2 = 4.7 | 32.6-35.2 = -2.6 | 21.1-35.2 =-14.1 |
| T = 30 | 39.9-39.4 = 0.5 | 32.6-39.4 = -6.8 | 21.1-39.4 = -18.3 | 36.0-39.4 = -3.2 |
| 2_12_CMAVG/NF1 *MAE* 1.6 | | 1.4 | 1.7 | 1.6 |
| 2_12_CMAVG/NF1 *MSE* 1.9 | | 2.2 | 1.,9 | 2.4 |

Figure 3.5 - NAÏVE_1 (NF1) fit versus forecast errors, and comparison 2_12_CMAVG / NF1 mean absolute error (*MAE*) and mean square error (*MSE*) for monthly Champagne sales. (*Source*: Data in Figure 3.2; *n* = 36).

## *Predictive Visualization Techniques*

**Predictive Visualization** techniques for forecast accuracy measurement provide a perspective on how serious a forecasting bias may be. If the bias exceeds a designated threshold, a "red flag" is raised concerning the forecasting approach. The forecaster should then reexamine the data to identify changes in the trend, seasonal, or other business patterns, which in turn suggest some adjustment to the forecasting approach.

## Ladder Charts

By plotting the current year's monthly forecasts on a ladder chart, a forecaster can determine whether the seasonal pattern in the forecast looks reasonable. The ladder chart in Figure 3.6 consists of six items of information for each month of the year: average over the past 5 years, the past year's performance, the 5-year low, the 5-year high, the current year-to-date, and the monthly forecasts for the remainder of the year. The 5-year average line usually provides the best indication of the seasonal pattern, assuming this pattern is not changing significantly over time. In fact, this is a good check for reasonableness that can be done before submitting the forecast for approval.

The level of the forecast can be checked for reasonableness relative to the prior year (dashed line in Figure 3.6). The forecaster can determine whether or not the actuals are consistently overrunning or underrunning the forecast.

In this example, the forecast errors are positive for 3 months and negative for 3 months. The greatest differences between the actual and forecast values occur in March and April, but here the deviations are of opposite signs; additional research should be done to uncover the cause of the unusual March-April pattern. The forecasts for the remainder of the current year look reasonable, although some minor adjustments might be made. The ladder chart is one of the best predictive visualization tools for quickly identifying the need for major changes in forecasts.

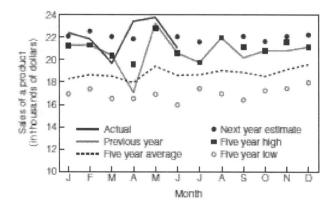

Figure 3.6 A ladder chart.

> *A ladder chart is a simple yet powerful tool for monitoring forecast results.*

## Prediction-Realization Diagram

Another useful visual approach to monitoring forecast accuracy is the prediction-realization diagram introduced in 1958 by the economist Henri Theil (1924–2000). If the predicted values are indicated on the vertical axis and the actual values on the horizontal axis, a straight line with a $45^0$ slope will represent perfect forecasts. This is called the line of perfect forecasts (Figure 3.7). In practice, the prediction-realization diagram is sometimes rotated so that the line of perfect forecasts appears horizontal.

The diagram has six sections. Points falling in sections II and V are a result of turning-point errors. In Section V, a positive change was negative predicted, but the actual change was negative. In Section II, a change was predicted, but positive change occurred.

The remaining sections involve predictions that were correct in sign but wrong in magnitude. Points above the line of perfect forecasts reflect actual changes that were less than predicted. Points below the line of perfect forecasts represent actual changes that were greater than predicted.

The prediction-realization diagram can be used to record forecast results on an ongoing basis. Persistent overruns or underruns indicate the need to adjust the forecasts or to re-estimate the model. In this case, a simple error pattern is evident and we can raise or lower the forecast based on the pattern and magnitude of the errors.

The prediction-realization diagram (Figure 3.8) shows at a glance how well you did in getting the direction of a forecast correct. The original diagram can be enhanced to include an assessment of whether the forecasts can be improved by comparisons with naïve (no-change) forecasts. Professor Roy Pearson (personal communication) has added a line, labeled U=1, where U is the Theil statistic used in economic forecasting *https://www.youtube.com/watch?v=fhjJWl7rw2A*). This line has a slope of two times the actual change. Predictions falling on this line have the same error as predictions from a no change forecast, which is frequently referred to as a naïve or NAÏVE_1 forecast. Points along the horizontal axis (other than the origin itself) also are outcomes where U=1, since the forecaster is predicting no change, exactly the same as a naive forecast.

> *The prediction-realization diagram indicates how well a model or forecaster has predicted turning points and also how well the magnitude of change has been predicted given that the proper direction of change has been forecast.*

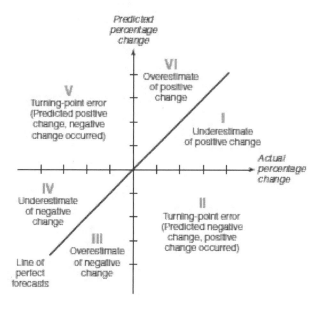

Figure 3.7 Prediction-realization diagram.

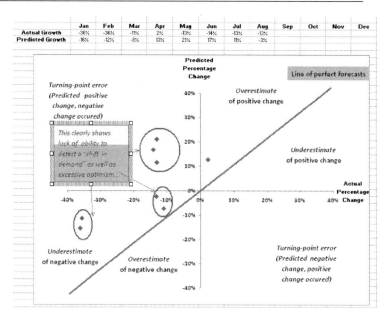

Figure 3.8 An application of the Prediction-realization diagram.

More importantly, the diagram indicates turning-point errors that may be due to misspecification or missing variables in the model. The forecaster may well be at a loss to decide how to modify the model forecasts. An analysis of other factors that occurred when the turning-point error was realized may result in inclusion of a variable in the model that was missing from the initial specification.

# Empirical Prediction Intervals for Time Series Models

A major shortcoming in much of today's practice in demand forecasting is the lack of use of error bounds on forecasts. However, with the availability of cheap computing power and a proven State Space Forecasting methodology for time series forecasting, the demand forecaster should be incorporating prediction limits to reflect conventional symmetrical (+/- x %), as well as the new, asymmetrical (+ x%, -y%) error bounds on forecasts. Why is this important? A simple example will make the point.

When no error distribution can be assumed in a method, as is generally the case with moving averages and simple smoothing, we can construct empirical prediction intervals using an approach by Goodman and Williams in a 1971 article entitled *"A simple method for the construction of empirical confidence limits for economic forecasts"* in the Journal of the American Statistical Association. To construct empirical prediction limits, we go through the ordered data, making forecasts at each time t. Then, the comparisons of these forecasts with the actuals (that are known) yield an empirical distribution of forecast errors. If the future errors are assumed to be distributed like the empirical errors, then the empirical distribution of these observed errors can be used to set prediction intervals for subsequent forecasts. In practice, the theoretical size and the empirical size of the intervals have been found to agree closely.

> *Prediction intervals are used as a way of expressing the uncertainty in the future values that are derived from models, and they play a key role in tracking forecasts from these models.*

In regression models, it is generally assumed that random errors are additive in the model equation and have a normal distribution with zero mean and constant variance. The variance of the errors can be estimated from the time series data. The estimated standard deviation (square root of the variance) is calculated for the forecast period and is used to develop the desired prediction interval.

Although 95% prediction intervals are frequently used, the range of forecast values for volatile series may be so great that it might also be useful to show the limits for a lower level of probability, say 75%.

This would narrow the interval. It is common to express prediction intervals about the forecast, but in the tracking process, it is more useful to deal with prediction intervals for the forecast errors on a period-by-period or cumulative basis.

*In typical forecasting situations, prediction intervals are probably too conservative or narrow.*

A forecaster often deals with aggregated data and would like to know the prediction intervals about an annual forecast based on a model for monthly or quarterly data. The annual forecast is created by summing twelve (independent) monthly (or four quarterly) predictions. Developing the appropriate probability limits requires that the variance for the sum of the prediction errors be calculated. This can be determined from the variance formula

$$\text{Var}\left(\sum e_i\right) = \sum \text{Var}(e_i) + 2 \sum \text{Cov}(e_i, e_j)$$

If the forecast errors have zero covariance (Cov)--in particular, if they are independent of one another--the variance of the sum equals the sum of the prediction variances.

The most common form of correlation in the forecast errors for time series models is positive autocorrelation. In this case, the covariance term is positive and the prediction intervals derived would be too small. In the unusual case of negative covariance, the prediction intervals would be too wide. Rather than deal with this complexity, most software programs assume the covariance is small and inconsequential.

## Prediction Interval as a Percentage Miss

Some forecast users find the expression of prediction intervals obtuse. In such cases, the forecaster may find more acceptance of this technique if the prediction intervals for forecasts are expressed in terms of percentages. For example, a 95% prediction interval for a forecast might be interpreted that we are 95% confident that the forecast will be within ± 15% (say) of the actual numerical value. The percentage miss associated with any prediction interval can be calculated from the formula:

Percentage miss = [(Estimated standard error of the forecast) ($t$ factor) x 100%] / (Predicted value)

where t is the tabulated value of the Student's t distribution for the appropriate degrees of freedom and confidence level. This calculation provides the percentage miss for any particular period. Values can be calculated for all periods (e.g., for each month of the year), resulting in a band of prediction intervals spanning the year.

It is also useful to determine a prediction interval for a cumulative forecast error. Under the assumption that forecast errors are independent and random, the cumulative percentage miss will be smaller than the percentage miss for an individual period because the positive and negative errors will cancel to some extent. As an approximate rule, the average period (say monthly or quarterly) percentage miss is calculated by dividing the average monthly percentage miss by $\sqrt{12}$ (the square root of the number of periods of the forecast) or the average quarterly percentage miss by $\sqrt{4}$ (=2).

## Prediction Intervals as Early Warning Signals

One of the simplest tracking signals is based on the ratio of the sum of the forecast errors to the mean absolute error. It is called the cumulative sum tracking signal (CUSUM). For certain CUSUM measures, a threshold or upper limit of $|0.5|$ suggests that the forecast errors are no longer randomly distributed about 0 but rather are congregating too much on one side (i.e., forming a biased pattern).

More sophisticated tracking signals involve the taking of weighted or smoothed averages of forecast errors. The best-known standard tracking signal, due to Trigg Leach dates back to 1964 and will be described shortly. Tracking signals are especially useful when forecasting a large number of products at a time, as is the case in repair parts inventory management systems.

> *A tracking signal is a ratio of a measure of bias to a companion measure of accuracy.*

Warning signals can be visualized by plotting the forecast errors over time together with the associated prediction intervals and seeing whether the forecast errors continually lie above or below the zero line. Even though the individual forecast errors may well lie within the appropriate prediction interval for the period (say monthly), a plot of the cumulative sum of the errors may indicate that their sum lies outside its prediction interval.

> *An early warning signal is a succession of overruns and underrun.*

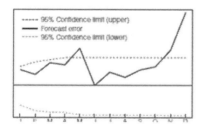 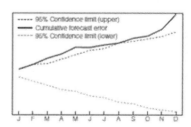

Figure 3.9 (*left*) Monthly forecast errors and associated prediction intervals for a time series model.

Figure 3,10 (*right*) Cumulative forecast errors and associated cumulative prediction intervals for a time series model.

A type of warning signal is evident in Figures 3.9 and 3.10. It can be seen that the monthly forecast errors lie well within the 95% prediction interval for 9 of the 12 months, with two of the three exceptions occurring in November and December. Figure 3.12 suggests that the individual forecast errors lie within their respective prediction intervals. However, it is apparent that none of the misses are negative - certainly, they do not form a random pattern about zero. Hence, there appears to be a bias. To determine whether the bias in the forecast is significant, we review the prediction intervals for cumulative sums of forecast errors.

The cumulative prediction interval (Figure 3.10) confirms the problem with the forecast bias. The cumulative forecast errors fall on the outside of the prediction interval for all twelve periods. This model is clearly under-forecasting. Either the model has failed to capture a strong cyclical pattern during the year or the data are growing rapidly and the forecaster has failed to make a proper specification in the model.

Using these two plots, the forecaster would probably be inclined to make upward revisions in the forecast after several months. It certainly would not be necessary to wait until November to recognize the problem.

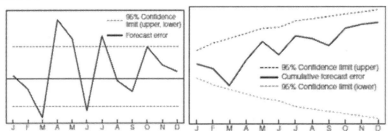

Figure 3.11 (*left*) Monthly forecast errors and prediction intervals for a time series model.
Figure 3.12 (*right*) Cumulative forecast errors and cumulative prediction intervals for a time series model.

Another kind of warning signal occurs when too many forecast errors fall outside the prediction intervals. For example, with a 90% prediction interval, we expect only 10% (approximately 1 month per year) of the forecast errors to fall outside the prediction interval. Figure 3.11 shows a plot of the monthly forecast errors for a time series model. In this case, five of the twelve errors lie outside the 95% interval. Clearly, this model is unacceptable as a predictor of monthly values. However, the monthly error pattern may appear random and the annual forecast (cumulative sum of twelve months) might be acceptable. Figure 3.12 shows the cumulative forecast errors and the cumulative prediction intervals. It appears that the annual forecast lies within the 95% prediction interval and is acceptable.

The conclusion that may be reached from monitoring the two sets of forecast errors is that neither model is wholly acceptable, and that neither can be rejected. In one case, the monthly forecasts were good but the annual forecast was not. In the other case, the monthly forecasts were not good, but the annual forecast turned out to be acceptable. Whether the forecaster retains either model depends on the purpose for which the model was constructed.

It is important to note that, by monitoring cumulative forecast errors, the forecaster was able to determine the need for a forecast revision more quickly than if the forecaster were only monitoring monthly forecasts. This is the kind of early warning advice that management should expect from the demand forecaster.

## *How You Can Monitor Forecasts*

Suppose that we are using simple exponential smoothing, a model with a level forecast profile. Now, assume that a trend develops. We have a problem because the exponential smoothing forecasts will not keep up with a trend. How do we detect this problem?

One answer is to periodically test the data for trends and other patterns. Another is to examine a graph of the forecast errors each time that we add new data to our model. Both methods quickly become cumbersome, especially when we forecast a large number of product SKUs by locations. Visually checking all these data after every forecast period is out of the question!

### Trigg Tracking Signal

The tracking signal, a simple quality control method, is just the tool for the job. When a forecast for a given time period is too large, the forecast error has a negative sign; when a forecast is too small, the forecast error is positive. Ideally, the forecasts should vary around the actual data and the sum of the forecast errors should be near zero. But if the sum of the forecast errors departs from zero in either direction, the forecasting model may be out of control.

The tracking signal proposed by D. W. Trigg in 1964 indicates the presence of nonrandom forecast errors; it is a ratio of two smoothed errors $E_t$ and $M_t$. The numerator $E_t$ is a simple exponential smooth of the forecast errors $e_t$, and the denominator $M_t$ is a simple exponential smooth of the absolute values of the forecast errors. Thus,

$$T_t = E_t / M_t$$

$$E_t = \alpha\, e_t + (1 - \alpha)\, E_{t-1}$$

$$M_t = \alpha \, |e_t| + (1 - \alpha) \, M_{t-1}$$

where $e_t = Y_t - F_t$ the difference between the observed value $Y_t$ and the forecast $F_t$.

Trigg shows that when $T_t$ exceeds 0.51 for $\alpha = 0.1$ or 0.74 for $\alpha = 0.2$, the forecast errors are nonrandom at the 95% probability level. Figure 3.13 shows a sample calculation of the Trigg tracking signal for an adaptive smoothing model of seasonally adjusted airline passenger data. The tracking signal correctly provides a warning at period 15 after five consecutive periods in which the actual exceeded the forecast. Period 11 has the largest forecast error, but no warning is provided because the sign of the forecast error became reversed. It is apparent that the model errors can increase substantially above prior experience without a warning being signaled as long as the errors change sign. Once a pattern of over- or under forecasting is evident, a warning is issued.

| Time | Error | Smoothed Error | Smoothed Absolute Error | Tracking Signal |
|------|-------|----------------|-------------------------|-----------------|
| 1 | −1.58 | | | |
| 2 | 2.54 | −1.17 | 1.68 | −0.70* |
| 3 | 5.24 | −0.53 | 2.04 | −0.26 |
| 4 | −0.51 | −0.53 | 1.89 | −0.28 |
| 5 | 0.59 | −0.42 | 1.76 | −0.24 |
| 6 | 2.26 | −0.15 | 1.81 | −0.08 |
| 7 | 1.49 | 0.01 | 1.78 | 0.01 |
| 8 | 1.31 | −0.14 | 1.73 | 0.08 |
| 9 | 0.43 | 0.17 | 1.6 | 0.11 |
| 10 | −7.73 | −0.62 | 2.21 | −0.28 |
| 11 | 11.57 | 0.6 | 3.15 | 0.19 |
| 12 | 8.98 | 1.44 | 3.73 | 0.39 |
| 13 | 3.82 | 1.68 | 3.74 | 0.45 |
| 14 | 4.17 | 1.93 | 3.78 | 0.51 |
| 15 | 1.06 | 1.84 | 3.51 | 0.53† |

* Starting value—ignore.
† Exceeds 0.51—warning!

Figure 3,13 Trigg's tracking signal ($\alpha = 0.1$) for an adaptive smoothing model of seasonally adjusted airline data.

In this book we discuss a variety of forecasting models, from simple exponential smoothing to multiple linear regression. Once we implement one of these models, we cannot expect it to supply good forecasts indefinitely. The pattern of our data may change, and we will have to adjust our forecasting assumptions and perhaps select a new model better suited to the data.

Just how large should the sum of the forecast errors grow before we act? To answer this, we need a basis for measuring of the relative dispersion, or scatter, of the forecast errors. If forecast errors are widely scattered, a relatively large sum of errors is not unusual. A standard measure of variability such as the standard deviation could be used as a measure of dispersion, but more commonly the mean absolute error (MAE) is used to define the tracking signal

Tracking signal = (Sum of forecast errors) / (MAE)

Typically, the control limit on the tracking signal is set at ±4.0. If the signal goes outside this range, we should investigate. Otherwise, we can let our forecasting model run unattended. There is a very small probability, less than 1% that the signal will go outside the range ±4.0 due to chance.

## The Tracking Signal in Action

Figure 3.14 is a graph of actual sales and the forecasts produced by simple exponential smoothing. For the first six months, the forecast errors are relatively small. Then, a strong trend begins in month 7. Fortunately, as shown in Figure 3.15, the tracking signal sounds an alarm immediately.

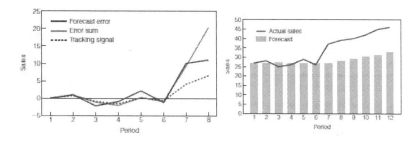

Figure 3.14 (*left*) Monthly forecasts and sales for a time series model.

Exponential Smoothing with Tracking Signal
Weight = 0.1     Control Limit = 4.0

| Month | Actual Sales | Fcst. Sales | Actual Error | Abs. Error | MAE | Error Sum | Tracking Signal | | |
|---|---|---|---|---|---|---|---|---|---|
| | | | | | 1.4 | 0.0 | 0.0 | | |
| 1 | 27 | 27.0 | 0.0 | 0.0 | 1.3 | 0.0 | 0.0 | | |
| 2 | 28 | 27.0 | 1.0 | 1.0 | 1.3 | 1.0 | 0.8 | | |
| 3 | 25 | 27.1 | -2.1 | 2.1 | 1.4 | -1.1 | -0.8 | | |
| 4 | 26 | 26.9 | 0.9 | 0.9 | 1.3 | -2.0 | -1.5 | | |
| 5 | 29 | 26.8 | 2.2 | 2.2 | 1.4 | 0.2 | 0.1 | | |
| 6 | 26 | 27.0 | -1.0 | 1.0 | 1.4 | -0.8 | -0.6 | | |
| 7 | 37 | 26.9 | 10.1 | 10.1 | 2.2 | 9.3 | 4.2 ALARM | ALARM IN MONTH 7 --> | |
| 8 | 39 | 27.9 | 11.1 | 11.1 | 3.1 | 20.3 | 6.5 ALARM | | |
| 9 | 40 | 29.0 | 11.0 | 11.0 | 3.9 | 31.3 | 8.0 ALARM | | |
| 10 | 42 | 30.1 | 11.9 | 11.9 | 4.7 | 43.2 | 9.2 ALARM | | |
| 11 | 45 | 31.3 | 13.7 | 13.7 | 5.6 | 56.9 | 10.2 ALARM | | FORECAST |
| 12 | 46 | 32.7 | 13.3 | 13.3 | 6.4 | 70.2 | 11.9 ALARM | ACTUAL SALES | |
| 13 | | 34.0 | | | | | | | |

Figure 3.15 (right) Monthly forecast errors and tracking signal.

Figure 3.16 Actuals, forecasts, and forecast tracking signal.

Column F in Figure 3.16 contains the mean absolute error. This is updated each month to keep pace with changes in the errors. Column G contains the running sum of the forecast errors, and column H holds the value of the tracking signal ratio. A formula in column I displays the label ALARM if the signal is outside the range ±4.0.

## Creating Waterfall Charts for Tracking Biases in Point Forecasts

A rolling simulation results in multiple forecasts at virtually every lead time. For the forecasting example shown in Figure 4.14, the rolling simulation resulted in 11 one-period-ahead forecasts, 10 two-period-ahead forecasts, nine three-period-ahead forecasts, and a single 11-period-ahead forecast (Figure 3.17).

| | | | | | | | | | | |
|---|---|---|---|---|---|---|---|---|---|---|
| T=52 | | | | | | | | | | |
| $F_{52}(1)$ | T=53 | | | | | | | | | |
| F(2) | $F_{53}(1)$ | T=54 | | | | | | | | |
| F(3) | F(2) | $F_{54}(1)$ | T=55 | | | | | | | |
| F(4) | F(3) | F(2) | $F_{55}(1)$ | T=56 | | | | | | |
| F(5) | F(4) | F(3) | F(2) | $F_{56}(1)$ | T=57 | | | | | |
| F(6) | F(5) | F(4) | F(3) | F(2) | $F_{57}(1)$ | T=58 | | | | |
| F(7) | F(6) | F(5) | F(4) | F(3) | F(2) | $F_{58}(1)$ | T=59 | | | |
| F(8) | F(7) | F(6) | F(5) | F(4) | F(3) | F(2) | $F_{59}(1)$ | T=60 | | |
| F(9) | F(8) | F(7) | F(6) | F(5) | F(4) | F(3) | F(2) | $F_{60}(1)$ | T=61 | |
| F(10) | F(9) | F(8) | F(7) | F(6) | F(5) | F(4) | F(3) | F(2) | $F_{61}(1)$ | T=62 |
| F(11) | F(10) | F(9) | F(8) | F(7) | F(6) | F(5) | F(4) | F(3) | F(2) | $F_{62}(1)$ |

Figure 3.17 Generating a waterfall chart with forecasts generated by a rolling simulation.

| | T=53 | T=54 | T=55 | T=56 | T=57 | T=58 | T=59 | T=60 | T=61 | T=62 | T=63 | T=64 | T=65 |
|---|---|---|---|---|---|---|---|---|---|---|---|---|---|
| Hold-out ACTUALS | 313 | 1568 | 283 | 56 | 83 | 31 | 1165 | 29 | 24 | 1846 | 359 | | |
| | 2 | -49 | -48 | 13 | 20 | -15 | 33 | 9 | 4 | -55 | 43 | | |
| FCST | | -74 | -52 | 13 | 20 | -15 | 16 | 9 | 4 | -84 | 39 | | |
| | | | -51 | 13 | 20 | -15 | 20 | 9 | 4 | -76 | 40 | | |
| E | | | | 13 | 20 | -15 | 19 | 9 | 4 | -69 | 45 | | |
| R | | | | | 20 | -16 | 18 | 9 | 4 | -66 | 45 | | |
| R | | | | | | -16 | 18 | 8 | 3 | -66 | 43 | | |
| O | | | | | | | 19 | 9 | 4 | -70 | 44 | | |
| R | | | | | | | | 9 | 4 | -72 | 44 | | |
| | | | | | | | | | 3 | -62 | 48 | | |
| | | | | | | | | | | -58 | 49 | | |
| | | | | | | | | | | | 50 | | |
| ME | | | -50 | 13 | 20 | -15 | 20 | 9 | 4 | -68 | 45 | | |
| MdE | | | -51 | 13 | 20 | -15 | 19 | 9 | 4 | -68 | 44 | | |
| | | | Week 3 | | | Week 6 | | | | Week 10 | | | |

Figure 3.18 Waterfall chart with model forecasts untransformed to original scale of sales units.

Because the **Mean Error (ME)** and **Median Error (MdE)** for the seasonal peak period (T=62) are so close, we find no credible evidence of unusual values in the biases: the seasonal peak appears to be over forecasted (Actual < Forecast), which may not be aligned with an historical fit (Actual > Fit). For a future period, it might be possible to adjust the seasonal peak forecast by the ME. Similar adjustments in the forecast might be suggested for other periods showing a systematic bias, upward or downward.

For example, the forecast for Period 3 can be adjusted down by 50 units to compensate for the over-forecast of 50 units. Likewise, Periods 6 and 10 would be adjusted down by 15 and 68 units, respectively. Similarly, for the under-forecasted periods, but not without discussing with marketing about possible root causes. Small adjustments should be avoided as all forecasts are uncertain.

To get an indication of the accuracy in the seasonal peak, we calculate the **A**bsolute **P**ercentage **E**rrors (**APE**) in a third waterfall chart. As a good practice, we also calculate a non-conventional measure of accuracy like the **Med**ian of the **A**bsolute **P**ercentage **E**rrors (**MdAPE**).

|       | Hold-out | S    | A    | L    | E    | S    |      |      |      |      |      |     |
|-------|----------|------|------|------|------|------|------|------|------|------|------|-----|
|       | ACTUALS  | F    | O    | R    | E    | C    | A    | S    | T    |      |      |     |
| T=53  | 46       | 44   |      |      |      |      |      |      |      |      |      |     |
| T=54  | 1568     | 1617 | 1642 |      |      |      |      |      |      |      |      |     |
| T=55  | 283      | 331  | 335  | 334  |      |      |      |      |      |      |      |     |
| T=56  | 56       | 43   | 43   | 43   | 43   |      |      |      |      |      |      |     |
| T=57  | 83       | 63   | 63   | 63   | 63   | 63   |      |      |      |      |      |     |
| T=58  | 31       | 46   | 46   | 46   | 46   | 47   | 47   |      |      |      |      |     |
| T=59  | 1165     | 1132 | 1149 | 1145 | 1146 | 1147 | 1147 | 1146 |      |      |      |     |
| T=60  | 29       | 20   | 20   | 20   | 20   | 20   | 21   | 20   | 20   |      |      |     |
| T=61  | 24       | 20   | 20   | 20   | 20   | 20   | 21   | 20   | 20   | 21   |      |     |
| T=62  | 1846     | 1901 | 1930 | 1922 | 1915 | 1912 | 1912 | 1916 | 1918 | 1908 | 1904 |     |
| T=63  | 359      | 316  | 320  | 319  | 314  | 314  | 316  | 315  | 315  | 311  | 310  | 309 |

Figure 3.19 Waterfall chart of forecast errors for the holdout sample in original domain of sales units. (Forecast error FE = ACTUAL − FCST). (Source: Figure 3.18)

|                 | T=53 | T=54 | T=55 | T=56 | T=57 | T=58 | T=59 | T=60 | T=61 | T=62 | T=63 | T=64 | T=65 |
|-----------------|------|------|------|------|------|------|------|------|------|------|------|------|------|
| Hold-out ACTUALS| 313  | 1568 | 283  | 56   | 83   | 31   | 1165 | 29   | 24   | 1846 | 359  |      |      |
|                 | 1%   | 3%   | 17%  | 23%  | 25%  | 47%  | 3%   | 32%  | 17%  | 3%   | 12%  |      |      |
| FCST            |      | 5%   | 18%  | 22%  | 24%  | 49%  | 1%   | 31%  | 16%  | 5%   | 11%  |      |      |
|                 |      |      | 18%  | 22%  | 24%  | 49%  | 2%   | 31%  | 16%  | 4%   | 11%  |      |      |
| E               |      |      |      | 22%  | 24%  | 49%  | 2%   | 30%  | 16%  | 4%   | 13%  |      |      |
| R               |      |      |      |      | 24%  | 50%  | 2%   | 30%  | 15%  | 4%   | 13%  |      |      |
| R               |      |      |      |      |      | 51%  | 2%   | 29%  | 14%  | 4%   | 12%  |      |      |
| O               |      |      |      |      |      |      | 2%   | 30%  | 16%  | 4%   | 12%  |      |      |
| R               |      |      |      |      |      |      |      | 30%  | 16%  | 4%   | 12%  |      |      |
|                 |      |      |      |      |      |      |      |      | 14%  | 3%   | 13%  |      |      |
|                 |      |      |      |      |      |      |      |      |      | 3%   | 14%  |      |      |
|                 |      |      |      |      |      |      |      |      |      |      | 14%  |      |      |
| MAPE            |      |      | 18%  | 23%  | 24%  | 49%  | 2%   | 30%  | 16%  | 4%   | 12%  |      |      |
| MdAPE           |      |      | 18%  | 22%  | 24%  | 49%  | 2%   | 30%  | 16%  | 4%   | 12%  |      |      |

Figure 3.20 Waterfall chart of forecast percentage errors in original scale of sales units (absolute percentage error APE = 100% *Abs (FE)/Actual).

# Why Moving Average Forecasting Needs to Be Swept into the Dustbin

In the past, when computing power was expensive and data storage very limited, a forecaster did not have enough resources to run statistical forecasting models efficiently. A Moving Average (MAVG) forecast was, then, a convenient and easy to implement solution using only a calculator. While the MAVG method is still used widely, it results in limited forecast profiles that are always level, independent of what the historical data patterns represent.

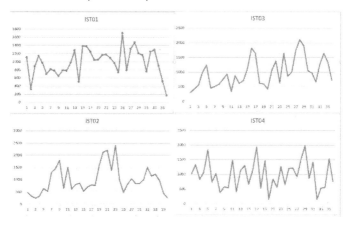

Figure 3.21 Time plots of four monthly time series IST01, IST02, IST03 and IST04.

Figure 3.21 shows four time series (IST01, IST02, IST03, and IST04) each with three years (36 months) of real-world historical data. The context of the data is not important here because a MAVG forecast does not make use of any additional information about the data. The four monthly series have been normalized so that the overall average in each series is the same (=985).

In a MAVG forecast, a smoothing window of twelve periods is used, because the data are monthly and could be seasonal. Applying the MAVG Method, the forecasts for periods 36, 37, 38, etc. are equal to the average of the latest twelve values in the history (periods 25 – 36). In this case, we get 1045 (for IST01), 879 (for IST02), 1273 (for IST03), and 1052 (for IST04), even though the average of each series is the same. This may seem reasonable, but certainly not credible, if you are expecting non-trending forecasts.

To get some insight into demand variability, we can decompose the variation into three components using a data analysis Add-in available in Excel (Two-way ANOVA without Replication). Figure 3.22

shows the four decompositions summarized graphically with bar charts. More than 50% of the variation can be attributed to seasonality (either multiplicative or additive, yet to be determined), with dominant seasonality in IST04. The trend variation does not stand out, but what is an exception is that actual consumer/customer-driven demand profiles are generally not level. Added to that, we observe that the uncertainty factor (labelled irregular) is not small, except in IST04. The uncertainty factor has a direct bearing on estimating the width and skewness of prediction intervals (error bounds) from statistical models. High uncertainty means we should forecast broad and varying prediction intervals, and this pre-modeling analysis suggests that the MAVG forecasting method should not even be considered.

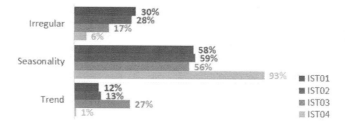

Figure 3.22 Bar charts of four monthly time series Trend/Seasonal/Irregular decompositions for IST01, IST02, IST03 and IST04.

It is a much smarter forecasting practice to always take some exploratory data analysis steps **prior, during, and after** a forecast modeling exercise. With consumer-driven demand, we should be able to recognize seasonality (i.e., consumer/customer habits), trend (i.e., consumer/customer demographics) and an uncertainty factor (that includes all other variation not explained by trend and seasonality) as the primary variation in this context.

The next step is to run the models. We already know that trend and seasonality are the primary drivers of demand in supply chain environments. To be credible and effective, we should start with statistical models providing **trend/seasonal forecast profiles**. The *ErrorTrendSeasonal* (**ETS**) models (Chapter 8) have been accessible since the mid-1990s in a unified State-Space Forecasting methodology for both exponential smoothing and ARIMA models). These models have the flexibility to do the job more accurately and automatically. You can find software for them online in open-source R-libraries. The ETS models can distinguish between additive and multiplicative profiles in the trend, seasonal and error components.

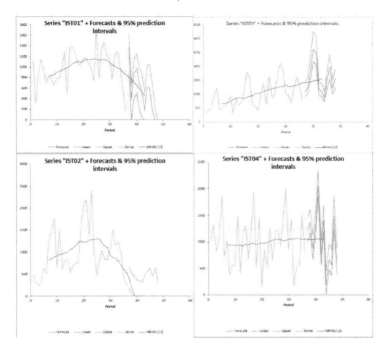

Figure 3.23 Predictive visualization charts of four monthly time series showing Trend/Seasonal/Irregular variation for IST01, IST02, IST03 and IST04.

The corresponding MAVG forecast profiles are not included, but it should be clear where we would have been led, had we applied the MAVG method instead a statistical modeling approach with prediction intervals. The charts show the ETS profiles fluctuating as expected, reproducing seasonality in a credible way, and also presenting a range, embodying the uncertainty we have about the future of each data set. The MAVG forecasts, on the other hand, would extend resolutely into the future, with its typical level profile, with zero response to trend, seasonality and uncertainty, drawing a completely unlikely profile for real-world` supply chain demand forecasting, so the MAVG Method could very well be relegated to the dustbin.

A MAVG forecast is a heuristic *method*, not a *statistical model*. With a statistical modeling approach, prediction limits (error bounds) can be obtained to characterize the uncertainty factor. This is not possible with a heuristic method.

Many business planners and managers often produce forecasts using some variation of weighted average smoothing, known as **simple**

**smoothing.** Simple smoothing is the familiar name for simple exponential smoothing that produce *level* forecast profiles. In Chapter 8, exponential smoothing is shown to be more than a single, simple Method. There are more general exponential smoothing models that produce *level, trend and seasonal* profiles, and have the additional advantage of producing prediction intervals with the forecasts.

There are at least two reasons for the popularity of these exponential smoothing methods. First, the computations are relatively simple, even in a spreadsheet. Second, smoothing methods and models can be accurate and compare very favorably to more complex forecasting models, even for a volatile series like the demand a for a repair part.

The aim of the simple smoothing method is to make a typical point forecast - a point estimate of the level or average value of the data. This estimate should be used only as a short-range forecast and can be continuously adjusted to keep pace with changes. Simple smoothing is easy to automate, so the method was widely used in the early days of forecasting service parts for manufactured products when there are a large number of forecasts to process on a regular basis with limited computer power.

Forecasting bias and accuracy at each lead time were assessed by determining the typical one-period-ahead forecast error, percentage error, and absolute percentage error by summaries with means and medians by lead-time. The typical value for each selected error measure (e.g., ME, MdE, MAPE, MdAPE, and MSE, RMSE), and relative error measures should be reported separately for each lead time and on an ongoing basis.

For example, the forecast errors for three periods are obtained by summing $F(1) +F(2) +F(3)$ separately for each time origin (each column) and subtracting each total from the sum of the actuals in the corresponding periods. The multi-period forecast errors can then evaluated in terms of **bias** and **accuracy**. If this is done on an ongoing basis, a performance tracking can be adequately recorded and assessed. Multiple error measures should be reported separately for each multi-period needed.

## Takeaways

Understanding multiple approaches is fundamental to the selection of a useful forecasting technique. To succeed, the demand forecaster should be able to perform (1) an exploratory data analysis on historical data to gain insight into the dominant drivers of demand, (2) a screening procedure that reduces the list of all available extrapolative techniques to a list of those approaches that are capable of handling the data patterns under investigation, (3) a thorough examination of the assumptions required for using techniques that are considered to be the most appropriate for the given context, (4) the final selection of not just one "best" technique, but **validation runs with more than one technique** that can be considered  appropriate and reliable for the given situation.

# 4

# Taming Uncertainty: Measuring Forecast Accuracy

*Television won't be able to hold on to any market it captures after the first six months. People will soon get tired of staring at a plywood box every night.*

A WELL-KNOWN MOVIE MOGUL IN THE EARLY DAYS OF TV

This chapter describes
- why it is necessary to start first with an unambiguous definition of forecast error
- what bias and dispersion mean for accuracy measurement
- how, when and why to make accuracy measurements
- the systematic steps in a forecast evaluation process.

`After reading this chapter, you should be able to
- distinguish between fit and forecast errors
- recognize that there is not one best measure of accuracy for products, locations and summary hierarchies
- understand why simple averaging is one of the worst best practices for summarizing accuracy measurements. The use of accuracy measures that make use of the arithmetic mean (as in the case of the MAPE, MAD, MASE) for (*non-outlier-resistant*) forecast performance measurement can yield misleading results
- engage with forecast users and demand managers to identify appropriate accuracy standards for the business.

## *The Need to Measure Forecast Accuracy*

The Institutional Broker's Estimate System (I/B/E/S), a service that tracks financial analysts' estimates, reported that forecasts of corporate yearly earnings that are made early in the year are persistently optimistic, that is to say, upwardly biased. In all but two of the 12 years studied (1979–1991), analysts revised their earnings forecasts downward by the end of the year. In a *New York Times* article (January 10, 1992), Jonathan Fuerbringer wrote that this pattern of revisions was so clear that the I/B/E/S urged stock market investors to take early-in-the year earnings forecasts with a grain of salt.

It is generally recognized in most organizations that accurate forecasts are essential for achieving measurable improvements in business operations. Developers of forecasting models use accuracy measures, and accuracy at all levels is relevant to the users of forecasts in a company.

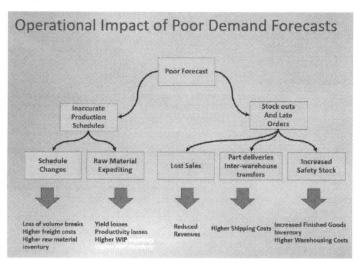

Figure 4.1 Operational impact of poor forecasts. (*Source*: Simon Conradie, Noetric Business Consulting, RSA)

Will the model prove reliable for forecasting units or revenues over a planned forecast horizon, such as item-level product demand for the next 12 weeks or aggregate revenue demand for the next four quarters? Will it have a significant impact on marketing, sales, budgeting, logistics and production activities? Will it have an effect on inventory investment or customer service? In a nutshell, inaccurate forecasts can have a direct effect on setting inadequate safety stocks, ongoing capacity problems, massive rescheduling of manufacturing plans, chronic late shipments to customers, and adding expensive manufacturing flexibility resources (Figure 4.1).

In addition, the Income Statement and Balance Sheet are also impacted by poor demand forecasts for financial planning (Figure 4.2).

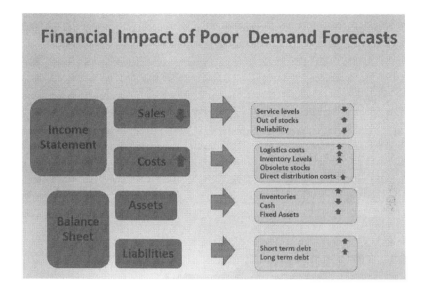

Figure 4.2 Financial impact of poor forecasts. (*Source*: Noetric Business Consulting. RSA)

## Analyzing Forecast Errors

Whether a method that has provided a good fit to historical data will also yield accurate forecasts for future time periods is an unsettled issue. Intuition suggests that this may not necessarily be the case. There is no guarantee that past patterns will persist in future periods. For a forecasting technique to be useful, we must demonstrate that it can forecast reliably on ongoing basis and with consistent accuracy. It is not credible to simply produce a model that performs best only in a historical (within sample) fit period.

Because of ever-present outliers and non-normality, the demand forecaster must also measure forecasting performance with multiple measures, not just with a single measure, like the Mean Absolute Percentage Error (MAPE) or weighted MAPE. At the same time, the users of a forecast need forecasting results in a timely fashion. Using a forecasting technique and waiting one or more periods for history to unfold in future periods is not practical because our advice as forecasters will not be agile.

Two important aspects of forecast accuracy measurement are bias and dispersion. **Bias** is a problem of direction: Forecasts are typically too low (downward bias) or typically too high (upward bias). **Dispersion** is an issue of magnitudes: Forecast errors can be too large (in either direction) using a particular forecasting technique. Consider first a simple situation - forecasting a single product or item. The attributes that should satisfy most forecasters include lack of serious bias, acceptable dispersion, and superiority over naive models.

## Lack of Bias

If forecasts are typically too low, we say that they are downwardly biased; if too high, they are upwardly biased. If over-forecasts and under-forecasts tend to cancel one another out (i.e., if an average of the forecast errors is approximately zero), we say that the forecasts are unbiased.

> *Bias refers to the tendency of a forecast to be predominantly toward one side of the truth.*

If bias is a problem of direction, we can think of forecasting as aiming darts at a target; then a bias implies that the aim is off-center. That is, the darts land repeatedly away from the target.

## What Is an Acceptable Dispersion?

Imprecision is a problem if the forecast errors tend to be too dispersed. The precise forecast is generally right around a target (Figure 4.3).

Figure 4.3 Dispersion in forecasts.

> *Precision refers to the dispersion among the forecasts as a result of using a particular forecasting procedure and the corresponding actual values.*

But what is a forecast error? It is not unusual to hear inconsistent definitions and interpretations among practitioners, even within the same company.

Figure 4.4 illustrates the measurement of bias for three hypothetical forecasting techniques. In each case, the fit period is periods 1 - 20. Shown in the top row of the table in Figure 4.4 *(left)* are actual values for the last four periods (21 – 24). The other three rows contain forecasts using forecasting models X, Y, and Z. These are shown in a bar chart in Figure 4.4 (*left*). What can we say about how good these forecast models are? On the left graph, the three forecasts do not look all that different,

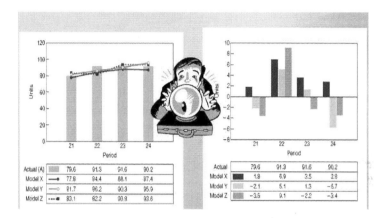

| Actual (A) | | 79.6 | 91.3 | 91.6 | 90.2 |
| Model X | —• | 77.8 | 94.4 | 88.1 | 87.4 |
| Model Y | —○ | 81.7 | 96.2 | 90.3 | 95.9 |
| Model Z | ---◆ | 83.1 | 82.2 | 93.9 | 93.6 |

| Actual | | 79.6 | 91.3 | 91.6 | 90.2 |
| Model X | | 1.8 | 6.9 | 3.5 | 2.8 |
| Model Y | | −2.1 | 5.1 | 1.3 | −5.7 |
| Model Z | | −3.5 | 9.1 | −2.2 | −3.4 |

Figure 4.4 Bar charts and tables showing actuals (A), forecasts, and forecast errors for three forecasting techniques.

Figure 4.4 (*right*) records the deviations between the actuals and their forecasts. Each deviation represents a **forecast error** (or forecast miss) for the associated period:

$$\text{Forecast error } (\textbf{E}) = \text{Actual } (\textbf{A}) - \text{Forecast } (\textbf{F})$$

If (F–A) is the preferred use in some organizations but not others, then demand forecasters and forecast users should name it something else, like **forecast variance**, a more conventional meaning among revenue-oriented planners. The distinction is important because of the interpretation of bias in under- and over forecasting situations. Contrast this with a fit error (or residual) of a model fit over a historical period, which is Fit error = Actual (**A**) - Model fit (**F**).

*Forecast error is a measure of forecast accuracy. Fit error (or residual) is a measure of model adequacy.*

In Figure 4.4 (*right*), the forecast errors shown for model X is 1.8 in period 21. This represents the deviation between the actual value in forecast period 21 (= 79.6) and the forecast using model X (= 77.8). In forecast period 22, the forecast using model X was lower than actual value for that period resulting in a forecast error of 6.9.

The period 24 forecast using model Z was higher than that period's actual value; hence, the forecast error is negative (- 3.4). When we **over-forecast**, we must make a *negative* adjustment to reach the actual value. Note that if the forecast is less than the actual value, the miss is a positive number; if the forecast is more than the actual value, the miss is a negative number.

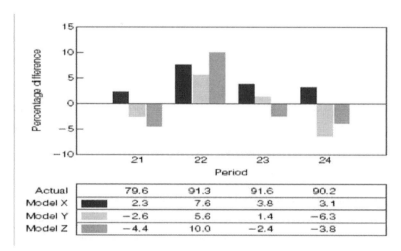

| | 21 | 22 | 23 | 24 |
|---|---|---|---|---|
| Actual | 79.6 | 91.3 | 91.6 | 90.2 |
| Model X | 2.3 | 7.6 | 3.8 | 3.1 |
| Model Y | −2.6 | 5.6 | 1.4 | −6.3 |
| Model Z | −4.4 | 10.0 | −2.4 | −3.8 |

Figure 4.5 Bar chart and table of the forecast error as percentage error (PE) between actuals and forecasts for three models.

To identify patterns of upward- and downward-biased forecasts, we start by comparing the number of positive and negative misses. As Figure 4.5 shows, Model X under-forecasts in all four periods, indicative of a persistent (downward) bias. Model Y under-forecasts and over-forecasts with equal frequency; therefore, it exhibits no evidence of bias in either direction. Model Z is biased slightly toward overforecasting. As one measure of forecast accuracy (Figure 4.5), we calculate a percentage error PE = 100% * (A − F)/A.

To reduce bias in a forecasting technique, we can either (1) reject any technique that projects with serious bias in favor of a less-biased alternative (after we have first compared the dispersion and complexity of the techniques under consideration) or (2) investigate the pattern of bias in the hope of devising a bias adjustment; for example, we might take the forecasts from method X and adjust them upward to try to offset the tendency of this method to under-forecasts certain periods. Also, forecasts for Models Y and Z could be averaged after placing Forecast X aside for the current forecasting cycle.

> *A forecast accuracy measure should be devised with data from holdout samples before selecting a final model for use.*

## Ways to Evaluate Accuracy of Point Forecasts

 A number of forecasting competitions have been held to assess the effectiveness of statistical forecasting techniques and determine which techniques are among the most useful. Starting with the original M competition in 1982, Spyros Makridakis (*left*) and his academic collaborators compared the accuracy of about 20 forecasting techniques across a sample of 111 time series—a very small dataset by today's standards. A subset of the methods was tested on 1001 time series. The last 12 months of each series were held out and the remaining data were used for model fitting. Using a range of measures on a holdout sample, the *International Journal of Forecasting* (IJF) conducted a competition in 1997 comparing a range of forecasting techniques across a sample of 3003 time series. Known as the M3 competition, these data and results can be found at the website *www.maths.monash.edu.au/~hyndman/forecasting/*. A number of IJF papers have been written summarizing the results of these competitions. These competitions have become the basis for how we should measure forecast accuracy in practice.

> *Forecast accuracy measurements are performed in order to assess the accuracy of a forecasting technique.*

## The Fit Period versus the Holdout Period

Generally, business forecasters are interested in *multi-step-ahead* (lead time) forecasts because lead times longer than one period are required for business to act on a forecast.

In measuring forecast accuracy, a portion of the historical data is withheld, and reserved for evaluating forecast accuracy. Thus, the historical data are first divided into two parts: an initial segment (the **fit period**) and a later segment (the **holdout sample**).

The fit period is used to develop a forecasting model. Sometimes, the fit period is called the within-sample training, initialization, or calibration period. Next, using a particular model for the fit period, model forecasts are made for the later segment. Finally, the accuracy of these forecasts is determined by comparing the projected values with the data in the holdout sample. The time period over which forecast accuracy is evaluated is called the **test period**, validation period, or holdout-sample period.

To minimize confusion, we introduce some common notation for the concepts used in these calculations: $Y_t(1)$ as the **one-period-ahead** forecast of $Y_t$ and $Y_t(m)$ the **m-period-ahead** forecast. A forecast for $t = 25$ that is the one-period-ahead forecast made at $t = 24$ is denoted by $Y_{24}(1)$ and the a two-period-ahead forecast for the same time, $t = 25$, made at $t = 23$ is denoted by $Y_{23}(2)$.

We use the following conventions for a time series:

- $\{Y_t, t = 1, 2, ... T\}$ the historical dataset up to and including period t = T
- $\{\hat{Y}_t, t =1, 2, . . . T\}$ the data set of fitted values that result from fitting a model to historical data
- $Y_{T+m}$ the future value of $Y_t$, m periods after t = T
- $\{Y_T(1), Y_T(2), ..., Y_T(m)\}$, the one- to m-period ahead-forecasts made from t = T

Consequently, we see that forecast errors and fit errors (residuals) refer to

- $Y_1 - \hat{Y}_t, Y_2 - \hat{Y}_2, ..., Y_T - \hat{Y}_T$ the fit errors or residuals from a fit
- $Y_{T+1} - Y_T(1), Y_{T+2} - Y_T(2), ... Y_{T+m} - Y_T(m)$ the forecast errors (*not* to be confused with the residuals from a fit)
- 

*When dealing with forecast accuracy, it is important to distinguish between forecast errors and fitting errors.*

## Goodness of Fit versus Forecast Accuracy

We need to assess forecast accuracy rather than just calculate overall **goodness of fit** statistics, for several reasons:

- **Goodness of fit** statistics may appear to give better results than forecasting-based calculations, but goodness of fit statistics measure model adequacy over a fitting period that may not be representative of the forecasting period.
- When a model is fit, it is designed to reproduce the historical patterns as closely as possible. This may create complexities in the model that capture insignificant patterns in the historical data, which may lead to over-fitting.
- By adding complexity, we may not realize that insignificant patterns in the past are unlikely to persist into the future. More importantly, the unexpected patterns of the future are unlikely to have revealed themselves in the past.

- Exponential smoothing models are based on updating procedures in which each forecast is made from smoothed values in the immediate past. For these models, goodness of fit is measured from forecast errors made in estimating the next time period ahead from the current time period. These are called one-period-ahead forecast errors (also called one-step-ahead forecast errors). Because it is reasonable to expect that errors in forecasting the more distant future will be larger than those made in forecasting the next period into the future, we should avoid accuracy assessments based exclusively on one-period-ahead errors.

*When assessing forecast accuracy, we may want to know about likely errors in forecasting more than one period-ahead.*

## Item Level versus Aggregate Performance

Forecast evaluations are also useful in multi-series comparisons (see Chapter 8). Production and inventory managers typically need demand or shipment forecasts for hundreds to tens of thousands of items (SKUs) based on historical data for each item at a number of locations. Financial forecasters need to issue forecasts for dozens of budget categories in a strategic plan on the basis of past values of each source of revenue. In a multi-series comparison, the forecaster should appraise the method based not only on its performance for the individual item but also on the basis of its overall accuracy when tested over various summaries of the data by product category and location segment. In the next section, we discuss various measures of forecast accuracy.

## Absolute Errors versus Squared Errors

Both the perspective based on absolute errors and that based on squared errors are useful. There is a good argument for consistency in the sense that a model's forecasting accuracy should be evaluated on the same basis used to develop (fit) the model. The standard basis for model fit is the least-squares criterion that is minimizing the mean-square-error MSE between the actual and fitted values. To be consistent, we should evaluate forecast accuracy based on squared error measures, such as the root mean squared error (RMSE). It is useful to test how well different methods do in forecasting using a variety of accuracy measures. Forecasts are put to a wide variety of uses in any organization, and no single forecaster can dictate on how they will be used and interpreted.

Sometimes costs or losses due to forecast errors are in direct proportion to the size of the error - double the error leads to double the cost. For example, when a soft drink distributor realized that the costs of shipping its product between distribution centers was becoming prohibitive, it made a study of the relationship between under-forecasting (not enough of the right product at the right place, thus requiring a transshipment, or backhaul, from another distribution center) and the cost of those backhauls.

As shown in Figure 4.6, over-forecasts of 25% or higher appeared strongly related to an increase in the backhaul of pallets of product. In this case, the measures based on absolute errors are more appropriate. In other cases, small forecast errors do not cause much harm and large errors may be devastating; then, we would want to stress the importance of (avoidance of) large errors, which is what squared-error measures accomplish.

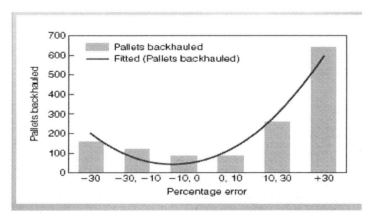

Figure 4.6. Backhauls in pallets versus forecast percentage error.

## Measures of bias

There are two common measures of bias. The **Mean Error** (ME) is the sum of the forecast errors divided by the number of periods in the forecast horizon ($h$) for which forecasts were made:

$$\text{ME} = [\sum (A_t - F_t)] / h \quad \text{sum from } t = T+1 \text{ to } t = T+h$$
$$= [\sum (A_i - F_i)] / h \quad \text{sum from } i = 1 \text{ to } i = h$$

The **Mean Percentage Error** (MPE) is

$$\text{MPE} = 100 * [\sum (A_t - F_t) / A_t] / h \quad \text{sum from } t = T+1 \text{ to } t = T+h$$

$$= 100 * [\sum (A_i - F_i) / A_i] / h \quad \text{sum from } i = 1 \text{ to } i = h$$

The MPE and ME are useful supplements to a count of the frequency of under- and over-forecasts. The ME gives the average of the forecast errors expressed in the units of measurement of the data; the MPE gives the average of the forecast errors in terms of percentage and is unit-free.

If we examine the hypothetical example in Figures 4.4 and 4.5, we find that for model X, ME = 3.8, and MPE = 4.2%. This means that, using model X, we underforecast by an average of 3.8 units per period. Restated in terms of the MPE, this means that the forecasts from model X were below the actual values by an average of 4.2%. A positive value for the ME or MPE signals negative bias in the forecasts using model X.

**The two most common measures of bias are the mean error (ME) and the mean percentage error (MPE).**

Compared to model X, the ME and MPE for model Y are much smaller. These results are not surprising. Because model Y resulted in an equal number of under-forecasts and overforecasts, we expect to find that the average error is close to zero.

On the other hand, the low ME and MPE values for model Z are surprising. We have previously seen that model Z over-forecasts in three of the four periods. A closer look at the errors from model Z shows that there was a very large under-forecast in one period and relatively small over-forecasts in the other three periods. Thus, the one large underforecast offset the three small over-forecasts, yielding a mean error close to 0. The lesson here is that averages can be distorted by one or just a few unusually large errors. One should always consider calculating non-conventional measures like the **Median Error** (MdE) and the **Median Percentage Error** (MdPE), because unusual values are not that unusual.

**We should always use multiple error measures as a supplement to the analysis of the individual errors.**

## Measures of Point Forecast Accuracy

Certain indicators of accuracy are based on the absolute values of the forecast errors. By taking an absolute value, we eliminate the possibility that under-forecasts and over-forecasts negate one another. Therefore, an average of the absolute forecast errors reveals simply how far apart the forecasts are from the actual values. It does not tell us if the forecasts are biased.

The most familiar averages of absolute values are the **M**ean **A**bsolute **E**rror (MAE), **M**ean **A**bsolute **P**ercentage **E**rror (MAPE), and **M**ed**i**an **A**bsolute **P**ercentage **E**rror (MdAPE). Interpretations of the averages of absolute error measures are straightforward. In Figure 4.7, we calculate that the MAE is 4.6 for model Z, from which we can conclude that the forecast errors from this technique average 4.6 per period. The MAPE, from Figure 4.8, is 5.2%, which tells us that the period forecast errors average 5.2%. The MdAPE for model Z, from Figure 4.8, is approximately 4.1% (the average of the two middle values: 4.4 and 3.8). Thus, half the time the forecast errors are expected to exceed 4.1%, and half the time smaller than 4.1%.

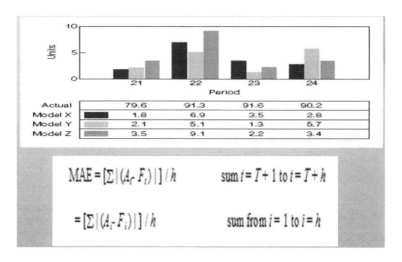

Figure 4.7 Bar chart and table showing forecast error as absolute difference |E| between actuals and forecasts for three models. |E|= |(A −F)|

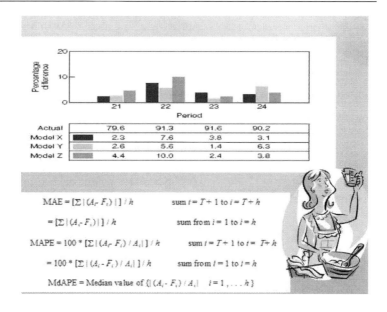

Figure 4.8 Bar chart and table showing forecast error as absolute percentage difference |PE(%)| between actuals and forecasts for three models. |PE(%)|= 100* |(A −F)|/A

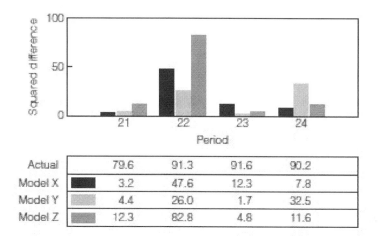

| | | | | |
|---|---|---|---|---|
| Actual | 79.6 | 91.3 | 91.6 | 90.2 |
| Model X | 3.2 | 47.6 | 12.3 | 7.8 |
| Model Y | 4.4 | 26.0 | 1.7 | 32.5 |
| Model Z | 12.3 | 82.8 | 4.8 | 11.6 |

Figure 4.9 Bar chart and table showing forecast error as squared difference ($E^2$) between actuals and forecasts for three models.

When there is a significant outlier among the forecast errors, as with model Z, it is useful to know the MdAPE in addition to the MAPE because medians are less sensitive than mean values to distortion from outliers. This is why the MdAPE is a full percentage point below the MAPE for model Z. Sometimes, as with model Y, the MdAPE and the MAPE are virtually identical. In this case, we can safely report the MAPE because it is the far more common measure.

In addition to the indicators of accuracy calculated from the absolute errors, certain measures are commonly used that are based on the squared values of the forecast errors (Figure 4.9), such as the MSE and RMSE. (RMSE is the square root of MSE.) A notable variant on RMSE is the **Root Mean Squared**

**Percentage Error** (RMSPE), which is based on the squared percentage errors (Figure 4.10).

$$MSE = [\sum (A_t - F_t)^2] / h \qquad \text{sum from } t = T+1 \text{ to } t = T+h$$

$$= [\sum (A_i - F_i)^2] / h \qquad \text{sum from } i = 1 \text{ to } i = h$$

$$RMSPE = \sqrt{100 * [\sum \{(A_t - F_t) / A_t\}^2] / h} \qquad \text{sum } t = T+1 \text{ to } t = T+h$$

$$= 100 * [\sum \{(A_i - F_i) / A_i\}^2] / h \qquad \text{sum from } i = 1 \text{ to } i = h$$

To calculate RMSPE, we square each percentage error in Figure 4.10. The squares are then averaged, and the square root is taken of the average. The RMSPE is the percentage version of the RMSE (just as the MAPE is the percentage version of the MAE). Because the RMPSE for model Y equals 4.5%, we may suggest that "the forecasts of model Y have a standard or average error of approximately 4.5%."

The MSE is expressed in the square of the units of the data. This may make it difficult to interpret when referring to dollar volumes, for example. By taking the square root of the MSE, we return to the units of measurement of the original data.

> *The RMSE can be interpreted as a standard error of the forecasts.*

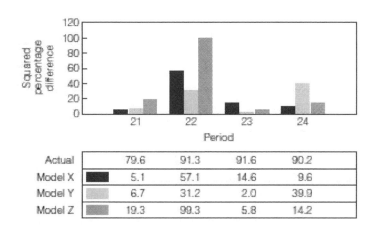

| | Period | | | |
|---|---|---|---|---|
| | 21 | 22 | 23 | 24 |
| Actual | 79.6 | 91.3 | 91.6 | 90.2 |
| Model X | 5.1 | 57.1 | 14.6 | 9.6 |
| Model Y | 6.7 | 31.2 | 2.0 | 39.9 |
| Model Z | 19.3 | 99.3 | 5.8 | 14.2 |

Figure 4.10 Bar chart and table showing forecast error as squared percentage difference between actuals and forecasts for three models.

Figure 4.10 Bar chart and table showing forecast error as squared percentage difference PE(%)2 between actuals and forecasts for three models. We can simplify the interpretation of RMSE and present it as if it were the mean absolute error (MAE); the forecasts of model Y are in error by an average of 4. There is little real harm in doing this; just keep in mind that the RMSE is generally somewhat larger than the MAE. (Compare Figures 4.8 and 4.10).

Some forecasters present the RMSE within the context of a prediction interval. Here is how it might sound: "Assuming the forecast errors are normally distributed, we can be approximately 68% confident that model Y's forecasts will be accurate to within 4.0 on the average." However, it is best to not to make these statements too precise because it requires us to assume a normal distribution of forecast errors.

If we desire a squared error measure in percentage terms, the following shortcut is sometimes taken. Divide the RMSE by the mean value of the data over the forecast horizon. The result can be interpreted as the standard error as a percentage of the mean of the data and is called the **coefficient of variation** (because it is a ratio of a standard deviation to a mean). Based on model Y, average actual values over periods 21–24 were 88.2 (Figure 4.5), and the RMSE for model Y was found to be 4.0 (Figure 4.9). Hence, the coefficient of variation is 4/88.2 = 4.5%, a result that is virtually identical to the RMSPE, in this case.

## Comparing with Naive Techniques

After reviewing the evidence of bias and accuracy, we may want to select model Y as the most useful of the three candidates. Based on the evaluation, model Y's forecast for periods 21–24 shows no indication of bias - two under-forecasts and two over-forecasts - and proves slightly more precise than the other two models, no matter which measure of accuracy is used. The MAE for model Y reveals that the forecast errors over periods 21–24 average approximately 3.5 per period, and the MAPE indicates that these errors come to just under 4% on average.

To provide additional perspective on model Y, we might contrast model Y's forecasting record with that of a very simplistic procedure, one requiring little or no thought or effort. Such procedures are called naive techniques. The continued time and effort investment in model Y might not be worth the cost if it can be shown to perform no better than a naïve technique. Sometimes the contrast with a naive technique is sobering. The forecaster thinks an excellent model has been developed and finds that it barely outperforms a naive technique.

*If the forecasting performance of model Y is no better or is worse than that of a naive technique, it suggests that in developing model Y we have not accomplished very much.*

A standard naive forecasting technique has emerged for data that are yearly or otherwise lack seasonality; it is called a NAIVE_1 or Naive Forecast1 (NF1). We see later that there are also naïve forecasting techniques for seasonal data.

A NAIVE_1 forecast of the following time period is simply the value in effect during this time period. Alternatively stated, the forecast for any one time period is the value observed during the previous time period.

*A NAIVE_1 is called a no change forecasting technique, because its forecasted value is unchanged from the previously observed value.*

Figure 4.11 shows the forecast for our example (Figure 4.5). Note that one-period-ahead forecasts for periods 22 - 24 are the respective actuals for periods 21 - 23. The forecast for period 21 (=73.5) is the actual value for period 20. When we appraise NAIVE_1's performance, we note it is biased. It underestimated periods 21 - 23 and overestimated period 24.

| Period | Actual | NAIVE_1 |
|--------|--------|---------|
| 21 | 79.6 | 73.5 |
| 22 | 91.3 | 79.6 |
| 23 | 91.6 | 91.3 |
| 24 | 90.2 | 91.6 |
| MAE | 3.6 | 4.9 |
| MAPE | 4 | 5.60% |
| RMSE | 4 | 6.6 |
| RMSPE | 4.5 | 7.50% |

(*Source*: Exhibit 5.3)

Figure 4.11 Actuals and NAIVE_1 (one-period-ahead) forecasts for model Y. (Source: Figure 4.5)

By always projecting no change, a NAIVE_1 underforecasts whenever data are increasing and overforecasts whenever the data are declining. We do not expect a NAIVE_1 to work at all when the data are steadily trending in one direction.

The error measures for NAIVE_1 in Figure 4.11 are all higher than the corresponding error measures for model Y, indicating that model Y was more precise than NAIVE_1. By looking at the relative error measures, we can be more specific about the advantage of model Y over NAIVE_1.

Because a naive technique has no prescription for a random error term, the NAIVE_1 technique can be viewed as a **no-change, no-chance** method (in the sense of our demand forecasting objectives in Chapter 1) to predict *change* in the presence of uncertainty (*chance*). Hence, it is useful as a benchmark-forecasting model to beat.

## Relative Error Measures

A **relative error measure** is a ratio; the numerator is a measure of the accuracy of a forecasting method; the denominator is the analogous measure for a naive technique.

| | RAE | FC |
|--------|--------|--------|
| RAE | 0.73 | 0.27 |
| MAPE | 0.71 | 0.29 |
| RMSE (Theil's U2) | 0.61 | 0.39 |
| RMSPE | 0.60 | 0.40 |

(*Source*: Exhibit 5.3)

Figure 4.12 Relative error measures for model Y relative to NAIVE_1. (*Source*: Figure 4.5)

Figure 4.12 provides a compendium of relative error measures that compare model Y with the NAIVE_1. The first entry (=0.73) is the ratio of the MAE for model Y to the MAE for the NAIVE_1 (3.55/4.87 = 0.73). It is called the **relative absolute error** (RAE). The RAE shows that the average forecast error using model Y is 73% of the average error using NAIVE_1. This implies a 27% improvement of model Y over NAIVE_1.

Expressed as an improvement score, the relative error measure is sometimes called a **forecast coefficient** (FC), as listed in the last column of Figure 4.12 When FC = 0, this indicates that the technique in question was no better than NAIVE_1 technique. When FC < 0, the technique was in fact less precise than the NAIVE_1, whereas when FC > 0 the forecasting technique was more precise than NAIVE_1. When FC = 1, the forecasting technique is perfect.

The second row of Figure 4.12 shows the relative error measures based on the MAPE. The results almost exactly mirror those based on the MAE, and the interpretations are identical. The relative error measure based on the RMSE (which is the RMSE of model Y divided by RMSE of the NAIVE_1) was originally proposed by the economist Henri Theil in 1966 and it is known as Theil's U or Theil's U2 statistic. As with the RAE, a score less than 1 suggests an improvement over the naive technique.

The relative errors based on the squared-error measures, RMSE and RMSPE, suggest that model Y in Figure 4.12 was about 40% more precise than the NAIVE_1. The relative errors based on MAE and MAPE put the improvement at approximately 25 – 30%. Why the difference?

Error measures based on absolute values, such as the MAE and MAPE, give a weight (emphasis) to each time period in proportion to the size of the forecast error. The RMSE and RMSPE, in contrast, are measures based on squared errors and squaring gives more weight to large errors. A closer look at Figure 4.11 shows that the NAIVE_1 commits a very large error in forecast period 22.

## Using Rolling Forecast Evaluations

The first step in a forecasting performance evaluation to divide the historical data between a **fit period** and a **test** or **holdout period.** Typically, the fit period starts at the beginning of the historical data and continues to some point in the recent past.

## Choosing the Holdout Period

In Figure 4.13, a weekly time series spans periods 1–63 and the fit period could be chosen to be periods 1–52. The last eleven periods of data are treated as the **holdout sample** to provide a test of the model's forecasting accuracy over an eleven-week forecast horizon (lead time).

Here are some guidelines to decide how much of the historical data should be held out from the fit period to use in evaluating forecasting accuracy,

*The choice of how much data to use in a holdout period is a matter of achieving an acceptable balance between data availability and length of the forecasting horizon.*

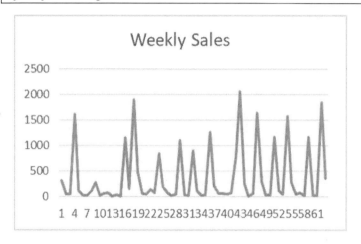

Figure 4.13 Time plot of weekly sales data. (*Source*: Figure 11.24)

Suppose the forecasting lead-time horizon ($h$) is eleven periods, so that we wish to make projections for a lead-time period (64–74). We should aim, at minimum, to withhold the previous eleven periods (53–63) from the fit period. The accuracy with which a model will forecast the next eleven periods (53–63) can then be gauged by measuring how accurately the model forecasts the previous eleven periods (after using only the data from the fit period for the model, through period 52).

*Forecasting horizon: From the present, how long into the future do we need to forecast?*

In a demand forecasting context, an adequate holdout sample should be based on practical business considerations. For instance, if we have a 12–18-month budget cycle for which rolling forecasts are desired, we would need at least 36 periods to fit a model (to adequately model seasonality) and the remaining 12 to 18 periods to test the model's forecasting accuracy. Because estimating seasonality requires a minimum two-season (24-month) sample, it is preferable to start with at least a third year.

*Holdout period: The number of time periods held out from the model fit should be at least as large the length of our forecasting horizon.*

## Rolling Origins

A rolling-origin simulation involves successively updating the forecasting origin and creating forecasts from each new origin. Rolling simulations begin the same way as fixed-origin simulations: Data from periods 1 through $T$ are used to fit a model. Then, starting at the origin period $t = T$, forecasts $F_T(1)$, …, $F_T(h)$ are generated for periods $T + 1$ through $T + h$. The rolling simulation takes the actual data value for period $T + 1$ and adds it to the fit period. The model is updated and revised based on the data, which now includes period $T + 1$. Using period $t = T + 1$ as the origin, new forecasts are made for periods $T + 2$ through $T + h$.

The updating process continues and should be maintained in an ongoing process as part of the monthly or periodic forecasting cycle. The actual data value for period $T + 2$ is added to the fit period, the model revised once again, and, from the new origin, $T + 2$, additional forecasts are generated. The process stops after the next-to-last period $(T + h - 1)$ has done its stint as the origin.

## *Evaluating Profile Forecasting Performance*

What should be a "useful" Method in a particular Supply Chain forecasting application? We regard a Method as **Useful** if it is both 1) **effective** (*doing the right things fulfilling the requirements of a particular application*), as well as (2) **efficient** (*doing things right in converting inputs to outputs*). We can validate the performance of a forecasting Method by creating an "effectiveness score" and an associated "efficiency rating". Next, we set up an objective performance evaluation procedure that can be implemented with just spreadsheet calculations and predictive visualizations.

| Time Origin $T = 24$ | Actual Demand | Simple Smoothing Projection (206) Error | NAÏVE_1 Projection (266) Error |
|---|---|---|---|
| 25 | 162 | - 44 | -104 |
| 26 | 275 | 69 | 9 |
| 27 | 280 | 74 | 14 |
| 28 | 227 | 21 | - 39 |
| 29 | 234 | 28 | - 32 |
| 30 | 288 | 82 | 22 |
| 31 | 226 | 20 | -40 |
| 32 | 200 | - 6 | -66 |
| 33 | 279 | 73 | 13 |
| 34 | 196 | -10 | -70 |
| 35 | 246 | 40 | -20 |
| 36 | 293 | 87 | 27 |
| Mean Square Error (MSE) | | 2930 | 2190 |

Figure 4.14 NAÏVE_1 method **one-step** ahead point-forecast errors versus simple smoothing Method **one-step** ahead point-forecast errors for demand for a repair dataset. ($n = 24$, m = 12).

By withholding the last 12 months of a repair dataset in Year 3 (Figure 4.14), we can investigate and validate the performance of a Method over the holdout period. For the fitted 24 values, the **M**ean **S**quared **E**rror (MSE) is 1502. The MSE is calculated by averaging the squared residuals (actual minus fitted values). The same MSE calculation can be made for the forecast errors over the hold-out period, but with a different interpretation.

Based on the MSE calculated over the withholding/validation period, it appears that a one-step ahead simple smoothing method has not done a very good job of forecasting Year 3. Had we used a smoothing parameter of 0.13, the projections would be 218, the MSE over the **fit period** would be larger (1621 vs. 1502), but the MSE over the forecast period would be reduced (2206 vs. 2930) but still worse than the NAÏVE_1 method in this particular situation. How can we do better?

In contrast, if we focus on the **pattern** of the actuals and *lead-time* forecasts over the holdout period, we note that the forecast profile for the holdout period is level (=206) based on the simple smoothing Method. The projection for the NAÏVE_1 Method is the last observed value (=266) for month 12 of Year 2.

## What is a Profile Analysis?

In practice, we should be comparing a *forecast* **profile** with the *historical* or actual **profile** and assess how the model is able to reproduce the primary **patterns** representing level, trend and seasonality. Following that, we might take another step using **S**tatistical **L**earning (SL) algorithms (a.k.a. **M**achine **L**earning (ML) algorithms when SL is combined with computing algorithms) to gain further insights based on the residual profile errors. It should also be evident that a context-free algorithmic approach, like ML, would be insufficient for dealing with trend and seasonal consumer demand patterns.

It is generally not useful to try to find a **best** forecasting Method. Rather, what should be a *useful* forecasting Method in a particular Supply Chain application? We will regard a **M**ethod as **Useful** if it is both 1) **effective** (*doing the right things fulfilling the requirements of a particular application*), as well as (2) **efficient** (*doing things right in converting inputs to outputs*).

We can validate the performance of a forecasting Method by creating an "effectiveness score" and an associated "efficiency rating". Next, we set up an objective procedure that can be implemented with just spreadsheet calculations and predictive visualizations.

A profile analysis of a forecasting Method can be derived from well-established, information-theoretic concepts that you can also find in climatology and machine learning applications. In an information-theoretic approach, forecast accuracy can be defined by the miss or 'divergence' between the profiles of the actuals and the forecasts for a prescribed lead-time evaluation horizon or time period.

A Forecast Profile Error (FPE) is given by

$$(a_i \ln a_i) \quad \text{minus} \quad (f_i \ln f_i)$$

where the $a_i$ are the components of an **A**ctual **A**lphabet **P**rofile (AAP) and the $f_i$ are the components of the **F**orecast **A**lphabet **P**rofile (FAP). In the formula, *ln* stands for the natural logarithm. The units of FPE are '*nats*', in contrast to *bits* when we use the logarithm to the base 2.

Lead-time demand forecasts are widely used by supply chain practitioners for inventory planning, budget forecasting, and S&OP planning. Once a baseline forecast has been put together, many planners and managers contribute their expertise to create more useful planning forecasts with judgmental overrides or by incorporating more current data and planning objectives.

To create a profile, individual forecasts and holdout sample actuals are 'encoded' or transformed into corresponding FAP and AAP without changing the underlying data pattern of the forecasts and actuals. This is accomplished by dividing the *Lead-time Total* into each component of the respective profiles. Thus, for a given forecast, a FAP is created by dividing each *forecast value* by the sum of the forecasts over a fixed time horizon *m*.

Likewise, the AAP is calculated by dividing each *actual* by the sum of the actuals over the predetermined time horizon.

In Figure 4.15, you can immediately note a discrepancy in the peaks at period 4 and 5 between the forecasts and the actuals that can be attributed to an unusual December 2015 seasonal peak (Figure 3.22). When switching December 2015 (=49786) with January 2016 (=73079), the profiles line up more credibly. Period 9 (= May 2016) is also worth investigating **before** proceeding with a performance evaluation.

The sum of the forecast profile error FPE over a lead-time of *m* periods is called the **Profile Miss** (FAP Miss) and can be interpreted as a measure of ignorance about the forecast profile error:

$$FAP\ Miss = \sum_{i=1}^{m}(a_i \ln a_i) - \sum_{i=1}^{m} (f_i \ln f_i)$$

The closer to zero the better.

The accuracy of a FAP is given by the **Profile Accuracy** measure D(a|f), which is always positive and equal to zero if and only if forecast and actual profiles are identical. That is, when AAP = FAP:

$$D(a|f) = \sum_{i=1}^{m} \left( a_i \ln \left( \frac{a_i}{f_i} \right) \right)$$

When D(a|f) = 0, the alphabet profiles overlap, which represents 100% accuracy.

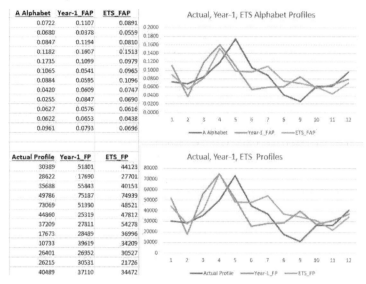

| A Alphabet | Year-1_FAP | ETS_FAP |
|---|---|---|
| 0.0722 | 0.1107 | 0.0891 |
| 0.0680 | 0.0378 | 0.0559 |
| 0.0847 | 0.1194 | 0.0810 |
| 0.1182 | 0.1607 | 0.1513 |
| 0.1735 | 0.1099 | 0.0979 |
| 0.1065 | 0.0541 | 0.0965 |
| 0.0884 | 0.0595 | 0.1096 |
| 0.0420 | 0.0609 | 0.0747 |
| 0.0255 | 0.0847 | 0.0690 |
| 0.0627 | 0.0576 | 0.0616 |
| 0.0622 | 0.0653 | 0.0438 |
| 0.0961 | 0.0793 | 0.0696 |

| Actual Profile | Year-1_FP | ETS_FP |
|---|---|---|
| 30389 | 51801 | 44123 |
| 28622 | 17690 | 27701 |
| 35688 | 55843 | 40153 |
| 49786 | 75187 | 74939 |
| 73069 | 51390 | 48521 |
| 44860 | 25319 | 47812 |
| 37209 | 27811 | 54278 |
| 17673 | 28489 | 36996 |
| 10733 | 39619 | 34209 |
| 26401 | 26952 | 30527 |
| 26215 | 30531 | 21726 |
| 40489 | 37110 | 34472 |

Figure 4.15 The alphabet and data profiles of actuals and forecast profiles (FP) for Year-1 naïve method and an ETS statistical model.

The D(a|f) accuracy measure, also known as the *Kullback-Leibler divergence*, is greater than zero and equals zero if and only if $a_i = f_i$, for all *i*. In other words, when the forecast pattern is identical to the pattern of the actuals, then D(a|f) = 0. A profile bias is represented by the ratio of the Lead-time actual Total to the Lead-time forecast Total,

| | A | B | C | D | E | F | G | H | I | J | K | L | M | N |
|---|---|---|---|---|---|---|---|---|---|---|---|---|---|---|
| 1 | Forecast Review Data | | | | | | | | | | | | | |
| 2 | Values: Units | | | | | | | | | | | | | |
| 3 | Data Scope: TOTAL PRODUCT: 99, TOTAL COMPANY: 10 | | | | | | | | | | | | | |
| 4 | Last Demand: 8/15 | | | | | | | | | | | | | |
| 5 | Data Type: Demand | | | | | | | | | | | | | |
| 6 | | Sep. | Oct. | Nov. | Dec. | Jan. | Feb. | Mar. | Apr. | May | Jun. | Jul. | Aug. | Total |
| 7 | 2012 | 0 | 0 | 0 | 0 | 55060 | 71365 | 70350 | 49375 | 20403 | 35518 | 27454 | 35430 | 364955 |
| 8 | 2013 | 41336 | 24871 | 21162 | 80025 | 33755 | 57809 | 58769 | 35496 | 39467 | 24332 | 13731 | 34915 | 465668 |
| 9 | 2014 | 41356 | 41328 | 42273 | 75694 | 61779 | 49478 | 68117 | 36155 | 40483 | 34373 | 11157 | 31158 | 533357 |
| 10 | 2015 | 51801 | 17898 | 55843 | 75187 | 51390 | 25319 | 27811 | 28489 | 39619 | 26952 | 30531 | 37110 | 467742 |
| 11 | 2016 | 30389 | 28622 | 35688 | 49786 | 73069 | 44860 | 37209 | 17673 | 10733 | 26401 | 26215 | 40489 | 421134 |
| 12 | 2017 | | | | | ??????? | | | | (Weak May 2016) | | | | 0 |
| 13 | | | | | | | | | | | | | | |
| 14 | Holdout_AAP | 0.07216 | 0.067964 | 0.084743 | 0.118219 | 0.173505 | 0.106522 | 0.088354 | 0.041965 | 0.025486 | 0.06269 | 0.062249 | 0.096143 | SUM = 1 |

Figure 4.16 A spreadsheet example of a monthly historical data set (2012 – 2015) and a 12-month hold-out sample (2016), containing an unusual January and a weak May month.

In Figure 4.16, the twelve months starting September, 2016 were used as a lead-time holdout sample or training dataset for forecasting with three univariate forecasting Methods: (1) the previous year's twelve-month actuals (**Year-1**), a *judgmental* Method, (2) a trend/seasonal *exponential smoothing* Model **ETS (A, A, M)**, a *statistical* Method and (3) a twelve-month *moving average* (**MAVG-12**), a *heuristic* Method. The twelve-month lead-time forecasts constitute a **Forecast Profile** (FP). The results (Figure 4.17) show in columns F-H that the three MAPEs are around 50%, not great but probably typical, especially at a SKU-location level. For comparison, the Naive1 Method is used as a benchmark Method in an effectiveness analysis; it has a MAPE of 50%, which turns out to be slightly better than MAVG-12 and YEAR-1 Methods, in this case.

| | B | C | D | E | F | G | H | I |
|---|---|---|---|---|---|---|---|---|
| 1 | Holdout Actuals | Year-1 | ETS | MAVG-12 | APE_Year-1 | APE_ETS | APE_MAVG-12 | |
| 2 | 30389 | 51801 | 44123 | 38979 | 70% | 45% | 28% | |
| 3 | 28622 | 17690 | 27701 | 38979 | 38% | 3% | 36% | |
| 4 | 35688 | 55843 | 40153 | 38979 | 56% | 13% | 9% | |
| 5 | 49786 | 75187 | 74939 | 38979 | 51% | 51% | 22% | |
| 6 | 73069 | 51390 | 48521 | 38979 | 30% | 34% | 47% | |
| 7 | 44860 | 25319 | 47812 | 38979 | 44% | 7% | 13% | |
| 8 | 37209 | 27811 | 54278 | 38979 | 25% | 46% | 5% | |
| 9 | 17673 | 28489 | 36996 | 38979 | 61% | 109% | 121% | |
| 10 | 10733 | 39619 | 34209 | 38979 | 269% | 219% | 263% | |
| 11 | 26401 | 26952 | 30527 | 38979 | 2% | 16% | 48% | |
| 12 | 26215 | 30531 | 21726 | 38979 | 16% | 17% | 49% | |
| 13 | 40489 | 37110 | 34472 | 38979 | 8% | 15% | 4% | |
| 14 | 421134 | 467742 | 495457 | 467742 | 56% | 48% | 54% | MAPE |

Figure 4.17 The MAPE comparisons among four Methods (Source: Figure 4.15; n = 24, m = 12).

> *A Method is called **useful**, if it is both effective and has a high efficiency rating.*

For the four Methods in this example, it appears that ETS (A, A, M) results in a more accurate forecast, because the point forecast accuracy measure MAPE is the smallest.

The **MAPE Skill score (=1 - [MAPE(**Method)**/MAPE(**Benchmark)**]**, which measures the contribution of the data to the effectiveness of a Method, yields the following results (in the brackets) with the Naive1 as Benchmark Method:  MAVG-12 (1- [0.54/0.50] = - 0.08), YEAR-1 (1- [0.56/0.50] = - 0.12), and only ETS (A, A, M) has a *positive* MAPE Skill Score (1- [0.48/0.50] = + 0.04), showing a *positive* benefit or advantage over the Naive1 benchmark Method for this example.

131

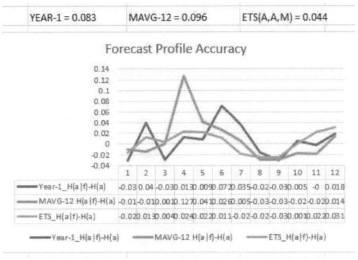

| YEAR-1 = 0.083 | MAVG-12 = 0.096 | ETS(A,A,M) = 0.044 |

Forecast Profile Accuracy

| | 1 | 2 | 3 | 4 | 5 | 6 | 7 | 8 | 9 | 10 | 11 | 12 |
|---|---|---|---|---|---|---|---|---|---|---|---|---|
| Year-1_H(a\|f)-H(a) | -0.03 | 0.04 | -0.03 | 0.013 | 0.009 | 0.072 | 0.035 | -0.02 | -0.03 | 0.005 | -0 | 0.018 |
| MAVG-12 H(a\|f)-H(a) | -0.01 | -0.01 | 0.001 | 0.127 | 0.041 | 0.026 | 0.005 | -0.03 | -0.03 | -0.02 | -0.02 | 0.014 |
| ETS_H(a\|f)-H(a) | | -0.02 | 0.013 | 0.004 | 0.024 | 0.022 | 0.011 | -0.02 | -0.02 | -0.03 | 0.001 | 0.022 | 0.031 |

Figure 4.18 The Profile Accuracy calculation for three Methods: Year-1, MAVG-12 and ETS (A, A, M)

Using the profile accuracy measure D(a|f) in Figure 4.18 results in a sharper distinction in accuracy performance for the three Methods, MAVG-12 (= 0.096), YEAR-1 (= 0.083), and ETS (A, A, M) = 0.044. For lead-time forecasting performance with multiple series, the overall **effectiveness** of a Method can be measured by the **positive data** contributions using the D(a|f) profile accuracy in the *Levenbach* **L-Skill score (= 1 - [D(a|f)**(Method)**/ D(a|f)**(Benchmark)]**

The MAPE Skill score (=1 - [MAPE(Method)/MAPE(Benchmark)], which measures the contribution of the data to the effectiveness of a Method, yields the following results (in the brackets) with the Naive1 as Benchmark Method:   MAVG-12 (1- [0.54/0.50] = - 0.08), YEAR-1 (1- [0.56/0.50] = - 0.12), and only ETS (A, A, M) has a positive MAPE Skill Score (1- [0.48/0.50] = + 0.04), showing a positive benefit or advantage over the Naive1 benchmark Method for this example.

Next, we create an efficiency rating for a profile forecasting Method.

# How to Evaluate the Efficiency of a Profile Forecasting Method

**Step 1**. Using the information-theoretic formulae for Profile Miss and Profile Accuracy, it is apparent that Profile Accuracy of a time series can be decomposed into (1) Profile Miss plus (2) a second measure, called Relative Skill, where Profile Miss + (Relative Skill) = Profile Accuracy. Because D(a|f) > 0, we can write 1 = [Profile Miss/D(a|f)] + [Relative Skill/D(a|f)].   This decomposition suggests that by using the

Pythagorean theorem to label Profile Miss/ D(a|f) and Relative Skill/ D(a|f) as the sides of a right triangle, we can create coordinates on a unit circle with the hypotenuse of the triangle as a radius.

The Profile Miss/D(a|f) and Relative Skill/D(a|f) can be seen as directional statistics. Each time series defines a direction and a resulting point on the unit circle; a collection of time series creates a distribution on the circle, called the **Efficiency Frontier** for the Method (Figure 3.25). A measure of central tendency (in radians) in the circular distribution is the **Efficiency** of the Method.

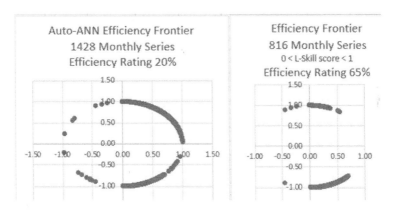

Figure 4.19 The Efficiency Frontier of a Method and the Efficiency Frontier of an Effective Method (with positive L-Skill scores)

**Step 2**. Using x=0, y=1 as the reference direction on the unit circle in the X-Y plane, the 'average efficiency' is represented by an angle on the unit circle relative to the reference direction, where 0 < angle (series) < $2\pi$. To visualize this, if we do not hit the bulls-eye but rather an off-center 'bulls-eye', we can have a highly "efficient" (or very precise process) Method (left frame). On the other hand, if we aim and strike the target at similar distances from the bullseye, but in different directions, then we have an inefficient (high variance process) Method (right frame). When a Method is used with many SKUs or demand items, a point of central tendency on the distribution on the circle is a measure of an 'average efficiency' of the Method. Because of the possibility of positive and negative directions, it means you need to be careful when creating the square roots of the sides of the right triangles.

**Step 3**. Figure 4.20 summarizes the calculations needed for displaying an **Efficiency Frontier**. Firstly, the series are ranked by the **L-Skill** effectiveness score. The spreadsheet shows the results for the top ten and the bottom ten monthly time series from the M3 competition dataset:

| | A | B | C | D | E | F | G | H | I | J | K | L |
|---|---|---|---|---|---|---|---|---|---|---|---|---|
| 1 | SERIES | D(a|f) | (N2) L-Skill Score | PMISS/D(a|f) | RelSkill/D(a|f) check | Sqrt(D) | Sqrt(E) | Angle | x | y | check |
| 2 | | | | | | TOP 10 | | | | | | |
| 3 | N1906 | 0.00194 | 0.99 | 12.33 | 11.33 | 1 | 3.51 | -3.37 | -2.34 | 0.69 | -0.72 | 1 |
| 4 | N2592 | 0.00003 | 0.97 | 8.94 | 7.94 | 1 | 2.99 | -2.82 | -2.33 | 0.69 | -0.73 | 1 |
| 5 | N2663 | 0.00021 | 0.97 | 8.07 | 7.07 | 1 | 2.84 | -2.66 | -2.32 | 0.68 | -0.73 | 1 |
| 6 | N2694 | 0.00001 | 0.93 | 6.18 | 5.18 | 1 | 2.49 | -2.28 | -2.31 | 0.68 | -0.74 | 1 |
| 7 | N2777 | 0.00001 | 0.93 | 6.08 | 5.08 | 1 | 2.47 | -2.25 | -2.31 | 0.67 | -0.74 | 1 |
| 8 | N2570 | 0.00001 | 0.99 | 6.00 | 5.00 | 1 | 2.45 | -2.24 | -2.31 | 0.67 | -0.74 | 1 |
| 9 | N2814 | 0.00017 | 0.92 | 5.70 | 4.70 | 1 | 2.39 | -2.17 | -2.31 | 0.67 | -0.74 | 1 |
| 10 | N2320 | 0.00001 | 0.82 | 4.95 | 3.95 | 1 | 2.22 | -1.99 | -2.30 | 0.67 | -0.75 | 1 |
| 11 | N2581 | 0.00010 | 0.91 | 4.85 | 3.85 | 1 | 2.20 | -1.96 | -2.30 | 0.67 | -0.75 | 1 |
| 12 | N2716 | 0.00002 | 0.89 | 4.77 | 3.77 | 1 | 2.18 | -1.94 | -2.30 | 0.66 | -0.75 | 1 |
| 13 | | | | | | BOTTOM 10 | | | | | | |
| 14 | N2809 | 0.00019 | 0.41 | -2.87 | -3.87 | 1 | -1.69 | 1.97 | 0.71 | 0.76 | 0.65 | 1 |
| 15 | N2829 | 0.00118 | 0.29 | -3.29 | -4.29 | 1 | -1.81 | 2.07 | 0.72 | 0.75 | 0.66 | 1 |
| 16 | N2736 | 0.00268 | 0.87 | -3.69 | -4.69 | 1 | -1.92 | 2.17 | 0.73 | 0.75 | 0.66 | 1 |
| 17 | N2504 | 0.00056 | 0.93 | -3.98 | -4.98 | 1 | -2.00 | 2.23 | 0.73 | 0.75 | 0.67 | 1 |
| 18 | N2487 | 0.00004 | 0.94 | -3.99 | -4.99 | 1 | -2.00 | 2.23 | 0.73 | 0.75 | 0.67 | 1 |
| 19 | N2219 | 0.00005 | 0.82 | -4.59 | -5.59 | 1 | -2.14 | 2.36 | 0.74 | 0.74 | 0.67 | 1 |
| 20 | N2816 | 0.00031 | 0.89 | -4.72 | -5.72 | 1 | -2.17 | 2.39 | 0.74 | 0.74 | 0.67 | 1 |
| 21 | N2776 | 0.00000 | 0.89 | -5.57 | -6.57 | 1 | -2.36 | 2.56 | 0.74 | 0.74 | 0.68 | 1 |
| 22 | N2804 | 0.00062 | 0.91 | -6.10 | -7.10 | 1 | -2.47 | 2.66 | 0.75 | 0.73 | 0.68 | 1 |
| 23 | N2571 | 0.00002 | 0.96 | -8.18 | -9.18 | 1 | -2.86 | 3.03 | 0.76 | 0.73 | 0.69 | 1 |
| 24 | | | | | | | | Sum | | 644 | 133 | 658 |
| 25 | | | | | | | | Angle A(Z) | 0.20 | 0.98 | 0.20 | 1.00 |
| 26 | | | | | | | | | | | | |
| 27 | | | | | | | | | | | | |
| 28 | | | | | | | | | | 339 | -260 | 427 |
| 29 | | | | | | 0 < L-Skill < 1 | | Angle A(Z) | -0.65 | 0.79 | -0.61 | 1.00 |

Figure 4.20 The calculations for displaying an Efficiency Frontier (Figure 4.19).

- he calculations for PMISS/D(a|f) are displayed in column C followed by Relative Skill/D(a|f) in column D. These are the two sides of a right triangle with hypotenuse = 1.
- The calculation is checked in column F to verify that PMiss + RelSkill = D(a|f) as interpreted from the information-theoretic entropy measures: $[H(f) - H(a)] + [H(a|f) - H(f)] = H(a|f) - H(a)$.
- The calculations in columns G and H are the horizontal and vertical lengths, respectively, of the right triangle intersecting on the unit circle.
- The sine of the values in column H, or equivalently the cosine of the values in column G define the Angles in column I.
- Columns J and K show the X-Y coordinates of the Efficiency Frontier on the unit circle.
- Column L is a check that the coordinates for each series are on the unit circle $(x^2 + y^2 = 1)$ creating a directional distribution of efficiency ratings on the unit circle for the Method.
- The sums in cell J24 and cell K24 are squared, and the square root of the sum is posted in cell L24. This represents the length of the Method's 'efficiency vector'. The longer the efficiency vector, the tighter the distribution of efficiency ratings around its central tendency (the Method **Efficiency Rating**).
- When the sums in cell J24 (= 644) and cell K24 (= 133) are divided by cell L24 (= 658), we obtain coordinates (0.98, 0.20) in cell J25 and cell K25 for the Method's **Efficiency Rating** in radians on the unit circle. The corresponding angle in radians on the unit circle for Method Efficiency is found in cell I25 (=0.20).

## *The Myth of the MAPE . . . and how to Mitigate It*

Planners and managers in supply chain organizations are accustomed to using the **M**ean **A**bsolute **P**ercentage **E**rror (MAPE) as their best (and sometimes only) answer to measuring the accuracy of point forecasts. It is so ubiquitous that it is hardly questioned. Even a basic definition of forecast error is not commonly understood among practitioners in supply chain organizations I have encountered around the world in my professional development workshops (http://cpdftraining.org/galleryLogo.htm). For most, Actual (A) minus Forecast (F) is the forecast error, for others just the opposite.

**Bias** is the other component of accuracy, but is not consistently defined. If Actual (A) minus Forecast (F) is the forecast error, what should the sign be of a reported under-forecast or over-forecast? Who is right and why? For example, Figure 4.6 shows pallets of soft drinks shipped versus forecast error. Is under- or overforecasting the dominant issue in this situation?

Outliers in forecast errors and other sources of unusual data values should never be ignored in the accuracy measurement process. For a measurement of bias, for example, the calculation of the mean forecast error ME (the arithmetic mean of Actual (A) minus Forecast (F)) will drive the estimate towards the outlier. An otherwise unbiased pattern of performance can be distorted by just a single unusual value.

What should a demand planner do in practice? What is a typical bias in an analysis of forecast errors? Although the arithmetic mean is the conventional estimator of central tendency, forecasters and business planners should not accept it uncritically.

As our example in Chapter 2 (Figure 2.10) illustrates, one outlier can have an undesirable effect on the arithmetic mean and pull an estimate of the bulk of data away from a typical or representative bias value. It is always best to compare and present multiple measures for the same quantity to be estimated, just to be sure that you are not misled by unusual values lurking in the data and distorting the meaning of the measure.

Forecast evaluations are also needed in multi-series comparisons. Production and inventory planners typically need demand or shipment forecasts for hundreds to tens of thousands of items (SKUs) based on historical data for each item. Financial planners need to issue forecasts for numerous budget categories in a strategic plan on the basis of past values of each source of revenue. In a multi-series comparison, the forecaster should appraise the method based not only on its performance for the individual item but also on the basis of its overall accuracy when tested over various Period/Place/Product summaries of the data. Rather than a one-number summary, it is more informative to display five-number box plots as well, particularly for the critical items and groupings of products. How to create the most effective predictive visualizations will depend on the context of the forecasting problem and can, in general, not be stipulated in advance.

## A Measurement Model for Forecast Error - The SIB Approach

If we want to measure forecast accuracy for a *single* forecast, most practitioners would agree that the forecast error (**FE** = **A**ctual *A* minus **F**orecast *F*) is the common, acceptable way to do that. It is only a measurement so the exact difference is subject to some measurement error. We can view this process as a black box model, in which the measurement error $\varepsilon$ enters the box from the right and the observed difference, or bias $\beta$, is the outcome of a *translation* of an unknown constant $\beta$ while the dispersion $\sigma$ is an unknown constant that *scales* the measurement error; these constants are commonly referred to as *parameters* in a model.

This particular model is called a *Structured Inference Base* (**SIB**) model, because it offers a pathway to probability forecasts. The **SIB** model can also be represented by an equation **FE** = $\beta$ + $\sigma$ $\varepsilon$, where $\beta$ and $\sigma$ are unknown constants and $\varepsilon$ is the measurement error which has a known or assumed distribution. As we have seen so far, we should be sensitive to outliers (even just a few) or unusual variation with real world data, so with the SIB modeling approach we can shy away from the normal (Gaussian) distribution

Rather than following the *Gaussian mindset*, the SIB approach assumes a *family* of distributions, known as the **Exponential Family**, for the measurement error distribution. The *exponential family*, not to be confused with exponential smoothing, contains many familiar distributions including the normal (Gaussian) distribution, as well as others with thicker tails and skewness. However, the approach is fundamentally algorithmic, driven by the data, and the data are examined first within the context of a particular problem, without assuming a data-generation-process with normally distributed errors.

## What Can Be Learned from a Forecast Error Measurement Process? |

The **S**tructured **I**nference **B**ase (SIB) model for forecast error measurement is a *location-scale model*. The SIB model shows that the output FE is a translation of a random input error $\varepsilon$ shifted by an amount $\beta$, and where the random errors are scaled by a positive constant $\sigma$. In practice, we have multiple measurements $\mathbf{FE} = \{FE_1, FE_2, FE_3., \ldots, FE_n\}$ of observed forecast errors as output of the SIB model:

$$FE_1 = \beta + \sigma\, \varepsilon_1,$$
$$FE_2 = \beta + \sigma\, \varepsilon_2,$$
$$FE_3 = \beta + \sigma\, \varepsilon_3,$$

$$\cdot$$
$$\cdot$$
$$\cdot$$

$$FE_n = \beta + \sigma\, \varepsilon_n,$$

where $\boldsymbol{\varepsilon} = \{\varepsilon_1, \varepsilon_2, \varepsilon_3., \ldots, \varepsilon_n\}$ represent *n realizations* of measurement errors from an assumed distribution in the exponential family.

The question now is what information can we uncover about the forecast error measurement process. This is where it gets interesting, and perhaps a somewhat unfamiliar for those who have been through a course on *statistical inference*.

As a data detective, we would discover that, based on the observed data, there is now information uncovered about the unknown, but *realized* measurement errors $\boldsymbol{\varepsilon}$. This revelation will guide us to an important and necessary SIB modeling step, namely a reduction in the dimensionality of the measurement error distribution. This revelation will guide us to the next important step, namely a parsing or decomposition of the measurement error distribution into two components: (1) a marginal distribution for the *observed* components and (2) a two-dimensional conditional distribution (*conditioned* on the observed components) for the remaining unknown measurement error distribution.

The conditional distribution is a two-dimensional unknown measurement error distribution, which becomes the source of a lead-time forecast probability distribution.

Consider the location and scale measures denoted by $m(\mathbf{FE})$ and $s(\mathbf{FE})$, respectively. Typically, we can select a location measure $m(.)$, such as. min $FE_i$, or the arithmetic mean), and a scale measure s(.), such as. the range, or standard deviation. Then, we can make a calculation that yields observable information about the measurement process. The SIB modeling process reveals (with substitution and some manipulation) that

$$[FE_1 - m(\mathbf{FE})]/\, s(\mathbf{FE}) = [\beta + \sigma\, \varepsilon_1 - m(\beta + \sigma\, \boldsymbol{\varepsilon})]/\, s(\sigma\, \boldsymbol{\varepsilon})$$
$$= [\beta + \sigma\, \varepsilon_1 - \beta - m(\sigma\, \boldsymbol{\varepsilon})]/\, \sigma\, s(\boldsymbol{\varepsilon})$$
$$= \sigma\, [\varepsilon_1 - m(\boldsymbol{\varepsilon})]/\, \sigma\, s(\boldsymbol{\varepsilon}) = [\varepsilon_1 - m(\boldsymbol{\varepsilon})]/\, s(\boldsymbol{\varepsilon})$$

$$[FE_2 - m(FE)]/\,s(FE) \quad = [\varepsilon_2 - m(\varepsilon)]/\,s(\varepsilon)$$
$$[FE_3 - m(FE)]/\,s(FE) \quad = [\varepsilon_3 - m(\varepsilon)]/\,s(\varepsilon)$$

$$[FE_n - m(FE)]/\,s(FE) \quad = [\varepsilon_n - m(\varepsilon)]/\,s(\varepsilon)$$

The *left-hand* side of each equation can be calculated from the *observed* forecast errors, so the *right-hand* side is known information about a *realized* measurement error and its distribution. What is known we can *condition on* so we can derive a *conditional* distribution of $m(\varepsilon)$] and $s(\varepsilon)$ given a known $(n\text{-}2)$ dimensional error component and a marginal distribution for the realized $(n - 2)$ dimensional error component.

This is clearly no longer a data-generation modeling approach. The critical step in the SIB analysis is to note that the n left-hand sides of the equations are observed quantities named $d(FE)$ that are equal to $d(\varepsilon)$, the right-hand side of the equations. We call this array of numbers the observed **d-vector**, because it plays an important role in the construction of a *posterior probability distribution*.

> *The essential conditioning step is somewhat like what a gambler can do knowing the odds in a black jack game. The gambler can make calculations and should base inferences from what is observed in the dealt cards. We do something similar here with the "SIB game" box.*

We do not need to go further into details at this time, as it will get much beyond the scope of this book. The full inferential process can be computed; it will lead to practical inferences about the parameters. The **location-scale measurement model** and its generalizations were worked out over four decades ago by University of Toronto Professor D.A.S. Fraser in a book entitled **Inference and Linear Models** (1979), as well as numerous peer-reviewed papers in the statistical literature. Because the results do not lend themselves to easy-to-derive theoretical answers (except for the normal (Gaussian) distribution), this inferential approach has not seen much use in practice because the modeling requires machine learning/statistical learning (ML/SL) algorithms such as bootstrapping and MCMC, and extensive computing capabilities. In other words, it can become a practical approach with today's computing resources. With modern computing power, we can also show what we *should* do with the data, not necessarily what we *could* do based on a traditional Gaussian mindset.

There are also a number of peer-reviewed journal papers on statistical inference on the subject. It is not mainstream inferential thinking and it is not a Bayesian approach. There are, in fact, no "priors" involved, which are basic to the Bayesian approach, Also, not relying on normally distribution assumptions is key as it achieves **unique** estimates and confidence bounds procedures for the parameters without normality assumptions.

## Application of SIB Modeling for Inventory Planning

In Chapter 8, we introduced a SIB model for lead-time demand forecasting. To proceed with the inferential process, we need to derive *posterior distributions* for the unknown parameters β and σ in the SIB model in Figure along with posterior prediction limits. The derivations and formulae are obtained from University of Toronto Professor D.A.S. Fraser's 1979 book **Inference and Linear Models**, Chapter 2, as well a number peer-reviewed journal articles dealing with statistical inference and likelihood methods. These are not mainstream results in modern statistical literature, but that does not diminish their value in practice.

*Statistical inference refers to the theory, methods, and practice of forming judgments about the parameters of a population and the reliability of statistical relationships*

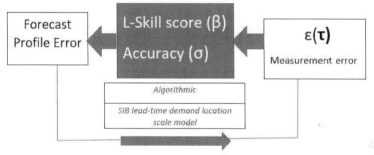

Today, the algorithms can be implemented in a forecast decision support platform, which was not the case more than four decades ago when I was first exposed to them in graduate school. With normal (Gaussian) error distribution assumptions, there are closed form solutions (i.e., solvable in a mathematical analysis) that have a semblance to more familiar Bayesian inference solutions.

**Application to Inventory Planning.** The SIB inferential analysis will yield a POSTERIOR distribution (conditional on the observed **d-vector** for the unknown parameters β and σ from which we can derive unique confidence bounds for β (Profile Relative Skill) and σ (Profile Accuracy). These confidence bounds will give us the service levels we require to set **desired level of safety stock**.

Using the ETS(A,A,M) model and data example, the reduced error distribution for location measure $m(\varepsilon)$ and scale measure $s(\varepsilon)$ conditional on observed $d = (d_1, d_2, \ldots, d_{12})$ is:

- Location component:     $m(\varepsilon) = [m(FPE) -\beta]/ \sigma = [0.00 -\beta]/ \sigma$
- Scale component:     $s(\varepsilon) = s(FPE)/ \sigma = 0.044/ \sigma$

Define Safety Factor SF= $\sqrt{12}\ m(\varepsilon)/s(\varepsilon)= \sqrt{12}\ \{0.001- \beta_0\}/ 0.044$, where $\beta_0$ = max β under a selected contour boundary. Then, $\beta_0 = 0.001+SF* 0.044/ \sqrt{12}$ Is the desired level of safety stock for the service level you select.

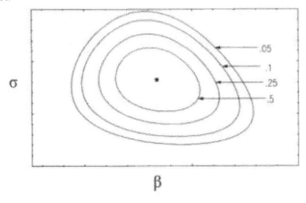

σ

β

***

## *Takeaways*

➤ One goal of an agile demand forecasting strategy is to improve forecast accuracy through the use of reliable forecast performance measurement. Demand forecasters should use **multiple accuracy measures** to evaluate the relative performance of forecasting models and assess alternative forecast scenarios.

➤ It should always be good practice to report accuracy measures in pairs to insure against misleading results. When the pair make sense (for practical use), then report the traditional result. Otherwise, go back and investigate the data going into the calculation, using domain knowledge whenever possible

➤ We recommend the use of **relative error measures** to see how much of an improvement is made in choosing a particular forecasting model over some benchmark or "naive" forecasting technique. Relative error measures also provide a reliable way of ranking forecasting models on the basis of their usual accuracy over sets of time series.

➤ Test a forecasting model with hold out samples by splitting the historical data into two parts, using the first segment as the fit period. Then, the forecasting model is used to make forecasts for a number of additional periods (the forecast horizon).

Because there are actual values withheld in the holdout sample, one can assess forecast accuracy by comparing the forecasts against the known figures. Not only do we see how well the forecasting technique has fit the more distant past (fit period) but also how well it would have forecast the test period.

➢ **Tracking signals** can be useful when large numbers of items must be monitored for accuracy. This is often the case in inventory systems. When the tracking signal for an item exceeds the threshold level, the forecaster's attention should be promptly drawn to the problem. The tracking of results is essential to ensure the continuing relevance of the forecast. By properly tracking forecasts and assumptions, the demand forecaster can advise management when a forecast revision is required. It should not be necessary for management to instruct the demand forecaster that something is wrong with the forecast. Through tracking, we can better understand the models, their capabilities, and the uncertainty associated with the forecasts derived from them

➢ Beware of the Myth of the MAPE. This could be among the worst "best practices" in accuracy measurement.

➢ The useful information we can derive from a Structured Inference Base (SIB) model is a decomposition of a measurement error distribution. The analysis yields a (conditional) posterior distribution for the unknown parameters $\beta$ and $\sigma$ from which we can derive unique confidence intervals and related useful inferences.

➢ The location-scale model is an application of a Structured Inference Base (SIB) approach that can be generalized to a wide range of applications, not just for accuracy measurement.

➢ Most importantly, when determining forecast accuracy, **uncertainty is a certain factor**.

# 5

# Characterizing Demand Variability: Seasonality, Trend, and the Uncertainty Factor

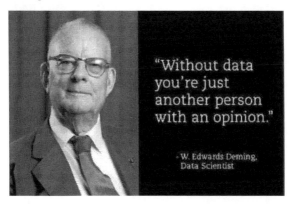

"Without data you're just another person with an opinion."

- W. Edwards Deming, Data Scientist

In chapter 2, we saw why exploratory data analysis is so basic to the demand forecasting process. We now focus on data that are ordered sequentially in time, better known as **time series**. When sales volumes, inventory counts, and such are reported as a time series, the data may contain important components that we can effectively visualize, quantify, and create models for. Time series analysis is a useful tool for

- identifying essential components in historical data so that we can select a good starting model

- comparing a number of traditional and innovative analytical tools to increase our understanding of data that are typical or representative of the problem being studied (such data are accurate in terms of reporting accuracy and also have been adjusted, if necessary, to eliminate nonrepresentative or extreme values)

This chapter will present techniques that help you prepare historical data in a variety of graphical ways, allowing you to see that

- not only do data summaries help explain historical patterns, but the requirements of an appropriate modeling strategy can also be visualized
- analysis of deseasonalized, detrended, smoothed, transformed data (e.g., logarithms and square roots), fitted values, and residuals can all be most effectively presented graphically,

## How Business-Cycle Data Analysis Can Lead to More Insightful Forecasts of Upcoming Economic Downturns

*As to the propriety and justness of representing sums of money, and time, by parts of space, tho' very readily agreed to by most men, yet a few seem to apprehend that there may possibly be some deception in it, of which they are not aware.*

WILLIAM PLAYFAIR

The first known time series using economic data was William Playfair's *Commercial and Political Atlas*, published in London in 1786 and beautifully reprinted in Ed Tufte's masterful *The Visualization of Quantitative Information* (1983). Playfair (1759–1823), an English political economist, preferred graphics (Figure 5.1) to tabular displays because he could better show the shape of the data in a comparative perspective. In one example, he plotted three parallel time series—prices, wages, and the reigns of British kings and queens, noting:

> **The purpose of analyzing time series data is to expose and summarize its components as a prelude to a model-building process.**

*You have before you, my Lords and Gentlemen, a chart of the prices of wheat for 250 years, made from official returns; on the same plate I have traced a line representing, as nearly as I can, the wages of good mechanics, such as smiths, masons, and carpenters, in order to compare the proportion between them and the price of wheat at every different period.* (Quoted in Tufte, 1983, p. 34)

Business forecasters commonly assume that variation in a time series can be expressed in terms of several basic components: a long-term trend plus an economic cycle, seasonal factors, and an irregular or random term. For a given time series, it may not be possible to observe a particular component directly due to the existence of other components that are more dominant. If appropriate, it is also desirable to correct, adjust, and transform data before creating forecasting models (see Chapters 5, 8, and 9).

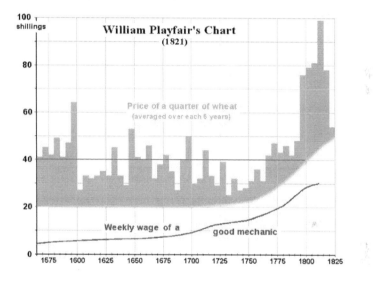

Figure 5.1 Playfair's 1821 chart comparing the "weekly wages of a good mechanic" and the "price of a quarter of wheat" over time.

## Trends and Cycles

It is not unusual for practicing forecasters to use the term trend when referring to a straight-line projection. But a trend does not need to be a straight-line pattern; a trend may fall or rise and can have a more complicated pattern than a straight line. The U.S. Federal Reserve Board (FRB) index of industrial production (Figure 5.2), highlighting the shaded areas for business recession periods, is a good example of a time series that is predominantly upward trending. The industrial production index measures output in the manufacturing, mining, and electric and gas utilities industries; the reference period for the index is 2007.

> *In a time series, a trend is seen as the tendency for the same pattern to be predominantly upward or downward over time.*

How do we know a time series is trending? The inspection of a time series plot often indicates strong trend patterns. Then fitting trend lines is a simple and convenient way of exposing detail in data.

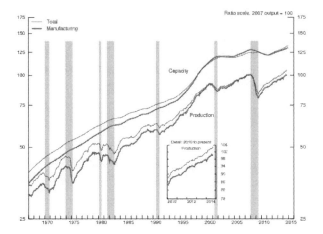

Figure 5.2 Time plot of FRB index of industrial production. (Source: Board of Governors of the Federal Reserve System, http://www.federalreserve.gov/feeds/g17.html)

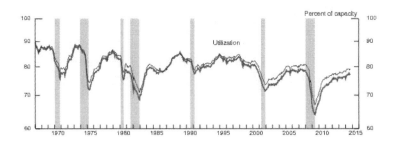

Figure 5.3 Time plot of the FRB index as a percentage of capacity. Shaded areas show periods of business recession as defined by the U.S. National Bureau of Economic Research (NBER). (*Source*: Figure 5.2)

A useful way of presenting the FRB index is to compare it to some trend line, such as an exponential or straight-line trend. This type of analysis brings out sharply the cyclical movements of the FRB index, and it also shows how the current level of output compares with the level that would have been achieved had the industrial sector followed its historical growth rate.

Although this may not be the best or final trend line for the data, the straight-line trend is a simple summary tool. In order to assess the value of this simple procedure, the deviations of the data (like peeling a layer from the onion) from this trend line of the FRB data are known as **residuals.**

In Figure 5.3, the FRB index is shown as a percent of another trending series. It is evident that elimination of trend in the data now reveals a cyclical component that appears to correspond to economic expansions and contractions. Modeling can often be thought of as a process of stripping away the essential variation to expose some hidden detail.

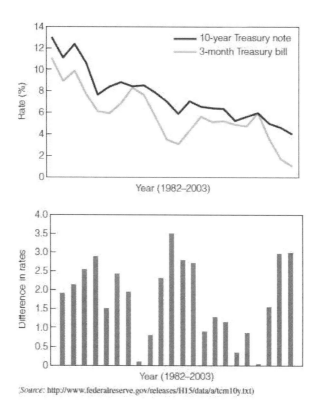

(Source: http://www.federalreserve.gov/releases/H15/data/a/tcm10y.txt)

Figure 5.4 Time plots (top) of the three-month and 10-Year U.S. Treasury rates; bar plot (bottom) of the differences between three-month and 10-Year U.S. Treasury rates

> *In practice, trend and cycle are often considered as a single component, known as the trend-cycle.*

Some financial data can also be useful for analyzing and predicting economic cycles. Figure 5.4a shows time plots of U.S. Treasury rates (a plot of the interest rates paid on U.S. securities ranging from three-month bills to 30-year bonds), which have been used by investors and market analysts to decide which Treasury bond or note offers the best interest rate. Typically, 10-year notes yield between one and two percentage points more than 3-month bills and the yield curve bends up. However, if long-term rates fall below the short-term rates, the curve inverts and arcs downward.

Economist Frederic Mishkin (b. 1951) of the Federal Reserve Bank of New York has discovered that every time the yield curve has inverted, a recession followed a year or so later. A way of looking at this is to plot the difference between the 3-month and 10-year Treasury rates. As shown in Figure 5.4b, every time the difference has sunk below zero, a recession followed roughly 12 months later. Business cycle analysis, leading indicators and a method of cycle forecasting are taken up in Chapter 7.

The definition of a cycle in demand forecasting is somewhat specialized in that the duration and amplitude of the cycle are not constant. This characteristic is what makes cycle forecasting so difficult. Although a business cycle is evident in so many economic series, modeling is one of the most challenging problems in time series analysis.

Other time series data that are not strongly dominated by seasonal and trend effects, such as the University of Michigan Survey Research Center's (SRC) index of consumer sentiment (Figure 5.5). In this case, the dominant pattern is a cycle corresponding to contractions and expansions in the economy. Of course, a large irregular component is present in this series because there are many unknown factors that significantly affect the behavior of consumers and their outlook for the future.

Based on an exploratory STI_Classification method, we determine that the total variability in the consumer sentiment index (Figure 5.5) is made up of 80% trend-cycle effect, 3% seasonal and 17% other (unknown). When using this index as a factor in a useful forecasting model, the driver would not have to be seasonally adjusted, while the demand variable to be forecasted may need to be seasonally adjusted first.

Similar consumer sentiment indices are available on the Internet for many countries. In this situation, the dominant pattern is a cycle corresponding to contractions and expansions in the economy. (Contrast Figure 5.5 with the index of industrial production (Figure 5.3). Of course, a large irregular component present in this series because there are other unknown factors that can significantly affect the behavior of consumers and their outlook on future spending.

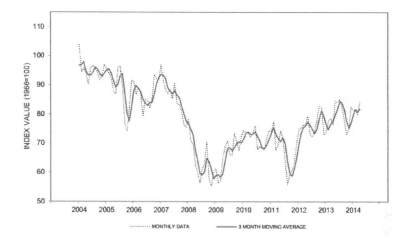

Figure 5.5 Time plot of the SRC index of consumer sentiment (monthly) from 2004-1 to 2014-4. (*Source*: University of Michigan Survey Research Center, *http://www.sca.isr.umich.edu/*)

## Seasonality

Certain sales data show strong peaks and troughs within the years, corresponding to a seasonal pattern. Consumer habits, like family holidays and festivals, give rise to seasonal patterns. When seasonality is removed from these data, secondary patterns reveal themselves that may still be useful and informative.

Figure 5.6 depicts a time series strongly dominated by seasonal effects, namely, monthly changes in telephone access lines connections and disconnections some years ago; today, this would be more like TV/Internet cable connections and disconnections to the home. The seasonality results from the installation of access lines coincident with school openings and removal of access lines with school closings each year as families relocate. Thus, the seasonal peaks and troughs appear with regularity each year.

The positive trend in telephone access lines used to be related to the growth in households and the increasing use of telephone services by former nonusers. Today, such relationships may not be the same in the telecommunications industry. Thus, both trend and seasonal components are superimposed on one another, as well as some residual effects, which are not readily discernible from the raw data.

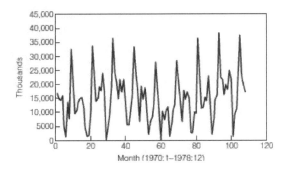

Figure 5.6 Time plot of monthly fluctuations in telephone access lines over a 9-year period.

Figure 5.7 Time plot of monthly new privately owned housing units started over the same period as that shown in Figure 5.6 (1970-1 to 1978-12). (*Source*: *http://www.census.gov/const/C20/startsua.xls*)

Although seasonality is the dominant pattern, there is also some changing variability in the highs and lows with trend. The seasonality also appears to be additive in the sense that the seasonal deviations from a trend for the same period each year appear relatively constant.

Contrast this seasonal pattern with that of the monthly housing starts shown in Figure 5.7. This economic time series is the result of survey data reported by contractors and builders for use by government and private industry. Based on an exploratory STI_Classification, we see that the total variability in the data is made up of 38% seasonal effect, 50% trend-cycle effect and 12% other (unknown or uncertain).

In the consumer goods industry, housing starts can be used as a driver of the demand for hard goods (e.g., refrigerators, dishwashers and washing machines). The housing starts over time are also subject to the business cycle fluctuations as do consumer hard goods. Even visually, there appears to be a close association between Figures 5.6

and 5.7. There are other industries where demand forecasters can establish such linkages with economic or demographic factors.

Using a visual assessment, the seasonality appears to be *additive* when the repeating seasonal effect in the data is represented by *constant amounts* around a trend-cycle.

> **Most commonly, seasonality refers to regular periodic fluctuations that recur every year with about the same timing and intensity. Seasonality can also occur as fluctuations that recur during months, weeks or days.**

When we see the seasonal variation around a trend appear more like constant percentages, we say this represents a *multiplicative* seasonality. Sales data for fast moving consumer goods may fall in this category.

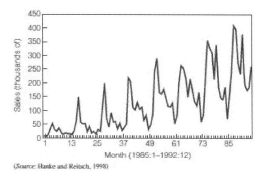

(Source: Hanke and Reitsch, 1998)

Figure 5.8 Time plot of monthly sales of formal-wear rentals over an 8-year period. (Source: J. E. Hanke and A. G. Reitsch, Business Forecasting, 1998)

In contrast to the patterns in Figures 5.6 and 5.7, the sale of formal-wear rentals (Figure 5.8) has a pronounced multiplicative seasonal component because seasonality tends to increase with the increase of the level of the data.

Based on the preliminary STI_Classification, we determine that the total variability in the formal wear rental data is made up of 57% trend effect, 31% seasonal effect and 12% other (unknown or uncertain). This should not be misinterpreted because the ANOVA procedure assumes additivity in trend and seasonal impact. Later, we will have a test for non-additivity between the trend and seasonal effect.

When looking for useful forecasting models, the most dominant driver should be considered first. Any characterization of the uncertainty factor should be based on the residuals after removing the effect of the dominant factors. We will also contrast additive and multiplicative seasonal patterns using a diagnostic test for non-additivity to highlight the difference between additive and multiplicative (non-additive) seasonality.

Many economic series show seasonal variation. For example, income from a farm in the United States may rise steadily each year from early spring until fall and then drop sharply. In this case, the main use of a seasonal adjustment procedure is to remove such fluctuations to expose an underlying trend-cycle. Many industries also have to deal with similar seasonal fluctuations.

To make decisions about price and inventory policy and about the commitment of capital expenditures, the business community wants to know whether changes in business activity over a given period of time were larger or smaller than normal seasonal changes. It is important to know whether a recession has reached bottom, for example, or whether there is any pattern in the duration, amplitude, or slope of business cycle expansions or contractions.

The semiconductor industry, for instance, plays a crucial role in the size, growth, and importance of information technology. The industry is subject to a number of forces that influence growth and cyclical behavior. Competitive forces, economic climate, pricing, and political events have a way of making demand forecasting a complex process.

In addition, seasonal patterns are frequently present in the monthly sales demand and unit-shipment figures because of the need for chips in the consumer electronics products and the fast-growing markets for hand-held devices.

A closely watched indicator of the strength and weakness of this market is the book-to-bill ratio, which compares orders with shipments of semiconductors - a number above 1 indicates positive growth and a ratio of 1.22 indicates that, for every $100 of chips shipped during the month, $122 of chips were ordered.

Clearly, to make sense of this indicator we require a seasonal adjustment of the ratio or a seasonal adjustment of the components of the ratio. Seasonal adjustment procedures are treated in Chapter 6.

## Irregular or Random Fluctuations

Irregular fluctuation is the catchall category for all patterns that cannot be associated with trend-cycle, or seasonality. Except for some cyclical fluctuations, the plot of the consumer sentiment index (Figure 5.5) does not suggest any systematic variation that can be readily identified. Irregular fluctuations most often create the greatest difficulty for the demand forecaster because they are generally unexplainable. A thorough understanding of the source and accuracy of the data is required to get full benefit of their use in modeling.

An example of an irregular fluctuation, an unusual or rare event arising in a time series, is depicted in Figure 5.9, which shows a monthly record of landline telephone installations in Montreal over a 10-year period. Although a predominantly trend and seasonal pattern, the unusually low September 1967 figure is greatly reduced because of the influence of the 1967 world's fair held in that city. At the time, residential telephone installations normally accompanied a turnover (by law) of apartment leases during September; however, a large number of apartments were held for visitors (like myself) to the world's fair that year. The dotted line depicts what might have happened under normal conditions (in the absence of this unusual event).

 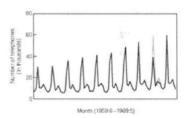

Figure 5.9 Impact of Expo '67 on monthly installations of landline telephones in Montreal, Quebec.

We may also see these kinds of unusual events in consumer demand data affected by holidays, festivals, fairs and popular events. In a more current example, an inventory shortfall in residential refrigerators created a backlog of sales during a peak selling season (Figure 5.10 *left*). We will want to know how to adjust (Figure 5.10 *right*) or normalize the data so that trend-seasonal models will function properly.

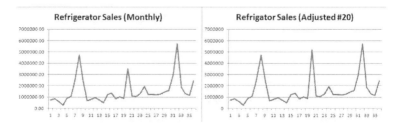

Figure 5.10 Refrigerator sales during a Ramadan holiday selling season, original (*left*) and adjusted (*right*) for period #20

Figure 5.11 shows how an administrative decision can influence a time series. The series represents the number of access lines (telephones for which separate numbers are issued) in service in a specific region. The saturation (or filling-up) of a neighboring exchange for a period necessitated a transfer of new service requests from that exchange to the one depicted in Figure 5.11, distorting the natural growth pattern.

Any useful modeling effort based on these data must be preceded by an adjustment to the historical data to account for this unusual event. There are many other examples like this where openings and closings of retail stores or hospitals, shifts of production among manufacturing or distribution centers as a result of natural disasters can create distortions in historical data.

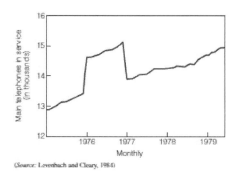

(Source: Levenbach and Cleary, 1984)

Figure 5.11 Time plot of access lines in service in a telephone exchange.

Many time series do not illustrate any seasonality, whereas others, such as weather data, are not affected by the business cycle. In practice, we may a need to be able to identify and describe additional patterns in data, such as sales cycles, promotions, and other calendar variation that will impact how we use models for forecasting purposes.

*The irregular component consists of atypical values, which may be caused by unusual or rare events, errors of transcription, administrative decisions, and random variation.*

## Visualizing Daily Patterns

Data visualization with an explorative STI_Classification method is a useful technique to describe the month and year effects in monthly data or quarter and year effects in quarterly data. The same technique can be used to capture a day-of-the-week effect in daily data. It is part of smart forecasting to visualize data patterns before selecting a forecasting approach. The daily data, shown in Figure 5.12, appear volatile and to the inexperienced eye not even forecastable. With very granular data, however, it might be useful to explore patterns visually before including any effects in a model

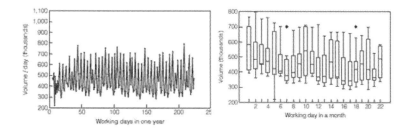

Figure 5.12 (*left*) Time plot of the daily volume of bank transactions. (*Source*: Figure 5.13); (*right*) Box plot of the daily volume of bank transactions by working day of month.

|  | Monday | Tuesday | Wednesday | Thursday | Friday | Row Average |
|---|---|---|---|---|---|---|
| Jan | 477,917 | 409,518 | 379,047 | 393,664 | 452,449 | 418,000 |
| Feb | 636,680 | 432,902 | 394,166 | 408,315 | 498,308 | 464,222 |
| Mar | 706,768 | 420,468 | 340,188 | 369,720 | 538,977 | 478,260 |
| Apr | 682,889 | 438,742 | 362,521 | 413,258 | 497,603 | 476,059 |
| May | 705,511 | 411,623 | 372,164 | 391,595 | 577,121 | 478,848 |
| Jun | 695,630 | 404,631 | 332,660 | 375,995 | 521,897 | 466,163 |
| Jul | 658,762 | 369,258 | 357,572 | 338,208 | 469,491 | 445,289 |
| Aug | 669,210 | 364,905 | 317,892 | 369,743 | 528,029 | 449,859 |
| Sep | 680,885 | 380,473 | 360,015 | 371,994 | 509,277 | 464,742 |
| Oct | 669,066 | 382,439 | 361,079 | 392,102 | 522,753 | 447,327 |
| Nov | 714,527 | 401,480 | 392,144 | 385,208 | 545,422 | 485,524 |
| Dec | 666,161 | 400,921 | 361,410 | 384,294 | 518,274 | 461,053 |
| Results: | | | | | | |
| Day of week | 91% | | | | | |
| Time of year | 3% | | | | | |
| Irregular | 6% | | | | | |

Figure 5.13 Month-by-week display for of the daily volumes of bank transactions.

In Figure 5.13, a two-way-table displays the daily volume of Bank transactions over 220 working days; the rows are months and the columns are because of their unusually high volume. These can be treated as exceptions to the primary effects we are looking for.

In the spreadsheet, each cell contains the average volume for that day of week in the particular month. For example, the Jan/Monday cell contains the average of all Monday volumes in the month of January. For demand forecasting purposes, it may be easier to forecast the daily volumes first and add a percentage for days following the major holidays.

The STI_Classification results show 91% day-of week effect, 3% time-of-year effect, and 6% everything else affecting the volumes (Excel

Addin > DataAnalysis > ANOVA:Two-way without replication>View SS column in Percents ).

## Visualizing Trading-Day Patterns

When trying to forecast future volumes for each business day in the next year, we can see that daily volumes experience a yearly pattern also that closely follow the average monthly retail seasonality.

Displaying box plots of the daily volumes for the working days of a month (Figure 5.12, *right*) allows us to note a downward trend in pattern, in that the first part of the month is much heavier than the last. The fifth working day of each month has the greatest amount of variability and the tenth working day shows a higher overall volume than its neighboring days.

Figure 5.14 Scatter diagram of the daily volumes of bank transactions by working day of week.

Tuesdays (marked with asterisks) can also experience some unusually high volumes, perhaps following a holiday on a Monday

Furthermore, when we look at a scatter diagram of the daily volumes by day of week (Figure 5.14), we note that the pattern is somewhat parabolic in shape, indicating that the heaviest volumes are on Mondays, the lightest volumes occur midweek, and volume increases again by end of week. These displays are the basis of our analysis of the daily volumes for forecast modeling,

Evidently, the fact that Monday is the big volume day, followed by a midweek low, plays a strong role is the description of this time series and should be reflected in any forecasting model. If we used only the time plot of the data or the spreadsheet display, we might not have recognized that the day of the week was a key factor.

Based on an exploratory STI_Classification, we discovered that the total variability in the bank transactions data is made up of 91% day of week effect, 3% time of year effect and 6% irregular (unknown or uncertain). When looking for appropriate forecasting models, the most dominant driver should be considered first. Any measurement of the uncertainty factor should be based on the residuals after removing the primary driver effects.

## Visualizing Weekly Patterns and Seasonality

Weekly promotions are frequently used to increase sales of consumer goods, such as canned beverages (Figure 5.15). Sharp peaks might be attributed to periods during which the price of the product was sharply reduced, thereby increasing demand data are examined when we quantify the impact of price changes on quantities demanded with elasticities.

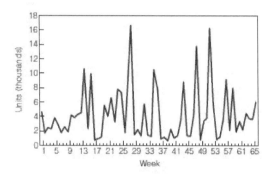

Figure 5.15 Time plot of weekly shipments of a canned beverage data.

When viewed on a monthly basis, such weekly shipment patterns can appear to have a seasonal pattern because of the periodic nature of many marketing promotions. Weekly seasonality, on the other hand, does not lend itself as well to established Error-Trend-Seasonal (ETS) modeling approaches, and in those situations, we will have to resort to customized causal models.

> *It is important for forecasting demand to clearly differentiate between the seasonality associated with general consumer behavior and the induced seasonal pattern arising from scheduled promotions.*

## Exploring Components of Variation

NUMBER OF YEARS OF DATA = 8
GRAND MEAN OF DATA = 125,872.188

| Month | Year | | | | | | | | |
|---|---|---|---|---|---|---|---|---|---|
| | 1 | 2 | 3 | 4 | 5 | 6 | 7 | 8 | |
| | 1985 | 1986 | 1987 | 1988 | 1989 | 1990 | 1991 | 1992 | AVG |
| 1 | 6,028 | 16,850 | 15,395 | 27,773 | 31,416 | 51,604 | 58,843 | 71,043 | 34,869 |
| 2 | 5,927 | 12,753 | 30,826 | 36,653 | 48,341 | 80,366 | 82,386 | 152,930 | 56,273 |
| 3 | 10,515 | 26,901 | 25,589 | 51,157 | 85,651 | 208,938 | 224,803 | 250,559 | 110,514 |
| 4 | 32,267 | 61,494 | 103,184 | 217,509 | 242,673 | 263,830 | 354,301 | 409,567 | 210,603 |
| 5 | 51,920 | 147,862 | 197,608 | 206,229 | 289,554 | 252,216 | 328,263 | 394,747 | 233,550 |
| 6 | 31,294 | 57,990 | 68,600 | 110,081 | 164,373 | 219,566 | 313,647 | 272,874 | 154,803 |
| 7 | 23,573 | 51,318 | 39,909 | 102,893 | 160,608 | 149,082 | 214,561 | 230,303 | 121,531 |
| 8 | 36,465 | 53,599 | 91,368 | 128,857 | 176,096 | 213,888 | 337,192 | 375,402 | 176,608 |
| 9 | 18,959 | 23,038 | 58,781 | 104,776 | 142,363 | 178,947 | 183,482 | 195,409 | 113,219 |
| 10 | 13,918 | 41,396 | 59,679 | 111,036 | 114,907 | 133,650 | 144,618 | 173,518 | 99,090 |
| 11 | 17,987 | 19,330 | 33,443 | 63,701 | 113,552 | 116,946 | 139,750 | 181,702 | 85,801 |
| 12 | 15,294 | 22,707 | 53,719 | 82,657 | 127,042 | 164,154 | 184,546 | 258,713 | 113,604 |
| Monthly average per year | 22,012 | 44,603 | 64,842 | 103,610 | 141,381 | 169,432 | 213,866 | 247,231 | |

Figure 5.16 Month-by-year display for monthly sales (in dollars) of formal-wear rentals over an 8-year period. (*Source*: Figure 5.8)

Consider the display of eight years of formal-wear rentals (Figure 5.8) in a two-way table, or spreadsheet, as shown in Figure 5.16. In this display, the rows represent months and the columns years. Each row shows the trending pattern, if any, for a given month. If a seasonal component is present, this is revealed by a regularity of the pattern in each column.

It is also informative to display the monthly averages per year and the averages (and medians) per month over eight years as additional rows/columns, respectively. By looking at the yearly totals it is possible to detect a trend component if the annual sums are steadily increasing or decreasing. The high and low seasonal months can be determined by comparing the values to the monthly averages.

*A two-way table is a spreadsheet in which the data are arranged in a rectangular array allowing for the display of trend and seasonal components.*

## Contribution of Trend and Seasonal Effects

Consider various graphical displays of the information in Figure 5.16. In Figure 5.17, we show a plot of each column in the table in a multiple-tier chart. Note how a similar pattern (the seasonal pattern within the year) is shown when the tiers stack on top of another.

We can further summarize these by creating a box plot of the values for each month (rows) (Figure 5.18, *top*). For a given month, the variation is generally smaller than the variation between months, suggesting an almost constant effect for each month. This is known as the **seasonal component**.

By plotting the values of each month (row) for the formal-wear data in Figure 5.18, we note a seasonality peaking in the fourth and fifth months and also much variability within months. On the other hand, the box plots by years (Figure 5.18) (*bottom*) clearly depict an upward trend, the unusually high months of May in Years 2 and 3, and increasing variability with increasing years. Hence, we note a relationship occurring (1) between the values for successive months in a particular year and (2) between the values for the same month in successive years. This observation will be useful when we consider exponential smoothing models and multiplicative versus additive trend/seasonal models.

There is still about 12% of the variation **not** explained by trend and seasonality. As we will see a trend, multiplicative seasonal time series model (e.g., Holt-Winters exponential smoothing models (Chapter 8) or the 'airline' ARIMA (011) (011)$_{12}$ model (Chapter 9)) should do quite well for these data. The remaining 12% contains the uncertainty factor and undetermined variation yet to be uncovered through running models on the residuals.

Through a root-cause analysis (Chapter 11), we begin to get a sense of the nature of "change & chance" in the data. We should not have to look so hard at so many different models, because it is the nature of the uncertainty in the model residuals that suggests how well we can measure (*tame*) the uncertainty factor.

The STI_Classification method is a simple mechanism for quantifying row and column effects in terms of their relative contributions to the total variation in a data table. When used to learn about time series, the TSI_ Classification method is a descriptive tool and is not an extrapolative technique.

This type of analysis might be useful for characterizing (roughly) the dominant components in the data, identifying potential modeling problems if the irregular component (residual percent) is relatively large, correlating with data with similar structures, and suggesting an appropriate transformation to check for the additivity of trend and seasonality.

As randomness increases, forecasting becomes more difficult. Because of possible outliers and the unidentified variation, data with an irregular component exceeding 15–20% may need to be scrutinized more carefully.

When the irregular component is quite high, it might be reduced through an adjustment of outliers prior to creating a forecasting model. As a rule of thumb, experience suggests that monthly and quarterly time series that show more than 40% in the irregular component should be forecasted with as simple a model as possible. A best practice is to handle such data with simpler models that can offer some insight into the variability of outliers or unusual values.

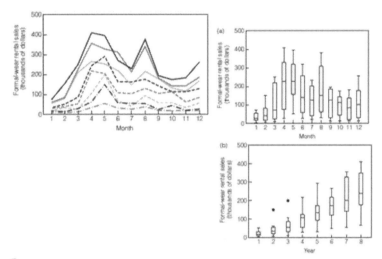

Figure 5.17 (*left*) Monthly tier plots for formal-wear rentals data. (Source: Figure 5.16);

Figure 5.18 (*right*) Box plots of formal-wear data showing row (*top frame*) and column (*bottom frame*) variation. (*Source:* Figure 5.16)

> *The results of an exploratory STI_Classification can provide an important clue to which data patterns can be handled as part of the criteria for technique selection*.

This tool works with quarterly data, as well. Figure 5.19 is similar to Figure 5.16 but for a quarterly automobile time series. A strong seasonal presence (= 68.2%) is noted because new car introductions occur in the same quarter every year in the US. Irregular component contributed only 4.6% to the total variation. Hence, for modeling purposes, we would be focusing on drivers or factors characterizing the seasonality as well as some market growth factors.

## Interpreting the Residual Table

Now that we can visualize trends and seasonality graphically, how can we create a decomposition of a time series in terms of a trend and seasonal variations? From the analysis in this section, we will gain insight into the relative strength of these components as well as a measure of the difficulties likely to be encountered in modeling and forecasting. This measure, called the percent residual effect, may turn out to be high because the presence of outliers or other variation in the data, not explained by trend and seasonal variation.

The method by which a two-way table is constructed is not complex, but the notation can become somewhat cumbersome; however, it is necessary in order to follow the calculations. A two-way table is a spreadsheet in which values $Y_{ij}$ ($i$ = month, $j$ = year) are displayed in a rectangular array, where $i = 1, 2 \ldots I$ ($I$ = 12 for monthly data), and $j = 1 \ldots J$ ($J$ = number of years).

This representation can also be used for quarterly data, and then $i = 1, 2, 3, 4$. The data must be in **complete arrays**, that is complete years and months. The procedure is available in the Data Analysis Excel Add-in as well as any comprehensive statistics package.

The dominant components generally found in forecasting demand are the trend, cycle, and seasonal components. At times, it is impractical to distinguish trend and cycle as distinct components. So, in many demand forecasting applications, we speak of trend-cycle as a single source of variation in which the two factors are inseparable.

In the discussion here it is instructive to consider trend and cycle as separate components. By removing or subtracting both trend and seasonal effect from a time series, it is possible to examine the residual variation for more subtle patterns; that is,

$$\text{Residuals} = \text{Data} - \text{Fit}$$
$$= \text{Data} - (\text{Trend} + \text{Seasonal effects})$$

The $(i,j)$th residual represents the deviation from the grand mean less the $i$th month seasonal effect and the $j$th year's trend effect. Thus, the $(i,j)$th residual is the $(i,j)$th value corrected for seasonal and trend effect in the sense of a two-way ANOVA decomposition. For example, we can examine the residual variation to show the effects of cyclic down-turn consistent with empirical data or economic theory. If so, a trend-seasonal decomposition would best describe the dominant patterns in the data.

The analysis also shows whether the seasonal pattern is stable from year to year. Have school openings and closing perhaps been shifting, thereby shifting the seasonality of the data? Have holiday (e.g., pre-Christmas, Ramadan, etc.) buying patterns of shoppers shifted, thus affecting sales data? Do nontypical values destroy the underlying trend and/or seasonal pattern? All these questions may be reasonably explored with a preliminary STI_Classification.

Other useful quantities can be derived from the residual two-way table. The residual variance is the total variation corrected for trend and seasonal effects. This provides a measure of variation for all the residuals. The residual column variance $S_j^2(C)$ provides a variance measure for each column and the residual row variance $S_i^2(R)$ provides a variance measure for each row. Large differences among the residual column variances may indicate some outliers or special events in a year that has a large deviation. Large differences among the residual row variances for various months may suggest the relative difficulty of forecasting months with large variability and may also indicate the presence of outliers in certain months.

ANALYSIS OF VARIANCE: QUARTERLY DATA
TITLE1:                 AUTOMOBILE SALES IN QUEBEC CITY
TITLE2:                 1960-1964
X-AXIS:                 QUARTER
Y-AXIS:                 THOUSANDS

| Year | Qtr | Per | Data | SOURCE OF VARIATION | PERCENT |
|------|-----|-----|------|---------------------|---------|
| 1960 | 1 | 1 | 27.304 | TREND | 27.20% |
| | 2 | 2 | 42.773 | SEASONALITY | 68.20% |
| | 3 | 3 | 24.798 | IRREGULAR | 4.60% |
| | 4 | 4 | 27.365 | | |
| 1961 | 1 | 5 | 28.448 | TOTAL | 100.00% |
| | 2 | 6 | 43.531 | | |
| | 3 | 7 | 26.728 | | |
| | 4 | 8 | 31.590 | | |
| 1962 | 1 | 9 | 36.824 | | |
| | 2 | 10 | 54.115 | | |
| | 3 | 11 | 26.708 | | |
| | 4 | 12 | 34.313 | | |
| 1963 | 1 | 13 | 36.232 | | |
| | 2 | 14 | 58.323 | | |
| | 3 | 15 | 28.872 | | |
| | 4 | 16 | 42.496 | | |
| 1964 | 1 | 17 | 43.681 | | |
| | 2 | 18 | 61.855 | | |
| | 3 | 19 | 36.273 | | |
| | 4 | 20 | 40.244 | | |
| 1965 | 1 | 21 | | | |
| | 2 | 22 | | | |
| | 3 | 23 | | | |
| | 4 | 24 | | | |
| 1966 | 1 | 25 | | | |

Figure 5.19 Layout for quarterly ANOVA of automobile sales in Quebec

# A Diagnostic Plot and Test for Additivity

When the data depart systematically from an additive structure, as is the case with the formal-wear data, it may be desirable to re-express the $Y_{ij}$ ($i$ = month, $j$ = year) using a transformation (e.g., logarithmic transformation). For this ANOVA formulation, Tukey introduced the **diagnostic plot** in *Exploratory Data Analysis* (1977) for suggesting a transformation for additivity. Understanding the nature of additive patterns may also help in constructing the appropriate linear regression and ARIMA forecasting models.

> *By selecting the appropriate transformation, we are assured that the underlying modeling assumptions can be approximated as closely as possible.*

In addition to having a few unusual values, the data might also systematically depart from an additive structure (e.g., Data = {Trend + Seasonal} + Error). The diagnostic plot consists of a scatter diagram between the residuals in the table and the corresponding comparison values $cv_{ij}$ defined by

$$cv_{ij} = S_i T_j / m$$

where $T_j$ is the row effect (trend), $S_i$ is the column effect (seasonal) and m is the grand mean. If the diagnostic plot reveals no consistent trend or pattern, we can conclude that the data do not depart systematically from an additive model. If the slope of the diagnostic plot is k, then simple powers near $(1 - k)$ may be used to provide useful transformations.

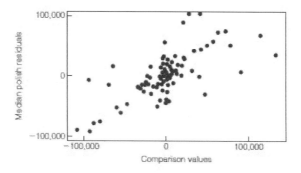

Figure 5.20 Scatter diagram of the residuals from a median polish against comparison values for formal-wear rental sale (*Source*: Figure 5.16).

Figure 5.20 displays a scatter diagram of the residuals from a median polish against the corresponding comparison values. This diagnostic plot has a straight-line slope of k = 0.64. Hence, we may want to try a cube root transformation (k = 0.66) on the data before modeling.

> *The diagnostic plot is designed to let us judge the extent to which there is any non-additivity in the trend and seasonal components.*

## The Median Polish

An outlier-resistant approach for analyzing additivity in two-way tables is the median polish described in a chapter entitled *"Analysis of Two-Way Tables by Medians"* in Hoaglin, Mosteller, and Tukey, *Understanding Robust and Exploratory Data Analysis* (1983).

The median polish is designed to replace the original table by an associated residual table for which outlier-resistant medians (as opposed to the conventional arithmetic means, which are not outlier-resistant) for each row and each column are 0. This procedure for taking out medians is an iterative, ad hoc procedure in the sense that the procedure depends on whether we start with rows or columns. However, as a complementary tool to the STI_Classification, it is effective in prescreening data for unusual values that can distort the importance of the underlying additivity of trend and seasonal effects.

Figure 5.21 (left) Box plots of the differences in residuals from a median polish and STI_Classification against months for residuals from a two-way table decomposition for the formal-wear rental sales data. (Source: Figure 5.16)

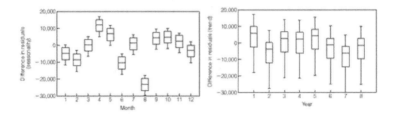

Figure 5.21 (*right*) Box plots of the differences in residuals from a median polish and STI_Classification against *years* for residuals from a two-way table decomposition for the formal-wear rental sales data. (*Source*: Figure 5.16)

Figure 5.21 (*left*) displays a box plot of the differences in the residuals from a two-way median polish of the formal-wear rental sales (Figure 5.17) data and the corresponding residuals from the ANOVA decomposition against months. Figure 5.21 (*left*) suggests that, for the months April and August, the residuals from the STI_Classification differ significantly from the corresponding residuals from a median polish. Because the median polish is resistant to outliers, this suggests that the monthly effect may be biased in the STI_Classification for the trend and seasonal components. If differences were small, we expect to see box plots around a zero line. Furthermore, it appears that Quarter 2 and Quarter 3 are not represented well in the STI_Classification, due to the rather large variation in the differences.

Figure 5.21 (*right*) displays the box plots of these residuals against years, in which the outliers point to Year 7 as the most unusual. In addition, the variations in the box plots are negatively skewed, so that there may be a tendency for trend (annual averages) to be understated.

## *Unusual Values Need Not Look Big or Be Far Out*

We use the Ratio-to-Moving Average (RMA) decomposition method (described later in this chapter) as an exploratory tool for detecting unusual values using some domain knowledge. Figure 5.22 shows both a flow chart as a model to visually depict a demand model for e-books and seven years of monthly sales for a popular e-book.

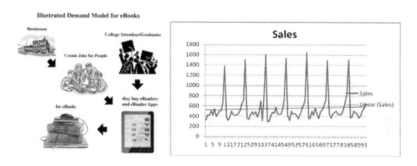

Figure 5.22 (*left*) Flow chart of demand model for e-books, and (*right*) time plot of monthly sales of a popular e-book. (Source: Figure 5.23, *left*)

| | 1990 | 1991 | 1992 | 1993 | 1994 | 1995 | 1996 |
|---|---|---|---|---|---|---|---|
| 1 | 320 | 375 | 356 | 292 | 406 | 350 | 447 |
| 2 | 423 | 318 | 338 | 295 | 314 | 361 | 364 |
| 3 | 414 | 378 | 428 | 408 | 503 | 502 | 437 |
| 4 | 506 | 497 | 490 | 480 | 438 | 417 | 478 |
| 5 | 419 | 433 | 434 | 460 | 453 | 565 | 504 |
| 6 | 544 | 426 | 487 | 576 | 417 | 432 | 438 |
| 7 | 392 | 421 | 381 | 436 | 352 | 353 | 429 |
| 8 | 449 | 448 | 472 | 436 | 439 | 495 | 439 |
| 9 | 502 | 519 | 699 | 437 | 533 | 528 | 544 |
| 10 | 520 | 638 | 310 | 556 | 618 | 612 | 671 |
| 11 | 689 | 714 | 795 | 747 | 706 | 715 | 848 |
| 12 | 1377 | 1501 | 1605 | 1531 | 1647 | 1487 | 1504 |

Figure 5.23 (*left*) Table of monthly sales of a popular eBook, and (*right*) ANOVA table decomposition of the data.

The exploratory STI_Classification (Figure 5.23, *right*) shows 96.5% Seasonality, 0.2% Trend and 3.3% Other. This should be easy to forecast, but is there any other information that could distort the modeling process and be used to tame the uncertainty factor?

An additive RMA decomposition (explained in the next section) leads to a decomposition of the data $Y_t$ as the sum of Trend-Cycle (TC), Seasonal (S) and Irregular (I). If we subtract the trend-cycle and seasonal components from the data, we end up with a residual series (Figure

165

5.26). Upon examining the residuals visually, it appears that some values, say outside +/- 100 limits, could be unusual.

$$Y_t = TC + S + I$$

It may be desirable to have a more formal method, but in the spirit of data exploration, it appears that #33 (September 1992) and #34 (October 1992) are respectively the highest and lowest residual. The conventional outlier detection method (Mean +/- 3 Std Dev) gives the limits (- 167, 167). Two nonconventional (outlier resistant) methods, described in Chapter 2, give limits (-132, 110) and (-122, 125). Unusual values #33 (170) and #24 (-240) are detected by the nonconventional methods, but the conventional outlier limits just barely reached the positive value (#33).

With the help of a domain expert, we uncovered the reasons for the unusual values; there was over reporting of sales in one month and then adjusting for it in the next month. A practical approach is to adjust the two residuals to their respective limits (Adjusted Residual) and calculate Adjusted Actual = Fit + Adjusted Residual.

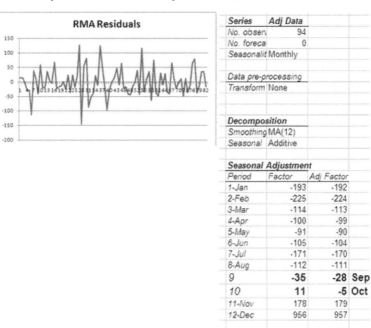

| Series | Adj Data | |
| --- | --- | --- |
| No. observ | 94 | |
| No. foreca | 0 | |
| Seasonalit | Monthly | |
| | | |
| Data pre-processing | | |
| Transform | None | |
| | | |
| | | |
| Decomposition | | |
| Smoothing | MA(12) | |
| Seasonal | Additive | |

| Seasonal Adjustment | | |
| --- | --- | --- |
| Period | Factor | Adj Factor |
| 1-Jan | -193 | -192 |
| 2-Feb | -225 | -224 |
| 3-Mar | -114 | -113 |
| 4-Apr | -100 | -99 |
| 5-May | -91 | -90 |
| 6-Jun | -105 | -104 |
| 7-Jul | -171 | -170 |
| 8-Aug | -112 | -111 |
| 9 | -35 | -28 Sep |
| 10 | 11 | -5 Oct |
| 11-Nov | 178 | 179 |
| 12-Dec | 956 | 957 |

Figure 5.24 (*left*) Residual plot from an RMA decomposition of sales of a popular eBook. (Source: Figure 5.23, *left*); (*right*) Comparison of additive seasonal factors from RMA decompositions of monthly sales of a popular eBook.

In these situations, seasonal factors can also appear distorted as a result of outliers or unusual values. Figure 5.24 (*right*) is a comparison of the (additive) seasonal factors obtained with the RMA method for the unadjusted and adjusted data (#33, 34) using a nonconventional outlier detection scheme. The key months in question (September and October) are affected by unusual values. The adjusted factors should be more typical and representative of what the seasonal influences are for those months, especially for October.

The results would be even more dramatic if the unusual values were adjusted to their fitted values, but that may not be easily justified. Unusual values should never be simply removed.

## The Ratio-to-Moving-Average Method

In the 1920s and early 1930s, the US Federal Reserve Board and the US National Bureau of Economic Research were heavily involved in the smoothing of economic time series. Many basic time series such as the monthly manufacturers' shipments, inventories, and orders and retail sales and housing starts needed to be seasonally adjusted and published for use by other government agencies and the public. In 1922, the U.S. National Bureau of Economic Research developed the ratio-to-moving-average method in a study done at the request of the Federal Reserve Board. Simplicity in the decomposition calculations was a basic necessity in the early days of seasonal-adjustment because of the lack of computing power.

> *The ratio-to-moving average-method is a simple way to determine seasonal factors in seasonal data.*

A general multiplicative decomposition method takes the form

$$Y_t = TC \times S \times TD \times I$$

where TC = trend-cycle, S = seasonal, TD = trading day, and I = irregular are the components of the original data. (The irregular component includes effects such as strikes, wars, floods, other unusual events and random errors.)

Many practitioners and their managers find the decomposition of a time series into components intuitively appealing and practical as a forecasting method. It allows them to explain the variations inherent in the data and create forecasts of changes in sub patterns in ways that are easy to interpret. Because they are able to relate their knowledge of related economic and industry patterns to the forecasting process, managers not only use the method for forecasting, but also consider it as a means for making management adjustments to forecasts.

### Step 1: Trading-Day Adjustment

Because trading days are variations that are attributable to the composition of the calendar and that can be measured, the trading-day adjustment TD is usually removed as a component. Typical trading-day factors are obtained by dividing the number of trading days for a given month by the average number of trading days for the same month over a period of the time series. The adjustment ratio is applied by dividing the original monthly value by its adjustment ratio. This seasonal-adjustment procedure is attributed to Frederick R. Macaulay (1882–1970), but those before the Census X-11 variant did not deal with the problem of trading-day variations. It simply used the number of working days in a month. This results in an adjustment of the original data, and so the data are assumed to take the form

$$Y_t = TC \times S \times I$$

## Step 2: Calculating a Centered Moving Average

Many forecasters use the moving average technique as a means of smoothing seasonal patterns and generating a level projection from an average of the most recent $p$ values in a time series $Y_t$. For creating a seasonal decomposition, a centered moving average plays a key role. The $p$-term *centered* moving average P_CMAVG is given by

$$P\_CMAVG_t = (Y_{t-m} + Y_{t-m+1} + \ldots + Y_{t-1} + Y_t + Y_{t+1} + \ldots + Y_{t+m})/p$$

where the $Y_t$ values denote the actual (observed) values and $p$ is the number of values included in the average. In this formula, $p$ is an odd integer and $m = (p - 1)/2$. In other words, we are using $(p - 1)/2$ values on either side of $Y_t$ to produce a smoothed value of $Y_t$. In particular, the three-term centered moving average 3_CMAVG has the formula

$$3\_CMAVG_t = (Y_{t-1} + Y_t + Y_{t+1})/3$$

The larger the value of $p$, the smoother the moving average becomes. If $p$ is even, as is the case in smoothing quarterly data ($p = 4$) or monthly data ($p = 12$), there is no middle position to place the smoothed value. In that case, we place it to the right of the observed value or take another centered two-period moving average.

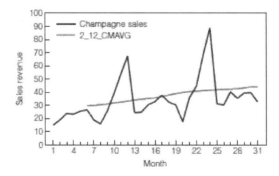

Figure 5.25 Time plot of monthly champagne sales: Two-term of a 12-term moving average.

To illustrate this calculation, we show the time plot in Figure 5.25 that illustrates the smoothness of the final result. The data are 36 values of monthly champagne sales in the first column of Figure 5.26.

> *A centered moving average can be used to smooth unwanted fluctuations in a time series*

### Step 3: Trend-cycle and Seasonal Irregular Ratios

The next step in the RMA method is to obtain an estimate of the trend and cyclical factors by use of a p-month centered moving average, where $p$ is the length of the seasonal period. This moving average is divided into the trading-day adjusted data to yield a series of seasonal-irregular ratios:

$$Y_t = S \times I = (TC \times S \times I)/TC$$

Averaging the SI ratios for a given month over a number of years produces an estimate of the seasonal factor or seasonal index. The irregular factor is assumed to cancel out in the smoothing process.

| Champagne | 12_CMAVG | 2_12_CMAVG |
|---|---|---|
| 15 | | |
| 18.7 | | |
| 23.6 | | |
| 23.2 | | |
| 25.5 | | |
| 26.4 | | 29.75 |
| 18.8 | 29.75 | 29.9115 |
| 16 | 30.3958 | 30.3677 |
| 25.2 | 30.9292 | 30.9646 |
| 39 | 31.6042 | 31.6625 |
| 53.6 | 32.5125 | 32.475 |
| 67.3 | 33.2708 | 33.2625 |
| 24.4 | 33.9958 | 33.951 |
| 24.8 | 34.5417 | 34.5344 |
| 30.3 | 35.0583 | 35.101 |
| 32.7 | 35.7458 | 35.7875 |
| 37.8 | 36.6 | 36.7625 |
| 32.3 | 38.1042 | 38.0198 |
| 30.3 | 39.2708 | 39.1042 |
| 17.6 | 39.7708 | 39.8073 |
| 36.0 | 40.4167 | 40.3875 |
| 44.7 | 40.9458 | 40.8563 |
| 68.4 | 41.1167 | 41.1698 |
| 88.6 | 41.5 | 41.5073 |
| 31.1 | 41.9125 | 41.8698 |
| 30.1 | 42.1542 | 42.1302 |
| 40.5 | 42.3 | 42.3406 |
| 35.2 | 42.6083 | 42.6885 |
| 39.4 | 43.2375 | 43.3177 |
| 39.9 | 44.1875 | 43.95 |
| 32.6 | | 44.1875 |
| 21.1 | | |
| 36.0 | | |
| 52.1 | | |
| 76.1 | | |
| 103.7 | | |

Figure 5.26 Monthly champagne sales: Calculation of a two-term of a 12-term centered average.

## Step 4: Seasonally Adjusted Data

The final seasonally adjusted data are obtained by dividing each monthly value by the seasonal index for the corresponding month. This corresponds to a multiplicative seasonal-adjustment procedure.

# GLOBL Case Example: Is the Decomposition Additive or Not?

In Chapter 2, we performed an exploratory STI_Classification of GLOBL consumer electronics Product Line B for Region A. It shows 51% Seasonality, 4% Trend, and 45% Other (unknown and the uncertainty factor). We realize that there are two scenarios:  an *additive* and *multiplicative* option with the RMA decomposition method to contrast additive versus multiplicative seasonal adjustments.

We perform both and create the seasonal factors as well:

| Decomposition | | Decomposition | |
|---|---|---|---|
| Smoothing MA(12) | | Smoothing MA(12) | |
| Seasonal Additive | | Seasonal Multiplicative | |
| | | | |
| Seasonal Adjustment | | Seasonal Adjustment | |
| Period | Factor | Period | Factor |
| Jan | 8626 | Jan | 1.5 |
| Feb | 9066 | Feb | 1.5 |
| Mar | 4620 | Mar | 1.3 |
| Apr | -6054 | Apr | 0.7 |
| May | -5686 | May | 0.7 |
| Jun | -3171 | Jun | 0.8 |
| Jul | -5548 | Jul | 0.7 |
| Aug | -5745 | Aug | 0.7 |
| Sep | -1427 | Sep | 0.9 |
| Oct | -1635 | Oct | 0.9 |
| Nov | 402 | Nov | 1.0 |
| Dec | 6552 | Dec | 1.4 |
| | | | |
| | 0 | | 12 |

> Using the data table, create a two-way decomposition table and verify the percentage variation attributable to the trend, seasonal, and irregular components for GLOBL Product Line B/Region A.
> Can you find a couple of reasons what factors drive the dominant pattern in the data?
> Perform two RMA decompositions and contrast the additive and multiplicative seasonal factors, shown below.

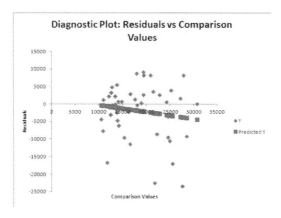

➤ Calculate the Comparison Values and display the Diagnostic plot. What inferences do you make about the non-additivity of the seasonal and trend components in the STI_Classification method? *Answer*: Slope of line − 0.2 (t = -1, not significantly different from zero. This suggests there is no sufficient evidence of non-additivity found. We should prefer the additive model in this case for making seasonal adjustments.

## APPENDIX: A Two-Way ANOVA Table Analysis

We now describe a year-by-month ANOVA table as a means of constructing the trend and seasonal contribution to the total variation in a time series. It is an example of an exploratory method for visualizing the characteristics of trend and seasonal time series data. This two-way ANOVA (without replication) algorithm has been used from the beginning to provide an intuitive way of illustrating components of variation while introducing the useful concepts of additivity, median smoothing and residual analysis. Although many statistical software packages and Excel Add-in tools will allow you to perform this kind of analysis from a menu selection, it is nevertheless instructive to work this out as a spreadsheet exercise.

Recall that the basic premise underlying a decomposition approach is that a time series can be represented by a number of distinctly interpretable, albeit *unobservable*, components. Two-way table decompositions can give us a preliminary feel for the *relative* contributions and additivity of seasonal, trend-cycle, and irregular variations to the total variation in a demand time series. This helps the demand forecaster identify the two key sources of variability driving demand and thereby helps in the selection of suitable drivers of demand and forecasting techniques.

To begin, the **grand mean** (average of all the data values) is computed first. Then the differences between each data value and the grand mean are squared and summed' this is, called the **total variation.** This measures the overall variation due to trend, seasonal, and irregular components.

The variation due to trend alone is found as well as the variation due to seasonality. Remember, for this analysis to work, we must use complete years of data in a two-way data table. You should use a minimum of 3 (season) years. For a graphical summary, you may also want to consider a pie chart instead of a bar chart in management presentations.

The method by which a two-way table is constructed is not complex, but you may feel the notation is somewhat cumbersome. By working carefully through the analysis, you should be able to understand how to create the analysis on a spreadsheet.

A two-way table is a spreadsheet in which the values $Y_{ij}$ ($i$ = month, $j$ = year) are displayed in a rectangular array, where $i$ = 1, 2 . . . , I (I = 12 for monthly data) and $j$ = 1, 2. . . , J (J = number of years). This representation can also be used for quarterly data, but then $i$ = 1, 2, 3, 4.

When the data are arranged in a spreadsheet with I (=12) columns (for the months) and J rows (for the years), an additive model that describes a typical value in terms of a seasonal component $S_i$, a trend or yearly component $T_j$, and a residual error term (irregular component $\varepsilon_{ij}$) is given by

$$Y_{ij} = \mu + S_i + T_j + \varepsilon_{ij}$$

where $\mu$ denotes a mean effect or typical value. Because row averages ($\bar{Y}_i. = Y_i. /J$) and column average ($\bar{Y}.j = Y.j /12$) in the table represent average seasonal and trend effects, respectively, variations of these averages from the grand mean ($\bar{Y}.. = \sum\sum Y_{ij} = \sum \bar{Y}.J = \sum Y_i.$) reflect the respective variation due to an average seasonal pattern and trend. The following notation summarizes certain totals and averages of interest in the analysis:

$Y.j = \sum Y_{ij}$ is the total of year j, which has been summed over 12 rows, and $\bar{Y}.j = Y.j / 12$

represents the average per month for year j.

Thus, {Y.j ; j = 1, . . . , J} are annual totals, which are used to summarize the trend over J years. Summing across columns corresponding to the number of years gives $\bar{Y}i. = \sum Y_{ij}$, which is the total of month i (sum over J years). Then, $\bar{Y}_i. = Y_i. /J$ is the average per month of month I. Thus $\{\bar{Y}_i . ; i = 1 \ldots ,J\}$ are monthly averages, which are used to summarize the average seasonal pattern over J years.

To get overall totals, define $\bar{Y} . . = \sum \sum Y_{ij} = \sum \bar{Y}. j = \sum Y_i ..$ The quantity $\bar{Y} . . = \sum \sum Y_{ij} = \sum \bar{Y}. J = \sum Y_i .$ is known simply as the grand total, and $\bar{Y} . . = Y. ./12 J$ is the average per month over J years, or the grand mean.

It is now possible to describe the various contributions to the total variation in the data. The total variation (as measured from the grand mean) is given by

$$SST = [\sum \sum (Y_{ij} - \bar{Y} . . )^2 ]/ (12J - 1)$$

This is a measure of the overall variation in the data, which is due to trend, seasonal, and irregular patterns. Specific entries within each row (month) can be measured against the row mean to give a measure of variation for the given month. This variation may be due to trends and changes in the seasonal patterns as well as irregularity. Thus,

$$SSRow = \sum (Y_{ij} - \bar{Y} i . )^2 / (J - 1)$$

$$SSCol = \sum (Y_{ij} - \hat{Y} . j )^2 / 11$$

is a measure of the variation within column J (year) measured from the column mean. This variation may be due to seasonal patterns and changes in trend as well as irregularity. Because the row and column means represent average seasonal and trend effects, variations of these averages reflect the respective variation due to average seasonal pattern and trend. Thus,

$$SSSeas = \sum (\bar{Y} i . - \bar{Y} . . )^2 / 11$$

$$SSTrend = \sum (\bar{Y} . j - \bar{Y} . . )^2 / (J - 1)$$

represent variation in row (monthly) means and column (yearly) means, respectively.

## Percent Contribution of Trend and Seasonal Effects

It is also possible to quantify the proportion of variability due to seasonal effects, S, by the ratio $R^2_{Seas} = SS_{Seas} / SST$:

$$R^2_{Seas} = J \sum (\bar{Y} i. - \bar{Y}..)2 / \sum \sum (Y_{ij} - \bar{Y}..)2$$

and the proportion of variability due to trend effects, T by $R^2_{Trend} = SS_{Trend} / SST$:

$$R^2_{Trend} = 12 \sum (\bar{Y}.j - \bar{Y}.)^2 / \sum \sum (Y_{ij} - \bar{Y}.)^2$$

Ideally, or for an extreme case, if there is no trend in the data, the column means equal the grand mean and the proportion of variability that is due to trend equals zero. The foregoing computations can be readily made using a statistical package or spreadsheet software that offers a two-way ANOVA (without replication) capability.

By performing an STI_Classification on the formal-wear sales data., we find an STI_Classification of the data into the seasonal and trend components. Trend 56.9%, Seasonality 31.3%, and Other 11.8%. Jointly the two primary factors appear to explain almost 90% of the total variation. In this case, we look for models with trend/seasonal forecast profiles (Chapters 8 and 9) for modeling and forecasting. On the other hand, in Figure 5.16, the STI_Classification yields a seasonal component that is quite dominant by itself (almost 70%). Hence, in this case, we look for seasonal and trend/seasonal forecast profiles (Chapters 8 and 9) for modeling and forecasting.

## *Takeaways*

➢ Many analysts and researchers proceed by seeing how *alike* things are. Others proceed by trying to understand why things are *different*. A **residual analysis** is consistent with the latter approach.

➢ The unplanned findings often yield the most interesting and important results in a forecasting study.

➢ In general, the difference between the STI_Classification and the median polish are that an analysis using arithmetic means tends to produce fewer residuals with large magnitudes, fewer residuals whose magnitudes are close to 0, and more residuals of moderate size. The advantage of the median polish is that it generally produces substantial residuals for the likely outliers.

# 6

# Dealing with Seasonal Fluctuations

 "Nature has established patterns originating in the return of events, but only for the most part. New illnesses flood the human race, so that no matter how many experiments you have done on corpses, you have not thereby immposd a limit on the nature of events so that in the future they could not vary."

Von Leibniz, 1703

Many business time series show seasonal fluctuations. Time series data have been adjusted for seasonal fluctuations in business and financial applications for about a century. Businesses may need to know when a change in a time series is due to more than the typical seasonal variation. Government agencies adjust statistical indicators for seasonality before publication and distribution to the public.

There are generally three distinct uses of seasonal adjustment: the historical adjustment of available past data, the current adjustment of each new value, and the predicted seasonal factors for future adjustment. This chapter describes how seasonal effects can be removed and adjusted for in historical data. We examine how the centered moving average and related smoothers play a central role in a number of widely used seasonal-adjustment procedures.

The X-13ARIMA-SEATS seasonal adjustment programs from the U.S. Census Bureau are accepted standards for the large-scale analysis of publicly reported seasonal adjustments of monthly and quarterly data. These data-driven seasonal adjustment procedures involve smoothing data to eliminate unwanted irregular variation from the patterns that are meaningful to the analyst.

## *Seasonal Influences*

One of the first people to study periodicity in economic time series was the British astronomer William Herschel (1738–1822), *left*, who tried to find a relationship between sunspots and wheat prices. Another

was the banker James W. Gilbart (1794–1863), *right*, who discovered that the Bank of England notes were in high demand in January, April, July, and October due to the payment of dividends in these months. He used this information to

argue against attempts by smaller country banks to issue their notes during these periods.

Today we see many examples of seasonality in economic time series and tourism demand series. Anyone who shops at the end of the calendar year realizes that retail, toy, and card stores have a surge in demand at year end. Some businesses have 25% or most of all their yearly sales in December. In other countries, it can peak at a different religious holiday. Even Peruvian anchovy production shows seven-year repeating patterns caused by recurring changes in ocean currents.

In Chapter 5, we defined **seasonality** as periodic fluctuations that recur every year with about the same timing and intensity. For example, farm income from all farms in the United States may rise steadily each year from early spring until fall and then drop sharply. For agricultural economists, it is important to determine whether a recession has reached bottom or whether there is a predictable pattern in the duration, amplitude, or slope of the business cycle expansions and contractions. In this case, the main use of techniques for seasonally adjusting farm income data is to remove any seasonal fluctuations in order to expose an underlying trend-cycle pattern.

> *Seasonality is described by periodic fluctuations that recur every year with about the same timing and intensity.*

Many business time series are recorded over calendar months, which create a seasonal movement because the number of working days varies from month to month. The timing of major public holidays (e.g., Christmas, Ramadan and Easter, etc.), school openings and closings, dividend payments by corporations, and fiscal tax years all contribute seasonal effects, because these events tend to occur at similar times each year.

Often companies have to deal with seasonal fluctuations when making decisions about price and inventory policy or the commitment of capital expenditures. In these situations, the demand forecaster wants to know whether changes in business activity over a given period were larger or smaller than normal.

Business forecasters are not in general agreement on how best to deal with seasonality in forecasting. Some advocate using data-driven methodologies for seasonally adjusting data before forecasting them; others advocate using model-driven approaches for making seasonality explicit in a model for the data. Because, advanced model-driven approaches to seasonal adjustments are beyond the scope of this book, we follow a hybrid model-based, data-driven approach in this chapter.

There may be times when seasonally adjusted data are the only data readily available. For instance, computerized data banks containing a wide variety of seasonally adjusted economic data, both global and regional are available on the Internet. It often makes sense to use commercially available sources rather than adjusting many of these series ourselves, even if the unadjusted data are available. For adjusting internal data, the Census Bureau programs are available at no charge with a user-friendly interface program.

## Identifying Seasonality Visually

If at least two or more seasonal cycles are available, seasonality can usually be identified visually. We can perform a preliminary TSI-Classification (see Figure 5.25) and look for the percentage variation attributable to seasonality. We can check to see if the peaks (troughs) occur during the same quarter or month of every year in a tier chart (see Figure 5.17).

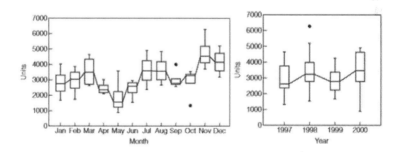

Figure 6.1 (left) Box plots by month for series N410 from IJF-M3 competition. (Fifty monthly values from the MICRO set; Source: www.maths.monash.edu.au/~hyndman/forecasting/)

Figure 6.2 (*right*) Box plots by year for series N410 from IJF-M3 competition. (Fifty monthly values from the MICRO set; *Source: www.maths.monash.edu.au/~hyndman/forecasting/*)

Further, we can trace yearly peaks and yearly troughs visually (see Figure 5.19); if they are widening over time, this signals that seasonality is multiplicative, and if they are relatively constant, this suggests additive seasonality.

Other visual displays include box plots by month (each box plot representing the values for a given month), which can point to a pattern of seasonality (Figure 6.1). The medians in the box plots are connected to indicate a typical seasonality. The height of the box plot indicates the variability of the seasonal period. On the other hand, **box plots by year** (each box representing one year's values) can be helpful in isolating unusual values and variability in seasonality with trend (Figure 6.2). The medians are connected in the box plots, which suggest little or no trend in the data. There is an unusual value in one of the years (1998).

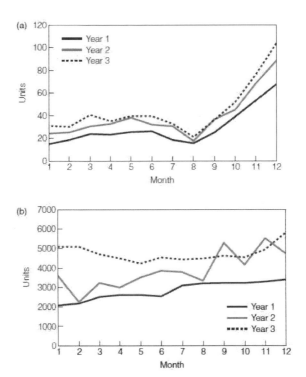

Figure 6.3 Time plots of intra-year variation for (a) a seasonal time series and (b) a nonseasonal time series.

Sometimes, the appearance of intra-year fluctuations in a time plot may not indicate seasonality, in that the peaks (or troughs) do not recur at the same time each year. Selecting a seasonal model for such a series is not advisable because the underlying sources of the fluctuations, miscast as seasonal, go unmodeled. One visual aid to help with this is the tier chart (see Figure 5.17), in which the horizontal axis displays the seasons of the year (in quarters or months) and the values for the seasons of any one year are connected.

In Figure 6.3a, the evidence of seasonality is clear, whereas in Figure 6.3b the intra-year variation is too irregular to be modeled as a seasonal index.

> *Keep the following rule in mind when planning to run additive or multiplicative seasonal models on seasonal demand history: If the data are inventory volumes, intermittent demands, or without trends, running and comparing multiple additive seasonal models is recommended; in other situations, multiplicative seasonal models may be appropriate.*

Volatility in a time series makes it difficult not only to identify seasonal influences in a time series but to distinguish trend as well. Smoothing the seasonal fluctuations of a volatile series may be necessary to permit the identification of the underlying trend. The following visual rules have been recommended by Tashman and Kruk (from "*The use of protocols to select exponential smoothing procedures: A reconsideration of forecasting competitions,*" **International Journal of Forecasting** [1996]):

1.  If the recent trend in the time series is unstable (defined as a change in direction from growth to decline or vice versa), use a constant level method.
2.  If the recent trend is stable and appears flatter (slower) than the global trend, use a damped trend method.
3.  If the recent trend is stable and appears as steep as or steeper than the global trend, use a linear or exponential trend method.

If the data are seasonal, these rules can be applied to the deseasonalized data.

When the main source of variation in a time series is due to seasonality, the time series can be smoothed by seasonal adjustment. This suggests that the demand forecaster should examine a plot of the deseasonalized data or the annualized data. Alternatively, the use of an appropriate moving average of the time series (a four-period moving average for quarterly data or a 12-period moving average for monthly data) may be useful.

## Removing Seasonality by Differencing

In Chapter 7, we introduce differencing as a means of removing trends from data. For example, a first difference (also called a regular difference of period 1) of the time series $Y_t$ results in a new time series $Z_t$ of successive changes defined by $Z_t = Y_t - Y_{t-1}$. Successive values are separated by one period. This can be seen by visualizing a set of points lying on a straight line. The first difference is a horizontal line (= the slope, no trend).

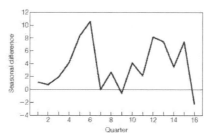

| Sales | Seasonal difference of period 4 |
|---|---|
| 27.304 | * |
| 42.773 | * |
| 24.798 | * |
| 27.365 | * |
| 28.441 | 1.137 |
| 43.531 | 0.758 |
| 26.728 | 1.93 |
| 31.59 | 4.225 |
| 36.824 | 8.383 |
| 54.115 | 10.584 |
| 26.708 | −0.02 |
| 34.313 | 2.723 |
| 36.232 | −0.592 |
| 58.323 | 4.208 |
| 28.872 | 2.164 |
| 42.496 | 8.183 |
| 43.681 | 7.449 |
| 61.855 | 3.532 |
| 36.273 | 7.401 |
| 40.244 | −2.252 |

Figure 6.4 Quarterly automobile sales: time plot (top) of seasonal differences of period 4 (bottom). (Source: Figure 4.20)

In Figure 5.20, we noted that the seasonal contribution in a quarterly series of automobile sales in Quebec City was 68.2%. With the differenced data, the seasonal contribution to the total variability is reduced to 4.3%, for trend = 11.5% and irregular = 84.2 %. A time plot and the calculation for the seasonal difference of period 4 for these data are in Figure 6.4.

The differencing operation needed to remove seasonal fluctuations in monthly data is the seasonal difference of period 12:

$$Z_t = Y_t - Y_{t-12}$$

*In addition to removing trends, differencing can also be used to remove seasonal influences from data.*

For the following data on the sales of a weight-control product and expenditures on monthly advertising, an exploratory STI_Classification (described in Chapter 5) resulted in the following interpretation for the trend and seasonal contributions:

**Sales: trend = 20%, seasonality = 47%, irregular = 33%**

**Advertising: trend = 7%, seasonality = 51%,    irregular = 42%**

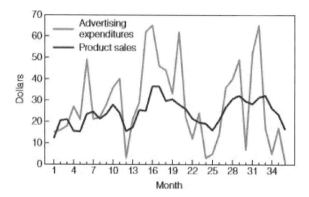

Figure 6.5 Time plots of monthly sales and advertising expenditures over 36 months. (*Source*: Cryer and Miller, *Statistics for Business*, 1994; SALESADS.DAT)

When developing formal regression models with these variables, a relatively high noise component suggests that much of the variation is not explainable by trend and seasonal influences alone. The time plots in Figure 6.5 clearly show the seasonal patterns in the two series, as well as the greater volatility in the advertising expenditures. In addition, peaks and troughs appear to correlate reasonably well. These are important considerations when modeling the data.

With the seasonal differenced data, the seasonal contribution to the total variability in the differenced sales is only approximately 17% (irregular = 64%, trend = 19%). The results for the differenced advertising variable now show: trend = 23%, seasonal = 36%, and irregular = 41%.

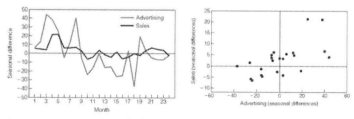

Figure 6.6 Time plots (*left*) and scatter diagram (*right*) of seasonal differences for sales and advertising.

Although the seasonal contribution to sales and advertising has been reduced by differencing, this analysis has its weaknesses. The relative scarcity of data (only 24 values of differenced data) does not support drawing strong conclusions about the actual strength of these components in the data; it only helps us to quantify their relative influences.

Figure 6.6 depicts time plots and a scatter diagram for the seasonal differences of period 12 for the sales and advertising data. With the seasonal influences removed, an apparent association still exists between the two variables. We are interested in exploring other patterns, such as a lag relationship, in the data. This is dealt with again in Chapter 10 where we develop a linear regression model.

In a forecasting model, the objective is to predict product sales from advertising expenditures. To do this, we can correlate

- unadjusted sales and unadjusted advertising expenditures
- seasonally adjusted sales and seasonally adjusted advertising expenditures
- seasonal differenced sales and seasonal differenced advertising expenditures

In addition, we can use the previous approaches with log-transformed sales and log transformed advertising expenditures as well as with lagged advertising expenditures. Each of these approaches will lead to different models and hence different forecasts. Only experimentation and experience can uncover the most appropriate models.

> *A typical objective of a seasonal decomposition procedure is to measure typical or average seasonal movements in monthly or quarterly data.*

## Seasonal Decomposition

There are a wide variety of factors that influence economic data, so it is often difficult to determine precisely the way seasonal influences affect changes in a time series. The more commonly used methods of seasonal decomposition for large-scale adjustments are data-driven; they are less frequently based on formal statistical models. These methods use smoothing procedures extensively. However, most methods are based on assumption that seasonal fluctuations can be measured in terms of a constant set of factors that can be identified apart from underlying trend-cycle and other fluctuations.

If the magnitude of the seasonal increase or decrease is assumed to be essentially constant and independent of the level of the time series, an additive decomposition is appropriate:

$$\text{Data} = \text{Trend-cycle} + \text{Seasonal} + \text{Irregular}$$

Recall that irregular is the catch-all word for all unexplained 'noisy' variations including random error.

More often, the magnitude of the seasonal change tends to increase or decrease with level, so that seasonality might be assumed to be proportional to the level of the time series. This leads to the multiplicative decomposition:

$$\text{Data} = \text{Trend-cycle} \bullet \text{Seasonal} \bullet \text{Irregular}$$

Even in this circumstance, an additive decomposition could be used if we transform the original time series with logarithms (provided there are no zeros or negatives in the data).

A logarithmic transformation of the data tends to stabilize the magnitude of the seasonal pattern and allows us to use additive decomposition on the transformed series. One major limitation of using the log-transformed model, however, is that the constraint that annual sums of the seasonal factors must be 0 in an additive model does not give the same result as the constraint that the product of seasonal indices must be 1 for the log additive model.

Because all methods have their limitations, the demand forecaster needs to be aware of the pros and cons of seasonal-adjustment procedures in the context of the particular application. One desired feature of a good seasonal-adjustment procedure is that the seasonal component not change too much over time. The choice between an additive or multiplicative method may be important here. There are also methods that make simultaneous additive and multiplicative adjustments.

## Uses of Seasonal Adjustment

Consider the following simplified example showing how a forecaster uses seasonal factors. Seasonal factors can be used to identify turning points that are not apparent in the raw data, and adjust seasonality out of the data so that forecasting techniques that cannot handle seasonally unadjusted data (e.g., exponential smoothing models found in Chapter 8) can be applied to the seasonally adjusted data.

Figure 6.7 shows three rows of numbers. The first row shows the actual demand for a product during a given year. The second row shows seasonal factors that were developed, based on historical data and projected for the same year. The third row shows the seasonally adjusted data under an assumed additive decomposition:

$$\text{Data} - \text{Seasonal factor} = \text{Trend-cycle} + \text{Irregular}$$

In this example, the actual values decline from January through May. The seasonal factors indicate that the first three months are generally strong, April has no significant seasonality, and May is generally weak. After adjusting for the seasonal effect, we can see that the adjusted demand grows after February. This might be a result of an economic recovery that is not apparent in the actual values.

Figure 6.7 also highlights the importance of assuring ourselves that the seasonal factors are appropriate. Otherwise, inappropriate conclusions can be drawn from a faulty seasonal adjustment.

| Description¤ | Jan.¤ | Feb.¤ | Mar.¤ | Apr.¤ | May¤ |
|---|---|---|---|---|---|
| Actual·data¤ | 2000¤ | 1900¤ | 1700¤ | 1300¤ | 1100¤ |
| Seasonal·factors¤ | 1000¤ | ·900¤ | ·600¤ | ·0¤ | -·400¤ |
| Seasonally·adjusted·data¤ | 1000¤ | 1000¤ | 1100¤ | 1300¤ | 1500¤ |

Figure 6.7 Using seasonal factors to adjust a data set.

In Figure 6.8, the same actuals are used, but a different seasonal pattern is assumed. After we adjust for the seasonal effect, the data show a flat demand pattern. In contrast, in Figure 6.6, the same actuals are used, but the seasonal factors have been distorted as a result of severe outliers in the prior year's actuals.

Thus, the seasonal factors in Figure 6.8 are correct, but the method used to derive the seasonal factors in Figure 6.9 has incorrectly handled the outliers in the prior year. These distorted factors have then been projected into the current year, altering the April and May seasonal factors. In the seasonally adjusted data, it appears that demand is falling off when it really is not.

| ·¤ | Jan.¤ | ···Feb.¤ | Mar.¤ | Apr.¤ | May¤ |
|---|---|---|---|---|---|
| Actual·data¤ | 2000¤ | ··1900¤ | 1700¤ | 1300¤ | 1100¤ |
| Seasonal·factors¤ | 500¤ | ···400¤ | 200·¤ | -·200¤ | -··400¤ |
| Seasonally·adjusted·data·¤ | 1500¤ | ···1500¤ | 1500¤ | 1500¤ | 1500¤ |

Figure 6.8 Using different seasonal factors to adjust the data.

| ¤ | Jan.¤ | Feb.¤ | Mar.¤ | Apr.¤ | May¤ |
|---|---|---|---|---|---|
| ¤ | ¤ | ¤ | ¤ | ¤ | ¤ |
| Actual·data¤ | 2000¤ | 1900¤ | 1700¤ | 1300¤ | 1100¤ |
| Seasonal·factors¤ | ··500¤ | ···400¤ | ··100¤ | ·0¤ | ·100¤ |
| Seasonally· adjusted data·¤ | 1500¤ | 1500¤ | 1500¤ | 1300¤ | 1200¤ |

Figure 6.9 Using seasonal factors that have been impacted by outliers in the prior year's data to adjust the data set.

## Multiplicative and Additive Seasonal Decompositions

We can gain some insight from a seasonal decomposition into the model building considerations with forecasting models. A strong seasonal pattern suggests that particular attention should be paid to accurately representing the seasonal influences in the data.

## Decomposition of Monthly Data - Multiplicative

A multiplicative seasonal adjustment is appropriate when the range of seasonal fluctuations each year increases as the trend in the data increases. Figure 6.10 shows a multiplicative decomposition of monthly champagne sales in a spreadsheet calculation. The data are highly seasonal, which is supported by the two-way table decomposition (Chapter 5): trend = 7%, seasonality = 91%, and irregular = 2%. Figure 6.14 (later in the chapter) shows a multiplicative decomposition of quarterly gas grill sales (trend = 14%, seasonality= 75%, irregular = 11%). These are clearly time series with strong seasonal influences.

We also gain insight from this decomposition into the modeling complexities when building formal forecasting models. The dominant seasonality suggests that particular attention should be paid to models with seasonal forecast profiles that can accurately represent the seasonal influences in the data.

Filename: SEASADJ.XLS
Worksheet: MULTIMON

| | A | B | C | D | E | F | G | H | I | J | K |
|---|---|---|---|---|---|---|---|---|---|---|---|
| 1 | MULTIPLICATIVE SEASONAL ADJUSTMENT, MONTHLY DATA | | | | | | | | | | |
| 2 | TITLE1: MULTIPLICATIVE SEASONAL ADJUSTMENT | | | | | | | | | | |
| 3 | TITLE2: CHAMPAGNE SALES | | | | | | | | | | |
| 4 | X-AXIS: MONTH | | | | | | | | | | |
| 5 | Y-AXIS: MILLIONS OF CASES | | | | | | | | | | |
| 6 | | | | | | | | | | | |
| 7 | | | Actual | Moving | | | Sum of | # of | Avg. | Seas. | Adj. |
| 8 | Year | Mon | Per | Data | Avg. | Ratio | Ratios | Ratios | Ratio | Index | Data |
| 9 | 2000 | 1 | 1 | 15.0 | 0.0 | 0.00 | 1.47 | 2 | 0.736 | 0.728 | 20.60 |
| 10 | | 2 | 2 | 18.7 | 0.0 | 0.00 | 1.44 | 2 | 0.718 | 0.711 | 26.32 |
| 11 | | 3 | 3 | 23.6 | 0.0 | 0.00 | 1.83 | 2 | 0.916 | 0.907 | 26.02 |
| 12 | | 4 | 4 | 23.2 | 0.0 | 0.00 | 1.75 | 2 | 0.877 | 0.868 | 26.74 |
| 13 | | 5 | 5 | 25.5 | 0.0 | 0.00 | 1.97 | 2 | 0.984 | 0.974 | 26.18 |
| 14 | | 6 | 6 | 26.4 | 0.0 | 0.00 | 1.78 | 2 | 0.892 | 0.883 | 29.90 |
| 15 | | 7 | 7 | 18.8 | 29.4 | 0.64 | 2.14 | 3 | 0.715 | 0.708 | 26.57 |
| 16 | | 8 | 8 | 16.0 | 30.1 | 0.53 | 0.98 | 2 | 0.488 | 0.483 | 33.13 |
| 17 | | 9 | 9 | 25.2 | 30.7 | 0.82 | 1.72 | 2 | 0.861 | 0.852 | 29.57 |
| 18 | | 10 | 10 | 39.0 | 31.2 | 1.25 | 2.34 | 2 | 1.172 | 1.160 | 33.62 |
| 19 | | 11 | 11 | 53.6 | 32.0 | 1.68 | 3.34 | 2 | 1.671 | 1.653 | 32.42 |
| 20 | | 12 | 12 | 67.3 | 33.0 | 2.04 | 4.19 | 2 | 2.095 | 2.073 | 32.46 |
| 21 | 2001 | 1 | 13 | 24.4 | 33.5 | 0.73 | | | Sum 12.124 | 12.000 | 33.50 |
| 22 | | 2 | 14 | 24.8 | 34.5 | 0.72 | | | | | 34.90 |
| 23 | | 3 | 15 | 30.3 | 34.6 | 0.88 | | | | | 33.40 |
| 24 | | 4 | 16 | 32.7 | 35.5 | 0.92 | | | | | 37.69 |
| 25 | | 5 | 17 | 37.8 | 36.0 | 1.05 | | | | | 38.80 |
| 26 | | 6 | 18 | 32.3 | 37.2 | 0.87 | | | | | 36.59 |
| 27 | | 7 | 19 | 30.3 | 39.0 | 0.78 | | | | | 42.82 |
| 28 | | 8 | 20 | 17.6 | 39.6 | 0.45 | | | | | 36.45 |
| 29 | | 9 | 21 | 36.0 | 40.0 | 0.90 | | | | | 42.24 |
| 30 | | 10 | 22 | 44.7 | 40.8 | 1.09 | | | | | 38.53 |
| 31 | | 11 | 23 | 68.4 | 41.1 | 1.67 | | | | | 41.37 |
| 32 | | 12 | 24 | 88.6 | 41.2 | 2.15 | | | | | 42.74 |

Figure 6.10 Monthly champagne sales—multiplicative decomposition.

The first step (Figure 6.10, column E) is to compute a 12-month centered moving average of the data. The first moving average, covering January to December, is always placed next to month 7. The second moving average, for February to January, is placed opposite month 8 and so on. The result of this procedure is that there is no moving average for the first 6 months and the last 6 months of the data (not shown).

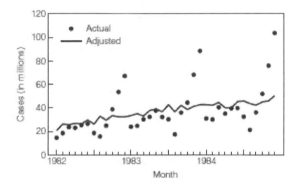

Figure 6.11 Time plot of monthly champagne sales and seasonally adjusted values by multiplicative seasonal decomposition. (*Source*: Figure 6.10, column D)

The second step is to use the centered moving averages to compute seasonal indexes. If we *divide* each data value by its moving average, the result is a preliminary seasonal index. Ratios are computed in column F; each ratio is simply actual sales in column D divided by the moving average in column E. The ratios for the same month in each year vary somewhat, so they are summed in column G and averaged in column I.

The average ratios can be interpreted as follows. Sales in January are predicted to be 73.6% of average monthly sales for the year. Sales for December are predicted to be 209.5% above the average. For this interpretation to make sense, the average ratios must sum to 12 (called normalization) because there are 12 months in the year. The average ratios actually sum to 12.12 because rounding is unavoidable. Thus, the formulas in column J normalize the ratios to sum to 12.

The last step is to adjust the sales data. Each actual value in column D is divided by the seasonal index applicable to that month to obtain the adjusted data in column K. The graph is shown in Figure 6.11.

## Decomposition of Quarterly Data - Additive

An additive procedure can be developed in a manner analogous to the multiplicative decomposition. The worksheet in Figure 6.12 is similar to the worksheet in Figure 6.10 except that it removes a quarterly seasonal pattern from the data instead of a monthly seasonal pattern.

Filename:    SEASADJ.XLS
Worksheet:   ADDITQTR

1  ADDITIVE SEASONAL ADJUSTMENT, QUARTERLY DATA
2  TITLE1: ADDITIVE SEASONAL ADJUSTMENT
3  TITLE2: CALCULATOR SALES
4  X-AXIS: QUARTER
5  Y-AXIS: THOUSANDS OF UNITS

| | A | B | C | D | E | F | G | H | I | J | K |
|---|---|---|---|---|---|---|---|---|---|---|---|
| 6 | | | | Actual | Moving | | Sum of | # of | Avg. | Seas. | Adj. |
| 8 | Year | Qtr | Per | data | Avg. | Diff. | Diffs. | Diffs. | Diff. | Index | Data |
| 9 | 1978 | 1 | 1 | 73.9 | 0.0 | 0.00 | -7.45 | 2 | -3.725 | -3.778 | 77.7 |
| 10 | | 2 | 2 | 76.8 | 0.0 | 0.00 | -4.55 | 2 | -2.275 | -2.328 | 79.1 |
| 11 | | 3 | 3 | 77.7 | 78.8 | -1.10 | -3.67 | 3 | -1.225 | -1.278 | 79.0 |
| 12 | | 4 | 4 | 86.8 | 79.3 | 7.50 | 14.88 | 2 | 7.438 | 7.384 | 79.4 |
| 13 | 1979 | 1 | 5 | 75.9 | 79.8 | -3.85 | | | Sum 0.213 | 0.000 | 79.7 |
| 14 | | 2 | 6 | 78.6 | 80.4 | -1.78 | | | | | 80.9 |
| 15 | | 3 | 7 | 80.2 | 80.8 | -0.63 | | | | | 81.5 |
| 16 | | 4 | 8 | 88.6 | 81.2 | 7.38 | | | | | 81.2 |
| 17 | 1980 | 1 | 9 | 77.5 | 81.1 | -3.60 | | | | | 81.3 |
| 18 | | 2 | 10 | 78.1 | 80.9 | -2.78 | | | | | 80.4 |
| 19 | | 3 | 11 | 79.3 | 81.3 | -1.95 | | | | | 80.6 |
| 20 | | 4 | 12 | 90.1 | 0.0 | 0.00 | | | | | 82.7 |
| 21 | 1981 | 1 | 13 | | 0.0 | 0.00 | | | | | 0.0 |
| 22 | | 2 | 14 | | 0.0 | 0.00 | | | | | 0.0 |
| 23 | | 3 | 15 | | 0.0 | 0.00 | | | | | 0.0 |
| 24 | | 4 | 16 | | 0.0 | 0.00 | | | | | 0.0 |
| 25 | 1982 | 1 | 17 | | 0.0 | 0.00 | | | | | 0.0 |
| 26 | | 2 | 18 | | 0.0 | 0.00 | | | | | 0.0 |
| 27 | | 3 | 19 | | 0.0 | 0.00 | | | | | 0.0 |
| 28 | | 4 | 20 | | 0.0 | 0.00 | | | | | 0.0 |
| 29 | 1983 | 1 | 21 | | 0.0 | 0.00 | | | | | 0.0 |
| 30 | | 2 | 22 | | 0.0 | 0.00 | | | | | 0.0 |
| 31 | | 3 | 23 | | 0.0 | 0.00 | | | | | 0.0 |
| 32 | | 4 | 24 | | 0.0 | 0.00 | | | | | 0.0 |

Figure 6.12 Quarterly calculator sales—additive seasonal decomposition.

The first step in column E is to compute a 12-month moving average of the data. The first moving average, covering January to December, is always placed next to month 7. The second moving average for February to January is placed opposite month 8 and so on. The result of this procedure is that is no moving average for the first six months and the last six months of the data. The second step is to use the moving averages to compute seasonal indexes. If we subtract each moving average from its actual value, the result is a preliminary seasonal index.

The differences are computed in column F (the actual sales in column D minus the moving average in column E). The differences for the same month in each year vary somewhat, so they are summed in column G and averaged in column I.

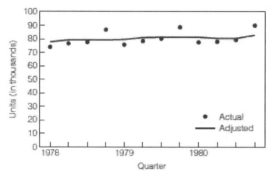

Figure 6.13 Time plot of quarterly calculator sales and seasonally adjusted values by additive decomposition. (*Source*: Figure 6.12, column D)

The average differences can be interpreted as follows. The data in January are predicted to be 8.68 units less than the average monthly data for the year. The data in July are predicted to be 22.43 units more than the average. For this interpretation to make sense, the average differences must sum to zero. The average differences actually sum to 2.23 because rounding is unavoidable. Thus, the formulas in column J normalize the differences to sum to zero. The last step is to adjust the data. The final seasonal index is subtracted from each actual data value in column D to obtain the adjusted data in column K.

## Seasonal Decomposition of Weekly Point-of-Sale Data

With scanner technology, point-of-sale (POS) data has become the basic data to improve the forecasting accuracy for detailed product sales by store in the retail industry. POS data are typically summarized in weekly periods for product detail at a store (referred to as "door" in the retail industry) level. We describe here an analysis of weekly cycles and show how weekly demand forecasts can be effectively combined with monthly seasonal patterns to improve the forecasts of very short-term trends.

The retail industry is faced with increasingly shortened lead-time demands due to changing consumer-supplier relationships and overall competitive and profitability pressures. Various industry initiatives, such as **Quick Response** (QR)), **Efficient Consumer Response** (ECR), **Continuous Replenishment Programs** (CRP), and **Vendor-Managed Inventory** (VMI), have surfaced but share a similar goal: To make every order count. Retail and consumer goods manufacturers, in particular, strive for a seamless flow of product from manufacturers to retailers through tightly integrated information systems.

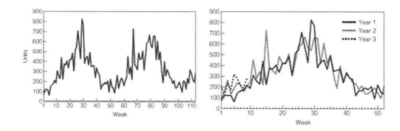

Figure 6.14 (*left*) Time plot of weekly sales of clips for sunglasses.
Figure 6.15 (*right*) Ladder chart of seasonal patterns in weekly sales of clips for sunglasses.

> ***Typical weekly POS data are characterized by volatile patterns consisting of calendar effects, promotional spikes, and seasonality.***

Figure 6.14 depicts a sample of POS data over a 112-week period that shows seasonality according to a monthly cycle, promotional peaks for a duration of one to three weeks, an outlier due to an isolated unexplained event, and minimal trend. The demand forecasting challenge is to isolate these patterns and determine their relationships to the underlying dynamics of location-specific consumer demand. By structuring patterns according to readily understood factors driving consumer demand at a store level, demand forecasters can help improve the ordering and inventory planning processes for the large numbers of SKUs required for replenishment and production planning.

Practice suggests that promotion patterns consist of a pre-promotion dip, a promotional peak, and then forward-buy dip. Such patterns are difficult to discern in real data because of the inherent volatility of weekly patterns. Although calendars for promotions can be documented, consistent patterns are nevertheless difficult to see in POS data for promoted products. With little trending evident in the disaggregated data, seasonality can be displayed by showing a week as a percentage of the annual average of weekly sales. Shown over the same period, this can lead to patterns in which the weekly variation can easily overshadow the underlying seasonal cycle in the data. Plotting the weekly sales for 52 weeks for each year in a ladder chart can also show this pattern. (Figure 6.15).

However, when we view the same data in monthly periods the seasonal pattern is much clearer, suggesting that seasonal patterns in POS data might be better analyzed at an aggregated level, such as months.

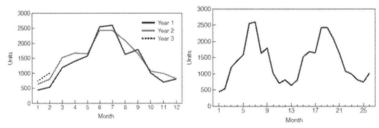

Figure 6.16 (left) Ladder chart of seasonal pattern in monthly sales of clips for sunglasses.
Figure 6.17 (*right*) Time plot of seasonal pattern in monthly sales of clips for sunglasses.

Figure 6.16 illustrates a year-over-year pattern for monthly aggregates; after aggregating the weeks into months we show the data as a time plot in Figure 6.17. The seasonal peaks and troughs within a year appear smoother and are not overshadowed by the weekly fluctuations within months.

For instance, it is a common practice to create monthly aggregates based on a 4-4-5-4-4-5-4-4-5-4-4-5 pattern for the 52 weeks in a year. When weeks are aggregated into months according to a 4-4-5 pattern, it means that month 1 is the sum of the first four weeks, month 2 is the sum of the next four weeks, and month three is the sum of the next five weeks. This pattern is repeated for each quarter in the year.

***Promotions are characterized by a pattern consisting of a pre-promotion dip, a promotional peak, and then a forward-buy dip.***

To start the decomposition, we make a seasonal adjustment of the monthly aggregated POS data, either in a multiplicative or additive mode. Because POS data tend to have small values and are generally not strongly trending, the additive decomposition might be most useful. Using the ratio-to-moving-average additive decomposition (RMA) method (as in Figure 6.12) on the monthly data results in a set of 12 additive indices or factors {-629, 9, 168, 216, 1064, 874, 288, 329, -340, -623, -635, -712} for January through December. To complete an additive decomposition, the monthly seasonal components can be applied to the weeks within the months by reversing the operation we used to translate weeks to months and using proportional week/month ratios from the same month that the adjustments are applied to. This results in a set of weekly seasonal components and a seasonally adjusted weekly series.

Once a weekly POS time series has been adjusted using the weekly seasonal components, we can continue to analyze the residual pattern for a secondary seasonal pattern.

For example, a pattern may be found that reflects the consumers' monthly buying behavior or an account manager's efforts to meet sales goals. Using a decomposition approach in which weekly cycles are analyzed within quarter seasons (by using 13 periods per quarter as seasonality), it is at times possible to reveal these consumer patterns. If properly interpreted, they can be useful in improving forecasting accuracy by improving our understanding of the buying behavior of consumers and the selling pressures of account managers.

In fact, such a secondary pattern in the POS data was found for a costume-jewelry manufacturer. The pattern showed a rise in the second week of the month when consumers may have more discretionary income for nonessentials than in the last week of a month. Moreover, there appeared to be a strong increase in sales at the end of the quarter, perhaps due to sales efforts to reach quotas.

## *Census Seasonal Adjustment Method*

Government agencies adjust statistical indicators for seasonality before publication and distribution to the public. In many industries, it is vital to use an accepted standard high-quality approach to seasonal adjustment. In regulated industries, the regulatory bodies may require this kind of reliability for the economic and cost studies submitted as part of a hearing. For example, in the semiconductor industry regional bookings and billings data are of interest to monitor changes in the book-to-bill ratio, a leading indicator for the industry. The book-to-bill ratio, reported on a seasonally adjusted basis, compares orders with shipments: a value above 1 indicates positive growth, and a value of 1.22 indicates that for every $100 of chips shipped during the month, $122 of chips were ordered. The U.S., European, Japanese, and Asian markets experienced shifts in their quarterly patterns as the industry became more global and the U.S. market share declined during the 1980s.

> *Seasonal adjustments are very important in the analysis of economic business cycles and short-term trends and the development of large-scale econometric models.*

## The Evolution of the X-13ARIMA-SEATS Program

In 1954, Julius Shiskin (1912–1978), *left*, first developed a computerized approach (known as Method I) at the U.S. Census Bureau for decomposing large numbers of time series. An improved Method II, which essentially contained refinements to the ratio-to-moving-average method, followed the first Census program very closely. Subsequent experimental variants of

Method II (known as X-1, X-2 and so on) included moving seasonal-adjustment factors and smoother and more flexible trend-cycle curves. Adjustments for variations in the number of working days were included in the last major release of the program (the X-11 variant), which appeared in 1965. Variable holidays (such as Easter) were later included in the X-11ARIMA/88 from Statistics Canada and X-13-ARIMA programs from the Census Bureau.

An important development since 1965 combines ARIMA models with the X-11 seasonal-adjustment procedure to produce future seasonal factors. To circumvent the need to apply asymmetric moving averages for the last few values, Estela Bee Dagum, *right*, at Statistics Canada developed a useful modification to the procedure in 1975, enlarging the original time series by an additional year with forecasts from ARIMA models.

This enhancement allowed for symmetric moving averages to be applied and resulted in improved estimates of current seasonal factors. The technique has shown demonstrable improvements over the X-11 method, and the X-11-ARIMA/88 implementation from Statistics Canada is being widely used now.

There have also been releases of X-12ARIMA and X-13ARIMA versions by the U.S. Census Bureau, a complete regression and time series modeling language has been added as an integral part of the program. However, for the basic seasonal decomposition, the programs produce essentially identical outputs (*https://www.census.gov/srd/www/x13as/*).

Additional releases have become available at no charge, such as X-13ARIMA-SEATS, which integrates an enhanced version of X-12ARIMA with an enhanced version of SEATS, developed by the Bank of Spain, to provide both X-11 method seasonal adjustments and ARIMA model-based seasonal adjustments and diagnostics.

The Census Bureau programs are widely used by government agencies, central banks, and corporations around the world, creating a standardized way to obtain deseasonalized data for publishing official statistics and to use in regulatory studies. These programs have seasonally adjusted a vast amount of economic and demographic time series reported by federal agencies for public use. There are separate programs to deal with monthly and quarterly data.

> *The basic goal of the X-13-ARIMA method is to estimate seasonal factors from seasonal data.*

# Why Use the X-13ARIMA-SEATS Seasonal Adjustment Program?

Sometimes unusual variation can appear in ordinary situations in demand forecasting applications. For instance, in a hotel/motel room demand data for Washington, D.C. metropolitan area (Figure 1.14), the basic seasonal decomposition can lead to a series of seasonal-irregular ratios in which the variation for a particular month (January) appears much larger than the variation for ratios in the remaining months. Let us look carefully at the causes that lead to this situation.

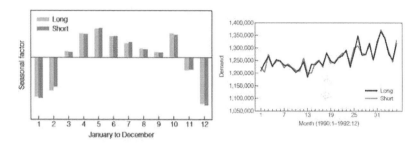

Figure 6.18 *(left)* Bar chart of seasonal factors for hotel/motel room demand (Long, 1987–1994, with two inaugural years; Short, 1990:1–1992:12, with no inaugural year). (Source: D. C. Frechtling, Practical Tourism Forecasting, 1996, Appendix 1)

Figure 6.19 *(right)* Time plot of seasonally adjusted hotel/motel room demand. (Long, 1987–1994, with two inaugural years; Short, 1990:1–1992:12, with no inaugural year)

Figure 6.18 depicts the seasonal factors for a ratio-to-moving-average (multiplicative decomposition) seasonal-adjustment process for two periods: "Long" is the period 1987–1994, in which two U.S. presidential inaugurations (January 1989 and January 1993) took place and "Short" is the period 1990–1992, in which no inaugurals took place. March, August, and September are the typical months for these data; they are right on trend. The winter months November through February run 8%–30% below trend on average. The remaining five months run 10–20% above trend.

Figure 6.19 shows the resulting seasonally adjusted data for the two decompositions. Although most seasonal factors remain fairly constant (except for February), the January inauguration following an election year appears to have an influence on the stability of the seasonal pattern. Evidently, there are significant differences in the adjusted values for the months adjacent to each January. To provide a consistent, reliable picture of the seasonal impact on the industry, we may have to rely on more sophisticated approaches, such as X-13ARIMA-SEATS, than a basic ratio-to-moving average decomposition method

## A Forecast Using X-13ARIMA-SEATS

To forecast the hotel/motel room demand data, there are now a few options:

- Create a forecast for the trend-cycle component with a trending technique, such as nonseasonal State Space forecasting (introduced in Chapter 8), nonseasonal ARIMA models (introduced in Chapter 9), or linear regression (introduced in Chapter 10). Then, re-seasonalize the point forecasts with seasonal factors derived from X-13ARIMA-SEATS.

- Create forecasts for the original data with State Space models with a trend/seasonal forecast profile (discussed in Chapters 8 and 9). Contrast the seasonal factors derived from each of these approaches.

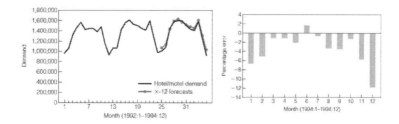

Figure 6.20 (*left*) Time plot of the 12-month forecast for monthly hotel/motel room demand using X-12ARIMA; (*right*) Bar chart of forecast percentage errors over the holdout period (1994:1–1994:12).

Figure 6.20 displays the results of a point forecast for monthly hotel/motel room demand using the last 12 months of data (1994:1–1994:12) as a holdout sample. Using data through 1993:12, we derived point forecasts for the 12 months of 1994 using the X-12 program. A comparison of these forecasts and holdout sample is shown along with the percentage errors for the months of 1994 (Figure 6.24). It appears that the projections are mostly higher than the actuals, with the greatest forecast errors in the winter months. This suggests that the impact of the two presidential inaugurations may not have been adequately discounted in the analysis.

194

## *Resistant Smoothing*

A resistant smoothing procedure is used to estimate a typical value within a range of data as a sliding window across the data. To illustrate we have used a short section of logarithms of "airline data" compiled in Box, Jenkins and Reinsel's book *Time Series Analysis: Forecasting and Control* (1994, *series G*). Figure 6.21 shows a plot of the data along with three outliers that were arbitrarily inserted for June 1957, September 1958, and July 1959 (7.0, 8.0, 3.0) to illustrate how such extreme values can be handled.

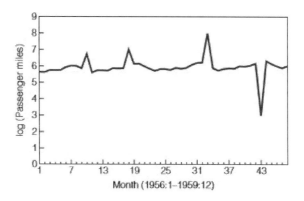

Figure 6.21 Time plot of the logarithms of the airline data, showing three inserted outliers. (*Source*: Box et al., 1994, series G)

Figure 6.22 shows the monthly values for 1956-1959. Column 1 contains the basic data and column 2 contains a 12-month moving median of the data. To compute the medians, the data have been re-sequenced (put in order from smallest to largest, 12 months at a time) and the average of the sixth and seventh values has been taken in every 12-month period.

In column 3 of Figure 6.22, a 12-month moving average of the median is calculated. The first entry in this column is positioned between the sixth and seventh moving median entries in the December 1956 row. A 3-month moving average of the means (column 4) further smoothes the data and results in a new time series with exactly 1 year of data missing at the beginning and end of the original data.

> *Resistance to outliers is also important in the smoothing of seasonal time series, in which underlying trends should not be unduly distorted by extreme values in the pattern.*

Next, a tapered moving average (tapered smooth) is used. This involves calculating weighted moving averages in which the weights diminish with distance from the month for which the calculation is being made. A scheme is used in which the weights follow a Bisquare function, of the form

$$B(u) = (1 - u^2)^2 \qquad \text{if } |u| \le 1$$
$$= 0 \qquad \text{if } |u| > 1$$

The user selects the amount of trend smoothing required. For a small, medium, and large amount of smoothing, the recommended smooth window is 7, 15, and 31, respectively. The calculation of the weights for a seven-period window bisquare weighting function is illustrated to the right.

The tapered mean is calculated by (1) multiplying the values by the appropriate weights, (2) summing up the weighted values, and (3) dividing by the sum of the weights. A sample calculation is shown in Figure 6.23. Here the months of January through July in 1957 figure into the tapered mean for April 1957. Column 5 of Figure 6.26 was compiled in this manner and shows the tapered moving averages of the values given in column 4. The tapered mean is resistant to outliers because it is an arithmetic mean of medians, which are themselves resistant to the distortion of extreme values.

$$W(t) = B\left[t/(T+1)\right] \quad t = -T, \ldots, 0, \ldots T$$

$$W(-3) = B\left(-\frac{3}{4}\right) = \left[1 - \left(-\frac{3}{4}\right)^2\right]^2 = 0.191$$

$$W(-2) = B\left(-\frac{2}{4}\right) = \left[1 - \left(-\frac{2}{4}\right)^2\right]^2 = 0.563$$

$$W(-1) = B\left(-\frac{1}{4}\right) = \left[1 - \left(-\frac{1}{4}\right)^2\right]^2 = 0.879$$

$$W(0) = B(1-0) = \left[1 - (-0)^2\right]^2 = 1.0$$

$$W(1) = B\left(\frac{1}{4}\right) = 0.879$$

$$W(2) = B\left(\frac{2}{4}\right) = 0.563$$

$$W(3) = B\left(\frac{3}{4}\right) = 0.191$$

Figure 6.22 can be extended to include additional columns. Figure 6.23 shows the continuation of the calculations involved to develop a more refined trend smooth. Here, column 6 is the moving average (column 4 of Figure 6.22) minus the tapered moving average (column 5). This result can be viewed as a systematic noise pattern about the trend and is similar to autocorrelated residuals about a regression line.

These residual values are then smoothed (column 7) and added to the trend approximation (tapered moving average in column 5) to develop the initial trend smooth that represents trend-cycle (column 8).

The seasonal values are computed next. They are then subtracted from the original data to yield trend plus irregular (T + I). The T + I series can then be smoothed to produce a resistant approximation of trend T.

*A tapered smooth, like a Bisquare, is a weighted moving average in which weights diminish with distance from the month for which the calculation is being made.*

| | | (1) | (2) | (3) | (4) | (5) |
|---|---|---|---|---|---|---|
| Year | Month | Data | 12-Mo Moving Median of (1) | 12_MAVG of (2) | 3_MAVG of (3) | Tapered MAVG of (4) |
| 1956 | Jan | 5.649 | | | | |
| | Feb | 5.624 | | | | |
| | Mar | 5.759 | | | | |
| | Apr | 5.746 | | | | |
| | May | 5.762 | | | | |
| | Jun | 5.924 | 5.753 | | | |
| | Jul | 6.023 | 5.756 | | | |
| | Aug | 6.004 | 5.756 | | | |
| | Sep | 5.872 | 5.758 | | | |
| | Oct | 6.724 | 5.807 | | | |
| | Nov | 5.602 | 5.862 | | | |
| | Dec | 5.724 | 5.862 | 5.822 | | |
| 1957 | Jan | 5.753 | 5.862 | 5.831 | 5.831 | 5.84 |
| | Feb | 5.707 | 5.862 | 5.84 | 5.84 | 5.844 |
| | Mar | 5.875 | 5.862 | 5.849 | 5.849 | 5.848 |
| | Apr | 5.852 | 5.862 | 5.858 | 5.856 | 5.854 |
| | May | 5.872 | 5.862 | 5.862 | 5.861 | 5.858 |
| | Jun | 7* | 5.862 | 5.863 | 5.863 | 5.862 |
| | Jul | 6.146 | 5.862 | 5.864 | 5.864 | 5.864 |
| | Aug | 6.146 | 5.862 | 5.865 | 5.865 | 5.865 |
| | Sep | 6.001 | 5.862 | 5.865 | 5.865 | 5.866 |
| | Oct | 5.849 | 5.862 | 5.866 | 5.866 | 5.867 |
| | Nov | 5.72 | 5.872 | 5.868 | 5.868 | 5.869 |
| | Dec | 5.817 | 5.872 | 5.871 | 5.871 | 5.871 |
| 1958 | Jan | 5.829 | 5.872 | 5.873 | 5.873 | 5.873 |
| | Feb | 5.762 | 5.872 | 5.875 | 5.875 | 5.876 |
| | Mar | 5.892 | 5.872 | 5.877 | 5.877 | 5.879 |
| | Apr | 5.852 | 5.888 | 5.88 | 5.881 | 5.883 |
| | May | 5.894 | 5.888 | 5.886 | 5.887 | 5.889 |
| | Jun | 6.075 | 5.888 | 5.896 | 5.896 | 5.896 |
| | Jul | 6.196 | 5.889 | 5.906 | 5.904 | 5.903 |
| | Aug | 6.225 | 5.889 | 5.911 | 5.911 | 5.91 |
| | Sep | 8* | 5.89 | 5.917 | 5.917 | 5.917 |
| | Oct | 5.883 | 5.938 | 5.922 | 5.923 | 5.924 |
| | Nov | 5.737 | 5.994 | 5.931 | 5.931 | 5.932 |
| | Dec | 5.82 | 5.994 | 5.939 | 5.94 | 5.941 |
| 1959 | Jan | 5.886 | 5.934 | 5.949 | 5.949 | 5.95 |
| | Feb | 5.835 | 5.934 | 5.959 | 5.959 | 5.959 |
| | Mar | 6.006 | 5.934 | 5.969 | 5.969 | 5.969 |
| | Apr | 5.981 | 5.994 | 5.98 | 5.979 | 5.977 |
| | May | 6.04 | 5.994 | 5.988 | 5.987 | 5.985 |
| | Jun | 6.157 | 6.005 | 5.992 | 5.992 | 5.993 |
| | Jul | 3* | 6.008 | 5.995 | 5.998 | 6.001 |
| | Aug | 6.326 | 6.008 | 6.008 | 6.008 | 6.01 |
| | Sep | 6.138 | 6.021 | 6.02 | 6.02 | 6.021 |
| | Oct | 6.009 | 6.036 | 6.033 | 6.033 | 6.031 |
| | Nov | 5.892 | 6.036 | 6.045 | 6.045 | 6.039 |
| | Dec | 6.004 | 6.036 | 6.056 | 6.056 | 6.045 |
| | | | | 6.067 | | |

*Original values: June 1957, 6.045; September 1958, 6.008; July 1959, 6.306. (MAVG, moving average)

Figure 6.22 Logarithms of the monthly airline data for 1956–1959, with three outliers (MAVG, moving average).

| Month | Data* | Weight | Weighted Values | Tapered Moving Average |
|---|---|---|---|---|
| Jan | 5.831 | 0.191 | 1.114 | |
| Feb | 5.84 | 0.563 | 3.288 | |
| Mar | 5.849 | 0.879 | 5.141 | |
| Apr | 5.856 | 1 | 5.856 | 5.854 |
| May | 5.861 | 0.879 | 5.152 | |
| Jun | 5.863 | 0.563 | 3.301 | |
| Jul | 5.864 | 0.191 | 1.12 | |
| Total | 4.266 | 24.972 | | |

Tapered mean = 24.972/4.266 = 5.854

Figure 6.23 Calculation for a tapered mean of log-transformed airline data for April 1957.

| Year | Month | (6) (4) − (5) | (7) Tapered MAVG of (6) | (8) Initial Trend Smooth (7) + (5) | (9) Data Trend (1) − (8) (= T + 1) |
|------|-------|------|------|------|------|
| 1956 | Jan | | | | |
| | Feb | | | | |
| | Mar | | | | |
| | : | | | | |
| | Oct | | | | |
| | Nov | | | | |
| | Dec | | | | |
| 1957 | Jan | −0.009 | −0.004 | 5.836 | −0.083 |
| | Feb | −0.004 | −0.003 | 5.84 | −0.133 |
| | Mar | 0.001 | −0.001 | 5.847 | 0.026 |
| | Apr | 0.002 | 0 | 5.854 | −0.002 |
| | May | 0.003 | 0.001 | 5.859 | 0.013 |
| | Jun | 0.001 | 0.001 | 5.863 | 1.137 |
| | Jul | 0 | 0.001 | 5.865 | 0.281 |
| | Aug | 0 | 0 | 5.865 | 0.281 |
| | Sep | −0.001 | −0.001 | 5.865 | 0.136 |
| | Oct | −0.001 | −0.001 | 5.866 | −0.017 |
| | Nov | −0.001 | −0.001 | 5.868 | −0.148 |
| | Dec | 0 | −0.001 | 5.87 | −0.053 |

Figure 6.24 Continuation of the calculation for a tapered mean of log-transformed airline data for April 1957.

## Mini Case: A PEER Demand Forecasting Process for Turkey Dinner Cost

*Prepared by Jared Endicott following his participation in a CPDF Workshop in Istanbul.*

The CPDF® industrial professional development workshops (*http://cpdftraining.org/*) and the follow-up certification designation to become a Certified Professional Demand Forecaster are great learning experiences, helping participants to understand in a practical way what are often complex forecasting concepts and techniques. The names of these concepts alone are extremely daunting for those not initiated in statistical jargon and notation, like Holt-Winters exponential smoothing, autoregressive integrated moving averages (ARIMA), median absolute deviation from the median (MdAD), and the merits of using the nonconventional robust correlation coefficient of standardized sums and differences r*(SSD) over the traditional Pearson's product moment correlation coefficient r are prime examples of how intimidating these forecasting tools sound. The CPDF® industrial training workshops and certification spreadsheet exercises can help one come to grips with the above concepts by showing how to put them to use in practice.

The core framework for the CPDF® training is the PEER forecasting process. This is a structured, systematic and iterative process to maintain forecasting excellence with four phases: Preparation, Execution, Evaluation, and Reconciliation.

- In the preparation phase, the forecaster must gauge the needs and requirements, get a grasp on the business environnement, seek out reliable data sources, locate predictive factors and use a feedback process to review and prioritize these factors.
- In the execution phase, the forecaster applies forecasting methodologies by choosing quantitative and qualitative approaches, building and selecting models, and producing forecasts with these models.
- In the evaluation phase, the forecaster measures the relative accuracy of the various models, backtests with hold-out sample simulations, and observes performance through ongoing examination of model accuracy in an iterative cyclical process of structured judgment.
- In the reconciliation phase, the forecaster must bring together the findings into a final model and forecast selection with an articulate presentation to decision makers and stakeholders.

On an annual forecasting cycle, the process starts with gathering information of the relevant factors and theory that pertains to Thanksgiving Dinner prices (evaluation), then followed by developing and utilizing forecasting models (execution), monitoring and analyzing the accuracy and errors of the previous year's forecasts (evaluation), and providing presentations and explanations of findings in forecast presentations (reconciliation). This is basically the PEER process.

For now, we move to the evaluation stage in order to consider last year's forecast of the 2013 cost for Thanksgiving dinner. The price survey comes from the **American Farm Bureau Federation** (AFBF), and it is the average cost of Thanksgiving dinner for 10 people. In the application, an increase of 3.6% was predicted, but average prices actually fell by 0.9%, so with a forecast $51.26, the cost went down to $49.04. The miss was favorable in terms of the consumer, but falling prices can also be a troubling sign of deflation and a weakening economy. The AFBF analysis does not indicate weakness in the economy though, with most factors simply unchanged, although the biggest factor—price of turkey is down. Deputy Chief Economist for the AFBF John Anderson says, "Slightly higher turkey production for much of the year coupled with an increase in birds in cold storage may be responsible for the moderate price decrease our shoppers reported." (Grondine and Sirekis, 2013)

Upon further evaluation, the actual number fell outside the measured 95% prediction interval. This seemed odd, since the forecast was off by only 4.5%, which is a better performance than the previous two attempts, and those higher errors were within the 68% prediction interval. The prediction interval should not have been symmetrical (same percentage high as low, especially in light of the higher probability of price declines than price increases, which have occurred eight times of the last twenty-seven years. The measurement of prediction intervals through modeling should have more focus in future forecasts.

In previous years, the absolute percent errors (APEs) and mean absolute percent error (MAPE) were calculated, but it was stressed in the Istanbul workshop this year that it is good to consider other evaluation measures as well, such as median absolute percent error (MdAPE). The Absolute Percentage Errors (APE) were 9.9%, 4.8%, and 4.5% for 2011, 2012, and 2013 respectively. This works out to a MAPE of 6.4% and a MdAPE of 4.8%. It is good to look at multiple measures of performance, with the MdAPE being particularly helpful because it is more robust and less sensitive to outliers. We will cover what can be learned about robust methods in more detail in a later section.

## Applying ARIMA Models

Understanding how to use ARIMA models for forecasting frequently stumps the practitioner, because of its mathematical formulation and use of notation. While one does not need to be an expert statistician by any means, a demand forecaster can be much more comfortable with the theory, concepts, and appropriate use of ARIMA models with some practical training through examples.

This is a time series technique in which the historical patterns of the data are being analysed and forecasted through a formal model building process. The major benefit of ARIMA models over Exponential Smoothing (ES) models or a seasonal decomposition method is the way that this alternative approach takes into account autocorrelations. Autocorrelation is the momentum in the data that correlates the current value to past values. The standard strategy to ARIMA modeling is called Box-Jenkins (named after the developers of the methodology), and it involves a three-part iterative process of identification, estimation, and diagnostic checking.

It is not the intent here to provide details of these techniques, but rather to demonstrate some of what was used for the Thanksgiving Dinner forecasts. Given that Thanksgiving Dinner forecasts are annual, and we really need to use a seasonal ARIMA model for understanding

200

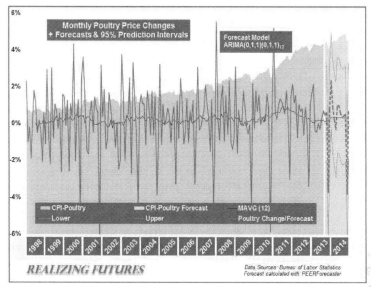

the seasonal nature of the problem, it necessary to forecast the monthly price changes for poultry. First thing to do is visualize and explore the historical data to determine if there is a seasonal and trend pattern that can be modeled. For this, one might just look at the time plot of the monthly data. Or, to have a more reliable indication of pattern, we can use an exploratory method by constructing an ANalysis Of VAriance (ANOVA) decomposition that measures how much of the differences between the data points belong to seasonality, trend, or irregular factors [Excel Data Analysis Add-in: Analysis Tools > ANOVA: Two Factor without Replication].

For ARIMA, the identification phase is typically carried out with autocorrelation functions (ACFs) and partial autocorrelation functions (PACFs). Next with estimation, the model parameters are inferred from the data, and once preliminary models are chosen the forecasts produced from them can be checked diagnostically with an analysis of the residuals between the model data and the actual data.

The model building process of identification, estimation, and diagnostic checking is iterated until the residuals from the model resemble randomly distributed white noise. For the first iteration of poultry price forecasts, I used a common benchmark, ARIMA $(0,1,1)(0,1,1)_{12}$, the so-called "Airline Model" used by Box and Jenkins to demonstrate their seasonal method with airline passenger mile data. It turns out this is the best performer compared to three alternative seasonal ARIMA models I tried, in terms of testing against a hold-out sample of actual data, with monthly simulations evaluated using a waterfall display. An illustration of the poultry price data and forecasts are shown in the chart below.

In tjis chart there is a distinct seasonal pattern in the month over month change in poultry prices, with a dramatic drop in price every November. This seems a contrary to economic assumptions at first glance. The law of demand suggests that if there is an increase in demand of something, say turkey for Thanksgiving dinner, then the price will be driven up, all other things the same. During Thanksgiving turkeys sell at prices well below cost, with the mark down being a strategy by competitive retailers to get customers in the door in order to capture the sales on other items (Sullivan, 2013). The laws of supply and demand are still contingent, and the competitive custom of displaying the holiday bird as an enticing loss leader becomes an extenuating circumstance that defies normal price behavior. The turkey price reverses course in December, going back up, and over time the trend is generally a higher price for poultry each year, as illustrated by the chart below.

# Learning About Robust/Resistant Methods

Another technique found in the CPDF training is the use of transformations to handle nonlinear data. Following the CPDF II

### Thanksgiving Dinner Price Changes Correlation Matrix (1999-2012)

| Robust Correlation Matrix | Thanksgiving Dinner | Food | Consumer Prices | Poultry-Nov | Oil | M1 Money |
|---|---|---|---|---|---|---|
| Thanksgiving Dinner | 1.00 | | | | | |
| Food | 0.79 | 1.00 | | | | |
| Consumer Prices | 0.24 | 0.52 | 1.00 | | | |
| Poultry-Nov | -0.31 | -0.25 | -0.18 | 1.00 | | |
| Oil | -0.47 | -0.02 | 0.32 | 0.50 | 1.00 | |
| M1 Money | 0.26 | 0.16 | -0.54 | 0.29 | 0.06 | 1.00 |
| Ordinary Correlation Matrix | Thanksgiving Dinner | Food | Consumer Prices | Poultry-Nov | Oil | M1 Money |
| Thanksgiving Dinner | 1.00 | | | | | |
| Food | 0.54 | 1.00 | | | | |
| Consumer Prices | 0.47 | 0.68 | 1.00 | | | |
| Poultry-Nov | 0.49 | 0.58 | 0.47 | 1.00 | | |
| Oil | -0.05 | 0.13 | 0.66 | 0.31 | 1.00 | |
| M1 Money | 0.32 | 0.29 | -0.19 | 0.66 | -0.54 | 1.00 |

*REALIZING FUTURES*

Data Sources: American Farm Bureau Federation, Bureau of Labor Statistics, Federal Reserve, InflationData.com

Workshop in Istanbul in 2013, we started using nonconventional methods of analysis, techniques that are robust and more suited for data that do not conform to the conventional assumptions. In terms of statistical models,

it is conventional to use measures of central tendency and dispersion that are derived from the mean and the standard deviation. In a linear and symmetric world, where error distributions are assumed to conform to the normal bell curve. These methods are optimal, but in the real world where we are often confronted with data that are nonlinear these methods can be ill suited. It is these nonlinear situations that call for nonconventional solutions.

The most conventional and familiar statistical techniques, in terms of data analysis and forecasting, derive from the mean and the standard deviation. This is the method of calculating a simple average or arithmetic mean from a set of numbers and then using that average to calculate the spread of the data around the average. After the mean and the standard deviation are analysed, one or more data sets can be related using ordinary correlation and linear regression. If the underlying data are linear and normally distributed, then the conventional methods are most appropriate. Conventional methods of analysis may provide misleading results when applied to nonlinear data, because these methods are sensitive (not resistant) to outliers and unusual distortions. When these problematic situations arise, it is advisable to adjust or transform the data into a linear perspective, by handling outliers, calculating differences, or converting to logarithms. Massaged data can then be input into the conventional models to better effect.

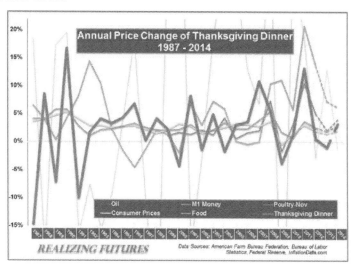

Rather than simply locate and adjust or remove outliers, another approach is to complement the conventional methods involving means and standard deviations with nonconventional robust methods that work better non-normal data. Instead of using the mean as the measure of central tendency, the median will not be affected as much by outliers and is said to be more resistant. Rather than use standard deviation or mean absolute deviation from the mean (MAD) to estimate the scale, or spread, we use median absolute deviation from the median (MdAD).

Along with using the product-moment correlation coefficient r, we can also relate two or more variables by using a robust correlation coefficient, called the standardized sums and differences r*(SSD). Below are two correlation matrices that display the correlation coefficients of the prices changes of Thanksgiving dinner against related variables, one produced by the ordinary correlation coefficient r and the other with a robust method. After that scatter plots of these factors are shown, with straight line fits associated with the ordinary correlation coefficient *r*.

The changing price of Thanksgiving dinner is most closely associated with the price of food more generally, and is also the only variable that showed an improved view of the correlation with the robust method. The association with changes in consumer prices is much weaker with the robust correlation, and poultry prices in November show a different direction of the correlation altogether, going from positive in the ordinary method to negative in the robust method. The reversal of signs between the two measures of correlation between Thanksgiving Dinner and November poultry prices is worthy of a closer analysis as to the root cause.

## Forecasting Thanksgiving Dinner Inflation for 2014

For my primary forecasting task of predicting the price of Thanksgiving Dinner next year I tested out a few different methods and models. Times series methods are one possible approach, like the ARIMA example discussed earlier, or exponential smoothing, which both use the historical values of the same data for forecasting. These models allow for seasonal and trend effects to indicate a likely future course. On the other hand, linear regression is a tool by which we leverage correlations and causal relationships, using independent variables to estimate future values of a forecast variable, using both linear regression and robust regression modeling.

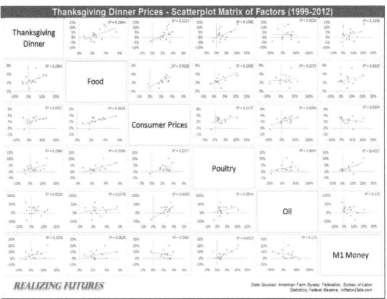

There are pros and cons to each approach, depending on the forecasting situation, such as whether leading indicators are available or unusual patterns are found in the historical data. With this in mind, I blended a few approaches. Combining forecasts from diverse models has merits, including robustness, which I discuss in more depth in the article Macroeconomic Forecasting with Diverse Predictions.

The forecast for the cost of Thanksgiving dinner in 2014, as measured by the American Farm Bureau Federation, is $50.63. This is a 3.2% lift from the 2013 cost of $49.04. With 68% confidence, we estimate that prices will come in between $48.10 and $53.43. Alternatively, with 95% confidence, we predict that prices will land between $45.58 and $56.23. The prediction intervals are wider than were set for the 2013 forecast, and this should allow for greater contingency in the price movements. We are expecting consumer prices to grow by 2.1% and food prices to grow by 3.0%, and I expect the change in price for turkey dinner to move in the same direction with a modest magnitude.

## Works Cited

1. "Cost of Classic Thanksgiving Dinner Down for 2013". American Farm Bureau Federation . Contacts: Tracy Taylor Grondine and Cyndie Sirekis. 14 Nov. 2013. Web. 14 Nov. 2013.
2. Sullivan, Paul. "In the Labyrinthe of Turkey Pricing, a Reason Under Every Giblet." The New York Times. 8 Nov 2011.

## Postscript

The biggest lesson learned in Istanbul, Turkey is not one that we applied to forecasting Thanksgiving Dinner, but it is one that gives the greatest hope about this magnificent nation's future. This forecaster fell in love with Istanbul in the short time he was there, which was a relatively serene week the month before the Taksim Square protests over Gezi Park broke out, a situation I covered in the article, Taksim: Tranquility before the Tumult.

I marveled in the history of the Byzantine and Ottoman Empires with visits to Galata Tower, Blue Mosque, Aya Sofya, Topkapı Palace, Basilica Cistern, and a relaxing cruise down the Bosphorus Strait with my friend Sinan. We even visited the Grand Bazaar where I picked up a necklace for my wife, and spent some time negotiating over carpets. While enjoying cay, tasty kebabs, and Turkish coffee, I encountered a culture that has preserved and honored its rich heritage while also embracing modernity and a dynamic future. In an interesting coincidence for this forecasting trip, I also had a chance to see a relic from the Oracle of Delphi, a piece of the Pythia's tripod located on the site of Constantinople's old Hippodrome which is now in front of the Blue Mosque.

## *Takeaways*

➤ Seasonal adjustment is a useful procedure that helps identify turning points in the economy or the trends in the demand for products and services.

➤ Knowledge of the seasonal pattern also helps in planning employee workloads and inventory levels. If we can remove seasonality from a time series, we can apply a number of forecasting techniques that otherwise would not handle seasonal data (e.g., some of the State Space forecasting models with non-seasonal forecast profiles, to be discussed in Chapter 8).

➤ The X-13ARIMA-SEATS is a widely used seasonal adjustment software program produced, distributed at no cost, and maintained by the U.S. Census Bureau (*https://www.census.gov/srd/www/x13as/*). The program provides a proven, standardized procedure for deseasonalizing and creating trend-cycle decompositions for thousands of time series data in government and business. These programs are capable of mass-processing data and producing detailed analyses of seasonal factors and of trend-cycle and irregular variations; they can be run in an additive or multiplicative form for quarterly or monthly data.

➤ The use of resistant smoothing techniques is demonstrated in the calculation of a tapered smooth. Twelve-month moving medians of a time series eliminate the influence of extreme values. Bisquare weights (which diminish in magnitude with distance from the time for the calculation) are calculated and then used to smooth these medians.

# 7

# Trend-Cycle Forecasting with Turning Points

*The only function of economic forecasting is to make astrology look respectable.*

EZRA SOLOMON (1920–2002), although often attributed to

JOHN KENNETH GALBRAITH (1908–2006)

This chapter describes how to

- use economic leading indicators as trend-cycle factors of demand
- characterize the variability in trending patterns
- identify serial correlation in trend-cycle data patterns
- detect and remove non-stationary trending behavior in time series

So far, we have seen how economic time series show historical patterns primarily in terms of trend, business cycle, and to a lesser extent seasonality. In this chapter, we consider how a lack of time dependence in the average behavior and variability relates to the uncertainty factor in demand forecasting.

When statistical techniques are combined with economic theory, it makes up what is known as **econometrics**. Econometric techniques have been widely applied as a way to model a macro economy. Macroeconomic demand analysis and econometric methods are used extensively in forecasting, structural and policy analysis in a wide variety of business planning applications. In this chapter, we offer an overview, without much technical detail, of the uses and pitfalls of econometric analysis in demand forecasting.

We discuss the method of **leading indicators** as the most important aspect of any macroeconomic forecasting activity dealing with business forecasts of the levels of economic indicators in econometric models.

We also discuss the measurement of the impact of expansions and contractions on businesses, government, or public sector organizations; and policy studies to assess the impact of changing economic and demographic assumptions on business and public programs.

## *Demand Forecasting with Economic Indicators*

Before creating forecasting models for products and services, demand forecasters need to identify the important features, uses, and interpretations of the factors that model the macroeconomy so that maximum benefit can be derived from these techniques in practical situations. The goal is to acquire the information needed to select the indicators that will help structure a framework for demand forecast modeling and judgment from a macro or top-down perspective.

Econometric techniques have been widely applied as a way to model the macroeconomy. Macroeconomic demand deals with the aggregates of income, employment, and price levels. The uses of econometric modeling and analysis techniques can be classified by the way outputs are required. The outputs produce three classes of applications for econometric modeling (structural models, policy analysis and forecasting), of which the most widely applicable use is that of **econometric forecasting**.

*Applications of econometrics include structural models, policy analysis, and forecasting.*

In econometric forecasting, the general focus is the development of a set of equations based on economic rationale, whose parameters are estimated using a statistical methodology. The model is designed to provide the business variable(s) with some explanatory underpinnings, but is also able to generate extrapolative values for future periods. That is, the model offers predictive values for the output variable(s) outside the sample of data actually observed. In practice, the statistical estimation procedures are evaluated from the perspective of forecasting performance through the up- and downturns of business cycles and using leading indicators.

## Origin of Leading Indicators

 The method of leading indicators dates back to the sharp business recession of 1937–1938. At that time, an effort was initiated by the US National Bureau of Economic Research (NBER) to devise a system that would signal the end of a recession. Arthur F. Burns (1904–1987), *left*, and Wesley C. Mitchell (1874–1948 *right*, first developed a comprehensive description of business cycle activity in the economy that became the foundation of classical methods of business cycle analysis.

| BUSINESS CYCLE REFERENCE DATES | | DURATION IN MONTHS | | | |
|---|---|---|---|---|---|
| Peak | Trough | Contraction | Expansion | Cycle | |
| Quarterly dates are in parentheses | | Peak to Trough | Previous trough to this peak | Trough from Previous Trough | Peak from Previous Peak |
| | December 1854 (IV) | -- | -- | -- | -- |
| June 1857(II) | December 1858 (IV) | 18 | 30 | 48 | -- |
| October 1860(III) | June 1861 (III) | 8 | 22 | 30 | 40 |
| April 1865(I) | December 1867 (I) | 32 | 46 | 78 | 54 |
| June 1869(II) | December 1870 (IV) | 18 | 18 | 36 | 50 |
| October 1873(III) | March 1879 (I) | 65 | 34 | 99 | 52 |
| March 1882(I) | May 1885 (II) | 38 | 36 | 74 | 101 |
| March 1887(II) | April 1888 (I) | 13 | 22 | 35 | 60 |
| July 1890(III) | May 1891 (II) | 10 | 27 | 37 | 40 |
| January 1893(I) | June 1894 (II) | 17 | 20 | 37 | 30 |
| December 1895(IV) | June 1897 (II) | 18 | 18 | 36 | 35 |
| June 1899(III) | December 1900 (IV) | 18 | 24 | 42 | 42 |
| September 1902(IV) | August 1904 (III) | 23 | 21 | 44 | 39 |
| May 1907(II) | June 1908 (II) | 13 | 33 | 46 | 56 |
| January 1910(I) | January 1912 (IV) | 24 | 19 | 43 | 32 |
| January 1913(I) | December 1914 (IV) | 23 | 12 | 35 | 36 |
| August 1918(III) | March 1919 (I) | 7 | 44 | 51 | 67 |
| January 1920(I) | July 1921 (III) | 18 | 10 | 28 | 17 |
| May 1923(II) | July 1924 (III) | 14 | 22 | 36 | 40 |
| October 1926(III) | November 1927 (IV) | 13 | 27 | 40 | 41 |
| August 1929(III) | March 1933 (I) | 43 | 21 | 64 | 34 |
| May 1937(II) | June 1938 (II) | 13 | 50 | 63 | 93 |
| February 1945(I) | October 1945 (IV) | 8 | 80 | 88 | 93 |
| November 1948(IV) | October 1949 (IV) | 11 | 37 | 48 | 45 |
| July 1953(II) | May 1954 (II) | 10 | 45 | 55 | 56 |
| August 1957(III) | April 1958 (II) | 8 | 39 | 47 | 49 |
| April 1960(II) | February 1961 (I) | 10 | 24 | 34 | 32 |
| December 1969(IV) | November 1970 (IV) | 11 | 106 | 117 | 116 |
| November 1973(IV) | March 1975 (I) | 16 | 36 | 52 | 47 |
| January 1980(I) | July 1980 (III) | 6 | 58 | 64 | 74 |
| July 1981(III) | November 1982 (IV) | 16 | 12 | 28 | 18 |
| July 1990(III) | March 1991(I) | 8 | 92 | 100 | 108 |
| March 2001(I) | November 2001 (IV) | 8 | 120 | 128 | 128 |
| December 2007 (IV) | June 2009 (II) | 18 | 73 | 91 | 81 |

| Average, all cycles: | | | | | |
|---|---|---|---|---|---|
| 1854-2009 (33 cycles) | | 17.5 | 38.7 | 56.2 | 56.4* |
| 1854-1919 (16 cycles) | | 21.6 | 26.6 | 48.2 | 48.9** |
| 1919-1945 (6 cycles) | | 18.2 | 35.0 | 53.2 | 53.0 |
| 1945-2009 (11 cycles) | | 11.1 | 58.4 | 69.5 | 68.5 |

\* 32 cycles
\*\* 15 cycles

Figure 7.1 Business cycle referece dates, 1857–2009. (*Source*: NBER)

A considerable amount of data, assembled by the NBER since the 1920s, has been analyzed to gain a better understanding of business cycles. These data, which included monthly, quarterly, and annual series on prices, employment, and production, resulted in a collection of 21 promising economic indicators that were selected on the basis of past performance and to the first recession in a decade and the tenth since World War II.

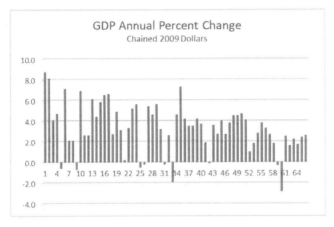

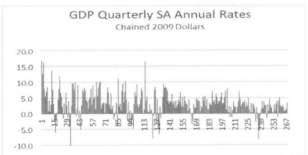

Figure 7.2 Coincident indicator of the U.S. economy: (*top*) Bar chart of GDP annual percent change in billions of chained 2009 dollars for 1950 to 2015; (*bottom*) percentage change of GDP quarterly seasonally adjusted annual rates for 1950: I–2016: III. (*Source: https://www.bea.gov/*)

This recession lasted eight months, ending in November 2001. Figure 7.1 illustrates business cycle turning points for historical U.S. data from future promise as reliable indicators of business revival. Over the years, this effort has been greatly expanded to other public and private agencies. To this day, the NBER publishes turning points of business cycle peaks and troughs. The longest economic expansion on record ended in March 2001 and gave way the mid-1800s to 2009.A number of time series, such as employment, indexes of consumer and producer prices, and manufacturers' orders, are published in newspapers, business journals and websites. As indicators of the nation's economic health, professional economists and the business community follow them very closely, especially during periods of rapid change in the pace of business activity.

For convenience of interpretation, economic indicators have been classified into three groups: leading, coincident, and lagging. **Leading indicators** are those that provide advance warning of probable changes in economic activity. Indicators that confirm changes previously indicated are known as **lagging indicators**. **Coincident indicators** are those that reflect the current performance of the economy. Coincident indicators provide a measure of current economic activity. They are the most familiar and include GDP, industrial production, personal income, retail sales, and employment.

> *Economic indicators are classified as leading, lagging or coincident with changes in economic activity.*

Figure 7.2 (*top*) shows the annual GDP percentage changes in billions of chained 2009 dollars from 1950 to 2015. The GDP is mostly trending, but the economic cycles are nevertheless in evidence. To highlight the quarter-to-quarter changes, Figure 7.2 (*bottom*) depicts the percentage changes in seasonally adjusted annual rates for the period 1950: I–2016: III. The GDP is a coincident indicator of the U.S. economy.

## Use of Leading Indicators

It would be very useful to demand forecasters and planners to have some advance warning of an impending change in the local, national, or world economy. Whereas **coincident indicators** are used to indicate whether the economy is currently experiencing expansion, recession, or inflation, leading indicators help forecasters to assess short-term trends in the coincident indicators. In addition, leading indicators help planners and policy makers anticipate adverse effects on the economy and examine the feasibility of taking corrective steps.

In individual sectors, such as agriculture, leading indicators have played a major part in short-term production forecasting. For example, the estimation of the number of acres planted to spring wheat is a good indication of harvested acreage. Economic indicator analysis has also been used to assist investors in optimizing the rate of return in their asset allocation between stocks and fixed income securities.

> *Knowledge of current economic conditions can be found in the duration, rate, and magnitude of recovery or contractions in business cycles.*

Among the leading indicators in business forecasting, housing starts, new orders for durable goods, construction contracts, formation of new business enterprises, hiring rates, and average length of workweek are the most commonly mentioned. In recent times, weekly initial employment claims, expressed in terms of a 4-week moving average, are getting a great deal of attention in the media. Housing starts, a key leading indicator plotted in Figure 7.3, tend to lead fluctuations in overall economic activity.

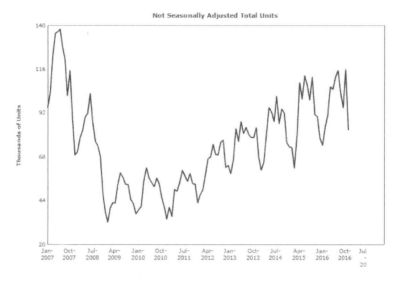

Figure 7.3 Time plot of monthly housing starts (total housing units started), January 2007–November 2016. (*Source*: *http://www.census.gov/econ/currentdata/*

A useful set of indicators for revealing and explaining the economy's broad cyclical movements includes manufacturers' shipments and orders (Figure 7.4). These are comprehensive indicators of industrial activity and are especially important to demand forecasters because the durable goods sector (plant equipment and durable machinery, automobiles, etc.) is the economy's most volatile component.

Figure 7.4a displays total manufacturers' shipments and the 3-month moving average in billions of dollars for the time period May 1999 to May 2001, Figure 7.4b shows total manufacturers' orders, Figure 7.4c shows total inventory, and Figure 7.4d displays the ratios of unfilled orders and total inventory to shipments.

Shipments are an indicator of current economic activity, measuring the dollar value of products sold by all manufacturing establishments.

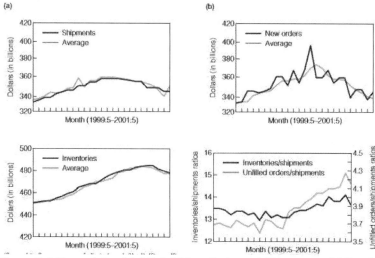

Figure 7.4 Time plots of (a) Total Manufacturers' Shipments, (b) Total Manufacturers' Orders, (c) Total Inventory, and (d) ratios of Unfilled Orders and Total inventory to Shipments in billions of seasonally adjusted current dollars for May 1999 to May 2011.

Orders, on the other hand, are a valuable leading indicator. They measure the dollar value of new orders and the net order cancellations received by all manufacturers. The two series are distorted by inflation because there is no relevant price index to convert it to real terms. It is the difference between shipments and orders, which shows what is happening to the backlog of unfilled orders that gives insight into the degree of sustainability of current national output.

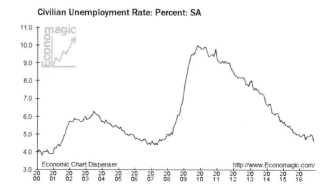

Figure 7.5 Time plot of U.S. civilian unemployment rates, January 2000–November 2016.

213

The data are widely used by private economists, corporations, trade associations, investment consultants, and researchers for market analysis and economic forecasting; and by the news media in general business coverage and specialized commentary.

An example of a lagging indicator is the unemployment rate (Figure 7.5). Although it is frequently quoted in the press, demand forecasters should realize that the unemployment rate is not an indicator of future or even current labor market conditions.

> *A composite indicator provides a single measure of complicated economic activities that experience common fluctuations.*

## Composite Indicators

Economists have developed composite indicators to reduce the number of series that must be reviewed and at the same time not lose a great deal of information. These series provide single measures of complicated economic activities that experience common fluctuations. The procedure involved includes amplitude adjustment, in which the month-to-month percentage change of each series in the composite is standardized so that all series are expressed in comparable units. The average month-to-month change, without regard to sign, is 1.0. The score it receives from the scoring plan weights each individual series.

If an index shows an increase of 2.0 in a month, it is rising twice as fast as its average rate of change in the past. If an index increases by 0.5, it is rising only one-half as fast as its historical rate of increase. Composite indicators have been developed for the leading, coincident, and lagging series.

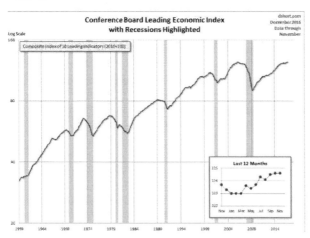

Figure 7.6 Time plot of a composite index of leading indicators with recessions highlighted, January 1959–November 2016.

One problem with interpreting an index of leading indicators is that its month-to-month changes can be erratic (Figure 7.5); however, comparing movements of the index over a longer span helps to bring out the underlying cyclical movements. For example, Figure 7.7 shows the percentage change in the current level of the leading index from the average level of the preceding 12 months. On that basis, the leading indicators have declined (i.e., fallen below zero) before every one of the seven recessions since 1970.

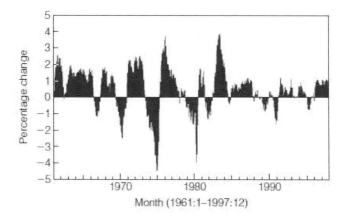

Figure 7.7 Time plot of the percentage change in the current level of the leading index from the average level of the preceding 12 months, January 1961–December 1997.

## Reverse Trend Adjustment of the Leading Indicators

Economists have been concerned about two aspects of the leading indicators: (a) the lead at the business cycle peak is much longer than the lead at the trough, and (b) leading indicators do not have the long-term trend that the economy has, as measured by coincident indicators.

Because the objective of macroeconomic forecasting is to predict current levels rather than detrended levels, the reverse trend adjustment procedure adds a trend to the leading indicators (rather than removing the trend from the coincident indicators). First, however, it is necessary to eliminate whatever trend already exists in the leading indicators. Then the trend of the coincident indicators (based on full cycles) is added to the detrended leading indicators.

The effect of reverse trend adjustment is to shorten the lead time at business-cycle peaks and increase the lead time at troughs. It also tends to reduce the number of false signals of recession that are evident when the unadjusted index turns down but a recession does not occur.

Because reverse trend adjustment helps to reduce the lead time at peaks and increase the lead time at troughs, it makes the two lead times more equal. This lessens the reaction time at the peak, however. Even with reverse trend adjustment, the lead at the peaks is approximately one or two months longer, on the average, than the lead at the troughs.

In forecasting with regression models (to be discussed in Chapter 12), the generally different lead times must be reckoned with before regression models are used. Because regression models do not offer us a simple solution to vary the lead or lag times in the explanatory variables at different periods in the cycle, the indicators tend to average the impact of the lesser lead or lag at either the peak or the trough. It is possible to have one model in which the indicator has as its lead time the appropriate lead for a peak and a second model that has as its lead time the appropriate lead for a trough. Then, either the first or second model is used to generate forecasts, depending on the state of the business cycle.

## Sources of Indicators

On a monthly basis, the U.S. Conference Board publishes current data for many different indicators. The charts and graphs cover the national income and product accounts series, cyclical indicators, series on anticipations and intentions, analytical measures, and international comparisons. The series are usually seasonally adjusted and the NBER reference dates for recessions and expansions are shown. It is apparent from the plots that business contractions are generally shorter than business expansions. The average peacetime cycle is slightly less than 4 years.

## Selecting Indicators

Specified criteria have been applied by the NBER to hundreds of economic series from which a list of indicators could be selected. A score can be given for each of six criteria, and those series with the highest scores can then be retained. The scoring is subjective in many aspects.

**Economic significance**. Some aspects of criteria of significance have already been discussed - that is, the role a given economic process has in theories that purport to explain how business cycles come about or how they may be controlled or modified.

A consideration in indicator selection and scoring is the breadth of coverage. A broad indicator covers all corporate activity, total consumption, or investment. A narrow indicator relates to a single industry or to minor components of the broad series.

A broad economic indicator (e.g., nonfarm employment) may continue to perform well even if some components deteriorate because of technological developments, changes in customer tastes, or rapid growth or decline of single products or industries. Therefore, a broad indicator receives a higher score than a narrow indicator.

Criteria for selecting indicators include economic significance, statistical adequacy, historical conformity to business cycles, consistency of lead or lag, smoothness of the data, and timeliness of the data.

**Statistical adequacy**. The characteristics we should consider in evaluating the statistical adequacy of a series include a good reporting system and good coverage; that is, the data should cover the entire period they represent, benchmarks should be available, and there should be a full account of survey methods, coverage, and data adjustments.

A good reporting system is one based on primary rather than indirect sources or estimates. Some important series, such as the index of industrial production, the index of net business formation, and GDP, are based largely on indirect sources. Employment and retail sales are based on direct reporting from primary sources.

Good coverage means that if sampling is required, it should be a probability sample with stated measurement error regarding sample statistics. Moreover, coverage means, for example, that monthly data should include all days and not be a figure based on one day or week. In addition, the availability of benchmark is important as a check on the accuracy of data. For example, the U.S. Census provides a benchmark for estimates of population.

**Historical conformity to business cycles**. The NBER developed an initial index to measure how well the fluctuations in a series conformed to business cycle variations. A series that rose through every business expansion and declined during every contraction received an index score of 100. This particular index did not include extra cycles, such as occurred in 1966–1967, which are not classified as recession troughs. The index did not indicate whether the lack of conformity occurred early in the data or later; and it did not take into account the amplitude of the cycles. The scoring system subsequently developed by Julius Shiskin and Geoff. H. Moore in 1967 takes these considerations into account.

**Consistency of timing**. A number of considerations govern scoring a series on the basis of consistency of timing. The first is the consistency of lead or lag time relative to cycle peak or trough. The second is the variability about the average lead or lag time. A third consideration is the difference in lead-time for a peak compared to the lead-time for a trough. A final consideration is whether there has been any recent departure from historical relationships. Leading indicators have a median lead-time of two or more months; lagging indicators have a median lag of two or more months. Coincident indicators have a median timing of - 1, 0, or + 1 months. Occasionally, median leads of +2 months are possible when the lead or lag is not constant over many cycles.

**Smoothness and timeliness of data**. The factors that are weighed in arriving at a score for smoothness and timeliness include prompt availability of data and their smoothness. It is easier to identify changes in direction in a smooth series than in an irregular series. Generally speaking, because of irregularity of data, comparisons over spans greater than one month must usually be made to detect cyclical changes. Smoothing of some irregular series may result in some delay but may still provide a longer lead-time than for other series that are less irregular but have shorter lead times.

Generally speaking, leading indicators are the most erratic; lagging indicators are the smoothest. Coincident indicators have the shortest publication lag and the highest conformity scores. For example, corporate profits after taxes received an average score of 68 in the NBER index.

This indicator also received fairly high scores for economic significance, statistical adequacy, conformity, and timing. However, it received a score of 60 for smoothness, because it is irregular, and only 25 for timeliness, because it is a quarterly series subject to slow reporting.

Leading indicator methodology is not without its problems. Some basic limitations of leading indicators are that they are too focused on manufacturing, whose importance is declining; they can produce many false signals for turning points; they may not be available on a timely basis; thereby reducing their lead-advantages.

# Using Elasticities
Two important determinants of a firm's profitability—indeed its survival—are cost and the demand for its products or services. Demand must exist or be created if the business is to survive. It must also be high enough at least to cover fixed costs. Because of its key role, all business-planning activities require a careful analysis of demand over time. Demand forecasters also need to be aware of the relationship between quantity demanded and price.

*Demand forecasters play an important role in helping to make pricing decisions by estimating price elasticities for products and services with regression models.*

## Price Elasticities

The demand for gasoline in a market is routinely measured by analysis of oil imports (Figure 7.8) or of gasoline consumption (gross expenditure divided by the price index) (Figure 7.9). Figure 7.8 shows that U.S. oil demand rose steadily from 1984 through the early 2000s, peaking in 2004 before decreasing in conjunction with rising oil prices. Depicting U.S. gas consumption for the years 1960–1995,

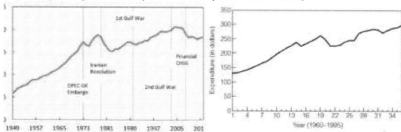

Figure 7.8 (*left*) Time plot of U.S. oil demand, 1949–2013. (*Source: https://www.weforum.org/agenda/2015/07/the-surprising-decline-in-us-petroleum-consumption/*)
Figure 7.9 (*right*) Time plot of U.S. gasoline consumption, 1960–1995.

Figure 7.9 indicates that consumption of gasoline in the U.S. market rose steadily through the 1960s as gasoline price fell in real terms and incomes rose. The dips in years 15, 20, 21, and 31 reflect the formation OPEC, the Iranian revolution, and the war in Iraq, respectively. Slow recovery in the early 1980s occurred during a severe recession in the U.S. economy. So, the market appears to have become very unstable after 1974 in comparison to the market of the 1960s.

Variables determining the consumption of gasoline include (a) the price indexes for gasoline, new and used cars, and public transportation; (b) the general price indexes for consumer durables, consumer nondurables, and consumer services; and (c) per capita income.

The quantity demanded for a product will increase as the price of the product decreases, all other determinants held constant (known as the *ceteris paribus* condition). As price falls, a product becomes cheaper relative to its substitutes, and thus it becomes easier for the product to compete for the consumer's dollar. The relationship is known as the **demand curve**.

> *The forecast of the quantity that is demanded at various price levels is important to businesses, since it permits them to maximize profitability by considering price and cost trade-offs.*

> **If a good is both a necessity and without a substitute, demand will tend to be very inelastic.**

For the weekly shipments of a canned beverage, shown in figures 8.8 – 8.10 in the next chapter, in relation to the price of a can of the beverage for that week, there is a general increase in shipments with declining prices. The element missing from such demand illustrations is *elasticity,* which explains the responsiveness of changes in demand to changes in prices or any of the other variables.

Most often we make note of a price elasticity, defined as the percentage change in the quantity demanded Q as a result of a given percentage change in price P:

$$\frac{\text{Percentage change in Q}}{\text{Percentage change in P}} \ \boxed{=} \ \frac{\Delta Q/Q}{\Delta P/P}$$

An important condition in the definition of elasticity is that all factors influencing demand other than **own price** (price of the item under consideration) are held constant (*ceteris paribus* condition) while own price is varied. In general, price elasticity is determined by at least four factors:

- whether or not the good is a necessity
- the number and price of close substitutes
- the proportion of the budget devoted to the item
- the length of time the price change remains in effect

If the product or service is a necessity, its demand will be **inelastic**; consumers will pay any reasonable price for a necessity. Lack of substitutes for a product will also cause demands to be inelastic. If substitutes are available, consumers will switch their purchases to those substitutes that have not increased in price. If the proportion of income spent for a good is small, price changes may not have too great an impact on the demand for the good. If the proportion of the income is large, price increases will cause postponements in demand or reductions in the quantity demanded.

The longer a price change remains in effect, the more elastic the demand for a product. Consumers become aware of price changes and adjust their consumption habits to the new circumstances.

Elastic as used here is a relative term. Demand becomes more elastic as time goes by; but it could still be inelastic, i.e., less than unity. Other factors influencing price elasticity are the frequency of purchases and the presence or absence of complements (e.g., automobiles and gasoline). Frequently purchased and relatively inexpensive products may be more inelastic than infrequently purchased expensive items.

# Price Elasticity and Revenue Demand Forecasting

Because revenue equals unit price multiplied by quantity demanded, a price change can result in an increase, in no change, or in a decrease in total revenue. (Figure 7.10). Consider first the impact of own-price elasticity on revenue by means of an example, deferring the impact of cross-elasticity until later. Suppose a forecast for a service predicts $1000 in revenues for a particular future year. Assume the own-price elasticity $E$ is −0.2. If $P$ = the existing price, $Q$ = the forecast of quantity demanded at the existing price, and $R$ = the forecast of revenue at the existing price, then $R = P \times Q = \$1000$. How will a 10 percent price increase in the service under consideration, effective at the start of the future year, impact demand for the service?

(a)

| Behavior of model | Unitary | Inelastic | Elastic |
|---|---|---|---|
| Price rise | Total revenue remains the same | Total revenue increases | Total revenue decreases |
| Price decline | Total revenue remains the same | Total revenue decreases | Total revenue increases |
| Gain versus loss | Gain = Loss | Gain > Loss | Gain < Loss |

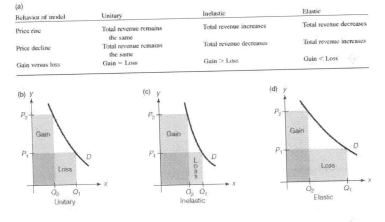

Figure 7.10 (a) Table and (b–d) graphs showing the relationship of price to revenue.

The new price is clearly just 1.10 $P$, but the quantity demanded will be somewhat less than before. With $E$ = −0.2, a 10 percent price increase will result in approximately a 2 % loss. Hence, the new demand will be approximately 0.98 $Q$, and the revenue $R'$ after the price change will be

$$R' = (1.10\ P)\ (0.98\ Q) = 1.08\ R$$

Thus, a 10% price increase will increase revenues by 8%, in this example.

In general, the own-price elasticity effect will cause an X% price increase to yield less than an X% increase in revenues. The reprice value of a rate or price increase is the incremental revenue that would result if there were no demand reaction, it is $100 in the example. The amount by which revenues fall short of the reprice value, $20 here, is called revenue repression.

A *revenue repression factor* may be defined as the ratio of revenue repression to reprice value. In this example, it is 0.2. An elasticity of −

0.2 implies a minimum revenue repression factor of 0.2, e.g., at least $20 for a price increase worth $100 on a reprice basis. The revenue repression factor often goes up with the magnitude of the price change.

Price elasticities can be used as a root cause to show how price changes are likely to affect total revenue.

To continue with the $1000 service example, suppose it has been determined that this service must produce $1100 to enable the company to each its profit objective. A 10% price increase will not be sufficient, owing to the revenue repression of $20 (revenue repression factor 0.2). Evidently, to net $100 in incremental revenues, almost 12.5% increase in price will be necessary. The reprice value ($1000 x 1.125) of such an increase is $1125. A repression of $25 (0.2 x $125) leaves a net of $1100.

## Cross-Elasticity

Goods and services are frequently affected by the availability or prices of other goods or services. **Cross-elasticity** measures the percentage change in the demand for good A as a result of a given percentage change in the price of good B. If a good has a close substitute, a price increase for one will create increased demand for the other.

When airfares increase, for instance, travelers may find it more desirable to travel by train, bus, or automobile. When products are complementary (used together), a decrease in the price of one will lead to an increase in demand for both products.

For example, in the travel industry, "nearby" destinations, such as Australia and New Zealand, are complementary in that package tours frequently package such destinations together at more attractive prices than the destinations individually. The cross-elasticity is positive for substitutes, and negative for complementary goods. As before, this is a dimensionless number, since it is defined in terms of percent changes.

A cross-elasticity coefficient is a measure of the interaction effect between the price of a good and prices of other goods.

## Other Demand Elasticities

The focus here so far has been concentrated on price elasticity. However, there is elasticity associated with each independent variable in the demand equation. Income is another determinant of demand that also receives attention. For most goods and services, one would expect a positive relationship between demand and income. **Income elasticity** is the percentage change in demand divided by the percentage change in income. However, the elasticity for normal goods is now positive instead of negative. If the demand for a good is income-inelastic, the increase in demand will not be proportional to the percentage increase in income. As national income rises, for instance, a business firm will not experience a proportional growth in revenues, and its share of national income will decline.

Income elasticity is a double-edged sword. If the economy contracts and income declines, the revenues of an income-inelastic firm will shrink less than the revenues for an income-elastic firm. The firms whose goods are income-elastic should be more concerned with anticipating the business cycle expansions and contractions.

Another useful elasticity to consider in sales-driven, 'push' supply chains would be **salesforce elasticity**.

## Estimating Elasticities

In forecasting retail sales of durable goods (plant equipment and durable machinery, automobiles, etc.), one might expect monthly retail sales to be very sensitive to changes in gross earnings of workers and to the **Consumer Price Index** (CPI) for durable goods. If earnings rise, one can expect retail sales to increase. On the other hand, if the CPI rises, one expects retail sales to fall. Because the explanatory variables in a demand equation can change simultaneously, a general model for the retail sales of product Y may take the form

$$Q_Y = Q\ (P_Y,\ I,\ P_X,\ ,\ A,\ B,\ \varepsilon)$$

where the quantity demanded $Q_Y$ is a function of the (deflated) price $P_Y$ of the product, income $I$, the price $P_X$ of a competing (complementary) product, the market potential $A$, advertising $B$, and any number of other variables, and a random error term $\varepsilon$.

Demand theory does not help us with the specific form for $Q$. However, several forms appear to give a useful interpretation of the elasticity. In the application of demand models, the additive and multiplicative forms are the most commonly used. Elasticities can be derived for either model, but the multiplicative form gives a particularly simple result. A **multiplicative demand model** takes the form

$$Q_Y = \beta_0\,(P_Y)^{\beta_1}\,(I)^{\beta_2}\,(P_X)^{\beta_3}\,(A)^{\beta_4}\,(B)^{\beta_5}\,e^{\varepsilon}$$

where the $\beta_i$ are parameters and $e^\varepsilon$ is a multiplicative error term.

The estimation of these parameters from data is performed by regression analysis. The important point to note here is that the price elasticity (formally the partial derivative of ln $Q_Y$ with respect to ln $P_Y$) is the *constant* $\beta_1$. Hence, it is called the **constant elasticity model**.

*Elasticities can be estimated from additive and multiplicative demand models.*

The theory can be applied to determine the responsiveness of tax revenues (TAX_REV) to changes in either the tax rate (RATE) or the tax base (BASE) in a state's budget. For example, if a (hypothetical) model takes the form

Log$_e$ TAX_REV = −3.8 − 0.6 Log$_e$ RATE + 1.4 Log$_e$ BASE,
then a suitably qualified statement could be made that says: (1) a 1%
increase in the tax rate will lead to a 0.6 % decrease in tax revenues;
and (2) a 1% increase in the taxable base, retail sales, will increase
revenues by 1.4%.

Getting back to the earlier gasoline consumption example, Figure
7.11 shows the results of an analysis for the parameters in a constant
elasticity model. The coefficients are elasticities. For example, the price
elasticity of demand is estimated to be −0.518 and the income elasticity
is 1.222. All else being equal, we would expect consumption to increase
0.89% per year. Since the coefficients for the price indexes for new
automobiles are less than zero, these are complementary products with
gasoline. The elasticity for consumer durables as a group are closer to
unity than the elasticities for a more narrowly defined category of new
automobiles, which is consistent with economic theory.

| | |
|---|---|
| Constant | −23.34 |
| log Price index for gasoline | −0.518 |
| log Per-capita Income | 1.222 |
| Year (time trend) | 0.009 |
| log Price index for new cars | 0.038 |
| log Price index for used cars | −0.119 |
| log Price index for public transportation | 0.125 |
| log General price index for consumer durables | 1.058 |
| log General price index for consumer nondurables | 1.149 |
| log General price index for consumer services | −1.362 |

Figure 7.11 Elasticities of a constant elasticity model for the
consumption of gasoline in the United States, 1960–1995. (*Source*:
Figure 7.8)

| | Price | Income |
|---|---|---|
| Short run | Coeff of X$_1$ = - 0.402 | Coeff of X$_2$ = 0.597 |
| Long run | Coeff of X$_1$/(1-Coeff of X$_3$) = - 0.651 | Coeff of X$_2$/(1-Coeff of X$_3$) = 0.967 |

Figure 7.12 Determining short- and long-term elasticities for the
consumption of gasoline in the United States, 1960–1995. (*Source*:
Figure 7.9)

To distinguish long-term from short-term elasticities, we can
construct a constant elasticity model with a lagged term for the
dependent variable gasoline consumption. Using multiple linear
regression analysis, the resultant coefficient estimates are shown in
Figure 7.12 for this dataset. This conforms to the theory that demand

becomes more elastic as time goes by; but it could still be inelastic, that is, less than unity.

## *Characterizing Trending Data Patterns*

When data are ordered sequentially, as in a time series, data sequences one or more time periods apart are often statistically related. As a result of the chronological ordering of historical data, most time series exhibit a mutual dependence of successive values, called **serial correlation**.

For example, in a trending series there is a close association between successive periods because adjacent values follow a very similar pattern. In particular, successive changes are constant for values on a straight line. That is, if $Y_t$ is a straight line given by $Y_t = a + b\,t$, then the first difference of $Y_t$ results in a new series $Z_t = [a + b\,t] - [a + b(t-1)]$ of constant values equal to the slope b; this means that the first differences $Z_t$ of a straight line trend are constant and not dependent on time t. This condition is part of the central concept of **stationarity**.

This effect can also be shown among values that are not successive. For example, when we look at the periodic pattern of highs and lows in a seasonal time series over a number of years, we note a similarity of values four, six, or 12 periods apart. More generally, this effect is known as **autocorrelation**.

### Autocorrelation Analysis

An objective of autocorrelation analysis is to describe correlation in time series. Autocorrelations are also used frequently in the analysis of residuals (actual minus fit) from a forecasting model. In this situation, the demand forecaster seeks an *absence* of autocorrelation, namely a purely random pattern in the residuals. We will also frequently use autocorrelation analysis in the identification of ARIMA models for the Box-Jenkins model-building strategy (Chapter 9). And as we'll see, it also plays a significant role in the analysis of residuals in ARIMA forecasting models and regression modeling applications (Chapters 10 and 11).

> *Most time series exhibit a mutual dependence of successive values, known as serial correlation.*

### First Order Autocorrelation

The calculation of the first-order autocorrelation coefficient is analogous to calculating the ordinary or Pearson product moment correlation coefficient r between $Y_t$ and $Y_{t-1}$ (Correlation is introduced in Chapters 11 and 12 in connection with regression analysis).

For the mortgage rate data this is done by creating two columns in a spreadsheet where the first column is the original and the second column is a shifted (one row down) version of the first, when $Y_{t-1}$ is positioned adjacent to $Y_t$ (Figure 7.13). The first difference is the original rate minus the lagged rate. The changes in successive values (known as first differences) are seen to vary around zero (Figure 7.13). The Lagged 1 column shows the mortgage rates shifted down one row and the First Difference column is the difference between Mortgage Rates column and Lagged 1 column. The mean and standard deviation of the First Differences column are 0.11 and 0.88, respectively.

> *Through autocorrelation analysis, we measure the effects of mutual dependence in values of a time series. First differences are changes in successive values in a time series.*

| Mortgage Rates | Lagged 1 | First Difference |
|---|---|---|
| 5.8 | | |
| 5.75 | 5.8 | −0.05 |
| 5.74 | 5.75 | −0.01 |
| 6.14 | 5.74 | 0.4 |
| 6.33 | 6.14 | 0.19 |
| 6.83 | 6.33 | 0.5 |
| 7.66 | 6.83 | 0.83 |
| 8.27 | 7.66 | 0.61 |
| 7.59 | 8.27 | −0.68 |
| 7.45 | 7.59 | −0.14 |
| 7.78 | 7.45 | 0.33 |
| 8.71 | 7.78 | 0.93 |
| 8.75 | 8.71 | 0.04 |
| 8.77 | 8.75 | 0.02 |
| 8.8 | 8.77 | 0.03 |
| 9.33 | 8.8 | 0.53 |
| 10.49 | 9.33 | 1.16 |
| 12.26 | 10.49 | 1.77 |
| 14.13 | 12.26 | 1.87 |
| 14.49 | 14.13 | 0.36 |
| 12.11 | 14.49 | −2.38 |
| 11.88 | 12.11 | −0.23 |
| 11.09 | 11.88 | −0.79 |
| 9.74 | 11.09 | −1.35 |
| 8.94 | 9.74 | −0.8 |
| 8.83 | 8.94 | −0.11 |
| 9.77 | 8.83 | 0.94 |
| 9.68 | 9.77 | −0.09 |
| 9.01 | 9.68 | −0.67 |
| | Mean = 0.114643 | |
| | SD = 0.884913 | |

Figure 7.13 Annual mortgage rates, rates time-lagged one period, and first differences.

To calculate the first-order autocorrelation coefficient (Figure 7.14), we first create the standardized values of the mortgage rates and the shifted values. Then, we place the product of the 28 common values in the next column. Finally, we simply calculate the arithmetic mean of the values in the last column to obtain an estimate of first-order autocorrelation coefficient $r_1$.

| Mortgage Rates | Lagged Mortgage Rates | Standardized Mortgage Rates | Standardized Lagged Mortgage Rates | Column 3 × Column 4 |
|---|---|---|---|---|
| 5.75 | 5.80 | −1.4572 | −1.3265 | 1.93 |
| 5.74 | 5.75 | −1.4615 | −1.3472 | 1.97 |
| 6.14 | 5.74 | −1.2905 | −1.3513 | 1.74 |
| 6.33 | 6.14 | −1.2093 | −1.1863 | 1.43 |
| 6.83 | 6.33 | −0.9956 | −1.1079 | 1.10 |
| 7.66 | 6.83 | −0.6409 | −0.9017 | 0.58 |
| 8.27 | 7.66 | −0.3802 | −0.5593 | 0.21 |
| 7.59 | 8.27 | −0.6708 | −0.3077 | 0.21 |
| 7.45 | 7.59 | −0.7307 | −0.5882 | 0.43 |
| 7.78 | 7.45 | −0.5896 | −0.6459 | 0.38 |
| 8.71 | 7.78 | −0.1922 | −0.5098 | 0.10 |
| 8.75 | 8.71 | −0.1751 | −0.1262 | 0.02 |
| 8.77 | 8.75 | −0.1665 | −0.1097 | 0.02 |
| 8.80 | 8.77 | −0.1537 | −0.1014 | 0.02 |
| 9.33 | 8.80 | 0.0728 | −0.0891 | −0.01 |
| 10.49 | 9.33 | 0.5686 | 0.1296 | 0.07 |
| 12.26 | 10.49 | 1.3250 | 0.6080 | 0.81 |
| 14.13 | 12.26 | 2.1242 | 1.3381 | 2.84 |
| 14.49 | 14.13 | 2.2781 | 2.1095 | 4.81 |
| 12.11 | 14.49 | 1.2609 | 2.2580 | 2.85 |
| 11.88 | 12.11 | 1.1626 | 1.2763 | 1.48 |
| 11.09 | 11.88 | 0.8250 | 1.1814 | 0.97 |
| 9.74 | 11.09 | 0.2480 | 0.8555 | 0.21 |
| 8.94 | 9.74 | −0.0939 | 0.2987 | −0.03 |
| 8.83 | 8.94 | −0.1409 | −0.0313 | 0.00 |
| 9.77 | 8.83 | 0.2609 | −0.0767 | −0.02 |
| 9.68 | 9.77 | 0.2224 | 0.3110 | 0.07 |
| Mean = 9.16 | 9.02 | 0 | 0 | 0.90 |
| SD = 2.34 | 2.42 | 1 | 1 | |

Figure 7.14 Calculation of first-order autocorrelation coefficient of annual mortgage rates. (Source: Figure 7.13)

The standard deviation of column 1 = 2.34 (based on 28 values) and standard deviation of column 2 = 2.42 (based on 28 values); the two column averages are 9.16 and 9.02. This gives $r_1 = 0.90$. The coefficient can take on values between +1 and -1, so $r_1 = 0.9$ suggests a strong positive association between mortgage rates and a lagged 1 version of itself as shown in a scatter diagram (Figure 7.15).

In practice, the formula used in software packages for autocorrelation at lag 1 has some technical differences (a factor $\sqrt{n}/n-1$) but yields the same interpretation from the data. We introduce a more commonly used formula later in this chapter when dealing with autocorrelation plots.

*A time series is said to be lagged if it is a time-shifted version of itself.*

In an autocorrelation analysis, a time series is related to lagged versions of itself. To illustrate the association between successive values in the mortgage rates series, we have depicted the mortgage rate column and Lagged 1 column in Figure 7.13 as a scatter plot or scatter diagram in Figure 7.15. There is evidence of a strong positive (almost linear) association between the values in the two columns of data. This dependency on past values is used to measure the strength of the relationship between the values of a time series and values *one or more* time periods away. We depict this mutual dependence in a time series with a set of autocorrelation coefficients.

In Chapter 2 (Figure 2.9) we show the relationship between changes in one variable (housing starts) and changes in another variable (mortgage rates) in a scatter diagram. The downward sloping scatter suggests a negative association between the two variables. In other words, as changes in mortgage rates increase, the corresponding changes in housing starts decrease.

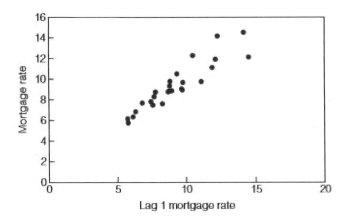

Figure 7.15. Scatter diagram of mortgage rates versus lagged 1 values. (*Source*: Figure 7.13)

To use this for forecasting housing starts, we want to measure the strength of this relationship with lagged values of the mortgage rates variable. Figure 7.11 shows the values of the mortgage data for 29 years. The scatter diagram (Figure 7.16) shows the same negative association between the variables as Figure 2.9, but is there any difference between the first order autocorrelation coefficients? When used in a regression model in Chapter 10, we will see that lagging variable will let us use actual data, rather than forecasted data for the forecast profile in the relationship.

## The Correlogram

A useful way to visualize the effect of autocorrelation is to display the sample autocorrelation function, known as the ordinary **correlogram**.

The ordinary correlogram is determined by correlating a time series with versions of itself in which the dimension of time has been shifted. This yields a set of coefficients, which can be plotted successively, corresponding to each time shift or lag. The ordinary or autocorrelogram is simply a plot of the estimated autocorrelation

| Datum Numbers | Housing Starts (1963–1991) |
|---|---|
| 1 | 1603.2 |
| 2 | 1528.8 |
| 3 | 1472.8 |
| 4 | 1164.9 |
| 5 | 1291.6 |
| 6 | 1507.6 |
| 7 | 1466.8 |
| 8 | 1433.6 |
| 9 | 2052.2 |
| 10 | 2356.6 |
| 11 | 2045.3 |
| 12 | 1337.7 |
| 13 | 1160.4 |
| 14 | 1537.5 |
| 15 | 1987.1 |
| 16 | 2020.3 |
| 17 | 1745.1 |
| 18 | 1292.2 |
| 19 | 1084.2 |
| 20 | 1062.2 |
| 21 | 1703.0 |
| 22 | 1749.5 |
| 23 | 1741.8 |
| 24 | 1805.4 |
| 25 | 1620.5 |
| 26 | 1488.1 |
| 27 | 1376.1 |
| 28 | 1192.7 |
| 29 | 1014.5 |

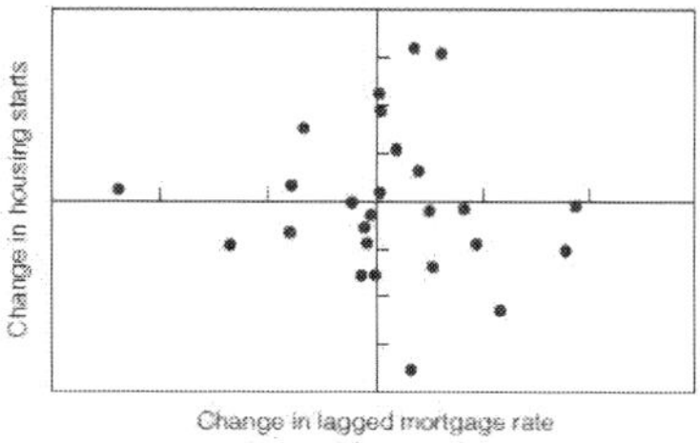

coefficients.

Figure 7.16 (*left*) Annual housing start s for a 29-year period.
Figure 7.17 (*right*) Scatter diagram of changes in annual housing starts versus changes in annual mortgage rates lagged one period. (*Source:* Figures 7.13 and 7.14)

The interpretation of a correlogram is more an art than a science and requires substantial experience. Correlograms are commonly used for time series with the following characteristics: pure randomness, low-order serial correlation, trend, seasonality, and alternating and rapidly changing fluctuations.

Given $n$ values of a time series $\{Y_t, t = 1, 2, \ldots, n\}$, a commonly used formula for the first sample autocorrelation coefficient $r_1$ is

$$r_1 = \Sigma \ (Y_t - \bar{y}) \ (Y_{t-1} - \bar{y}) \ / \ \Sigma \ (Y_t - \bar{y})^2$$

where $\bar{y}$ is the average (arithmetic mean) of the $n$ values of the time series. The subscript $t$ in the value $Y_t$ denotes the time; thus, $Y_{t-1}$ is the value of the series one period earlier.

In a similar fashion the formula for the sample autocorrelation coefficient $r_j$ between values of the time series separated $j$ periods is

$$r_j = c_j \ / \ c_0 \qquad \text{for } j = 0, 1, 2, 3, \ldots, k \text{ where}$$

$$c_j = 1/n \ \Sigma \ (Y_t - \bar{y}) \ (Y_{t-j} - \bar{y}) \text{ , summed } t = j + 1 \text{ to } t = n$$

For large $n$, $r_k$ is approximately normally distributed with a mean of 0 and variance $1/n$. Thus, approximate 95% confidence limits for autocorrelation coefficients can be plotted at $\pm 1.96 \ / \ \sqrt{n}$. The observed values of $r_j$ that fall outside these limits suggest that the corresponding autocorrelation coefficient is significantly different from 0 at the 5% level. If the first 20 values of the correlogram are plotted, we expect one significant value even if the $r_j$ values are random.

In practice, the number of $r_j$ values calculated for a correlogram varies with the length of the series and the length of the seasonal cycle. Generally, for a 12-month seasonal series, approximately 36 - 60 monthly values are appropriate. No more than approximately $n/4$ to $n/3$ correlations should be calculated for a series of length $n$. Otherwise, there will not be enough terms in the calculation for higher lags for any inferences to be meaningful. It is desirable that $n > 50$.

*An (ordinary) correlogram is a display of the sample autocorrelation coefficients. Autocorrelation coefficients measure the degree of association between lagged values of a time series.*

Correlograms should be interpreted, with caution, in terms of the patterns of autocorrelation coefficients more than the behavior of individual values of the coefficients.

A purely random time series is one in which there is no time dependence between values any number of time periods (lags) apart and thus no systematic pattern that can be exploited for forecasting. Thus, autocorrelation coefficients for a purely random time series should be 0 at all lags, except at lag 0. At lag 0, the time series is perfectly related to itself and has the maximum value 1.

*A random time series is one in which there is no time dependence between values that are any number of time periods apart.*

For a sampled random series, a correlogram shows sample estimates of autocorrelations of the data. Hence, the correlogram of a random series is 1 at lag 0 and nearly 0 for all lags different from lag 0.

Hence, the correlogram shown in Figure 7.13 is unity at lag 0 and very close to 0 for all nonzero values k of the lag (there are 15 of these plotted on the abscissa.)

Note that a random series is not necessarily normally distributed. A normal probability plot of the 60 numbers does not support a normal distribution assumption for the data (Figure 7.19, *top*), but, in fact, the random series was generated from a lognormal distribution (Figure 7.19, *bottom*).

As we will see in Chapter 9, patterns found in a correlogram can be used to analyze associated patterns in the basic data, such as seasonal periods, which is useful for the specification of ARIMA time series models.

> *Patterns of autocorrelation coefficients can give insight into the structure or characteristics of a time series.*

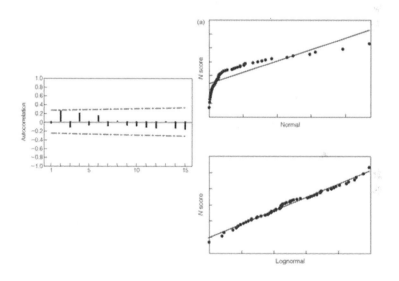

Figure 7.18 (*left*) Correlogram of a random time series.
Figure 7.19 (right, *top*) Normal and (*bottom*) lognormal probability plots of the random series.

## Low-Order Autocorrelation

Many time series, even after a certain amount of differencing, exhibit short-term correlations (or memory) in their pattern. Thus, autocorrelation at shorter lags is greater than autocorrelation at longer lags.

> *For a time series having low-order dependence, a correlogram shows a decaying pattern.*

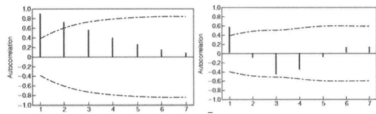

Figure 7.20 Correlograms of (*left*) annual housing starts and (*right*) annual mortgage rate data. (*Source*: Figures 7.16 and 7.13)

Figure 7.20 (*left*) shows a correlogram of the annual housing starts data, and Figure 7.21 (*right*) shows a correlogram of the annual mortgage rate series. Note that the spikes tend to get progressively smaller.

Once inside the bounds (roughly, 2 /√n, n = 29), the spikes cannot be interpreted as significant. In this case, the trending in the data induces a memory pattern, and the correlogram corroborates this. Thus, a correlogram can help identify structure in the data, but the pattern is not unique to the individual time series.

## Trend-Variance Analysis

The data displayed in Figure 7.21 represent the number of bags (pieces of checked luggage) lost per 100,000 passenger miles by a certain airline over a 12-year period. To check for trend, we compute the differences between successive data values. The first-difference values are in column E for Years 2 through 12 along with the original data. If a trend exists, the variance of the difference values will be smaller than the variance of the original data. To see this, recall that a (sample) variance is a measure of the degree to which individual values in a set of data differ from the average of all values. Because the original data contain a trend, values near the beginning and end of the data differ radically from their average. By computing the differences between data values, we eliminate the trend and the difference values cluster around their average.

At this point, we know that a trend exists in the number of bags lost but we do not know the type of trend. We can narrow the possibilities by computing the differences between differences, that is, the second difference (column F).

If the set of second differences has a smaller variance than the first, we may conclude that there is a strong trend in the data, either linear or exponential. If the set of second differences does not reduce the variance, we conclude that the trend is moderate, probably a damped trend. That would help in the preliminary steps of model profile selection. The spreadsheet example that follows shows the details of these calculations.

To explain the rationale for the trend test, we analyze the bags lost data shown in Figure 7.21. We calculate the variance of the original data, variance of the differences between successive values and variances of differences between are shown in the row labeled VARIANCE (Figure 7.22). The row labeled VARIANCE INDEX converts the variances to indexes to make them easier to interpret.

Spreadsheet:    TRENDIFF
1  TREND CLASSIFICATION MODEL
2  TITLE1: TREND ANALYSIS
3  TITLE2: BAGS LOST PER 100,000 PASSENGER MILES
4  X-AXIS: YEAR
5  Y-AXIS: THOUSANDS OF BAGS
6
7  MEAN: 0.8375 0.0563 −0.012
8  VARIANCE: 0.0379 0.0040 0.0088
9  VARIANCE INDEX: 100% 10% 23%
10 TYPE OF TREND: MODERATE
11

| | A | B | C | D | E | F |
|---|---|---|---|---|---|---|
| 12 | | | | | | |
| 13 | | | | | Differences | Differences |
| 14 | | | | Original | between | between |
| 15 | Year | Mon | Per | Data | Data | Differences |
| 16 | 1978 | NA | 1 | 0.50 | NA | NA |
| 17 | 1979 | | 2 | 0.64 | 0.14 | NA |
| 18 | 1980 | | 3 | 0.69 | 0.05 | −0.09 |
| 19 | 1981 | | 4 | 0.79 | 0.10 | 0.05 |
| 20 | 1982 | | 5 | 0.76 | −0.03 | −0.13 |
| 21 | 1983 | | 6 | 0.73 | −0.03 | 0.00 |
| 22 | 1984 | | 7 | 0.80 | 0.07 | 0.10 |
| 23 | 1985 | | 8 | 0.91 | 0.11 | 0.04 |
| 24 | 1986 | | 9 | 0.93 | 0.02 | −0.09 |
| 25 | 1987 | | 10 | 1.08 | 0.15 | 0.13 |
| 26 | 1988 | | 11 | 1.10 | 0.02 | −0.13 |
| 27 | 1989 | | 12 | 1.12 | 0.02 | 0.00 |

(Mon, month; NA, not available; Per, period)

Figure 7.21 Spreadsheet layout of the trend analysis for bags lost per 100,000 passengers.

The variance of the original data is taken as a base of 100%. The row labeled TYPE OF TREND is a reminder of the trend indicated when the variance in that column is the minimum. Thus, the difference values display a much smaller variance from their average than the original data.

This is the basis of the test for trend. If computing the differences reduces the variance, a trend exists; otherwise, there is no trend.

```
TREND CLASSIFICATION MODEL
TITLE1:              TREND ANALYSIS
TITLE2:              BAGS LOST PER 100,000 PASSENGER MILES
X-AXIS:              YEAR
Y-AXIS:              THOUSANDS OF BAGS

MEAN:                        0.8375          0.056364        −0.012
VARIANCE:                    0.03793         0.003965        0.00884
VARIANCE INDEX:              1               0.104548        0.233064
TYPE OF TREND:                               MODERATE
```

Figure 7.22 computing the variances of differences for bags lost per 100,000 passengers.

| Minimum Variance Occurs In | Trend Indicated | Recommended Forecasting Technique |
|---|---|---|
| Original data | Nonexistent | Simple exponential smoothing |
| Differences between data observations | Moderate | Damped-exponential trend |
| Differences between differences | Strong | Linear or exponential trend |

Figure 7.23 Summary of trend analysis for use in model selection.

In Figure 7.22, we compare variances for the original data in Figure 7.21 and two sets of differences: between the years (between values in column D), and between differences (between values in column E). The smallest variance indicates the type of trend. With a moderate trend, the variance of the differences between years is smallest. With a strong trend, computing the second differences is necessary to achieve the smallest variance

Get into the habit of testing data before forecasting. We suspect that many practitioners would simply choose a straight-line trend in a graph of the number of bags lost by the airline. However, a test suggests otherwise (Figure 7.23).

## Using Pressures to Analyze Business Cycles

Some observers of economic patterns believe that the business cycle is dead and that recessions are a thing of the past. Others state that the U.S. Federal Reserve Board has been able to avoid recessions by bringing the economy in for a "soft landing" during periods of declining growth. During a time of economic uncertainty, analyzing cycles in business data may still prove to be a valuable addition in a demand forecaster's toolkit.

Information about business cycles is extremely valuable for business planning, especially developing a budget, an inventory plan, or a production schedule. The technique can be applied to any demand-related data collected at monthly time intervals.

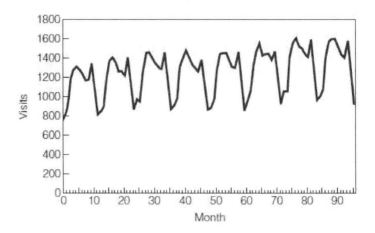

Figure 7.24 Time plot of monthly hotel/motel room demand in Washington, D.C.

We can use **pressures analysis** to analyze company or industry sales, orders, shipments, inventories, production, and so on. As in all forecasting work, the more data the better, although many supply chain planning organizations try to get by with only a couple of years of history.

> ***The aims of pressures analysis are to detect changes in the rate of growth in data and to identify the turning points (peaks and troughs) of cycles.***

The hotel/motel room industry experienced a slump in the early 1990s in the eastern part of the United States. Figure 7.24 illustrates the use of pressures for the Washington, D.C., hotel/motel room demand series to identify an approximate turning point.

A **pressure** is a ratio calculation between two points in time. The three graphs in Figures 7.25 and 7.26 illustrate the 1/12, 3/12, and 12/12 pressures. How should we interpret the behavior of hotel/motel room demand? Will growth pick up again? Has a turning point occurred? To help answer these questions, a ratio is calculated of the demand in each month compared to the same month a year before. If the index for a given month is 100%, the demand for that month is unchanged from a year before; if the index is greater than 100%, demand has grown from a year before. Such index numbers are called **1/12 pressures**.

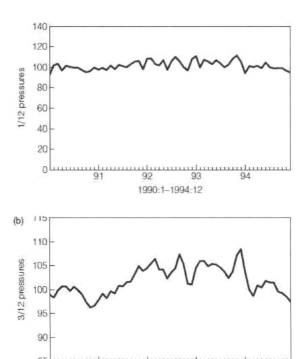

Figure 7.25 Pressures for hotel/motel room demand data for Washington, D.C.: (*top*) 1/12 pressures, (*bottom*) 3/12 pressures. (*Source*: Figure 7.24)

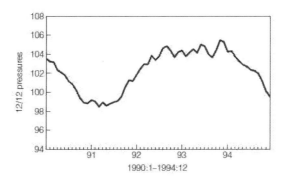

Figure 7.26 Pressures for hotel/motel room demand data for Washington, D.C.: 12/12 pressures. (*Source*: Figure 7.24)

In the 1/12 pressures graph (Figure 7.25a), there is little evidence of a turning point. In the **3/12 pressures** graph (Figure 7.25b), which compares three-month totals with the same period the previous year, a minimum begins to appear toward the end of 1990. This is further confirmed in the **12/12 pressures** graph (Figure 7.26). Does the decline in 1994 suggest another downturn, and when will it turn up again? If tourism demand is driver of demand in your business, consults with the experts in the tourism industry for their views.

If the timings of the possible turning points are substantially different, we should be more cautious about the future. Pressures analysis is not foolproof and randomness may prevent us from seeing any definite patterns.

1/12, 3/12, and 12/12 are the pressures most used in practice, but we may also want to look at 6/12 and 9/12 pressures when the results are ambiguous. For quarterly data, we would use ¼, 2/4, and 4/4, and for weekly data use 1/52, 4/52, 13/52, and 52/52 pressures.

Demand forecasters may want to temper or boost their projections when a turning point appears in the pressures. We should also keep an eye on the trends in pressures; for example, projections of strong growth in sales are less likely when the recent trend in pressures is down.

## Alternative Approaches to Using Seasonally Adjusted Data in Forecast Modeling

Strong arguments against the use of seasonally adjusted data for econometric regression models have been made in the literature. The objections are related, in part, to the fact that we cannot be quite sure what the statistical properties of the residuals are after we have subjected the series to a seasonal adjustment procedure. This practice has an impact on the inferences that can be drawn—specifically for establishing prediction limits (measured uncertainty) about forecasts. In the cycle forecasting approach, the subjective nature of the forecast and the intentional omission of prediction intervals recognize that this is a highly subjective approach.

As we will see in Chapters 9 and 10, an alternative to modeling seasonally adjusted data is modeling appropriately differenced data. We can also take differences of economic data and correlate the patterns of deviations from trend of the two series, thereby developing business cycle forecasts. A final step is to "undifference" the series by adding the predicted differences to the appropriate actual (and later predicted) values of the series.

## *Takeaways*

➤ Autocorrelation—describing the association or mutual dependence between values within the same data at different time periods—is a key aspect of any projection technique using historical data.

➤ While modeling techniques can be very versatile, they all have their limitations, and this should be recognized early. Unless examined and accounted for, changes in trend, cycle, seasonal, calendar, promotion, and irregular variations, and possibly their interactions, can cause significant modeling problems. Recognizing these characteristics is a first step to reducing their effect.

➤ The number of times that the original series must be differenced before stationary series results is termed **the order of homogeneity** of the series. For most economic data, differences should be taken at most twice. As a first step, it is important to identify *the minimum* amount of differencing required to create a stationary series. Modeling can rarely compensate for overdifferencing.

➤ Approaches to cycle forecasting are based on the decomposition of a time series into trend, cyclical, seasonal, and irregular components.

  o Seasonally adjusted data are required to help identify the trend-cycle component.

  o The trend-cycle component is correlated with economic indicators to relate turning points in the economy with the demand for products and services.

# 8

# Big Data: Baseline Forecasting with Exponential Smoothing Models

PREDICTION·IS·VERY·DIFFICULT,·ESPECIALLY·IF·IT·IS·ABOUT·THE·FUTURE·¶

NIELS·BOHR·(1885-1962),·Nobel·Laureate·Physicist¶

Exponential smoothing models provide a viable framework for forecasting large volume, disaggregate demand patterns. For short-term planning and control systems, these techniques are extremely reliable and have more than adequate track record in forecast accuracy with trend/seasonal data.

This chapter deals with the description and evaluation of techniques that

- are widely used in the areas of sales, inventory, logistics, and production planning as well as in quality control, process control, financial planning and marketing planning
- can be described in terms of a state-space modeling framework that provides prediction intervals and procedures for model selection that are well-suited for large-scale, automated forecasting applications, because they require little forecaster intervention, thereby releasing the time of the demand forecaster to concentrate on the few problem cases
- are based on the mathematical extrapolation of past patterns into the future, accomplished by using forecasting equations that are simple to update and require relatively small number of calculations

- capture level (a starting point for the forecasts), trend (a factor for growth or decline) and seasonal factors (for adjustment of seasonal variation) in data patterns

## *What is Exponential Smoothing?*

In chapter 3, we introduced forecasting with simple and weighted moving averages as an exploratory smoothing technique for short-term forecasting of level data. With exponential smoothing models, on the other hand, we can create short-term forecasts with prediction limits for a wider variety of data having trends and seasonal patterns; the modeling methodology offers prediction limits (ranges of uncertainty) and prescribed forecast profiles. Exponential smoothing provides an essential simplicity and ease of understanding for the practitioner, and has been found to have a reliable track record for accuracy in many business applications.

Exponential smoothing was invented during World War II by Robert G. Brown (1923–2013), *left*, who was involved in the design of tracking systems for fire-control information on the location of enemy submarines. Later on, the principles of exponential smoothing were applied to business data, especially in the analysis of the demand for service parts in inventory systems in Brown's book *Advanced Service Parts Inventory Control* (1982).

As part of the state-space forecasting methodology, exponential smoothing models provide a flexible approach to weighting past historical data for smoothing and extrapolation purposes. This exponentially declining weighting scheme contrasts with the equal weighting scheme that underlies the outmoded simple moving average technique for forecasting.

> *Exponential smoothing is a forecasting technique that extrapolates historical patterns such as trends and seasonal cycles into the future.*

There are many types of exponential smoothing models, each appropriate for a particular forecast pattern or **forecast profile**. As a forecasting tool, exponential smoothing is very widely accepted and a proven tool for a wide variety of short-term forecasting applications. Most inventory planning and production control systems rely on exponential smoothing to some degree.

We will see that the process for assigning smoothing weights is simple in concept and versatile for dealing with diverse types of data. Other advantages of exponential smoothing are that the methodology takes account of trend and seasonal patterns in time series; embodies a weighting scheme that gives more weight to the recent past than to the distant past; is readily automated, making it especially useful for large-scale forecasting applications; and can be described in a modeling framework needed for deriving useful statistical prediction limits and flexible trend/seasonal forecast profiles.

> **When selecting a model for demand forecasting, focus on plausible forecast profiles, rather than fit statistics and model coefficients.**

For demand forecasting, the disadvantages are that exponential smoothing models do not easily allow for the inclusion of explanatory variables into a forecasting model and cannot handle business cycles. Hence, when forecasting economic variables, such techniques are not expected to perform well on business data that exhibit cyclical turning points.

## Smoothing Weights

To understand how exponential smoothing works, we need first to understand the concept of exponentially decaying weights. Consider a time series of production rates (number of completed assemblies per week) for a 4-week period in the table below. In order to predict next period's $(T + 1)$ production rate without having knowledge of or information about future demand, we assume that the following week will have to be an average week for production. A reasonable projection for the following week can be based on taking an average of the production rates during past weeks. However, what kind of average should we propose?

| : Week | Production |
| --- | --- |
| Three periods ago (T - 3) | 266 |
| Two periods ago (T - 2) | 411 |
| Previous (T - 1) | 376 |
| Current t = T | 425 |

**Equally Weighted Average**. The simplest option. Described in Chapter 3, is to select an equally weighted average, which is obtained by given equal weight to each of the weeks of available data:

$$(425 + 376 + 411 + 266) / 4 = 370$$

This equally weighted average is simply the arithmetic mean of the data, the same basis underlying the moving average. The forecast of next week's production rate is 370 assemblies. Implicitly, we are assuming that events of 2 and 3 weeks prior (i.e., the more distant past) are as relevant to what may happen next week as were events of the most current and prior week.

In Figure 8.1, a weight is denoted by $w_i$, where the subscript $i$ represents the number of weeks into the past. For an equally weighted average, the weight given to each of the terms is $1/n$, where $n$ is the number of time periods. With $n = 4$, each weight in column 3 is equal to 1/4.

| Week | Weights | Equal | Naïve_1 | Linear Decay | Exponential Decay | Adjusted Weights |
|------|---------|-------|---------|--------------|-------------------|------------------|
| $T-3$ | $w_4$ | 0.25 | 0 | 0.1 | 0.0625 | 0.0667 |
| $T-2$ | $w_3$ | 0.25 | 0 | 0.2 | 0.125 | 0.1333 |
| $T-1$ | $w_2$ | 0.25 | 0 | 0.3 | 0.25 | 0.2667 |
| $T$ | $w_1$ | 0.25 | 1 | 0.4 | 0.5 | 0.5333 |
| Sum | | 1.00 | 1.00 | 1.00 | 0.9375 | 1.0000 |

Figure 8.1 Smoothing weights.

If we consider only the latest week, we have another option, shown in column 4 of Exhibit 8.1, which is the Naïve_1 forecast; it places all weight on the most recent data value. Thus, the forecast for next week's production rate is 425, the same as the current week's production. This forecast makes sense if only the current week's events are relevant in projecting the following week. Whatever happened before this week is ignored.

**Exponentially Decaying Weights.** Most business forecasters find a middle ground more appealing than either of the two extremes, equally weighted or Naïve_1. In between lie weighting schemes in which the weights decay as we move from the current period to the distant past.

$$w_1 > w_2 > w_3 > w_4 > \ldots$$

The largest weight, $w_1$, is given to the most recent data value. This means that to forecast next week's production rate, this week's figure is most important; last week's is less important, and so forth.

Many other patterns are possible with decaying weight schemes. As illustrated by column 5 of Figure 8.1, the weight starts at 40% for the most recent week and declines steadily to 10% for week $T - 3$. Our forecast for week $t = T + 1$ is the weighted average with decaying weights:

$$425 \times 0.4 + 376 \times 0.3 + 411 \times 0.2 + 266 \times 0.1 = 392$$

This weighted average gives a production rate forecast that is more than that of the equally weighted average and less than that of the Naïve_1, in this case.

> *An exponentially weighted average refers to a weighted average of the data in which the weights decay exponentially.*

The most useful example of decaying weights is that of exponentially decaying weights, in which each weight is a constant fraction of its predecessor. A fraction of 0.50 implies a decay rate of 50%, as shown in column 6 of Figure 8.1. In forecasting next period's value, the current period's value is weighted 0.5, the prior week half of that at 0.25, and so forth with each new weight 50% of the one before. (These weights must be adjusted to sum to unity as in column 7.) From Figure 8.1, we can see that the adjusted weights are obtained by dividing the exponential decay weights by 0.9375.

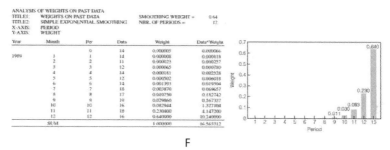

F

Figure 8.2 (*left*) Calculation of weighted averages of past data.
Figure 8.3 (*right*) Exponentially decaying weights for simple exponential smoothing.

Figure 8.2 illustrates the weighted average of all past data, with recent data receiving more weight than older data. The most recent data is at the bottom of the spreadsheet. The weight on each data value is shown in Figure 8.3. The weights decline exponentially with time, a feature that gives exponential smoothing its name.

# The Simple Exponential Smoothing Method

All exponential smoothing techniques incorporate an exponential-decay weighting system, hence the term exponential. Smoothing refers to the averaging that takes place when we calculate a weighted average of the past data. To determine a one-period-ahead forecast of historical data, the projection formula is given by

$$Y_t(1) = \alpha\, Y_t + (1 - \alpha)\, Y_{t-1}(1)$$

where $Y_t(1)$ is the smoothed value at time $t$, based on weighting the most recent value $Y_t$ with a weight $\alpha$ ($\alpha$ is a smoothing parameter) and the current period's forecast (or previous smoothed value) with a weight $(1 - \alpha)$. By rearranging the right-hand side, we can rewrite the equation as

$$Y_t(1) = Y_{t-1}(1) + \alpha\, [Y_t - Y_{t-1}(1)]$$

which can be interpreted as the current period's forecast $Y_{t-1}(1)$ adjusted by a proportion $\alpha$ of the current period's forecast error $[Y_t - Y_{t-1}(1)]$.

> *The simple exponential smoothing method produces forecasts that are a level line for any period in the future, but it is not appropriate for projecting trending data or patterns that are more complex.*

We can now show that the one-step-ahead forecast $Y_t$ (1) is a weighted moving average of all past values with the weights decreasing exponentially. If we substitute for $Y_{t-1}$ (1) in the first smoothing equation, we find that:

$$Y_t (1) = \alpha\, Y_t + (1 - \alpha)\, [\alpha\, Y_{t-1} + (1 - \alpha)\, Y_{t-2} (1)]$$

$$= \alpha\, Y_t + \alpha\, (1 - \alpha)\, Y_{t-1} + (1 - \alpha)^2\, Y_{t-2} (1)$$

If we next substitute for $Y_{t-2}(1)$, then for $Y_{t-3}(1)$, and so, we obtain the result

$$Y_t (1) = \alpha\, Y_t + \alpha\, (1 - \alpha)\, Y_{t-1} + \alpha\, (1 - \alpha)^2\, Y_{t-2} + \alpha\, (1 - \alpha)^3\, Y_{t-3} + \alpha\, (1 - \alpha)^4\, Y_{t-4}$$

$$+ \dots + \alpha\, (1 - \alpha)^{t-1}\, Y_1 + (1 - \alpha)^t\, Y_0 (1)$$

| Weight Assigned to: | $\alpha = 0.1$ | $\alpha = 0.3$ | $\alpha = 0.5$ | $\alpha = 0.9$ |
|---|---|---|---|---|
| $Y_T$ | 0.1 | 0.3 | 0.5 | 0.9 |
| $Y_{T-1}$ | 0.09 | 0.21 | 0.25 | 0.09 |
| $Y_{T-2}$ | 0.081 | 0.147 | 0.125 | 0.009 |

| Week | $Y$ | Actual | $Y_t(1)$ | Formula | Error $Y_t - Y_{t-1}(1)$ |
|---|---|---|---|---|---|
| $T-3$ | $Y_{T-3}$ | 266 | 266 | $Y_{(t-3)}(1) = Y_{(t-3)}$ | |
| $T-2$ | $Y_{T-2}$ | 411 | 339 | $Y_{(t-2)}(1) = 0.5 \times Y_{(t-2)} + 0.5 \times Y_{(t-3)}(1)$ | 72 |
| $T-1$ | $Y_{T-1}$ | 376 | 357 | $Y_{(t-1)}(1) = 0.5 \times Y_{(t-1)} + 0.5 \times Y_{(t-2)}(1)$ | 19 |
| $T$ | $Y_T$ | 425 | 391 | $Y_t(1) = 0.5 \times Y_t + 0.5 \times Y_{(t-1)}(1)$ | 34 |

Figure 8.4 Updating an exponentially weighted average.

The one-step-ahead forecast $Y_T(1)$ represents a weighted average of all past values. For four selected values of the parameter $\alpha$, the weights that are assigned to the past values are shown in the following table:

In Figure 8.4, we calculate a forecast of the production data, assuming that $\alpha = 0.5$. (The production data are repeated in Figure 8.4, in the Actual column.) To use the formula, we need a starting value for the smoothing operation - a value that represents the smoothed average at the earliest week of our time series, here $t = T - 3$. The simplest choice for the starting value is the earliest data point.

In this example, the starting value for the exponentially weighted average is the production rate for week $t = T - 3$, which was given as

266. The final result, $Y_T(1) = 391$ (rounded) for week $t = T$, is called the current level. It is a weighted average of 4 weeks of data, where the weights decline at a rate of 50% per week.

We defined a one-period-ahead forecast made at time $t = T$ to be $Y_T(1)$. Likewise, the $m$-period-ahead forecast is given by $Y_T(m) = Y_T(1)$, for $m = 2, 3, \ldots$. For a time series with a relatively constant level, this is a good forecasting technique. We called this simple smoothing in Chapter 3, but it is generally known as the simple exponential smoothing.

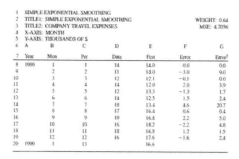
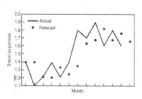

Figure 8.5 (*left*) Forecasting with simple exponential smoothing – company travel expenses.
Figure 8.6 (*right*) Simple exponential smoothing: company travel expenses and one-period ahead forecasts.

---

**The forecast profile of the simple exponential smoothing method is a level horizontal line.**

---

Simple exponential smoothing works much like an automatic pilot or a thermostat. At each time period, the forecasts are adjusted according to the sign of the forecast error (actual data minus forecast.) If the current forecast error is positive, the next forecast is increased; if the error is negative, the forecast is reduced.

To get the smoothing process started (Figure 8.5), we set the first forecast (cell E8) equal to the first data value (cell D8). We can also use the average of the first few data values. Thereafter, the forecasts are updated as follows: In column F, each error is equal to actual data minus forecast. In column E, each forecast is equal to the previous forecast plus a fraction of the previous error. This fraction is called the **smoothing weight** (cell I2).

But how do we select the smoothing weight? The smoothing weight is usually chosen to minimize the mean square error (MSE), a statistical measure of fit. This smoothing weight is called *optimal*, because it is our best estimate based on a prescribed criterion (MSE). Forecasts, errors, and squared errors are shown in columns E, F, and G.

The one-step-ahead forecast (=16.6 in cell E20) extends one period into the future. The travel expense data, smoothed values, and the one-period-ahead forecast are shown graphically in Figure 8.6.

## Forecast Profiles for Exponential Smoothing Methods

A system of exponential smoothing models can be classified by the type of trend and/or seasonal pattern generated as the forecast profile. The most appropriate technique to use for any forecasting should match the profile expected or desired in an application. Figure 8.7 shows the extended Pegels classification for 12 forecasting profiles for exponential smoothing developed by Everette S. Gardner (1944–2023), in a seminal paper *Exponential smoothing: The state of the art*, Journal of Forecasting. 1985.

> **A Pegels classification of exponential smoothing methods gives rise to 12 forecast profiles for trend and seasonal patterns.**

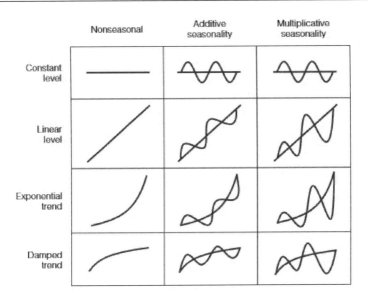

Figure 8.7 Pegels' classification of exponential smoothing forecast profiles including the damped trend technique.

After a preliminary examination of the data from a time plot, we may be able to determine which of the dozen models seems most suitable. In Figure 8.7, there are four types of trends to choose from (Nonseasonal column), and two types of seasonality (Additive and Multiplicative).

Each profile can be directly associated with a specific exponential smoothing model, as described in the next section (some of which are referred to by a common name attributed to their authors). We now explain how each model works to generate forecasts; that is, we describe how each model produces the appropriate forecasting profile.

| Model Name | Trend Profile | Seasonal Profile | State Space Classification |
|---|---|---|---|
| Simple (single) | **N**one | **N**one | (N, N) |
| Holt | **A**dditive (Linear) | **N**one | (A, N) |
| Holt-Winters | **A**dditive (Linear) | **A**dditive or **M**ultiplicative | (A, A) or (A, M) |

> *For a downwardly trending time series, multiplicative seasonality appears as steadily diminishing swings about a trend. For level data, the constant-level multiplicative and additive seasonality techniques give the same forecast profile.*

## Smoothing Levels and Constant Change

An exponential smoothing method comprises one or more of the following components: the current level, the current trend, and the current seasonal index.

- The *current level* serves as the starting point for the forecast. It is calculated to represent an exponentially weighted average of the time series at the end of the fit period. We can regard the current level as the value the time series would now have if there were nothing at all unusual going on at present. An alternative is to use the last value as the starting point, but doing so might set the forecasts off at the wrong level if the most recent data is abnormal.

- The *current trend* represents the amount by which we expect the time series to grow or decline per time period into the future. It is often calculated as an exponentially weighted average of past period-to-period changes in the level of the series. In this way, recent growth or decline in the time series is given more weight than changes farther back in time.

- The *current seasonal index* is interpreted the same way as a conventional seasonal index – as the amount or degree by which the season's value tends to exceed or fall short of the norm. Recall that in the classical decomposition of a time series, a (multiplicative) seasonal index measured the norm as a moving average (see Chapter 6).

The determination of the current seasonal index, a key part of Holt-Winters' method, differs from the conventional indexes in two respects:

> **Difference in weighting years**. In a ratio-to-moving-average (RMA) method, the data used over the years to determine a monthly or quarterly index are weighted equally. In contrast, the Holt-Winters method takes an exponentially weighted average of the ratios to level, thus giving more weight to recent years than to those of the past.

1. **Representing the norm**. The Holt-Winters method uses the current level of the series instead of a moving average of four quarters or 12 months.

The interpretation and estimation of the parameters in the smoothing algorithms is a complex matter that we will not deal with. The algorithms to describe the current level, trend, and seasonal indexes can be found in Hyndman, Koehler, Ord and Snyder's book *Forecasting with Exponential Smoothing*, (2008). It describes in detail the state space framework for forecasting time series with exponential smoothing models.

Optimal or near-optimal parameter settings are derived using prescribed criteria for optimal selection found in modern forecasting software tools, such as the *R* forecast package: *robjhyndman.com/software/forecast.*

In addition, combinations of multiple parameter values severely limit an intuitive feel for their impact on the forecasts. Moreover, for inventory replenishment planning purposes, a demand forecaster needs to rely on automatic forecasting features of modern software because of the very large volume of data involved.

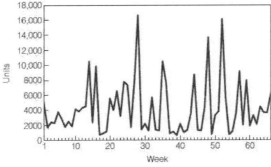

Figure 8.8 Time plot of weekly shipments of a canned beverage (66 weeks) – no trend or seasonality. (Source: Figure 8.9).

We now illustrate the use of the smoothing equations for (1) calculating the current level, trend, and seasonal indexes and (2) combining these values into the forecasting formula. Figure 8.8 is a time plot of weekly shipments of a canned beverage for 66 weeks, shown previously in Chapter 6.

The series is highly variable but not trending. The average level is approximately 4000 - 5000 units per week with a standard deviation of 3639. Some of the high peaks may be attributed to promotions, but we will choose to forecast it using simple exponential smoothing. This technique is appropriate for data lacking trend and seasonality.

The simple exponential smoothing algorithm is used to fit to all 66 weeks and point forecasts are calculated for 4 weeks. The optimal estimate (based on the MSE criterion) of the smoothing parameter is 0.62 with MSE = 1669. The multi-period point forecasts are a constant level (= 5129). Thus, it represents a "typical" level. Figure 8.9 displays the most recent 20 weeks of historical shipments, 20 weeks of fitted values, and the four forecasts.

Because simple exponential smoothing views the future of the time series as lacking both trend and seasonality, the forecasting equation does not contain these terms, leaving the current level as the sole component.

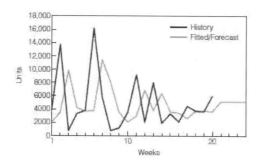

Figure 8.9 Fit and forecast profile for canned beverage shipments: simple exponential smoothing: no trend, no seasonality.

*The current level $L_t$ is calculated by an equation for an exponentially smoothed average of the past data: $Y_T(m) = L_t$.*

Consider annual car registrations data as another example. Because the data are annual, the time series is necessarily nonseasonal. The global trend appears to be linear, although there are a number of local variations on the trend.

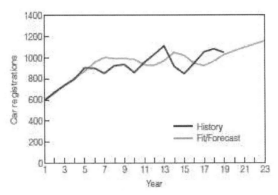

Figure 8.10 Time plot of annual car registrations for a 19-year period, fit and the forecast profile from the Holt method – linear trend, no seasonality.

Figure 8.10 shows the straight-line forecast profile from the Holt method (A, N) – linear trend, no seasonality. We see that from the vantage point of Year 19, the current level of car registrations is estimated to be 1034 and the current trend is estimated to be an increase of 31 registrations per year.

For nonseasonal data, the seasonal index terms are not present in the forecasting algorithm. What remains in the Holt method, however, is the forecasting equation for a linear trend:

$$Y_T(m) = [L_t + m \times T_t]$$

The forecast for year 22 is 1126, based on calculating a 3-year-ahead projection from the base year T = 19:

$$Y_{19}(3) = [1033.62 + 3 \times 30.78] = 1126$$

## Damped and Exponential Trends

For seasonal patterns, the trend component, if one is present, is assumed to be linear. Trends can also be nonlinear. For example, damped (upward) trend assumes that the series will continue to grow but that the growth gradually dampens out. An exponential growth trend assumes that the series will grow by a progressively larger amount. Exponential growth is equivalent to a constant percentage rate of growth. As the base grows over time, the constant percentage increase on the base translates into larger and larger increments in volume, in the manner of compound-interest growth on an investment.

In the case of a downward trend, the damped and exponential forecast profiles are similar. During a phase out or decline under adverse market conditions, a forecast profile will be decaying without becoming negative. We may refer to the pattern of shipments of a cosmetic product (Figure 8.11) either as a downwardly damped trend or as exponential decay.

Like a no-trend or linear trend, the exponential trend may be used in conjunction with multiplicative, additive, or no seasonality patterns. We use the nonseasonal case here to illustrate damped and exponential trends. (When seasonality is included, it is called the Holt-Winters procedure, discussed later.)

Both damped and exponential trends can be represented in a single forecasting equation, given by

$$Y_T(m) = L_t + \sum \varphi^i \times T_t$$

where $m$ is the length of the forecast horizon. The symbol $\phi$ is called the **trend-modification parameter**. Depending on the value of $\phi$, the forecast profile can be an exponential trend, linear trend, damped trend, or constant level. Here are the cases:

If $\phi > 1$ trend is *exponential.*

If $\phi = 1$ trend is *linear.*

If $\phi < 1$ trend is *damped.*

If $\phi = 0$ there in *no trend.*

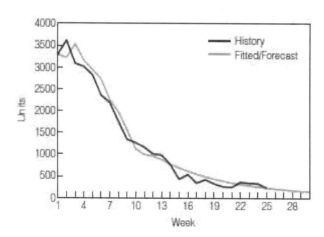

Figure 8.11 Time plot of weekly shipments of a cosmetic product – damped trend exponential smoothing.

Figure 8.12 shows the historical and forecast profiles for a damped trend and exponential trend model of the annual car registration series.

The growth in the forecasts, the change from the prior year's forecast, has dampened. With $\phi$ = 0.83, the forecasted trend is slowing by 1 - 0.83 = 0.17 or 17% per period. The estimates of level and trend weights are 0.6 and 0.2, respectively.

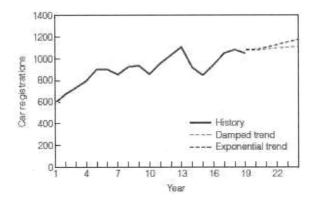

Figure 8.12 Time plot for annual car registrations with two exponential smoothing forecast profiles – damped trend and exponential trend. 12)

> **The damped trend exponential smoothing approach offers forecasters a well-tested and consistently top performing approach to trend-seasonal time series forecasting.**

We can illustrate how the point forecast was obtained for Year 20 (= $T$ + 1); the fitted value for year 19 is 1078.55, $L_t$ = 1060.86, and $T_t$ = 18.75. Setting $m$ = 1,

$$Y_{19}(1) = L_t + \phi \times T_t$$

$$= 1060.86 + 0.83^1 \times (18.75) = 1076.42$$

The Year-21 point forecast is calculated as follows:

$$Y_{19}(2) = L_t + (\phi + \phi^2) \times T_t$$

$$= 1060.86 + (0.83 + 0.83^2) \times (18.75) = 1089.34$$

Alternatively, we can obtain the point forecast for $T$ + 2 by calculating $Y_T(2) = Y_T(1) + \phi^2 \times T_t$

## Some Forecast Profile Examples

**Annual Sales of a Cosmetic Product.** Consider the trending data for the yearly sales of a cosmetic product. The sales for this cosmetic product, for the period 1978 - 2002, show a declining trend.

The forecast profile declines exponentially, modeled by a nonlinear trend exponential smoothing method. Exhibit 8.13 presents a graphical comparison of a linear trend and damped trend exponential trend method for the cosmetic product.

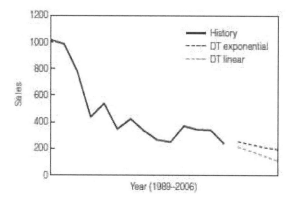

Figure 8.13 Forecast models for a cosmetic product: damped and linear trend exponential smoothing.

Note that the minimizing MSE may not be the only criterion for selecting a model; the eventual profile should also be considered. In this case, the linear trend with the lowest MSE also yields much lower point forecasts over the forecast period than the damped trend approach. It may require informed judgment on the part of the demand planner and forecaster to determine the most useful profile for the data at hand.

To illustrate how the damped exponential trend point forecast was obtained for the year 2005 (= T + 3), we set m = 3 and T = 2002:

$$Y_{2005}(3) = L_t + (\phi + \phi^2 + \phi^3) \times T_t$$

$$= 279.85 + (0.88 + 0.88^2 + 0.88^3) \times (-29.86) = 210.10$$

| Period | Linear Trend LT (0.64, 0.34, 1.0) | Damped Trend DT (0.64, 0.34, 0.88) | Linear Trend LT (0.81, 0.18, 1.0) |
|---|---|---|---|
| 2002 actual | 236 | 236 | 236 |
| 2003 | 255 | 253 | 214 |
| 2004 | 228 | 230 | 180 |
| 2005 | 201 | 210 | 144 |
| 2006 | 174 | 192 | 109 |

Figure 8.14 A four-period forecast comparison for sales of a cosmetic product: linear and damped trend exponential smoothing.

The difference in the forecast profiles for the linear trend and damped trend arises from the value of the trend modification parameter, which is below unity ($\phi$ = 0.88) for the damped trend. This value of $\phi$ leads to a decrease over prior year's forecast and is characteristic of an exponential decline. On the other hand, the damped exponential trend model, for which the trend modification parameter is constrained to $\phi = 1$, gives rise to a linear trend forecast profile.

Comparing the results with the corresponding forecasts from the damped trend exponential method (DT) in Figure 8.15 we find that the log-transform approach yields point forecasts that are slightly lower than those shown in Figure 8.13; however, both depict a forecast profile with a negative exponential trend.

By taking a transformation of the data, exponential growth patterns can also be modeled by applying a linear trend (Holt method) to the natural logarithm of the time series. The results are shown in Figure 8.15. The point forecasts are calculated first in terms of the logarithm of the series and then transformed into the original data by exponentiation. To illustrate how the forecast was obtained for the year 2006 $(t = T + 4)$, we set $m = 4$ and $T = 2002$:

$$\text{Forecast for } \log_{10} (T + 4) = 2.44 + 4 \times (-0.04) = 2.28$$

Transform back to original data $= 10^{2.28} = 190$.

Comparing the results with the corresponding forecasts from the damped trend exponential method (DT) in Figure 8.15 we find that the log-transform approach yields point forecasts that are slightly lower than those shown in Figure 8.13; however, both depict a forecast profile with a negative exponential trend.

| Period | LT (0.64, 0.38, 1.0) (log-transformed data) | Linear Trend model (untransformed column 1) | DT (0.64, 0.38, 0.8) (from Exhibit 8.21) |
|---|---|---|---|
| 2002 Actual | 2.373 | 236 | 236 |
| 2003 | 2.40 | 251 | 253 |
| 2004 | 2.36 | 229 | 230 |
| 2005 | 2.32 | 209 | 210 |
| 2006 | 2.28 | 190 | 192 |

Figure 8.15 Forecast model for sales of a cosmetic product (logarithmic transformation): linear trend.

Depending on the context in which these projections are used in practice, the differences could become substantial. This illustrates the limitation of using these types of techniques for extrapolating highly trending annual time series for more than a couple of periods. More important, when we calculate prediction limits on the forecasts, these two approaches also give different interpretations.

*In general, the damped trend techniques appear better suited for smoothing short-term patterns for operational forecasting in inventory and production planning than for smoothing long-term forecasting.*

## Trend-Seasonal Profiles with Prediction Limits

The forecasting equations for additive and multiplicative seasonality are:

$$\text{Additive:} \quad Y_T(m) = L_t + m \times T_t + \text{Seasonal index}$$
$$\text{Multiplicative:} \quad Y_T(m) = [L_t + m \times T_t] \times \text{Seasonal index}$$

where $Y_T(m)$ denotes a forecast made at time $T$, the final season in the fit period, for $m$ periods into the future. This technique is known as the Holt-Winters procedure. Unlike the nonseasonal exponential smoothing techniques, seasonality brings in a complexity that makes interpreting the smoothing equations directly less intuitive. Fortunately, these algorithms are available in some software, such as $R$ forecast package: *robjhyndman.com/software/forecast.*, so we show only here that the forecast for $m$ periods ahead can be compiled using the steps:

1. Start at the current level, $L_t$.
2. Add the product of current trend, $T_t$, and the number of periods $m$ ahead that we are projecting trend.
3. Adjust the resulting sum of level and trend for seasonality through a multiplicative or additive seasonal index.

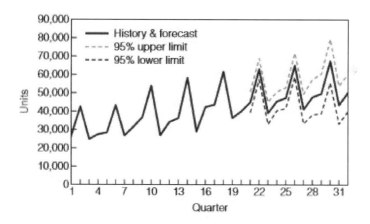

Figure 8. 16 A time plot with 95% prediction limits of a quarterly automobile sales series.

Figure 8.16 is a time plot of a quarterly automobile sales time series. An STI_Classification shows that approximately 68% of the total variation was attributed to seasonality. The trend appears to be linear with seasonal peaks occurring in the second quarter of each year.

A **proper Skill score** is 1 - [(MSE of your model)/(MSE of Naïve_4)] and can be computed as follows:

1. The series is deseasonalized so that the seasonal pattern is removed.
2. The preliminary forecast for each period is taken as the seasonally adjusted value from the previous period.
3. The final forecasts are computed by reseasonalizing the preliminary forecasts.
4. Forecast errors are computed by subtracting final forecasts from actual data.

The low seasonal peak in Year 2 was not adjusted because it occurred very early in the dataset and would have minimal weight in the exponential smoothing calculations.

The prediction limits are shown in Figure 8.16. These 95% prediction limits indicate that we are 95% sure that the true (in the sense that the model is correct) forecasts will lie within these limits. The prediction limits do not appear symmetrical around the forecast, which suggests that the model errors are multiplicative. The forecasts are more likely to be high than low, which makes sense with the consistent upward trend in the historical data.

The smoothing weights (level = 0.02, trend = 0.115 and seasonal = 0.00) are an indication of the relative emphasis given to the data from the recent and more distant past in the calculation of the current level, trend, and seasonal indexes. The values for the current level, trend, and seasonal indexes are called final values. Note that period $T$ is the second quarter (spring) of Year 6. To forecast from this time origin, the current level is 46,841, the current trend is 561.8 (units per quarter), and each season has its own seasonal index. The summer index (Q3= -2225.8) indicates that automobile sales during the summer tend to be approximately 2226 units below the norm.

In Figure 8.16, starting from spring Q2 of Year 6, the automobile sales forecast for Q3 is (setting m = 1):

$$Y_T(m) = [L_t + m \times T_t] + \text{Seasonal index}$$
$$Y_T(1) = [46{,}841 + 561.8] + (-2225.8)$$
$$= 45{,}178 \text{ units}$$

To forecast three periods ahead to winter Q1 of Year 7, we set $m$ = 3 and use the seasonal index for Q1:

$$Y_T(3) = [L_t + 3 \times T_t] + \text{Seasonal index}$$
$$= [46{,}841 + 3 \times 561.8] + (-9602.5) = 38{,}925 \text{ units}$$

The point forecast for the winter of Year 7 is lower than that for the previous summer for two reasons. First, the trend is only growing by approximately 562 units per quarter. Second, and more substantially, the seasonal index for winter is 7377 units lower than in summer. The multiplicative seasonal model produces the following forecast for the winter quarter of Year 7

$$Y_T(3) = [L_t + 3 \times T_t] \times \text{Seasonal index}$$

$$= [46{,}961.5 + 3 \times 957.1] \times 0.755 = 37{,}624$$

In this example, the two versions of Holt-Winters procedure give very similar values for the current level and trend. The seasonal indexes are in a different form and result in different projections. The additive index for the summer season tells us that summer sales tend to be approximately 15000 units above the norm; this will be a constant amount for all future years. In contrast, the multiplicative index for the summer season is estimated to be approximately 39% above the norm, which represents an increasing amount as long as the data are trending up.

Which model is most useful? From purely statistical considerations, the multiplicative model has the preferred summary results. However, this may not necessarily mean that forecast performance will be better as well.

# The Pegels Classification for Trend-Seasonal Models

The state-space models (Figure 8.17) that underlie the exponential smoothing techniques come in two forms: models with additive error assumptions and models with multiplicative errors. Although the forecast profiles for a given model formulation are identical, there are important differences in the prediction limits produced by the additive and multiplicative error assumptions. With this distinction in error structure, the **Error-Trend-Seasonal** (ETS) state-space framework today effectively describes 30 models in the Pegels classification, by creating triplets, like (A, N, N) and (M, N, N) for the entry (N, N) in the follwoing table:

| Model Name | Error | Trend Profile | Seasonal Profile | State Space Classification |
|---|---|---|---|---|
| Simple (single) | Additive | None | None | (A, N, N) |
| Holt | Additive | Additive (Linear) | None | (A, A, N) |
| Holt-Winters | Additive | Additive (Linear) | Additive or Multiplicative | (A, A, A) or (A, A, M) |

There are differences in their use as well. The new **multiplicative error** models are not well defined if there are zeros or negative values in the data. Similarly, additive error models should not be used with **multiplicative trend** or multiplicative seasonality if any data value is zero.

*A Pegels classification of exponential smoothing profiles in a state-space modeling framework gives rise to 30 trend-seasonal forecast profiles with prediction limits for trend and seasonal patterns*

| | Seasonal Component | | |
|---|---|---|---|
| **Trend** | N | A | M |
| **Component** | (None) | (Additive) | (Multiplicative) |
| N (None) | (N,N) | (N,A) | (N,M) |
| A (Additive) | (A,N) | (A,A) | (A,M) |
| A_d (Additive damped) | (A_d,N) | (A_d,A) | (A_d,M) |
| M (Multiplicative) | (M,N) | (M,A) | (M,M) |
| M_d (Multiplicative damped) | (M_d,N) | (M_d,A) | (M_d,M) |

Some of these methods we have already seen:

| | | |
|---|---|---|
| (N,N) | = | simple exponential smoothing |
| (A,N) | = | Holts linear method |
| (M,N) | = | Exponential trend method |
| (A_d,N) | = | additive damped trend method |
| (M_d,N) | = | multiplicative damped trend method |
| (A,A) | = | additive Holt-Winters method |
| (A,M) | = | multiplicative Holt-Winters method |
| (A_d,M) | = | Holt-Winters damped method |

Figure 8.17 Classification of the exponential smoothing methods for State Space forecasting. (*Source*: Hyndman, et al *Forecasting with Exponential Smoothing – The State Space Approach.* (2008).

# Outlier Effect on Prediction Limits

Figure 8.18 depicts a time series of a product in which the seasonal peak (value #31) for the third year is diminished. What could be the root-cause and how should we clean this data?

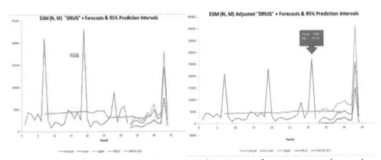

Figure 8.18 *(left)* A predictive visualization of a seasonal peak adjustment, unadjusted value #31.
Figure 8.219 *(right)* An improved predictive visualization (with a seasonal peak adjustment in period #31).

If not adjusted, an automatic exponential smoothing algorithm (State-Space model (N, M)) produced forecasts and prediction limits (Figure 8.19) for period's #32 - #43 (12 months). It clearly does not look credible. The issue is not with the no-trend, multiplicative seasonal exponential smoothing model, but rather the impact that an outlier can have on the forecast profile.

For exponential smoothing models it is important that data are cleaned before modeling especially when the unusual values are so close to the most current period. The one-step-ahead forecast for value #31 is 5740, based on the (N, M) model for the first 30 values. With this value (or any value within the prediction limits) replacing the original value with 27036 yielded a much-improved forecast profile with prediction limits in Figure 8.19 (Note the change in the vertical scale).

# Predictive Visualization of Change and Chance – Hotel/Motel Room Demand

| Fit Statistics | (A, A) | (A, M) |
|---|---|---|
| Level (alpha) | 0.238 | 0.233 |
| Trend (beta) | 0.1 | 0.1 |
| Season (gamma) | 0.1 | 0.1 |
| MAPE (Mean Absolute Percentage Error) | 2.2% | 1.9% |
| AIC | 2269 | 1973 |
| ME (Mean Residual Error) | -2231 | -696 |
| MdE (Median Residual Error) | -2511 | -73 |
| MAD (Mean Absolute Deviation | 25202 | 23237 |
| MdAD (Median Absolute Deviation) | 19852 | 18790 |

Figure 8.20 Model-fitting summary for monthly hotel/motel room demand - additive trend, additive seasonality model (A, A) and additive trend, multiplicative seasonality model (A, M).

In the examples above, we demonstrate how to calculate point forecasts with exponential smoothing equations. In Figure 8.20, we provide a model fitting summary and model performance comparison for an additive seasonal (A, A) and multiplicative seasonal (A, M) exponential smoothing model of the monthly time series of hotel/motel room demand). The smoothing parameters come from minimizing MSE over the fit period.

Based on the fit statistics alone, the multiplicative seasonal version (A, M) appears to have the better summary results. However, fit may not be a good indication of post-sample forecast accuracy. In practice, it would always be advisable to maintain several models on an ongoing basis at all times for a post sample forecasting performance analysis.

| | | YEAR | | | | | | | |
|---|---|---|---|---|---|---|---|---|---|
| | | 1987 | 1988 | 1989 | 1990 | 1991 | 1992 | 1993 | 1994 |
| | Jan | 786152 | 839670 | 974188 | 903905 | 885370 | 959456 | 1063319 | 1001666 |
| | Feb | 887466 | 886806 | 955943 | 974746 | 971191 | 1059044 | 1061060 | 1073196 |
| | Mar | 1179318 | 1220361 | 1269982 | 1317009 | 1282507 | 1321280 | 1417406 | 1421423 |
| M | Apr | 1279396 | 1376184 | 1455327 | 1414099 | 1440099 | 1468333 | 1556240 | 1577321 |
| O | May | 1317952 | 1408277 | 1463003 | 1484942 | 1457659 | 1561624 | 1608882 | 1600991 |
| N | Jun | 1277096 | 1361691 | 1411940 | 1421063 | 1456850 | 1425970 | 1524063 | 1594481 |
| T | Jul | 1239127 | 1262819 | 1348487 | 1342884 | 1362356 | 1442066 | 1503225 | 1510052 |
| H | Aig | 1170964 | 1267118 | 1307840 | 1301696 | 1309305 | 1444047 | 1448443 | 1436164 |
| | Sep | 1177436 | 1225871 | 1289197 | 1261578 | 1302742 | 1380209 | 1416191 | 1404978 |
| | Oct | 1349938 | 1405643 | 1458479 | 1368512 | 1466332 | 1473327 | 1593538 | 1585409 |
| | Nov | 1054226 | 1125935 | 1159213 | 1113859 | 1181893 | 1146961 | 1274462 | 1234848 |
| | Dec | 813315 | 863217 | 869957 | 869067 | 854615 | 920010 | 969445 | 923115 |

Figure 8.21 Historical data of monthly hotel/motel room demand. (*Source*: D. C. Frechtling, *Practical Tourism Forecasting* 1996, Appendix. 1)

> *The most useful way to simulate forecast accuracy is by creating a holdout period and distinguishing a fit period (to estimate parameters) from a forecast period (to determine forecast accuracy).*

Because our primary interest is in forecasting performance of models, we started with a holdout period of the latest 12 months and created forecasts based on the first 84 monthly values.).

The evaluation results for an automatic, optimally selected model: suggest that we have a credible (A, M) model. The data are clearly seasonal. This is a static test with a multiplicative trend/seasonal forecast profile (Holt-Winters model) in the sense that all forecasts were made from a single time point ($T = 1984$) for a fixed time horizon ($m = 12$).

For the forecasting evaluations (Figure 8.22) we are using the ME and MdE for bias and MAPE and MdAPE for accuracy. The 12 forecast errors are all negative, implying that the model is biased (i.e., over-forecasting). The average of the 12 forecast errors is − 63716 and the median error is − 65395 indicating overforecasting the entire year. The MAPE and MdAPE are both 5%, so there is no evidence in any unusual monthly over-forecast.

The hold-out sample evaluation of forecasts in Figure 8.23 is a dynamic test: both starting point and horizon change. For one-period-ahead forecasts (lead-time = 1), there are 12 possible forecasts that could generated. The average of the 12 one-period-ahead absolute forecast percentage errors is 2.4%, a measure of accuracy. This suggests that, on average, one-period-ahead forecasts can be accurate within 3% or so. For longer horizons, the accuracy decreases, but still within 10%, based on the test. The lead 12 accuracy is based on only one forecast, so the improved accuracy is an anomaly.

| Exponential Smoothing/State Space - Model (A,M) | | | | | | |
|---|---|---|---|---|---|---|
| **Forecasts & 95% prediction intervals** | | | | | | |
| Period | Forecast | Lower | Upper | Actual | ForecastError | AbsolutePctError ForecastSqError |
| 85 | 1053875 | 995598 | 1124032 | 1001666 | -52209 | 5.2% | 2725796337 |
| 86 | 1110008 | 1050767 | 1178340 | 1073196 | -36812 | 3.4% | 1355115686 |
| 87 | 1470395 | 1404213 | 1540855 | 1421423 | -48972 | 3.4% | 2398215654 |
| 88 | 1632686 | 1563852 | 1708082 | 1577321 | -55365 | 3.5% | 3065331226 |
| 89 | 1686319 | 1610548 | 1762291 | 1600991 | -85328 | 5.3% | 7280918502 |
| 90 | 1616734 | 1538055 | 1691889 | 1594481 | -22253 | 1.4% | 495174886.4 |
| 91 | 1558806 | 1477801 | 1638322 | 1510052 | -48754 | 3.2% | 2376993543 |
| 92 | 1517417 | 1434450 | 1599909 | 1436164 | -81253 | 5.7% | 6602118260 |
| 93 | 1483846 | 1395880 | 1568649 | 1404978 | -78868 | 5.6% | 6220234506 |
| 94 | 1660834 | 1559909 | 1754568 | 1585409 | -75425 | 4.8% | 5688876400 |
| 95 | 1323055 | 1233145 | 1408416 | 1234848 | -88207 | 7.1% | 7780418497 |
| 96 | 1014265 | 931560.7 | 1092019 | 923115 | -91150 | 9.9% | 8308252033 |

|  | BIAS ==> | Mean Error= | -63716 |  | MSE= 4524767128 |
|---|---|---|---|---|---|
|  |  | Median Error= | -65395 |  | RMSE= 67267 |
|  |  |  |  | MAPE= 4.9% |  |
|  |  | PRECISION | MdAPE= 5.0% |  |  |

Figure 8.22 Monthly hotel/motel room demand series - linear trend, multiplicative seasonality model (A, M). Forecast bias and accuracy over 12-month horizon.

When we repeat this dynamic simulation for the additive seasonal (A, A) version of Holt-Winters model (not shown), the range of MAPEs is between 2.5% and 14%. Hence, the multiplicative model still seems to be the better choice for this forecast period

| Date | Actual | Forecast | Error | Level | Trend | Index |
|---|---|---|---|---|---|---|
| 1994—1 | 1,001,666 | 1,063,949 | −62,283 | 1,326,148 | −2660 | 0.77 |
| 1994—2 | 1,073,196 | 1,045,975 | 27,221 | 1,345,926 | −623 | 0.79 |
| 1994—3 | 1,421,423 | 1,398,118 | 23,306 | 1,359,538 | 337 | 1.04 |
| 1994—4 | 1,577,321 | 1,578,977 | −1656 | 1,358,871 | 178 | 1.16 |
| 1994—5 | 1,600,991 | 1,614,232 | −13,241 | 1,352,017 | −256 | 1.19 |
| 1994—6 | 1,594,481 | 1,537,137 | 57,344 | 1,383,392 | 1525 | 1.14 |
| 1994—7 | 1,510,052 | 1,502,676 | 7376 | 1,388,664 | 1250 | 1.09 |
| 1994—8 | 1,436,164 | 1,456,457 | −20,293 | 1,377,391 | 186 | 1.05 |
| 1994—9 | 1,404,978 | 1,412,361 | −7383 | 1,373,012 | −117 | 1.02 |
| 1994—10 | 1,585,409 | 1,593,154 | −7745 | 1,368,758 | −303 | 1.16 |
| 1994—11 | 1,234,848 | 1,261,615 | −26,767 | 1,350,392 | −1179 | 0.92 |
| 1994—12 | 923,115 | 951,879 | −28,764 | 1,324,091 | −2162 | 0.70 |

Figure 8.23 Performance evaluation of the hotel/motel room demand series - damped trend, multiplicative seasonality model (Ad, M). Evaluation of dynamic rolling forecasts).

| Lead | Number of Forecasts | MAD | MAPE | RMSE |
|---|---|---|---|---|
| 1 | 12 | 30,871 | 2.40% | 37,779 |
| 2 | 11 | 43,041 | 3.09% | 55,160 |
| 3 | 10 | 48,202 | 3.43% | 60,343 |
| 4 | 9 | 52,679 | 3.75% | 68,680 |
| 5 | 8 | 70,180 | 5.19% | 98,091 |
| 6 | 7 | 72,493 | 5.56% | 99,852 |
| 7 | 6 | 72,736 | 5.12% | 99,632 |
| 8 | 5 | 93,286 | 7.23% | 119,237 |
| 9 | 4 | 116,838 | 9.08% | 149,592 |
| 10 | 3 | 93,531 | 8.31% | 122,273 |
| 11 | 2 | 88,349 | 9.11% | 103,814 |
| 12 | 1 | 44,061 | 4.77% | 44,061 |

Figure 8.24 One-period-ahead forecasts over the holdout period for the hotel/motel room demand series - damped trend, multiplicative seasonality model (Ad, M).

The one-step-ahead forecast errors play a special role in the analysis of forecast performance because prediction limits are based on them. Figure 8.24 displays the 12 period-ahead forecasts with the upper and lower prediction limits over the holdout period made with the damped trend, multiplicative seasonal model (Ad, M). These forecasts are compared with the actuals in the holdout sample and forecast errors are calculated. The final level and trend components are shown, along with the seasonal index for the month. Evidently, the peak month is May (index = 1.187), meaning that May is almost 19% above norm. This may be attributable to the attractions of the spring season in this location. As expected for these data, the low months are in the winter.

## *Lead-time Profile Forecasting with State Space Models*

In Chapter 4, we approached multi-step ahead point forecasting for unspecified horizons. For **fixed** horizons, a multi-step ahead forecast is called a **lead-time forecast**. to contrast it to one-step ahead or short-term forecasts. A lead-time forecast is commonly used in practice for regular and intermittent demand forecasting applications, when

- planning product mix based on future patterns of demand at the item, product group and store level
- setting safety stock levels for SKUs at multiple locations
- conducting S&OP and annual budget planning meetings
- validating methods in forecasting competitions

Lead-time demand forecasts are widely used by supply chain practitioners for inventory planning, budget forecasting, and S&OP planning. Once a baseline forecast has been put together, planners and managers can contribute their expertise in creating planning forecasts by adding judgmental overrides or including another forecasting method based on more current information or planning objectives.

For this kind of forecast, an objective approach based on information-theoretic concepts can be used to measure the accuracy and performance of both regular and intermittent lead-time demand forecasts.

| | Sep. | Oct. | Nov. | Dec. | Jan. | Feb. | Mar. | Apr. | May | Jun. | Jul. | Aug. | Total |
|---|---|---|---|---|---|---|---|---|---|---|---|---|---|
| 2012 | 0 | 0 | 0 | 0 | 55060 | 71365 | 70350 | 49375 | 20403 | 35518 | 27454 | 35480 | 364955 |
| 2013 | 41336 | 24871 | 21162 | 80025 | 33755 | 57809 | 58769 | 35496 | 39467 | 24332 | 13731 | 34915 | 465668 |
| 2014 | 41356 | 41328 | 42273 | 75694 | 61779 | 49478 | 68117 | 36155 | 40489 | 34373 | 11157 | 31158 | 533357 |
| 2015 | 51901 | 17690 | 55843 | 75187 | 51390 | 25319 | 27811 | 28489 | 39619 | 26952 | 30531 | 37110 | 467742 |
| 2016 | 30389 | 28622 | 35688 | 49786 | 73069 | 44860 | 37209 | 17673 | 10733 | 26401 | 26215 | 40489 | 421134 |
| 2017 | | | | | | | | | | | | | 0 |

Holdout_AAP: 0.07216 0.067964 0.084743 0.118219 0.173505 0.106522 0.088354 0.041965 0.025486 0.06269 0.062249 0.096143 SUM=1
LN AAP: -2.62887 -2.68878 -2.46814 -2.13522 -1.75155 -2.2394 -2.4264 -3.17091 -3.66963 -2.76955 -2.77662 -2.34192

Figure 8.25 A dataset of monthly demand with test period used for forecast profile performance evaluation.

In figure 8.25, a fiscal, budget or planning year does not necessarily have to start in January, so lead-time or forecasting cycle Totals are shown for a dataset to assess forecasting performance with the test or holdout data (shown in *italics*) in the row for year 2016. For a twelve-month test (holdout) period (Sep 2016 – Aug 2017), three forecasts were created by using (1) judgment, (2) a method and (3) a statistical model. For a JUDGMENT forecast, the previous year actuals (Sep 2015 – Aug 2016) were used as the forecast for the hold-out sample year. This forecast profile is labeled **Year-1.** It is also known as the Naive12 method. For a METHOD forecast, a level point- forecast (**MAVG_12**), is simply the average of previous 12-months of history repeated over the forecast horizon. The MODEL forecast is based on the State Space forecasting model **ETS (A,A,M)**, which is an exponential smoothing model with a local level and multiplicative seasonal forecast profile.

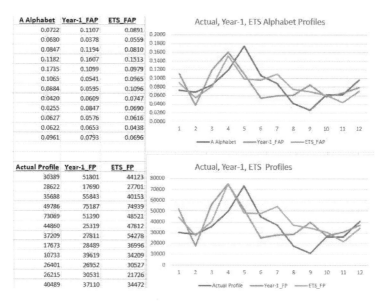

Figure 8.26 Actuals, forecasts and Actual Alphabet Profile (AAP) and Forecast Alphabet Profiles (FAP) for three forecasting approaches: (1)'same as last year' judgment, (2) '12-month moving average' method and (3) 'state space ETS' model.

For lead-time demand forecasting, a useful idea is to code or map a lead-time demand *forecast profile* into a *forecast alphabet profile* (FAP), which looks identical to the original data except that the pattern of the profile has been rescaled (Figure 8.26), so that the profile components become weights that sum to one. That makes alphabet profiles comparable for performance evaluations across series as well as product/location hierarchies.

A profile performance analysis of the forecasts is based on concepts in information theory that are widely used in in climatology and machine learning applications. In this approach, consider a forecast error to be the miss or 'spread' between the *profile* of the actuals and the forecast profile, like the patterns in Figure 8.27). A **Forecast Profile**

**Error** (FPE) for each of the three forecasting approaches ('same as last year' judgment, '12-month moving average' method and 'state space ETS' model) are shown in Figure 8.26.

The forecast profile errors are calculated with the formula

$$(a_i \ln a_i) \quad minus \quad (f_i \ln f_i)$$

where the $a_i$ are the components in the *Actual Alphabet Profile* (AAP) and $f_i$ are the components in the *Forecast Alphabet Profile* (FAP). and *ln* stands for the natural logarithm.

The sums of the rows (**FAP Miss**) can be interpreted as a measure of ignorance about the *forecast profile error* .

$$\textbf{FAP } Miss = \sum_{i=1}^{m}(a_i \ln a_i) - \sum_{i=1}^{m} (f_i \ln f_i)$$

The closer to zero the better, and the sign indicates over or under forecasting. The units are known as 'nats' (for natural logarithms).

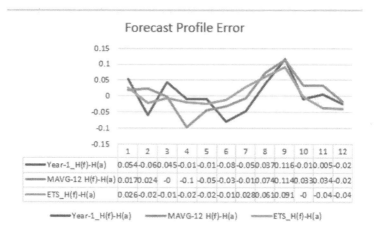

Figure 8.27 Forecast Profile Error (Miss) results for three forecasts.

## Assessing the Accuracy of a Forecast Profile

The accuracy of a Forecast Alphabet Profile FAP is given by the **Profile Accuracy** measure D(a|f).

$$D(a|f) = \sum_{i=1}^{m} \left(a_i \ln \left(\frac{a_i}{f_i}\right)\right)$$

When D(a|f) = 0, the alphabet profiles overlap, or what we might consider as **100% accuracy**. It is always positive and equal to zero if and only if AAP = FAP. The sums of the rows in Figure 8.28 can be interpreted as a measure of ignorance or uncertainty about profile accuracy. In this instance, it appears that ETS (A,A,M) is the more accurate of the three .

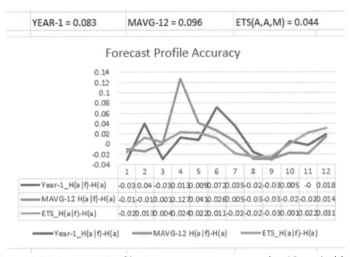

| YEAR-1 = 0.083 | MAVG-12 = 0.096 | ETS(A,A,M) = 0.044 |

**Forecast Profile Accuracy**

| | 1 | 2 | 3 | 4 | 5 | 6 | 7 | 8 | 9 | 10 | 11 | 12 |
|---|---|---|---|---|---|---|---|---|---|---|---|---|
| Year-1_H(a|f)-H(a) | -0.03 | 0.04 | -0.03 | 0.013 | 0.009 | 0.072 | 0.035 | -0.02 | -0.03 | 0.005 | -0 | 0.018 |
| MAVG-12 H(a|f)-H(a) | -0.01 | -0.01 | 0.001 | 0.127 | 0.041 | 0.026 | 0.005 | -0.03 | -0.03 | -0.02 | -0.02 | 0.014 |
| ETS_H(a|f)-H(a) | -0.02 | 0.013 | 0.004 | 0.024 | 0.022 | 0.011 | -0.02 | -0.02 | -0.03 | 0.001 | 0.022 | 0.031 |

Year-1_H(a|f)-H(a)     MAVG-12 H(a|f)-H(a)     ETS_H(a|f)-H(a)

Figure 8.28 Forecast Profile Accuracy pattern over the 12-period lead-time for three models.

# How to Create and Use Error Bounds on Profile Accuracy

The ETS model is useful for setting error bounds on the Profile Accuracy by plugging in the ETS prediction limits as lower fLPL and upper forecast profiles in the D(a|f) accuracy formula, as follows: D(a|f) ETS_LL = D(a|fLPL) and D(a|f) ETL_UL = D(a|fUPL). The final column (Figure 8.29, *top*) shows the values to be plotted as horizontal lines on the scatter plot "ETS Model Accuracy vs Actual Profile H(a)

| Period | 45 | 46 | 47 | 48 | 49 | 50 | 51 | 52 | 53 | 54 | 55 | 56 | Sum | Sum'12 |
|---|---|---|---|---|---|---|---|---|---|---|---|---|---|---|
| Month | Sep. | Oct. | Nov. | Dec. | Jan. | Feb. | Mar. | Apr. | May | Jun. | Jul. | Aug. | | |
| D(a|f) ETS | -0.0152 | 0.0133 | 0.0038 | 0.0236 | 0.0223 | 0.0105 | -0.0190 | -0.0242 | -0.0254 | 0.0011 | 0.0218 | 0.0311 | 0.0439 | 0.0037 |
| D(a|f) ETS_LL | -0.0242 | 0.2162 | 0.0109 | -0.0822 | -0.0044 | -0.0133 | -0.0512 | -0.0100 | -0.0093 | 0.0886 | 0.2896 | 0.0936 | 0.5045 | 0.0420 |
| D(a|f) ETS_UL | -0.0140 | 0.0043 | 0.0028 | 0.0472 | 0.0271 | 0.0143 | -0.0128 | -0.0255 | -0.0269 | -0.0044 | 0.0077 | 0.0265 | 0.0466 | 0.0039 |

Figure 8.29 Profile Accuracy calculations.

There appear to be four to five accuracy components outside the limits worthy of further investigation. The points refer to periods 53 (May), 52 (April), 51 (March) and 45 (September prior year). The first three points refer to the periods where the FAP deviates the most from the AAP, perhaps suggesting a change or 'break in pattern' in the Actual profile as would happen in a change in trend in the data, for instance. Getting some insights into the forecast in a holdout period could be useful for forecasting the lead-time demand for the next horizon.

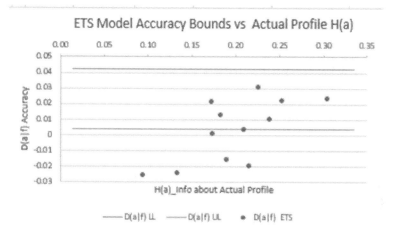

Figure 8.30 A scatter plot between Profile Accuracy components and Actual Alphabet Profile.

## Assessing the Effectiveness of the Forecasting Process

A forecast alphabet Profile Miss measures how different a forecast profile differs from a profile of actuals over a fixed horizon. For alphabet profiles, there is a measure of information H(a) that gives the information about the actual alphabet profile (AAP) and a measure H(f) that gives the information about a forecast alphabet profile (FAP). Thus, FAP Miss = H(f) – H(a).

$$\boldsymbol{FAP\ Miss} = \sum_{i=1}^{m}(a_i \ln\ a_i) - \sum_{i=1}^{m} (f_i \ln\ f_i)$$

There is also a measure of information H(a|f) about the FAP GIVEN we have the AAP information. Accuracy of the forecast profile is also known as the Kullback-Leibler divergence measure, so that D(a|f) = H(a|f) – H(a). By adding and subtracting H(a|f), I now rewrite D(a|f) = [H(a|f) – H(f)] + [H(f) – H(a)]. This results in a decomposition of profile accuracy into two components: (1) a **Forecast Profile Error** = H(f) – H(a) and (2) a **Profile Relative Skill measure** [= H(f) - H(a|f)], which is the negative of the first bracketed term in the expression for the **Profile Accuracy** measure D(a|f).

267

Another way of looking at this is using **Profile Accuracy = Profile Forecast Error - Profile Relative Skill.** In words, this means that accurately hitting the bullseye involves both skill at aiming and measuring how far from the bullseye the darts strike the board.

The **Profile Relative Skill** is in absolute value greater than zero, but **does not** include zero, unless the forecast profile error is zero. The smaller, in absolute value, the better the relative skill. When a FAP is constant, as is the case with the Croston methods, SES and MAVG-12-point forecasts, the relative skill = 0, meaning that with those methods, obtaining a Profile Forecast Error of zero (perfect forecast, except for lead-time Total bias) is clearly not possible. Thus, level point forecasts should not be used for lead-time forecasting.

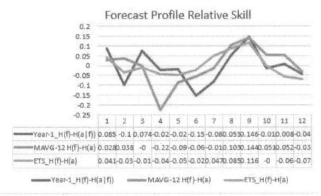

Figure 8.31 The relative skill for the three models over the 12-month holdout period.

For monitoring forecasts on an ongoing basis, it is useful to create a Profile *Skill* score defined by |Profile Relative Skill|/Profile Accuracy] and track the methods, models and judgmental overrides over multiple lead-time forecast horizons.

## Data Quality Matters Because Bad Data Will Beat a Good Forecast Every Time

With experience, we can get smarter at forecasting when we monitor data quality throughout the entire forecasting process. You may have noticed that both Dec 2016 (=49786) and Jan 2017 (= 73096) look unusual. It is plausible because of the seasonality evident in previous years that these numbers should have been interchanged as it appears like a data recording error. This small change results in a peak in AAP in period 4, rather than period 5. The results before the change are shown in Figure 8.32 (top). After adjustment, the Adjusted Performance table in Figure 8.32 (*bottom*) shows that the ETS(A,A,M) model had the best performing profile of the three given the AAP.

H(f) - H(a) = (Profile Relative Skill + Profile Accuracy)

| Performance Measures | MAVG-12 Naïve | Year-1 Method | ETS(A,A,M) Model |
|---|---|---|---|
| Profile Relative Skill: H(f) – H(a⏐f) | 0.0 (constant level always zero!) | -0.087 | *-0.023* |
| Profile Accuracy: D(a⏐f) | 0.096 | 0.104 | *0.068* (most accurate) |
| Profile Miss: H(f) – H(a) | 0.096 (overforecasting) | 0.017 (overforecasting) | 0.045 (overforecasting) |
| Relative Skill score = Profile Relative Skill/D(a⏐f) | = 0.0/ 0.096 = 0.0 (least useful) | = -0.087.104 = - 0.837 | *= -0.023/0.068 = 0.338* (most useful) |

| Adjusted Performance | MAVG-12 Naïve | Year-1 Method | ETS(A,A,M) Model |
|---|---|---|---|
| Profile Relative Skill: H(f) – H(a⏐f) | 0.00 (constant level always zero!) | -0.066 | *-0.001* |
| Profile Accuracy: D(a⏐f) | 0.096 | 0.083 | *0.044* (most accurate) |
| Profile Miss: H(f) – H(a) | 0.096 (overforecasting) | 0.017 (overforecasting) | 0.045 (overforecasting) |
| Relative Skill score = Profile Relative Skill/D(a⏐f) | = 0.0/ 0.096 = 0.0 (least useful) | = -0.066/0.083 = - 0.795 | *= -0.001/0.044 =- 0.023* (most useful) |

Figure 8.32 Leadtime forecast performance measures before and after adjustment of an unusual value in period 4.

## *A Structured Inference Base (SIB) Model for Forecast Profile Error*

A SIB modeling approach leads to a measurement model for the Forecast Profile Error (FPE) as FPE = $\beta + \sigma\ \varepsilon$, where $\beta$ and $\sigma$ are unknown constants or parameters and $\varepsilon$ has a known error distribution from the Exponential Family.

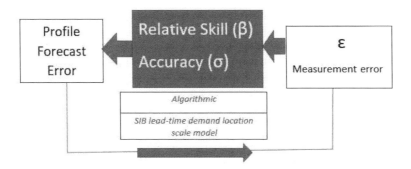

Figure 8.33 The Structured Inference Base (SIB) model for lead-time demand forecast profile error.

This SIB model is known as a location-scale measurement model because of its structure. The FPE model shows that the observed FPE data result from a translation and scaling of an input measurement error ε. Characterizing lead-time data with SIB structured inference base models can mitigate the impact of the "Gaussian mindset" in that a data-driven SIB modeling approach differs fundamentally from the conventional data-generating models in real-world forecasting applications.

## What Can Be Learned About the Measurement Process given the Forecast Profile Errors and the Observed Data?

**Step 1. Setting up the model with real data.** In practice, we have multiple measurements of observed forecast profile errors over a lead-time horizon ($m = 12$ in the spreadsheet example): And where $\varepsilon = \{\varepsilon_1, \varepsilon_2, \varepsilon_3, \ldots \varepsilon_{12}\}$ are now 12 *realizations* of measurement errors from an assumed distribution in the Exponential family.

$$\mathbf{FPE} = \{FPE_1, FPE_2, FPE_3., \ldots, FPE_{12}\}, \text{ where}$$

$$FPE_1 = \beta + \sigma\varepsilon_1$$

$$FPE_2 = \beta + \sigma\varepsilon_2$$

$$FPE_3 = \beta + \sigma\varepsilon_3$$

$$FPE_{12} = \beta + \sigma\varepsilon_{12}$$

**Step 2. A data reduction step critical to the inferential procedure.** What information can we uncover about the forecasting process? Like a detective, we can explore a SIB model and find that, based on the observed data, there is a clue revealed now about the unknown, but *realized* measurement errors ε. This is evidence that will guide us to the next important SIB modeling step: It points to a decomposition of the measurement error distribution into two components: (1) a *marginal distribution* for the observed components and (2) a *conditional distribution* (based on the observed components) for the remaining unknown measurement error distribution This conditional distribution depends on the parameters β and σ.

what are these observed components of the error distribution that are uncovered?

The essential information is gleaned from the *structure* of the model and the *recorded* forecast profile error data. If we now select a suitable Location-invariant measure $m(.)$, and a scale-invariant measure $s(.)$, we can make a calculation that yields important observables about the measurement process for each forecasting technique used. The SIB model shows, with some elementary algebraic manipulations, that the observables can be expressed by the equations (using a 12-month lead-time):

If we set $d = (d_1, d_2, ... , d_{12})$ to represent the left hand-side and right-hand side equations ,then we can *reduce* the dimension of the SIB model from twelve to only two equations with two unknown variables $m(\varepsilon)$ and $s(\varepsilon)$ that represent the remaining unknown information in the

$$[FPE_1 - m(FPE)]/ S(FPE) = [\varepsilon_1 - m(\varepsilon)]/ S(\varepsilon)$$

$$[FPE_2 - m(FPE)]/ S(FPE) = [\varepsilon_2 - m(\varepsilon)]/ S(\varepsilon)\}$$

$$FPE_{12} - m(FPE) / S(FPE) = [\varepsilon_{12} - m(\varepsilon)]/ S(\varepsilon)\}$$

measurement error model. The arithmetic mean is a location-invariant measure, so it can be used for representing $m(\varepsilon)$, and the standard deviation is a scale-invariant measure that can be used for $s(\varepsilon)$.

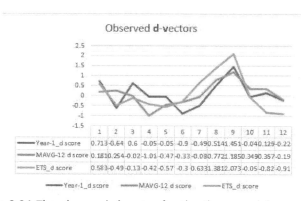

Observed d-vectors

| | 1 | 2 | 3 | 4 | 5 | 6 | 7 | 8 | 9 | 10 | 11 | 12 |
|---|---|---|---|---|---|---|---|---|---|---|---|---|
| Year-1_d score | 0.713 | -0.64 | 0.6 | -0.05 | -0.05 | -0.9 | -0.49 | 0.514 | 1.451 | -0.04 | 0.129 | -0.22 |
| MAVG-12 d score | 0.181 | 0.254 | -0.02 | -1.01 | 0.47 | -0.33 | -0.08 | 0.772 | 1.185 | 0.349 | 0.357 | -0.19 |
| ETS_d score | 0.583 | -0.49 | -0.13 | -0.42 | -0.57 | -0.3 | 0.633 | 1.38 | 12.073 | -0.05 | -0.82 | -0.91 |

Figure 8.34 The observed *d*-vector for the three models over the 12-month holdout period

**Step 3. Conditioning on what you know to be true.** We cannot go any further with a statistical inference procedure until we make an assumption an error distribution in the Exponential Family. However, we can infer that the conditional distribution (given the observed vector $d = (d_1, d_2, ... , d_{12})$, (Figure 8.34 for the variables $m(\varepsilon)$ **and** $s(\varepsilon)$ can be derived from the second equation using an assumed distribution for $\varepsilon$.

$$FPE = m(FPE) + s(FPE)* d$$

$$\varepsilon = m(\varepsilon) + s(\varepsilon)* d$$

**Step 4. Constructing confidence intervals for the unknown parameters β and σ.** The SIB inferential proves yields a **posterior distribution** for the parameters β and σ, *conditional* on the observed vector **d** = (d₁, d₂, ... , d₁₂). From this posterior distribution we can derive unique confidence bounds for parameters β and σ.

## *Takeaways*
This chapter provides an introduction to a *family* of exponential smoothing models highly useful for forecasting trending and seasonal data with prediction limits:

> ➤ The components can describe a current level, trend, and seasonal index. The current level is the starting point, the trend is the growth or decline factor, and seasonal index is the adjustment for seasonality
> ➤ All three components are exponentially weighted averages, rather than equally weighted averages, of the historical data. In calculating the current level, an exponentially weighted average is taken of the past data. The current trend is an exponentially weighted average of the past changes in the level and each seasonal index is an exponentially weighted average of the past ratios of data to level.

A strict emphasis on the estimation and manipulation of parameter values to improve forecasting accuracy is not productive because:

> ➤ In practical situations, estimates can vary widely without significantly affecting the forecast profile created by the algorithm
> ➤ Optimal or near optimal parameter settings are readily derived with automated software algorithms
> ➤ Combinations of multiple parameter values can limit an intuitive feel for their impact on the forecast profile
> ➤ In large database applications, the forecaster needs to be able to rely on the automatic forecasting features of ML software because of the very large volumes of data involved.
> ➤ When assessing forecasting performance, conventional measures of forecast accuracy used in practice can be misleading because of a lack of robustness in normality (Gaussianity) assumptions. With real data, just a single outlier or a few unusual values in the underlying numbers making up an accuracy measure (e.g., **MAPE**) will make the result unrepresentative and misleading.

> ➤ The arithmetic mean algorithm, used widely in calculating accuracy measures should only be trusted as representative or typical when data are normally distributed, so assumptions need to be always validated. An arithmetic mean can quickly become a very unreliable measure of central tendency even for slight departures from normality, hence the need for nonconventional methods.

> ➤ In the context of a multistep-ahead forecasting process with a **fixed** horizon, we can assess the usefulness of a method, model or forecaster in the performance of a profile forecasting process with the *Profile Relative Skill Score*.

> ➤ In theory, statistical forecasting models are designed to be unbiased, but that theoretical consideration may not be valid in practice for 'fixed horizon' lead-time demand forecasts. Moreover, *multiple one-step ahead* point forecasts have limited practical value in demand forecasting as the lead-time is the 'frozen' time window during which operational changes can usually not be made.

# 9

# Short-Term Forecasting with ARIMA Models

*All models are wrong, some are useful*

GEORGE E. P. BOX (1919 – 2013)

In this chapter, we introduce a class of techniques, called ARIMA (for **A**uto-**R**egressive **I**ntegrated **M**oving **A**verage), which can be used to describe stationary time series and nonstationary time series with changing levels. For seasonal time series, the nonstationary ARIMA process is extended to account for a multiplicative seasonal component. These models form the framework for

- expressing various forms of stationary (level) and nonstationary (mostly trending and seasonal) behavior in time series
- producing optimal forecasts with prediction limits for a time series from its own current and past values
- developing a practical and useful modeling process

The topics covered include:

- what an ARIMA forecasting model is used for

- why stationarity is an important concept for ARIMA processes
- how to select ARIMA models through an iterative three-stage procedure
- how, when, and why we should use the Box Jenkins modeling methodology for ARIMA forecasting models
- its relationship to the modern State Space forecasting methodology

## *Why Use ARIMA Models for Forecasting?*

In chapter 2, we constructed a year-by-month STI_Classification as an exploratory, data-driven technique for examining trend and seasonal variation in a time series. This led us to estimate many coefficients for the monthly and yearly means in the rows and columns of a table. (e.g., In Excel, run Data Analysis Add in > Anova: Two factor without replication). Although the results were not intended for generating projections, the STI_Classification provides a useful preliminary view of the data. Figure 9.1 shows (a) a time plot of the classical Series G Box-Jenkins airline passenger miles data and (b) pie chart representing the contribution in the total variation due to Seasonality (83%), Trend (14%) and Other (3%). These data consist of monthly totals of airline passenger miles from January 1949 to December 1960.

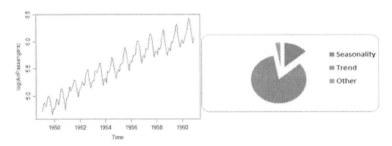

Figure 9.1 (a) Time plot and (b) pie chart of STI_Classification of monthly totals of airline passenger miles from January 1949 to December 1960 ($n$ = 144). (Seasonality 83%, Trend 14%, Other 3%)

The ARIMA modeling approach offers a *model-driven* technique to time series forecasting by using a theoretical framework developed by George E.P. Box (1919–2013) and Gwilym M. Jenkins (1932–1982). The theory was first published in a seminal book titled *Time Series Analysis – Forecasting and Control* (1976),

Many studies have shown that forecasts from simple ARIMA models have frequently outperformed larger, more complex econometric systems for a number of economic series. Although it is possible to construct ARIMA models with only 2 years of monthly historical data, the best results are usually obtained when at least 5 to 10 years of data are available - particularly for seasonal time series.

A significant advantage of univariate ARIMA approach is that useful models can be developed in a relatively short time with automated State Space Forecasting algorithms. Therefore, a practitioner can often deliver significant results with ARIMA modeling early in a project for which adequate historical data exist. Because of the sound theoretical underpinnings, the demand forecaster should always consider ARIMA models as an important forecasting tool whenever these models are relevant to the problem at hand.

A drawback of univariate models is that they have limited explanatory capability. The models are essentially sophisticated extrapolative devices that are of greatest use when it is expected that the underlying factors causing demand for products, services, revenues, and so on, will behave in the future in much the same way as in the past. In the short term, this is often a reasonable expectation, however, because these factors tend to change slowly; data tend to show inertia in the short term. However, there are extensions of the ARIMA approach that incorporate explanatory factors for including information such as price, promotions, strikes, and holiday effects. These models are called transfer function (or **dynamic regression**) models, but are beyond the scope of this book.

Much more time is usually required to obtain and validate historical data than to build the models. Therefore, a practitioner can often deliver significant results with ARIMA modeling early in a project for which adequate historical data exist. The forecaster should always consider ARIMA models as an important option in a forecasting toolbox whenever trend/seasonal models are relevant to the problem at hand.

> *The ARIMA models have proved to be excellent short-term forecasting models for a wide variety of time series.*

## The Linear Filter Model as a Black Box

The application of ARIMA models is based on the idea that a time series in which successive values are highly dependent (i.e. having "memory" of the past values) can also be thought of as having come from a process involving a series of independent errors or shocks, $\varepsilon_t$. The general form of a (discrete) linear process is:

$$Z_t = \mu + \varepsilon_t + \psi_1 \varepsilon_{t-1} + \psi_2 \varepsilon_{t-2} + \ldots + \psi_n \varepsilon_{t-n} + \ldots$$

where $\mu$ and all $\psi_j$ are fixed parameters and the $\{\varepsilon_t\}$ is a sequence of identically, independently distributed random errors with zero mean and constant variance.

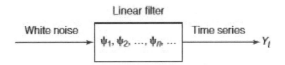

Figure 9.2 Black-box representation of the linear random process.

Why is it called a linear filter? The process is linear because $Z_t$ is represented as a linear combination of current and past shocks. It is often referred to as a black box or filter, because the model relates a random input to an output that is time dependent. The input is filtered, or damped, by the equation so that what comes out of the equation has the characteristics that are wanted.

A linear process can be visualized as a black box as follows (Figure 9.2). **White noise** or purely random error $\{\varepsilon_t\}$ is transformed to an observed series $\{Y_t\}$ by the operation of a linear filter; the filtering operation simply takes a weighted sum of previous shocks. For convenience, we henceforth write models in terms of $Y_t$, which has been mean adjusted, that is, $Y_t = Z_t - \mu$. The weights are known as $\psi$ (psi) coefficients. For $Y_t$ to represent a valid **stationary process**, it is necessary that the coefficients $\psi_j$ satisfy the condition $\sum \psi_j^2 < \infty$.

---

*A linear process is capable of describing a wide variety of practical forecasting models for time series. It can be visualized as a black-box equation transforming random inputs into the observed data.*

---

It can be shown that any linear process can be written formally as a weighted sum of the current error term plus all past shocks. In many problems, such as those in which it is required that future values of a series be predicted; it is necessary to construct a parametric model for the time series. To be useful, the model should be physically meaningful and involve as few parameters as possible. A powerful parametric model that has been widely used in practice for describing empirical time series is called the mixed autoregressive moving-average (ARMA) process:

$$Y_t = \phi_1 Y_{t-1} + \phi_2 Y_{t-2} + \ldots + \phi_p Y_{t-p} + \varepsilon_t - \theta_1 \varepsilon_{t-1} - \theta_2 \varepsilon_{t-2} - \ldots - \theta_q$$
$$\varepsilon_{t-q}$$

where p is the highest lag associated with the data, and q is the highest lag associated with the error term. The ARMA processes are important because they are mathematically tractable and they are capable of providing prediction limits for uncertainty measurement. The inputs to the black box (Figure 9.3) are the shocks $\varepsilon_t$ and the output is the observed historical data or time series $Z_{t..}$

There are some special versions of the ARMA process that are particularly useful in practice. If that weighted sum has only a finite number of nonzero error terms, then the process is known as a moving average (MA) process. It can be shown that the linear process can also be expressed as a weighted sum of the current shock plus all past observed values. If the number of nonzero terms in this expression is finite, then the process is known as an autoregressive (AR) process. The origin of the AR and MA terminology are described a little later with specific examples.

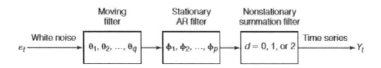

Figure 9.3 Black-box representation of the ARMA process (with a nonstationary filter).

It turns out that an MA process of finite order can be expressed as an AR process of infinite order and that an AR process of finite order can be expressed as an MA process of infinite order. This duality has led to the *principle of parsimony* in the Box-Jenkins methodology, which recommends that the practitioner employ the smallest possible number of parameters for adequate representation of a model. In practice, it turns out that relatively few parameters are needed to make usable forecasting models with business data.

It may often be possible to describe a stationary time series with a model involving fewer parameters than either the MA or the AR process has by itself. Such a model will possess qualities of both autoregressive and moving average models: it is called an ARMA process. An ARMA (1, 1) process, for example, has one prior observed-value term of lag 1 and one prior error term:

$$Y_t = \phi_1 Y_{t-1} + \varepsilon_t - \theta_1 \varepsilon_{t-1}$$

The general form of an ARMA (p, q) process of autoregressive order p and moving average order q looks like:

$$Y_t = \phi_1 Y_{t-1} + \phi_2 Y_{t-2} + \ldots + \phi_p Y_{t-p} + \varepsilon_t - \theta_1 \varepsilon_{t-1} - \theta_2 \varepsilon_{t-2} - \ldots - \theta_q \varepsilon_{t-q}$$

In short, the ARMA process is a linear random process. It is linear if $Y_t$ is a linear combination of lagged values of $Y_t$ and $\varepsilon_t$. It is random if the errors (also called shocks or disturbances) are introduced into the system in the form of white noise. The random errors are assumed to be independent of one another and to be identically distributed with a mean of zero and a constant variance $\sigma_\varepsilon^2$.

> *The ARMA process is important because it is mathematically tractable and can be shown to produce a wide variety of useful forecasting profiles for time series.*

## A Model-Building Strategy

The Box-Jenkins approach for ARIMA modeling provides the demand forecaster with a very powerful and flexible tool. Because of its complexity, it is necessary to establish procedures for coming up with practical models. Its difficulty requires a fair amount of sophistication and judgment in its use. Nevertheless, its proven results in terms of forecasting accuracy and understanding processes generating data and forecast accuracy can be invaluable in the hands of a skilled user.

The Box-Jenkins procedure consists of the following three stages.

1.  *Identification* consists of using the data and any other knowledge that will tentatively indicate whether the time series can he described with a **moving average** (MA) model, an **autoregressive** (AR) model, or a mixed autoregressive – moving average (ARMA) model.

2.  *Estimation* consists of using the data to make inferences about the parameters that will be needed for the tentatively identified model and to estimate values of them.

3.  *Diagnostic checking* involves the examination of residuals from fitted models, which can result in either no indication of model inadequacy or model inadequacy, together with information on how the series may be better described.

The procedure is iterative. Thus, residuals should be examined for any lack of randomness and, if we find that residuals are serially correlated, we use this information to modify a tentative model. The modified model is then fitted and subjected to diagnostic checking again until an adequate model is obtained.

> *Although a Box-Jenkins methodology is an excellent way for forecasting a time series from its own current and past values, it should not be applied blindly and automatically to all forecasting problems.*

## Identification: Interpreting Autocorrelation and Partial Autocorrelation Functions

The primary tool for identifying an ARMA process is with autocorrelation functions (ACFs) and partial autocorrelation functions (PACFs). ACFs are quantities used for describing the mutual dependence among values in a time series.

Extreme care should be taken in interpreting ACFs, however; the interpretation can be complex and requires some ongoing experience with real data. Attention should be directed to individual values as well as to the overall pattern of the autocorrelation coefficients.

In practice, the autocorrelations of low-order ARMA processes are used to help identify models with the Box-Jenkins methodology.

> *Autocorrelation analysis can be a powerful tool for deciding whether a process shows pure autoregressive behavior or moving average behavior in ARMA models.*

## Autocorrelation and Partial Autocorrelation Functions

The ACF and PACF are widely used in identifying ARMA models. The corresponding ordinary and partial correlograms are the sample estimates of the ACF and PACF. They play an important role in the identification phase of the Box-Jenkins methodology for forecasting and control applications. Some examples follow, but to simplify writing model equations, we use a notational device known as the **back-shift** operation.

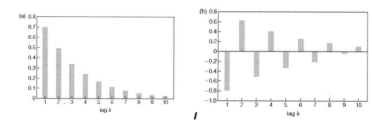

Figure 9.4 (a) ACF an AR (1) process ($\phi_1$ = 0.70); (b) ACF of an AR (1) process ($\phi_1$ = - 0.80.).

For example, the ACF of an AR (1) process is depicted in Figure 9.4. There is a decaying pattern in the ACF; the decay is exponential if $0 < \phi_1 < 1$ (Figure 9.4a). For $-1 < \phi_1 < 0$ (Figure 9.4b), the ACF is similar but alternates in sign. The PACF shows a single positive value at lag 1 if $0 < \phi_1 < 1$ and a negative spike at lag 1 if $-1 < \phi_1 < 0$.

The PACF is more complex to describe. It measures the correlation between $Y_t$ and $Y_{t-k}$ adjusted for the intermediate values $Y_{t-1}$, $Y_{t-2}$, . . . ., $Y_{t-k+1}$ (or the correlation between $Y_t$ and $Y_{t-k}$ not accounted for by $Y_{t-1}$, $Y_{t-2}$, . . . , $Y_{t-k+1}$).

If we denote by $\phi_{kj}$ the $j$th coefficient in an AR($k$) model, so that $\phi_{kk}$ is the last coefficient, then it can be shown that the $\phi_{kj}$ will be nonzero for $k \leq p$ and zero for $k > p$, where $p$ is the order of the autoregressive process. Another way of saying this is that $\phi_{kk}$ has a cutoff or truncation after lag *p*. For example, the PACF of an AR (1) process has one spike at lag 1. It has the value $\phi_1$.

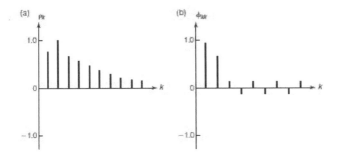

Figure 9.5 (*left*) ACF and (*right*) PACF of an autoregressive AR (2) model with parameters $\phi_1 = 0.3$ and $\phi_2 = 0.5$.

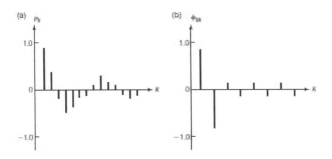

Figure 9.6 (*left*) ACF and (*right*) PACF of an autoregressive AR (2) model with parameters $\phi_1 = 1.2$ and $\phi_2 = - 0.64$.

Another basic process that occurs fairly often in practice is the AR (2) process. In this case there are two autoregressive coefficients $\phi_1$ and $\phi_2$. Figure 9.5 shows the ACF and PACF of an AR (2) model with $\phi_1 = 0.3$ and $\phi_2 = 0.5$. The PACF shows positive values at lags 1 and 2 only. The PACF is very helpful because it suggests that the process is autoregressive and, more important, that it is second-order autoregressive.

If $\phi_1 = 1.2$ and $\phi_2 = - 0.64$, the ACF and PACF have the patterns shown in Figure 9.6. The values in the ACF decay in a sinusoidal pattern; the PACF has a positive value at lag 1 and a negative value at lag 2. There are a number of possible patterns for AR (2) models. A triangular region describes the allowable values for $\phi_1$ and $\phi_2$ in the stationary case: $\phi_1 + \phi_2 < 1$, $\phi_2 - \phi_1 < 1$, and $-1 < \phi_2 < 1$. If $\phi_1^2 + 4\phi_2 > 0$, the ACF decreases exponentially with increasing lag. If $\phi_1^2 + 4\phi_2 < 0$, the ACF is a damped cosine wave.

The ACF) of a MA ($q$) process is 0, beyond the order $q$ of the process (i.e., it has a cutoff after lag $q$). For example, the ACF of a MA (1) process has one spike at lag 1, the others are 0. It has the value $\rho_1 = -\theta_1/(1 + \theta_1^2)$ with $|\rho_1| \leq \frac{1}{2}$.

The PACF of the MA process is complicated, so in Figure 9.7 we display the ACF and PACF of an MA (1) model with positive $\theta_1$. There is a single negative spike at the lag 1 in the ACF. There is a decaying pattern in the PACF. The ACF of an MA(1) process with negative $\theta$ (Figure 9.8) shows a single positive spike, but the PACF shows a decaying pattern with spikes alternating above and below the zero line.

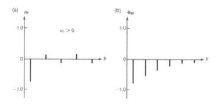

Figure 9.7 (*left*) ACF and (b) PACF of a MA (1) model with positive parameter $\theta$.

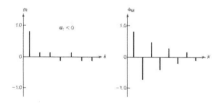

Figure 9.8 (*right*) ACF and (b) PACF of a MA (1) model with negative parameter $\theta$.

## An Important Duality Property

One important consequence of the theory is that the ACF of an AR process behaves like the PACF of an MA process and vice versa. This aspect is known as a **duality property** of the AR and MA processes. If both the ACF and the PACF attenuate, then a mixed model is called for.

It turns out that the ACF of the pure MA ($q$) process truncates, becoming 0 after lag $q$, whereas that for the pure AR ($p$) process is of infinite extent. MA processes are thus characterized by truncation (spikes ending) of the ACF, whereas AR processes are characterized by attenuation (gradual decay) of the ACF. Derivations of this kind are beyond the scope of this book.

For an AR process, the ACF attenuates and the PACF truncates; conversely, for an MA process, the PACF attenuates and the ACF truncates.

The mixed ARMA (p, q) model contains $p$ AR coefficients ($\phi_1$, $\phi_2$ . . . $\phi_p$) and $q$ MA coefficients ($\theta_1$, $\theta_2$, . .,$\theta_q$). This model is useful in that stationary series may often be expressed more parsimoniously (with fewer parameters) in an ARMA model than as a pure AR or pure MA model. In practice, for **mixed ARMA** processes, you should create a catalog of ACF and PACF patterns to establish the orders $p$ and $q$ of the autoregressive and moving average components. The estimated autocorrelation functions, or correlograms, are then matched with the cataloged patterns in order to establish a visual identification of the most useful model for a given situation. Usually, more than one model suggests itself, so that we may tentatively identify several similar models for a particular time series.

Some useful rules for identification are:

- If the **correlogram** cuts off at some point, say $k = q$, then the appropriate model is MA ($q$).
- If the **partial correlogram** cuts off at some point, say $k = p$, then the appropriate model is AR ($p$).
- If neither diagram cuts off at some point, but does decay gradually to zero, the appropriate model is ARMA ($p'$, $q'$) for some $p'$, $q'$.

The ACF and PACF of an ARMA ($p$, $q$) model are more complex than either the AR ($p$) or MA ($q$) models. The ACF of an ARMA ($p$, $q$) process has an irregular pattern at lags 1 through $q$, then the tail diminishes. The PACF tail also diminishes.

The best way to identify an ARMA process initially is to look for decay or a tail in both the ACFs and PACFs.

In practice, it is sufficient to recognize the basic structure of the ACF and PACF for values of $p = 1$, 2 and $q = 1$, 2. The coefficients of the ACF and PACF for the ARMA (1, 1) process can vary over a range of values of $\phi_1$ ($-1 < \phi_1 < 1$) and $\theta_1$ ($-1 < \theta_1 < 1$).

The ACF and PACF of an ARMA (1, 1) process with $\phi_1 = 0.7$ and $\theta_1 = -0.6$ are shown in Figure 9.9. The value at lag 1 in the ACF is high. The remaining values show an exponential decay. The PACF also shows a decay or tail.

The ACF and PACF of the same ARMA (1, 1) process, but with the signs of $\phi_1$ and $\theta_1$ reversed, shows alternating decaying values in the ACF (Figure 9.10). In the PACF, there is a large negative value at lag 1 followed by an exponential decay in the remaining values.

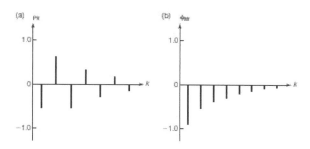

Figure 9.9 (a) ACF and (b) PACF of an ARMA (1, 1) process with parameters $\phi_1 = 0.7$ and $\theta_1 = -0.6$.

In practice, it can be challenging to identify the process just by looking at empirical ACF and PACF based on real data. There are many possible parameter values to choose from that result in similar-looking patterns in the ACF and PACF. Even when performed by computer, the ranges of permissible values for the coefficients are limited. Consequently, the demand forecaster should focus on the forecast profile generated by the model and use automatic estimation procedures for determining 'optimal' parameter values. It is not practical to be 'playing' with changing parameter values in search of the 'best' model for forecasting.

## Seasonal ARMA Process

For the pure seasonal AR process $(1, 0, 0)_s$, the ACF and PACF have similar patterns for the corresponding ACF and PACF for the regular AR process (1, 0, 0), except the spikes are $s$ lags apart. Similarly, the autocorrelation patterns of the pure seasonal MA process $(0, 0, 1)_s$ is similar to the patterns found for the corresponding regular MA process (0, 0, 1) with $s$ lags apart.

> *In most cases, seasonal time series are modeled best with a combination of regular and seasonal parameters.*

A more useful model that we look at later is the general multiplicative model, in which nonstationarity is removed through regular $(1 - B)^d$ and seasonal differencing $(1 - B^s)^D$, where d = 0, 1, or 2 and D = 0, 1, or 2. The ACF and PACF for these models have a mixture of the regular and seasonal patterns in them and, hence, tend to be somewhat complex to construct and identify. For monthly time series, s = 12, and the various seasonal spikes appear at lags 12, 24, and so on, requiring a fairly long time series for reliable identification. Hence, in practice, we encounter seasonal ARIMA models with very low AR and MA structure (usually P = 0, 1; p = 0. 1 and/or Q = 0, 1; q = 0, 1).

Another process that occurs in practice is the combination of regular and seasonal autoregressive components. Figure 9.11 shows the ACF of a particular regular AR (1) and a seasonal AR (12) process (1, 0, 0) (1, 0, 0)$_s$. A pattern in which the values reach a peak at multiples of 12 is noticeable, as are buildups to and decays from that peak at the other lags.

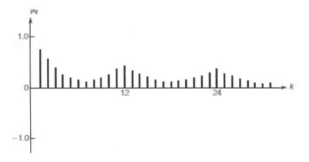

Figure 9.10 (*left*) ACF and (*right*) PACF of an ARMA (1, 1) process with parameters $\phi_1$ = - 0.7 and $\theta_1$ = 0.6.

Figure 9.11 ACF of a combined regular and seasonal AR model: $(1 - \phi_1 B)$

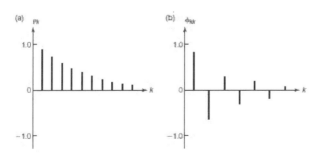

$(1 - \phi_{12} B^{12}) \, Y_t = \phi_1 \, Y_{t-1} + \phi_{12} \, Y_{t-12} \ - \phi_1 \, \phi_{12} \, Y_{t-13} + \varepsilon_t.$

There are a large variety of patterns that can emerge in the modeling process. The Box-Jenkins approach is so general that it is impossible to catalog all possibilities. Therefore, it is essential to follow an iterative procedure in developing successful forecasting models.

In later sections, we treat the identification of an appropriate ARIMA model based on real data. The first step is to transform and/or difference the data to produce a stationary series, thereby reducing the model to one in the ARMA class. Then, the ordinary and partial correlograms for the various patterns of differencing that are found in the adjusted data are displayed and compared to the basic catalog of theoretical autocorrelation functions already described. We first look at identifying the regular ARIMA models that are appropriate for nonseasonal data.

## *Identifying Nonseasonal ARIMA Models*

This section describes the identification of nonseasonal ARIMA models, also known as regular ARIMA models. These nonstationary models are appropriate for many business and economic time series that are nonseasonal, are seasonally adjusted, or have strong trends.

> *Nonstationarity typically includes periodic variations and systematic changes in mean (trend) and variance.*

## Identification Steps

In the previous chapter we described the main features of the ARIMA $(p, d, q)$ process:

$$(1 - \phi_1 B - \phi_2 B^2 - \ldots - \phi_p B^p) (I - B)^d Y_t = (1 - \theta_1 B - \theta_2 B^2 - \ldots \theta_q B^e) \varepsilon_t.$$

where the $\varepsilon_t$ 's are white noise (a sequence of identically distributed uncorrelated errors). Using the backshift operator B again, this expression can be simplified to:

$$\phi (B) (I - B)^d Y_t . = \theta (B) \varepsilon_t.$$

where the AR($p$) terms are given by the polynomial $\phi (B) = (1 - \phi_1 B - \phi_2 B^2 - \ldots - \phi_p B^p )$ and the MA(q) terms are $\theta (B) = (1 - \theta_1 B - \theta_2 B^2 - \ldots \theta_q B^q)$. For example, the ARIMA (1, 1, 1) process takes the form

$$(1 - \phi_1 B) (I - B)^d Y_t . = (1 - \theta_1 B) \varepsilon_t.$$

To identify one of these ARIMA models we need to

- Determine the order of differencing ($d = 0, 1,$ or at most 2) required to produce stationarity. This occurs when the ACF of the differenced series decays relatively quickly.
- Determine preliminary estimates of the $\phi$ and $\theta$ coefficients in the resulting ARMA model. Viewing the cut-off 'and' decay patterns of the ACF and PACF does this.

> *The three letters p, d, and q give the order of a regular (nonseasonal)*
> *ARIMA model. By convention, the order of the autoregressive*
> *component is p, the order of differencing needed to achieve*
> *stationarity is d, and the order of the moving average part is q.*

## Models for Forecasting Stationary Time Series

What kinds of historical patterns do we get with ARMA models and what sort of forecast profiles (projections) do they produce? Once a time series is assumed stationary, it can be used with a linear filter in order to devise a forecast. Once an appropriate ARMA model (linear filter) has been fit to the series, an optimal forecasting procedure follows directly from the theory.

The ARMA process is designed for stationary time series, that is, series whose basic statistical properties (e.g., means, variances, and covariances) remain constant over time. Thus, in order to build ARMA models, non-stationarity must first be identified and removed through differencing.

The technical definition of stationarity is a complex one. For practical purposes, a stochastic process is said to be weakly stationary if the first and second moments of the process are time-independent. This assumption implies, among other things, that the mean, variance and covariances of the data are constant and finite.

Another critical assumption in describing stationary time series comes as a result of the chronological order of the data. The difference between conventional regression methods and time series modeling of the sort possible with ARMA models is that independence of the values cannot be assumed in practice; in fact, in ARMA, modeling derives its strength from the mutual dependence among values that is found in time series data.

## White Noise and the Autoregressive Moving Average Model

Consider a process $Y_t = \varepsilon_t$, $t = 0, \pm1, \pm2$, where $\varepsilon_t$ is independent of all other values $\varepsilon_{t-1}$, $\varepsilon_{t-2}$, ..., $\varepsilon_{t+1}$, $\varepsilon_{t+2}$, . This process is called **purely random**. If all $\varepsilon_t$ are normally distributed as well, the process is said to be white noise. The reason is that the next value, $\varepsilon_t$, of white noise is unpredictable even if all previous values $\varepsilon_{t-1}$, $\varepsilon_{t-2}$, ..., $\varepsilon_{t-q}$ and subsequent values $\varepsilon_{t+1}$, $\varepsilon_{t+2}$, ... are known. The counts of radioactive decay from a long-lived sample and even the changes in the level of stock prices are examples of data that are stationary and can be regarded as white noise.

> *The concept of white noise is of central importance to forecasting time*
> *series, just as independent random error is of central importance to*
> *forecasting with regression models.*

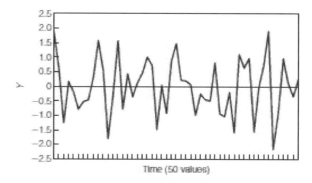

Figure 9.12 Realization of an MA (1) process ($\theta_1 = 0.25$).

One simple linear random process that we encounter in practice is the MA process. For example, a sample of a computer-generated first-order MA process (MA (1)) with $\theta_1 = 0.25$ is given in Figure 9.12. There is no discernible pattern in the numbers.

The term *moving average* has been a convention for this model and should not be confused with the moving average MAVG, introduced in Chapter 2 for smoothing time series.

Another simple linear random process is the AR process. This model, also known as a Markov process, states that the value $Y_t$ of the process is given by $\phi_1$ multiplied by the previous value plus a random error $\varepsilon_t$. Computer-generated realizations of an AR (1) process with $\phi_1$ = +0.55 and $\phi_1$ = -0.55 are shown in Figure 9.13.

*The term autoregression that is used to describe such an AR process arises because an AR(p) model is much a like a multiple linear regression model.*

The corresponding correlograms are shown in Figure 9.14. Both correlograms have significant spikes (outside the bands) at lag 1 (= 0.47 and −0.38). Theoretically, these two spikes are +0.55 and −0.55. Other spikes appear to be within the confidence bands. Note that the AR process with positive $\phi_1$ coefficient has some positive memory of itself in that the plot displays a tendency to retain the pattern of its own immediate past. There are practical examples of data that follow a Markov process.

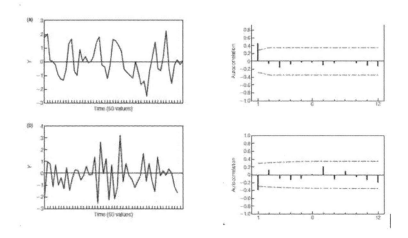

Figure 9.13 *(left)* Realizations of an AR (1) process: (a) $\phi_1$ = 0.55; (b) $\phi_1$ = - 0.55.

Figure 9.14 (*right*) Correlograms of the data in Figure 9.13: (a) $\phi_1$ = 0.55; (b) $\phi_1$ = - 0.55.

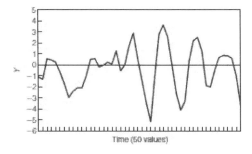

Figure 9.15 Realization of an AR (2) process ($\phi_1$ = 1.0, $\phi_2$ = - 0.50).

## One-Period Ahead Forecasts

What are the forecast profiles for these models? As a first example, consider an AR (1) process with $\phi_1$ = 0.5 given by $Y_t = 0.5\, Y_{t-1} + 2.0 + \varepsilon_t$. We have generated an artificial example (Figure 9.16) and noted the current value at time $t = T$ as well as the previous four observed values. The random errors are calculated from $\varepsilon_t = Y_t - 0.5\, Y_{t-1} - 2.0$ for $t = T$ - 3 to $t = T$. We assume now that the true parameters of the model are known, and that the current time is $t = T$ - 4 so that we can examine the pattern of the one-step-ahead forecasts. The forecast error at time $t = T - 3$ is $Y_{T-3} - \hat{Y}_{T-4}\,(1) = 4 - [0.5 * 10 + 2.0] = -3.0$.

290

At the next period, when the current time is t = T - 3, the forecast error at time $t = T - 2$ is $Y_{T-2} - \hat{Y}_{T-3}(1) = 5 - [0.5 * 4 + 2.0] = 1.0$. Finally, when the current time is $t = T - 1$, the forecast error at time $t = T$ is $Y_T - \hat{Y}_{T-1}(1) = 6 - [0.5 * 8 + 2.0] = 0$. Note that the random errors are the same as the one-step-ahead forecast errors.

| Time Origin | Data $Y_t$ | Residuals |
|---|---|---|
| $T-4$ | 10.0 | −3.0 |
| $T-3$ | 4.0 | 2.0 |
| $T-2$ | 5.0 | 1.0 |
| $T-1$ | 8.0 | 0 |
| $T$ | 6.0 | 2.0 |

Figure 9.16 Sample data (hypothetical) for forecasting with $Y_t = 0.5Y_{t-1} + 2.0 + \varepsilon_t$.

The one-step-ahead forecast is given by $\hat{Y}_T(1) = 0.5\ Y_{T+2}$. Because the random errors $\varepsilon t$ are assumed to have zero mean and constant variance $\sigma_\varepsilon^2$, our best estimate of $\varepsilon_{T+1}$ is 0.

# L-Step-Ahead Forecasts

The two- and three-step-ahead forecasts are derived through the following procedure.

1.  Replace $T$ by $T + 2$ in the formula $Y_t = 0.5\ Y_{t-1} + 2.0 + \varepsilon_t$ ; then

$$Y_{T+2} = 0.5\ Y_{T+1} + 2.0 + \varepsilon_{T+2}$$

2.  Use the one-step-ahead forecast $\hat{Y}_T(1)$ in place of $Y_{T+1}$ because the latter is not known.

3.  Assume $\varepsilon_{T+2} = 0$. Then the two-step-ahead and three-step-ahead forecasts are, respectively,

$$\hat{Y}_T(2) = 0.5\ \hat{Y}_T(1) + 2.0 + 0 = 4.5$$

$$\hat{Y}_T(3) = 0.5\ \hat{Y}_T(2) + 2.0 + 0 = 4.25$$

Notice that the forecast of $Y_{T+h}$ with $h \geq 1$ is made from a time origin, designated T, for a lead time or horizon, designated h. This forecast, denoted by $\hat{Y}_T(h)$ is said to be a forecast at origin T, for lead time h. It is called the minimum mean square error (MSE) forecast. When $\hat{Y}_T(h)$ is regarded as a function of h for a fixed T, it is referred to as the forecast function or profile for an origin T.

*A forecast profile can be generated by plotting the h-step-ahead forecasts for a fixed time horizon, h = 1 , 2 , 3 , . . . .*

The forecast error for the lead time $h$,
$$e_T(h) = Y_{T+h} - \hat{Y}_T(h)$$
has zero mean; thus, the forecast is unbiased.

It is also important to note that any linear function of the forecasts $\hat{Y}_T(h)$ is a minimum MSE forecast of the corresponding linear combination of future values of the series. Hence, for monthly data, the best year-to-date forecast can be obtained by summing the corresponding 1-, 2-, ..., h-step-ahead forecasts.

It can be seen from Figure 9.17 that for this example there is a geometrical decay to a mean value; the mean equals the constant term divided by $(1 - \phi_1)$. In this case, the mean is 4.0. The equation for the h-step-ahead forecast $\hat{Y}_T(h)$ is then given as

$$\hat{Y}_T(h) = 4.0 + 0.5^h (Y_T - 4.0)$$

In effect, forecasts from AR (1) models with positive parameter will decay (up or down) to a mean level and be level thereafter. AR (1) models with a positive parameter occur much more frequently in practice than ones with a negative parameter.

In the same manner as the AR (1) model, the forecasts for the MA (1) model can be developed. Suppose the MA (1) model is given by $Y_t = 3.0 + \varepsilon_t - 0.5 \varepsilon_{t-1}$. Once again $t = T$ is replaced by $T + 1$, and all future errors are set to zero. Then, $Y_{T+1} = 4.0$ and all $Y_{T+I}$ values $(I = 2, 3, \ldots)$ are equal to 3.0.

The forecast profile for an MA (1) model is rather simple. It consists of one estimate based on the last period's error (= 4.0 in the example), followed by the constant mean (= 3.0 in the example) for all future periods. This makes sense intuitively because the ACF of the MA (1) model has nonzero correlation only at lag 1 and hence a memory of only one period. In effect, the MA (1) process will yield level forecast profiles.

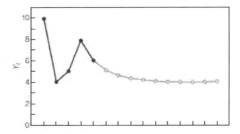

Figure 9.17 Forecast profile for the AR (1) model: $Y_t = 0.5\, Y_{t-1} + 2.0 + \varepsilon_t$.

The forecast profile for a MA $(q)$ can be generalized rather easily. It consists of values at $h = 1, 2. \ldots q$ that are determined by the past errors and then equals the mean of the process for periods greater than $q$.

## Three Kinds of Short-Term Trend Profiles

Many time series exhibit trends. It is instructive to compare the characteristics of several simple forecasting models that deal with trends. Figure 9.18 shows three alternative approaches to forecasting a trending series. The first model uses time as an independent variable in a simple linear regression model (Chapter 10). As new actuals are added, the forecasts do not change, unless the model is updated. The slope and the intercept of the line of forecasts are constant.

| | | Characteristic of updated forecasts | |
| --- | --- | --- | --- |
| Model Type | Equation | Intercept | Slope |
| Deterministic trend | $Y_t = \alpha + \beta t + \varepsilon_t$ | Constant | Constant |
| ARIMA *with* deterministic trend constant | $Y_t - Y_{t-1} = \alpha + \varepsilon_t$ or $(1 - B)Y_t = \alpha + \varepsilon_t$ | Varies | Constant |
| ARIMA *without* deterministic trend constant | $(1 - B)^2 Y_t = \alpha + \varepsilon_t$ | Varies | Varies |

Figure 9.18 Three models for forecasting a trending time series: straight-line trend versus ARIMA (0, 1, 0).

The second is a first difference model and is an extension of the first:

$$Y_t - Y_{t-1} = \mu + \varepsilon_t$$

This model has a slope $\mu_t$ which must be estimated from the data. The forecasts from this model are updated as new actuals become available. This has the effect of changing the intercept of the line of future forecasts but with a constant slope.

The third model is an AR(2) model and can be written

$$Y_t = 2Y_{t-1} - Y_{t-2} + \varepsilon_t$$

Both the slope and the intercept of the lines of updated forecasts will change as new values become available. The trend can change direction with this model.

Unless there is reason (business or theoretical) to believe that a deterministic relationship exists, autoregressive models are more adaptive or responsive to recent values than straight-line models are. The choice of taking first differences with trend constant or second differences without a trend constant should depend on the data.

> *Because it is not helpful to over-difference a time series, second differences should be used only when first differences do not result in a stationary series.*

## A Comparison of an ARIMA (0, 1, 0) Model and a Straight-Line Model

We now show how the forecasts of an ARIMA (0, 1, 0) model differ from straight-line models, which are commonly used to model trends. Consider a (seasonally adjusted) quarterly economic time series that is generally increasing in trend (Figure 9.19). Moreover, the series contains several up- and downturns corresponding to economic business cycles.

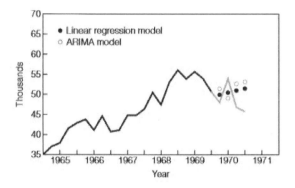

Figure 9.19 Comparison of forecasts generated by the ARIMA (0, 1, 0) model and the straight-line regression model for Year 6.

The correlogram (not shown) of the time series has a gradual decay that confirms nonstationarity in the data due to the trend. Thus, first differences of the quarterly data are recommended; a plot of the first differences (not shown) suggests a constant mean and there is no sign of increasing variability. The correlogram and partial correlogram (not shown) of the first differences also confirm that there are no significant patterns in either diagram. Therefore, an ARIMA (0, 1, 0) model of the seasonally adjusted quarterly data seems appropriate as a starting model:

$$Y_t - Y_{t-1} = \alpha + \varepsilon_t$$

The first differences have a mean value that is 1.35 standard deviations from zero, so a deterministic trend constant is included; the fitted model is given by

$$Y_t = Y_{t-1} + 332.0$$

This is perhaps one of the simplest time series models covered so far. Note that a one-period-ahead forecast is simply the data value for the current quarter plus 332.0. All information before the last value has no effect on the one-period-ahead forecast. Past data were used to determine that the trend constant should be 332.0.

To compare the forecast profile of the ARIMA (0, 1, 0) model with a simple linear regression model with time as the independent variable, a straight-line fit to the data results in:

$$Y_t = 7165.2 + 60.8\,t \qquad\qquad t = 1, 2\,\ldots$$

We can see that the forecast profile of this model is a straight line with a slope = 60.8. Because the slope is positive in this model, the forecasts are always increasing with time.

To compare the response of new data on the forecasts from the two models, four straight-line regressions were performed. The first regression was performed through the fourth quarter of Year 5 (next to the last year); in other words, 4 quarters of the data were kept as a holdout sample for evaluating forecast accuracy.

Next, four quarterly forecasts were produced for the holdout sample (i.e., for Year 6). Subsequent regressions and forecasts were also generated by adding another period before fitting the model, and so on. In this manner, ten forecasts were produced, four for quarter 1, three for quarter 2, two for quarter 3, and one for the last quarter of the holdout sample.

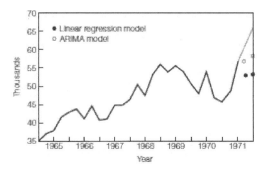

Figure 9.20 Changes in model predictions for Q3 and Q4 of (a) Year 6 (b) Year 7.

The effect of new data on the predictions of the two models can be seen in Figure 9.19, which shows the one-step-ahead predictions by the two models for the 4 quarters of Year 6. The predictions show that the straight-line regression model is closer to the actuals for each of the 4 quarters when the fit period ends in the fourth quarter of Year 5.

When two more quarters of data are included and the third and fourth quarters of Year 6 are predicted, the straight-line model predictions are again closer to the actual values.

When the first two quarters of Year 6 are added, the changes in the predictions made by the models for the last two quarters of Year 6 are as shown in Figure 9.20(a). Clearly, the ARIMA model responds to the new data (upturn in $Q_2$ of Year 6) by a much greater amount than does the straight-line model. In fact, for this ARIMA model, the forecasts equal the latest data value plus a constant. Notice that the second quarter of Year 6 is somewhat unusual; this influenced the forecasts for the remainder of Year 6.

Next, two more quarters ($Q_3$ and $Q_4$ of Year 6) are added to the fit period and the 4 quarters of Year 7 are predicted. Now the predictions of the straight-line model were once again superior to the ARIMA model (Figure 9.20b).

Lastly, a fit with actuals through the second quarter of Year 7 is done. This time, the plot of the data shows a sharp turn upward. The model forecasts are shown in Figure 9.21. Once again, the ARIMA model reacts much more quickly to changing conditions. Figure 9.21 shows that this time the ARIMA model is correct because the data were indeed continuing upward.

(a)

| Year 6 | ARIMA | Straight Line |
|---|---|---|
| Quarter 3 | 2756 | 96 |
| Quarter 4 | 2807 | 100 |

(b)

| Year 7 | ARIMA | Straight Line |
|---|---|---|
| Quarter 3 | 233 | 116 |
| Quarter 4 | 11,499 | 118 |

Figure 9.21 Comparison of point forecasts generated by the ARIMA (0, 1, 0) model and the straight-line regression model for the last two quarters of Year 7.

The forecast test just described is not done to claim that either model is superior. Rather, it shows how differently the ARIMA (0, 1, 0) model and straight-line regression models react to new data. There is almost no change in the forecasts from a straight-line model (vs. time) when new data are introduced. However, ARIMA models respond significantly to recent data. Which model we should select depends more on the expected forecast profile of the application and not so much on the summary statistics from fitting the models.

- If future demand in a given year is expected to be substantially above or below trend (say, based on economic rationale), then the forecast of a straight-line model must be modified. A turning point analysis or a trend-cycle curve-fitting approach may be the best way of supplementing our judgment about the cycle to a straight-line model (see Chapter 7).
- If we assume that the current short-term trend in the data is likely to continue, an ARIMA model should be seriously considered.

Univariate ARIMA models cannot predict turning points, however. If the economy is near a turning point, extreme care should be exercised in using the ARIMA models. Regression models with explanatory variables, econometric models, and transfer function models may be a more appropriate way of sensitizing forecasts to take into account changes in the business cycle.

## Seasonal ARIMA Models

Many of business and economic time series reported in business periodicals and online news services are already seasonally adjusted. Corporate and government forecasters use seasonally adjusted data in models for items strongly influenced by business cycles in which a seasonal pattern would otherwise mask the information of primary interest. Because seasonal variation is seldom unchanging, seasonal adjustment procedures based on simplistic smoothing procedures may leave some seasonal pattern of unknown nature in the data. In these situations, it may be preferable to take a model-based approach to seasonal adjustment and forecasting. Seasonal ARIMA models are well suited for these situations.

Other times, forecasts of seasonal data are required. In airline-traffic design, for example, average traffic during the months of the year when total traffic is greatest is of central importance. Clearly, monthly traffic data rather than the seasonally adjusted traffic data are required.

Sometimes seasonality shifts with time, as with Easter and Ramadan holidays. For example, changes in school openings and closing during the year can affect a variety of time series, such as energy demand. If the seasonal change persists, models based on unadjusted data rather than seasonally adjusted data are likely to be more flexible and useful.

If changing seasonality is expected, it is therefore better to take account of it through the development of a properly specified seasonal ARIMA model.

## A Multiplicative Seasonal ARIMA Model

Models incorporating both regular and seasonal components can be used for forecasting a typical 12-month seasonal series with positive trend ($Y_t$ = Hotel/motel room demand; Figure 9.22a). To remove the linear trend from such a series requires at least one first difference (Diff 1 = $Y_t - Y_{t-1}$; Figure 9.22b). The resultant series still shows strong seasonality, with perhaps some residual trend pattern.

This result may call for taking a first-order seasonal difference for the residual series (series $Y_t - Y_{t-12}$; Figure 9.22c). A first differences followed by a seasonal difference often give data appearing stationary. Figure 9.22d is essentially free from the trend and seasonal pattern.

It turns out that the order in which the differencing operations are applied to $Y_t$ in Figure 9.22a is immaterial and that the operation of successive differencing is *multiplicative* in nature. That is, series $Y^*_t = Y_t - Y_{t-12}$ in Figure 9.22c is the first-order seasonal difference of $Y_t$. Then, the first difference of $Y^*_t$ is the time plot in Figure 9.22d.

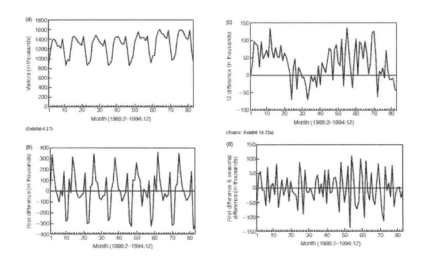

Figure 9.22 (a) Hotel/motel room demand; (b) first differences; (c) seasonal differences; (d) first and seasonal differences. (Source: Frechtling's 1996 book Practical Tourism Forecasting is source of the hotel/motel room demand data)

For seasonal ARIMA models, seasonality is introduced into the model multiplicatively. Although this may seem arbitrary, it can be intuitively explained by our example; if a month – say January – is related to the December preceding it and to the previous January, then it is also related to the December 13 months previous.

The combined operation suggests that if the residual series resembles a random process, or white noise, then a model of the original data could have the form

$$Y_t = Y_{t-1} + Y_{t-12} - Y_{t-13} + \varepsilon_t$$

A forecast from this model is the sum of the values for the same month ($Y_{t-12}$) in the previous year and the annual change in the values of the previous months ($Y_{t-1} - Y_{t-13}$).

This is a special case of an autoregressive model in that past values have been given a constant weight of ± 1. It also shows that those weights given to $Y_{t-1}$ and $Y_{t-13}$ are equal but have opposite signs.

Frequently both seasonality and trend are present in data. Hence an AR (13) model of the form

$$Y_t = \phi_1 Y_{t-1} + \phi_2 Y_{t-12} + \phi_3 Y_{t-13} + \varepsilon_t$$

can be used to interpret this underlying structure. If the coefficients at lags 1 and 13 are approximately equal and have opposite sign and $\phi_2$ equals approximately 1, then the resultant model

$$Y_t = \phi_1 Y_{t-1} + Y_{t-12} - \phi_1 Y_{t-13} + \varepsilon_t$$

is a more parsimonious model. These are good representations for strongly seasonal series of period 12:

$$Y_t - Y_{t-12} = \phi_1 (Y_{t-1} - Y_{t-13}) + \varepsilon_t$$

For time series that contain a seasonal periodic component that repeats every $s$ values, a supplement to the nonseasonal ARIMA model can be applied. In a seasonal process with seasonal period $s$, values that are $s$ time intervals apart are closely related. This is analogous to the regular ARIMA process in which adjacent ($s = 1$) values are closely related.

For a time series with seasonal period $s$, $s = 4$ for quarterly data and $s = 12$ for monthly data. In a manner very similar to the regular ARIMA process, seasonal ARIMA (P, D, Q) models can be created for seasonal data (to differentiate between the two kinds, it is customary to use capital letters P, D, and Q when designating the order of the parameters for the seasonal models).

## Identifying Seasonal ARIMA Models

As with regular ARIMA models, seasonal ARIMA models can be classified as autoregressive and moving average. The seasonal MA process is analogous to the regular MA process. It differs from a regular MA process of order 12 where there could be significant values at lags 1 *through* 12 in the ACF. If there is a single dominant value at 12, this indicates a seasonal MA process.

*In most cases, seasonal time series are modeled best with a combination of regular and seasonal parameters.*

In practice, it is not unusual to find significant spikes at other lags of, say 5 or 9 in the correlogram of a residual series. Generally, these are spurious and may not suggest a secondary seasonal pattern. Their removal through a lag structure generally has little impact on forecasts generated from such a model. They may have more to do with unusual values, such as an outlier. It is important, however, to isolate and interpret seasonal lags corresponding to interpretable periodicities.

The seasonal AR process is also analogous to the regular AR process. However, the pattern of decay that is evident in the ACF is noticed at multiples of the period. For example, the ACF of a first-order seasonal (monthly) AR process has a decaying pattern in the values at multiples of 12. The PACF has a single value at lag 12. It is worth noting that pure monthly seasonal models look like 12 independent series, so that the ACF and PACF are approximately 0, except at multiples of 12.

The ACF of a particular simple combined regular and seasonal moving average process is depicted in Figure 9.23. On expanding the factors in the model, it becomes apparent that the current error and errors 1, 12, and 13 periods back in time affect $Y_t$. The pattern that results in the ACF is a large value at lags 1 and 12 and smaller values at lags 11 and 13. As a general rule, there will be less significant values at lag 12 plus or minus each regular moving average parameter. For example, if the process is a regular MA (2), there will be smaller values at lags 10, 11, 13, and 14.

The easiest way to identify the order of combined MA processes is to introduce a seasonal moving average parameter in the model. The order of the regular MA parameter will then be apparent from the correlogram of the residuals.

> *The ACF of a pure seasonal MA process has a single value at the period of the seasonality. The PACF shows a decaying pattern at multiples of 12 if the seasonality has a 12-month period.*

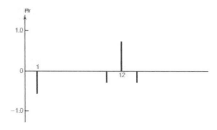

Figure 9.23 ACF a combined regular and seasonal MA model: $Y_t = \varepsilon_t - \theta_1 \varepsilon_{t-1} - \theta_{12} \varepsilon_{t-12} + \theta_1 \theta_{12} \varepsilon_{t-13}$ .

## *Diagnostic Checking: Validating Model Adequacy*

The third and last stage of the model-building strategy is called **diagnostic checking**, in which analytical techniques are used to detect inadequacies in the model and to suggest model revisions. It may be necessary to introduce new information into the model after this stage and to initiate another three-stage procedure for assessing the new model.

Diagnostic checking involves examining the statistical properties of the residuals. Tests should be designed to detect departures from the assumptions on which the model is based and to indicate how further fitting and checking should be performed. When the model is adequate, the residual series should be independently and randomly distributed about 0. Any dependence or non-randomness indicates the presence of information that could be exploited to improve the reliability of the model.

> *In the diagnostic checking phase, analytical techniques are used to detect inadequacies in the model and to suggest model revisions.*

To ensure that a valid forecasting model has been obtained, it is important to examine the residuals from the fitted model. If the model is ultimately selected for use as a forecasting tool, the empirical performance of the model should also be monitored periodically during its use so that it can be updated when appropriate.

We consider two ways in which a fitted model can be checked for adequacy of fit. First, the model can be made intentionally more complex by overfitting; those parameters whose significance is in question can be tested statistically. Second, in a more technical test, correlogram estimates can be tested individually or in an overall chi-squared test.

**Overfitting.** When a tentatively identified model is to be enhanced, an additional parameter can be added to the model (overfitting) and the hypothesis that the additional parameter is 0 can be tested by a *t* test. Thus, overfitting with an AR (2) model or an ARMA (1, 1) model for instance, could test an AR (1) model.

The estimate $s_\varepsilon^2$ of the square of the residual standard error can also be used for diagnostic checking. A plot of $s_\varepsilon^{\ 2}$ (adjusted for degrees of freedom) against the number of additional parameters should decrease with improved fitting. When overfitting, the improvement, if any, in decreased $s_\varepsilon^2$ may be inconsequential.

**Chi-Squared Test.** Correlograms and partial correlograms are probably the most useful diagnostic tools available. If the residuals are not random, these diagrams may suggest residual autocorrelations that can be further modeled.

A chi-squared test can be used to evaluate whether the overall correlogram of the residuals exhibits any systematic error. When the chi-squared statistic exceeds the threshold level, the residual series contains more structure than would be expected for a random series. The test statistic, due to Box and Pierce, is known as the Ljung-Box test, is given by the formula

$$Q = n\,(n + 2) \sum (n - k)^{-1}\, r_k^2$$

where $r_k$ ($k = 1, \ldots, m$) are residual autocorrelations selected (typically $m = 20$); $n$ is the number of values used to fit the model, and $m$ is usually taken to be 15 or 20. Then, $Q$ has an approximate chi-squared distribution with ($m$ - p - $q$) degrees of freedom. For an ARIMA ($p$, $d$, $q$) model, $n$ is the number of terms in the differenced data. This is a general test of the hypothesis of model adequacy, in which a large observed value of $Q$ points to inadequacy. Even if the statistic $Q$ is not significant, a review of the residual time series for unusual values is still appropriate.

> *A chi-squared test statistic is used to evaluate whether the overall correlogram of the residuals exhibits any systematic error.*

It may also appear practical to examine individual values in the correlogram of the residuals relative to a set of confidence limits. Those values that fall outside the limits are examined further. Upon investigation, appropriate MA or AR terms can be included in the model.

Just as there are for the ordinary correlation coefficient, there are approximate confidence limits for the theoretical autocorrelation coefficients that establish which autocorrelation coefficient can reasonably be assumed to be 0. As a rough guide for determining whether or not theoretical autocorrelations are 0 beyond lag $q$, it is known that, for a sample of size $n$, the standard deviation of $r_k$ (an estimated standard error to be plugged into a confidence interval statement) is approximately

$$n^{-\frac{1}{2}} [\, 1 + 2 \,(\, r_1{}^2 + r_2{}^2 + \ldots + r_q{}^2 \,)]^{\frac{1}{2}} \qquad \text{for } k > q$$

The theory also offers us that, for a $p$th-order autoregressive model, the standard errors of the partial autocorrelogram estimates $\phi_{kk}$ are approximately $n^{-\frac{1}{2}}$ for $k > p$. Assuming normality for moderately large samples, the limits of plus or minus two standard errors about 0 should provide a reasonable guide in assessing whether or not the autocorrelation coefficients are effectively different from 0. For details about the origins of these theoretical results, the reader is referred to Box, G.E.P., G.M. Jenkins, and G.C. Reinsell (1994) *Time Series Analysis: Forecasting and Control*, 3$^{rd}$ ed.

# *Implementing a Trend/Seasonal ARIMA Model for Tourism Demand*

Let us examine a more detailed example to illustrate the use of trend/seasonal ARIMA models. This analysis will result in a forecast of hotel/motel room demand; the data have been previously referred to in this book. An exploratory ANOVA (Two-Factor without Replication) decomposition suggests that the variation due to trend, seasonality and irregularity accounts for 12.1%, 86.6%, and 1.3%, respectively, of the total variation about the overall mean. The Box-Jenkins methodology for fitting ARIMA models provides a sound framework for embracing both change and chance: optimal forecasts (change) along with associated prediction limits (chance) for assessing the uncertainty factor in the forecasts.

## Preliminary Data Analysis

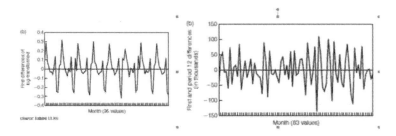

Figure 9.24 (*left*) Time plot of first differences of the log of hotel/motel room demand (series B). (*Source:* Figure 9.22a)

Figure 9.25 (*right*) Time plot of the first and period 12 differences of the hotel/motel room demand (Series C). (*Source*: Figure 9.22a).

A time plot of the historical data and various differenced and log transformed data are shown in Figures 9.22, 9.24, and 9.25. These give us a basis for creating several competing models for the data. Series A is the first difference of the basic data (Figure 9.24a). Series B is the first difference of the log-transformed data (Figure 9.24b). Series A behaves like changes in the data, whereas series B acts much like percentage changes. We will seek seasonal ARMA models for series A and B.

The original data (Figure 9.22a) shows a positive trend in the historical data and slightly increasing dispersion in the seasonal variation over time. The increasing dispersion is the motivation behind taking logarithms. The seasonal volatility can be validated in the first differences of the data (Figure 9.22b). Note that the seasonality appears slightly more uniform in the first differences of the log-transformed data (Figure 9.24) than in the untransformed version (Figure 9.22b). The period 12 differences show a cyclical pattern (Figure 9.22c). The combination of differences of period 1 and 12 finally appear almost stationary (Figure 9.25); the latter is designated series C.

Taking logarithms can reduce the increasing dispersion in the data over time. Another stationary series (series D) is obtained by taking differences of period 1 and 12 after log-transforming the data. For purposes of the analysis, it appears adequate to model the differenced data (of periods 1 and 12 together) with and without the logarithmic transformation.

## Step 1: Identification

The next step is to examine the ordinary and partial correlograms and match them with a catalog of ACF and PACF patterns. Figure 9.26 shows seasonality in the pattern and, hence, the underlying data are seasonal (not surprising).

Along with the partial correlogram, we may conclude that series **B** is much like a seasonal AR (1) model. The significant spikes at lag 1 in both correlograms can be interpreted as either a regular AR or MA term.

For balance in the model, we will opt for the MA (1) term. The same result applies to series **A** because the ordinary correlogram for series **B** (Figure 9.26a) and series **A** (not shown) look essentially the same.

## Step 2: Estimation

A tentative (seasonal autoregressive) model with a regular MA (1) term was fit to series **A** and **B**, and the correlograms of the residuals were plotted (not shown). The coefficient for the seasonal AR1 parameter (= 0.99; $t$ = 35) in series **B** suggests that a seasonal difference is in order – when expressed in backshift notation, a seasonal AR1 parameter is $(1 - 0.99B^{12})$, which is very close to a seasonal difference $(1 - B^{12})$. The regular MA1 coefficient was significant ($\theta_1$= 0.75; $t$ =10.4).

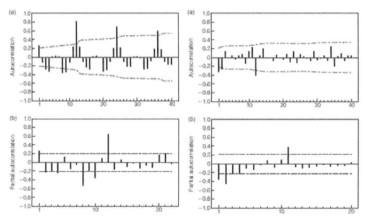

Figure 9.26 (*left*), (a) Ordinary and (b) partial correlograms of aeries B: first difference of log-transformed of the hotel/motel room demand series. (*Source*: Figure 9.24a).

Figure 9.27 (*right*). (a) Ordinary and (b) partial correlograms of series D: (first and period 12 differences of the log-transformed hotel/motel room demand series. (*Source*: Figure 9.24a).

The ordinary and partial correlograms of series **D** (the first and period 12 differences of the log-transformed hotel/motel room demand) was examined next (Figure 9.27). These patterns can have a couple of interpretations.

Recall, that we are not necessarily interested in only a single 'best' model. It serves us better to have a few different, but competing, models for developing and tracking forecasts on an ongoing basis. Consequently, the decaying pattern in the estimated PACF suggests an ARMA (0, 2) model, assuming the estimated ACF truncates at lag 2. On the other hand, a decaying pattern in both the estimated ACF and PACF suggests an ARMA (1, 1) model.

The resultant estimated parameters for the first instance turn out to be MA1 = 0.3 and $t$ = 5.7, and MA2 = 0.3 and $t$ = 1.1. Apparently, the MA2 parameter is not necessary, so the ARMA (0, 1) is sufficient.

The ARMA (1, 1) model turns out to have estimated parameters AR1 = 0.08 and $t$ = 0.5 (not significant), and MA1 = 0.77 and $t$ = 7.7. We end up with an ARMA (0, 1) model for series **D** with estimated MA1 coefficient = 0.75 and $t$ = 9.8. This result is consistent with our analysis of series **B**.

## Step 3: Diagnostic Checking

After fitting the ARMA (0, 1) model to series **D**, we plotted ordinary and partial correlograms of the residuals. These are shown in Figure 9.28. There is still a significant (negative) spike at lag 12 in both correlograms. We will opt for a seasonal MA (1) term to account for it. Figure 9.29 displays the ordinary and partial correlograms after taking this last modeling step. There is no more evidence of any useful structure to be extracted from the data.

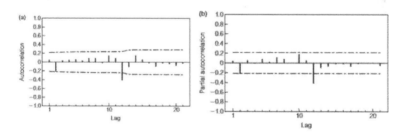

Figure 9.28. (a) Ordinary and (b) partial correlograms of the residuals from the ARMA (0, 1) model for series D (with 95% confidence limits

We have run a number of ARIMA models. Using the backshift notation, these models are estimated from the ARIMA processes shown in Figure 9.30. Model E is attributed to Frechtling's 1996 book *Practical Tourism Forecasting* and comes from the source of the hotel/motel room demand data. How different are these models in terms of forecasting performance? Although summary statistics can be helpful in creating the model, the acid test is a forecast evaluation with a holdout sample.

We have run a number of ARIMA models. Using the backshift notation, these models are estimated from the ARIMA processes shown in Figure 9.30. Model E is attributed to Frechtling's 1996 book *Practical Tourism Forecasting* and comes from the source of the hotel/motel room demand data. How different are these models in terms of forecasting performance? Although summary statistics can be helpful in creating the model, the acid test is a forecast evaluation with a holdout sample.

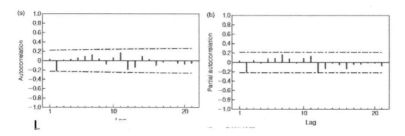

Figure 9.29 (a) Ordinary and (b) partial correlograms of the residuals from a seasonal MA (1) and ARMA (0, 1) model for series D (with 95% confidence limits).

Forecast tests were performed for all the models. By holding out Year 8, the following lead-time demand forecasts are obtained: 12 one-month-ahead forecasts were generated in Year 8; 11 two-month-ahead forecasts, and so on, until we have one 12-month-ahead forecast.

The **Waterfall** chart is shown for model **D** in Figure 9.31, displaying the percentage errors (PE =100 * (Actual - Forecast)/Actual) and the MAPE (average of absolute PE) for each row. Note the overforecasting bias in Month 3 and Months 6 -12. Because the latter months have fewer forecast percentage errors, it is important to maintain forecast errors on an ongoing basis. It should be possible, however, to use the waterfall chart to 'anticipate' a positive or negative bias in a future month and use that as an adjustment of the forecast.

| Series A | $(1 - \phi_{12} B^{12})(1 - B) Y_t. = (1 - \theta_1 B) \varepsilon_t.$ |
|---|---|
| Seriesl B | $(1 - \phi_{12} B^{12})(1 - B) \text{Ln } Y_t. = (1 - \theta_1 B) \varepsilon_t..$ |
| Series C | $(1 - B^{12}) (1 - B) Y_t. = (1 - \theta_1 B) (1 - \theta_{12} B^{12}) \varepsilon_t$ |
| Series D | $(1 - B^{12}) (1 - B) \text{Ln } Y_t. = (1 - \theta_1 B) (1 - \theta_{12} B^{12}) \varepsilon_t.$ |
| Frechtling (1996): | $(1 - B^{12}) (1 - B) (1 - \phi_1 B) Y_t. = (1 - \theta_1 - \theta_2 B) \varepsilon_t$ |

Figure 9.30 ARIMA models for hotel/motel room demand in backshift notation. (Source: Figure 9.22a).

| DCTOUR Hold-Out | 1 | 2 | 3 | 4 | 5 | 6 | 7 | 8 | 9 | 10 | 11 | 12 | MAPE (%) Model D |
|---|---|---|---|---|---|---|---|---|---|---|---|---|---|
| 1001666 | -5.38 | -2.22 | -1.28 | -0.70 | -2.33 | 2.53 | -0.36 | -2.60 | -1.72 | -0.06 | -2.12 | -4.07 | 2.1 |
| 1073196 | -3.85 | -1.95 | -1.08 | -2.55 | 1.86 | 0.41 | -2.72 | -2.52 | -0.59 | -2.14 | -4.73 | | 2.2 |
| 1421423 | -3.58 | -1.75 | -2.94 | 1.65 | -0.27 | -1.92 | -2.62 | -1.36 | -2.66 | -4.75 | | | 2.4 |
| 1577321 | -3.37 | -3.62 | 1.28 | -0.49 | -2.64 | -1.83 | -1.48 | -3.46 | -5.29 | | | | 2.6 |
| 1600991 | -5.27 | 0.62 | -0.88 | -2.85 | -2.54 | -0.70 | -3.58 | -6.12 | | | | | 2.8 |
| 1594481 | -0.96 | -1.55 | -3.24 | -2.75 | -1.39 | -2.77 | -6.23 | | | | | | 2.7 |
| 1510052 | -3.16 | -3.93 | -3.16 | -1.61 | -3.49 | -5.41 | | | | | | | 3.5 |
| 1436164 | -5.58 | -3.84 | -2.00 | -3.71 | -6.14 | | | | | | | | 4.3 |
| 1404978 | -5.49 | -2.68 | -4.11 | -6.36 | | | | | | | | | 4.7 |
| 1585409 | -4.32 | -4.80 | -6.78 | | | | | | | | | | 5.3 |
| 1234848 | -6.46 | -7.49 | | | | | | | | | | | 7.0 |
| 923115 | -9.20 | | | | | | | | | | | | 9.2 |

Figure 9.31 Waterfall chart with holdout sample (Year 8 = 1994) for model D for hotel/motel room demand. (Source: Figure 9.22a).

MAPE

| Model A | Model B | Model C | Model D | Model E |
|---|---|---|---|---|
| 3.2 | 3.1 | 2.8 | **2.1** | 3.0 |
| 2.8 | 2.8 | 2.6 | **2.2** | 3.0 |
| 3.0 | 3.1 | 2.5 | **2.4** | 2.8 |
| 3.1 | 3.3 | 2.8 | **2.6** | 3.3 |
| 3.6 | 3.6 | 3.3 | **2.8** | 3.4 |
| 3.2 | 3.4 | 2.7 | **2.7** | 3.4 |
| 4.2 | 4.4 | **2.9** | 3.5 | 4.1 |
| 5.0 | 5.1 | **3.8** | 4.3 | 5.1 |
| 5.6 | 5.7 | **3.9** | 4.7 | 5.6 |
| 6.6 | 6.8 | **4.6** | 5.3 | 6.8 |
| 9.2 | 8.8 | 7.7 | **7.0** | 9.1 |
| 12.9 | 11.4 | 12.4 | **9.2** | 12.9 |

Figure 9.32 Forecast test results with holdout sample (Year 8 =1994) for the models A – E for hotel/motel room demand.

Figure 9.32 summarizes the results of the tests using the MAPE as the criteria; the MdAPE should have been included. Model **D** had the best results (when measured in terms of average absolute percent of forecast error), followed by Model **C**. Models **A**, **B**, and **E** can be safely discarded for now, because they are consistently outperformed and do not appear very competitive. That leaves the two models based on the regular and seasonal differencing. Some other values can be made about these results:

- All the models exhibit a seasonal forecast profile over the forecast horizon.
- All models tended to over-forecast Year 8.

- Rival models **C** and **D** are versions of the so-called airline model, a model commonly found in seasonal forecasting applications with the Box-Jenkins approach.
- Model **D** (log-transformed) was outperformed by model **C** only during July through October.
- Log-transformed data reduced seasonal volatility and yielded the best results.
- It should be possible to forecast each of the first six periods within 3% and the remaining six periods individually within 6 or 7%, on average.

If model D is true, 95% prediction limits can be constructed for the forecasts in the holdout period, based on a fitted model up to the holdout period. Figure 9.33 displays the forecasts and lower and upper prediction limits calculated as a percentage deviation from the actual hotel/motel room demand for the holdout period. As noted, the forecasts are greater than the actuals. Here, the actuals are within the 95% confidence limits for the forecast (except for December 1994). In practice, we should not recommend an override adjustment for the bias unless we can also find a rationale based on business factors. Also note that, because of the log transformation, the confidence limits are asymmetric and are wider for larger values of the forecast.

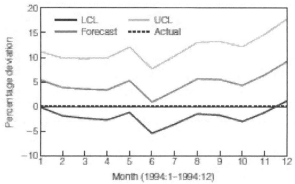

Figure 9.33. Model D 95% prediction interval for forecasts in holdout sample (Year 8 =1994); forecasts, lower confidence limit (LCL) and upper confidence limit (UCL) expressed as percentage deviation from the actual hotel/motel room demand. (*Source*: Figure 9.22a)

## ARIMA Modeling Checklist

| Green = YES    Yellow = SOMEWHAT    Red = NO |
| --- |

✓ Does the time plot show recognizable trend, seasonal or cyclical pattern?

✓ Is the series stationary?

✓ Do seasonal and regular differencing help to create stationarity?

✓ Does the trending series show increasing volatility in the seasonal pattern? Consider taking log transformations of the data first.

✓ Are you watchful of over-differencing? Be alert to the requirement that moving average parameters corresponding to the differencing that has been taken must achieve stationarity. For example, first differences may induce the need for a moving average parameter of order 1. Differencing with period 4 may induce the need for a seasonal moving average parameter in quarterly series. A check of the correlogram helps here. Over-differencing may be apparent if regular and seasonal moving average parameter estimates are very close to unity.

✓ Create ordinary and partial correlograms. Are patterns recognizable?

✓ Can correlogram patterns be matched to a theoretical ACF and PACF catalog?

✓ Have all the model parameters (i.e., terms) been included in the model as required?

✓ Have you examined the correlation matrix? There should not be a high degree of correlation between parameter estimates (e.g., over 0.7).

✓ Have you examined parameter estimates and their standard errors? The confidence interval for each parameter (including the trend constant if there is one) should not span zero but should be either positive or negative. If the confidence interval does include zero and the interval is basically symmetric about zero, then consideration should be given to eliminating the parameter.

✓ If a first-order regular autoregressive or seasonal autoregressive term is included in the model, the parameter estimates should not be close to 1.0 (e.g., over 0.90 or 0.95). If either is close to 1.0, a regular or seasonal difference should be tried in the model and a forecast test performed to determine whether the differenced model or the autoregressive model is better.

✓ Do the sum of squares of the errors and the standard error of the residuals become smaller as fits of the model improve?

✓ Does the chi-squared statistic fall below the critical value for the associated degrees of freedom? If so, this indicates white noise. (Note: A quick, conservative check for white noise is whether the model has a chi-squared statistic below the number of degrees of freedom.)

✓ Are there significant patterns in the correlograms of the residuals? Review the ordinary and partial correlograms for any remaining pattern in the residuals. Give primary emphasis to patterns in the correlogram. (Note: If the confidence limits on the correlogram and partial correlogram are approximately 95%, 1 spike in 20 can be expected to be outside the confidence limits due to randomness alone. Decaying spikes in the correlogram, which by visual inspection appear to originate at 1.0, indicate a regular autoregressive process; decaying spikes that originate at a lower level indicate a mixed autoregressive moving-average model.)

✓ Has a deterministic trend constant been estimated? It is suggested that a deterministic trend constant not be added until the very last step. Then, if the mean of the residuals of the final model is more than one standard deviation from zero, put a trend constant in the model and test it for significance. (There may be times when we do not want the model to put a trend in the forecasts.)

✓ There are some combinations of parameters that are unlikely to result within the same model. If these combinations are present, reevaluate the previous analysis of seasonal differences and seasonal autoregressive parameters, seasonal autoregressive and seasonal moving average parameters, and seasonal moving average parameters at other than lags 4 or 12 (or multiples of 4 and 12) for quarterly and monthly series, respectively.

## *Takeaways*

➤ The Box-Jenkins methodology presents a formally structured class of time series models that are sufficiently flexible to describe many practical situations. Known as ARIMA models, these are capable of describing various stationary and nonstationary (time-dependent) phenomena.

➤ The rule for identification is (1) If the correlogram cuts off at some point, say $k = q$, then the appropriate model is MA $(q)$; (2) if the partial correlogram cuts off at some point, say $k = p$, then the appropriate model is AR $(p)$; and (3) if neither diagram cuts off at some point, but does decay gradually to zero, the appropriate model is ARMA $(p', q')$ for some $p', q'$.

## *Postscript*

George Box (1919-2013) (*left*) and Gwilym Jenkins (1932-1982) (*right*) developed the unifying three-step Box-Jenkins modeling strategy during the 1960's. This strategy is the result of their direct experience with forecasting problems in business, economic, and control engineering applications. Since the 1990s, we have seen the development of **State Space Forecasting** as a unifying theoretical framework for exponential smoothing methods and ARIMA models; most of it attributed to the work of Rob J. Hyndman, Anne B. Koehler, J. Keith Ord and Ralph D. Snyder, all distinguished, contributing members of the *International Institute of Forecasters* (www.forecasters.org). Published in 2008, their book is entitled *Forecasting with Exponential Smoothing – The State Space Approach*.

The general theory of linear filters goes back almost a hundred years; much of the original work was done in the 1930s by the renowned mathematicians Andrei Nikolayevich Kolmogorov (1903-1987), (*left*) and Norbert Wiener (1894-1964) (*right*) for automatic control problems. However, as an approach to forecasting, these techniques became popular in the 1960s and beyond through the work of Box and Jenkins.

A special kind of linear filter, called the autoregressive (AR) process, goes back a little further: AR models were first used in the 1920s and in the next decade another kind of linear filter, called the moving average (MA) process was being applied in various applications with time series. Autoregressive moving average (ARMA) theory, in which these processes are combined, was developed in 1938 by Herman Wold (1908-1992) (*right*).

# 10

# Demand Forecasting with Regression Models

*I have seen the future and it is very much like the present,*
*only longer*

Kehlog Albran, *The Profit*

---

In this chapter, you will learn about
- the concept of a linear regression model and how to use it for describing and creating causal models for demand forecasting purposes
- preparing data to identify a regression model, and assumptions needed to validate model relationships involving appropriate drivers of demand elasticities, both own-price and cross-elasticity, as essential to understanding business growth as well as revenue-quantity relationships
- what role correlations and residuals play in validating modeling assumptions
- how a resistant measure of correlation can safeguard making unwarranted statements about causation

---

## *What Are Regression Models?*

The term regression has a rather curious origin in studies of inheritance in biology, which showed that whereas tall (or short) fathers had tall (or short) sons, the sons were *on average* not as tall (or

as short) as their fathers. This phenomenon was discovered by Sir Francis Galton, (1822-1911), and is called *regression toward the mean*. Thus, Galton observed that the average height of the sons tended to move toward the average height of the overall population of fathers rather than toward reproducing the height of the parents. It has since been observed in a wide spectrum of settings from economic behavior and athletic performance to demand forecasting. Regression analysis is the principal method of causal modeling in demand forecasting.

Demand forecasters begin a regression analysis by identifying the factors or drivers of demand (Chapter 1), called **independent**, causal or explanatory variables – that they believe have influenced and will continue to influence the variable to be forecast (the **dependent** variable).

It is useful to categorize causal variables as internal or external. **Internal variables**, also called policy variables, can be controlled to a substantial degree by managerial decisions, and their future values can be set as a matter of company policy. Examples include product prices, promotion outlays, and methods of distribution. **External** or environmental variables are those whose level and influence are outside organizational control. Included here may be variables that measure weather and holidays, demographics such as the age and gender of consumers in the market area, decisions made by competing enterprises, and the state of the macro economy as measured by rates of economic growth, inflation, and unemployment. Normally a regression analysis will attempt to account for both internal and external causal variables.

The forecaster's beliefs about the way a dependent variable responds to changes in each of the independent variables is expressed as an equation, or series of equations, called a **regression model**. A regression model also includes an explicit expression of an error variable to describe the role of chance or underlying uncertainty.

*A model with a single independent variable is called a simple regression model. Multiple regression refers to a model with one dependent and two or more independent variables.*

A successful regression analysis provides useful estimates of how previous changes in each of the independent variables have affected the dependent variable. In addition, assuming that the underlying structure is stable, forecasts of the dependent variable can then be conditioned on assumptions or projections of the future behavior of the independent variables.

For example, suppose that a regression analysis of the demand for a product or service indicates that price increases in the past, holding other things constant, have been associated with less than proportional reductions in sales volumes (i.e., demand has been **price inelastic** – *see* Chapter 11). This knowledge may be useful both for forecasting future demand and for adjusting product-pricing policy.

The inelastic demand suggests that price increases might be improving profitability. Demand forecasts would then be made in light of the price changes that the company plans to institute.

Similar feedback can be obtained through regression analysis of the influence of external economic variables such as the Gross Domestic Product (GDP). Although the firm cannot control the rates of economic growth, projections of GDP growth can be translated via regression analysis into forecasts of product sales growth.

> *As a forecasting approach, regression analysis has the potential to provide not only demand forecasts of the dependent variable but useful managerial information for adapting to the forces and events that cause the dependent variable to change.*

Indeed, a regression analysis may be motivated as much or more by the need for policy information as by the interest in demand forecasting. It is important to note that no extrapolative forecasting method can supply policy information, such as how product sales respond to price and macroeconomic variables. When such information is desired, explanations are required, not merely extrapolations. The chapter-opening quotation suggests that Einstein would have preferred the empirical approach to demand forecasting, which analyzes the data ("experience") in terms of a model ("knowledge of reality") that relates the dependent and independent variables.

## The Regression Curve

A regression curve can be used to describe a relationship between a variable of interest and one or more related variables that are assumed to have a bearing on the demand forecasting problem. If data are plentiful, a curve passing through the bulk of the data represents the regression curve. The data are such that there is no functional relationship describing exactly one variable Y as a function of X; for a given value of the independent variable X, there is a *distribution* of values of Y. This relationship may be approximated by determining the average (or median) value of Y for small intervals of values of X.

> *A regression curve (in a two-variable case) is defined as that "typical" curve that goes through the mean value of the dependent variable Y for each fixed value of the independent variable X.*

In many practical situations, there are not enough values to "even pretend that the resulting curve has the shape of the regression curve that would arise if we had unlimited data", according to Mosteller and Tukey in their *Data Analysis and Regression* book (1977, p. 266). Instead, the values result in an approximation. With only limited data, a shape for the regression curve (e.g., linear, or exponential) is assumed and the curve is fitted to the data by using a statistical technique such as the **method of least squares.** This method is explained shortly.

## A Simple Linear Model

Because regression analysis seeks an algebraic relationship between a dependent variable $Y$ and one or more independent variables, the deterministic (*change*) component of the model describes the mean (expected) value for Y given a specific value of X:

Deterministic component = Mean $Y$,

when $Y$ is some function of $X$. In practice, there is considerable variability in $Y$ for a given $X$ around a mean value. This mean value is an unknown quantity that is commonly denoted by the Greek letter $\mu$ with a subscript $Y(X)$ to denote its dependence on $X$:

$$\mu_{Y(X)} = \beta_0 + \beta_1 X$$

> *One key assumption in the linear regression model is that for any value of X, the value of Y is scattered around a mean value.*

The straight line may be approximately true; the difference between $Y$ and the straight line is ascribed to a random error (*"chance"*) component. Thus, the observed values of $Y$ will not necessarily lie on a straight line in the $XY$ plane but will differ from it by some random errors.

$$Y = \beta_0 + \beta_1 X + \text{Random errors}$$

Thus, the **simple linear regression model** (SLR) for $Y$ can be expressed by the sum of a deterministic component $\mu_{Y(X)}$ and a random component $\varepsilon$:

$$Y = \mu_{Y(X)} + \varepsilon$$

$$= \beta_0 + \beta_1 X + \varepsilon$$

where the mean (expected) value of random errors $\varepsilon$ is assumed to be zero. The intercept $\beta_0$ and slope $\beta_1$ are known as the regression parameters. The model is linear in the parameters, both $\beta_0$ and $\beta_1$ are unknown parameters to be estimated from the data. As a standard statistical convention, it is useful to designate unknown parameters in models by Greek letters, to distinguish them from the corresponding statistics $b_0$ and $b_1$ (in Roman letters) estimated from the data.

As demand forecasters, we can view the deterministic component as describing a systematic *change,* whereas the random errors depict measured *chance* in the sense of our notion of embracing **both** "change & chance" for demand forecasting best practices. In a particular application of the model, the demand forecaster has data that are assumed to have arisen as a realization of the hypothetical model. The next step is to come up with a rationale for estimating the parameters, $\beta_0$ and $\beta_1$, in the model from a given set of data.

## The Least-Squares Assumption

There are many techniques around for estimating parameters from data, but the method of **ordinary least squares** (OLS) is the most common and it has a sound basis in statistical theory. This is not to say that other techniques have little merit.

In fact, weighted least-squares techniques of several kinds have been found to have increased importance in practical applications of outlier-resistant data analysis techniques and robust regression (cf. C. Fred. Mosteller and John W. Tukey, *Data Analysis and Regression,* 1977).

> ***The method of least squares is the most widely accepted criterion for estimating parameters in a model.***

| $Y_i$ | $X$ | $y_i = (Y_i - \bar{Y})$ | $x_i = (X_i - \bar{X})$ | $y_i x_i$ | $x_i^2$ |
|---|---|---|---|---|---|
| 3 | 1 | −5 | −2 | 10 | 4 |
| 5 | 2 | −3 | −1 | 3 | 1 |
| 7 | 3 | −1 | 0 | 0 | 0 |
| 14 | 4 | 6 | 1 | 6 | 1 |
| 11 | 5 | 3 | 2 | 6 | 4 |
| Sum 40 | 15 | | | 25 | 10 |

Average: $\bar{Y} = 8$  $\bar{X} = 3$
$b_1 = 25/10$
$b_0 = \bar{Y} - b_1 \bar{X} = 8 - 2.5(3) = 0.5$
Fitted equation: $\hat{Y} = 0.5 + 2.5X$

Figure10.1 Example illustrating the calculation of regression coefficients in a simple linear regression.

Consider now one reasonable criterion for estimating $\beta_0$ and $\beta_1$ from data in a simple linear regression model. OLS determines values $b_0$ and $b_1$ (Notation is important now because parameters will be estimated from data, so we "plug in" lower-case Roman letters $b_0$ and $b_1$ to replace the Greek symbols $\beta_0$ and $\beta_1$), so that the sum of squared vertical deviations (squared residuals) between the data and a fitted line is less than the sum of the squared vertical deviations from any other straight-line fit that could be drawn through the data:

$$\text{Minimum of } \Sigma(\text{Data - Fit})^2 = \Sigma(\text{Residuals})^2$$

Recall Residual = Data - ($b_0 + b_1 X$). A vertical deviation is the vertical distance from an observed data point to the line. Each deviation in the sample is squared and the least-squares line is defined to be the straight line that makes the sum of these squared deviations a minimum. The notation for this is as follows.

Consider the data pairs ($Y_i, X_i$) for ($i = 1, \ldots, n$). Let $y_i = Y_i - \bar{Y}$ and $x_i = X_i - \ddot{X}$, where $\bar{Y} = (\Sigma Y_i)/n$, and $\ddot{X} = (\Sigma X_i)/n$. The symbol $\Sigma$ denotes the summation over $n$ values. Then $\Sigma D^2 = \Sigma (Y_i - b_0 - b_1 X_i)^2$ is minimized. Figure 10.1 shows the calculations of $b_0$ and $b_1$ for a small set of data.

## CASE: Sales and Advertising of a Weight Control Product

The VP of Sales has called you into her office to help plan for an upcoming advertising campaign. To date, much of the planning has used a seat-of-the-pants approach and not entirely satisfactory. To help improve the situation, you recommend investigating some quantitative approaches to the problem. You want to gain some familiarity with some methodologies you find in a search on the Internet, and you embark on a preliminary analysis of an existing data set. It is hoped that this investigation will lead to some insights that will help tackle your company's data.

| Year 1 | | | | | | | | | | | |
|---|---|---|---|---|---|---|---|---|---|---|---|
| Sales | 12.0 | 20.5 | 21 | 15.5 | 15.3 | 23.5 | 24.5 | 21.3 | 23.5 | 28.0 | 24.0 | 15.5 |
| Adv | 15 | 16 | 18 | 27 | 21 | 49 | 21 | 22 | 28 | 36 | 40 | 3 |
| Year 2 | | | | | | | | | | | |
| Sales | 17.3 | 25.3 | 25 | 36.5 | 36.5 | 29.6 | 30.5 | 28.0 | 26.0 | 21.5 | 19.7 | 19.0 |
| Adv | 21 | 29 | 62 | 65 | 46 | 44 | 33 | 62 | 22 | 12 | 24 | 3 |
| Year 3 | | | | | | | | | | | |
| Sales | 16.0 | 20.7 | 26.5 | 30.6 | 32.3 | 29.5 | 28.3 | 31.3 | 32.2 | 26.4 | 23.4 | 16.4 |
| Adv | 5 | 14 | 36 | 40 | 49 | 7 | 52 | 65 | 17 | 5 | 17 | 1 |

Figure 10.2 Sales versus advertising example. (*Source*: F. M. Bass and D. G. Clarke (1972), *Testing distributed lag models of advertising effect*, J. Marketing Research, pp. 298 - 308)

Figure 10.3 shows a scatter diagram of the sales (dependent variable) and lag 1 advertising (independent variable). A good fit is no surprise, because the correlation coefficient between $Y$ and $X$ is relatively high ($r = 0.67$). The correlation between Y and X (without lag 1) is 0.64, supporting our decision to use a lagged independent variable.

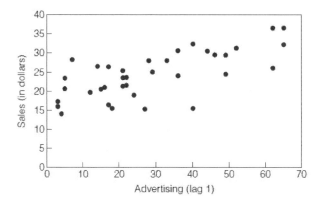

Figure 10.3 Scatter diagram of sales and advertising variables (lag 1). (Source: Figure 10.2)

Because *X* is a lagged value of the data, it allows us to forecast the first period based on an actual value of advertising. Note that the slope coefficient in the equation $Y = 18.28 + 0.22\,X$ is 0.22 (Figure10. 4). The other parts will be covered more fully later. In Figure 10.2, the dependent variable Y is the sales of a weight-control product; the independent, explanatory variable is monthly advertising expenditures (lagged 1 period earlier).

**Regression Statistics**

| | |
|---|---|
| Multiple $R$ | 0.67 |
| $R^2$ | 0.45 |
| Adjusted $R^2$ | 0.44 |
| Standard error | 4.42 |
| Observations | 35 |

ANOVA

| | df | SS | MS | F |
|---|---|---|---|---|
| Regression | 1 | 537.55 | 537.55 | 21.49 |
| Residual | 33 | 645.38 | 19.56 | |
| Total | 34 | 1182.93 | | |

| | Coefficients | Standard Error | *t* Statistic | Lower 95% | Upper 95% |
|---|---|---|---|---|---|
| Intercept | 18.28 | 1.42 | 12.89 | 15.4 | 21.17 |
| X variable 1 | 0.22 | 0.04 | 5.26 | 0.13 | 0.3 |

Figure 10.4 Computer output for a simple linear regression model of sales versus (lagged) advertising; (a) intercept and X variable 1 coefficients. (*Source*: Figure 10.2)

## The Role of Correlation Analysis in Regression Modeling

When demand forecasters have reason to believe that more than one factor (driver of demand) is required to solve a demand forecasting or econometric analysis problem, they turn to multiple linear regression models. To make forecasts with a multiple linear regression model, one needs to provide forecasts of more than one independent (explanatory) variable. When multiple variables are involved, the modeling effort can easily become more involved, so it is necessary to start with exploratory data analysis tools to get proper insight into the forecast-generating process.

By focusing only on the fit of the equation, you may discover a useful description of a forecast profile (*change*) but at the same time mis specify the uncertainty (*chance*), because error assumptions are needed in using the equation for forecasting. Also, accurate forecasts of the drivers of demand are needed, and if the underlying model errors are not normally distributed, as is usually assumed, there is a need for identifying root causes and exceptions. So, there is always a trade-off between the goodness of fit and the quality of fit in the use of regression models for forecasting applications.

Recall, in a **multiple linear regression** (MLR) analysis, the deterministic component (*change*) takes the form of an equation,

$$\mu_{Y(X)} = \beta_0 + \beta_1 X_1 + \ldots + \beta_k X_k$$

where $X_1, \ldots, X_k$ are $k$ independent variables (or regressors), and $\beta_0$, $\beta_1, \ldots, \beta_k$ are called **regression parameters**. This regression equation arises when the variation in the dependent variable $Y$ is assumed to be affected by changes in more than one independent variable. Thus, the *expected (or average) value* of $Y$ is said to depend on $X_1, X_2, \ldots, X_k$. The dependence on $X$ is henceforth suppressed in the notation; Let $\mu_{Y(X)} = \mu_Y$. In this case, one speaks of a multiple linear regression of $Y$ on $X_1 \ldots X_k$.

The regression equation is called a **model** when a random error (*chance*) term is added to the equation, which then becomes $Y = \mu_{Y(X)} + \varepsilon$, where $\varepsilon$ commonly has an assumed normal error distribution.

While the formal theory of normal multiple linear regression analysis is extensive and is dealt with in many business statistics textbooks, of interest here are its application and interpretation in demand forecasting problems and those derivations and algorithms that are directly applicable to the interpretation of the analysis.

Adequacy of the model assumptions can be examined through a variety of methods, frequently graphical and mostly involving residuals (Actual minus Fit). One must be aware of a range of regression pitfalls to be avoided. These include trend collinearity, overfitting, extrapolation, outliers, nonnormal distributions, multicollinearity, and invalid assumptions regarding the model errors (e.g., independence, constant variance, and, usually, normality). Such inadequate assumptions often point to the root causes of not-so-credible forecasts.

But how does one put a model together? The first step in beginning a regression analysis for demand forecasting is to identify the **drivers of demand**—called factors—independent or explanatory variables that are believed to have influenced and expected to continue to influence the (dependent) variable to be forecast. The **scatter diagram** is a useful graphical tool for exploring the relationships among such factors.

The second step is to create a regression model by estimating the coefficients in the model by the method of least squares. This will give us a fitted equation from which we can determine the forecast profile.

## Linear Association and Correlation

When the values of one time series (or variable) are paired with corresponding values of a related time series (or variable), a relationship between the variables can be depicted in a **scatter diagram** with one variable is plotted on the horizontal scale and the other is plotted on the vertical scale. Such a plot is a valuable tool for studying the relationship between a pair of variables.

When two series have a strong positive association, the scatter diagram reveals a pattern of points along a line of positive slope. A negative association shows up as a scatter pattern along a line with negative slope. A conventional measure of such linear association between a pair of variables $Y$ and $X$ is given by the *Pearson* **product moment correlation coefficient** $r$, where $r$ is an averaging formula using the sample mean and sample standard deviation of the two variables, respectively.

> *The product moment correlation coefficient is a conventional measure of linear association between two variables.*

Although forecasting and statistical software programs routinely calculate $r$, it is useful to view it as the result of an averaging process; namely, of the average of a product of standardized variables: Average {(Standardized $Y_t$)*(Standardized $X_t$)}, with a divisor of $(n-1)$ instead of $n$, where $n$ is the common number of $X$, $Y$ pairs. When a variable is standardized, it has a zero mean and a unit standard deviation, which is useful for making comparisons and correlations between variables that have very different sizes or scales of measurement.

> *A standardized value is obtained by subtracting the sample mean from the data and dividing by the sample standard deviation.*

Figure 10.5 shows a spreadsheet calculation for obtaining the product moment correlation between annual housing starts and mortgage rates. The coefficient can vary between +1 and −1, so that $r =$ −0.20 suggests a weak negative association between housing starts and mortgage rates.

Although the product moment correlation coefficient for housing starts versus mortgage rates data shown in the figure is only about − 0.20, the correlation coefficient for the respective annual change in these variables turns out to be −0.57. Both are negative, as expected, but the latter reflects a much stronger linear association. This suggests that the strength of the relationship between housing starts and mortgage rates is reflected in their respective growth rates, not so much the actual levels.

## The Scatter Plot Matrix

Creating scatter diagrams to validate a **linear association** between the dependent variable and each of the independent variables, as well as between pairs of independent variables, is an essential step in exploratory data analysis for larger datasets. Doing so can save you time when questions arise about root causes and exceptions with flawed models. At the same time, the diagrams can provide a better understanding of the data-generating process in the underlying relationships.

An arrangement of scatter diagrams between multiple pairs of variables is called the **scatter plot matrix**. We can summarize this by creating a correlation matrix of **product moment correlations** between pairs of variables.

The diagonal of a correlation matrix consists of 1s because each variable is perfectly correlated with itself. At the intersection of each row and column is the correlation coefficient relating the row variable to the column variable.

Because the matrix is symmetrical, it is useful to display the product moment correlation coefficient r on one side of the diagonal and an outlier-resistant version of correlation called r* (SSD)—defined in the next section—on the other. To distinguish it from other types of correlation measures, the term ordinary correlation coefficient is here used interchangeably with the term Pearson product moment correlation coefficient.

In this way, the demand forecaster gets the necessary insight from the augmented correlation matrix for constructing regression relationships. Contrasting r with r* (SSD) may indicate departures from linearity due to outlying or non-typical data, so the demand forecaster then needs to review the underlying data for nonlinearity in the patterns. An outlier may not necessarily appear visually extreme from the bulk of the data in these situations.

> *A scatter plot matrix is an array of associations between pairs of variables.*

| Housing Starts | Mortgage Rates | Col 1 × Col 2 |
|---|---|---|
| 0.168898 | −1.384396 | −0.233822 |
| −0.051812 | −1.405769 | 0.072836 |
| −0.217938 | −1.410043 | 0.307302 |
| −1.131335 | −1.239058 | 1.401789 |
| −0.755474 | −1.157839 | 0.874718 |
| −0.114703 | −0.944107 | 0.108292 |
| −0.235737 | −0.589311 | 0.138923 |
| −0.334226 | −0.328558 | 0.109813 |
| 1.500873 | −0.619234 | −0.929391 |
| 2.403886 | −0.679079 | −1.632429 |
| 1.480404 | −0.538016 | −0.796480 |
| −0.618717 | −0.140474 | 0.086913 |
| −1.144684 | −0.123375 | 0.141226 |
| −0.026003 | −0.114826 | 0.002986 |
| 1.307751 | −0.102002 | −0.133393 |
| 1.406240 | 0.124554 | 0.175153 |
| 0.589850 | 0.620413 | 0.365951 |
| −0.753694 | 1.377025 | −1.037857 |
| −1.370734 | 2.176384 | −2.983244 |
| −1.435998 | 2.330271 | −3.346265 |
| 0.464958 | 1.312906 | 0.610447 |
| 0.602902 | 1.214589 | 0.732279 |
| 0.580060 | 0.876850 | 0.508650 |
| 0.768732 | 0.299815 | 0.230477 |
| 0.220219 | −0.042157 | −0.009284 |
| −0.172550 | −0.089178 | 0.015388 |
| −0.504802 | 0.312639 | −0.157821 |
| −1.048865 | 0.274167 | −0.287564 |
| −1.577502 | −0.012234 | 0.019300 |
| 0.000000 | 0.000000 | r = −0.201611 |
| 1.000000 | 1.000000 | |

Figure 10.5 Calculation of the product moment correlation coefficient between annual housing starts and mortgage rates. (*Source*: Figure 7.12 Housing starts data; Figure 7.8 Mortgage rates data)

# The Need for Outlier Resistance in Correlation Analysis

The robust estimator of correlation, known as $r^*$(SSD), is less sensitive to outliers than the ordinary correlation coefficient $r$. It is derived from the standardized sums and differences of two variables, say $Y$ and $X$, as introduced in a 1975 *Biometrika* paper entitled "*Robust Estimation and Outlier Detection with Correlation Coefficients*," by Susan J. Devlin, Ram Gnanadesikan, and Jon R. Kettenring.

The first step in obtaining $r^*$(SSD) is to standardize both $Y$ and $X$ robustly by constructing two new variables $Y$ and $X$:

$$\bar{Y} = (Y - Y^*)/S_Y^* \text{ and } \ddot{X} = (X - X^*)/S_X^*$$

where $Y^*$ and $X^*$ are robust/resistant estimates of location and $S_Y^*$ and  $S_X^*$ are robust/resistant estimates of scale.

Now, let $Z_1 = \bar{Y} + \ddot{X}$ and $Z_2 = \bar{Y} - \ddot{X}$, the sum and differences vectors, respectively. Then the robust variance of the sum vector $Z_1$ and difference vector $Z_2$ are calculated; they are denoted by $V_+^*$ and $V_-^*$, respectively. These variances are used in the calculation of the robust correlation estimate $r^*$(SSD given by

$$r^*(SSD = (V_+^* - V_-^*) / (V_+^* + V_-^*).$$

The justification for this formula can be seen by inspecting the formula for the variance of the sum of two variables:

$$Var(Z_1) = Var\,(\bar{Y}) + Var\,(\ddot{X}) + 2\,Cov\,(\bar{Y}, \ddot{X})$$

where Cov denotes the covariance between $\bar{Y}$ and $\ddot{X}$.

Because $Y$ and $X$ are standardized, centered about zero, with unit scale, the expected variance of $Z_1$ is approximately

$$Var(Z_1) \approx 1 + 1 + 2\,\rho\,(\bar{Y}, \ddot{X}) = 2\,(1 + \rho)$$

where $\rho$ is the theoretical correlation between $\hat{Y}$ and $X$.

Similarly, for $Z_2$,

$$Var\,(Z_2) \approx Var\,(\bar{Y}) + Var\,(\ddot{X}) - 2\,Cov\,(\bar{Y}, \ddot{X})$$

$$= 1 + 1 - 2\,\rho\,(\bar{Y}, \ddot{X}) = 2\,(1 - \rho).$$

Notice that $\rho$ is given by the expression

$$[Var\,(Z_1) - Var\,(Z_2)] / [Var\,(Z_1) + Var\,(Z_2)] \approx [2(1 + \rho) - 2(1 - \rho)] / [2(1 + \rho) + 2(1 - \rho)] = \rho.$$

Some robust estimates of the (square root of the) variance, required in the formula for $r^*$ were discussed in Chapter 2; these include the unbiased median absolute deviation from the median (UMdAD = MdAD/0.6745) and the unbiased interquartile range (UIQR = IQR/1.349).

## *Creating Multiple Linear Regression Models*

When we have reasons to believe that more than one explanatory variable is required to solve a demand forecasting problem, the simple regression model will no longer provide the appropriate representation and we need to develop a linear regression model for forecasting a dependent variable from a projection of more than one explanatory variable. In this case, we are extending the simple linear regression model with one explanatory variable to a model that can encompass multiple explanatory variables. The most direct extension is the multiple linear regression model.

> **A multiple linear regression model relates a dependent variable to more than one explanatory variable.**

In multiple linear regression, the regression function $\mu_{Y(X)}$ is the deterministic component of the model and takes the form

$$\mu_{Y(X)} = \beta_0 + \beta_1 X_1 + \ldots + \beta_k X_k$$

where $X_1, \ldots, X_k$ are explanatory variables *(or regressors)* and $\beta_0, \beta_1, \ldots, \beta_k$ are called regression parameters.

Explanatory variables are also commonly termed independent variables, and demand forecasters use these terms interchangeably. This model arises when the variation in the dependent variable $Y$ is assumed to be impacted by changes in more than one explanatory variable. Thus, the average value of $Y$ is said to depend on $X_1, X_2, \ldots, X_k$. The dependence on $X$ is henceforth suppressed in the notation; let $\mu_{Y(X)} = \mu_Y$. In this case, we speak of a multiple regression of $Y$ on $X_1, \ldots, X_k$.

A multiple linear regression model may be used to fit a polynomial function, such as

$$\mu_Y = \beta_0 + \beta_1 X + \beta_2 X^2 + \ldots + \beta_k X^k$$

By letting $X_1 = X$, $X_2 = X^2$, $\ldots X_k = X^k$ , we obtain the form of the linear regression model.

Often $X$ is used to represent a time scale (weeks, months, or years). It is worth emphasizing that the regressors may be any functional form; there need only be linearity in the $\beta$ parameters. What is meant by **linearity**? Examples of linearity in the parameters include $\mu_Y = \beta_0 + \beta_1 t$, $\mu_Y = \beta_0 + \beta_1 e_t$ and $\mu_Y = \beta_0 + \beta_1 \ln X$. On the other hand, functional forms for a regression model, such as $\beta_1 \sin(\gamma_1 t) + \beta_2 \cos(\gamma_1 t)$ and $\beta_1 \exp(\gamma_1 t) + \beta_2 \cos(\gamma_2 t)$, are *not* linear in the $\beta$ and $\gamma$ parameters A linear combination has the form  "parameter times variable" *plus* "parameter times variable", etc., which defines a linear equation.

## Using Linear Regression to Estimate Elasticities and Promotion Effects

Scanner data are routinely obtained at the checkout counter of many stores. Large amounts of data are created this way, and stores have been investigating these data for analysis and forecasting purposes. For example, grocery stores use scanner data to evaluate its promotional activities. This information is critically useful to demand forecasters who need to make overrides (adjustments) to a baseline forecast. Scanner data can be combined with data on promotions, such as in-store displays and flyer distribution activities. In order to get an idea of the amount of scanner data the chain of stores is collecting, it should be realized that (1) there are many franchised stores, (2) in each store, data are collected on thousands of individual products (e.g. supermarkets commonly carry at least 4000 SKUs) and data are collected on a weekly basis.

| | Price / Unit | Unit Sales | Log Sales | Log Price | Flyer Promotion | Display Promotio |
|---|---|---|---|---|---|---|
| 6 | | | | | | |
| 7 | 1.01 | 323 | 2.51 | 0.00 | 0 | 1 |
| 8 | 1.55 | 48 | 1.68 | 0.19 | 0 | 1 |
| 9 | 1.52 | 58 | 1.76 | 0.18 | 0 | 0 |
| 10 | 0.88 | 1612 | 3.21 | -0.06 | 1 | 1 |
| 11 | 1.13 | 122 | 2.09 | 0.05 | 0 | 0 |
| 12 | 1.67 | 27 | 1.43 | 0.22 | 0 | 0 |
| 13 | 1.66 | 31 | 1.49 | 0.22 | 0 | 0 |
| 14 | 1.37 | 115 | 2.06 | 0.14 | 0 | 0 |
| 15 | 1.09 | 280 | 2.45 | 0.04 | 0 | 1 |
| 16 | 1.67 | 24 | 1.38 | 0.22 | 0 | 1 |
| 17 | 1.45 | 70 | 1.85 | 0.16 | 0 | 0 |
| 18 | 1.37 | 80 | 1.90 | 0.14 | 0 | 0 |
| 19 | 1.73 | 16 | 1.20 | 0.24 | 0 | 0 |
| 20 | 1.55 | 42 | 1.62 | 0.19 | 0 | 0 |
| 21 | 1.82 | 15 | 1.18 | 0.26 | 0 | 0 |
| 22 | 0.97 | 1155 | 3.06 | -0.01 | 1 | 1 |
| 23 | 1.1 | 155 | 2.19 | 0.04 | 0 | 0 |
| 24 | 0.85 | 1892 | 3.28 | -0.07 | 1 | 1 |
| 25 | 0.95 | 481 | 2.68 | -0.02 | 0 | 1 |
| 26 | 1.35 | 62 | 1.79 | 0.13 | 0 | 1 |
| 27 | 1.35 | 58 | 1.76 | 0.13 | 0 | 1 |
| 28 | 1.35 | 139 | 2.14 | 0.13 | 0 | 0 |
| 29 | 1.46 | 76 | 1.88 | 0.16 | 0 | 0 |
| 30 | 0.99 | 841 | 2.92 | -0.00 | 1 | 1 |
| 31 | 1.28 | 204 | 2.31 | 0.11 | 0 | 0 |
| 32 | 1.37 | 77 | 1.89 | 0.14 | 0 | 0 |
| 33 | 1.61 | 29 | 1.46 | 0.21 | 0 | 0 |
| 34 | 1.7 | 58 | 1.76 | 0.23 | 0 | 0 |
| 35 | 0.99 | 1098 | 3.04 | -0.00 | 1 | 1 |
| 36 | 1.68 | 34 | 1.53 | 0.23 | 0 | 0 |
| 37 | 1.64 | 20 | 1.30 | 0.21 | 0 | 0 |
| 38 | 0.98 | 904 | 2.96 | -0.01 | 1 | 1 |
| 39 | 1.23 | 113 | 2.05 | 0.09 | 0 | 0 |

Figure 10.11 Original and transformed data; values 1 - 39. (*Source*: U. Menzefricke, *Statistics for Managers*, 1995, sec 10.8).

As a starting point, we decide to concentrate on one store and one product category, beverages. The promotions change weekly and are mainly of two types; flyers that were distributed outside the stores and in-store displays

The process of deriving this model is *iterative*, a layer at a time, much like peeling an onion. Definition of variables used in the model are: SALES, sales in units (abbreviated as S); PRICE, price in dollars (abbreviated P); FLYER, flyer promotion (1= YES, 0= NO); DISPLAY, display promotion (1= YES, 0= NO)

## A Four-Step Procedure

Draw scatter plots of pairs of variables, and describe the nature of the relationship among the variables

1.  Find the least-squares regression fit, and plot the residuals versus the fitted values. Interpret the coefficients in the context of this application
2.  Assuming the other variables remain essentially unchanged, what would you estimate to be the impact of a 3% change in PRICE on the SALES
3.  Calculate the residuals (Actual – Fit) and draw a scatter plot of the residuals versus each independent variable.
4.  Complete the checklist:

Figure 10.12 *(left)* Scatter plot of sales versus price. (*Source*: Figure 10.11)

Figure 10.13 (*right*) Scatter plot of log sales versus log price. (*Source*: Figure 10.11)

### Step 1 – Preliminary Data Analysis

To check for linearity in the relationship between Sales and Price, we display two scatter plots.  Figure 10.12 shows a nonlinear relationship between sales and price. As price increases, the sales decrease.

The same holds if the data are transformed with logarithms, but this pattern (Figure 10.13 is linear, however. As part of an exploratory analysis, the 52 weeks can be organized into four 13-week buckets and examined for within-quarter periodicities. The preliminary

STI_Classification yields for **Sales** 23% seasonality, 5% trend and 72% other. For **Price** the results show 21% seasonality, 4% trend and 74% other.

A discussion with a domain expert in the marketing department might give insight into a seasonal pricing pattern by quarter. Scatter diagrams of $\text{Log}_e$ Sales vs. $\text{Log}_e$ Price by quarter would indicate the stability of the constant elasticity by quarter. For the 52-week period, the constant price elasticity estimate of $\beta_1$ is −4.66 (Figure 10.12).

| M1 | Coeff | Std Error | t-Stat |
|---|---|---|---|
| Intercept | 2.76 | 0.036036 | 76.56353 |
| Log Price | -5.94 | 0.239734 | -24.7762 |

| M2 | Coeff | Std Error | t-Stat |
|---|---|---|---|
| Intercept | 2.54 | 0.047147 | 53.95927 |
| Log Price | -4.71 | 0.25775 | -18.2847 |
| Flyer Promotion | 0.45 | 0.06586 | 6.87911 |
| Display Promotion | -0.04 | 0.045029 | -0.9323 |

| M3 | Coeff | Std Error | t-Stat |
|---|---|---|---|
| Intercept | 2.52 | 0.042283 | 59.70899 |
| Log Price | -4.66 | 0.250843 | -18.5733 |
| Flyer Promotion | 0.43 | 0.0618 | 6.991004 |

Figure 10.14 Model coefficients and price elasticity estimates for models 1, 2, and 3. (*Source*: Figure 10.11)

**Step 2 - Model 1**:

Log (Sales) = $\beta_0 + \beta_1$log (Price) + $\varepsilon$, where $\varepsilon$ is the random error.

A summary output for Model 1 is shown in Figure 10.14. The fitted equation is

Log (Sales) = 2.76 − 5.94 log (Price)

Incorporate promotional factors to the, the model by adding two qualitative variables - **Flyer** (flyer promotion) and **Display** (display promotion). The form of the augmented model is:

**Step 3 - Model 2**:

Log (Sales) = $\beta_0 + \beta_1$log (Price) + $\beta_2$Flyer + $\beta_3$Display + $\varepsilon$

The fitted equation (Figure 10.14) is

Log (Sales) = 2.54 − 4.71 log (Price) + 0.45 Flyer - 0.04 Display

The Intercept and X Variables, except **Flyer**, have coefficients with t Stat > |2| and are deemed statistically significant, indicating valid effects. Generate a multiple linear regression model adding only **Flyer**, in addition to **Price**.

**Step 4 - Model 3**:

$$\text{Log (Sales)} = \beta_0 + \beta_1 \log (\text{Price}) + \beta_2(\text{Display}) + \varepsilon$$

For the final model (with **Price** and **Flyer**), work out the residuals (Sales minus Model Fit) and the expected sales for each of the 3 Models (Figure 10.14). The price elasticity of -4.66 suggests that leaving **Flyer** promotion fixed, a 1% decrease (increase) in Price will lead to a 4.7% increase (decrease) in Sales.

$$\text{Log (Sales)} = 2.52 - 4.68 \log (\text{Price}) + 0.43 \text{ Flyer Promotion}$$

# Some Examples of Multiple Linear Regression Models

**A Consumption Model**. Consider an economics illustration of a **multiple linear regression model** with two explanatory variables. The dependent variable, Y, measures annual consumption in the United States, $X_1$ measures national disposable income, and $X_2$ is the value of the nation's wealth in the form of corporate stocks. All variables are expressed per capita (i.e., divided by the U.S. population at end of year).

The essence of the consumption model is to see if the dependent variable consumption (what consumers spend) can be predicted on the basis of income (what consumers earn), and wealth (what consumers own). The model is:

$$\text{Consumption} = \beta_0 + \beta_1 \text{ Income} + \beta_2 \text{ Wealth} + \varepsilon$$

For a sample of recent years, coefficients were determined that resulted in a fitted equation given by:

$$\text{Fitted consumption} = -176 + 0.935 \text{ Income} + 0.047 \text{ Wealth}$$

The estimate of $\beta_1$ is $b_1 = 0.935$, and this suggests that, if wealth does not change, then every $1 increase in income will raise consumption on the average by 93.5 cents. (The economist John Maynard Keynes (1883 – 1946) called this coefficient the **marginal propensity to consume**.) So, the evidence is that consumers spend most of their additional earnings; in contrast, from the estimate of $\beta_2$ ($b_2 = 0.047$), consumers seem to save most of their added wealth. The constant term has no economic significance here, again because it represents an estimate of consumption during a hypothetical year in which both income and wealth are zero.

For future years, forecasts of consumption levels can be made from projections of income and wealth, as follows:

$$\text{Consumption forecast} = -176 + 0.935 * \text{Projected income} + 0.047$$
$$\text{Projected wealth}$$

The accuracy of these forecasts depends on the quality of the income and wealth projections as well as on the magnitude of random variation in consumption.

**Log-Linear Models.** Multiple linear regression models can be readily adapted to incorporate cases in which the response rate of the dependent variable to one or more explanatory variables is believed to be damping, growing exponentially, or changing in other nonlinear ways. The linear model can also be adapted to suit a common economic assumption of constant elasticities of response. All these can be accomplished using transformations to the explanatory and/or dependent variables.

One of the most common transformations leads to the log-linear model

$$\ln Y = \ln \beta_0 + \beta_1 \ln X_1 + \beta_2 \ln X_2 + \ldots + \ln \varepsilon$$

where ln refers throughout to a natural logarithm ($\log_e$). Because a one-unit change in the log of a variable can be viewed as a 1% change in the level of the variable, each coefficient represents the $\beta$% response in the dependent variable to a 1% increase in an explanatory variable. Economists refer to such ratios of percentage changes as **elasticities**. We give a detailed example in the next chapter. Through this model, the demand forecaster expresses the belief that each elasticity is a constant (does not vary with the level of $X$ or level of $Y$). This is in contrast with the assumption in the consumption model that each response rate - $\Delta Y / \Delta X$ is viewed as a constant.

For example, if $Y$ denotes sales volume and $X$ is price, the linear model in the same form as the consumption model assumes that there is a single number representing the average response to a $1 change in price. If, however, we believe that the effect of a $1 change in price is one thing if the original price is $10 (and hence the price change is 10%) and quite another if the original price is $100, then the log-linear model may be more appropriate. In the log-linear model, demand is scaled to the percentage change, not the absolute change, in price.

An example of a **log-linear regression model** in which the demand for a product $Y$ is related to three explanatory variables, product price $X_1$, advertising budget $X_2$, and sales force support $X_3$, is:

$$\ln \text{Demand} = \beta_0 + \beta_1 \ln \text{Price} + \beta_2 \ln \text{Advertising} + \beta_3 \ln \text{Salesforce} + \varepsilon^*$$

where $\ln \varepsilon$ is rewritten as $\varepsilon^*$. The fitted equation has the form

$$\text{Fitted } \ln \text{Demand} = -2.0 * \ln \text{Price} + 0.125 \ln \text{Advertising} + 0.250 \ln \text{Salesforce}$$

The estimate of the price elasticity $\beta_1$ is $b_1 = -2.0$, which indicates that each 1% price increase, holding the advertising and sales force budgets constant, is estimated to reduce demand by 2%. Similarly, the advertising elasticity $\beta_2$ is estimated by $b_2 = 0.125$, which denotes an estimated 1/8 of 1% increase in demand per 1% increase in advertising, holding price and sales force budget constant. Alternatively stated, it is estimated to take an 8% increase in advertising to raise demand by 1%.

Forecasts of future demand can use the estimated regression as a forecasting formula and then convert the final result from log to level. For example, if a forecast for In Demand is calculated to be 8.5, the reversal of the log transformation is $e^{8.5} = 2.7188.5 = 4915$ units. Most forecasting software should make such a reverse transformation unnecessary by presenting the forecasts in the original units of the dependent variable.

## A Linear Regression with Two Explanatory Variables

During a year, a pizza restaurant used two types of advertising, newspaper ads and radio spots (Figure 10.15). The number of ads per month is listed in column D of a spreadsheet, the number of minutes of radio advertising is shown in column E, the monthly sales in hundreds are shown in column F, and the estimated values of $Y$ based on the regression relationship appear in column G. Column H shows fit errors (= Actual Sales (column F) – Estimate (column G)).

The multiple linear regression model has two X coefficients $X_1$ and $X_2$. The fitted equation for pizza sales is derived from the data in Figure 10.15 and is given by:

$$\hat{Y} = 65.84 + 6.25 \text{ (News ads)} + 21.39 \text{ (Radio time)}$$

Y-axis: Sales (000)

| A | B | C | D | E | F | G | H |
|---|---|---|---|---|---|---|---|
| Year | Month | Period | News ads $X_1$ | Radio time $X_2$ | Sales $Y$ | $\hat{Y}$ | Error |
| 20XX | 1 | 1 | 12 | 13.9 | 436 | 438.1 | −2.1 |
| | 2 | 2 | 11 | 12 | 380 | 391.21 | −11.21 |
| | 3 | 3 | 9 | 9.3 | 301 | 320.97 | −19.97 |
| | 4 | 4 | 7 | 9.7 | 353 | 317.03 | 35.97 |
| | 5 | 5 | 12 | 12.3 | 464 | 403.88 | 60.12 |
| | 6 | 6 | 8 | 11.4 | 342 | 359.64 | −17.64 |
| | 7 | 7 | 6 | 9.3 | 302 | 302.23 | −0.23 |
| | 8 | 8 | 13 | 14.3 | 407 | 452.9 | −45.9 |
| | 9 | 9 | 8 | 10.2 | 385 | 333.97 | 51.03 |
| | 10 | 10 | 6 | 8.4 | 226 | 282.98 | −56.98 |
| | 11 | 11 | 8 | 11.2 | 376 | 355.36 | 20.64 |
| | 12 | 12 | 10 | 11.1 | 352 | 365.72 | −13.72 |

-Figure 10.15 Pizza sales versus newspaper advertisements and radio spots. (*Source*: E.S. Gardner, Jr. – private communication)

The first coefficient (for newspaper ads) is poor because the $|t$ Statistic$| < 2$. The second coefficient (for radio time) is better, but still not significant. However, this regression model is not as bad as it looks.

You can also test the effect of both X coefficients considered together with the F Statistic. This is really a test on the entire regression equation.

The F Statistic = 9.74 suggests that the overall regression equation is significant (F > 4 is the rule of thumb). This result is not unusual; often the regression equation looks good, but individual coefficients do not. We refer the reader to review the derivation of these test statistics in a business statistics book. For now, we only need to get a sense as to how they are used in practice. Why are the *t Statistics not* significant (< |2|) when the *F* Statistic is significant (>4)? This usually happens when the *X* variables are highly correlated with one another (Figure 10.8). The correlation coefficient is 0.89. In this case, the variables tend to increase and decrease at the same time, which is known as **multicollinearity**.

| Regression Statistics | |
|---|---|
| Multiple $R$ | 0.83 |
| $R^2$ | 0.68 |
| Adjusted $R^2$ | 0.61 |
| Standard error | 39.89 |
| Observations | 12 |

ANOVA

| | df | SS | MS | F | Significance F |
|---|---|---|---|---|---|
| Regression | 2 | 30998.6 | 15499.3 | 9.74 | 0.01 |
| Residual | 9 | 14320.1 | 1591.12 | | |
| Total | 11 | 45318.7 | | | |

| | Coefficients | Standard error | $t$ Statistic | $p$ Value |
|---|---|---|---|---|
| Intercept | 65.84 | 85.42 | 0.77 | — |
| $X_1$ | 6.25 | 11.2 | 0.558 | 0.30 |
| $X_2$ | 21.39 | 14.7 | 1.45 | 0.09 |

Figure 10.16 Regression summary of pizza sales model. (*Source*: Figure 10.15)

Correlated *X* variables make it difficult for the regression calculations to isolate the individual effects of each variable. Nevertheless, together the *X* coefficients do a reasonable job in predicting *Y*. To improve this model, we would need to look at the variables one at a time in simple linear regression models and select the model yielding the higher goodness of fit $R^2$ statistic. Additionally, we could seek an explanatory variable that was not highly correlated with radio time and news ads, but that we have reason to believe might help explain pizza sales.

Figure 10.18 shows the pizza sales and fitted values as a time plot. The historical pattern is tracked quite well, but how well will this model forecast? That will depend on the quality and accuracy of the explanatory variables. To forecast, we simply plug in values for $X_1$ and $X_2$ in the previous equation and determine the forecast $\hat{Y}$.

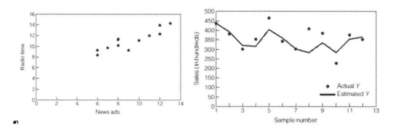

Figure 10.17 (*left*) Scatter diagram of radio time versus news ads. (*Source*: Figure 10.15)

Figure 10.18 (*right*) Time plot of pizza sales and fitted values. (*Source*: Figure 10.15)

## *Indicators for Qualitative Variables*

There are times a demand forecaster must apply special treatments to a regression model because the variables represent a specific statistical problem. Solutions to these problems include the use of indicator variables for qualitative factors and for seasonal and outlier adjustment and the use of lagged variables to describe effects that unfold over time.

### Use of Indicator Variables

Indicator variables, better known as dummy variables, are useful for extending the application of independent variables to represent various special effects or factors: one-time or fixed-duration qualitative factors or effects, such as wars, strikes, and weather conditions; significant differences in intercepts or slopes for different consumer attributes, such as race and gender; discontinuities related to changes in qualitative factors; seasonal variation; the effects of outliers; and the need to let the intercept or slope coefficients vary over different cross sections or time periods.

> *Dummy, or indicator variables, are used to indicate the existence or absence of an attribute or condition of a variable.*

### Qualitative Factors

In addition to quantifiable variables of the type discussed in earlier chapters, the dependent variable may be influenced by variables that are essentially qualitative in nature. Changes in government or public policy, wars, strikes, and weather patterns are examples of factors that are either non-quantifiable or very difficult to quantify. However, the presence of such factors can influence consumer demand for products and services.

For example, suppose that for any given income level, the sales $Y$ of a product to females exceed the sales of the same product to males. Also, suppose that the rate of change of sales relative to changes in income is the same for males and females. A dummy variable can be included in the sales equation to account for gender. Let D = 0 for sales to males and D = 1 for sales to females. Then

$$Y_i = \beta_0 + \beta_1 D_t + \beta_2 (\text{Income})_t + \varepsilon_t$$

For this example (Figure 10.19), the base or control condition will be "males" ($D_i = 0$). The prediction $Y$ of sales to males is therefore

$$Y_i = \beta_0 + \beta_2 (\text{Income})_t \qquad \text{for } D_t = 0$$

and the prediction of sales to females is

$$Y_i = \beta_0 + \beta_1 + \beta_2 (\text{Income})_t \quad \text{for } D_t = 1$$

The coefficient $\beta_1$ is called the differential intercept coefficient. It indicates the amount by which sales to females exceed sales to males at a given level of income. A $t$ test can be used to determine whether $\beta_1$ is significantly different from zero. Figure 10.19 shows a plot of the two regression lines for this example.

Similarly, the mean sales of a product in one geographical area may show the *same* rate of change relative to an economic variable that the sales in another area shows; yet the total sales for each state may be *different*.

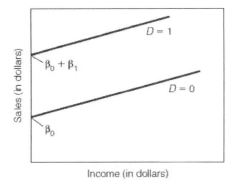

Figure 10.19 Plot of two regression lines.

*Models that combine both quantitative and qualitative variables, as both of the foregoing examples do, are called analysis-of-covariance models.*

We must always be careful to introduce one less dummy variable than the number of categories represented by the qualitative variable. In the best case, the two categories (males, females) can be represented by a single dummy variable.

## Dummy Variables for Different Slopes and Intercepts

In our example, suppose we want to know whether the intercepts and slopes are different for females and males. This can be tested in a regression model of the form

$$Y_i = \beta_0 + \beta_1 D_t + \beta_2 (\text{Income})_t + \beta_3 D (\text{Income})_t + \varepsilon_t$$

Then

$$Y_t (\text{Males}) = \beta_0 + \beta_2 (\text{Income})_t \qquad \text{for } D_t = 0$$

Likewise,

$$Y_t (\text{Females}) = (\beta_0 + \beta_1) + (\beta_1 + \beta_3)(\text{Income})_t, \qquad \text{for } D_t = 1$$

It should be noted that the test for the differences between intercepts and slope for males and females are significance tests to see whether $\beta_1$ and $\beta_3$ are different from zero.

> *The use of a dummy variable in the additive form allows us to identify differences in intercepts. The introduction of the dummy variable in the multiplicative form allows us to identify different slope coefficients.*

## Measuring Discontinuities

A change in a government policy or a change in a price may alter the trend of a revenue series. In the case of a price change, the preferable course of action is to develop a price index. Suppose that for any of a variety of reasons, such as lack of time or data, this is not possible. A dummy variable may be introduced into the model as follows. Let

$$Y_t = \beta_0 + \beta_1 X_t + \beta_2 D_t + \varepsilon_t,$$

where $D_t = 0$ for $t < T^*$ and $D_t = 1$ for $t \geq T^*$; $T^*$ is the time of the policy or price change; $D_t$ is a dummy variable with a value of 0 for all time less than $T^*$ and a value of 1 for all time greater than or equal to $T^*$; and $X_t$ is an explanatory variable.

In this example, the predicted values of revenues are:

$$Y_t = \beta_0 + \beta_1 X_t \qquad \text{if } t < T^*$$

and

$$Y_t = (\beta_0 + \beta_2) + \beta_1 X_t \qquad \text{if } t \geq T^*$$

Another situation that often occurs involves a "yes-no" or "on-off"' possibility. For example, the demand for some business services (communications, transportation, hotel accommodations) can be strongly affected by presidential and congressional elections, held in even-numbered years. Storefront campaign offices and candidates' headquarters are established; in the USA, there is a large increase in the demand for business services in September and October; and then, in November, the services related to the election campaign are discontinued. In odd-numbered years, local political elections are held; local politicians do not have the financial resources to establish as many campaign offices.

Consequently, the impact on demand is not as great in odd-numbered years. Aside from this, we can be sure that elections occur in odd- and even-numbered years alike. Therefore, it is possible to use a dummy variable that assumes that one-half of the business is attributable to an election occurs in September, the other half occurs in October, and it all disappears in November.

In this case, for a given year, the important consideration in assessing election-influenced business demand is whether there is or is not an election. This is what is meant by a "yes-no", "on-off", or categorical variable. The categorical variable does not continue to take on different values for an extended time and, in this sense, is not quantitative.

## Adjusting for Seasonal Effects

A demand forecaster may decide to use dummy variables to account for seasonality in quarterly data. In these situations, a dummy variable is omitted for one of the quarters. The interpretation of the coefficients is most revealing when the omitted quarter is the one that stands out as being different. For housing starts, it makes sense to not exclude a dummy variable for the first quarter. The seasonal effect of the first quarter is then captured by the constant term in the regression equation

$$Y_t = \beta_0 + \beta_1 D_{1t} + \beta_2 D_{2t} + \beta_3 D_{3t} + \beta_4 X_{1t} + \beta_5 X_{2t} + \varepsilon_t$$

where $D_{1t} = 1$ for the second quarter, $D_{2t} = 1$ for the third quarter, and $D_{3t} = 1$ for the fourth quarter. For monthly data, *eleven* dummy variables would be used (February through December, for example), and then the January seasonality would be captured by the constant term in the regression equation. On the other hand, the fourth quarter should be omitted for most retail sales time series to show the difference between the stronger quarter and the others.

It is possible that only 1 month or quarter has a significant seasonal pattern. Usually, each month or quarter has a unique seasonal pattern.

> *Dummy variables for seasonal adjustment may be of limited value if the season changes over time, because the dummy variable approach assumes a constant seasonal pattern.*

## Eliminating the Effects of Outliers

To illustrate the use of dummy variables to eliminate the effect of outliers, consider the following situation. Let us say that in our data for cable access-line-gain there is a year in which there was a cable company strike in April and May and the disconnections of cable service because of nonpayment of some bills were not recorded for those months, distorting the annual totals.

When we choose a model for predicting cable-access line gain, we can decide to incorporate a dummy variable into the model. The dummy variable, in this case, is a variable that can generally be set equal to 0 for all values except an unusual event or outlier.

Thus, the values for the dummy variable are equal to 0 for all years except the strike year, when it has a value of 1. Because the dummy variable equals 0 for all periods except that in which the outlier appears, the dummy variable explains the outlier perfectly. That is, the predicted value equals the actual value for the outlier.

The use of such a dummy variable tends to reduce the estimated standard deviation of the predicted errors artificially, because what is, in fact, a period of wide variation has been assigned a predicted error of 0. For this reason, we recommend that dummy variables be used very sparingly for outlier correction. They tend to result in a regression model with a higher $R^2$ statistic than can perhaps be justified: The model will appear to explain more of the variation than can be attributed to the independent variables. In some cases, the outliers may be a result of random events, and we need to be aware of this. In the case of outliers caused by nonexistent values, it is usually preferable to estimate a replacement value based on the circumstances that existed at the time the outlier occurred.

Be especially cautious when dummy variables and lagged dependent variables occur in the same equation. For example, a dummy variable might be used to correct for a strike that could have a large negative impact on the quantity of a product sold. However, it is then necessary to adjust the value for the subsequent period, or the value of the lagged dependent variable will drive next period's predicted value too low.

A preferable alternative is to adjust the original series for the strike effect (if lagged dependent variables are included in the model).

In some circumstances, robust regression techniques may offer a method for estimating regression coefficients so that the results are not distorted by a few outlying values. The variability in the data will not be understated, and the very large residuals will readily indicate that the model, as presently specified, is incapable of explaining the unusual events.

On the other hand, residuals in a model in which dummy variables have been used for outliers suggest that unusual events be perfectly estimated. A robust regression alternative has considerable appeal from a forecasting viewpoint. Because it will not understate the variability in the data, there is less of a tendency to expect a greater degree of accuracy in the forecast period than can be achieved over the fitted period.

At times it may be necessary to introduce dummy variables because it is almost impossible to estimate a replacement value for a missing or extreme data value: There may be too many unusual events occurring at the same time. For example, a strike may coincide with the introduction of wage-price controls or an oil embargo. It would be extremely difficult to determine the demand for a product or service had there been no strike because too many other variables would also have changed.

## *How to Forecast with Qualitative Variables*

Many business forecasters use regression models based on quantitative variables such as dollar expenditures or numbers of sales persons. However, we can often improve forecast accuracy by adding qualitative independent variables to our regression models. Examples include the location of stores, the condition of real estate property, the season of the year, the set of features in a product, and the age or income categories in a sample of customers.

*Qualitative variables let us analyze the effects of information that cannot be measured on a continuous scale.*

Qualitative variables are especially easy to use in spreadsheet regression models. The basic idea is to devise independent variables using binary formulas that return only one of two values, 0 or 1. Different combinations of the 0-1 values classify qualitative information to help predict the dependent variable, the quantity we are trying to forecast.

## Modeling with a Single Qualitative Variable

Several examples will help illustrate using qualitative variables. Let us start with a problem in which a single qualitative variable is necessary. The data in Figure 10.20 are from a small chain of fast-food restaurants that wanted to predict weekly sales volume based on store location (street or mall) and the population of each store's trading area. Both sales and population data are stated in thousands. One way to make predictions is to run separate regressions for malls and street locations.

But this is the hard way. We make better predictions by consolidating all the data in one model.

Regression output:

| | | | | | |
|---|---|---|---|---|---|
| Constant | | 9.142 | | | |
| Std error of $Y$ estimate | | 0.782 | | | |
| $R^2$ | | 0.997 | | | |
| Number of observations | | 12 | | | |
| Degrees of freedom | | 9 | | | |
| $X$ coefficient(s) | | 10.765 (Male) | 0.084 (Area Population) | | |
| Std error of coefficient | | 0.455 | 0.002 | | |

| A | B | C | D | E | F |
|---|---|---|---|---|---|
| | | $X_1$ | $X_2$ | $Y$ Actual | $Y$ Estimate |
| 1 | Street | 0 | 151 | 22 | 21.8 |
| 2 | Mall | 1 | 220 | 39 | 38.3 |
| 3 | Street | 0 | 53 | 14 | 13.6 |
| 4 | Mall | 1 | 112 | 30 | 29.3 |
| 5 | Mall | 1 | 332 | 47 | 47.7 |
| 6 | Mall | 1 | 398 | 54 | 53.2 |
| 7 | Street | 0 | 241 | 29 | 29.3 |
| 8 | Mall | 1 | 60 | 24 | 24.9 |
| 9 | Street | 0 | 104 | 17 | 17.9 |
| 10 | Street | 0 | 153 | 23 | 22.0 |
| 11 | Mall | 1 | 162 | 33 | 33.5 |
| 12 | Street | 0 | 410 | 43 | 43.5 |

Figure 10.20 Linear regression model with one qualitative variable: analysis of restaurant sales.

**Step 1. Setting Up the Worksheet**. The first step is to enter formulas in column C that return the value 1 for a mall location and 0 otherwise. Next, execute the regression commands. Include both the mall indicators and the population data. The actual weekly sales in thousands are in Column E, and the corresponding fitted values are in Column F.

**Step 2. Performing the Analysis**. The regression equation is

Estimated weekly sales = 9.143 + 10.765 * $X_1$ (or mall indicator) +
0.084 * $X_2$ (or area population)

The coefficient 9.142 is the regression constant or intercept value, the base sales estimate when the mall indicator is 0 (when the store has a street location). The mall indicator coefficient is 10.765. We interpret this figure as the average increase in weekly sales produced by a mall location compared to a street location. The area population coefficient is 0.084, meaning that sales should increase by an average of $84 for each thousand population, regardless of store location.

When there is a single qualitative variable, the estimated values in column F can be plotted as two parallel lines (as graphed in Figure 10.19). When $X_1$ is 1, the mall location applies, and the result is the upper regression line. When $X_1$ is 0, the street location applies, and the result is the lower line. Thus, the actual effect of a qualitative variable is to shift the constant or intercept value. In this example, the constant shifts upward by 10.765 units, the value of the $X_1$ coefficient. Every point on the upper line is 10.765 units greater than the corresponding point on the lower line.

## Modeling with Two Qualitative Variables

Now let us look at the problem in Figure 10.21, where two qualitative variables are needed. The aim is to develop an equation to predict the selling price of apartment complexes based on the condition of the property and the number of units in each complex. The condition information is qualitative in nature, with A = excellent, B = good, and C = fair. Again, we could run separate regressions for each condition, but there is an easier way.

Regression output:

| Constant | 11,357 | | |
|---|---|---|---|
| Std error of $Y$ estimate | 11,485 | | |
| $R^2$ | 0.995 | | |
| Number of observations | 13 | | |
| Degrees of freedom | 9 | | |
| $X$ Coefficient(s) | 125,855 (excellent) | 81,322 (good) | 25,614 (units) |
| Std error of coefficients | 8,160 | 7,712 | 637 |

| A | B | C | D | E | F | G |
|---|---|---|---|---|---|---|
| | | $X_1$ | $X_2$ | $X_3$ | $Y$ Actual | $Y$ Estimate |
| Property number | Condition code | Excellent indicator | Good indicator | Number of units | Selling price | Selling price |
| 158 | A | 1 | 0 | 4 | 230,250 | 239,668 |
| 509 | A | 1 | 0 | 6 | 295,000 | 290,896 |
| 118 | A | 1 | 0 | 8 | 345,800 | 342,124 |
| 973 | A | 1 | 0 | 18 | 599,900 | 598,263 |
| 300 | B | 0 | 1 | 4 | 185,500 | 195,135 |
| 725 | B | 0 | 1 | 10 | 335,750 | 348,819 |
| 28 | B | 0 | 1 | 12 | 419,900 | 400,047 |
| 172 | B | 0 | 1 | 14 | 449,900 | 451,275 |
| 133 | B | 0 | 1 | 14 | 455,500 | 451,275 |
| 661 | C | 0 | 0 | 4 | 118,500 | 113,813 |
| 760 | C | 0 | 0 | 5 | 143,900 | 139,427 |
| 980 | C | 0 | 0 | 14 | 377,700 | 369,952 |
| 795 | C | 0 | 0 | 18 | 455,500 | 472,408 |

Figure 10.21 Linear regression model with two qualitative variables; analysis of apartment-complex sales prices.

Formulas in columns C and D convert the condition codes to 0-1 variables. If the property is in excellent condition, column C returns a 1; otherwise, it returns a 0. If the property is in good condition, column D returns a 1 and otherwise a 0. We could use a third indicator for fair condition, but it would be redundant; fair condition is already represented by $X_1 = 0$ and $X_2 = 0$.

The regression equation is:

Estimated selling price = 11,357 + 125,855 * $X_1$ (or excellent indicator)

+ 81,322 * $X_2$ (or good indicator) + 25,613 * $X_3$ (or number of units)

The value of the regression constant or intercept value is 11,357. This value is the base price when both $X_1$ and $X_2$ are 0, which is the base price for property in fair condition, regardless of the number of units in the complex. Property in excellent condition sells for a premium of 125,855, the $X_1$ coefficient, compared to property in fair condition. Property in good condition sells for a premium of 81,322, the $X_2$ coefficient, compared to property in fair condition. The $X_3$ coefficient, 25,613, is the amount that the price increases for each unit in the complex.

When there are two qualitative variables, the regression equation can always be plotted as three parallel lines. Again, the effect of the qualitative variables is to shift the constant or intercept values.

## Modeling with Three Qualitative Variables

When there are three qualitative variables, the regression equation can always be plotted as four parallel lines. Again, the effect of the qualitative variables is to shift the constant or intercept values.

Seasonal patterns complicate demand forecasting. These patterns can be removed from the data before forecasting by performing a seasonal adjustment (Chapter 6). If the range of seasonal fluctuation each year is relatively constant, that is the seasonal pattern is additive, we can also use qualitative variables to handle seasonality within the regression model itself.

An example of this is given in Figure 10.22, where we develop a model to predict the demand for plaster casts at a ski resort. An obvious independent variable is the number of visitors to the resort. This number is known well in advance because demand exceeds supply and reservations are required. A regression using only the number of visitors to predict the demand of casts (not shown) gives relatively poor results. The problem is that more visitors ski during the fall and winter so the resort needs variables to take the season of the year into account. In column E, formulas return 1 during the winter, quarter and 0 otherwise. Similar formulas in columns F and G mark the spring and summer quarters. We do not need an indicator for the fall quarter because this is represented by $X_2 = 0$, $X_3 = 0$, and $X_4 = 0$.

Analysis of Demand for Plaster Casts at a Ski Resort

Regression output:

| | | | | | |
|---|---|---|---|---|---|
| Constant | 14.22 | | | | |
| Std error of Y estimate | 2.57 | | | | |
| $R^2$ | 0.99 | | | | |
| Number of observations | 24 | | | | |
| Degrees of freedom | 19 | | | | |
| X coefficient(s) | 0.99 | 6.44 | −6.44 | −30.59 | |
| Std error of coefficient | 0.02 | 1.50 | 1.49 | 1.48 | |

| A | B | C | D | E | F | G | |
|---|---|---|---|---|---|---|---|
| | | $X_1$ | $X_2$ | $X_3$ | $X_4$ | Y | Y estimate |
| | | Visitors | Winter | Spring | Summer | Number | Number |
| Period | Year Quarter | (000s) | indicator | indicator | indicator | of casts | of casts |
| 1 | 1975 Winter | 33.63 | 1 | 0 | 0 | 53 | 54.0 |
| 2 | Spring | 36.46 | 0 | 1 | 0 | 41 | 44.0 |
| 3 | Summer | 41.18 | 0 | 0 | 1 | 24 | 24.5 |
| 4 | Fall | 43.16 | 0 | 0 | 0 | 57 | 57.0 |
| 5 | 1976 Winter | 46.45 | 1 | 0 | 0 | 70 | 66.8 |
| 6 | Spring | 50.63 | 0 | 1 | 0 | 60 | 58.0 |
| 7 | Summer | 54.41 | 0 | 0 | 1 | 41 | 37.6 |
| 8 | Fall | 58.66 | 0 | 0 | 0 | 77 | 72.4 |
| 9 | 1977 Winter | 62.52 | 1 | 0 | 0 | 81 | 82.7 |
| 10 | Spring | 65.55 | 0 | 1 | 0 | 70 | 72.8 |
| 11 | Summer | 69.62 | 0 | 0 | 1 | 50 | 52.7 |
| 12 | Fall | 72.92 | 0 | 0 | 0 | 87 | 86.6 |
| 13 | 1978 Winter | 74.64 | 1 | 0 | 0 | 94 | 94.7 |
| 14 | Spring | 80.31 | 0 | 1 | 0 | 86 | 87.5 |
| 15 | Summer | 80.97 | 0 | 0 | 1 | 64 | 64.0 |
| 16 | Fall | 87.75 | 0 | 0 | 0 | 99 | 101.3 |
| 17 | 1979 Winter | 88.07 | 1 | 0 | 0 | 109 | 108.0 |
| 18 | Spring | 94.00 | 0 | 1 | 0 | 101 | 101.0 |
| 19 | Summer | 96.16 | 0 | 0 | 1 | 77 | 79.0 |
| 20 | Fall | 96.98 | 0 | 0 | 0 | 110 | 110.4 |
| 21 | 1980 Winter | 103.90 | 1 | 0 | 0 | 123 | 123.8 |
| 22 | Spring | 107.77 | 0 | 1 | 0 | 120 | 114.7 |
| 23 | Summer | 110.42 | 0 | 0 | 1 | 95 | 93.2 |
| 24 | Fall | 114.91 | 0 | 0 | 0 | 126 | 128.2 |

Figure 10.22 Linear regression model with three qualitative variables; analysis of demand for plaster casts at a ski resort.

The regression equation is:

Estimated demand for casts = 14.22 + 0.99 * $X_1$ (or number of visitors) + 6.44 * $X_2$ (or winter indicator)- 6.44 * $X_3$ (or spring indicator)- 30.59 * $X_4$ (or summer indicator)

## A Multiple Linear Regression Checklist

The following checklist can be used as a scorecard to help identify gaps in the forecasting process that will need attention. It can be scored or color coded on three levels:

| | | |
|---|---|---|
| Green = YES | Yellow = SOMEWHAT | Red = NO |

✓ Is the relationship between the variables linear?
✓ Have linearizing transformations been tried?
✓ What is the correlation structure among the independent variables?

✓ Have seasonal and/or trend influences been identified and removed?

✓ Have outliers been identified and replaced when appropriate?

✓ Do the residuals from the model appear to be random?

✓ Are any changes in the variance apparent (is there heteroscedasticity)?

✓ Are there any other unusual patterns in the residuals, such as cycles or cup shaped or trending patterns?

✓ Have $F$ tests for overall significance been reviewed?

✓ Do the $t$ statistics indicate any unusual relationships or problem variables?

✓ Can the coefficients be appropriately interpreted?

✓ Have forecast tests been made?

## *Takeaways*

This chapter has

➤ explained the normal multiple linear regression model and its assumptions and the interpretation of key summary statistics

➤ provided an overview of common pitfalls to be avoided in building multiple linear regression models

➤ discussed modeling assumptions implicit in formulating a demand forecasting model, including robustness considerations

➤ emphasized the importance of the interpretation of the results in the light of the assumptions.

➤ Least squares estimation is sometimes inappropriate because it gives equal weight to outliers, thereby distorting the fit to the bulk of the data. In these circumstances, a robust regression and correlation serves as an alternative to the OLS regression.

➤ . Weighted least squares techniques, together with Huber and Bisquare weighting schemes, provide the capability to down weight extreme values so that the regression fit is not affected by them.

➤ If both OLS and robust methods yield similar results, use the OLS results with an added degree of confidence because OLS and normality assumptions are likely to be reasonable for these data..

# 11

# Gaining Credibility Through Root-Cause Analysis and Exception Handling

*Plurality which is not reduced to unity is confusion; unity which does not depend on plurality is tyranny.*

BLAISE PASCAL (1623–1662)

This chapter describes

- the diagnostic checking process, designed to reveal departures from underlying assumptions in a statistical forecasting model
- why transformations of data should be performed to improve your understanding of what the data are trying to tell you an important phase for demand planners and managers to learn about powerful visual tools for assessing the potential effectiveness of a forecasting model, isolating unusual values, identifying hidden patterns, and understanding the nature of randomness in historical data
- several analytical tools that are useful as regression model diagnostics and in situations where normality of the error distribution cannot be assumed.
- why nonconventional techniques are so important in improving the robustness of forecasting models in the face of uncertainty
- why forecast error patterns can give valuable insights into improving forecasting performance
- how forecasting techniques can also be applied effectively in presenting management with the results of a forecasting analysis

## The Diagnostic Checking Process in Demand Forecasting

Many demand forecasters, planners and managers proceed by seeing how alike things are. Others proceed by trying to understand why things are different. The *root-cause analysis* of residuals and forecast errors is consistent with the latter approach. The diagnostic checking process is designed to reveal departures from assumptions about the underlying distribution of random errors and model formulation. It is an important phase for demand forecasters to learn about, as it can be a powerful tool for assessing, often visually, the potential usefulness of a forecasting model, isolating and correcting unusual values, identifying hidden patterns, improving forecast credibility, and understanding the nature or uncertainty in historical data.

A residual analysis may suggest nonlinear relationships, the need for transformations, or a better understanding of patterns and events that may not be transparent in the bulk of the unexplored data. Forecast error patterns can give valuable insights into improving forecasting performance. And as we have seen in Chapter 10, the unplanned findings of correlation analysis in regression modeling will often yield the most interesting and important results in a forecasting application.

## Assessing Model Adequacy

Regression models are based on a number of statistical assumptions that are needed to derive inferences from such models. The adequacy of model assumptions can be examined through a variety of methods, many graphical and involving the analysis of residuals. There is a range of regression pitfalls that we must be aware of and avoid if possible. The pitfalls include trend collinearity, overfitting, extrapolation, outliers, non-normal distributions, and invalid assumptions regarding the model errors.

The standard assumptions about model errors (independence, constant variance, and normality) and the additivity of the model needs to be evaluated. If, for a particular set of data, one or more of these assumptions fail, it may help to transform the data. Transformations of data are often required to validate assumptions.

## Transformations and Data Visualization

One of the most important reasons for making transformations of data is that linear relationships among variables are desired. The theory of linear regression is widely used by forecasters to describe relationships among variables. Straight-line fits are the simplest forms to visualize. If more than one variable is assumed to be related to the variable to be forecasted, making a transformation that closely approximates a linear relationship among these variables has practical advantages.

Aside from the desire to apply linear regression models, there are other reasons why transformations are useful. By using a suitable transformation, we can uncover desired characteristics of the data, such as additivity of trend and seasonal components. In addition, changes in trend and percentage changes in growth can be visualized.

Many numbers that are reported for public use and to business managers, for example, deal with profits and sales. In reporting results, current sales may be compared with sales of the immediate past and with sales the same period 1 and 2 years earlier. This involves differencing of data. In addition, the expression of comparisons as percentages is consistent with the use of a logarithmic transformation because growth rates can be viewed as absolute changes in the logarithms of the data. Logarithmic transformations often tend to stabilize variance, in the sense that variability around a model is kept constant, which is an important assumption in many modeling situations.

> *By selecting the appropriate transformation, we are assured that the underlying modeling assumptions can be approximated as closely as possible.*

## Achieving Linearity

Rarely do time series have patterns that permit the direct application of standard statistical modeling techniques. Hence, before statistical forecasting models can be used, it is important to know how to put data in the proper form for modeling and to transform the data so that they will be consistent with modeling assumptions of a quantitative forecasting technique.

A very flexible family of transformations on a (positive) variable Y is the power transformations devised by G.E.P. Box and D.R. Cox in 1964. Known as the Box-Cox transformations, they are:

$$W = (Y^\lambda - 1)/\lambda \quad \text{for } \lambda \neq 0,$$
$$= \text{Ln } Y \quad \text{for } \lambda = 0.$$

The parameter $\lambda$ is estimated from the data, usually by the *method of maximum likelihood*. This procedure involves several steps:

1. Select a value of $\lambda$ is selected from within a reasonable range-bracketing zero, say (-2, 2). A    convenient set of values for $\lambda$ is $\{\pm 2, \pm 1\ 1/2, \pm 1, \pm 2/3, \pm 1/2, \pm 1/3, \pm 1/4, 0\}$.

2. For the chosen $\lambda$, evaluate the likelihood
$$\text{Lmax} (\lambda) = -n/2 \text{ ln } \sigma^2 (\lambda) + (\lambda - 1) \sum \text{ln } Y_i$$

$$= -n/2 \ln (\text{Residual SS}/n) + (\lambda - 1) \sum \ln Y_i$$

where $n$ is the total number of values, and SS denotes sum of squares.

3. Plot Lmax $(\lambda)$ against $\lambda$ over the selected range and draw a smooth curve through the points.
4. Select the value of $\lambda$ that maximizes Lmax $(\lambda)$ is the maximum likelihood estimate of $\lambda$.
5. For applications, round the maximum likelihood estimate to the nearest value that makes practical sense. This should have a minor impact on the results, especially if the likelihood function is relatively flat (as it is in many cases).
6. Determine an approximate 100 $(I - \alpha)$-percent confidence interval for $\lambda$ from the inequality

$$\text{Lmax} (\lambda) - \text{Lmax} (\lambda) \leq 1/2 \, \chi^2 \, (1 - \alpha),$$

where $\chi^2 \, (1 - \alpha)$ is the percentage point of the $\chi^2$ distribution with one degree of freedom, which leaves an area of $\alpha$ in the upper tail of the distribution.

7. Draw the confidence interval can be drawn on the plot of Lmax $(\lambda)$ against $\lambda$ by drawing a horizontal line at the level

$$\text{Lmax} (\lambda) - 1/2 \, \chi^2 \, (1 - \alpha)$$

of the vertical scale.

The two values of $\lambda$ at which this cuts the curve are the end points of the approximate confidence interval. Figure 11.1(a) shows the maximum likelihood estimates of four series used in a telecommunication forecasting model. The results suggest that for practical purposes it may be useful to consider a cube root for revenues, square roots for messages and business telephones, and no transformation for the employment data. However, for ease of interpretation, the logarithmic transformation $(\lambda = 0)$ could also be considered.

Box and Cox gave a somewhat more general version of the Box-Cox transformation:

$$W = [(Y + \lambda_2)^{\lambda_1} - 1)] / \lambda_1 \qquad \text{for } \lambda_1 \neq 0,$$
$$= \text{Ln} (Y + \lambda_2) \qquad \text{for } \lambda_1 = 0,$$

where $Y + \lambda_2 > 0$. It is assumed that, for some appropriate values of $\lambda_1$ and $\lambda_2$ the transformed time series can be well described by a model of the type discussed in this book. In the telecommunications example, the data were first detrended with straight-line trends. The resulting parameter estimates, determined by a maximum likelihood method, are shown in Figure 11.1(b). The logarithmic $(\lambda_1 = 0)$ and square root transformations $(\lambda_1 = 0.5)$ are generally the most frequently occurring in practice.

(a)

| Series Code | $\hat{\lambda}$ | Transformation close to |
|---|---|---|
| Toll revenues (TOLL_REV) | 0.36 | Cube root ($\lambda = 0.33$) |
| Toll messages (MSG) | 0.43 | Square root ($\lambda = 0.5$) |
| Business telephones (BMT) | 0.57 | Square root ($\lambda = 0.5$) |
| Nonfarm employment (NFRM) | 0.93 | No transformation ($\lambda = 1.0$) |

(b)

| Series Code | $\hat{\lambda}_1$ | $\hat{\lambda}_2$ | Transformation close to |
|---|---|---|---|
| Toll revenues (TOLL_REV) | 0.36 | −21.4 | Cube root ($\lambda = 0.33$) |
| Toll messages (MSG) | 0.43 | −7.5 | Square root ($\lambda = 0.5$) |
| Business telephones (BMT) | 0.57 | −490.8 | Square root ($\lambda = 0.5$) |
| Nonfarm employment (NFRM) | 0.93 | −6508 | No transformation ($\lambda = 1.0$) |

Figure 11.1 (a) Estimate of $\lambda$ in the Box-Cox transformation for a telecommunication forecasting model; (b) estimate of ($\lambda_1$, $\lambda_2$) in the Box-Cox transformation for the telecommunication example

## Some Perils in Regression Modeling

When the dependent and independent variables are time series, there are many pitfalls specific to time series to be aware of and avoid, if possible. The pitfalls include trend collinearity, overfitting, outliers, multicollinearity, and nonnormal distributions.

**Collinearity Due to Trends.** Suppose we are interested in forecasting the cyclical variation in one series on the basis of predictions of a related cyclical time series, such as business telephones and nonfarm employment. In the regression model, a high value of the $R^2$ statistic may result from what is known as trend collinearity.

*Trend collinearity* often occurs when both series have trends. It is quite possible that the trends are highly correlated but that the cyclical patterns are not. The dissimilarities in cycle may be masked by the strong trends. Similarly, when a regression model is built on raw time series, it is not clear just what information will result. If both series have rising trend and corresponding strong seasonality, the regression will very probably show a very high $R^2$ statistic. Alternatively, if there is a strong underlying relationship between variables but their seasonal patterns differ, the regression may appear insignificant.

In the case of a telephone revenue - message relationship, seasonality is not a primary factor, so we can use seasonally adjusted data. A high correlation now means that there may be a strong association in trend-cyclical patterns. In order to determine whether there is strong cyclical relationship, the appropriate procedure is to fit preliminary trend lines and correlate residuals from the fitted values.

In time series analysis, removing trend from each variable often greatly reduces trend collinearity. In the example in Figure 11.2, the product moment correlations of the differenced data for quarterly access-line gain, housing starts, and FRB index of industrial production are shown below the diagonal in the matrix. The entries above the diagonal in Figure 11.2 represent *robust* (outlier-resistant) versions r* (SSD) of the ordinary correlations. The robust correlations are all somewhat lower, possibly due to outliers or a few influential data values.

| | 1 Access-Line Gain | 2 Housing Starts | 3 FRB Index |
|---|---|---|---|
| 1 Access-Line Gain | 1. 00 | 0.32 | 0.47 |
| 2 Housing Starts | 0.72 | 1 | 0.36 |
| 3 FRB Index | 0.57 | 0.42 | 1 |

Figure 11.2 Ordinary and robust (outlier-resistant) correlations for a telephone access-line gain model involving housing starts and FRB index. (Based on *differenced* data).

These correlations can be compared to Figure 11.3, the matrix of correlations for the original (undifferenced) data. Although there are some significant correlations among the differenced independent variables, they are probably not large enough to introduce serious collinearity problems. The demand forecaster should become cautious, however, when simple correlations exceed values from 0.8 to 0.9. As a practical rule, we should adjust the data for possible sources of variation in which we are not interested in order to study the relationships with respect to those factors whose effects are of primary interest.

| | 1 Access- Line Gain | 2 Housing Starts | 3 FRB Index |
|---|---|---|---|
| 1 Access-Line Gain | 1 | 0.07 | 0.74 |
| 2 Housing Starts | 0.01 | 1 | 0.14 |
| 3 FRB Index | 0.47 | 0.32 | 1 |

Figure 11.3 Ordinary and robust correlations for an access-line gain model involving housing starts and FRB index. (Based on *original* data)

**Overfitting.** Another source of peril in regression analysis is overfitting. This occurs when too many independent variables are used to attempt to explain the variation in the dependent variable. Overfitting may also arise when there are not enough data values. If the number of independent variables is close to the number of values, a "good fit" to the values may be obtained but the coefficient and variance estimates will be poor. This often results in very bad estimates for new values.

**Extrapolation.** In forecasting applications, regression models are frequently used for purposes of extrapolation - that is, for extending the relationship to a future period of time for which data are not available. A relationship that is established over a historical time span and a given range of independent and dependent variables may not necessarily be

350

valid in the future. Thus, extreme caution must be exercised in using correlation analysis to predict future behavior among variables. There may be no choice in some cases, but the demand forecaster should recognize the risks involved.

**Outliers.** Outliers are another well-known source of complexity in correlation analysis. A single outlier can have a significant impact on a correlation coefficient.

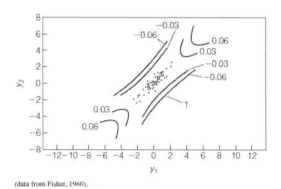

(data from Fisher, 1960).

Figure 11.4 Scatter plot with influence function contours for a sample of bivariate normal data with the added outlier (n = 60, r = 0.9, with outlier r = 0.84). (Data Source: Sir Ronald Fisher, *The Design of Experiments*, 1960).

Figure 11.4 shows a scatter diagram of 60 values from a simulated sample, from a bivariate normal distribution with population correlation coefficient $\rho = 0.9$. One point was moved to become an outlier. The empirical correlation coefficient is now calculated to be 0.84. This shows that, except for this single point, the scatter is quite linear and, in fact, with this outlier removed, the estimated correlation coefficient is 0.9. (*Source*: Susan R. Devlin, et al., *Robust estimation and outlier detection with correlation coefficients*, Biometrika, 1975). Robust alternatives offer some protection in these instances, as well as in others in which there is nonmorality in the error distribution.

**Multicollinearity.** Be aware of multicollinearity effects when forecasts are based on multiple linear regression models. Models with more than approximately five independent variables will often contain regressors that are highly mutually correlated.

Because it is likely that there are interrelationships among the variables, we find high pairwise correlations. Simply, one variable may serve as a proxy for another. In such cases, it may be beneficial to seek linear combinations of these variables as regressors, thereby reducing the dimension of the problem.

In its simplest form, multicollinearity arises whenever explanatory variables in a regression model are highly mutually correlated. We will find low t-values for one or more of the estimated regression coefficients, which suggests that some variable could be dropped from the equation. Multicollinearity is difficult to deal with because it is almost invariably a problem of degree rather than kind. Multicollinearity results in bias, inconsistency, and inefficiency of estimators, which are undesirable, at least from a theoretical viewpoint. In practice, remedies must be found so that the model assumptions can be made approximately true without completely destroying the statistical validity of the model.

Frequently, we would like to retain certain explanatory variables in the equation, even if associated t values suggest that such variables add little to the explanatory power of the equation. The problem is that the variables that are expected to be important have small t values (large standard errors) and lead to unstable estimation of the coefficients.

Some of the practical effects of multicollinearity include imprecise estimation. Although the concepts of bias, consistency, and inefficiency have very precise theoretical definitions, their effect on the inferences that are drawn from a model may be difficult to determine in every practical application.

Problems of multicollinearity also encourage the misspecification of the model if they are not carefully noted. The stability of coefficients can be severely affected, so that different segments or subsets of the data give rise to vastly different results. This lack of sensitivity precludes the possibility of making sound interpretations of model coefficients.

To examine the relationship among the explanatory variables, we can calculate a **variance inflation factor** (VIF) associated with each explanatory variable. When statistical software displays these VIFs, we can establish whether a variable is highly correlated with the remaining explanatory variables in the equation and whether dropping any of the variables will eliminate the collinearity effects.

> *Multicollinearity arises when the independent variables in a regression model are highly correlated.*

## Exception Handling: The Need for Robustness in Regression Modeling

In Chapter 10, we saw a close relationship between the correlation coefficient as a measure of linear association and the simple linear regression model as a confirmation (goodness-of-fit) of that linearity. Unfortunately, in multiple linear regression models, it is not as simple as that. However, least-squares estimation of regression coefficients must still be examined for sensitivity to outlying residuals and unusual values in the data.

## Why Use a Robust Regression Approach?

In least-squares estimation, regression coefficients are derived by minimizing the sum of the squares of the residuals (Residual = Data − Fit). In the minimization process, all residuals are given *equal* weight. Experience has shown, however, that outliers can have an unusually large influence on least squares estimators. That is, the outliers pull the least-squares fit toward them too much, and the resulting estimation of residuals may become misleading because the residuals corresponding to the outliers look smaller than the residuals from a robust fit—they do not seem to be outliers.

> *Robust methods have been created to modify least-squares regression procedures so that outliers have much less influence on the final estimate.*

Outliers and other sources of unusual data values should never be ignored. A robust procedure operates to reduce their impact on the regression estimates. Other advanced techniques, however, tackle outlier and unusual data problems directly—through **intervention models**—rather than through adjustments of a computational algorithm.

## M-Estimators

A family of robust estimators, called **M-estimators**, is obtained by minimizing a specified function of the residuals. Alternate forms of the function produce the various M-estimators. Generally, the estimates are computed by *iterated* weighted least squares.

One such function $\xi$ (.) of the residuals takes the form

$$\xi\,(e) = 0.5\,e^2 \qquad\qquad \text{if } |\,e\,| \leq c = Ks$$

$$= c\,|\,e\,| - 0.5\,e^2 \quad \text{if } |\,e\,| > c = Ks$$

where $s$ is a scale estimate, such as UMdAD, the unbiased median absolute deviation of the residuals from the median, divided by 0.6745 (see Chapter 2). If the data are normally distributed and the number of values is large, then divisor 0.6745 should be used because then $s$ approximates the standard deviation of the normal distribution.

Usually, the sample standard deviation is not used as a value because it itself is influenced too much by outliers and thus is not resistant against them. The constant $K$ is chosen to obtain a desired level of efficiency (as compared to least-squares regression if the data are assumed normal), and it is often set to between 1 and 2. If $K$ is sufficiently large, the M-estimate will be equivalent to ordinary least-squares estimates.

Minimizing $\xi(e)$ yields an estimate of the regression coefficients; the minimization requires *Huber weights*, defined by

$$W_i = 1 \qquad \text{if } |e_i| \leq c = Ks$$

$$W_i = Ks / |e_i| \qquad \text{if } |e_i| > c = Ks$$

The statistic $s$ approximates the standard deviation of a normal distribution, and the constant $K$ is chosen as some number close to 1.5 (based on empirical evidence). The iterative procedure has the following steps:

1. Obtain an initial estimate of the regression coefficients. The initial estimates can be obtained in a number of ways such as by OLS.
2. Compute residuals and calculate Ks = K * (UMdAD).
3. Compute the weights and perform the method of weighted least squares.
4. Repeat steps 1 through 3 until convergence or a reasonable number of iterations has been performed.

To distinguish robust regression coefficients from OLS coefficients, the robust coefficients for a simple linear regression, denoted by $\beta_0^*$ and $\beta_1^*$, are calculated using the weighted least squares.

A second *M*-estimator, called the *bisquare estimator*, gives zero weight to data whose residuals are quite far from zero. The bisquare weighting function is defined by

$$W_i = 0 \qquad \text{if } |e_i| > Ks$$

$$W_i = [1 - (e_i/Ks)^2]^2 \qquad \text{if } |e_i| \leq Ks$$

Note that the bisquare-weighting scheme is more severe than the Huber scheme. In the bisquare scheme, all data for which $|e_i| \leq Ks$ *will* have a weight less than 1. Data having weights greater than 0.9 are not considered extreme, data with weights less than 0.5 are regarded as extreme, and data with zero weight are, of course, ignored.

A recommended robust regression procedure begins with OLS estimates of the parameters. This is followed by several iterations of bisquare-weighted least squares. To avoid the potential problem of finding local minima, which can result from "bad" initial estimates, we recommend starting the bisquare procedure with a few iterations of the Huber scheme. In practice, we have found that one iteration of the Huber scheme followed by a couple of iterations of the bisquare scheme works quite well. For example, see my paper *Time Series Forecasting Using Robust Regression,* http://onlinelibrary.wiley.com/doi/10.1002/for.3980010304/abstract).

> *To counteract the impact of outliers, the bisquare estimator gives zero weight to data whose residuals are quite far from zero.*

## Calculating M-Estimates

It is instructive to take a closer look at the weighted least-squares calculations of *M*-estimates. These estimates can be substantially different when the data contain one or more outliers. For simplicity, consider the simple time series (2.5, 4.0, 5.5, 7.0, 8.5, 10.0, 11.5, 13.0, 14.5, 3.0), which is of the form $Y = 1.0 + 1.5 X$ for the first nine points if $X$ represents 1, 2, . . ., 10. Notice that the last value (3.0) is an outlier according to the model.

One iteration of a robust solution for these data, using Huber weights ($K = 1$), is given in Figure 11.5. This is analogous to downweighting residuals that are greater than one standard error from their central measure. Note that the initial estimates are obtained from the OLS solution $\hat{Y}_{(OLS)} = 3.60 + 0.79 X$.

Next, the residuals are computed in column 3. Column 4 shows the absolute deviations of the residuals from the median residual (= 0.595). The median value in column 4 is the MdAD statistic. Comparing column 3 with the UMdAD statistic (= MdAD/0.6745) derives column 5 (= 2.64), using the definition of the Huber weight function. The weight $W$ is 1.0 if the absolute value of the residual in column 3 is less than 2.64; otherwise, the weight is 2.64 divided by the absolute value of the residual. It is evident that the last three points receive a weight less than 1 for this iteration.

| (1) $X$ | (2) $Y$ | (3) $e_i = Y_i - \hat{Y}_{(OLS)}$ | (4) $|e_i - c_M|$ | (5) Huber weights ($K = 1$) | Iteration | $b_0^*$ | $b_1^*$ | Weights |
|---|---|---|---|---|---|---|---|---|
| 1 | 2.5 | −1.89 | 2.49 | 1 | 1 | 2.85 | | 0.62 |
| 2 | 4 | −1.18 | 1.78 | 1 | 2 | 2.26 | 1.16 | 0.38 |
| 3 | 5.5 | −0.47 | 1.07 | 1 | 3 | 1.83 | 1.27 | 0.24 |
| 4 | 7 | 9.24 | 0.56 | 1 | 4 | 1.54 | 1.33 | 0.15 |
| 5 | 8.5 | 0.95 | 0.36 | 1 | 5 | 1.34 | 1.41 | 0.09 |
| 6 | 10 | 1.66 | 1.07 | 1 | 6 | 1.21 | 1.44 | 0.06 |
| 7 | 11.5 | 2.37 | 1.78 | 1 | 7 | 1.13 | 1.46 | 0.03 |
| 8 | 13 | 3.08 | 2.49 | 0.86 | 8 | 1.08 | 1.48 | 0.02 |
| 9 | 14.5 | 3.79 | 3.2 | 0.7 | 9 | 1.05 | 1.49 | 0.01 |
| 10 | 3 | −8.5 | 9.1 | 0.31 | 10 | 1.03 | 1.49 | 0.01 |
| | | | | | 11 | 1.02 | 1.49 | 0 |
| | | | | | 12 | 1.01 | 1.5 | 0 |
| | | | | | 13 | 1.01 | 1.5 | 0 |

$\hat{Y}_{(OLS)} = 3.60 + 0.79X$
Median residual $c_M$ (median of column 3) = 0.595
MdAD (median of column 4) = 1.78
$s$ = UMdAD = MdAD/0.6745 = 2.64

Figure 11.5 (*left*) One iteration of sample data using Huber weights ($K = 1$) for fitting $Y = 1.0 + 1.5 X$.

Figure 11.5 (*right*) Thirteen iterations of the Huber ($K = 2$) solution to the fit in which the last point ($W_{10}$) is down weighted. (Weights are shown only for point $W_{10}$; weights for $W_1$ through $W_9$ are 1 for all iterations).

The first 13 Huber iterations using $K = 2$ are summarized in Figure 11.5. The coefficients are calculated by using the weighted least-squares formula set forth in the preceding section. As can be seen, only the last point (the weights column) received a weighting less than 1. With each iteration, the slope of the line gradually increases, as can be seen from the column under $b_1^*$ column. Notice that in this artificial example, the weight associated with the outlier becomes 0. With real data, however, the Huber weights rarely get smaller than 0.2.

| $Y_i$ | 2.5 | 4 | 5.5 | 7 | 8.5 | 10 | 11.5 | 13 | 14.5 | 3 |
|---|---|---|---|---|---|---|---|---|---|---|
| $W_i$ | 0.943 | 0.977 | 0.996 | 0.999 | 0.985 | 0.956 | 0.911 | 0.852 | 0.78 | 0.17 |

Figure 11.6 Calculation using bisquare weights (K = 4.2) for the first iteration of sample data. (Bisquare weights $W_i = [1 - (e_i /Ks)^2]^2$; s = UMAD = 2.64; residuals are given in Figure 11.5, column 3).

In Figure 11.6, a robust solution using bisquare weights (K = 4.2) is shown for the first iteration. The bisquare-weighting scheme downweighs all but the third ($W_3$) and fourth ($W_4$) points in the first iteration (Figure 11.7). We can see by looking at the coefficient estimates that the calculations converge after only three iterations to a final fit of the form $\hat{Y}_{BS} = 1.0 + 1.5X$.

| Regression coefficient ($b^*$) and weight ($W$) | Iteration | | | |
|---|---|---|---|---|
| | OLS | 1 | 2 | 3 |
| $b_0^*$ | 3.6 | 1.51 | 1 | 1 |
| $b_1^*$ | 0.79 | 1.36 | 1.5 | 1.5 |
| $W_1$ | 1 | 0.94 | 0.94 | 0.83 |
| $W_2$ | 1 | 0.97 | 0.98 | 0.91 |
| $W_3$ | 1 | 1 | 1 | 0.94 |
| $W_4$ | 1 | 1 | 1 | 0.99 |
| $W_5$ | 1 | 0.98 | 0.98 | 1 |
| $W_6$ | 1 | 0.95 | 0.95 | 1 |
| $W_7$ | 1 | 0.9 | 0.9 | 0.99 |
| $W_8$ | 1 | 0.84 | 0.83 | 0.94 |
| $W_9$ | 1 | 0.76 | 0.75 | 0.91 |
| $W_{10}$ | 1 | 0.12 | 0.00 | 0.00 |

Figure 11.7 Bisquare solutions to the fit in which all but the fifth and sixth values are downweighed.

## *Validating Modeling Assumptions: A Root-Cause Analysis*

Much of a residual analysis involving time series can be carried out effectively through a visual inspection of data patterns. If a problem pattern can be discerned in a residual plot, then these patterns typify a violation of one or more assumptions about randomness in a regression model.

A cyclical pattern (Figure 11.8) is often evident when we fit trending (nonstationary) models to economic time series data. If the nonstationarity with differences of order 12 (year-over-year changes) is removed, the result shows a cyclical pattern (Figure 11.9). This pattern should be related to contractions and expansions in the economy. An economic contraction or recession may be underway when the Industrial Production series plunges below the trend level (or residuals become negative). This economic variable could be valuable in creating an economic driver of demand for industrial products and services, such as construction or mining.

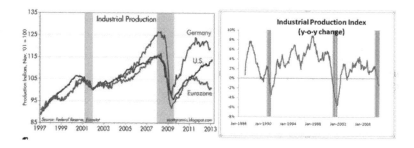

Figure 11.8 (*left*) Indices of German, U.S., and Eurozone industrial production (recession periods shaded).

Figure 11.9 (*right*) Index of industrial production (year-over-year changes; recessions in shaded portion).

In other situations, an economic index may not have a persistent trend but, rather, it may meander as it grows for certain fairly long periods but then drop over other long periods. Then, it is the first differences (or period-to-period changes) that may reveal the interesting secondary patterns.

For example, the monthly index for a regional commodity (Figure 11.10a) can meander, but it's month-to-month changes (Figure 11.11a) will behave more like a random residual series. The correlogram in Figure 11.10b declines gradually from $r_1 = 0.93$ to approximately 0 at lag 14, thereafter becoming negative. Note that an $r_1$ coefficient so close to 1 suggests that the series is highly correlated with its lagged 1 value, which is typical of a meandering series.

The sample autocorrelations of the differenced series in Figure 11.11b, on the other hand, show the behavior of a more random series; $r_1 = 0.14$, $r_2 = 0.00$, $r_3 = -0.03$, $r_4 = 0.06$, and $r_5 = 0.02$ are close to 0. A series whose period-to-period changes are random is known as a random walk. Random walk models are widely applied in finance for predicting price movements and in the development of an efficient markets theory.

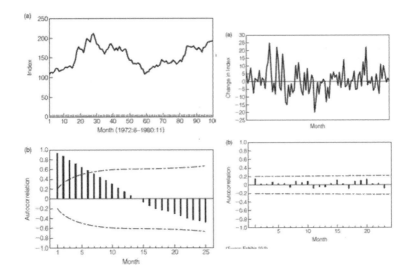

Figure 11.10 (*left*) (a) Time plot and (b) correlogram of 100 monthly values of flour price index at Buffalo, New York. (*Source*: BUFLOUR.DAT; Cryer and Miller, *Statistics for Business—Data Analysis and Modeling*, 1994)

Figure 11.11 (*right*) (a) Time plot and (b) correlogram of the month-to-month changes of a flour price index at Buffalo, New York. (*Source*: Figure 11.10a)

> ***A residual analysis is about revealing departures from the assumptions of a model and suggesting corrective steps.***

A time plot that has no visible pattern (Figure 11.12a) provides no evidence against the assumption that the errors in the model are random, have zero mean, and show constant variance.

It is worth pointing at this time the random data need not be normally distributed. Note that the correlograms of the differenced flour price index (Figure 11.13b) and the random lognormal data (Figure 11.12b) are indistinguishable. They both display the characteristics of a **random walk** model.

In fact, the normal probability plot of the differenced flour price index (Figure 11.13a) appears more normal (points lie along a straight line) than the random lognormal data (Figure 11.13b) (lognormal data are such that the logarithms of the data are normally distributed, not the d data itself.

> *A residual analysis may suggest relationships, transformations, or the need for a better understanding of events that may not be apparent in the bulk of the data.*

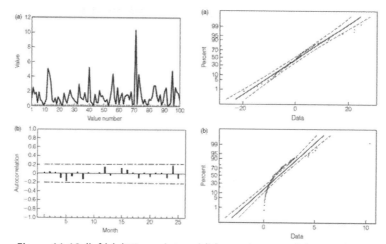

Figure 11.12 *(left)* (a) Time plot and (b) correlogram of data without any pattern. (One hundred random values generated from a random [lognormal] series.)

Figure 11.13 *(right)* (a) Normal probability plots for (a) the differenced flour price index data and the sample of random lognormal data.

## A Run Test for Randomness

Some tests indicative of randomness (or lack thereof) in residuals include tests based on first differences, rank correlation, and runs of signs. The first-differences test assumes that, if there is non-randomness in the form of trend, the number of positive first differences will be large for a residual series with an upward trend and small for a residual series with a downward trend.

In the **rank correlation test**, residuals are ranked in order depending on size and then correlated with a straight-line trend. The distribution of the test statistic is difficult to determine, so approximate tests based on the student's $t$ distribution are used.

The **runs-of-signs test** is a simple way to test for randomness by counting runs. A run is a string of pluses (+) or minuses (-) that accumulates when a plus (+) value is assigned to a value larger than the average value $K$ of the data and a minus (-) value is assigned to a value less than the average. In counting these runs, we let the number of consecutive runs of pluses be denoted by $r$; $n$ denotes the number of values in the sample. Then, the average number of runs over all possible sequences of runs is $1 + [2\,r\,(n - r)/n]$.

A measure of the expected dispersion of runs among different sequences that could have occurred is the standard error given by

$$\{2r\,(n - r)\,[2r\,(n - r) - n]/n^2\,(n - 1)\}^{1/2}$$

Thus, if the observed number of runs is within two standard errors of the expected (average) number of runs, then there is little evidence that the series is not random. The runs measure is a measure of conformity of the data to a model specification of randomness.

*It is often observed that changes in many stock prices behave essentially like a random series.*

The average (expected) number of runs and associated standard errors is 37 (± 3.6) for the differenced flour price index (Figure 11.13a) and is 36 (± 3.5) for the random lognormal data (Figure 11.12a). The observed value for number of consecutive runs of plusses is 24 for the differenced flour price index and 23 for the random lognormal data. Consequently, in both examples there is evidence that these series are not random according to the runs-of-signs test because the observed r is only 24 and 23 for the two series, respectively.

When runs-of-signs counting is applied to residuals, we expect that the number of consecutive positive or negative residuals will be neither small nor large for a random residual series. A straight-line trend with positive slope will have a run of negative signs followed by a run of positive signs. A wildly fluctuating series, on the other hand, will exhibit too many sign changes.

*The ordinary correlogram is the most widely used graphical tool for detecting the presence of first- or higher-order autocorrelation.*

## Nonrandom Patterns

Much of a residual analysis for time series models can be carried out effectively through a visual inspection of data patterns and correlograms. If a pattern can be discerned in a residual plot, then these patterns typify a violation of one or more assumptions about randomness in a regression model. First consider the identification of such patterns and some remedies. Five basic types of patterns are frequently observed in residual plots: no visible pattern, cyclical pattern (positively autocorrelated residuals), nonlinear relationships, increasing dispersion, and trend.

One reason for the appearance of nonrandom patterns is that a linear model is being fit to an inherently nonlinear phenomenon. For instance, a plot of sales of a new product may show a rate of growth that is faster than linear growth. Likewise, the income tax rate on individual earnings has a nonlinear relationship with earnings. When one attempts to fit such nonlinear relationships with a straight-line trend, the residuals often appear to have a cup-shape or inverted cup shape (Figure 11.14).

It often happens that the residuals from a nonlinear relationship may not look cup shaped over the entire regression period. However, in forecasts made from a straight-line model, the forecast errors might show increasing dispersion (Figure 11.15), known as **heteroscedasticity**.

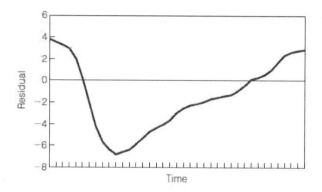

Figure 11.14 Time plot of residuals with a cup-shaped pattern.

*Heteroscedasticity refers to variability in data that is not constant or not homogeneous (nonconstant variance).*

If it does not become apparent that the data are nonlinear from analyzing the residuals over the entire regression period, the pattern of over- or underforecasting will certainly exhibit nonlinearity over a long enough period.

Finally, trends, up or down, may be apparent in the residuals (Figure 11.16). This pattern can also be the result of a nonlinear relationship between the variables.

It is important to distinguish between nonlinear growth in trend and nonlinear variations as a result of a short-term cycle. In the first case, the nonlinear relationship between two variables will continue in the same direction over a long time. In the case of a short-term cycle, the nonlinear relationship will change direction at the peaks and troughs of each cycle.

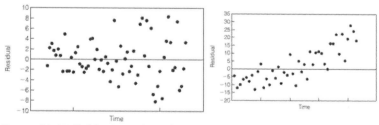

Figure 11.15 (left) Time plot of residuals with increasing dispersion.
Figure 11.16 (*right*) Time plot of residuals with trending pattern.

## Graphical Aids

In addition to the visual examination of residual plots for non-randomness, nonlinearities, and outliers, other graphical aids such as histograms, stem-and-leaf displays, box plots, and probability plots, can prove useful.

Figure 11.17 shows the box plots of the residuals for two competing ARIMA models. Both sets of residuals appear to be centered on 0, as expected, but the model 1 residuals appear to have a slightly broader distribution in the middle. Model 2 appears to have a longer right tail in the distribution. These two box plots of the residuals turn out to be similar; each shows a nonsymmetrical distribution in the residuals, with a longer tail for positive residuals. Because of the outliers, robust/resistant alternatives should be considered to complement the approach taken for these models.

We can also use box plots effectively to look at the distribution of the residuals for a particular period of the year. This may prove useful in determining which months are likely to create more difficulties in forecasting. Figure 11.18 displays the residuals for Model 1 in a box plot for each month.

Note the highly skewed distributions for June and October, which may be interpretable from the underlying date used in the model. January residuals appear to show the greatest variability and September residuals the least. March, July, and September have fairly symmetrically distributed residuals.

The residuals of a model should also be plotted against the explanatory variable to help detect outliers, assess non-homogeneity (nonconstancy) of variance, and determine if a transformation is required.

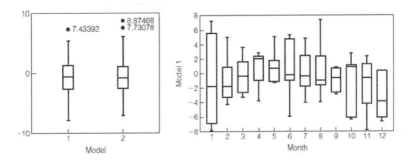

Figure 11.17 (*left*) Box plots of residuals for two competing models.
Figure 11.18 (*right*) Box plots of residuals for individual months. (Model 1)

> *Box plots offer an effective tool for graphically examining the distribution of residuals.*

## Identifying Unusual Patterns

When we look at residuals, it may become apparent that certain individual values or small sequences of them are in some sense unusual. When the objective is to extrapolate past results into the future with statistical models, outliers can severely affect the accuracy of forecasts, especially if they occur in the most recent time periods.

Outliers are not expected to recur or to influence the data in the same way again, so replacing them with values that are more typical should negate their effect on a model and forecast profile.

> *Outliers can adversely affect the accuracy of forecasts, especially if they appear during the most recent time periods.*

Looking at residuals resulting from the transformation and modeling steps may require discounting distortions caused by outliers. This is especially true if the method used is not resistant to outliers. Here are some examples:

- The outlier may be caused by an administrative decision. If so, the staff of the department responsible for corporate financial results should be consulted. This type of problem is common with revenues, in which retroactive billing distorts revenue data.
- Price changes produce another form of irregularity that requires adjustment. In this case, part of the entire series must be adjusted to put the data on a constant rate base. Alternatively, price indexes can be constructed and used.
- Irregular values may be due to a **Black Swan event**. If so, it should be documented so as to indicate why it was felt to be an **event** or occurrence that deviates beyond what is normally expected of a situation and is extremely difficult to predict; the term was popularized by Nassim Nicholas Taleb, a finance professor, writer and former Wall Street trader. Black swan events are typically random and are unexpected.

On the other hand, if we are attempting to build a model to explain past results, we should think long and hard before adjusting past data. The explanatory model may be designed to help us understand how extreme or unusual events affect the process of generating data. If we want to know the impact of severe weather on communication habits, the data will provide excellent indications and, as such, should not be adjusted. More often, however, the reasons for unusual values are not obvious or unknown and should be investigated.

> *Even with the assistance of statistical models, informed judgment and domain knowledge is always required to spot patterns and take innovative action to isolate a root-cause.*

## Residual Analysis

A residual analysis is a process designed to reveal departures from assumptions about the underlying distribution of random errors and model formulation. Because significance testing and setting confidence limits for model parameters depends on the validity of assumptions about the error distribution, residual analysis is, perhaps, the single most valuable diagnostic tool for evaluating forecasting models.

> *A recommended sequence of residual analysis begins with a plot of the residuals against the predicted values of the dependent variable.*

What steps could the demand forecaster follow to sort out all these different ways of analyzing residuals? Review the summary statistics (F, t, incremental F, and $R^2$ statistics). If the model passes these tests, review a residual plot for constancy of variance among residuals; patterns of increasing dispersion with increasing magnitude, as mentioned earlier, suggest that logarithmic or square-root transformations of the dependent variable should be made as a first attempt. Then re-estimate the model to accomplish this, and plot the residuals once again against predicted values.

Once a satisfactory transformation of the dependent variable has been obtained, if one is indeed required, plot the **partial residuals** versus each independent variable. At this time,

- Delete variables with low correlation (< 0.2) and re-estimate the model.
- Transform independent variables that exhibit nonlinear relationships (one at a time). After each transformation, re-estimate the model and generate a new set of partial residual plots.
- Perform additional analyses if all the plots show linear and significant (not horizontal) relationships.

For time series models, plot the residuals and a correlogram of the residuals. Test for serially correlated residuals. The plots may suggest additional variables for consideration. The techniques discussed in the next chapter may be required if the serial correlation problem remains.

Generate percentiles of the residuals versus the percentiles of a standard normal distribution. This will highlight potential outliers (review each end carefully) and indicate if there are departures from normally distributed residuals. Outliers should be investigated and replaced, if replacement is appropriate. Transformations of the dependent variable may be required; alternatively, robust regression may be appropriate if normally distributed residuals cannot be validated.

Although linear regression models based on nonlinearly related data may appear to give acceptable summary statistics, the inferences drawn from such models can be erroneous and misleading. Residual analysis is an effective tool for graphically demonstrating departures from model assumptions. When looking at regression residuals, keep the following in mind:

- A residual plot of constant variance with no visible pattern is consistent with the basic assumptions of the linear least-squares regression model. If the residuals are also normally distributed, a variety of significance tests can be performed. Also, the run test can be applied to test for no randomness.
- A residual pattern of increasing dispersion may suggest the need to transform one or more variables. The logarithmic and square root transformations are the most commonly used to solve this problem. A plot of the residuals versus the dependent variable also highlights the need for transformations.
- The normal probability plot is a convenient way to decide whether the residuals are normally distributed. In addition, outliers are readily detected at one or the other end of the plot.

## Forecasting with Intermittent Demand: The LZI Method

When the independence assumption between zero intervals and positive demand is not valid in the **Croston Methods**, what can you do? First, you can check the validity of independence assumption on which the Croston methods are based with the **Kullback-Leibler** divergence measure.

Next, you can forecast with intermittent demand history with the **LZI** method, which establishes a quantifiable relationship between zero interval durations and the non-zero demand. Then, the empirical conditional distribution of nonzero demand following a lag time duration of zero demand are used to create the forecasts by taking a **bootstrap sample** of lag time zero intervals and projects them over the required lead-time for inventory (e.g., 6), budgeting (e.g., 12) or operations (e.g., 18-24) applications.

From each zero interval, a one-step ahead projection of nonzero demand is generated from the associated conditional distribution of nonzero demand. This is followed by another bootstrap sample from the empirical distribution of zeroes. After the second interval create a projection of nonzero demands accordingly, and so on. The forecast has the same intermittency distribution as the historical data and independence is no longer an unvalidated assumption.

Intermittent Demand **(ID)** (also known as *sporadic demand*) comes about when a product experiences several periods of zero demand. Often in these situations, when demand occurs it is small, and sometimes highly variable in size. Forecasting intermittent demand occurs in practice, when

- creating lead time demand forecasts for inventory planning
- creating multiple forecasts of low volume items for a particular period in the future based on a rolling forecast horizon, as in an annual budget or production cycle
- creating forecasts for multiple periods in an 18-month business planning horizon.

Before creating any models for intermittent demand, the forecaster should first consider the validity of an assumption by examining the historical data in a real-world context. Figure 11.19 shows the demand series for a SKU and location in a population health forecasting application at a NYC area hospital from Jan 2015 to Apr 2018. The next 20 months are used as a test period, so that the results can be compared with the actuals for this period. We are asked to make a lead-time demand forecast for the year 2020. Similar data may be seen for hospital admissions in virus pandemics, retail sales at doors (stores) in different regions of the country, and more commonly in spare parts inventory management applications.

Forecast Review Data
Values: Units
Data Scope: SKU: 12520-1037 ^ 12520, TOTAL COMPANY: Region 20 + Region 50
Last Demand: 4/18
Data Type: Intermittent Demand

| | Jan. | Feb. | Mar. | Apr. | May | Jun. | Jul. | Aug. | Sep. | Oct. | Nov. | Dec. | Total |
|---|---|---|---|---|---|---|---|---|---|---|---|---|---|
| 2015 | 0 | 390 | 0 | 211 | 0 | 0 | 458 | 231 | 0 | 532 | 0 | 816 | 2638 |
| 2016 | 0 | 0 | 1035 | 0 | 120 | 281 | 334 | 134 | 737 | 0 | 0 | 275 | 2916 |
| 2017 | 959 | 0 | 1056 | 480 | 250 | 489 | 0 | 0 | 212 | 0 | 0 | 205 | 3651 |
| 2018 | 95 | 0 | 0 | 118 | | | | | | | | | |
| 2019 | | | | | | | | | | | | | |

Figure 11.19 Demand for a SKU by location for store level retail sales.

**Step 1**. *Explore the nature of the relationship between interdemand intervals* and the distribution of non-zero demand sizes. For instance, it may be surmised that for longer interdemand intervals, demand sizes could be increasing or decreasing in size over time.

Starting from Feb 2015, we examine the relationship between intervals and demand sizes with the **L**ag-time **Z**ero **I**nterval (LZI) method, considering the interval duration *preceding* a demand size. For this dataset the results show that there are three LZI interval durations.

For example, the first **LZI** interval has one zero preceding the demand size 211. The next **LZI** interval has two zeros preceding the demand size 458. The next one has none and so on. If the process started in Jan 2015 with a new product introduction, for instance, we could add demand size 390 in the single-zero LZI bucket. However, this should not make a material difference in forecasting in an ongoing intermittent demand forecasting process.

| LagtimeZI | ID* | | | | Ln Transformed ID* | | | |
|---|---|---|---|---|---|---|---|---|
| | 0 | 1 | 2 | 3 | 0 | 1 | 2 | 3 |
| | 231 | 390 | 458 | | 5.44 | 5.97 | 6.13 | |
| | 281 | 211 | 1035 | | 5.64 | 5.35 | 6.94 | |
| | 334 | 532 | 275 | | 5.81 | 6.28 | 5.62 | |
| | 134 | 816 | 212 | | 4.90 | 6.70 | 5.36 | |
| | 737 | 120 | 205 | | 6.60 | 4.79 | 5.32 | |
| | 959 | 1056 | 118 | | 6.87 | 6.96 | 4.77 | |
| | 480 | | | | 6.17 | | | |
| | 250 | | | | 5.52 | | | |
| | 489 | | | | 6.19 | | | |
| | 95 | | | | 4.55 | | | |
| | | | | | **Typical Projections** | | | |
| AVG | 399 | 521 | 384 | | AVG | 5.77 | 6.01 | 5.69 |
| MED | 308 | 461 | 244 | | MED | 5.72 | 6.12 | 5.49 |
| NF1 | 95 | 1056 | 118 | | NF1 | 4.55 | 6.96 | 4.77 |
| AVG_3 | 278 | 664 | 178.3 | | AVG_3 | 5.42 | 6.15 | 5.15 |
| | | | | | | 5.37 | 6.31 | 5.27 |
| | | | | | ID Fcst | 214 | 550 | 195 |
| | | | | | One-step | | | |

Figure 11.20 The empirical (conditional) distribution of nonzero demand volumes given interval sizes.

Examining the data first in this way differs from a **Croston-based method** which assumes that zero intervals and demand sizes are *independent*. The independence assumption needs to be validated in applications to intermittent demand forecasting.

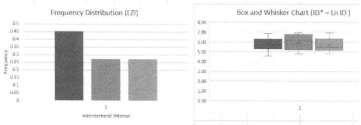

Figure 11.21 (*left*) The conditional empirical demand distribution given LZI as a frequency distribution and (*right)* as box and whisker plots

**Step 2**: *Determine the empirical interdemand interval distribution*. Each demand size is *preceded* by an interval of zeros. Adjacent demand sizes are separated by a zero lagtime interval LZI_0. In this dataset, there are three LZI intervals with the following distribution: LZI_0 has 10 occurrences, LZI_1 and LZI_2 each have 6 occurrences. Figure 11.21 shows the empirical frequency distribution of demand sizes given LZI.

# Forecasting Intermittent Demand Size Based on Lagged Zeros Dependence

We can continue to analyze the data for forecasting nonzero demand size ID as follows:

**Step 3**: *Each interdemand interval LZI is followed by a nonzero demand size ID*. Our measurement model is expressed in terms of ID* = Ln ID, (Figure 11.21). In Figure 11.21 (*right*), the box and whisker plot is a method for graphically depicting groups of numerical data through their quartiles. Box plots may also have lines extending vertically from the boxes (whiskers) indicating variability outside the upper and lower quartiles, hence the terms box-and-whisker plot. The three empirical frequencies corresponding to each interval size are not the same. The middle one has thicker tails than the first one, and the third box plot depicts a skewed distribution.

**Step 4**: *Create point forecasts for ID\* by interval size*. Unlike the Croston method, multistep forecasts are not assumed to have a level or flat forecast profile. In Figure 11.20, using an overall mean, median, last actual (naïve) or an average of the most recent three demand sizes as potential point forecasts, a typical projection can be obtained by averaging, for instance. Then exponentiate the typical projection to obtain a typical ID = exp (ln ID*) for each interval size LZI.

| Forecast Review Data | | | | | | | | | | | | |
|---|---|---|---|---|---|---|---|---|---|---|---|---|
| Values: Units | | | | | | | | | | | | |
| Data Scope: SKU: 12520-1037 ^ 12520, TOTAL COMPANY: Region 20 + Region 50 | | | | | | | | | | | | |
| Last Demand: 4/18 | | | | | | | | | | | | |
| Data Type: Intermittent Demand | | | | | | | | | | | | |
| | Jan. | Feb. | Mar. | Apr. | May | Jun. | Jul. | Aug. | Sep. | Oct. | Nov. | Dec. | Total |
| 2015 | 0 | 390 | 0 | 211 | 0 | 0 | 458 | 231 | 0 | 532 | 0 | 816 | 2638 |
| 2016 | 0 | 0 | 1035 | 0 | 120 | 281 | 334 | 134 | 737 | 0 | 0 | 275 | 2916 |
| 2017 | 959 | 0 | 1056 | 480 | 250 | 489 | 0 | 0 | 212 | 0 | 0 | 205 | 3651 |
| 2018 | 95 | 0 | 0 | 118 | 550 | 0 | 0 | 195 | 550 | 0 | 214 | 550 | 2272 |
| 2019 | 0 | 0 | 195 | 0 | 214 | 550 | 0 | 0 | 195 | 550 | 0 | 214 | 1918 |

Figure 11.22 The projected empirical intermittent demand based on a SIB modeling approach

**Step 5**: *Create enough interval projections to cover the lead-time or planning horizon*. By sampling the LZI distribution as an urn model, we obtain multistep ahead interdemand intervals. Each projected interdemand interval is *followed* by a projected demand volume associated with that interval size. The urn model in this example would contain 22 colored balls for the forecast horizon, each color associated with an interval duration [ten blue balls for LZI_0, six orange balls for LZI_1, and six grey balls for LZI_2]. In the sampling process, a ball is drawn from the urn, a color noted, the ball replaced in the urn, the urn shaken, and then another ball drawn, etc. until the forecast horizon (20 months) is covered. This sampling algorithm is programmable.

**Step 6.** *Create a forecast profile as needed.* For example, consider a sampled sequence of interval sizes to cover May 2018 through Dec 2019 (Figure 11.22): {LZI_0, LZI_2, LZI_0, LZI_1, LZI_0, LZI_2, LZI_1, LZI_0, LZI_2, LZI_0, LZI_1}. Each interval is followed by a demand size, so in this example, the projected intermittent demand profile starting in May 2018 is {550, 0, 0, 195, 550, 0, 214, 550, 0, 0, 195, 0, 214, 0, 0 , 195, 550, 0, 214}.

**Step 7.** *Embracing change and chance.* A SIB measurement model allows for an assessment of the *uncertainty* in terms of confidence bounds on a location parameter $\beta^*$, a posterior distribution for $\beta^*$, and likelihood analyses for the shape parameter $\lambda$ and typical "lagtime" interdemand interval $\tau$ in the measurement error $\varepsilon^*(\tau, \lambda)$. But, to fully embrace *change* (ID*) and *chance* ($\varepsilon^*$) with the intermittent data is a topic beyond the scope of this book.

# A Structured Inference Base (SIB) Modeling Approach for Intermittent Demand Forecasting

Structured Inference Base (SIB) models are algorithmic, data-driven inferential models, in contrast to the conventional data-generating models encountered in mainstream forecasting applications. A *bias measurement* model in forecasting is the simplest example of a SIB location measurement model.

**Step 8**: *A location measurement model for demand sizes.* If Ln refers to the natural logarithm, then the logarithm of the demand sizes can be described by a *location* measurement error model, known as a *simple measurement model*. The simple measurement model is known as a *location* model because of its structure.

Starting with a *location-scale* measurement model, the nonzero demand size ID in an intermittent demand history can be represented as the output ID = $\beta + \sigma\,\varepsilon$, in which $\beta$ and $\sigma$ are unknown constants and the input $\varepsilon$ is a measurement error with a known or assumed distribution. This equation can be rewritten as ID = $\beta\,(1 + \sigma/\beta\;\varepsilon)$. If Ln refers to the natural logarithm, then the logarithm of the nonzero demand sizes can be transformed into *location* measurement error model, known as a simple measurement model.

The location parameter is the unknown constant Ln $\beta$ in the equation Ln ID = Ln $\beta$ + {Ln $(1 + \sigma/\beta\;\varepsilon)$}. The term inside the curly brackets represents the measurement error in this model. Thus, Ln ID = $\beta^*$ + $\varepsilon^*$ is a SIB location measurement model with error $\varepsilon^*$ = Ln (1 + $\lambda$ $\varepsilon$) and location parameter $\beta^*$ = Ln $\beta$.

The parameter $\sigma/\beta$ is called a shape *parameter* $\lambda$ for the $\varepsilon^*$ distribution. This is a SIB location measurement model. In practice, when there are more interdemand interval durations, the error variable $\varepsilon^*$ may need to represented by a multivariate measurement error for each possible LZI duration in the data, but for now we will assume $\varepsilon^*(\tau)$ will depend on a typical LZI, represented by a single constant $\tau$.

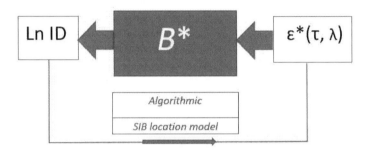

Figure 11.23 The SIB location measurement model for log transformed nonzero demand sizes.

The SIB model is *algorithmic and data-centric*. The SIB model uses algorithmic methods on observed data and treats the data as a feedback loop to the error measurement distribution. Keeping in mind the pervasive presence of outliers and non-normal (non-Gaussian) thick-tailed variation in real-world intermittent demand data, we shy away from the normal distribution assumptions and replace it with flexible family of error distributions, known as the **Exponential Family.** The exponential family contains many familiar distributions including the normal (Gaussian) distribution, as well as ones with thicker tails and skewness. There are also some technical reasons for selecting the exponential family, besides its flexibility.

The SIB model Ln ID = $\beta^*$ + $\varepsilon^*(\tau, \lambda)$ shows that the output Ln ID results from a translation of an input measurement error $\varepsilon^*(\tau, \lambda)$ shifted by a constant amount $\beta^*$, in which a conditioned measurement error distribution depends on a fixed shape parameter $\lambda$ and a typical lagtime interdemand interval $\tau$. This simple measurement model and its generalizations were worked out over four decades ago by Professor D.A.S. Fraser, whose 1979 book **Inference and Linear Models** documents the statistical inference and likelihood analyses.

*Statistical inference refers to the theory, methods, and practice of forming judgments about the parameters of a population and the reliability of statistical relationships.*

370

In practice, we have multiple measurements $\{ID_1, ID_2, ID_3., \ldots, ID_n\}$ of observed nonzero demand sizes over a time horizon $n$ (= 22 in the spreadsheet example). The output of the location measurement model is

$$Ln\ ID_1 = \beta^* + \varepsilon^*_1(\tau, \lambda)$$
$$Ln\ ID_2 = \beta^* + \varepsilon^*_2(\tau, \lambda)$$
$$Ln\ ID_3 = \beta^* + \varepsilon^*_3(\tau, \lambda)$$

$$Ln\ ID_n = \beta^* + \varepsilon^*_n(\tau, \lambda),$$

where $\varepsilon^*(\tau, \lambda) = \{\varepsilon^*_1(\tau, \lambda), \varepsilon^*_2(\tau, \lambda), \varepsilon^*_3(\tau, \lambda). \ldots, \varepsilon^*_n(\tau, \lambda)\}$ are now $n$ realizations of measurement errors from an assumed distribution with fixed shape parameter $\lambda$ and lag-time interdemand interval parameter $\tau$ in the exponential family. What information can we uncover about the SIB process?

The structure of the SIB model, given the data, shows that there is now information about the unknown, but realized measurement errors $\varepsilon^*(\tau, \lambda)$. The structure in the model directs us to a decomposition of the measurement error distribution into two components: (1) a *marginal* distribution for the *observed* components with fixed $(\tau, \lambda)$ and (2) a *conditional* distribution (based on the observed components) for the remaining *unknown* measurement error distribution. This is the insight or essential information gleaned from the structure of the black box and the recorded output data.

If we now select a location measure m(Ln ID) like the arithmetic mean, median, or smallest value (first order statistic), we can make a calculation that provides observable information about the measurement process. The model equations for Ln ID show (with substitution and some simple manipulations and leaving out the $(\tau, \lambda)$ notation), that

$$Ln\ ID_1 - m(Ln\ \mathbf{ID}) = \beta^* + \varepsilon^*_1 - m(\beta^* + \varepsilon^*) = \beta^* + \varepsilon^*_1 - \beta^* - m(\varepsilon^*)$$
$$= \varepsilon^*_1 - m(\varepsilon^*)$$
$$Ln\ ID_2 - m(Ln\ \mathbf{ID}) = \varepsilon^*_2 - m(\varepsilon^*)$$
$$Ln\ ID_3 - m(Ln\ \mathbf{ID}) = \varepsilon^*_3 - m(\varepsilon^*)$$

$$--------------$$

$$Ln\ ID_n - m(Ln\ \mathbf{ID}) = \varepsilon^*_n - m(\varepsilon^*)$$

The critical modeling step to note here is that the **left-hand** side of each equation can be calculated from the data, so the **right-hand** side is new information about a realized measurement error $\varepsilon^*$ and its distribution. What is now known we can condition on, so we can derive a one-dimensional *conditional* distribution given the known $(n - 1)$ dimensional error component and a *marginal* distribution for the observed error component with fixed shape parameter $\lambda$ and lagtime interdemand interval $\tau$ . This is computationally doable, but theoretically not tractable, except under the normality assumptions.

The argument for conditioning is necessary in the sense that it is somewhat like what a gambler can do knowing the odds in a black jack game. You can make calculations and inferences from what you observe in the dealt cards.

The above equations work, because for a location measure $m(.)$ as you add a constant amount to each component, a location measure $m(.)$, like a mean or median, is shifted by the same constant amount. In other words, $m(a + \ln \textbf{ID}) = a + m(\ln \textbf{ID})$, where a is a constant and $\ln \textbf{ID}$ = ($\ln \text{ID}_1$, $\ln \text{ID}_2$, $\ln \text{ID}_3$, ... $\ln \text{ID}_n$). It turns out that the choice of the measure $m$ is not important in the inferential procedure, as long as $m(.)$ has the location invariance property above. Some measures may turn out to be easier to process than others in the computations depending on the choice of the measurement error distribution. For example, the arithmetic mean is a natural choice under normality assumptions.

The useful information we can derive from this analysis is a decomposition of the measurement error distribution. The analysis will yield a (conditional**) posterior** distribution for the unknown parameter $\beta^*$ from which we can derive unique confidence bounds for the unknown constant and related likelihood inferences for the $(\tau, \lambda)$ parameters.

The location measurement model is well documented in two of D.A.S. Fraser's books along with a number of peer-reviewed academic papers. Because the results do not lend themselves to tractable theoretical formulae (except for the normal (Gaussian) distribution), they have not seen much daylight in practice until data science came into its own. Nowadays, inferential modeling can be dealt with in today's, empirically rich and fast, computing environment. In other words, SIB modeling is a practical approach, like machine learning algorithms.

> *With modern computing power, we can show what we should be doing for intermittent demand forecasting, not necessarily what we could do based on the mathematical elegance of unrealistic normality assumptions.*

## Takeaways
This chapter presented

> ➤ some statistical issues surrounding the benefit of routinely running **conventional methods** along with **nontraditional**

**methods**, which has not received adequate recognition among demand planners and forecasters.

➤ the use of *resistant* correlation and *robust* regression analysis to complement conventional regression methods that lack validity when unusual values are present and normality assumptions cannot be made.

➤ several analytical tools that are useful for the preliminary adjustment of data before confirmatory modeling steps are taken.

➤ Exploratory Data Analysis (EDA) as a tool for seeking evidence in the ARIMA lag structure of a model on the residuals, which could improve very short-term forecasts.

➤ residual analysis as a process designed to reveal departures from assumptions about the underlying distribution of random errors and model formulation.

➤ Advice to always involve domain expertise to find credible root-causes. Never simply delete bad data.

➤ the SIB measurement model Ln ID = $\beta^* + \varepsilon^*(\tau, \lambda)$ to show that the output Ln ID results from a translation or *shift* of an input measurement error $\varepsilon^*(\tau, \lambda)$ by a constant amount $\beta^*$, in which a *conditioned* measurement error distribution depends on a fixed shape parameter $\lambda$ and a typical "lagtime" interdemand interval $\tau$.

# 12

# The Final Forecast Numbers: Reconciling Change & Chance

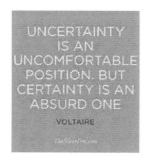

UNCERTAINTY
IS AN
UNCOMFORTABLE
POSITION, BUT
CERTAINTY IS AN
ABSURD ONE

VOLTAIRE

This chapter describes, first, the use of forecasting models to establish the credibility of demand forecasts, and second, the application of such information to supporting approval of recommended forecasts. The process requires not only preparing forecast scenarios but establishing credibility with accepted performance standards, evaluating the reliability of forecast scenarios using rolling forecasting simulations, and reconciling sales force and customer inputs where appropriate. A rigorous adherence to this process will allow you to recommend, with confidence, final forecast numbers for how much of what product will be needed in what place, at what time, and at what price. It also allows for you to package and present the forecast for approval.

The forecaster's checklist presented in this chapter allows for measurement of a specific forecast relative to generic standards. Use of the checklist by both demand forecasters and managers in the preparation and subsequent review of the forecast can greatly simplify and speed forecast evaluation.

## *Establishing Credibility*

One of the most perplexing problems that demand forecasters face is how to tell a good forecast from a bad one at the time it is presented for approval. Certainly, after the forecast time period has elapsed, anyone can look back and determine how closely the forecast predicted the actual results. Yet the demand forecaster wants to be confident that the forecast is reasonable and credible at the time it is prepared.

*tandards of performance for demand forecasting are necessary for establishing forecasting credibility*

## Setting Down Basic Facts: Forecast Data Analysis and Review

To be satisfied those basic facts have been adequately researched, a demand forecaster should expect to be able to produce tables and charts of historical data. The data should be adjusted to account for changes in geographic boundaries, organizational changes, product groupings, and customer segmentations, or other factors that will distort analyses and forecasts. If appropriate, the data should be seasonally adjusted to give a better representation of trend-cycle patterns. Outliers or other unusual data values should be explained and replaced, if this is warranted (see Chapter 2). It may be useful to indicate the National Bureau of Economic Research (NBER) reference dates for the peaks and troughs of business cycles that affect the company. This provides the demand forecaster with an indication of the extent to which a client's data are impacted by the national business cycles. Knowing this relationship will be helpful when the demand forecaster reviews the assumptions about the future state of the economy and assesses how these assumptions are reflected in the forecast.

Tables and plots of annual or period-to-period percentage changes provide an indication of the volatility of the historical data and can be useful later in checking the reasonableness of the forecast compared to history. If possible, ratios should be developed between the forecast series and other stable data series that are based on company or regional performance and shown in tables or plots. Once again, these ratios provide reasonableness checks. If some major change is expected in the forecast period, these ratios should help identify the change.

*The practice of forecast evaluation requires placing primary emphasis on the forecasting process rather than on the numbers. Meticulously following an effective forecasting process will lead to delivery of the best possible forecast.*

As much data as is feasible must be available for the demand forecaster's review. Most planning purposes involving 12–24-month budget cycles require a minimum of three seasons of history available (e.g., 36 months or 12 quarters). It may not be necessary to show this much history when presenting the demand forecast for review, but it is necessary to have such data available to analyze the impact of business cycles. Ideally, data going back several recessions should be available, though in many demand forecasting circumstances, data this old may no longer be relevant. Data covering several recessions (see Chapter 7) is desirable because this will reflect the timing, impact, and duration of the economic cycle on the business data.

> *Documentation of history is an important step that can serve as reference material for all future forecasts and forecasters.*

## Establishing Factors Affecting Future Demand

The next segment of the checklist is concerned with the factors likely to affect future demand and, therefore, the demand forecast. Assumptions have to be made about forward-looking factors for income, habit, price of a company's product, price of competing goods, availability of supply, and market potential. In addition, the forecaster should check to see that there is logical time integration between historical demand and the short- and long-term forecasts. Time plots are very useful here. In addition, related forecast items require logical time integration. The demand forecast should also be reasonably related to forecasts produced by other organizations in the company (if the demand forecasting function is not centralized in one organization) such as forecasts of economic conditions, revenues, and expenses.

> *Assumptions should be made about forward-looking factors influencing demand and the time integration between historical demand and the short- and long-term forecasts.*

## Determining Causes of Change and Chance

The first step toward determining causes of change and chance is to identify the trend in the data. Regression analysis is, as we've seen, an excellent tool for this (see Chapter 10). A straight-line fit against time, as a starting point, will provide a visual indication as to whether the trend is linear or nonlinear. The series and its fitted trend should be plotted on a scale of sufficient breadth to clearly identify deviations from trend. The reasons for the deviations should then be identified and root causes documented for future reference (see Chapter 11). These explanations must be specific. Was there any unusual competitive activity? Was there a change in promotion dates or prices? Did the deviation correspond to a regional or national economic pattern? What was the source of explanation—the demand forecaster or someone else? Finally, how certain is the demand forecaster that the reason or explanation stated is correct? Is the forecaster reasonably certain of the cause, or is there insufficient evidence to be confident that the true cause has been or can be identified? Documenting this is particularly helpful to a new forecaster and improves agility.

As noted, a record of demand forecasts and actual performance for at least the previous three years should be available. This allows the demand forecaster and manager to know how well the organization has done in the past and to gauge the possible reaction of management to changes in the forecast. It is also possible to determine from these data if any or all of the demand forecasters on the staff have a tendency to be too optimistic or too pessimistic over time.

*A record of forecast performance with actuals is useful in gauging the possible reaction of planners and managers to changes in the forecast and reduce the tendency of organizations to over- or underestimate demand.*

## Preparing Forecast Scenarios

After forecasting models have been developed, the demand forecaster reaches the stage where actual forecasts are produced, tested, and approved. This effort begins with the generation of scenarios from the models that have survived the selection process.

In addition to creating projections from models, the demand forecaster needs to create scenarios that provide estimates of the reliability of the forecast in terms of prediction limits around the forecast at specified levels of uncertainty. Alternatively, reliability can be expressed as the likely percentage (amount) of deviation between a forecast and actual performance.

For example, suppose that new car purchases for the year are forecast to be 1 million ± 70000 at a 90% confidence level. Another way of stating this is that, in a particular forecasting model, the average annual deviation (absolute value) between what is forecast and the actual new car sales is approximately 7%.

Demand forecasters should always test the validity of their models by simulating a forecast over a holdout period and generating scenarios from the models over time periods for which the actual results are known. In this way, it is possible to establish the likely forecast accuracy.

Figure 12.1 illustrates how a forecaster could summarize forecast errors in a model with actual data from Year 1 through Year 15. A projection from the model for Year 11 is generated, based on the historical data Year 1 to Year 10. The actual data through Year 10 show that the projection is 8.7% higher than the Year 11 actual value.

An additional year of actuals is then added to the model, and Year 12 is predicted. This time the projection is only 1.2% greater than the actual. This process can be continued and some typical performance can then be calculated. In this hypothetical example, the Mean Absolute 1-year-ahead forecast Percentage Error (MAPE) for five periods is 4.3%.

It might also be useful to consider the Median APE (MdAPE = 3.8%) as well to ensure that a very large miss in one year does not unduly distort the average value and that the distribution of APEs is not skewed. With this approach, the demand forecaster might expect the typical 1-year-ahead prediction to be within 4% of the actual value, on average.

| Historical Fit | Percentage Error |
|---|---|
| Year 1–Year 10 | −8.7 |
| Year 2–Year 11 | −1.2 |
| Year 3–Year 12 | 5.7 |
| Year 4–Year 13 | 3.8 |
| Year 5–Year 14 | −2.3 |
| MAPE | 4.3 |
| MdAPE | 3.8 |

Figure 12.1 Summary of one-year-ahead forecast errors from a hypothetical model with data for 15 years. (Percentage error = 100 x (actual – forecast)/actual))

## Analyzing Forecast Errors

Another checklist item requires analysis of the reasons for the differences between previous forecasts and actual results. This form of results analysis—where a forecast error is defined by convention as Actual minus Forecast—is useful for uncovering problem areas, identifying the need for new or improved methods, and determining the quality of the prior forecasts (see Chapter 11).

At this time, the demand forecaster or manager is looking for a pattern of overforecasting or underforecasting. The key to identifying the reasons for forecast deviations is to have written records of basic assumptions that can be reviewed.

These assumptions should then be tested for specificity against the standards shown on the checklist. Do the assumptions relate only to the future time periods? Has the demand forecaster used an assumption that states a positive assertion of facts that may hold true during the forecast period? Was the direction of expected impact stated? Presumably, the assumptions are both positive and negative in terms of their impact on the series being forecasted. Do the assumptions indicate the amount or rate of expected impact, the timing of the initial impact, and the duration of the expected impact?

Accompanying each assumption should be a rationale indicating why the assumption is necessary. The source of an assumption might be the demand forecaster, company economists, industry associations, government publications, online blogs, or newspaper or journal articles. The demand forecaster may be absolutely certain that the assumption will be proven correct. On the other hand, the demand forecaster may indicate that it is necessary to make the assumption but that considerable doubt exists as to whether it will prove to be accurate.

## Taming Uncertainty: A Critical Role for Informed Judgment

Statistical approaches can provide a framework of knowledge around which analytical skills and judgment can be applied in order to achieve agility in supporting a sound demand forecasting process. They have been around for a long time. To quote from Butler et al.'s *Methods and Techniques of Business Forecasting* (1974), "*In actual application of the scientific approaches, judgment plays, and will undoubtedly always play, an important role. The users of econometric models have come to realize that their models can only be relied upon to provide a first approximation—a set of consistent forecasts which then must be 'massaged' with intuition and good judgment to take into account those influences on economic activity for which history is a poor guide.*" This still sounds true today.

Continuing with the automobile sales analogy, consider that once the car buyer has purchased a car, subjective judgment comes into play if the car buyer realizes that the purchase was not a good decision. For example, during verification and confidence checks, suppose that the car buyer discovers a flaw so great that the dealer agrees either to repair the car or to exchange it for a comparable model—the buyer needs to exercise judgment not called for in the original forecast in order to reconcile expectations and reality.

In an actual demand forecasting situation, it may become apparent through rolling simulations that the actuals have exceeded the estimates for several successive periods, or that the forecasts for a given period under-predict the held-out actual value. Experience suggests that a model's projections be modified (adjusted upward or downward) by a given amount or percentage to account for the current deviation (bias) and the forecaster's expectation of whether that forecast profile pattern will continue.

Subjective judgment in demand forecasting should be based on all available information, including changes in company policy, changes in economic conditions and government regulations, and contacts with customers. Such judgment is a real measure of the skill and experience of the demand forecaster. For this reason, data and processes are only as good as the person interpreting them. To paraphrase George Box (Chapter 9), all data are wrong, some are useful. This judgment operates on many inputs to reach a final forecast.

Informed judgment is, by far, the most crucial element when we are trying to predict the future. Informed judgment is what ties the forecasting process and the extrapolative techniques into a cohesive effort that is capable of producing realistic predictions of future events or conditions.

> *Informed judgment plays a critical role in the determination of the final forecast numbers and, later on, in the determination of when a forecast should be revised.*

Informed judgment is an essential ingredient of the selection of the forecasting approach; the selection of data sources; the selection of the data collection and data cleaning methodologies; the selection of preliminary data analysis and extrapolative techniques; the use of exception-handling and root-cause analysis techniques during the forecasting process; the identification of forward-looking market and company factors that are likely to affect the future of the item to be forecast; the determination of how those factors will affect the item in terms of the direction, magnitude (amount or rate), timing, and duration of the expected impact; and the selection of the forecast presentation methodology.

> *Informed judgment plays a significant role in taming the uncertainty associated with demand forecasting.*

Automatic processes, models, and statistical algorithms are sometimes used in computing future demand from a set of key factors. However, no such approach should reduce substantially the reliance upon sound judgment. Judgment must be based on a comprehensive analysis of market activities and a thorough evaluation of basic assumptions and influencing factors.

The limitations of a purely statistical modeling approach should be kept clearly in mind. Statistics, like all tools, may be valuable for one job but of little use for another. An exploratory analysis of patterns is basic to demand forecasting and a number of different statistical procedures may be employed to make this analysis more meaningful (see Chapter 2). However, the human element is required to understand the differences between what was expected in the past and what actually occurred and to predict the likely outcome of future events.

# Forecast Adjustments: Reconciling Sales Force and Management Overrides

In many situations, the company's sales force and its trading partners can provide input to the demand forecasting process that can be of value to the creation of the final forecast numbers. This is particularly true when a limited number of customers account for a large share of the total business. It is likely that the sales manager has assigned a salesperson to an account and that a sales force composite process is used to identify and quantify future business opportunities. So specific situations may support an adjustment to the proposed forecast.

*With access to the sales forecaster's targets, the demand forecaster can determine whether the proposed forecast is aligned with sales plans.*

Although the existence of such sales force input is of great value, a few key factors may diminish its usefulness. At the beginning of the planning process for a given year, the sales quotas, on which sales compensation will be based, have not yet been set. The sales force is usually reluctant to identify all of its most likely opportunities in hopes that the quota will be set somewhat lower. Similarly, even after the quotas are set, the sales force is often reluctant to identify new opportunities later in the year for fear that the quota will be raised.

If the sales force believes the quota will not be revised, the sales force and the distributors have a tendency to like forecasts to be high to make sure that product will be available to their customers. Prompt delivery will increase customer satisfaction and make sure that business is not lost to competitors because of a delivery delay. On the other hand, when the sales force is unlikely to meet its quota and management find out, it may get more help than it wants from management.

In addition, the sales force may get this help every subsequent month. Therefore, there may be a tendency to hold to the business-plan target as the sales forecast until the last moment. The sales force is naturally optimistic and is unwilling to signal an inability to meet the plan until all possible options have been explored.

For these reasons, a statistical model may actually provide better final forecast numbers even lacking the intelligence that resides with the sales force. Some demand managers have attempted alternative sales force compensation systems that encourage better forecasts by maximizing a bonus based on increased sales and forecast accuracy. In any case, the statistical models are objective, reproducible, and provide a minimum level of credibility to the demand forecasting process.

> *The source of each assumption should be identified and the degree of confidence in the assumption should be stated.*

## Combining Forecasts and Methods

The combining of forecasts is treated extensively in the forecasting literature, such as the *International Journal of Forecasting (http://www.journals.elsevier.com/international-journal-of-forecasting/)*. Given that it is frequently difficult to know which smoothing technique to select, it may be useful to bypass a specific model selection procedure entirely. For instance, by automating the modeling process, we can fit a variety of exponential smoothing models and then average their individual forecasts to come up with a combined forecast as a typical forecast scenario. Different approaches for combining two or more forecasts into a composite forecast have led to some surprising improvements in the accuracy of forecasting results.

> *Combining forecasts is a technique that can be implemented completely automatically, making it useful for multiseries forecasting.*

One alternative to simple averaging or selecting a median is to base the weights on the accuracy of past forecasting or fitting performance. Another suggestion uses subjective weightings to form a composite forecast.

Practitioners might choose to weigh the forecast based on their informed judgments about which methods most closely reflect reality at the time. Clearly, some models may at times produce unusual projections distorting the MAPE, which would suggest supplementing the MAPE with a TAPE (Typical Absolute Percentage Error) measure (*see* Chapter 4). Unfortunately, there are no pat answers to combining forecasts, although some promising improvements in accuracy have been reported in the literature.

What is needed is a process that, if followed, will increase the likelihood of good forecasting performance. In other words, it is necessary to establish credibility by setting standards of performance for forecasters that will increase the likelihood of improved forecast accuracy.

At this time, the demand forecaster and demand manager can decide whether the forecasting methodologies used present the best methods available at the time (*see* Chapter 3). The methods presented in this book have been tested extensively in business applications and have proved to be practical.

> *The use of multiple methods to arrive at the final demand forecast is highly recommended.*

Within limits, it is very difficult for a demand forecaster or manager to fine-tune the numbers presented and have any degree of confidence that the changes are appropriate. However, the forecaster or manager can carefully review the forecast assumptions for reasonableness. Such assumptions are the heart of a forecast, and considerable probing of the assumptions can satisfy the forecaster as to their appropriateness for the forecast period.

The demand forecaster and forecast manager can also review the technical soundness of the analysis and be satisfied that no errors were made. Having performed these forecast evaluations, the demand forecaster and manager can discriminate between a good forecast and a bad one at the approval stage. This level of managerial involvement is generally required only for extremely sensitive or important forecasts, for training new forecasters, for reviewing exceptional cases, and for spot-checking to ensure that the processes are being followed.

After narrowing down the possible alternatives, a demand forecaster must determine the parameters of selected forecasting models. These parameters may be ratios such as housing units per acre or market penetration rates. Similarly, a potential car buyer double-checks the parameters that make a certain car seem right, including the specific model, color, engine size, and options.

Model parameters may also be coefficients estimated statistically from data by computer. Software solutions can provide immediate access to the flexibility and breadth of potentially useful forecasting techniques.

## Verifying Reasonableness

Continuing with the car-buying example, the car buyer attempts to validate the manufacturer's claims concerning ease of automatic parking, comfort of heated seats, engine noise level, active engine braking, and acceleration. Taking a road test does this. Likewise, the demand forecaster has number of analytical tools available (e.g., residual analysis and forecast simulations) to determine whether it is possible to improve on an initial model. These tools have been presented throughout the book.

As a result of the road test, the car buyer may decide to try a different make, model, or engine. Likewise, the demand forecaster might decide to add new data, try a different modeling approach, or replace a one-time series (e.g., the reciprocal of an unemployment rate) with another series (e.g., total employment in a revenue model).

*Forecasters validate models through diagnostic checking.*

The diagnostic checking stage usually requires a number of iterations. New variables can be considered and transformations of variables can be made to improve the models.

Likewise, some techniques should be rejected at this stage because of their inability to provide statistically defensible results and their inability to achieve the desired objectives of accuracy (in terms of bias and dispersion).

In evaluating alternatives, we will find patterns or characteristics of the models that will influence the final selection of the models for use. For example, which techniques are more reliable in predicting turning points? In predicting stable periods? Which techniques have the best overall accuracy in a rolling forecast simulation mode? Do some techniques tend to overpredict or under-predict in given situations? Are the short-term projections of one technique better than another? Do we actually need long-term predictions? Do the coefficients of one model seem more reasonable than those of another either in sign or magnitude?

## Selecting 'Final Forecast' Numbers

The final steps of the process entail relating projections from various models to the final forecast. The demand forecaster has several decisions to make. He or she recognizes that the various models are abstractions from the real world. The future will never be exactly like the past; the projections from the models must be viewed as job aids in making an informed judgment about the future.

In most cases, that advice is provided in the form of a "best bet" number that represent either values at some specific time or the cumulative values of series of data points at the end of a specific period of time.

The "best bet" numbers can be illustrated most effectively with the expected value of a random variable in a statistical model. There is a calculable chance that the future outcome will fall above or below that expected value. Its primary weakness, however, is that the demand/supply planning and decision-making processes assume that a demand forecast precisely describe the future when, in fact, it cannot perform such a feat.

> *Because future events and conditions cannot be predicted consistently with complete accuracy, the end product of the forecasting process might best be described as considered advice.*

Decision making involves the assessment and acceptance of risk. Therefore, demand forecasters can assist decision makers by providing forecast levels and associated prediction limits that indicate the chance of each of those levels being exceeded.

This does not mean that the demand forecaster takes a "shotgun" approach to predicting the future by incorporating the extreme alternatives at either end of the range. It simply means that the demand forecaster should provide the "best bet" figure and state the associated risk levels or range on each side of the "best bet." If a view of the future is presented in this format, the decision maker has much more information on which to assess the risk associated with decisions.

It is not realistic to assume that these risk levels are necessarily symmetrical. It is only that most software systems do not have the models to recognize asymmetrical prediction limits.

Creating probabilities associated with alternative views of the future is, of course, a highly subjective practice. In the social sciences, probabilities are developed through some form of scientific sampling process over a long period of time. Such is not the case when it comes to quantifying the probabilities of future events or conditions in a demand forecast. A multitude of influencing factors can enter into the picture after the forecast has been made and thereby completely change the course of future events.

The principle of using more than one extrapolative technique can again provide substance to the demand forecasting process by assigning a certain degree of objectivity in the development of risk levels. It is clear, therefore, that the extrapolative techniques play an important role in the decisions on the forecast level that is ultimately produced.

A high level of managerial involvement is generally required only for extremely sensitive or important forecasts, for training new forecasters, for reviewing exceptional cases, and for spot-checking to ensure that the processes are being followed.

The amount of analysis required in using extrapolative techniques may seem overwhelming. However, much of the data and graphic displays can often be generated and maintained with computer software in an agile forecasting process.

## *Gaining Acceptance from Management*

When a car buyer presents his or her selected car to friends and family, the buyer tries to convince them that the car is a beauty and that its cost does not exceed what had been planned for—besides, won't the neighbors be envious? The buyer seeks a form of approval, especially when his or her family has agreed to help in financing the purchase.

*It is necessary to obtain user acceptance and higher management approval of a forecast.*

The demand forecaster must also present a forecast for approval. With pride of authorship, the forecaster thinks the final forecast is a beauty and is worth what it cost to produce. The managers will approve it, hopefully, but never with much enthusiasm. After all, if things go wrong, it's the forecaster's forecast!

## The Forecast Package

After the demand forecast has been developed, it must then be documented and communicated to the people who need the information. The final forecast package should include

- the demand forecast with specified uncertainty
- a display of the forecast that analytically relates it to the past data (through a graphical and/or tabular display of the historical data and the forecast on the same page)
- appropriate statement of the rationale and assumptions regarding external and company factors that are likely to influence the item under study during the forecast period
- appropriate documentation on the approach that was used to make the forecast and on the extrapolative techniques used during the forecasting process
- a delineation of specific potential decision points related to planning risk levels and the significance of particular assumptions

*The purpose of the forecast package is to communicate the demand forecast to others and, at the same time, provide credibility to the demand forecast in the form of supporting documentation.*

The value of any forecast is a function of its usefulness to decision makers in the face of future uncertainty. Therefore, there is more to the demand forecaster's job than merely developing the forecast numbers. Because the product must also be sold to the planners and decision makers, the supporting documentation should emphasize the quality of the process, the inputs used during the process, and the judgment that was applied throughout the process.

The chore of maintaining support documentation can be minimized by advance planning and continuous record keeping. The demand forecaster's documentation is as essential to the forecast's success as the proof that a car has been serviced in compliance with its warranty is for someone wanting to buy or sell a used car. The forecaster must document all the specific steps taken and the assumptions made. Only with such documentation can the forecaster and the manager pursue a meaningful analysis of results, later, when the actual data are compared to the forecast data.

When forecast work has been documented, it is possible to specify a reason or set of reasons for the demand forecast's differing from actual accomplishments. These reasons will go a long way toward helping the manager evaluate the demand forecaster's performance. Without documentation, the forecaster cannot learn from past experiences in order to identify flaws in forecasting techniques.

From a manager's viewpoint, documentation also provides efficiencies in the face of staffing turnover. If the original demand forecaster is unavailable, a new demand forecaster will not have to reconstruct a forecast from scratch. Rather, a model or case study will already exist and a body of information will be available for use.

Finally, the users of the demand forecast will also appreciate the additional thorough documentation. Instead of simply having a set of numbers, they will have the kind of information they need to assist them in setting goals and making decisions about their area of responsibility.

> *A vital part of gaining credibility with management is quality documentation of the work at various stages of the process.*

## Forecast Presentations

In practice, there are normally far too many individual forecast variables to be reviewed and presented for approval. We suggest an approach that includes the following:

- Identify major changes from the last forecast.
- Review the forecasts for the strategic items that are most important to success. These are generally those items producing the greatest revenue. Pareto's law normally applies where approximately 20% of the items account for 80% of the business. However, there is generally a need to review the items that were only recently introduced and have not generated that much demand to date but that are expected to be the future flagship products for the company. This is particularly true for high-tech and fashion products where the product life cycles are short.
- Review the top 10 improvement opportunity items. These are the items will contribute to the greatest improvement in overall forecast accuracy. Because there are so many items, it may be desirable to weight the unit forecast miss (Actual – Forecast) by the percentage that the actual revenue for the item is of the total actual revenue. This places the greatest weight on the forecast accuracy of the items having the largest impact on total revenue. These items often have the most impact on the operation of the business.
- Review other major revenue items. These are the items that represent a large percentage of the total revenue and that have been forecast with a high degree of accuracy. Because they represent a large part of the revenue, they should not be overlooked.
- Compare the overall revenue forecast that results from multiplying the unit forecasts by their prices with overall top-down revenue

forecasting. This will demonstrate the degree of forecast alignment between the forecasts driving factory and purchasing decisions and the forecasts driving financial planning. This approach can also be used for major product groups.

- Summarize overall forecast accuracy trends. The use of a revenue-weighted accuracy measure is often used to summarize the performance of the numerous item forecasts. This will provide an indication of how well the demand forecaster, forecasting decision support system, and other relevant individuals (salesperson, sales manager, sales director, etc.) have done and where improvements are needed.

## A Demand Forecaster's Checklist

The following checklist can be used to help identify gaps in the demand forecasting process that will need your attention.  It can be scored or color-coded on three levels.

> (Green = YES,      Yellow = SOMEWHAT, and Red = NO)

**Step 1. Setting down basic facts about past trends and forecasts**
- ✓ Are historical tables and plots available?
- ✓ Are base-adjusted data available? (A constant base is needed. For example, have historical revenues been adjusted to today's price. Have data been adjusted for mergers and acquisitions?)
- ✓ Are seasonally adjusted data available?
- ✓ Have outliers and unusual values been identified, explained and corrected?
- ✓ Have NBER cyclical reference dates been overlaid?
- ✓ Are percentage changes shown in tables and plots?
- ✓ Have forecast-versus-actual comparisons been made for one or more forecast periods?

**Step 2. Determining factors likely to affect future demand**
- ✓ Do factors relate to the future?
- ✓ Do factors indicate the direction of impact?
- ✓ Do factors indicate the amount or rate of impact, the timing of the impact, and the duration of the impact on demand?
- ✓ Are there rationale statements for each factor?
- ✓ Are the sources of any rationale statement identified?

**Step 3. Determining causes of change in past demand trends**
- ✓ Is a trend identified?
- ✓ Is it linear or nonlinear?
- ✓ Are there plots of data and fitted trends?
- ✓ Is the scale of sufficient breadth to see deviations?
- ✓ Have the deviations been explained in writing?

   ✓   Are the explanations of causes specific?
   ✓   Has the source of the explanations been identified?
   ✓   Is the degree of certainty about the explanations noted?

**Step 4. Determining causes of differences between previous forecasts and actual data**

   ✓   Are differences explained?
   ✓   Are there any patterns to the explanations?
   ✓   Are there basic assumptions that can be reviewed?

**Step 5. Making forecasts for future periods**

   ✓   Time integration: Are the long-term forecast, short-term forecast, and history all shown on one chart?
   ✓   Item integration: Are the ratios of related items shown as well as their history through the long-term forecast?
   ✓   Functional integration: Are related forecasts identified and the relationships quantified?
   ✓   Have multiple methods been used for key items and have the results been compared?
   ✓   Has impact on the user of the forecast been considered?

## *Case: Creating a Final Forecast for the GLOBL Company*

In chapter 1, we introduce GLOBL (again, a fictitious company) as one of the leading international companies providing consumer technology products to a broad range of worldwide customers. GLOBL's mission is to provide

- development, manufacturing, and sales of educational technology products
- development and sales of the hardware and software systems to support these products
- a broad range of customer-support services ranging from installations, training, consulting, and ongoing maintenance.

Although GLOBL develops, manufactures, and sells a broad range of consumer products, there is one product line for which you will develop demand forecasts by region:

**Product Line B:** This is a family of consumer products for **academia and institutions of higher learning**. The customers for these products are students requiring specialized learning devices and educational materials to allow them to cope more effectively and competitively in a general academic environment.

**The Marketplace assumptions for GLOBL Products**. There are five major players in the worldwide educational technology marketplace, plus another dozen niche players. GLOBL has a centralized market intelligence staff that are responsible for overall marketplace trends and outlooks, keeping track of competitive activities and market share, and performing specialized marketplace studies as required by sales, marketing, and product development.

**GLOBL Product Development plans**. GLOBL does all development work on the three product lines. This means that GLOBL maintains a development staff whose responsibilities include evaluating and tracking customer requirements for educational products, determining and prioritizing what needs may be best pursued by GLOBL, designing and developing products to meet these needs, determining go-to-market strategies for these products, tracking GLOBL product performance versus objectives, and enhancing products as required to meet GLOBL objectives.

**GLOBL Sales Force and Channel Strategy**. GLOBL has a worldwide team of dedicated product sales specialists. Also, a number of business partners sell GLOBL products, often along with other products and services. There is a strong focus on increasing the use of Web-based facilities to exploit e-business sales.

**GLOBL Manufacturing**. GLOBL performs manufacturing activity for the products you forecast. Worldwide manufacturing supply/demand planning is performed centrally for all products, although there are several manufacturing sites for each product.

**GLOBL Product and Strategy Assumptions for Product Line B**: Product Line B sells into the academic market and institutions of higher learning. Although GLOBL has been in the market for quite a few decades, the original versions of this line were introduced just over 48 months ago. Sales have been normal for the past year. Two years ago, there was an unexpected upswing in demand in Quarter 3, which caused big manufacturing problems. A dedicated sales force does over 90% of sales and has grown significantly in size over the past 3 years.

There are currently plans for a further strengthening of the sales budget due to concern that GLOBL is still number 3 in this marketplace. This sales force operates off a quota system with sales contests scheduled approximately once a year, usually in the last quarter. Selling in this marketplace depends on establishing good relationships with the educational institutions. GLOBL's competitors appear to be more successful at this. You have difficulties getting solid information on the product line's sales activities from the sales force.

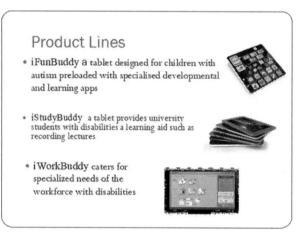

**Step 1**: Developing Factors (**PEER Prepare Stage**)

**Prepare the factors**. GLOBL has determined a number of internal and external factors that influence the demand for its products. These factors may be different across the product lines, but six factors appeared to have some common value. Unfortunately, these factors often display some similarities in their strength of impact on the demand. It is your responsibility to sort out the behavior of these factors and their influence on demand in order to obtain some quantification of this for presentation to your management.

      **Factor A Opportunity momentum index**: Because each sales situation can be characterized by its sell cycle status, win probability, revenue, and so forth, an index of opportunity momentum was created to measure the goodness of a sales opportunity by the end of its sales cycle.

      **Factor B Competitive pricing index**: Price levels for the product were tracked and compared against similar competitive product.

      **Factor C Product attractiveness index**: Product functionality was indexed with those of its major competitors.

      **Factor D Channel investment index**: This is the percentage of advertising/marketing spending on GLOBL product line as a percentage of total spend by business partners.

Factor E Industry investment index: This is the industry expenditure on web-based applications as a percentage of total industry expenditures on applications.

Factor F Gross Internet product: This is a measure, like the GDP, measuring e-industry output.

QUESTION 1: Developing Factors: Once you have defined a specific product and a name for each product line, suggest and define three more external (consumer-driven) factors for each product line to supplement factors A through F. How would you source the data for these factors? Characterize factors A through F as internal (consumer data-driven) or external (company-driven). See Chapter 1.

# Impact Change Matrix for the Factors Influencing Product Demand

An Impact Change Matrix is a table in which a measure of the impact on demand (during a time period relative to the current time period) is provided for each factor over a number of time periods in the product's life cycle. The table below is an example of an impact change matrix for a product line under a given set of assumptions about the business environment for GLOBL

| A | 3 | 3 | 4 | 4 | 5 | Index becoming more reliable |
| B | 3 | 4 | 4 | 5 | 5 | Index becoming more important as products are less differentiated |
| C | 5 | 3 | 4 | 3 | 4 | Competition has substantially caught up with GLOBL |
| D | 1 | 2 | 3 | 3 | 3 | Importance of larger customer is diminishing |
| E | 4 | 4 | 3 | 4 | 3 | Gradually decreasing importance as product life cycle is ending |
| F | 4 | 4 | 4 | 4 | 5 | Index is expected to increase in importance as the e-market matures |

This measure is on a scale of 1 to 5 (1= weaker, 2 = moderate, 3 = average, 4 = positive, 5 = stronger). The table is completed as follows:

- In Current Period, place the measure of impact the factor has on demand during the current period.
- In Prior Year column, place the measure to reflect the change of impact the factor has had on demand a year ago relative to its impact in the current period.
- In Immediate Past column, place the measure to reflect the change of impact the factor has had on demand in the past 3–6 months relative to its impact in the current period.

- In the Immediate Future column, place the measure to reflect the change of impact the factor is expected to have on demand in the next 3–6 months relative to its impact in the current period.
- In Next Year column, place the measure that reflects the change of the factor's expected impact on demand next year relative to its impact in the current period.

**QUESTION 2:** *Using assumptions about the GLOBL environment for the product line, how would you create impact change matrices? There are no unique answers to this.*

# The Impact Association Matrix for the Chosen Factors

An **Impact Association Matrix** is a table of correlations of the sequences in the impact change matrix. Because these sequences are very short, the ordinary correlation coefficient may not be adequate. Hence, we have used an outlier-resistant correlation coefficient r*(SSD) that is comparable to the ordinary correlation coefficient (see Chapter 11). Note that the association of a factor with itself is always unity (=1) and that the values can range between −1 and +1. The completed impact association matrix for the example matrix would look like this:

| IAM | A | B | C | D | E | F |
|-----|-----|-----|-----|-----|-----|-----|
| A | 1 | | | | | |
| B | 0.80 | 1 | | | | |
| C | 0.00 | −0.72 | 1 | | | |
| D | 0.80 | 0.95 | −0.28 | 1 | | |
| E | −0.80 | −0.34 | −0.47 | −0.70 | 1 | |
| F | 0.60 | 0.38 | 0.18 | 0.18 | −0.18 | 1 |

Aside from the direction of impact (positive or negative) on demand, there is a changing pattern of impact over time. When two factors display a similar *pattern of impact* on demand, these factors will be strongly associated. This high association can be positive or negative depending on whether the similarities in patterns move in the same or opposite directions. The importance of these associations may play out when you create models for demand over time using one or more of these factors. Having an early understanding of and insight into this, will help you with the modeling issues.

**QUESTION 3:** *Using assumptions about the GLOBL environment for your product lines, how could you evaluate the impact association matrices for the factors of your choice? This is a quantification of a subjective process to give specificity to your assumptions.*

**Factor F**, showing low association with several other factors might be used together with one or more good factors in a regression model. If this is successful, Factor F would be a good factor to use because the impact changes appear to be dissimilar from the others and thus providing a more independent influence on demand.

> **QUESTION 4:** *Reconcile the results found in Question 3 with the assumptions you made about the role of the factors in forecasting the demand for your product lines. (a) Factors A and E are strongly negatively associated. What implication does this have for their future inclusion in modeling demand for the product? (b) Factor A is strongly associated with most of the other factors. Why might this be so.*

## Exploratory Data Analysis of the Product Line and Factors Influencing Demand

> **UESTION 5:** *A seasonal decomposition – Can you create a trend-seasonal description (exploratory* STI_Classification*) and decomposition of the data using the RMA method? (See Chapter 2).*

1. Create an analysis of product line time series by identifying the trend and seasonal variation with a preliminary STI_Classification analysis and the Ratio-to-Moving Average (RMA) decomposition method. Document your results in a data sheet like the one given here for future use in reconciling multiple projection techniques.
2. Answer the following questions and in doing so, apply the Ratio-to-Moving Average (RMA) method (Chapter 5) to come up with an initial four-period projection (forecast horizon = 4 months).
3. 
   - What are the twelve seasonal factors?
   - What is the peak seasonal month?
   - What is the lowest seasonal month?
   - Do you notice any sub patterns (e.g., quarter by quarter)?
   - Is the RMA decomposition additive or multiplicative? How can you tell?
   - What is the average monthly change in trend (in level and percent)?
   - What is the projected trend over the forecast horizon assuming a straight-line trend?
   - What are the projected seasonal factors for the months in the forecast horizon?
   - What is the projection of demand over the four-period forecast horizon (as determined by combining trend and seasonal in a multiplicative formulation)?

> **QUESTION 6:** *Estimate preliminary projections using the RMA Decomposition Method. To do this, calculate: (a) the approximate slope of Tren1- What is the increment each period? (b) Four periods for the trend: 37, 38, 39, and 40. (c) Apply seasonal factor for each month to the trend and complete the table below. Which month is #37?*

**Sample Data Sheet: A Trend/Seasonal Decomposition for Product XYZ**

Seasonal Index (Multiplicative)

Accuracy of Model - Fit
MAPE:
75.6
MdAPE
:
88.9

| | |
|---|---|
| 1 | 0.279606 |
| 2 | 0.708010 |
| 3 | 1.30809 |
| 4 | 0.794871 |
| 5 | 1.09598 |
| 6 | 1.87311 |
| 7 | 0.921522 |
| 8 | 1.05525 |
| 9 | 0.928185 |
| 10 | 0.579209 |
| 11 | 0.781690 |
| 12 | 1.67447 |

| Month | CombSale | TREN1 | SEAS1 | DETR1 | DESE1 | FITS1 | RESI1 |
|---|---|---|---|---|---|---|---|
| 31 | 230 | 514.440 | 0.92152 | 0.44709 | 249.59 | 474.07 | -244.068 |
| 32 | 605 | 533.780 | 1.05525 | 1.13343 | 573.32 | 563.27 | 41.726 |
| 33 | 965 | 553.119 | 0.92819 | 1.74465 | 1039.66 | 513.40 | 451.603 |
| 34 | 450 | 572.459 | 0.57921 | 0.78608 | 776.92 | 331.57 | 118.427 |
| 35 | 460 | 591.798 | 0.78169 | 0.77729 | 588.47 | 462.60 | -2.603 |
| 36 | 765 | 611.138 | 1.67447 | 1.25176 | 456.86 | 1023.33 | -258.331 |

## Month Period  Projection

| Month | Period | Projection |
|-------|--------|------------|
| 1 | 37 | ------ |
| 2 | 38 | ------ |
| 3 | 39 | ------ |
| 4 | 40 | ------ |

**Notes for documentation**: In practice, you should always consider calculating a nonconventional (outlier resistant) alternative measure of correlation. The robust/resistant alternative is like an insurance policy. If the robust alternative is equal or very close to the ordinary correlation coefficient, then the forecaster has assurance of the validity of the correlation coefficient (*see* Chapter 11). However, when there are unusual values in the scatter diagram, the correlation coefficient is a deficient and unreliable measure of association. In such situations, the robust alternative and the ordinary correlation coefficient are not close. This can provide a valuable warning to the analyst to probe deeper into the nature of the deficiency

---

*QUESTION 7: Correlation analysis with the factors. Answer the following questions for each product line in the order that they appear below. In doing so, you will be creating scatter plots and the correlation measures for these factors. How do you interpret the scatter plots for the factors?*

---

| Scatter plot | Degree of scatter | Direction of scatter | Visually interpret linear association (-1, +1) |
|---|---|---|---|
| Factor A | Very narrow | Positive | 0.85 |
| Factor B | Narrow | Negative | −0.65 |
| Factor C | Broad | Positive | 0.38 |
| Factor D | -------- | | |
| Factor E | | -------- | |

| | Factor A | Factor B | Factor C | Degree and Direction of Scatter with B | Degree and Direction of Scatter with C |
|---|---|---|---|---|---|
| Factor A | XXXX | − 0.76 | 0.50 | | |
| Factor B | | XXXX | 0.26 | | |
| Factor C | | | XXXX | | |

**Step 2:** Creating Univariate and Multivariable Models for Product Lines (PEER Execute Stage)

Creating Three Exponential Smoothing (ESM) Scenarios for Product Line B, Region A

| ESM (A, A) | | ESM (A, M) | | ESM (At, A) | |
|---|---|---|---|---|---|
| *Summary Statistics* | | *Summary Statistics* | | *Summary Statistics* | |
| Log-Likelih | -378 | Log-Likelih | -380 | Log-Likelih | -378 |
| AIC | 763 | AIC | 765 | AIC | 765 |
| RMSE | 5021 | RMSE | 5172 | RMSE | 5039 |
| MAPE(%) | 29 | MAPE(%) | 30 | MAPE(%) | 29 |
| Sigma | 0.291 | Sigma | 0.295 | Sigma | 0.292 |
| | | | | | |
| *Smoothing parameters* | | *Smoothing parameters* | | *Smoothing parameter* | |
| alpha | 0.1 | alpha | 0.1 | alpha | 0.1 |
| beta | 0.1 | beta | 0.1 | beta | 0.1 |
| gamma | 0.1 | gamma | 0.1 | gamma | 0.1 |
| | | | | phi | 1 |
| *State parameters* | | *State parameters* | | *State parameters* | |
| Initial leve | 14853 | Initial leve | 16493 | Initial leve | 14941 |
| Initial gro | 130 | Initial gro | 212 | Initial gro | 144 |
| | | | | | |
| *Initial seasonals* | | *Initial seasonals* | | *Initial seasonals* | |
| ss(1) | 6829 | ss(1) | 1.36 | ss(1) | 7640 |
| ss(2) | 8221 | ss(2) | 1.46 | ss(2) | 8112 |
| ss(3) | 9866 | ss(3) | 1.54 | ss(3) | 9774 |
| ss(4) | -4438 | ss(4) | 0.75 | ss(4) | -4493 |
| ss(5) | -6761 | ss(5) | 0.60 | ss(5) | -6818 |
| ss(6) | -1344 | ss(6) | 0.92 | ss(6) | -1402 |
| ss(7) | -6885 | ss(7) | 0.62 | ss(7) | -6942 |
| ss(8) | -5255 | ss(8) | 0.73 | ss(8) | -5313 |
| ss(9) | -1928 | ss(9) | 0.93 | ss(9) | -1986 |
| ss(10) | -2644 | ss(10) | 0.89 | ss(10) | -2700 |
| ss(11) | -894 | ss(11) | 1.02 | ss(11) | -983 |
| ss(12) | 5232 | ss(12) | 1.20 | ss(12) | 5110 |

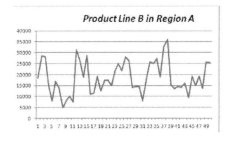

Product Line B in Region A

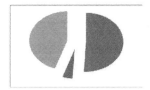

Reviewing a time plot, the exploratory STI_Classification and the Pegels diagram, we select three of the most appropriate exponential smoothing model profiles for GLOBL.

1. Three models (see ETS classification for State Space forecasting models:
   a. ETS (A, A)—Additive Trend, Additive Seasonality (Additive Holt-Winters)
   b. ETS (A, M)—Additive Trend, Multiplicative Seasonality (Multiplicative Holt-Winters)
   c. ETS ($A_t$, A)—Damped Trend, Additive Seasonality

4. Using the first 38 months of history to fit the model, we run forecasts for the remaining 12 months with prediction limits (95%). A 12-period centered moving average (12_CMAVG) through the history and forecasts shows trend-cycle behavior.
5. In order to compile background information, we summarize and interpret the model performance measures over the fit period.

**Notes for documentation:**
- Summary statistics are comparable—nothing to distinguish one model from another
- On the basis of the fit statistics, should ETS (A, A) be declared the "best" of the three? Would you think you can do better with another trend-seasonal model, like the ARIMA "airline" model?
- It does not appear that manipulating the parameters would lead to better forecasts
- February and March are peak season (about 50% above trend), May and July are lowest season (about 40% below trend), and November is a normal month (on trend)

**Notes for documentation: Product Line B, Region A series (50 monthly values: Seasonality = 51%, Trend Cycle = 4%, Unexplained = 45%).**

## Handling Exceptions and Forecast Error Analysis

6. Plot a correlogram of the residuals. Is there any suggestion of any nonstationarity in the residuals?

**Notes for documentation:** Correlogram looks like one for random numbers.

7. Use traditional, along with nonconventional, performance measures to evaluate forecasts for bias and accuracy over the 12-month holdout period.

8. Summarize performance measures and make a recommendation as to what model(s) should be retained for forecasting in the future. Give your rationale.

**Notes for documentation:** Generate waterfall chart showing ETS (A, A) model forecasts made by updating end-dates and shortening forecast horizons. (AA_11 means using historical data through period 39 and forecast the remaining 11 periods, AA_10 means using historical data through period 40 and forecast the remaining 10 periods in the holdout sample, etc.)

**Notes for documentation:** Forecasting model ETS (A, A) clearly over-forecasts the hold-out period. But how badly? By month, August (#44) and December (#48) around 100% over-forecast. The July forecast is the best, but four others are around 10% over-forecast. MPE overstates

| | Hold-out Actuals | AA_11 | AA-10 | ESM AA-09 | Model AA-08 | AA-07 | WaterFall Chart AA-06 | AA-05 | AA-04 | AA-03 | AA-02 | AA-01 |
|---|---|---|---|---|---|---|---|---|---|---|---|---|
| 39 | 15235 | | | | | | | | | | | |
| 40 | 13428 | 17816 | | | | | | | | | | |
| 41 | 14451 | 15681 | 15307 | | | | | | | | | |
| 42 | 14169 | 21079 | 20644 | 20590 | | | | | | | | |
| 43 | 16059 | 15719 | 15221 | 15153 | 14610 | | | | | | | |
| 44 | 9550 | 17799 | 17278 | 17195 | 16565 | 16698 | | | | | | |
| 45 | 19072 | 21399 | 20851 | 20766 | 20046 | 20197 | 19605 | | | | | |
| 46 | 14996 | 20862 | 20288 | 20201 | 19439 | 19609 | 18918 | 18885 | | | | |
| 47 | 19264 | 22889 | 22292 | 22202 | 21397 | 21578 | 20787 | 20745 | 20432 | | | |
| 48 | 13676 | 28869 | 28251 | 28160 | 27315 | 27508 | 26671 | 26620 | 26253 | 26164 | | |
| 49 | 25646 | 30590 | 29914 | 29811 | 28892 | 29100 | 28190 | 28134 | 27702 | 27593 | 26540 | |
| 50 | 25456 | 32552 | 31827 | 31715 | 30731 | 30954 | 29974 | 29913 | 29448 | 29321 | 28082 | 28022 |

the model bias, because of August and December (outlier) forecasts. Better to retain MdPE as well for comparisons. Should August and December actuals be reviewed (root-cause analysis) and adjusted before models run again to create forecasts for the following year?

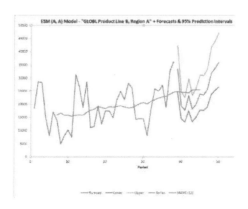

**Notes for documentation:** As for accuracy, MAPE and MdAPE for individual months give comparable results, in this case. However, the MAPE overstates model performance over holdout period, because of unusual August (#44) and December (#48) actuals. It is essential to retain MdAPE and not rely just on the MAPE. Options for adjustment – (1) Replace August (#44) and December (#48), by the one-period ahead forecast for that period or (2) replace with closest prediction limit. August (AA-07 forecast = 16698) and December (AA-01 forecast = 28022).

## Combining Forecasts from Most Useful Models

9.  With your best model (s), create forecasts for the 12 months following the last data period. Create a time plot of the full history, forecasts, and upper and lower prediction limits of your choice model for presentation to management.

**Notes for documentation:** There is some visual evidence from the prediction limits of the three models that the actuals for periods 51 through 68 are slightly more likely to be lower than higher than the forecast. In fact, the automatic model algorithm produced asymmetrical prediction limits, because the underlying model automatically found a multiplicative error assumption more valid than the conventional *additive error* formulation. (Note to IT: The multiplicative error version is generally not found in most if not all current commercial forecasting systems).

a.  If data adjustments are not justified, then the ETS (A, A) model produces the lower forecast below the "Average" forecast within the prediction limits. The "Average" forecast is based on combining by averaging the forecasts from the 3 ETS models (A, A), (A, M) and $(A_t, A)$, using outlier adjusted data values for periods 44 (August) and 48 (December).
b.  Assuming data adjusted for #44 and #48, the ETS (A, A) model produces the higher of the two forecasts with this model's prediction limits. A lower forecast is derived from the ETS (A, A) model using the original, unadjusted data.

## An Unconstrained Baseline Forecast for GLOBL Product Line B, Region A

We first create a predictive visualization chart of four ETS forecasts for Product Line B, Region A. Next, the Average Forecast is the average of the three outlier-adjusted ETS forecasts. The lower and upper prediction intervals are calculated from the average of the respective periods 51 through 68 may likely be higher than lower than the forecast lower and upper prediction intervals for the three outlier-adjusted ETS models. The limits are expressed as percentages below and above the

| Forecasts & 95% prediction intervals | | | |
|---|---|---|---|
| | | Average | |
| Period | Lower | Forecast | Upper |
| 51 | -25% | 25751 | 33% |
| 52 | -25% | 14791 | 33% |
| 53 | -26% | 13422 | 34% |
| 54 | -25% | 17280 | 34% |
| 55 | -27% | 13776 | 34% |
| 56 | -27% | 15467 | 33% |
| 57 | -26% | 18717 | 34% |
| 58 | -27% | 17182 | 34% |
| 59 | -28% | 19814 | 35% |
| 60 | -26% | 26012 | 34% |
| 61 | -27% | 26618 | 35% |
| 62 | -27% | 28027 | 35% |
| 63 | -29% | 25323 | 37% |
| 64 | -33% | 14464 | 38% |
| 65 | -35% | 13112 | 39% |
| 66 | -33% | 16941 | 38% |
| 67 | -37% | 13469 | 40% |
| 68 | -35% | 15145 | 40% |

Average Forecasts. Note that the prediction limits (1) widen for forecasts further into the future, and (2) indicate that the actuals for periods 51 through 68 may likely be higher than lower than the forecast

Consider that we have the data and that an analysis of each product has been created with time plots and scatter plots for factors A through E. Answer the following questions in the order that they appear. In doing so, you will be creating scatter plots and the association/correlation measures for these factors with each product.

> **QUESTION 8:** *Regression analysis. (See Chapters 10 and 11). Regression analysis determines whether one set of data (one or more factors or independent variables) has any relationship, or correlation, to another set of data (dependent variable). Can you make predictions once you create models for these relationships?*

I.  collect data for a period of time or multiple locations so you can perform a regression analysis. Predict future sales (dependent variable) based on the values specified for the key factors (independent variables) if the correlation between the key factors and sales are strong enough.

II.  What is your dependent variable and which factors will you be using for independent    variables? Build simple linear regression models for a product with one of its factors. Determine the equation and use the equation to project product demand for a particular value of the factor. Estimate a range of uncertainty.

**Example: Building a simple linear regression model for Product XYZ demand versus Factor A.** A regression with Product XYZ demand (dependent variable) against Opportunity Pipeline factor (independent variable) was run with the following results:

Regression output summary:

| | |
|---|---|
| Constant | -46.9 |
| Std error of $Y$ Estimate | 120.5 |
| $R^2$ | 0.79 |
| Number of observations | 34 |

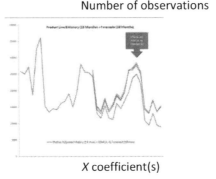

| | |
|---|---|
| $X$ coefficient(s) | 1.20 |

i.  Determine the equation.

*Answer*: The equation is **ProdXYZ demand = Constant + Xcoefficient * (Factor A) = – 46.9 + 1.20 (Factor A)**

ii.    Use the equation to project ProdXYZ Demand if Factor A = 110.
*Answer*: **ProdXYZ demand = - 46.9 + 1.20 *(110) = 673.1 = 673**

iii.    What is the estimated range on this projection?
*Answer*: Formula for calculating is:

$$\text{Projection } +/- 2 \text{ (Std error of } Y \text{ Estimate)}$$

$$\text{Range: } 673 - 2 \,(120.5) \text{ to } 673 + 2 \,(120.5) = [\textbf{432, 914}]$$

iv.    Build multiple linear regression models for each product with two of its factors. Determine the equation and use the equation to project product demand for a particular value of the factor. Estimate a range.

**Example: Building multiple linear regression models for Product XYZ demand versus Factor B and Factor C.**

Regression output summary:

| | |
|---|---|
| Constant | 3515.4 |
| Std error of $Y$ estimate | 195.0 |
| $R^2$ | 0.47 |
| Number of observations | 34 |
| $X$ coefficient(s) | 99.4 and 2899.5 |

i.    Determine the equation.
*Answer:* The equation is **ProdXYZ demand = Constant + $X_1$coefficient * (Factor B) + $X_2$coefficient * (Factor C) = 3515.4 + 99.4 (Factor B) – 2899.5 (Factor C)**

ii.    Use the equation to project ProdXYZ demand if Factor B = 1.4 and Factor C = 1.1.
*Answer*: **ProdXYZ demand = 3515.4 + 99.4 (1.40) – 2899.5 (1.23) = 465.2 = 465**

iii.    What is the estimated range on this projection?
*Answer*: Formula for calculating is:

$$\text{Projection } +/- 2 \text{ (Std error of } Y \text{ Estimate)}$$
$$\text{Range: } 465 - 2(195) \text{ to } 465 + 2(195) = [\textbf{75, 855}]$$

iv.    **Summarize the projections with ranges.** Complete the following table based on your results. (We will use these results in step 4 to reconcile ranges and recommend a final forecast.)

**Step 3**: Evaluating Model Performance Summaries **(PEER Evaluate Stage)**

| ES Model | MAPE | MAE | RMSE | Lower Limit | Projection | Upper Limit |
|---|---|---|---|---|---|---|
| Simple | 174 | 147 | 204 | 203 | 607 | 1011 |
| Linear Trend | 54 | 129 | 188 | 279 | 645 | 1015 |
| Damped Trend | 52 | 125 | 189 | 284 | 641 | 1021 |

---

**QUESTION 9:** *Summary of projections with ranges from exponential smoothing models. You are asked to recommend a projection and range from models for Product XYZ in a summary table.* The following results for exponential smoothing models based only on the historical data were determined for ProdXYZ. What is your recommended projection and range for each period in the forecast horizon? Give your reasons.

**QUESTION 10**: *Summarize the projections with ranges from regression models. The following results with the multi-variable regression models were found for ProdXYZ. What are the missing values?*

---

| Projections· and· Range:·· Product·XYZ·versus¤ | Lower·Limit·of·Range¤ | Projection¤ | Upper·Limit·of·Range¤ |
|---|---|---|---|
| Factor·¤ | ¤ | ¤ | ¶ ¶ ¤ |
| Factor¶ ¶ Projections· and· Range:·· Product·XYZ·versus¤ | ¶ ¶ Lower·Limit·of·Range¤ | ¶ ¶ Projection¤ | ¶ ¶ Upper·Limit·of·Range¤ |
| Factor·A¤ | Jan.:·432¶ Feb.:¶ Mar.:¤ | 673¤ | 914¤ |
| Factor·B·¤ | Jan.:·378¶ Feb.:¶ Mar.:¤ | 762¤ | 1146¤ |
| Factor·C·¤ | Jan.:·0¶ Feb.:¶ Mar.:¤ | 280¤ | 778¤ |
| Factor·D·¤ | Jan.:··105¶ Feb.:¶ Mar.:¤ | 491¤ | 1146¤ |
| Factor·B·and·Factor·C¤ | Jan.:·75¶ Feb.:¶ | 465¤ | 855¤ |

**Step 4**: Reconciling Model Projections with Informed Judgment (PEER Reconcile Stage)

| Model Projections and Range: XYZ versus | Lower Limit of Range | Projection | Upper Limit Range |
|---|---|---|---|
| Factor A | Jan.: 432<br>Feb.:<br>Mar.: | 673 | 914 |
| Factor B | Jan.: 378<br>Feb.:<br>Mar.: | 762 | 1146 |
| Factor C | Jan.: 0<br>Feb.:<br>Mar.: | 280 | 778 |
| Factor D | Jan.: 105<br>Feb.:<br>Mar.: | 491 | 877 |
| Factor B and Factor C | Jan.: 75<br>Feb.:<br>Mar.: | 465 | 855 |

| Judgment Factors | Projection Rationale | Range Assumptions |
|---|---|---|
| | | |
| | | |
| | | |
| | | |
| Demand Forecaster<br>Name ------------------<br>Date ----------- | Forecast Number | Range |
| <br><br>-----------------------<br>Forecaster Signature | Jan.:<br>Feb.:<br>Mar.: | {     ,     }<br>{     ,     }<br>{     ,     } |

QUESTION 11: What are your "Final Forecast Numbers?" Fill in the following table combining the results of the two major modeling approaches performed for this forecast: univariate exponential smoothing models based exclusively on the historical information in ProdXYZ and multivariable regression models based on the inclusion of factor information. Apply informed judgment to arrive at recommended forecast numbers and ranges.

## Takeaways

> This chapter dealt with determining the reliability of model forecasts by using rolling forecast simulations. The forecast simulations provide an understanding of how well the models would have predicted past demand history. In the case of regression models, it assumes that you can obtain accurate forecasts of the independent variables.

> Demand planners and forecast practitioners can increase the likelihood that the best forecast has been developed by using a forecast **checklist** to validate that a general forecasting process is practical and comprehensive.

> background of the audience must also be taken into account in deciding on the final presentation format.

# 13

# Creating a Database Framework for Agile Forecasting and Performance Management

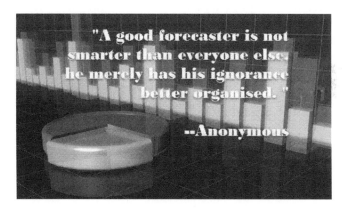

"A good forecaster is not smarter than everyone else; he merely has his ignorance better organised."

--Anonymous

This chapter describes a decision support framework for agile forecasting and planning in a data driven supply chain. We discuss (1) the role of the demand management process (2) why a cloud-based, database framework for demand forecasting is essential to its success, (3) how to identify the essential components of a forecast decision support platform (FDSP), and (4) when and how automatic forecasting should be used.

## Why Demand Managers Need to Manage a Demand Forecasting Process That is Independent of Plans and Targets

Successful demand management organizations are those that have discovered how to apply effective data management practices with **agile forecasting** and planning processes to what is essentially a nontraditional supply chain discipline (Figure 13.1, *right flowchart*). In the demand forecasting discipline, we do not have the power to *change* future demand, only to become **agile** by quickly and skillfully advising the sales target or demand plan to align it better with expected future demand.

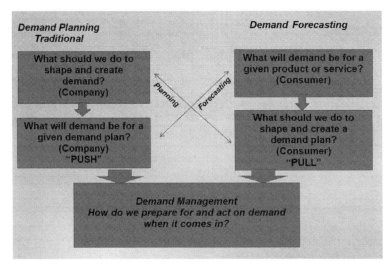

Figure 13.1 Traditional SC (Sell What You Can Make) versus consumer data-driven SC (Make What You Can Sell) (*left flowchart source*: Larry Lapide (MIT)) Also shown as Figure. 1.4 (Chapter 1).

Although the analogy of a chain is useful in visualizing the traditional "Sell What You Can Make" process, it is far too simplistic to describe what really happens with **demand forecasting**. Within the supplier/manufacturer, the supply chain includes forecasts of multiple sources of supply at every stage. In the distribution channel, multiple centers can supply multiple factories and provide service to multiple retail outlets.

In a modern consumer data-driven supply chain (Figure 13.2), which evolved over decades, consumer-demand information also flows back in the opposite direction, so that all operations have complete visibility to the whole supply and demand process).

Instead of being driven or supplied by the manufacturer, consumers are the drivers of demand, demanding cheaper, faster and higher quality products and services. A firm's success is a combination of a balanced supply chain, a sound infrastructure, and a focus on consumers.

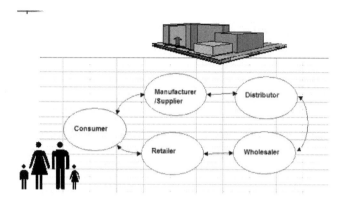

Figure 13.2 A consumer data- driven supply chain. (*Source*: L. Lapide, MIT, 2006)

The traditional supply chain model (Figure 13.3) includes a number of highly efficient processes for sourcing/suppliers (production, scheduling, and supply sourcing), distribution (channel management, transportation, and warehouse operations), and customer interface/point-of-sale (demand management, order management, inventory management, and store operations).

The manufacturing/distribution/retail pipeline starts with raw materials and purchased parts required by the manufacturing plant. At the manufacturing level, the fabricated components are added, subassemblies, and assemblies are used to produce the finished-goods inventory. At the distribution level, we generally have finished goods.

*A traditional supply chain is any sequential set of business operations leading from raw material through conversion processes, storage, distribution, and delivery to an end customer. In the integrated consumer data- supply chain, demand management's responsibility assures that demand information flows in the reverse direction as well.*

Demand planning systems have a similar underlying logic, but different factors/parameters affect the inventory plan at each point in this pipeline:

- **Manufacturing Resource Planning** (MRP) plans the raw materials, purchased parts, and components.

- **Master Production Scheduling (MPS)** plans the finished goods.
- **Distribution Resource Planning (DRP)** plans the finished goods at the distribution centers.

### Sell What You Can Make

• Assume predictable, continuous demand

• Efficient process

• No external drivers of demand

### Make What You Can Sell

• Assume unpredictable, discontinuous demand

• Adaptive process

• Both internal and external drivers of demand

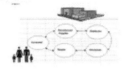

Figure 13.3 Traditional vs a consumer data-driven supply chains: "Sell What You Can Make." Versus "Make What You Can Sell" (*Source*: Figure 13.1)

## Data-Driven Demand Management Initiatives

There are a number of initiatives in the supply chain used to describe material flow from suppliers to the manufacturer through the distribution channel to the consumer. On the other hand, demand information flows in the reverse direction, from consumers to suppliers. **Quick Response** (QR), **Efficient Consumer Response** (ECR), and **Vendor Managed Inventory** (VMI) are all terms used in the trade for strategies for making manufacturers responsible for keeping the retailer in stock.

These acronyms represent industry initiatives to facilitate the flow of goods information in a timely manner. By implementing these management strategies, companies have reduced costs, increased sales, gained competitive advantage, and taken market share away from laggards.

The material flowing through a supply chain can be viewed from any one of three perspectives: the product view (SKUs), the customer view, the distribution view, or the supplier/manufacturer sourcing view. The product view defines the individual SKU, its contents including documentation and accessories, and its packaging and labeling. The customer view defines how the end customer (e.g., retailers and e-consumers) uses product descriptions, product numbers (SKUs), and product options to uniquely identify a complete product configuration. The supplier manufacturer view, like an engineering parts list, tends to consider a product or assembly to be complete without regard for the packaging documentation, software, or accessories that will make it a SKU. A complete customer configuration may require a shipment of many different SKUs

Figure 13.4 shows how a high-tech company looked at its business and realized how an overuse of demand hierarchies can add ineffective complexity to the demand forecasting process.

> *Material flow is from suppliers to the manufacturer through the distribution channel to the consumer. Demand information flow is in the reverse direction, from the consumer to the suppliers.*

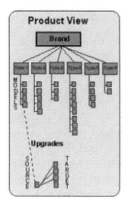 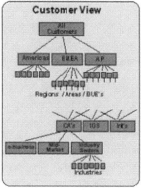 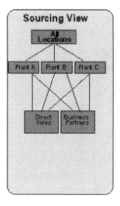

"They need the **SHIP** forecast for "Type 1" *upgrades* to "Type 2" for **EMEA** Manufacturing *Industry* Customers - sold through **Business Partners?**"

Figure 13.4 A product, customer, and sourcing view of the supply chain.

## Demand-Driven Information Flows

Manufacturing companies generally use forecasting systems to help synchronize production schedules and finished-goods inventory with actual customer/consumer sales. Therefore, they are more likely to feed forecast information to the **Materials Requirements Planning** (MRP) module of an **Enterprise Resource Planning** (ERP) system or even to an **Advanced Planning System** (APS). In addition, demand forecast data have become part of the **Sales and Operations Planning** (S&OP) process, which brings people from different functional areas together to collaborate on a "final forecast" that drives the activities of the entire enterprise.

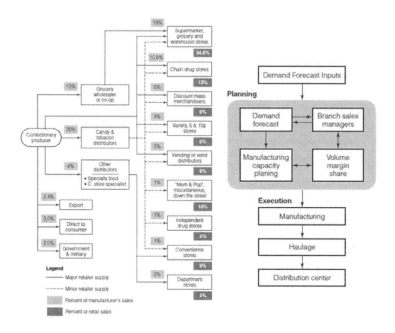

Figure 13.5 (*left*) A comprehensive view of a packaged goods producer: U.S. confectionary, shown previously in Chapter 1 (Figure 1.8).

Figure 13.6 (*right*) Demand forecasting drives crucial links in the supply chain. (*Source*: L. Lapide, MIT, 2006)

In Figure 13.5, the distinction between **customer** (light boxes) and **consumer** (dark boxes) is important in order to depict a comprehensive view of a supply chain for a packaged goods producer. The manufacturer produces a product for export, direct sales to consumers, the government, and the military; the product is sold to an extensive network of retailers. A grocery wholesaler or co-op retailer might distribute the product to supermarkets, grocery, and warehouse stores. Other distributors sell the product to chain drug stores, discount mass merchandisers, and variety stores.

> *The sales and operations planning (S&OP) process brings people from different functional areas in the organization together to collaborate on a single 'final forecast' and demand plan.*

Depending on the industry and business model, companies use forecasting systems in a variety of ways. For instance, distribution-oriented companies are likely to use systems to help organize the replenishment and flow of goods into distribution centers (Figure 13.6). These companies are also likely to send the output of forecasting systems to transportation management or other order-fulfillment systems.

Each industry has its own production and distribution needs. Information systems designed to manage the supply chain are focused on vertical markets in process manufacturing or discrete/repetitive/to-order manufacturing. Process manufacturers, which are predominantly batch-processing operations, include companies in the energy/petrochemical, chemical, and pharmaceutical industries. Electronics, fabricated metals, and automotive supplies are examples of discrete manufacturing markets.

In today's global market place, companies must achieve both in-stock levels and high *inventory turns*. In addition to competitive pressures, many companies have found it necessary to share demand information and forecasts with their business partners. Retailers, in particular, frequently share forecasting information with their supply chain partners.

Demand managers have also recognized the importance of data-based demand forecasting and top-down planning along with joint collaborations in forecasting with suppliers and customers. Because of the high volume of items involved and the uncertain nature in variability (see Chapter 5), data-driven analytics (see Chapter 2) and statistical forecasting techniques (see Chapters 3, 8, 9, and 10) are increasingly being adopted by demand planners and managers.

> *Demand management is the process of managing all independent demands for a company's product line and effectively communicating these demands to the master planner and top management production function.*

## Creating Planning Hierarchies for Demand Forecasting

Demand managers frequently discuss dependent and **independent demand** forecasts. Independent (unconstrained, unbiased) demand, which must be forecasted, comes from the customer/consumer and includes the demand for finished goods as well as service parts. In contrast, **dependent demand** applies to raw materials and other components that are used in production. The dependent demand for items need not be forecasted; it is calculated from the schedules of the item required for production and distribution.

At its core, demand planners establish a set of processes that produce plans or sets of time-phased numbers (e.g., forecasted orders) representing the best estimate of what demand is expected at a given time. For instance, a forecast for an item at a distribution center shows the expected demand over time, by the week or by the month, going forward. An order needs to be placed with the manufacturer or supplier against these requirements so that the requested item can arrive at the distribution center in time for shipment to the retailer or consumer. The timing of these orders is a function of the lead times of the items and the safety stock that assures adequate supply.

## What Are Planning Hierarchies?

Most planning functions in an organization are performed in time hierarchies, with strategic and rolling budget planning done once a year or more frequently and tactical planning done quarterly, monthly, weekly, daily, or hourly. Each of these planning horizons requires forecasts at different levels of product and location/customer aggregations.

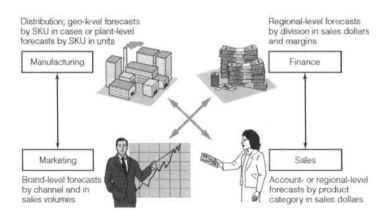

Figure 13.7 Demand forecasting and the cross-functional business process.

Through the functional organizations (Figure 13.7), we can view **dimensions of demand** from the perspective of marketing (brand-level forecasts by channel and sales currency and margins), sales (account- or regional-level forecasts by product category in sales currency), operations (distribution territory-level forecasts by SKU in cases or plant-level forecasts by SKU in units; incidentally, a SKU is the lowest level in which we might categorize a product, such as a bar code or product code that we might see on a box or the unit itself), and finance (regional-level forecasts by division in sales currency and margins).

*The level of planning being supported by the demand forecasting process impacts the data quality requirements and forecasting approaches needed.*

414

Each functional user group sets its own requirements. For example, market planners may want to review the demand forecast at a brand level in sales and margin rather than at the item level. Similarly, sales planners prefer reviewing the demand forecast in currency by region or customer account. To support these related requirements, forecasting approaches may need to be developed for multiple levels and the multiple forecasts reconciled.

Moreover, some functions need to view the demand forecast at the lowest level in a hierarchy, whereas others need to see it at higher levels. However, not all of these functions can necessarily be placed in the same hierarchy. These different types of planning requirements suggest the key database concepts that underlie a relational database system—*aggregation, allocation* and *data integrity*.

Because these requirements by the functional groups can occur at different levels, demand forecasters need to assure for quality data and effective and efficient forecasting methodologies to support a professional demand forecasting process.

All this is reflected in an operational demand plan, which assures that the right amount of the right product gets shipped to the right customer or location in the right time (and, of course, at the right price)—a bit of jargon, but nevertheless important to remember, because it provides the insight for the appropriate data framework requirements.

The differing functional views of a demand forecast are important for reaching consensus. The sales and operations planning function must first review the demand forecasts and then approve or modify them based on their view of the business: integrating sales, marketing, operations, and financial plans into a single demand plan; constantly balancing supply and demand; using company resources effectively throughout the enterprise; and making the results visible in inventory investment, product availability, and customer service.

## Operating Lead Times

Lead time influences inventory at different levels—the time it takes to get raw material, to manufacture, to ship product, and to process data all influence cumulative inventory and lead times. Although reducing cycle time is a major objective of **Supply Chain Management** (SCM), the variation in cycle times experienced by manufacturers and retailers can be quite substantial.

Typical cycle-time variations for product development can be between 5 days and 15 weeks, for production 5 days to 6 weeks, for inbound transportation from supplier to distribution center 1 day to 1.5 weeks, and for outbound transportation from distribution center to final destination 2 days to 1.5 weeks. Accurate forecasts are essential to the success of SCM in order to yield shorter lead times and, hence, higher turns and lower costs.

> *The amount of time it takes for demand information and goods to flow through a supply chain pipeline is known as cycle time; it is also called lead time.*

The safety stock for that same SKU is a plan for that component of inventory each week into the future. A replenishment plan for the same SKU shows the quantity of product arriving weekly at distribution center locations. A shipment plan for the same SKU shows the quantity of product that should be shipped to distribution center locations weekly.

# Distribution Resource Planning (DRP)—A Time-Phased Planned Order Forecast

Distribution planning managers face considerable complexities in managing inventory at various distribution points. Variables such as changing customer demand, transportation time, and shifting production schedules make it difficult to ensure correct inventory levels at the proper locations, at the proper time. DRP systems plan and manage the many variables that cause distribution problems.

A DRP system uses demand forecasts of independent demand—the demand of the consumer—instead of the dependent demand of the distribution center (DC) on the supplier/manufacturer. DRP starts with a forecast of consumer demand and calculates how long it will take to manufacture and move products through a distribution network to the consumer/customer.

> *DRP is part of the demand management function that creates long-term schedules designed to meet consumer/customer needs without holding excess inventory demand*

| | Period 1 | Period 2 | Period 3 | Period 4 | Period 5 | Period 6 | Period 7 |
|---|---|---|---|---|---|---|---|
| orecast | 100 | 100 | 100 | 100 | 100 | 100 | 100 |
| eceipts | | 200 | 100 | 100 | 100 | 100 | 100 |
| Order quantity | 200 | 100 | 100 | 100 | 100 | 100 | 100 |
| Inventory | 0 | 100 | 100 | 100 | 100 | 100 | 100 |
| Lead time | 1 period | | | | | | |
| Safety stock | 1 period | | | | | | |
| On-hand | 100 | | | | | | |

Figure 13.8 A basic DRP calculation.

Figure 13.8 shows a typical but simplified DRP allocation for a single product, in which the requirements needed are tied to the order quantity in a one-for-one relationship (i.e., need one, get one).

The forecasts are assumed to be 100 units per period (typically a month or a week). With an on-hand inventory of 100 units, the ending inventory in period 1 is 0, which is also the beginning inventory for period 2. In order to keep a one-period supply of safety stock, we need to order 200 units in period 1, which will be received in period 2 (because lead time = 1). This same logic is used for the future periods.

| | Period 1 | Period 2 | Period 3 | Period 4 | Period 5 | Period 6 | Period |
|---|---|---|---|---|---|---|---|
| orecast | 100 | 100 | 100 | 100 | 100 | 100 | 100 |
| eceipts | | 200 | | 200 | | 200 | |
| Irder quantity | 200 | | 200 | | 200 | | 200 |
| nventory | 0 | 100 | 0 | 100 | 0 | 100 | 0 |
| ead time | 1 period | | | | | | |
| afety Stock | 1 period | | | | | | |
| )n-hand | 100 | | | | | | |
| Minimum | 200 | | | | | | |

Figure 13.9 A basic DRP calculation with minimum order quantity of 200 units.

Figure 13.9 shows a DRP allocation with the added requirement that order quantity must be based on a minimum requirement (the lowest quantity that must be ordered). If the requirement is only one unit, the order must be 200 because the minimum is set to 200.

| | Period 1 | Period 2 | Period 3 | Period 4 | Period 5 | Period 6 | Period 7 |
|---|---|---|---|---|---|---|---|
| Forecast | 10 | 20 | 32 | 47 | 51 | 68 | 73 |
| Receipts | | 20 | 35 | 45 | 50 | 70 | 75 |
| Order quantity | 20 | 35 | 45 | 50 | 70 | 75 | |
| Inventory | 5 | 0 | 3 | 2 | 1 | 2 | 2 |
| Lead time | 1 period | | | | | | |
| On-hand | 15 | | | | | | |
| Minimum | 20 | | | | | | |
| Multiple | 5 | | | | | | |

Figure 13.10 A basic DRP calculation with minimum order quantity of 200 and multiples of five units.

Figure 13.10 shows a DRP allocation in which the requirements are tied to the order quantity based on a minimum requirement and multiple (quantities above and beyond the minimum amount). For example, if the total need is 22, the minimum is 20, and the multiple is 5, then the total order should be 25.

A manufacturing and distribution schedule, usually covering several weeks or months, is created to meet that order forecast. For example, a manufacturer of service parts may ship parts to several DCs that service dealers worldwide. If each DC tracks its own inventory and places orders independently, it will create a demand on the supplier/manufacturer that varies unpredictably.

By using DRP, the supplier/manufacturer obtains a greater visibility of upcoming orders. With accurate information about demand and inventory in each area, the DRP system can calculate a long-term plan for when each part should be produced and in what quantity, thus ensuring that each DC has the product it needs.

Benefits from a DRP system include reduced transportation costs; higher customer-service levels; fewer stock outs; improved communication among sales, distribution, and production; and having the right product at the right place at the right time.

## How to Create a Time-Phased Replenishment Plan Under Forecast Uncertainty

The basic function of DRP is to create a recommended order that is sent to manufacturing plants in order to plan production. Figure 13.11 shows the spreadsheet layout involved in forecasting the **Planned Orders** and **Months' Supply**. Here a number of inventory factors must be taken into account, such as on-hand, on-order, and backordered quantities.

| Min/Mult Example | May-01 | Jun-01 | Jly-01 | Aug-01 | Sep-01 | Oct-01 | Nov-01 | Dec-01 | Jan-02 | Feb-02 | Mar-02 | Apr-02 | May-02 | Jun-02 |
|---|---|---|---|---|---|---|---|---|---|---|---|---|---|---|
| Total Forecast | 1120 | 1689 | 1958 | 2210 | 3214 | 3225 | 3345 | 3578 | 3845 | 3895 | 3956 | 4012 | 4123 | 4231 |
| Prior Forecast | 1500 | | | | | | | | | | | | | |
| Other Forecast | | | | | | | | | | | | | | |
| Gross Requirements | 3020 | 1689 | 1958 | 2210 | 3214 | 3225 | 3345 | 3578 | 3845 | 3895 | 3956 | 4012 | 4123 | 4231 |
| Firm Planned Orders | | | | | | | | | | | | | | |
| Scheduled Receipts | | | | | | | | | | | | | | |
| Planned Receipts | | 5500 | 3200 | 3250 | 3358 | 3550 | 3650 | 3900 | 3950 | 4000 | 4150 | | | |
| Planned Orders | 5500 | 3250 | 3250 | 3550 | 3850 | 3900 | 3950 | 4000 | 4150 | 4250 | | | | |
| Projected Inventory | 380 | 4191 | 5433 | 6473 | 6609 | 6934 | 7439 | 7761 | 7886 | 7971 | 8165 | | | |
| On Hand | 2000 | | | | | | | | | | | | | |
| Months Coverage | 2 | | | | | | | | | | | | | |
| Lead Time | 1 month | | | | | | | | | | | | | |
| On Order | 1400 | | | | | | | | | | | | | |
| Minimum | 2000 | | | | | | | | | | | | | |
| Multiple | 50 | | | | | | | | | | | | | |

Figure 13.11 A basic DRP calculation with a minimum order quantity of 2000 and multiples of 50 units.

In addition, if you need to include the *uncertainty in the baseline forecast*, you can do that by plugging in the desired quantile of the statistical baseline forecast distribution, (using ETS State Space Forecasting algorithms, for example) into the Total Forecast line and recalculating the DRP calculation. You will end up with an estimate of the uncertainty in the Firm Planned Orders.

**Basic Distribution Resource Planning**. The basic DRP calculation starts with a demand forecast. The demand forecast (labeled "Total Forecast" in Figure 13.11) is the total forecast of independent demand, namely the (unbiased) statistical baseline forecast plus judgmental overrides made by the planners and management. Other forecasts may need to be included, such as a forecast from a division or region that is not part of the main forecasting system. Also samples, not for sale, are included here. These are handled in the lines below the final forecast.

In this spreadsheet, the **Gross Requirements** are the sum of the forecast lines. The gross requirements are determined for any practical number of periods into the future, with 12 to 18 months being typical.

Next, we determine **Planned Receipts**. At time T = 2 (June 01, in this case), the gross requirements over a lead-time of one period are 1689 and the ending Projected Inventory at T = 1 (May 01) is 380. The gross requirements over safety time (months coverage) starting at lead-time-period ahead are 4168 units (= 1958 + 2210). The Planned Receipts are calculated as follows:

> **Planned receipts = Gross requirements summed over lead times – Projected inventory + Gross requirements summed over safety times starting at lead-time-period ahead**

For example, the planned receipts for period T = 2 are (1689 - 380) + (1958 + 2210) = 5477. Next, the Planned Orders are offset one month back, determined by the lead time, so that the orders can be received as planned. Scheduled Receipts are already committed. The firm Planned Orders are the overridable receipts.

The projected (ending) inventory for this period is determined thus:

> **Projected inventory = Previous period ending inventory + Planned receipts – Gross requirements**

The projected inventory at the end of period T = 2 (Jun 01) is 4168 (= 380 + 5477 – 1689). Once the projected inventory has been determined, a calculation of Months Supply can be made as a measure of safety stock.

At the next period, the process repeats itself. Now, for T = 3 (Jun 01), the planned receipts are (1958 – 4168) + (2210 + 3314) = 3214. These are the planned orders offset to T = 2. The ending inventory is 5424 (= 4168+ 3214 – 1958).

For the very first period, things are a little different. The initial projected inventory is 380 (= 2000 + 1400 – 3020):

> **Projected inventory (initial period) = On-hand + On-order – Gross requirements**

**Minimum and Multiples**. When we take minimum quantities and multiples into account, the DRP calculation needs to be augmented. In this example (Figure 13.11), a minimum order is 2000 and additional orders are placed in multiples of 50. At T = 2 (Jun 01), the planned receipts previously calculated (= 5477) become 5500 because of the minimum and multiple conditions. The projected inventory now includes 23 additional units and becomes 4191 (= 4168 + 23). The remaining calculations remain the same, taking the minimum order quantity and multiples in consideration.

To fully balance the supply chain, an increased awareness and exchange of information must be established between the demand creation side of sales and marketing and the supply side of manufacturing and distribution. This should include both short-term communications about promotional programs that will affect demand and long-term communication for capacity planning. It is essential to keep the goal of balancing supply with demand in mind and to communicate it across all functional groups at the outset of each new sales initiative.

## *A Database Framework for Agility in Forecast Decision Support Applications*

One of the biggest paybacks of an effective demand management process is the creation of a *centralized* demand forecasting and decision support platform (**FDSP**) , in which sales, marketing, operations, and financial planners can then cooperatively view their own forecasts on their own terms with the knowledge that these forecasts will be centrally reconciled and synchronized to collaborating stakeholder organizations. This sharing of "one number" forecasts with other organizations, and more possibly, in the future, with business partners, results in a streamlined, agile demand forecasting process, allowing for reduced costs and increased sales and profits for the business.

Typically, in many firms across most industries there is a lack of **integrated business planning** (IBP) at the operational planning and business execution levels. Such systems have difficulty meeting the system requirements for demand forecasting, because the discipline requires a rather unique software architecture. Unexpected demands, which must be met at any location, wreak havoc on operations. At the higher levels of planning, such as strategic planning levels, demand forecasters have more options and more time to effect change. At the operational levels, however, forecasters are more strapped for quality data, modeling options, and effective software systems.

ERP systems support *transaction-based* processes for human resources, budgeting, and operations. A demand forecasting system, on the other hand, is better served by *databased-driven decision support* on a software environment that requires internal and external forecast data, can run complex analytical algorithms, and can quickly and easily analyze unstructured decisions so that managers can make business decisions more easily.

### The Need for Agile Demand Forecasting

The Internet is the perfect means for transforming conventional industry models because it constitutes an infrastructure that transcends traditional boundaries. In place of conventional planning systems based on sequential relationships, in which orders are placed with a supplier, inventory is consumed, and another order is placed, Web-enabled planning systems can now provide a near-instantaneous communications link among trading partners. The new ways to take account of customer and consumer preferences promote new views of point-of-sale replenishment solutions, so today we can communicate changing needs with greater agility to more entities.

Consumer orders may be placed directly with the supplier online, a new aspect of demand that must be taken into account when developing agile demand forecasting solutions. Suppliers can now reside in the center of a web of customers—all communicating needs and information via the Internet.

> *The single forecast of consumer/customer demand, at the item-location level, provides the unifying perspective from which to integrate all forecasting activities in the supply chain.*

Achieving the benefits of a one-number forecast (Chapter 12) requires the integration of clean data, quantifiable information, and predictive analytics across the whole business enterprise. The analytical database system to support these activities is the **Forecast Decision Support Platform** (FDSP). Demand forecasters need to build *database flexibility* **and** *agility* into their job functions, something that spreadsheet programs lack. The implementation of planning systems integrates the different levels of planning across the enterprise. FDSP is a flexible demand information and business intelligence processing environment in synch with the operational data processing environments used in a conventional ERP context.

> *Demand forecasting is performed at different levels of detail incorporating dimensions of period, place and product.*

## Dimensions of Demand

Effective demand planning and management requires that demand forecasters incorporate data into their forecasts, whatever their aggregation, to adequately support their clients and the sales, marketing, and financial and operations planners in the firm.

Before, in Figure 13.4, we show how a high-tech company looked at its business and realized how an overuse of demand hierarchies can add complexity to the demand forecasting process. Hence, demand forecasting is done at different levels of detail, involving:

- **Period** (time) *granularity* (annually, quarterly, monthly, weekly, daily, shifts, or hours)
- **Place** (geographical/customer/location) *segments* (global, national, market zone, channel, sales regions, warehouses, plants, zip codes, stores, and customers)
- **Product** (SKU) *hierarchy* (category, brand, product flavors, sizes, or special packs)

# A Database-Driven Forecast Decision Support Approach

In an integrated demand management system, projected demand plans are visible in a common database accessed by those along the supply chain. The source of the corporate (internal) data is a legacy database residing on a secure corporate server that can be accessed by its users via the cloud or through a network server. This enables the firm to guarantee the integrity and accuracy of the essential input information.

To collaborate with forecast users outside the firm, the forecasting system needs to be able to communicate with vendors' planning systems through an extranet or internet connection. In addition, when external information on economic, demographic, regulatory and competitive factors is required, demand forecasters can access many of these data sources through a dashboard.

> *The demand forecasting system needed to support a supply chain has a number of components for linking to data sources.*

Once quality data sources are in place, a demand forecaster can interact with the data through a presentation component (interface) of the forecasting system. The database management part of the system allows for flexible data input, data conversions, data cleaning and adjustment, prices, graphs, note pad, scheduled receipts, and on-hand inventory, data displays (year-to-date, percentages of annual totals), and communication.

Forecast information needs to be distributed to forecast users through a data-reporting component. This provides output in terms of standard reports, flexible user-defined reports, special studies, data export to SCM and ERP systems, and electronic messaging linkages with customers and suppliers.

**Period Granularity**. Depending on the forecasting environment, a forecasting system needs to be able to support multiple calendars. For typical SCM applications, the weekly and monthly period granularity (*time buckets*) are most frequently used for forecasting. Because weeks do not roll up neatly into months, there are different weekly patterns in use. For example, a 4-4-5 pattern means that the first month of a quarter is made up 4 weeks, the next month is 4 weeks, and the last month is 5 weeks. There are also firms that operate on a 13-period year.

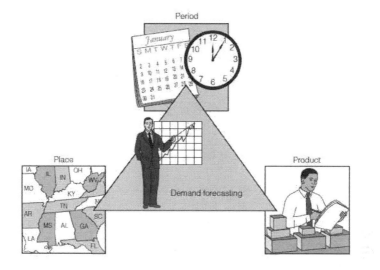

Figure 13.12 A multilevel, *relational* database forecasting decision support framework necessary for period (time), place (customer-location) and product (SKU). Forecasting.

The forecast dimensions of period, product, and place can be represented by a pyramid (Figure 13.12), in which each face depicts a separate hierarchy in a relational database (Figure 13.13).

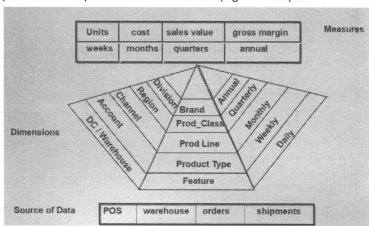

Figure 13.13 A three-tiered pyramid (relational database) structure for period (time) granularity, customer-location (place) segmentation and product (SKU) hierarchy.

Quarterly and yearly figures do not need to be stored because they accumulate naturally from months and can be readily rolled up in a database. In the energy utility industry, for example, a calendar is disaggregated even further into days, hours, and 30-minute time buckets.

In terms of period granularities,

- **forecast cycle** describes *how often* we should forecast. For many companies this is a monthly process, but with the higher service levels required to satisfy customers these days, it is not unusual to see a forecast cycle every week.
- **forecast horizon** tells *how far out* we should forecast. Many companies use a 12 to 18 month rolling forecast horizon. Today, with e-business, companies are shortening the horizon to 1 to 3 months to ensure that their businesses can respond to the increased volatility driven by new market dynamics.

The period granularity tells *how detailed* we should make the forecast. Commonly used quarterly granularity often does not provide the level of detail needed to address customer-service level requirements, efficient supply planning, or the need of marketing to respond to critical issues. Thus, demand and supply forecasting may need to implement a weekly forecast granularity for forecasts within critical **manufacturing lead times**.

**Place Segmentation.** Location/customer-specific information starts

with a designation of a lowest level location code. Typically, this is a customer account code that other segments can be mapped into. Additional fields might include description, discount rates, codes to map customer/locations into regions, channels, warehouses, and field sales accounts.

In addition, there may be conversions of the units of demand to sales revenue, profit margin, costs, pallets, cases, shift hours, and so on.

**Product Hierarchy.** To support a demand planning function, the FDSP

needs to maintain a variety of product-specific detail. The lowest level item identification is typically the Stock Keeping Unit (SKU). For each SKU, the system needs to maintain fields on unit price, unit costs (labor, material, etc., so as to be able to calculate margins), unit shipments (carton and pallet quantity, unit weight, and unit cube), lead time, and other attributes (description, promotion cut-in and cut-out dates, and summary category identifiers).

> *An agile forecast decision support platform (FDSP) is a cloud-based computing environment that supports the demand forecasting and sales & operations planning processes.*

## Dealing with Cross-Functional Forecast Data Requirements

The multilevel forecasting database requires that demand be collected, cleaned and stored at the **lowest** level of product and location so that accurate summaries can be obtained rapidly for product lines and families by customer locations and segments. For example, if a giant retailer has 5,000 stores and 100,000 items, and if a typical store carries a full line of items, the demand forecaster can potentially expect 500,000,000 lowest level records. In contrast, an online store carrying 35,000 items in one of six distribution centers can expect 210,000 lowest level records to manage and forecast.

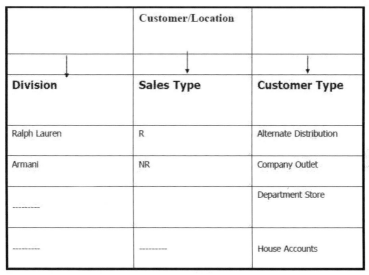

| | Customer/Location | |
|---|---|---|
| **Division** | **Sales Type** | **Customer Type** |
| Ralph Lauren | R | Alternate Distribution |
| Armani | NR | Company Outlet |
| ---------- | | Department Store |
| ---------- | ---------- | House Accounts |

Figure 13.14 Illustrative customer-location segmentation database table organized by division, sales type, and customer type.

> *The demand forecasting system needed to support a demand planning and management function has a number of components for linking to data sources, most efficiently and preferably in a relational database structure. A hierarchical structure may lead to expensive maintenance for companies with many new product introductions and product phase-outs.*

## Specifying Customer/Location Segments and Product Hierarchies

Using a cosmetic product manufacturer/distributor as an illustrative example, Figure 13.14 shows the summary levels for customer/locations as columns and the associated labels as rows in a database table (spreadsheet layout). For example, two sales type summaries are shown: R (Revenue) and NR (Nonrevenue). The other columns can have as many rows as there are summaries needed to specify the business operation. In practice, it is advisable to make sure the summary categories (columns) cover all the forecast reporting needs of the end user.

Likewise, in the initial specification of the relational database, demand forecasters need to obtain the user requirements for product summary categories (columns) and category labels (rows), as depicted in Figure 13.15. For this illustrative FDSP, seven product summary categories are needed to satisfy the end user requirements. Each summary category can have as many label rows as needed. Here, **All_ Product** represents the Summary category for **ALL** SKUs by location category or **Sales Plan** totals by location category. In this specification 43 **Brand** names and 34 **Family** names are available in the FDSP.

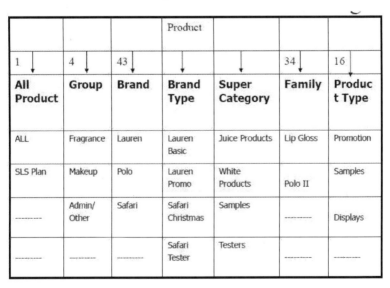

| | | | Product | | | |
|---|---|---|---|---|---|---|
| 1 | 4 | 43 | | | 34 | 16 |
| **All Product** | **Group** | **Brand** | **Brand Type** | **Super Category** | **Family** | **Product Type** |
| ALL | Fragrance | Lauren | Lauren Basic | Juice Products | Lip Gloss | Promotion |
| SLS Plan | Makeup | Polo | Lauren Promo | White Products | Polo II | Samples |
| --------- | Admin/ Other | Safari | Safari Christmas | Samples | --------- | Displays |
| --------- | -------- | --------- | Safari Tester | Testers | --------- | --------- |

Figure 13.15 An illustrative product hierarchy organized by All Product, Group, Brand, Brand Type, Super Category, Family, and Product Type.

## *Automating Statistical Model Selection for Baseline Demand Forecasting*

Typically, demand is collected so that baseline forecasts can be reviewed and adjusted by sales account, channel, or region. For example, a coupon program for a consumer product may be planned regionally; therefore, the impact on a product's forecast needs to be assessed from a regional perspective. If, for instance, a competitor plans a promotional event, a defensive change to a similar brand's forecast needs to be created. These are generally made as judgmental overrides to a baseline forecast by field forecast managers and consolidated into a consensus forecast.

> *An FDSP allows the practitioner to readily clean and analyze data, execute automatic modeling algorithms, evaluate multiple models and simulate forecasting performance, and reconcile a variety of forecast-related information and results for the purpose of driving a company's objectives for the future. It should also have the functionality to incorporate informed judgment and track forecast accuracy measures on an ongoing basis.*

Most companies go through a process to project their sales and operations plans for the next 1 to 3 years, which they use to create the budget. The assumptions and analyses are done at the macro level. Because annual sales levels are used to drive financial planning, demand forecasts are usually expressed in monetary terms, and the time granularity is typically expressed in months and quarters. The entities being forecast are often product categories or other product organizational groupings.

As the year progresses, the business also needs sales projections to plan financials as well as operations. During the monthly planning cycle, marketing may be responsible for a sales forecast—financial or unit volumes—by brand or product family. At the same time, the operations departments need to know demand at the SKU level for the next several weeks as inventories are produced, distributed, and delivered to customers.

Each functional group in the company has its own forecast data requirements, but not necessarily at the lowest product and customer-location level. For example, marketing may want to review the demand forecast at the brand level in sales and margin currency rather than in SKUs and unit volume level. Sales planners may find it more useful to see a demand forecast in currency by region or customer account. In support of these related requirements, forecasting approaches may need to be developed for multiple levels to support the reconciliation of these different forecasts.

> *A "best practice" demand forecasting process, striving to obtain the "single best number demand forecast" to drive the business, involves obtaining consensus among different functional planning organizations for enterprise FDSP database requirements.*

To work effectively, the demand forecasting process must generate views in terms that are familiar to each of the functions. These views need to be at different aggregation levels or dimensions as well as in different versions of the measure of demand. Some functions need to view the forecast in currency and some in units.

After a baseline (unbiased, unconstrained) demand forecast has been produced, other organizations in the company, as well as its trading partners, contribute to refining the forecast through a collaborative process such as **Collaborative Planning, Forecasting and Replenishment** (CPFR). The APICS society dictionary defines CPFR as (1) a collaboration process whereby supply chain trading partners can jointly plan key materials to production and delivery of final products to end customers, where collaboration encompasses business planning, sales forecasting, and all operations required to replenish raw materials and finished goods; (2) a process philosophy for facilitating endorsed by **Voluntary Interindustry Commerce Standards** (VICS). In the CPFR model, retailers and manufacturers extend collaboration from operational planning through execution. (**APICS** is the leading, non-profit association providing supply chain, operations, and logistics management research, publications, and education and certification programs; *www.apics.org*.)

# Automated Model Selection – The STI_Class Approach

To adequately perform the planning function, the forecaster needs to have ready access to multiple modeling algorithms and approaches. The modeling component of the system should allow for quantitative assessments (promotion analysis, statistical techniques, and data analysis), qualitative assessments (event management, field sales, and new product introductions), automated forecasting engine, best-performance evaluation criteria, analyst re-studies on useful models, outlier detection and correction, exception handling, root-cause analysis, integrated forecasting, and planning and user feedback.

> *For the high-volume forecasting needed for demand, inventory and production planning, a software system capable of running an automatic mode is essential to perform a best (i.e. useful) model selection.*

The STI Classification for month trend/seasonal data is an effective classification scheme of the data for model selection on an ongoing basis. Nowadays, forecasting systems frequently incorporate options for automatic forecast model selection. The particular implementation of an automated procedure may vary greatly among the software programs; even within an individual program, it can take on a number of different forms. In this section, we describe an approach for the univariate time series model selection used for baseline forecasting described in Chapter 8.

Starting with a Two-way ANOVA (without replication) algorithm, the Source of Variation (ANOVA) table is extended to show the SS column in terms of percentages in a decomposition into Season, Trend and Irregular (STI).

ANOVA

| Source of Variation | SS | df | MS | | |
|---|---|---|---|---|---|
| Rows | 8893762891 | 11 | 808523899.2 | Season | 91% |
| Columns | 536218254.5 | 4 | 134054563.6 | Trend | 6% |
| Error | 295720963.1 | 44 | 6720930.98 | Irregular | 3% |
| | | | | | |
| Total | 9725702109 | 59 | | | 100% |

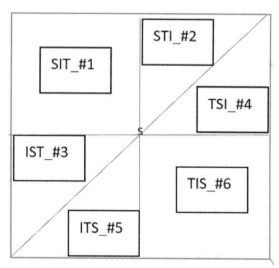

Define Seasonal Influence ISeas and Trend Influence ITrnd by
- ISeas = MS(Col)/MS(Err)
- ITrnd = MS(Row)/MS(Err)
- ITrnd+Seas = MS(Col+Row)/MS(Err), where MS(Row+Col)= SS(Row+Col)/(dfRow+dfCol)

It could be useful to transform the Influences into a **S**easonal Influence Factor (SIF) and Trend Influence Factor (TIF) by defining

- SIF= ISeas/ (df* + ISeas) , where df* = df(err)/df(seas)

- TIF= ITrnd/ (df** + ITrnd), where df** = df(err)/df(trnd)

*An SIF vs TIF scatter diagram* can be placed and labelled in a unit square diagram, as the ranges for SIF and TIF both fall between 0 and 1. Each STI class should be identified with the two or three of most effective methods in your toolkit.

- **SIT#1** (Seas% >Irregular %>Trend%)
- **STI#2** (Season% >Trend%> Irregular%)
- **IST#3** (Irregular% >Season% >Trend%)
- **TSI#4** (Trend% >Season% >Irregular%)
- **ITS#5** (Irregular %>Trend% >Season%)
- **TIS#6** (Trend% >Irregular% >Season%)

In most forecasting software systems, model choices for exponential smoothing can be made manually or through several levels of automation. In a manual mode, the user makes all choices, including model selections, estimates of smoothing parameters, and initializations. More typically, the forecaster's responsibility is to select a model, and the software will use an optimization procedure to find the best parameter values for the model fit.

Because Irregular factor is dominant in IST#3 and ITS#5, these two segments might be good candidates for identifying any unusual values that can provide an opportunity to improve overall data quality before model automation. When the TIF is higher than SIF, we might not be surprised to find that trending models would do well. Hence, an STI_Class classification before model selection could become helpful in practice.

The STI#2 and TSI#4 segments suggest that fitting multiplicative trend/seasonal-type models, for instance. The IST#3 and ITS#5 segments, on the other hand contain the dominant irregular series and might suggest damped trend/seasonal models. Once a classification can be validated with your company data, the STI_Class process could be implemented and maintained in an agile Forecast Decision Support System (**FDSS**) for automated forecasting and planning cycles.

The type of exponential smoothing forecast profile (Holt, Winters, or damped trend) depicted in a Pegels diagram (see Chapter 8) depends directly on the types of trend and seasonal patterns found in the historical data and the forecast profile expected in the forecast horizon (Figure 13.16).

*A Pegels classification of exponential smoothing techniques in a state-space modeling framework gives rise to 30 trend-seasonal forecast profiles with prediction limits for trend and seasonal patterns.*

Nowadays, forecasting systems frequently incorporate options for automatic forecast model selection. The particular implementation of an automated procedure may vary greatly among the software programs; even within an individual program, it can take on a number of different forms. In this section, we describe an approach for the univariate time series model selection used for baseline forecasting described in Chapter 8.

| | Seasonal Component | | |
|---|---|---|---|
| **Trend** | N | A | M |
| **Component** | (None) | (Additive) | (Multiplicative) |
| N (None) | (N,N) | (N,A) | (N,M) |
| A (Additive) | (A,N) | (A,A) | (A,M) |
| A$_d$ (Additive damped) | (A$_d$,N) | (A$_d$,A) | (A$_d$,M) |
| M (Multiplicative) | (M,N) | (M,A) | (M,M) |
| M$_d$ (Multiplicative damped) | (M$_d$,N) | (M$_d$,A) | (M$_d$,M) |

Some of these methods we have already seen:

| | | |
|---|---|---|
| (N,N) | = | simple exponential smoothing |
| (A,N) | = | Holts linear method |
| (M,N) | = | Exponential trend method |
| (A$_d$,N) | = | additive damped trend method |
| (M$_d$,N) | = | multiplicative damped trend method |
| (A,A) | = | additive Holt-Winters method |
| (A,M) | = | multiplicative Holt-Winters method |
| (A$_d$,M) | = | Holt-Winters damped method |

Figure 13.16 Classification of exponential smoothing models for automated state-space forecasting. (*Source*: Hyndman et al., *Forecasting with Exponential Smoothing—The State Space Approach*. (2008).

In most forecasting software systems, model choices for exponential smoothing can be made manually or through several levels of automation. In a manual mode, the user makes all choices, including model selections, estimates of smoothing parameters, and initializations.

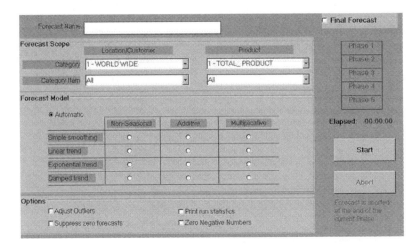

More typically, the forecaster's responsibility is to select a model, and the software will use an optimization procedure to find the best parameter values for the model fit. The type of exponential smoothing forecast profile (Holt, Winters, or damped trend) depicted in a Pegels diagram (see Chapter 8) depends directly on the types of trend and seasonal patterns found in the historical data and the forecast profile expected in the forecast horizon .

The values given by the smoothing weights determine the relative emphasis given to the immediate and distant past in the historical data. Initial values for level, trend, and seasonal indexes are usually required to start the updating process inherent in most smoothing algorithms.

Most commonly, automatic model selections involve some kind of a contest or tournament among a set of forecasting techniques (Figure 13.17). Each of the included models is used to forecast a particular time series, and the one that does so most accurately (according to preset criteria) is declared the most useful ("best"). Typically, each of several model profiles is fit to the entire time series, and the procedure that results in the best value of a performance statistic (e.g., MSE or MAD) is declared the most useful.

## Selecting Useful Models Visually

The first step in model selection is to visually display the salient features of the historical data. For well-behaved time series, the appropriate type of trend and/or seasonality pattern may be readily seen in a time or tier plot of the data (Chapter 5).

In some cases, it will be difficult to judge even visually whether the series is seasonal or nonseasonal. This can happen when the product was affected by special events, such as promotions, which as noted can be confounded with a seasonal pattern in monthly data. Turning points also complicate model identification because they may make models result in poor forecasts because conventional time series models are not designed for it.

**Outliers in Model Selection.** Finally, there are techniques for dealing with outliers and special events that can be automated (Chapter 2). An outlier may be due to a disruption of business (as a result of a catastrophic act of nature or a work stoppage), a windfall resulting perhaps from a legal ruling or business restructuring, a missed sale perhaps due to an out-of-stock inventory situation, or a simple data-entry error. If the outlying values are not identified and, in some way, reduced in influence, the underlying estimates of the level, trend, and seasonal profiles and uncertainty can be severely distorted. For example, an outlier toward the current end of the time series will change the current trend estimate and result in biased forecasts for the immediate future. It can also exaggerate the forecast errors and widen prediction intervals.

**Rolling Forecast Simulations.** The rolling forecast simulation is an evaluation procedure that involves a three-way split of the time series. First, a subset of the historical data is withheld from a time series to serve as a test period for evaluating forecasting accuracy. Next, the remaining period of fit is divided between the first $T_1$ values and the remaining $T_2$ values. We call the first $T_1$ values the **within sample** fit period and the $T_2$ values, from $T_1 + 1$ to $T_1 + T_2$, the **post-sample** fit period.

For each model under consideration, a pair of rolling forecast simulations are performed. The first rolling simulation is implemented using the post-sample fit period data to compute forecast error measures, which are used as error minimization criteria to optimize the smoothing weights and to select the best-performing model at each lead time. As a result, one model may be chosen to supply one-step-ahead forecasts while another is more useful for two-step-ahead ahead forecasts. The second rolling simulation is performed on the test period data, traditionally for the purpose of evaluating the accuracy of the forecasts made by the model selected.

> *The implementation of smoothing algorithms is complicated by the need for starting values or assumptions about the value of the level/trend/seasonal indexes as of the initial time period in the series. Because of this, implementations of the same model in different systems may show some small numerical differences in coefficients and results. However, the forecast profiles should look the same for different implementations of the same model.*

## Some Caveats on Automatic Model Selection

The drawbacks of fully automated systems for forecasting with smoothing procedures can become problematic if the data are very irregular (e.g. intermittent demand) or unusual data characteristics, such as unstable seasonality and outliers, go undetected. Even a few outliers, especially near the start of the forecast horizon, or patterns attributable to new product launches and product mix adjustments can have a significant impact on the eventual forecast profile. Hence, a visual inspection and numerical exploration of data as a first step in model evaluation and reconciliation is recommended.

When dealing with exceptional products or aggregates that are of particular importance to the business operation, some degree of manual oversight, especially with regard to adjusting outliers and useful model selection, is recommended

Very little is gained by manually selecting parameter values for the components, because their setting has relatively little impact on the forecast profile generated by the smoothing algorithm. Experience teaches that determination of the best smoothing weights should be left to the optimization (search) algorithms embedded in the forecasting software.

### Searching for Optimal Smoothing Procedures

Once a smoothing model has been selected, an algorithm is applied to find the optimal values of the smoothing weights. Once the weights are determined, the level, trend, and seasonal components of the forecasting equations are constructed to produce model extrapolations into the future.

The optimization algorithm itself requires some technical choices to be made, although many programs specify default values, often behind the scenes. The technical choices concern (1) which error-minimization criterion to use, (2) which search procedure to use, and (3) which starting values (also called initial values) to use for initiating the search procedure.

1. **Error-Minimization Criteria.** The error-minimization criterion defines what is best or optimal in an optimization procedure. In principle, any error measure can serve as a basis for optimization. In practice, software programs rely most commonly on a squared error measure: MSE or RMSE, the square root of MSE. In this procedure, calculations are made to keep the squared one-period-ahead forecast errors to a minimum. The choice of the error criterion, also interpretable as a loss function, could make a difference in practice. The most common alternative error-minimization measures are the Mean Absolute Deviation (MAD) and the Mean Absolute Percentage Error

(MAPE). In this case, the optimization criteria seek to keep the absolute errors to a minimum.

2. **Searching for Optimal Smoothing Weights.** Modern forecasting software can be expected to include at least one search procedure for optimizing the smoothing weights. The most common is the grid search. For example, by selecting a smoothing weight $\alpha$ in simple exponential smoothing, we can implement a crude grid search by setting $\alpha$ equal to designated values between 0 and 1, for example, the 100 values (0.01, 0.02, 0.03, . . . ,0.98, 0.99, 1.00). Then, for each $\alpha$ value, an error measure of choice is calculated. Finally, the $\alpha$ value, which keeps the defined measure to a minimum, can be found. Although this design might be adequate for a simple model, it may prove to be unacceptably slow for complex procedures such as the Winters method, which involves simultaneously optimizing three smoothing weights—one each for the level, trend, and seasonal components. Using the crude grid search for this would require not just 100 comparisons but 1 million. Therefore, certain shortcuts are typically employed to cut down on the number of comparisons that must be considered.

3. **Starting Values.** In order to initiate the grid search or simplex algorithm, starting values must be assigned to the level, trend, and seasonal components. A starting value is an estimate of that component's value during the initial time period in the historical series. The influence of the starting value gradually diminishes as the actual historical data are entered, and if the series is long enough, the impact becomes negligible. In many time series, especially seasonal series, starting values can make a difference in the smoothing weights and forecasts generated. The usual choices for starting values distinguish the seasonal component from the level and trend components.

What is the bottom line? Most forecasting practitioners do not find it practical to take time to adjust the technical settings in their software's computational algorithms to attempt to accommodate the particulars of individual time series. The comforting news is that empirical research suggests that reliance on the program's default settings is unlikely to be very harmful and is certainly cost-beneficial. But just as the user of an automatic camera might find it rewarding to go for manual overrides on specific occasions, so the demand forecaster may find occasional rewards for the extra effort in attending to the details.

> *The result of a collaborative forecasting process is a "one-number forecast" that becomes the basis for replenishment and production plans to meet customer needs in a timely and cost-effective way.*

**Computational Support for Management Overrides.** When making overrides to a baseline forecast, the integrity of the baseline forecast must be maintained at all times. This means that it remains a statistically generated forecast stored at the lowest levels and cannot be adjusted by the user. A manual override made at any product and or location summary gets prorated down to the lowest levels and stored as override amounts. For instance, an override of 35 in April 2003 (04/03) and 45 in July 2003 (07/03) should not change the statistical forecast but is allocated to the lowest level location codes for SKU 01540617 in direct proportion that the 10 forecasted units are allocated in the database for those periods. When aggregated, the sum of the statistical forecast and the override is labeled Stored Total Forecast in this dashboard example.

**Consolidating Multiple Overrides.** It is useful to create rules for making multiple overrides, such as (1) *Tier method.* The Tier method of overrides work as follows:

1. Override 3 dominates Override 2.
2. Override 2 dominates Override 1

For example, Marketing VP Tom makes adjustments in Override 3 line of the grid. This forecast would replace a forecast in Override 2 made by Product Manager Karen.

**Consolidating Multiple Overrides.** It is useful to create rules for making multiple overrides, such as (1) *Tier method.* The Tier method of overrides work as follows:

1. Override 3 dominates Override 2.
2. Override 2 dominates Override 1

For example, Marketing VP Tom makes adjustments in Override 3 line of the grid. This forecast would replace a forecast in Override 2 made by Product Manager Karen.

Likewise, the Product Manager's forecast in Override 2 would replace Override 1 made by a field sales forecaster Carl. (2) Composite method. In the Composite method, all overrides are given equal significance, and an unweighted average of the three forecasts for the period is taken. (3) Sum method. In the Sum method, all overrides are added as the sum of the three overrides entered for the particular period.

**Selecting an Adjustment Method.** It can be helpful to adjust options for calculating changes to forecasts, such as Add, Replace, Subtract, or Percent Change. This will affect how the numbers in the override rows are adjusted. Operations should be based on the baseline forecast or the adjusted (Total) forecast, but the table with the baseline forecast numbers must never be updated with changes from this.

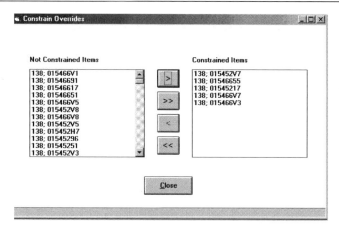

Figure 13.18 A dialog box for a Constrain option

- **Constraining Forecast Overrides**. Because overrides can be made at any level in the product and/or customer summaries, the FDSP needs to constrain an override to be applied to some but not all the location/customer codes making up the summary (Figure 13.19). The Constrain option that lets you select/deselect those customers not requiring the override (Constrained Items) can be listed in a dialog box, as shown. This example shows that certain 138 Canton customers will not have any overrides allocated when overrides are made for SKU codes 015452V7, 01546655, etc., shown under Constrained Items.

- **Reviewing the Override Audit Log**. The Override Audit Log (Figure 13.19) allows the user to view the overrides that were done for a particular SKU, Category, Region, or any combination of Location and Products. This view allows the user to see what was done for one forecast and apply this to a new forecast. The audit log as well as a report should be viewable in the FDSP on-screen as well.

| ID | ForNbr | User | OverrideDate | Col1 | Col2 | Col0 | Prod1 | Prod2 | Prod3 |
|----|--------|------|--------------|------|------|------|-------|-------|-------|
| 1 | 7 | Admin | 4/2001 3:30:55 PM | 2 - REGION | ER - Eastern Region | All - Items | 2 - BRAND | BR1 - Brand A | All - Items |
| 2 | 6 | Admin | 8/2001 7:57:11 PM | 1 - ALL CUSTOMERS | 999 - Total Company | All - Items | 1 - TOTAL_PRODUC | 000 - Total Product | 92120232 - Sprin 2( |
| 3 | 6 | Admin | 8/2001 8:00:23 PM | 1 - ALL CUSTOMERS | 999 - Total Company | All - Items | 1 - TOTAL_PRODUC | 000 - Total Product | 92120232 - Sprin 2( |
| 4 | 6 | Admin | 8/2001 8:03:34 PM | 1 - ALL CUSTOMERS | 999 - Total Company | All - Items | 1 - TOTAL_PRODUC | 000 - Total Product | 92120232 - Sprin 2( |
| 5 | 6 | Admin | 8/2001 8:04:08 PM | 1 - ALL CUSTOMERS | 999 - Total Company | All - Items | 1 - TOTAL_PRODUC | 000 - Total Product | 92120232 - Sprin 2( |
| 6 | 6 | Admin | 8/2001 8:04:37 PM | 1 - ALL CUSTOMERS | 999 - Total Company | All - Items | 1 - TOTAL_PRODUC | 000 - Total Product | 92120232 - Sprin 2( |
| 7 | 7 | Auto Copy | 8/2001 8:13:55 PM | | 66287 | | | | 4743801 |
| 8 | 7 | Auto Copy | 8/2001 8:13:55 PM | | 66287 | | | | 4743811 |
| 9 | 7 | Auto Copy | 8/2001 8:13:55 PM | | 66287 | | | | 4743831 |
| 10 | 7 | Auto Copy | 8/2001 8:13:55 PM | | 66287 | | | | 4743950 |
| 11 | 7 | Auto Copy | 8/2001 8:13:55 PM | | 66287 | | | | 4746801 |
| 12 | 7 | Auto Copy | 8/2001 8:13:55 PM | | 66287 | | | | 4746811 |

Figure 13.19. Display of an override audit log

## *Takeaways*

➤ Demand forecasting is part of an ongoing process affecting sales, marketing, inventory, logistics, production, and all other aspects of the supply chain. A bottom-up demand forecast incorporates a logical and coherent series of steps that, if performed in an organized management-supported fashion, can improve forecasting effectiveness, accuracy, and agility throughout the supply chain.

➢ Automated forecasting is a useful process when dealing with large volumes of end items by customer/location for the supply chain.

➢ Key functions supported by a Forecast Decision Support Platform (FDSP) include flexible, automated modeling including a statistical forecasting engine, database management, exploratory data analysis, outlier-resistant, data quality detection and correction procedures, multiple performance metrics and forecast error analyses, exception handling, and reporting.

➢ An effective, agile forecasting® process will result in lower costs and improved customer satisfaction. Inclusion of demand forecasting as a vital element in the supply chain is a requisite step toward the goal of having the right quantity of the right product at the right place at the right time (and at the right price)!

# 14

# Blending Agile Forecasting with an Integrated Business Planning Process

## a·gil·i·ty (əˈjilədē/)

noun
*Ability to move quickly and easily.*
*Ability to think and understand quickly.*

This chapter describes
- why a data-driven demand forecasting process is an essential component of effective demand planning and management practice
- how Agile Forecasting results from synchronizing database decision support, automated statistical forecast modeling, forecast uncertainty measurement, and ongoing forecast performance evaluation with a firm's business planning processes.

After reading this book, you should be able to
- understand the essential nature of a demand forecasting process in a consumer data-driven supply chain environment
- recognize the components of an efficient and smarter forecasting work cycle
- engage with potential forecast users to help define, formulate, execute, evaluate, and support their forecast data requirements and performance metrics

- provide advice on recommendations for forecast data-quality standards, forecast reviews, model checklists, performance measurement activities, and business planning integration.

# PEERing into the Future: Creating a Framework for Agile Forecasting

As demand managers we must strive to induce needed change—change in the way we deal with data, quantitative and qualitative techniques for forecasting, and the uncertainty factor. Change in encouraging planners and managers to rethink their goals for demand forecasting. Motivating them away from how they have always dealt with forecasting: *"Hey, forecaster, what are your final numbers?"* Getting them to take a different path, a new path. The question is, are we talking to the elephant or the rider?

## The Elephant and the Rider Metaphor

*The Elephant is the emotional side of motivation, while the Rider is the logical side. Perched atop the Elephant, the Rider holds the reins and seems to be the leader. But the Rider's control is precarious because the Rider is small relative to the Elephant. Anytime the six-ton Elephant and the Rider disagree about which direction to go, the Rider is going to lose. He's completely overmatched.*

We have to examine how these two internal motivations play together (or not). The most obvious examples we most can relate to are sticking to a diet, staying on an exercise program, or quitting smoking. We know it is the right thing to do (Rider) but we have a difficult time sticking to it (Elephant).

The Elephant and Rider are the yin and yang of our psyche. The Rider is the planner or manager (getting thin on a diet), while the Elephant is attracted to the short-term payoff (enjoying an ice cream cone).

> *Changes often fail because the Rider simply can't keep the Elephant on the road long enough to reach the destination.*

Recall that this book has advocated four key steps in an approach to solving demand forecasting problems. These same steps are key to forming an effective framework for an agile forecasting process.

1. **Prepare:** Define the purpose and role of the job or organization, define the major areas of responsibility, set objectives, and establish indicators of performance.

2. **Execute:** Define short-term goals and action plans, and carry out a plan for each area of responsibility.
3. **Evaluate:** Perform forecast monitoring (define objectives for the forecaster), know what to monitor, develop a measurement plan, develop metrics of forecast accuracy, and develop scores for performance.
4. **Reconcile:** Select the most credible approach, reconcile demand forecasts, support database forecast decision support in the cloud, and get top management involvement.

# Forecasting Does Not Need to Be the Enemy of Agility

**Purpose and Role.** What is the purpose of a demand forecasting job or organization? This requires considerable thought. It is difficult to be *agile* unless one knows what it is that needs to be accomplished (see Chapter 1). One role of a forecast manager is to serve as an advisor to a company's senior management and managers of end-user organizations. To fulfill the other part of the role, a forecast manager must manage colleagues and their work. Here is a mission statement:

*The responsibility of a demand forecasting organization is to provide top-quality advice—primarily about future demand for a firm's products and services under conditions of uncertainty.*

One can spend many hours wrestling with the purpose of the job. In addition, developing meaningful indicators of performance is no easy task and can give rise to many debates. Experience will cause us to reject some indicators and replace them with others that are more relevant. Naturally, both the indicators and attendant levels of performance will change over time as the business evolves.

**Major Areas of Responsibility.** These are the major areas of responsibility that should be defined in short one- or two-word statements. These might be product, revenue, capacity, or asset management forecasting. But almost all managers share some combination of professional self-development, forecasting staff/ personnel development, and resource management.

For forecast managers, the key areas of responsibility are likely to include forecast evaluation, measurement, monitoring, presentation, and forecaster appraisal and professional development. Forecaster performance appraisal/development is equally important, but the methods for achieving success in this area are not restricted to forecast managers. (The traditional management literature covers this topic adequately, and it is beyond the scope of this book.)

**Set Objectives.** Once one has determined the purpose and areas of responsibility of a forecasting discipline, the next step is to develop a long-range objective for each area of responsibility. These objectives should be general enough to have lasting significance, and they should contain an indication of the goal that the actual work should accomplish. Some examples are to

- improve the accuracy of X
- improve the productivity of X
- reduce the cost of X
- improve technical and managerial skills
- improve the credibility of the demand forecasting organization
- ensure the continuing relevance of X

Such objectives are important because they provide the managerial direction and focus that team members can embrace and strive to achieve. Demand forecasters can see how their activities are related to the achievement of organizational objectives. What is implicit in all of these objectives is a striving for improvement that can be translated into actual tasks.

**Establish Indicators of Performance.** How to define the indicators of performance for the organization? How will the organization know it is making progress toward the achievement of its objectives? What will be the yardsticks? For certain forecasts, one indicator might be the absolute percentage deviation between estimate and actual. For personnel development, indicators might be the demonstrated ability of a demand forecaster to use a new technique in effectively forecasting demand for a new product or service.

*Without an understanding of purpose and indicators of performance, we will find it difficult to manage effectively.*

**Define Short-Term Goals and Action Plan.** With indicators of performance in place, we can turn to the second major step of the Agile Forecasting process: executing a specific short-term goal and action plan for the next 6 to 12 months. If the goal is to improve the accuracy of a forecast item, a reasonable goal may be to improve the accuracy to within a given percentage, say 5 to 20%, depending on the item to be forecast. For professional development, the goal may be to assume responsibility for forecasting new revenues within the next 6 months.

**Carry Out a Plan for Each Area of Responsibility.** With areas of responsibility clearly stated, the forecast manager must establish specific activities that can lead to measurable results for the demand forecasting staff. Because results are evaluated, the action plan needs to be achievable and carried out in reasonable time frames (weeks or months, rather than years).

**Develop Objectives for the Demand Forecaster.** At the center of the agile demand forecaster's role are the analysis and actions that compose the evaluative process. A primary objective of forecast monitoring is to prevent surprising the company with news about unforeseen exceptions to a forecast. The firm should have sufficient time to evaluate alternative courses of action and not be forced to react to unpredicted yet predictable events.

A second objective of monitoring is to predict accurately a change in the direction of growth. This involves predicting the turning points in the business cycle and the demand for the firm's products. Quite often forecasters find it difficult to predict a decline in demand and instead call for an upturn too soon (see Chapter 7).

It is easy to see why few managers in business find the exercise of managerial control as challenging as the demand forecaster does. Demand forecasters are responsible for a function whose primary output is wholly related to the future environment. Unable to change the environment, the forecaster must instead be prepared to make revisions when it is evident that an original forecast or goal cannot be met with stated accuracy. In effect, the forecaster is changing some predetermined goal in order to more accurately predict expected performance.

The process of forecast monitoring provides the demand forecaster with an early indication that such changes in forecasts may be required. Through experience, an agile demand forecaster will develop an improved ability to anticipate change and to advise management so that the firm will have time to adjust operations to changing conditions. This, of course, is a valuable attribute in any forecaster.

At a more demanding level, the objectives of monitoring are to predict changes in the rate of growth, to predict the level of growth and to minimize the impact of forecast changes. The ability to predict any speeding up or slowing down of growth with uncertainty measurement helps management to decide on the proper timing of company plans and programs.

Accurate predictions of the level of growth—the forecast numbers themselves—allow management to make sizing decisions about investment in facilities, numbers of employees, and appropriate financing arrangements.

Last, it is necessary to minimize the internal disruption that results from changing forecasts too frequently. The demand forecaster could, after all, change a forecast every month so that the final forecast and the actual data are almost identical. However, this does not serve the needs of the firm. Using prediction limits, the demand forecaster must endeavor to minimize the need to override forecasts. The more carefully thought out and thoroughly researched the initial forecast is, the less likely the need for it to be revised or overridden.

**Know What to Monitor.** There should be a difference between what a demand forecaster monitors and what the forecast manager monitors. Demand forecasters monitor a predictive database that consists of time series, cross-sectional data, and assumptions for customer/geographic segments and product groupings. They are primarily interested in the numerical accuracy of the forecasts, reliable uncertainty measurement, and the credibility of the forecast assumptions.

The forecast manager monitors an enterprise database that is both more general and more selective. Included in this database are the exceptional cases that demand forecasters uncover as a result of their detailed monitoring. The manager is primarily concerned with the implications of the difference between the initial forecast and the evolving reality for the business for which the forecast is made. The manager should know more about that business and generally be more aware of the significance of forecast changes on business performance than need be the demand forecaster.

The specific items that demand forecasters select to monitor will naturally depend on their areas of responsibility. The indicators that are established in the organization's business plans are natural candidates for monitoring. With the items to be monitored selected, the demand forecaster should

- Consider monitoring composites, or groups of items. Composites often serve as indicators of overall forecast quality and are frequently used as a basis for decision making. They are resistant to individual deviations that may be measurement aberrations and not *managerially* significant. For example, a forecast of total revenues might be on target, although forecasts of revenues accruing from the sales of a product to residential or business users may need to be adjusted.
- Compare the sum of the components of a forecast to the whole helps to ensure that there is a reasonable relationship between the more stable aggregate forecast and the more volatile bottom-up forecast of many small components. For example, the sum of the individual product forecasts should be compared to a total product-line forecast. In this way, the forecaster can be assured that both upward and downward revisions in the component parts

are being made to keep them in reasonable agreement with the total forecast.

- Monitor ratios or relationships between different items. The ratio of a given geographic area's sales to the total corporate sales is an example of this approach. Another example is the ratio of sales to disposable personal income.

- Monitor time relationships. It may be appropriate to monitor changes or percentage changes over time. The use of seasonally adjusted annual rates is an example, as is the ratio of first quarter to total annual sales.

- Consider monitoring both on a period basis and on a cumulative basis. The sum of the actuals since the beginning of the year should be compared with the sum of the forecasts. This has the advantage of smoothing out irregular, random, month-to-month variations.

- Monitor external factors (drivers of demand). These are the basic key assumptions about business conditions or the economic outlook. Corporate policy assumptions also need to be monitored.

- Monitor user needs. It is possible that budgetary or organizational changes, new or discontinued products, or changes in management will cause changes in the forecast user's needs. Because demand forecasting is an advisory function, demand forecasters need to monitor user needs to be certain that the forecasting service being provided is consistent with evolving business needs. Questionnaires or periodic discussions with users will indicate whether such changes have occurred.

- Monitor similar forecasts in several geographic locations. This will help determine whether a pattern is developing elsewhere that may impact the company or area in the near future. Do any geographic areas of the market generally lead or lag the market as a whole? The forecaster may discover that his or her geographic area is not the only market area with weak or strong demand; a national pattern may be emerging that needs to be tracked.

*The items to be monitored should relate to the purposes and objectives of the organization.*

**Develop a Measurement Plan**. A major aspect of forecast process improvement is forecast measurement or results analysis. For any forecaster, improvement in organizational or staff effectiveness depends on measurement. A demand forecaster will find it useful to establish a forecast measurement plan to provide indications of overall performance that can be reviewed with upper management. A properly developed plan will show performance trends and highlight trouble areas.

The measurement plan will provide managers with a tool to assist in evaluating both forecasts and forecasters. When a measurement plan exists, demand forecasters know that they have to explain forecasts that miss the mark. This forces demand forecasters to structure and quantify their assumptions so that there will be documented reasons to explain deviations from forecasts and actuals.

> *The goal of a measurement plan is to develop meaningful ways of measuring the performance of the demand forecasting organization.*

More importantly, adequate documentation enables the demand forecaster to learn from past mistakes and successes. From reviews of these after-the-fact reports, it can be determined whether the assumptions were reasonable at the time they were made. Which assumptions turned out to be incorrect? Why? Did the forecaster do everything possible to obtain all the facts at the time the forecast was made? Were all sources of information reviewed? Were there any obvious breakdowns in communications? Was the forecast methodology appropriate for the particular problem? The answers to these questions provide the information needed to evaluate the demand forecast and the demand forecaster.

In reviewing forecasts that were particularly successful, it may be discovered that a demand forecaster has developed a new method or established new contacts that were responsible for the superior forecast performance. Perhaps the approach can be tried in areas where performance is not as strong. The documentation of both superior and substandard performance, which will result from the measurement plan, provides the needed inputs to determine areas where improvement in methods or data is required. This document can also be used to support requests for people, data, or other items needed to improve the performance of the organization.

The existence of a measurement plan will also be of value to the users of the forecasts. It will improve their understanding of the limitations that must be placed on the accuracy of the forecasts they receive. For example, suppose the demand forecaster considers a +2% miss to be a successful outcome for a given forecast, and the measurement plan takes this into account. A forecast user would then be foolish to plan on 0.5% accuracy, which for other reasons may be a desirable accuracy. By providing users with forecasting accuracy objectives, we are in effect providing a range forecast that can help users to scale their plans to differing degrees of forecast uncertainty.

> *The credibility of the demand forecasting organization will improve when it is capable of reporting on its own performance.*

446

**Develop Metrics of Forecast Accuracy**. The development of a measurement plan begins with selection of the metrics that will be used to measure forecast accuracy. Four widely used metrics are

- Absolute error = absolute value of forecast error (Actual - Forecast)
- Percentage error = 100 x (Forecast error)/Actual)
- Difference between total past sales and forecast, in percent
- Difference in growth rates

**Forecast accuracy** tends to be measured using averages and medians of either absolute or squared forecasting errors (see Chapter 4). By taking either the absolute values of the errors or by taking the squares of the errors, the possibility of negative and positive forecast errors offsetting one another is eliminated. The resulting averages then reveal how scattered the forecasts are typically around actual values rather than whether the forecasts tend to be too low or too high.

The most commonly used metric is the percentage deviation between the estimate and the actual. The actual demand, rather than the forecast, should be used in the denominator. This bases the deviation on actual performance. It is most useful when very large numbers are involved. However, when negative, zero, or relatively low levels of demand for a product are realized, the percentage deviation can become very large and not very meaningful. In those cases, the absolute difference or alternative metrics found in the literature are preferable.

The ratio of the deviation between forecast and actual to the in-service quantity of the series being forecast tends to put the forecast error in perspective. For example, a 100% deviation in forecasting the growth of sales may be only a 1-% miss in the total sales. Or a 100% miss in forecasting the growth rate of the GDP may be only a 4% miss in actual GDP. However, when dealing with very large numbers, such as the GDP, a 4% miss can be very significant. In such cases, a useful metric is the difference between the forecast and actual growth rates (Estimated percentage growth rate – Actual percentage growth rate). For example, the forecast could be for an 8% growth rate, while the actual growth rate is only 4%.

The forecast measurement periods are generally weekly, monthly, quarterly, annually, long term (5 to 6 years), or cumulatively. There will probably be different accuracy metrics depending on the use of the forecast. For example, for production planning, a 3-month cumulative forecast versus actual accuracy comparison may be appropriate. For evaluating budget plan performance, an annual or quarterly measure is typical. For financial reporting, quarterly and annual intervals apply. To be useful to management, the measurement plan should cover all areas for which demand forecasters have responsibility. The reports of forecast accuracy should include graphs and tables at various levels of reporting (e.g., SKU, product line, geography, and organization level).

Recognize that external or exogenous factors can affect forecast accuracy. For example, the forecast miss can be partially due to forecasting quality, but it could also be the result of breakdowns in production, inventory or distribution planning, or operations. Similarly, competitive actions or changed economic conditions can cause a forecast error. Therefore, the forecast error should trigger a root cause analysis or an exception handling investigation (see Chapter 11) to determine the reasons for the problems so that corrective action can be taken.

**Develop Scores for Performance**. The score a forecast error receives should not take into account the difficulty of forecasting. If difficulty is taken into account, it will generally not be possible to identify trouble spots; they will be hidden as a result of the scoring system. This means that the score is not a direct indication of the ability of the demand forecaster.

> *To identify trouble spots, it is necessary to have a uniform standard of performance.*

Some demand forecasters will be responsible for forecasting in series or geographic areas that are more difficult to forecast than others (see Figure 4.16). Such forecasts may receive low scores. However, it is better to identify low scores in difficult areas and know the reasons for the low performance than to have uniformly good scores and not know where the performance problems lie. Demand forecasters can be sure that the forecast users will know from past experience where performance problems are.

| (1) | (2) | (3) | (4) | (5) | (6) | (7) | (8) | (9) | (10) |
|---|---|---|---|---|---|---|---|---|---|
| | Units | | MAPE Abs. | 1-MAPE Percentage | Price | $(3)\times(6)$ Revenue | Revenue Weight | $(5)\times(8)/100$ Accur. $\times$ Rev | $(8)-(9)$ Impvnt |
| Item | Forecast | Actual | Diff (%) | Accuracy | (dollars) | (dollars) | (%) | (%)[a] | Opporty |
| 1 | 91 | 70 | 30 | 70 | 250 | 17,500 | 21.0 | 15.1 | 5.9 |
| 2 | 54 | 60 | 10 | 90 | 300 | 18,000 | 21.6 | 19.4 | 2.2 |
| 3 | 48 | 40 | 20 | 80 | 1200 | 48,000 | 57.4 | 45.9 | 11.5 |
| Total Wgtd | | | | | | 83,500 | 100 | 80.40 | 19.60 |

[a] Maximum score for an item = revenue weight (%). In this example, item 3 has greatest improvement opportunity even though the forecast accuracy is higher than item 1. This is because of item 3's high revenue percentage.

Figure 14.1 Revenue weighting in forecasting performance measurement.

Figure 14.1 illustrates the use of revenue weighting to calculate improvement opportunities. The same revenue weighting approach can be used to summarize overall forecasting performance in supply chain forecasting in which quantities of different products cannot be easily or meaningfully aggregated. In this case, the presumption is that lower revenue items are not as important as higher revenue products—which is generally the case. The demand forecaster can perform a separate analysis for strategic products that are more important than their revenue implies. Graphical plots of forecast accuracy at appropriate summary levels will provide overall measures of forecast accuracy. Because MAPE and MdAPE are used as the metrics, it is not possible to observe a bias toward overforecasting or underforecasting. A companion graph can be provided that indicates the percentage error (plus or minus). In addition, a summary statistic, such as the percentage of forecasts that exceeded actual results, can be added to the graph.

For internal use, management may also choose to develop a plan that measures the forecast accuracy of individual demand forecasters by attempting to incorporate a measure of difficulty into the scoring mechanism. One approach is to review the historical records of forecasts and actuals to determine the average miss and a measure of its variability (e.g., coefficient of variation) for each time series. It may be the case that the larger the variability, the more volatile and difficult the series is to forecast.

The advantage of this approach is that the current demand forecaster's accuracy can be compared with others who have predicted the same series. The difficulty is built into the index because difficult areas invariably have larger measures of variability of forecast misses. In practice, the measure of variability used in this process should be resistant to outliers (e.g., down-weighting of extreme deviations), so the outlier-sensitive standard deviation may not always be appropriate.

| Measurement | Area 1 (difficult area) | Area 2 (less difficult) |
|---|---|---|
| (Estimate – Actual) | 300 | 100 |
| Standard deviation of prior forecast miss | 300 | 100 |
| Accuracy ratio | 300/300 = 1 | 100/100 = 1 |

Figure 14.2 Using accuracy ratios to measure the demand forecaster.

Because the current miss is divided by a historical variability measure, a large miss will not necessarily penalize a forecaster. This is illustrated in Figure 14.2. The forecast miss in a given year in region 1 is 300, and the forecast miss in region 2 is 100. Region 1 had traditionally been more difficult to forecast than region 2, and their variability measures of misses are 300 and 100, respectively. The accuracy ratio in both cases equals 1 and both forecasters receive the same score. The resulting ratios can be graphed or averaged.

This approach measures only the relative forecast accuracy of forecasters. In assessing a forecaster's ability, several other responsibilities are also important. Management will want to judge a demand forecaster's ability to sell the forecast to users, documentation of the forecast work, development or testing of new methods, and overall productivity.

**Select Credible Forecasting Approaches**. The fourth and final major step of the Agile Forecasting process is to support processes of reconciliation, which begins with selecting credible forecasting approaches. Several approaches to demand forecasting can improve forecast accuracy. These include top-down versus bottom-up forecasting processes.

The bottom-up forecast provides the detail needed to manage operations. However, there is a tendency for the bottom-up forecast to overforecast aggregate demand. The top-down forecasts use aggregate data, which are less volatile and more amenable to a broader range of quantitative forecasting methods. For example, exponential smoothing may be used for lower-level operational forecasts. Regression and econometric methods may be created for product-line and total company forecasts. The bottom-up forecast of units is matched with the top-down forecast, and the reasons for any differences are investigated and reconciled. To mitigate intermittency, bottom-up forecasts can often be effectively derived from homogeneous groupings that are separately forecasted and then prorated to the bottom levels.

> *Develop top-down and bottom-up demand forecasts, and reconcile the multiple forecasting approaches.*

In demand forecasting for the supply chain, bottom-up unit forecasts are multiplied by average prices to develop revenue forecasts. This is compared to and reconciled with an aggregate revenue forecast that uses actual revenues as the data. Use the following guidelines:

- Develop the demand forecasts and the demand plan in parallel with reconciliation at several times. Capacity constraints that would limit demand should be taken into account in developing the final forecast and business plan (see Chapter 12).
- Use forecast accuracy metrics at various levels of the business to identify improvement opportunities (see Chapter 4).
- Encourage training in quantitative forecasting techniques and a better understanding of the business and its environment (see

Chapter 1). Also, provide training in the optimal use of the forecast decision support systems (see Chapter 13).

- Keep historical demands and price data current, and adjust unusual values as appropriate (see Chapter 2).
- Recognize and reward superior use of forecasting methodologies (see Chapters 3, 8, 9, and 10).

One possible approach to improving the accuracy of sales-force forecasts is to significantly link the proportion of such individuals' compensation packages to forecast accuracy ranges. To ensure that each person is measured against his or her own demand forecast, planners and managers who are authorized to override a forecast should have a separate forecast ownership and performance measurement standard.

*Recognition and rewards for improved forecast accuracy should take into account all the people responsible for contributing to the consensus process, not just the demand forecasting group.*

A complication related to this approach is the fact that sales-force members may hold back orders until they have an opportunity to predict them correctly. In addition, the business may take specific action related to lower revenue forecast (e.g., special deals, promotions, or incentives that result in improving revenues). When the business could have made the demand forecast in error by taking certain actions, it is not appropriate to penalize the sales force or demand forecasters for signaling the need for such action. Recognition is usually a simpler but less powerful approach because the specific form it takes is under more control by management.

When it is possible to obtain sales-force forecasting input, the following guidelines should be followed:

- Be sure the right people are assigned to and engaged in the forecasting process. Recognize that all sales personnel cannot sell all products (e.g., Asian, European, or South American products may be customized for specific markets). In addition, not all products are equally important. Consider three classes of products.
  - Class A items are high-revenue or strategic items and the forecasts are assigned to members of the sales force.
  - Class B items are more numerous and less important, and the forecasts are assigned to sales planners or forecasters, who use time series forecasting techniques extensively. Members of the sales force

are asked to identify any unusual factors that will impact sales of these items.

    o    Class C items are not sold and will not be sold in a given territory, and no forecast assignments are made.

- For major customers, try to include the customer in the demand forecasting process. Review the previous forecast-accuracy results with the customer. Review the assumptions and show them plots of history and forecasts (with prediction limits) and ask for their comments. Try to get them to quantify their input. If possible, get them to enter forecasts directly into the forecasting system; these forecasts still need to be reviewed for reasonableness by the sales team and adjusted if appropriate.

- Consider generating statistical baseline demand forecasts (with prediction limits) for review and adjustment by the sales force.

- Establish executive review sessions with the sales force to gain insights into the customers, competitors, and product migration plans that could modify demand forecast assumptions.

- Establish forecast approval points at which sales executives review key forecasts.

- Keep the number of demand forecast items that the sales team are asked to provide to a reasonable level (If you ask for too many, you will not get the attention you desire.) Identify items whose demand depends on other related items and consider using regression techniques to forecast dependent items rather than expanding the number of forecasts you ask the sales team to provide. Investigate whether more accurate demand forecasts of some class B items can be obtained by forecasting the items at a higher organizational level (region or company) where the data are less volatile rather than at an account level.

- Ask for input from the sales force about the language of what it sells and at the level that the salesperson experiences. Have the system translate from the sales-input level to the lower-level component demand forecasts using typical systems configurations.

Because there are a number of areas to consider, encourage the demand forecasters and users to identify the characteristics or criteria that will lead to excellence in demand forecasting (see Chapter 1). Rate current performance of the criteria elements on a six-point scale (0 = *Not done*, 1 = *Done infrequently*, 2 = *Done some/most of the time*, 3 = *Always done with opportunity for improvement*, 4 = *Always done with above-average quality*, 5 = *Always done with excellence*).

As a second exercise, rate the importance of the criteria (say from 1 to 10 if there are 10 criteria). Focus attention on the most important items with the lowest performance scores. Alternatively, try to identify areas of greatest potential for improvement.

> *Create an agile demand forecasting process that encourages communication, coordination, and collaboration among marketing, sales, product management, production, distribution, finance, and demand forecasting organizations.*

**Integrate Demand Forecasts.** In addition to selecting credible forecasting approaches, the acceptance and proper use of forecasts can improve the demand forecasting process. To prevent unnecessary disconnects between all the functional organizations that require forecasts, create a process to discuss and reach agreement or consensus on marketing and operational forecasts that are reasonably reconciled. The forecasting needs and requirements of all components of the organization are identified so that the agreed-on plan meets their critical needs and results in a synchronized business process.

It is desirable to identify a corporate demand forecasting process **champion** at the leadership level to encourage participation by all concerned. If possible, an independent demand forecasting group should be established to improve the overall forecasting process on an ongoing basis.

Within the overall process, different groups will be accountable for specific forecasts. It should be recognized that the initial demand forecast is unconstrained in terms of the company's ability to meet demand through its operations capabilities. At the subsequent stages of an integrated business-planning process, the forecast used to drive operations must to take into account the operational constraints that exist. For example, constrained production capacity information must be fed back to marketing and sales. Also, planned promotional programs must be communicated to production and distribution groups.

> *The consensus process must provide feedback to the functional organizations.*

**Enable Forecasting Decision Support Systems**. Improved computer systems are key to the demand forecasting process as well as the process of reconciliation. A hosted Web-based system architecture that allows for all impacted groups to interrogate and provide electronic input to an Agile Forecasting process is recommended. Information systems, based on client-server technology or corporate intranets should also be able to share information, make forecast accuracy metrics available in the cloud to appropriate groups, and provide descriptions of the products and linkages or translations between the product lines and SKUs.

By linking corporate information systems, manufacturing and distribution planning systems, and demand forecasting systems, it is possible to eliminate the inefficient transfer of data from one system to another, and the information used in the different functional organizations is better coordinated in multiple ways.

- Production planners can send out alerts to demand forecasters or sales teams identifying the most important or critical items for the forecasting cycle so that the forecast providers can focus on these items. A typical supply chain forecast contains so many items that it is not apparent when one or more items are most important at a particular point in time. The factory planners may be making production-capacity-enhancement decisions and require the best forecasts of selected items before investing capital for increased capacity.
- Higher-level summaries of demand history, demand forecasts, orders, and revenues can be to facilitate developing aggregate forecasts as reasonableness checks on lower-level forecasts.
- The products or SKUs that have been updated or changed since the last demand forecast cycle can be identified. Because there are potentially several thousands of individual items, it is not practical to expect the users to review all the items every forecast cycle.
- Major customers should be encouraged to enter their forecasts online or offline with an upload capability while retaining adequate security and confidentiality. Electronic data linkages with suppliers can provide information on parts availability.
- Higher-level management adjustments to the demand forecast should be made possible. However, all forecasts, not just the demand forecast, created at lower management levels need to be retained in an enterprise system. Then, contributors can retain ownership and be measured against their own forecasts, or plans, as the case maybe.

*The capability to improve the demand forecasting process is enhanced if the organization can enlist a forecasting process champion.*

**Get Top Management Involvement.** Last, but by no means least, a champion of the demand forecasting process needs to be identified at a high enough level in the firm to focus attention and resources on improved forecasting performance. This individual needs to have a stake in the outcome. Operations executives whose organizations depend on credible and accurate forecasts could be excellent champions. The champion does not need to manage the demand forecasting function, but does need to have a strong interest in sustaining an Agile Forecasting process. Once top management recognizes the importance of demand forecasting, both to the business and operational plans, it will increase its level of support.

> *Top management has a tendency to avoid dealing with forecasting issues because these issues have to do with mastering agility and navigating uncertainty rather than the areas of the business that management has greater control over.*

## *Creating an Agile Forecasting Implementation Checklist*

Managers in industry today can expect quantitative, data-based analytics in support of forecast-dependent decisions. This section provides guidelines for the implementation of an Agile Forecasting® process for demand forecasting and planning. The full implementation checklist is provided later in the chapter.

### Selecting Overall Goals

The first step of the implementation checklist is concerned with selecting overall goals for statistical forecast modeling. Clearly, it is difficult to be successful in any area of the business without having decided what it is that needs to be done (Chapter 1). Because quantitative and qualitative approaches can be used for many areas and the specific requirements of a company will determine which techniques are appropriate, it is important for a forecast manager to know the end user's needs.

> *Before starting a statistical modeling effort, the key point is to determine carefully the specific goals to be achieved.*

Elaborate statistical models are often constructed with the goal of improving forecast accuracy (Chapter 4). Because statistical models can give predictions with measured uncertainty that are potentially more accurate than corporate forecasts using judgmental approaches, we should be prepared to work with new models.

Planners and demand managers need to look for more than just a set of forecast numbers (Chapter 12). They need to understand the relationships that exist among the various series of interest and among corporate (internal) data (Chapter 2) and the external economic and market variables (Chapter 7), what the relevant relationships are (Chapter 10), and how they have been changing over time (Chapter 5).

Running models also provide management with the ability to explore alternative scenarios with associated risks. Most likely, optimistic, and pessimistic scenarios for economic or market forecasts can be used to assess the demand for a firm's products and services (Chapter 9). This helps management generate necessary contingency plans (Chapter 11) before they are needed.

The models can also provide estimates of advertising effectiveness and price elasticities (Chapter 11) that can be used to assess the impact that promotion and pricing strategies may have on revenues. There are numerous business situations in which extremely large numbers of forecasts have to be generated and seasonally adjusted (Chapter 6). Typically, tens of thousands of forecasts are required to determine the customer-specific requirements for products (SKUs) in inventory and production-planning systems on a periodic basis (Chapter 13).

For example, electricity demand forecasts are now being created in 30-minute intervals, where a forecasting work cycle is only 24 hours. To attempt to provide all of these forecasts in a spreadsheet environment or a manual, one-at-a-time basis is not practical. It requires a forecast-database decision support system (Chapter 13) with an automated statistical forecasting engine (Chapter 8) that can quickly and easily provide credible, reliable forecasts for the great majority of cases. The exceptions that warrant additional time and money can then be given the individual attention they deserve.

Demand forecasters may also want to develop documentation of useful forecasting techniques (Chapter 3) that work well in specific situations. When a request for a one-time forecast is received, the forecaster can review the documentation to determine the useful models that will most likely provide the best results. Unsuccessful attempts should also be noted to avoid the repetition of false starts.

> *Modeling may also be a way of increasing the productivity of a demand forecasting organization and reducing overall costs.*

A problem that demand planners and forecast practitioners face is the need to provide substantiation for the forecasts presented to management or regulatory authorities. Good documentation is often required to satisfy reviewers who question the demand forecasting job that has been done. Forecast tests, stability tests, and forecast simulations are a valuable part of the documentation package. In this regard, the demand forecaster can also use the forecast test as a criterion for automated model selection. If a given model's forecast test results in errors that are above the objective set by the demand forecaster, the model can be rejected.

## Obtaining Adequate Resources

Another prerequisite to the successful implementation of quantitative forecasting techniques is having adequate resources. First, the demand forecaster needs to be trained and experienced in the techniques that are available for use (Chapter 3). Special assistance may be required to gather, verify, input, and process the study data.

Access to computers and software is also required. Budgetary limitations on salary, equipment, training, and consulting will also need to be determined.

If we plan to build or purchase a forecasting decision support system, we can expect expenses and costs for computer-intensive work to build slowly at first but to increase rapidly as the modeling effort intensifies. This aspect of modeling is noted again, later in this chapter, in the section on computer-processing considerations.

## Defining Data

The demand forecaster is often faced with data-collection and data quality problems when attempting to build forecasting models. Even when the appropriate independent variables can be identified, it is not always possible to obtain independent projections for these variables. The availability of external data has significantly improved as the number of computerized data sources has grown. Many consulting firms and academic establishments are now forecasting a wide variety of national and regional economic/demographic time series on the Internet.

Many corporations and business firms have research-group staffs that provide forecasts of economic/demographic variables for internal use. These departments provide services to the company's management that enhance and balance the often-conflicting forecasts from outside sources. The advantage of using an internal organization is that company forecasts can be made consistent with the corporate business outlook.

Governments are also good data sources. Statistical agency publications, like the monthly U.S. Business Conditions Digest, vital statistics data from the Department of Health, and publications of the Federal Reserve Banks are all helpful and readily accessible online. In addition, county and regional planning boards and associations are often interested in economic and demographic projections in connection with funding from the federal government based on population, employment, unemployment, income, and other statistics. Finally, the National Bureau of Economic Research (NBER) provides an analysis of the economic cycles and determines official dates for the beginning and ending of recessions.

*Forecasts of independent variables should be carefully reviewed to be certain that they provide a consistent viewpoint.*

## Forecast Data Management

It is not the intent here to recommend ways to create a demand forecasting system involving system analysis, system design, and system implementation. However, certain data management considerations are worth mentioning. Very early in a forecasting project, the need for standardized naming and coding conventions for data will become obvious. As more and more models are created and new time series added, lack of standard data organization and warehousing can hamper agility significantly. As time goes on, the demand forecaster will not be able to remember what the various time series names anymore and undocumented output will become useless.

When models become part of the everyday demand forecasting process, it will be useful to establish a relational database containing the models and the data organized by product hierarchy and customer/location specific segments. In this way, forecasters are able to maintain a consistent database in which the models and new forecasts are available in a quick, efficient, and cost-effective manner.

When establishing a forecasting system, it is advisable to establish password, security conventions and access restrictions. This prevents unauthorized people from accidentally or intentionally using private information, changing forecasts, or destroying data.

Experience also suggests that historical data updates and maintenance should come from official corporate information resources. Otherwise, there is no accountability for data integrity, which results in duplication, excess storage for items no longer necessary, and out-of-date product/customer data forecasts.

## Selecting Forecasting Software

Statistical software and spreadsheet packages are widely used for the design, modeling, analysis, and implementation of forecasting applications. Demand forecasters should investigate the availability, quality, and performance of these as well as their ability to satisfy their needs for demand forecasting and business planning. No package or system will be everything to everybody.

And consider costs before selecting the appropriate software. For example, packages provide economies of scale and considerable savings in time, effort, and cost. The acquisition cost of software may be nominal; however, the investment in learning how to make effective use of it can often be substantial, as the cost of keeping up with its enhancements. The alternative, independent software development is a major investment that may be beyond the means of most individual organizations.

## Forecaster Training

This book has emphasized that most forecasting techniques, no matter how sophisticated, are only as good as the underlying data and the skill-level of the user. However, basic quantitative and judgmental forecasting techniques should be taught along with studies of best practices. With quality data, the value of these techniques will become more evident to management, and managers can absorb and will use the tools that work for them.

Quantitative analysis is an endeavor in which two minds are better than one. Members of the group should be encouraged to brainstorm alternative approaches to problem solving. They should also share the results of their work with others, because progress is synergistic.

Periodic training and professional development workshops are ideal mechanisms to coordinate quantitative modeling approaches. Participants should be encouraged to make presentations of their latest work. In this way successes can be transmitted throughout the firm, misconceptions can be corrected, and, equally valuable, approaches that have not worked can be discussed. The designation of technical coordinators, whose responsibility it is to assist all model builders, has proved to be a successful way of keeping the implementation project on schedule.

## Documenting for Future Reference

The documentation of results is one of the key aspects of any endeavor. It is also the area that is most disliked and easiest to postpone, because it is often done after a forecast has been made. A documentation system such as that covered in the checklist **in this chapter** is an effective way of solving the documentation problem. Documentation that takes place while the project is progressing can be planned ahead of time and monitored throughout the project. The establishment of literature, model, data, forecasts, software, and billing files will go a long way toward organizing the project and demonstrating to management the necessary control mechanisms for cost effectiveness.

## Presenting Models to Management

The presentation of the modeling approaches for evaluation by managers is an important part of the implementation of quantitative techniques. Experience has shown that it is best to do this in two different presentations.

The first presentation should explain the approach taken, the alternatives considered, and the results from the model when only actual data are used. The purpose of this meeting is to assure management that the methodology is reasonable. Management should be encouraged to ask questions so that it understands the strengths and weaknesses of the particular quantitative approach or approaches presented.

The first meeting should not be one in which higher management is asked to approve a demand forecast based on an unfamiliar methodology. There may be a natural reluctance to accepting the methodology because it is tied in with a presentation that is essentially the selling of a demand forecast. For these reasons, management's acceptance of the quantitative approach should, ideally, take place in a separate meeting. After gaining acceptance of methodology, the demand forecaster can incorporate the model results into the normal presentation of the demand forecast to management.

*The primary concern of management will be the strategic impact of the forecast numbers, an assessment of risk, and their implications for the firm's performance in the future.*

## Engaging Agile Forecast Decision Support

There will always be consulting firms and organizations that specialize in market/product forecasting, predictive analytics, statistical modeling and data analysis, data sources, system integration, and training. These outside sources fill an important niche, providing new, improved, and more sophisticated forecasting services consisting of economic forecasts, demographic projections, long-term trend (futures) scenarios, software systems, computer applications, technical assistance in model building, and training or educational services. Every day more of these services are being hosted through cloud service centers.

## Economic/Demographic Data and Forecasting Services

Until recent times, demand forecasters faced a great problem in obtaining accurate data and quality forecasts for economic variables for use with econometric model building. After expending effort in selecting the best factors to include in quantitative models, demand forecasters lacked the expertise needed to generate consistent and credible forecasts of the economic variables.

Forecasts for many national economic and demographic variables are readily available from a number of online services or consulting firms. At the local or regional level, however, there are fewer organizations routinely issuing forecasts of economic/demographic variables. The manager should consider obtaining consulting help to generate the necessary forecasts if desired variables are inadequate. It is best to check with peers within one's company for such knowledge before looking outside.

Demographic forecasts are also commonly available online at the national and regional levels and increasingly so at the local level. Because the funding for an increasing number of government programs depends on the local makeup of the population, local and regional planning agencies are developing expertise in preparing forecasts of births, deaths, migrations, and racial composition.

460

Unfortunately, the forecasts prepared by these agencies may not always be objective because the demographic projections depend on federal funding. In many models, the market potential is determined as a function of the size of the population, the number of households, or the age distribution of the population. Therefore, demographic forecasts are increasingly important and some caution should be exercised in using them.

Even when economic and demographic forecasts are available, they may not be published when the demand forecasting organization is in greatest need for them. Local or regional forecasts are seldom provided as frequently as national economic variables are. Therefore, the need for timeliness may require the assistance of outside resources.

## Data and Database Management

Most quantitative forecasting techniques rely on the availability of quality data and computer software. As the scope of the forecasting job expands, the Big Data issue surfaces and data management becomes a serious challenge. Consultants can sometimes recommend improved, integrated systems for storage and access, which can help reduce costs.

Most large corporations have in-house organizations that develop or acquire software for using quantitative forecasting techniques. Fortunately, there are also open-source libraries of application programs or hosted software rental services. If a demand forecasting organization requires a specific kind of program that is not generally available, consulting assistance may be required.

## Modeling Assistance

In most cases, only a small number of demand forecasters in an organization at one location will routinely use quantitative approaches. When it is not possible to participate in industry conferences or training workshops for demand forecasters, outside audit assistance may be desirable to ensure that the analyses being performed remain objective, defensible and technically sound. This approach may be more useful than outsourcing technical problems because demand forecasters will likely improve their numerical literacy in the quantitative disciplines and raise skill levels through exposure to outside experts.

## Training Workshops

The forecast manager should be concerned about preventing technological obsolescence and "modeling" complacency in the organization. Therefore, some form of periodic training will be required to maintain and enhance quantitative skills. For larger organizations, this training id often available at corporate training centers. For all organizations, however, professional associations can provide cost-effective training and professional development workshops.

A demand forecasting organization should be cautious in evaluating consulting services by thoroughly vetting the potential services it receives for benefits it expects. Failure to specify exactly which services are required can be a costly mistake. Generally speaking, the consultant must first understand the specific industry and the markets it serves, learn about the firm's operations, and become familiar with the data and variables to be forecast. This is frequently learned at the company's expense before any productive work is forthcoming. Be sure to evaluate a consultant's reputation and track records in solving the organization's kind of forecasting problems.

> *The role of outside experts in quantitative forecasting approaches is to help a company implement models or techniques that will improve the quality and credibility of the forecast.*

Outside experts often sell the use of specific data, forecasts, or software programs. The best way to avoid needless expense and undesirable outcomes is to define the services required very carefully ahead of time and to monitor the consultant's progress with specific indicators of performance in a consulting agreement.

## *The Forecast Manager's Checklists*

The following checklists for forecast implementation, software selection, and automated demand forecasting can be used to help identify gaps in the demand forecasting process that will need your attention. They can be scored or color coded on three levels

> Green = **YES**    Yellow = **SOMEWHAT**    Red = **NO**

### Forecast Implementation Checklist

**Step 1. Identify a task or product (What are your needs?)**
- ✓  Are models to be used for short-term or long-term forecasts?
- ✓  Are models to be used to solve "what if" questions?
- ✓  Are models to be used to determine elasticities?
- ✓  Are models needed at all?

**Step 2. Priorities (Identify these on the basis of your needs)**
- ✓  Which quantitative techniques are useful?
- ✓  Should they be implemented?
- ✓  In what order?
- ✓  What is the implementation schedule?
- ✓  How does qualitative analysis fit into total job responsibility?

**Step 3. Identification of resources**
- ✓  Is management interest and support available?

- ✓ Is money available for computer expenses?
- ✓ Do job responsibilities allow time to meet implementation schedules?
- ✓ Is adequate support available to maintain files?
- ✓ Is economic/demographic data available for modeling?
- ✓ Is modeling expertise available for consultation?

**Step 4. Database management**

- ✓ How will the forecast database be updated?
- ✓ Who will identify and correct outliers in data?
- ✓ Will an ongoing program of documentation of outliers and unusual values be implemented?
- ✓ Will appropriate time series be base-adjusted, if necessary, on an ongoing basis?
- ✓ Will seasonally adjusted data be created and updated periodically?
- ✓ Will data be maintained at the local, regional, or company level?

**Step 5. Intracompany coordination of modeling techniques**

- ✓ How many individuals in the company will be qualified to manage quantitative modeling techniques?
- ✓ Can intracompany communications through training seminars reduce redundant efforts and increase agility with automated forecasting and quantitative modeling?

**Step 6. Documentation of modeling work for future references**

- ✓ Will modeling work be documented for future reference by others engaged in predictive analytics and visualizations?
- ✓ Will publications be organized for different aspects of modeling work?
  - **Literature:** for publications about work in the modeling field, including trade journals and textbooks on mathematics, statistics, and economics; literature from vendors; modeling studies done by others; and so on
  - **Models:** about types of models developed, any changes and reasons for the changes, including information on statistical tests, estimation of parameters, forecast tests, and simulations
  - **Data:** about types, quality, and sources of data, as well as explanations of adjustments and transformations
  - **Forecasting:** containing records on forecasts, forecast errors and monitoring information, and any reports of forecast error analyses
  - **Software:** about evaluations of available software programs and services

- **Billing and Related Expenses:** about costs related to modeling work

## Step 7. Presentation of modeling work for evaluation
- ✓ What kind of feedback on modeling results should be sent for management evaluation
- ✓ How should this be done, and how often?

## Software Selection Checklist

### Step 1. Identify needs
- ✓ What level and detail is being forecasted (product hierarchy, customer/geography segmentation, time granularity)?
- ✓ Are the end-user needs well understood?
- ✓ Are models to be used to solve forecasting problems?
- ✓ What are the available sources of data?
- ✓ Are staffing and their staff qualifications adequate?

### Step 2. Establish goals and objectives
- ✓ Have you established your goals and objectives for the forecasting process?
- ✓ What are the strengths and weakness of the information systems?
- ✓ Are there requirements for both hardcopy and online forecasting output?
- ✓ Have you set up a planned approach to implementation?

### Step 3. Determine functional requirements for decision support
- ✓ Have you determined the scope of the system in terms of number of forecasts, size of historical database, system interfaces and hardware/software performance criteria?
- ✓ What is the environment under which the system is expected to work?
- ✓ What are the time and cost factors related to realizing a forecast decision support system?
- ✓ How are support issues for the system going to be handled?

### Step 4. Establish selection criteria
- ✓ What are the program features and capabilities required to support the demand forecasting process?
- ✓ Have the reporting and export functions been identified?
- ✓ Have performance and maintenance standards been established?

### Step 5. Review products
- ✓ What type of systems will be reviewed (mainframe, PC, client-server, intranet, other)?
- ✓ Have you established and prioritized a list of requirements and options?

✓ What features, modeling, and reporting capabilities are available?

✓ Can you identify pros and cons of each system under review?

✓ Are purchase price, implementation/support time, and costs provided by vendor?

**Step 6. Evaluate systems**

✓ Have systems been reviewed based on established criteria?

✓ Have you established a short list of potential solution providers that fit your needs?

✓ Is there a clear set of evaluation standards prepared for the vendor presentations?

✓ Can the system be customized, and by whom and at what cost?

✓ Are there options to develop a system in an alternative environment?

**Step 7 Check references**

✓ Have you checked functionality against your requirements?

✓ Can you obtain adequate system documentation?

✓ Have you established implementation, training, and support schedules?

✓ Can you test the system with live data from your own company?

✓ Can you review the operating in another environment or company

**Step 8 Acquire the system**

✓ Have you developed a purchasing recommendation?

✓ Can you provide a time, cost, and implementation schedule?

✓ Have you established performance criteria with system providers?

✓ Are contracts, nondisclosure agreements, and payment schedules in place?

## Automated Demand Forecasting Checklist

✓ Is timely data available for modeling, analysis, and exception handling in

- POS data for early warning of rapid shifts in demand?
- electronic promotion calendars for dealing with scheduled marketing/sales events?
- periodic demand history to establish baseline trends?
- seasonal and calendar factors to adjust for predictive patterns?

✓ Are demand forecasts adequately segmented and aggregated to serve marketing, financial, and operational needs of the business?

✓ Do customers and business partners collaborate on their business plans and demand projections on a regular basis?

✓ Are there electronic links (Internet, intranet, etc.) established to facilitate data communication with information providers, customers, and data suppliers?

✓ Have service and performance measurements been implemented to monitor forecast performance in terms of

- equipment change-over times?
- manufacturing cycle times?
- work-in-process (WIP) inventory balances?
- order backlogs?
- product obsolescence?
- transshipment costs?
- revenue objectives?

✓ Has a forecasting system implementation been evaluated in terms of

- employee understanding, acceptance and use?
- system features meeting expectations?
- system performance being acceptable?

## *Takeaways*

Improving the overall demand forecasting process can result from a number of well-planned activities.

- **Preparing demand information systems** supports demand forecasters as well as multiple users and allows for integrated databases so that manual or semi-automatic data transfers are eliminated. The systems should be able to provide online as well as reports on data quality and forecast accuracy. It should allow for judgmental management overrides (management adjustments) and results reporting at each level where a forecast was entered. The systems should allow for direct input of forecasts by customers and of material availability by suppliers.

- **Measuring forecasting performance** with multiple accuracy measures is important in identifying areas for improvement, understanding accuracy limitations and developing credibility with users. Two generic approaches can be pursued: (1) Measure only the demand forecast and make no allowance for difficulty (this approach identifies trouble spots), and (2) measure the demand forecaster by taking into account the relative difficulty of the forecasting environment.

- **Monitoring forecast performance** consists of activities designed to prevent surprise for a company by highlighting the need for a change in the forecast. These activities include monitoring composites or groups of items, the sum of the parts to the whole, ratios of related items, monthly and cumulative results, company and external factors, results in other locations, and user needs.

- **Reconciling multiple forecasting approaches** includes *top-down* and *bottom-up* forecasting with sales-force and/or customer input. Develop the demand forecast at the same time the business plan is developed with periodic reconciliation; training in forecasting techniques, the business environment, and the forecast decision support systems; and recognition and reward.
- **Forecast integration** refers to the need to encourage communication, collaboration, and coordination among all the organizations involved with demand forecasting, including the demand planning organization, marketing, sales, production, logistics, finance, and product management. It involves understanding the needs of all the organizations and developing a process to facilitate information sharing and consensus on the final forecast numbers that are used in business planning and operations.

This book has recommended a disciplined approach for implementing new forecasting techniques or process improvements. A specific methodology should be selected for on-the-job implementation; deadlines should be established, and the resources that will be made available to complete the project should be specified.

An implementation plan should indicate the techniques to be implemented and indicators of progress to ensure that the plan does not die from lack of follow-up. Considerations that should be incorporated into the plan are highlighted in the manager's checklists included in this final chapter.

Training courses can improve the likelihood that new techniques will be implemented, though the value of training is often dissipated because of lack of specific on-the-job reinforcement.

*The philosophy of an agile forecasting® discipline is one in which primary emphasis is placed on the process rather than the number generation. If the demand planner and forecast practitioner has meticulously followed a structured process, the end result will be as accurate and credible a forecast as can be developed. If not, a manager may need to find a better-trained forecast advisor*